A/CN.4/SER.A/2006/Add.1 (Part 2)

YEARBOOK OF THE INTERNATIONAL LAW COMMISSION

2006

Volume II
Part Two

Report of the Commission to the General Assembly on the work of its fifty-eighth session

UNITED NATIONS
New York and Geneva, 2013

NOTE

Symbols of United Nations documents are composed of capital letters combined with figures. Mention of such a symbol indicates a reference to a United Nations document.

References to the *Yearbook of the International Law Commission* are abbreviated to *Yearbook* ..., followed by the year (for example, *Yearbook ... 2006*).

The *Yearbook* for each session of the International Law Commission comprises two volumes:

Volume I: summary records of the meetings of the session;

Volume II (Part One): reports of special rapporteurs and other documents considered during the session;

Volume II (Part Two): report of the Commission to the General Assembly.

All references to these works and quotations from them relate to the final printed texts of the volumes of the *Yearbook* issued as United Nations publications.

A/CN.4/SER.A/2006/Add.l (Part 2)

UNITED NATIONS PUBLICATION

Sales No.: 12.V.13 (Part 2)
ISBN 978-92-1-133798-3
eISBN 978-92-1-055658-3

ISSN 0082-8289

CONTENTS

DOCUMENT A/61/10*

Report of the International Law Commission on the work of its fifty-eighth session (1 May–9 June and 3 July–11 August 2006)

CONTENTS

* Initially distributed as *Official Records of the General Assembly, Sixty-first Session, Supplement No. 10.*

ABBREVIATIONS

APEC	Asia–Pacific Economic Cooperation
BIT	bilateral investment treaty
CERN	European Organization for Nuclear Research
DNA	deoxyribonucleic acid
ECOWAS	Economic Community of West Africa
EIA	environmental impact assessment
FAO	United Nations Food and Agriculture Organization
GEF	Global Environment Facility
GPS	Global Positioning System
IAEA	International Atomic Energy Agency
IAH	International Association of Hydrogeologists
ICC	International Criminal Court
ICJ	International Court of Justice
ICRC	International Committee of the Red Cross
ICSID	International Centre for Settlement of Investment Disputes
ICTs	information and communication technologies
IGRAC	International Groundwater Resources Assessment Centre
IFRC	International Federation of Red Cross and Red Crescent Societies
ILO	International Labour Organization
IOPC	International Oil Pollution Compensation (Funds)
ISDN	integrated services digital network
ITC	International Tin Council
INTERPOL	International Criminal Police Organization
ITLOS	International Tribunal for the Law of the Sea
ITU	International Telecommunication Union
IUCN	International Union for Conservation of Nature
PCIJ	Permanent Court of International Justice
NATO	North Atlantic Treaty Organization
NGO	non-governmental organization
OAS	Organization of American States
OAU	Organization of African Unity
OCHA	Office for the Coordination of Humanitarian Affairs
OECD	Organisation for Economic Co-operation and Development
OHCHR	Office of the High Commissioner for Human Rights
RFID	radio frequency identification
SADC	Southern African Development Community
SDR	Special Drawing Rights
UNAT	United Nations Administrative Tribunal
UNCC	United Nations Compensation Commission
UNCITRAL	United Nations Commission on International Trade Law
UNECE	United Nations Economic Commission for Europe
UNEP	United Nations Environment Programme
UNESCO	United Nations Educational, Scientific and Cultural Organization
UNESCO-IHP	UNESCO International Hydrological Programme
UNHCR	United Nations High Commissioner for Refugees
UNMIK	United Nations Interim Administration Mission in Kosovo
UNRIAA	United Nations Reports of International Arbitral Awards
WSIS	World Summit on the Information Society
WTO	World Trade Organization

*

*   *

AJIL	*American Journal of International Law* (Washington, D.C.)
BYBIL	*The British Year Book of International Law*
I.C.J. Reports	ICJ, *Reports of Judgments, Advisory Opinions and Orders*
ILM	*International Legal Materials* (Washington, D.C.)
ILR	*International Law Reports*
P.C.I.J., Series A	PCIJ, *Collection of Judgments* (Nos. 1–24: up to and including 1930)
P.C.I.J., Series A/B	PCIJ, *Judgments, Orders and Advisory Opinions* (Nos. 40–80: beginning in 1931)
UNRIAA	United Nations, *Reports of International Arbitral Awards*

*

* *

In the present volume, the "International Tribunal for the Former Yugoslavia" refers to the International Tribunal for the Prosecution of Persons Responsible for Serious Violations of International Humanitarian Law Committed in the Territory of the Former Yugoslavia since 1991, and "International Tribunal for Rwanda" refers to the International Criminal Tribunal for the Prosecution of Persons Responsible for Genocide and Other Serious Violations of International Humanitarian Law Committed in the Territory of Rwanda and Rwandan Citizens Responsible for Genocide and Other Such Violations Committed in the Territory of Neighbouring States between 1 January and 31 December 1994.

*

* *

NOTE CONCERNING QUOTATIONS

In quotations, words or passages in italics followed by an asterisk were not italicized in the original text.

Unless otherwise indicated, quotations from works in languages other than English have been translated by the Secretariat.

*

* *

The Internet address of the International Law Commission is **www.un.org/law/ilc/**.

MULTILATERAL INSTRUMENTS CITED IN THE PRESENT VOLUME

	Source
Pacific Settlement of International Disputes	
Covenant of the League of Nations (Versailles, 28 April 1919)	League of Nations, *Official Journal*, No. 1, February 1920, p. 3.
General Act of Arbitration (Pacific Settlement of International Disputes) (Geneva, 26 September 1928)	*Ibid., Treaty Series*, vol. XCIII, No. 2123, p. 343.
Protocol Relating to the Mechanism for Conflict Prevention, Management, Resolution, Peace-keeping and Security (Lomé, 10 December 1999)	*Journal of Conflict and Security Law*, vol. 5, Issue 2 (June 2000), pp. 231–259.
Privileges and Immunities, Diplomatic and Consular Relations, etc.	
Convention on the Privileges and Immunities of the United Nations (New York, 13 February 1946)	United Nations, *Treaty Series*, vol. 1, No. 4, p. 15 and vol. 90, p. 327.
Vienna Convention on Diplomatic Relations (Vienna, 18 April 1961)	*Ibid.,* vol. 500, No. 7310, p. 95.
Vienna Convention on Consular Relations (Vienna, 24 April 1963)	*Ibid.,* vol. 596, No. 8638, p. 261.
Optional Protocol to the Vienna Convention on Consular Relations concerning the Compulsory Settlement of Disputes (Vienna, 24 April 1963)	*Ibid.,* No. 8640, p. 487.
Convention on special missions (New York, 8 December 1969)	*Ibid.,* vol. 1400, No. 23431, p. 231.
Convention on the prevention and punishment of crimes against internationally protected persons, including diplomatic agents (New York, 14 December 1973)	*Ibid.,* vol. 1035, No. 15410, p. 167.
Vienna Convention on the Representation of States in Their Relations with International Organizations of a Universal Character (Vienna, 14 March 1975)	*Ibid., Juridical Yearbook 1975* (Sales No. E.77.V.3), p. 87. See also A/CONF.67/16, p. 207.
United Nations Convention on Jurisdictional Immunities of States and Their Property (New York, 2 December 2004)	*Official Records of the General Assembly, Fifty-ninth Session, Supplement No. 49* (A/59/49), vol. I, resolution 59/38, annex (A/RES/59/38).
Human Rights	
Convention on the Prevention and Punishment of the Crime of Genocide (New York, 9 December 1948)	United Nations, *Treaty Series*, vol. 78, No. 1021, p. 277.
Convention for the Protection of Human Rights and Fundamental Freedoms (European Convention on Human Rights) (Rome, 4 November 1950)	*Ibid.*, vol. 213, No. 2889, p. 221.
Protocol No. 6 to the Convention of 4 November 1950 for the Protection of Human Rights and Fundamental Freedoms, concerning the abolition of the death penalty (Strasbourg, 28 April 1983)	*Ibid.,* vol. 1496, No. 2889, p. 281.
Protocol No. 11 to the Convention for the Protection of Human Rights and Fundamental Freedoms of 4 November 1950, restructuring the control machinery established thereby (Strasbourg, 11 May 1994)	*Ibid.,* vol. 2061, No. 2889, p. 7.
Convention on the Political Rights of Women (New York, 31 March 1953)	*Ibid.,* vol. 193, No. 2613, p. 135.
Supplementary Convention on the Abolition of Slavery, the Slave Trade, and Institutions and Practices Similar to Slavery (Geneva, 7 September 1956)	*Ibid.,* vol. 266, No. 3822, p. 3.
Convention against discrimination in education (Paris, 15 December 1960)	*Ibid.,* vol. 429, No. 6193, p. 93.

International Convention on the Elimination of All Forms of Racial Discrimination (New York, 7 March 1966)	*Ibid.*, vol. 660, No. 9464, p. 195.
International Covenant on Civil and Political Rights (New York, 16 December 1966)	*Ibid.*, vol. 999, No. 14668, p. 171.
Optional Protocol to the International Covenant on Civil and Political Rights (New York, 16 December 1966)	*Ibid.*
International Covenant on Economic, Social and Cultural Rights (New York, 16 December 1966)	*Ibid.*, vol. 993, No. 14531, p. 3.
European Convention on the adoption of children (Strasbourg, 24 April 1967)	*Ibid.*, vol. 634, No. 9067, p. 255.
American Convention on Human Rights: "Pact of San José, Costa Rica" (San José, Costa Rica, 22 November 1969)	*Ibid.*, vol. 1144, No. 17955, p. 123.
Convention on the Elimination of All Forms of Discrimination against Women (New York, 18 December 1979)	*Ibid.*, vol. 1249, No. 20378, p. 13.
Optional Protocol to the Convention on the Elimination of All Forms of Discrimination against Women (New York, 6 October 1999)	*Ibid.*, vol. 2131, No. 20378, p. 83.
Convention for the protection of individuals with regard to automatic processing of personal data (Strasbourg, 28 January 1981)	*Ibid.*, vol. 1496, No. 25702, p. 65.
Additional Protocol to the Convention for the protection of individuals with regard to automatic processing of personal data, regarding supervisory authorities and transborder data flows (Strasbourg, 8 November 2001)	*Ibid.*, vol. 2297, No. 25702, p. 195.
African Charter on Human and Peoples' Rights (Nairobi, 27 June 1981)	*Ibid.*, vol. 1520, No. 26363, p. 217.
Convention against Torture and Other Cruel, Inhuman or Degrading Treatment or Punishment (New York, 10 December 1984)	*Ibid.*, vol. 1465, No. 24841, p. 85.
European Convention for the prevention of torture and inhuman or degrading treatment or punishment (Strasbourg, 26 November 1987)	*Ibid.*, vol. 1561, No. 27161, p. 363.
Convention on the rights of the child (New York, 20 November 1989)	*Ibid.*, vol. 1577, No. 27531, p. 3.
African Charter on the Rights and Welfare of the Child (Addis Ababa, 11 July 1990)	E/CN.4/2004/WG.21/5, p. 220. See also OAU, document CAB/LEG/24.9/49 (1990).
Convention for the Protection of Human Rights and Dignity of the Human Being with regard to the Application of Biology and Medicine: Convention on Human Rights and Biomedicine (Oviedo, 4 April 1997)	United Nations, *Treaty Series*, vol. 2137, No. 37266, p. 171.
Additional Protocol to the Convention for the Protection of Human Rights and Dignity of the Human Being with regard to the Application of Biology and Medicine, on the Prohibition of Cloning Human Beings (Paris, 12 January 1998)	*Ibid.*, vol. 2177, No. A-37266, p. 366.

Refugees and Stateless Persons

Convention on Certain Questions relating to the Conflict of Nationality Laws (The Hague, 12 April 1930)	League of Nations, *Treaty Series*, vol. CLXXIX, No. 4137, p. 89.
Convention relating to the Status of Refugees (Geneva, 28 July 1951)	United Nations, *Treaty Series*, vol. 189, No. 2545, p. 137.
Protocol relating to the Status of Refugees (New York, 31 January 1967)	*Ibid.*, vol. 606, No. 8791, p. 267.
Convention on territorial asylum (Caracas, 28 March 1954)	*Ibid.*, vol. 1438, No. 24378, p. 127.
Convention relating to the Status of Stateless Persons (New York, 28 September 1954)	*Ibid.*, vol. 360, No. 5158, p. 117.

Convention on the nationality of married women (New York, 20 February 1957)	*Ibid.*, vol. 309, No. 4468, p. 65.
Convention on the reduction of statelessness (New York, 30 August 1961)	*Ibid.*, vol. 989, No. 14458, p. 175.
OAU Convention governing the specific aspects of refugee problems in Africa (Addis Ababa, 10 September 1969)	*Ibid.*, vol. 1001, No. 14691, p. 45.
European Convention on Nationality (Strasbourg, 6 November 1997)	*Ibid.*, vol. 2135, No. 37248, p. 213.

International Trade and Development

Agreement on the temporary importation, free of duty, of medical, surgical and laboratory equipment for use on free loan in hospitals and other medical institutions for purposes of diagnosis or treatment (Strasbourg, 28 April 1960)	United Nations, *Treaty Series*, vol. 376, No. 5377, p. 111.
European Convention on International Commercial Arbitration (Geneva, 21 April 1961)	*Ibid.*, vol. 484, No. 7041, p. 349.
Convention on the settlement of investment disputes between States and nationals of other States (Washington, 18 March 1965)	*Ibid.*, vol. 575, No. 8359, p. 159.
International Convention on the simplification and harmonization of Customs procedures (Kyoto, 18 May 1973; Protocol of Amendment, Brussels, 26 June 1999)	*Ibid.*, vol. 950, No. 13561, p. 269, and vol. 2370, p. 27.
International Sugar Agreement (Geneva, 7 October 1977)	*Ibid.*, vol. 1064, No. 16200, p. 219.
Convention on temporary admission (Istanbul, 26 June 1990)	*Ibid.*, vol. 1762, No. 30667, p. 121.
General Agreement on Trade in Services (Annex to the Marrakesh Agreement Establishing the World Trade Organization) (Marrakesh, 15 April 1994)	*Ibid.*, vols. 1867–1869, No. 31874.
United Nations Convention on the Use of Electronic Communications in International Contracts (New York, 23 November 2005)	*Official Records of the General Assembly, Sixtieth Session, Supplement No. 49* (A/60/49), resolution 60/21, Annex.

Transport and Communications

Convention on International Civil Aviation (Chicago, 7 December 1944)	United Nations, *Treaty Series*, vol. 15, No. 102, p. 295.
Convention on damage caused by foreign aircraft to third parties on the surface (Rome, 7 October 1952)	*Ibid.*, vol. 310, No. 4493, p. 181.
Convention on offences and certain other acts committed on board aircraft (Tokyo, 14 September 1963)	*Ibid.*, vol. 704, No. 10106, p. 219.
Convention concerning International Carriage by Rail (Bern, 9 May 1980)	*Ibid.*, vol. 1397, No. 23353, p. 2.
Convention on Civil Liability for Damage caused during Carriage of Dangerous Goods by Road, Rail and Inland Navigation Vessels (CRTD) (Geneva, 10 October 1989)	United Nations publication (Sales No. E.90.II.E.39).

Navigation

Convention between Austria-Hungary, France, Germany, Great Britain, Italy, the Netherlands, Russia, Spain and Turkey respecting the Free Navigation of the Suez Canal (Constantinople Convention) (Constantinople, 29 October 1888)	AJIL, *Supplement*, vol. 3, p. 123.
International Convention for the unification of certain rules relating to penal jurisdiction in matters of collision or other incidents of navigation (Brussels, 10 May 1952)	United Nations, *Treaty Series*, vol. 439, No. 6332, p. 233.
Convention on facilitation of international maritime traffic (London, 9 April 1965)	*Ibid.*, vol. 591, No. 8564, p. 265.

International Convention for Safe Containers (CSC) (Geneva, 2 December 1972)	*Ibid.*, vol. 1064, No. 16198, p. 3.

Penal matters

Treaty on International Penal Law (Montevideo, 19 March 1940)	Organization of American States, *Treaty Series*, vol. 34, p. 71.
European Convention on Extradition (Paris, 13 December 1957)	United Nations, *Treaty Series*, vol. 359, No. 5146, p. 273.
Convention concerning judicial competence and the execution of decisions in civil and commercial matters (Brussels, 27 September 1968)	*Ibid.*, vol. 1262, No. 20747, p. 153. See the consolidated and updated version in ILM, vol. 29 (1990), p. 1413.
European Convention on the service abroad of documents relating to administrative matters (Strasbourg, 24 November 1977)	*Ibid.*, vol. 1299, No. 21537, p. 3.
Inter-American Convention on Extraterritorial Validity of Foreign Judgments and Arbitral Awards (Montevideo, 8 May 1979)	ILM, vol. 18 (1979), p. 1224.
International Convention against the taking of hostages (New York, 17 December 1979)	United Nations, *Treaty Series*, vol. 1316, No. 21931, p. 205.
European Convention on the compensation of victims of violent crimes (Strasbourg, 24 November 1983)	*Ibid.*, vol. 1525, No. 26456, p. 37.
Inter-American Convention on Jurisdiction in the International Sphere for the Extraterritorial Validity of Foreign Judgments (La Paz, 24 May 1984)	ILM, vol. 24 (1985), p. 468.
Convention on jurisdiction and the enforcement of judgements in civil and commercial matters (Lugano, 16 September 1988)	United Nations, *Treaty Series*, vol. 1659, No. 28551, p. 13.
Convention on the Safety of United Nations and Associated Personnel (New York, 9 December 1994)	*Ibid.*, vol. 2051, No. 35457, p. 363.
Optional Protocol to the Convention on the Safety of United Nations and Associated Personnel (New York, 8 December 2005)	*Official Records of the General Assembly, Sixtieth Session, Supplement No. 49* (A/60/49), resolution 60/42, Annex.
Rome Statute of the International Criminal Court (Rome, 17 July 1998)	United Nations, *Treaty Series*, vol. 2187, No. 38544, p. 3.
Convention on cybercrime (Budapest, 23 November 2001)	*Ibid.*, vol. 2296, No. 40916, p. 167.

Law of the Sea

Geneva Conventions on the Law of the Sea (Geneva, 29 April 1958)	
Convention on the Territorial Sea and the Contiguous Zone	United Nations, *Treaty Series*, vol. 516, No. 7477, p. 205.
Convention on the Continental Shelf	*Ibid.*, vol. 499, No. 7302, p. 311.
Convention on the High Seas	*Ibid.*, vol. 450, No. 6465, p. 11.
United Nations Convention on the Law of the Sea (Montego Bay, 10 December 1982)	*Ibid.*, vol. 1833, No. 31363, p. 3.
Agreement for the Implementation of the Provisions of the United Nations Convention on the Law of the Sea of 10 December 1982 relating to the Conservation and Management of Straddling Fish Stocks and Highly Migratory Fish Stocks (New York, 4 August 1995)	*Ibid.*, vol. 2167, No. 37924, p. 3.

Law applicable in Armed Conflict

Hague Conventions respecting the Laws and Customs of War on Land: Convention II (The Hague, 29 July 1899), Convention IV (The Hague, 18 October 1907) and Convention IX concerning Bombardment by Naval Forces in Time of War (The Hague, 18 October 1907)	*The Hague Conventions and Declarations of 1899 and 1907*, J. B. Scott (ed.), New York, Oxford University Press, 1918.
Regulations concerning the Laws and Customs of War on Land (annexes to the Hague Conventions II and IV of 1899 and 1907)	*The Hague Conventions and Declarations of 1899 and 1907*, J. B. Scott (ed.), New York, Oxford University Press, 1918.
Treaty of Peace between the Allied and Associated Powers and Germany (Treaty of Versailles) (Versailles, 28 June 1919)	*British and Foreign State Papers, 1919*, vol. CXII, London, HM Stationery Office, 1922, p. 1.
Treaty of Peace between the Allied and Associated Powers and Hungary (Treaty of Trianon) (Trianon, 4 June 1920)	*British and Foreign State Papers, 1920*, vol. CXIII, London, HM Stationery Office, 1923, p. 486.
Geneva Conventions for the protection of war victims (Geneva, 12 August 1949)	United Nations, *Treaty Series*, vol. 75, Nos. 970–973, pp. 31 *et seq.*
Geneva Convention for the Amelioration of the Condition of the Wounded and Sick in Armed Forces in the Field (Convention I) (Geneva, 12 August 1949)	*Ibid.*, No. 970, pp. 31 *et seq.*
Geneva Convention for the Amelioration of the Condition of Wounded, Sick and Shipwrecked Members of Armed Forces at Sea (Convention II) (Geneva, 12 August 1949)	*Ibid.*, No. 971, pp. 85 *et seq.*
Geneva Convention relative to the Treatment of Prisoners of War (Convention III) (Geneva, 12 August 1949)	*Ibid.*, No. 972, pp. 135 *et seq.*
Geneva Convention relative to the Protection of Civilian Persons in Time of War (Convention IV) (Geneva, 12 August 1949)	*Ibid.*, No. 973, pp. 287 *et seq.*
Protocol additional to the Geneva Conventions of 12 August 1949, and relating to the protection of victims of international armed conflicts (Protocol I) (Geneva, 8 June 1977)	*Ibid.*, vol. 1125, No. 17512, p. 3.
Protocol additional to the Geneva Conventions of 12 August 1949, and relating to the protection of victims of non-international armed conflicts (Protocol II) (Geneva, 8 June 1977)	*Ibid.*, No. 17513, p. 609.
Convention for the Protection of Cultural Property in the Event of Armed Conflict (The Hague, 14 May 1954)	*Ibid.*, vol. 249, No. 3511, p. 215.

Law of Treaties

Vienna Convention on the Law of Treaties (Vienna, 23 May 1969)	United Nations, *Treaty Series*, vol. 1155, No. 18232, p. 331.
Vienna Convention on succession of States in respect of treaties (Vienna, 23 August 1978)	*Ibid.*, vol. 1946, No. 33356, p. 3.
Vienna Convention on the Law of Treaties between States and International Organizations or between International Organizations (Vienna, 21 March 1986)	A/CONF.129/15.

Outer Space

Treaty on principles governing the activities of States in the exploration and use of outer space, including the moon and other celestial bodies (Moscow, London and Washington, 27 January 1967)	United Nations, *Treaty Series*, vol. 610, No. 8843, p. 205.

Telecommunications

European Convention on Transfrontier Television (Strasbourg, 5 May 1989)	United Nations, *Treaty Series*, vol. 1966, No. 33611, p. 265.
Tampere Convention on the Provision of Telecommunication Resources for Disaster Mitigation and Relief Operations (Tampere, 18 June 1998)	*Ibid.*, vol. 2296, No. 40906, p. 5.

Liability

Convention on third party liability in the field of nuclear energy (Paris, 29 July 1960)	United Nations, *Treaty Series*, vol. 956, No. 13706, p. 251.
Additional Protocol to the Convention on Third Party Liability in the field of Nuclear Energy (Paris, 28 January 1964)	*Ibid.,* p. 325.
Protocol to amend the Convention on Third Party Liability in the field of Nuclear Energy of 29 July 1960, as amended by the Additional Protocol of 28 January 1964 (Paris, 16 November 1982)	*Ibid.*, vol. 1519, Annex A, No. 13706, p. 329.
Protocol to amend the Convention on Third Party Liability in the field of Nuclear Energy of 29 July 1960, as amended by the Additional Protocol of 28 January 1964 and the Protocol of 16 November 1982 (Paris, 12 February 2004)	*Official Journal of the European Union*, No. L 97, 1 April 2004, p. 55.
Convention on the Liability of Operators of Nuclear Ships (Brussels, 25 May 1962)	IAEA, *International Conventions relating to Civil Liability for Nuclear Damage*, Legal Series No. 4, rev. ed., Vienna, 1976, p. 34.
Vienna Convention on civil liability for nuclear damage (Vienna, 21 May 1963)	United Nations, *Treaty Series*, vol. 1063, No. 16197, p. 265.
Protocol to amend the Vienna Convention on civil liability for nuclear damage (Vienna, 12 September 1997)	*Ibid.*, vol. 2241, No. 16197, p. 270.
International Convention on Civil Liability for Oil Pollution Damage (Brussels, 29 November 1969)	*Ibid.*, vol. 973, No. 14097, p. 3.
Protocol to amend the International Convention on Civil Liability for Oil Pollution Damage (London, 27 November 1992)	*Ibid.*, vol. 1956, No. 14097, p. 255.
Convention on the international liability for damage caused by space objects (London, Moscow and Washington D.C., 29 March 1972)	*Ibid.*, vol. 961, No. 13810, p. 187.
European Convention on Civil Liability for Damage Caused by Motor Vehicles (Strasbourg, 14 May 1973)	Council of Europe, *European Treaty Series*, No. 79.
International Convention on Civil Liability for Oil Pollution Damage resulting from the Exploration for and Exploitation of Seabed Mineral Resources (London, 1 May 1977)	ILM, vol. 16 (1977), p. 1451.
Convention on Civil Liability for Damage caused during Carriage of Dangerous Goods by Road, Rail and Inland Navigation Vessels (CRTD) (Geneva, 10 October 1989)	United Nations publication (Sales No. E.90.II.E.39).
Convention on Civil Liability for Damage resulting from Activities Dangerous to the Environment (Lugano, 21 June 1993)	Council of Europe, *European Treaty Series*, No. 150.
International Convention on Liability and Compensation for Damage in Connection with the Carriage of Hazardous and Noxious Substances by Sea (HNS Convention) (London, 3 May 1996)	*HNS Convention*, publication of the International Maritime Organization (Sales No. IMO-479E).
Basel Protocol on Liability and Compensation for Damage Resulting from Transboundary Movements of Hazardous Wastes and their Disposal (Basel, 10 December 1999)	UNEP/CHW.5/29, Annex III.
International Convention on Civil Liability for Bunker Oil Pollution Damage (London, 23 March 2001)	United Nations, *Juridical Yearbook 2001* (Sales No.: E.04.V.12), p. 310.

Disarmament

Treaty on the Non-Proliferation of Nuclear Weapons (London, Moscow and Washington, 1 July 1968)	United Nations, *Treaty Series*, vol. 729, No. 10485, p. 161.

Environment

International Convention on the establishment of an international fund for compensation for oil pollution damage (Brussels, 18 December 1971)	United Nations, *Treaty Series*, vol. 1110, No. 17146, p. 57.
Protocol of 1992 to amend the International Convention on the establishment of an international fund for compensation for oil pollution damage (London, 27 November 1992)	*Ibid.*, vol. 1953, No. 17146, p. 330.
Convention on the prevention of marine pollution by dumping of wastes and other matter (London, Mexico City, Moscow and Washington D.C., 29 December 1972)	*Ibid.*, vol. 1046, No. 15749, p. 138.
1996 Protocol to the Convention on the Prevention of Marine Pollution by Dumping of Wastes and Other Matter (London, 7 November 1996)	ILM, vol. 36 (1997), p. 7.
Convention on the protection of the environment (Stockholm, 19 February 1974)	United Nations, *Treaty Series*, vol. 1092, No. 16770, p. 279.
Convention on the protection of the Rhine against pollution by chlorides (Bonn, 3 December 1976)	*Ibid.*, vol. 1404, No. 23469, p. 59.
Additional Protocol to the Convention on the protection of the Rhine against pollution by chlorides (Brussels, 25 September 1991)	*Ibid.*, vol. 1840, No. 23469 p. 372.
Vienna Convention for the Protection of the Ozone Layer (Vienna, 22 March 1985)	*Ibid.*, vol. 1513, No. 26164, p. 293.
ASEAN Agreement on the Conservation of Nature and Natural Resources (Kuala Lumpur, 9 July 1985)	UNEP, *Selected Multilateral Treaties in the Field of the Environment*, vol. 2, Cambridge, Grotius, 1991, p. 343.
Convention on early notification of a nuclear accident (Vienna, 26 September 1986)	United Nations, *Treaty Series*, vol. 1439, No. 24404, p. 275.
Convention for the Protection of the Natural Resources and Environment of the South Pacific Region (Noumea, 25 November 1986)	UNEP, *Selected Multilateral Treaties in the Field of the Environment*, vol. 2, Cambridge, Grotius, 1991, p. 372. See also ILM, vol. 26 (1987), p. 41.
Convention on the Regulation of Antarctic Mineral Resource Activities (CRAMRA) (Wellington, 2 June 1988)	*Revue générale de droit international public*, vol. 93 (1989/1), p. 182. See also ILM, vol. 27 (1988), p. 859.
Basel Convention on the control of transboundary movements of hazardous wastes and their disposal (Basel, 22 March 1989)	United Nations, *Treaty Series*, vol. 1673, No. 28911, p. 57.
International Convention on oil pollution preparedness, response and cooperation (London, 30 November 1990)	*Ibid.*, vol. 1891, No. 32194, p. 51.
Bamako Convention on the Ban of the Import into Africa and the Control of Transboundary Movement and Management of Hazardous Wastes within Africa (Bamako, 30 January 1991)	*Ibid.*, vol. 2101, No. 36508, p. 177.
Convention on Environmental Impact Assessment in a Transboundary Context (Espoo, 25 February 1991)	*Ibid.*, vol. 1989, No. 34028, p. 309.
Convention on the Transboundary Effects of Industrial Accidents (Helsinki, 17 March 1992)	*Ibid.*, vol. 2105, No. 36605, p. 457.
Protocol on Civil Liability and Compensation for Damage caused by the Transboundary Effects of Industrial Accidents on Transboundary Waters (Kiev, 21 May 2003)	ECE/MP.WAT/11.

Convention on the Protection and Use of Transboundary Watercourses and International Lakes (Helsinki, 17 March 1992)	United Nations, *Treaty Series*, vol. 1936, No. 33207, p. 269.
Protocol on Water and Health to the 1992 Convention on the Protection and Use of Transboundary Watercourses and International Lakes (London, 17 June 1999)	*Ibid.*, vol. 2331, No. 33207, p. 202.
Convention on the Protection of the Marine Environment of the Baltic Sea Area (Helsinki, 9 April 1992)	*Ibid.*, vol. 2099, No. 36495, p. 195.
Convention on the protection of the Black Sea against pollution (Bucharest, 21 April 1992)	*Ibid.*, vol. 1764, No. 30674, p. 3.
United Nations Framework Convention on Climate Change (New York, 9 May 1992)	*Ibid.*, vol. 1771, No. 30822, p. 107.
Convention on Biological Diversity (Rio de Janeiro, 5 June 1992)	*Ibid.*, vol. 1760, No. 30619, p. 79.
Cartagena Protocol on Biosafety to the Convention on Biological Diversity (Montreal, 29 January 2000)	*Ibid.*, vol. 2226, No. 30619, p. 208.
Convention for the protection of the marine environment of the North-East Atlantic (OSPAR Convention) (Paris, 22 September 1992)	*Ibid.*, vol. 2354, No. 42279, p. 67.
Convention on cooperation for the protection and sustainable use of the river Danube (Sofia, 29 June 1994)	*Official Journal of the European Communities*, No. L 342, 12 December 1997, p. 19.
Convention to combat desertification in those countries experiencing serious drought and/or desertification, particularly in Africa (Paris, 14 October 1994)	United Nations, *Treaty Series*, vol. 1954, No. 33480, p. 3.
Convention for the Protection of the Marine Environment and the Coastal Region of the Mediterranean (Barcelona, 10 June 1995)	UNEP, *Selected Multilateral Treaties in the Field of the Environment*, vol. 2, Cambridge, Grotius, 1991, p. 448.
Convention on the Law of the Non-Navigational Uses of International Watercourses (New York, 21 May 1997)	*Official Records of the General Assembly, fifty-first session, Supplement No. 49* (A/51/49), vol. III, resolution 51/229, Annex.
Convention on Supplementary Compensation for Nuclear Damage (Vienna, 12 September 1997)	IAEA, doc. GOV/INF/822-GC(41)/INF/13 and Corr. (N5-52 Circ. [Depositary Notification]). See also ILM, vol. 36 (November 1997), p. 1473.
Convention on Access to Information, Public Participation in Decision-making and Access to Justice in Environmental Matters (Aarhus, 25 June 1998)	United Nations, *Treaty Series*, vol. 2161, No. 37770, p. 447.
Convention for the Protection of the Rhine (Bern, 12 April 1999)	*Official Journal of the European Communities*, No. L 289, 16 November 2000, p. 31.
Revised Protocol on Shared Watercourses in the Southern African Development Community (Windhoek, 7 August 2000)	S. Burchi and K. Mechlem, *Groundwater in International Law: Compilation of Treaties and Other Legal Instruments*, Rome, FAO/UNESCO, 2005, p. 102. See also ILM, vol. 40, No. 2 (March 2001), p. 321.
Programme for the Development of a Regional Strategy for the utilisation of the Nubian Sandstone Aquifer System—Terms of Reference for the Monitoring and Exchange of Groundwater Information of the Nubian Sandstone Aquifer System (Tripoli, 5 October 2000)	S. Burchi and K. Mechlem, *Groundwater in International Law: Compilation of Treaties and Other Legal Instruments*, Rome, FAO/UNESCO, 2005, p. 4.
Tripartite Interim Agreement Between the Republic of Mozambique, the Republic of South Africa and the Kingdom of Swaziland for Co-operation on the Protection and Sustainable Utilisation of the Water Resources of the Incomati and Maputo Watercourses (Johannesburg, 29 August 2002)	*Ibid.*, p. 158.

Framework Agreement on the Sava River Basin (Kranjska Gora, 3 December 2002)	United Nations, *Treaty Series*, vol. 2366, No. 42662, p. 479.
Framework Convention on the Protection and Sustainable Development of the Carpathians (Kiev, 22 May 2003)	S. Burchi and K. Mechlem, *Groundwater in International Law: Compilation of Treaties and Other Legal Instruments*, Rome, FAO/UNESCO, 2005, p. 119.
Convention on the sustainable management of Lake Tanganyika (Dar es Salaam, 12 June 2003)	United Nations, *Treaty Series*, vol. 2338, No. 41902, p. 43.
African Convention on the Conservation of Nature and Natural Resources (Maputo, 11 July 2003)	*International Environmental Law—Multilateral Treaties*, W. E. Burhenne (ed.), The Hague, Kluwer Law International, vol. IX, p. 52.
Protocol for Sustainable Development of Lake Victoria Basin (Arusha, 29 November 2003)	S. Burchi and K. Mechlem, *Groundwater in International Law: Compilation of Treaties and Other Legal Instruments*, Rome, FAO/UNESCO, 2005, p. 198.

Miscellaneous

Convention and Statute establishing an International Relief Union (Geneva, 12 July 1927)	League of Nations, *Treaty Series*, vol. CXXXV (1932–1933), No. 3115, p. 247.
Articles of Agreement of the International Monetary Fund (Washington D.C., 27 December 1945)	United Nations, *Treaty Series*, vol. 2, No. 20, p. 39.
Treaty establishing the European Economic Community (Rome, 25 March 1957)	*Ibid.*, vol. 294, No. 4300, p. 3. See also the consolidated version of the Treaty establishing the European Community, *Official Journal*, No. C 340, 10 November 1997, p. 173.
The Antarctic Treaty (Washington D.C., 1 December 1959)	United Nations, *Treaty Series*, vol. 402, No. 5778, p. 71.
Protocol on Environmental Protection to the Antarctic Treaty (Madrid, 4 October 1991, and Stockholm, 17 June 2005 (Annex VI))	ILM, vol. 30 (November 1991), p. 1461, and vol. 45 (January 2006), No. 1, p. 5.
Convention on the means of prohibiting and preventing the illicit import, export and transfer of ownership of cultural property (Paris, 14 November 1970)	United Nations, *Treaty Series*, vol. 823, No. 11806, p. 231.
Convention for the protection of the world cultural and natural heritage (Paris, 16 November 1972)	*Ibid.*, vol. 1037, No. 15511, p. 151.
Convention on assistance in the case of nuclear accident or radiological emergency (Vienna, 26 September 1986)	*Ibid.*, vol. 1457, No. 24643, p. 133.
Inter-American Convention to Facilitate Disaster Assistance (Santiago, 7 June 1991)	OAS, *Official Records*, OEA/Ser.A/49 (SEPF).
Convention for the Safeguarding of the Intangible Cultural Heritage (Paris, 17 October 2003)	United Nations, *Treaty Series*, vol. 2368, No. 42671, p. 3.
ASEAN Agreement on Disaster Management and Emergency Response (Vientiane, 26 July 2005)	ASEAN, *ASEAN Documents Series 2005*, Jakarta, ASEAN Secretariat, 2006, p. 157.

Chapter I

ORGANIZATION OF THE SESSION

1. The International Law Commission held the first part of its fifty-eighth session from 1 May to 9 June 2006 and the second part from 3 July to 11 August 2006 at its seat at the United Nations Office at Geneva. The session was opened by Mr. Djamchid Momtaz, Chairperson of the Commission at its fifty-seventh session.

A. Membership

2. The Commission consists of the following members:

Mr. Emmanuel Akwei ADDO (Ghana)

Mr. Husain AL-BAHARNA (Bahrain)

Mr. Ali Mohsen Fetais AL-MARRI (Qatar)

Mr. João Clemente BAENA SOARES (Brazil)

Mr. Ian BROWNLIE (United Kingdom of Great Britain and Northern Ireland)

Mr. Enrique CANDIOTI (Argentina)

Mr. Choung Il CHEE (Republic of Korea)

Mr. Pedro COMISSÁRIO AFONSO (Mozambique)

Mr. Riad DAOUDI (Syrian Arab Republic)

Mr. Christopher John Robert DUGARD (South Africa)

Mr. Constantin ECONOMIDES (Greece)

Ms. Paula ESCARAMEIA (Portugal)

Mr. Salifou FOMBA (Mali)

Mr. Giorgio GAJA (Italy)

Mr. Zdzislaw GALICKI (Poland)

Mr. Peter KABATSI (Uganda)

Mr. Maurice KAMTO (Cameroon)

Mr. James Lutabanzibwa KATEKA (United Republic of Tanzania)

Mr. Fathi KEMICHA (Tunisia)

Mr. Roman Anatolyevitch KOLODKIN (Russian Federation)

Mr. Martti KOSKENNIEMI (Finland)

Mr. William MANSFIELD (New Zealand)

Mr. Michael MATHESON (United States of America)

Mr. Teodor Viorel MELESCANU (Romania)

Mr. Djamchid MOMTAZ (Islamic Republic of Iran)

Mr. Bernd NIEHAUS (Costa Rica)

Mr. Didier OPERTTI BADAN (Uruguay)

Mr. Guillaume PAMBOU-TCHIVOUNDA (Gabon)

Mr. Alain PELLET (France)

Mr. Pemmaraju Sreenivasa RAO (India)

Mr. Víctor RODRÍGUEZ CEDEÑO (Bolivarian Republic of Venezuela)

Mr. Eduardo VALENCIA-OSPINA (Colombia) (see para. 3 below)

Ms. Hanqin XUE (China)

Mr. Chusei YAMADA (Japan)

3. At its 2867th meeting on 1 May 2006, the Commission elected Mr. Eduardo Valencia-Ospina (Colombia) to fill the casual vacancy caused by the election of Mr. Bernardo Sepúlveda to the ICJ.

B. Officers and Enlarged Bureau

4. At its 2867th meeting on 1 May 2006, the Commission elected the following officers:

Chairperson: Mr. Guillaume Pambou-Tchivounda

First Vice-Chairperson: Mr. Giorgio Gaja

Second Vice-Chairperson: Mr. Víctor Rodríguez Cedeño

Chairperson of the Drafting Committee: Mr. Roman A. Kolodkin

Rapporteur: Ms. Hanqin Xue

5. The Enlarged Bureau of the Commission was composed of the officers of the present session, the previous Chairpersons of the Commission[1] and the Special Rapporteurs.[2]

6. On the recommendation of the Enlarged Bureau, the Commission set up a Planning Group composed of the following members: Mr. Giorgio Gaja (Chairperson), Mr. Emmanuel Akwei Addo, Mr. Enrique Candioti, Mr. Pedro Comissário Afonso, Mr. Riad Daoudi, Ms. Paula Escarameia, Mr. Salifou Fomba, Mr. Zdzislaw Galicki, Mr. Peter Kabatsi, Mr. Maurice Kamto, Mr. James Lutabanzibwa Kateka, Mr. Fathi Kemicha, Mr. Roman Anatolyevitch Kolodkin, Mr. Teodor Viorel Melescanu, Mr. Djamchid Momtaz, Mr. Bernd Niehaus, Mr. Alain Pellet, Mr. Pemmaraju Sreenivasa Rao, Mr. Eduardo Valencia-Ospina, Mr. Chusei Yamada and Ms. Hanqin Xue (*ex officio*).

C. Drafting Committee

7. At its 2871st, 2874th, 2880th and 2881st meetings on 5, 11, 23 and 30 May 2006 respectively, the Commission established a Drafting Committee, composed of the following members for the topics indicated:

[1] Mr. João Clemente Baena Soares, Mr. Enrique Candioti, Mr. Zdzislaw Galicki, Mr. Peter Kabatsi, Mr. Djamchid Momtaz, Mr. Alain Pellet, Mr. Pemmaraju.Sreenivasa Rao and Mr. Chusei Yamada.

[2] Mr. Ian Brownlie, Mr. Christopher John Robert Dugard, Mr. Giorgio Gaja, Mr. Zdzislaw Galicki, Mr. Maurice Kamto, Mr. Alain Pellet, Mr. Pemmaraju Sreenivasa Rao, Mr. Víctor Rodríguez Cedeño and Mr. Chusei Yamada.

(*a*) Diplomatic protection: Mr. Roman Anatolyevitch Kolodkin (Chairperson), Mr. Christopher John Robert Dugard (Special Rapporteur), Mr. Ian Brownlie, Mr. Enrique Candioti, Mr. Choung Il Chee, Mr. Constantin Economides, Ms. Paula Escarameia, Mr. Giorgio Gaja, Mr. Fathi Kemicha, Mr. William Mansfield, Mr. Michael Matheson, Mr. Djamchid Momtaz, Mr. Chusei Yamada and Ms. Hanqin Xue (*ex officio*).

(*b*) International liability for injurious consequences arising out of acts not prohibited by international law (international liability in the case of loss from transboundary harm arising out of hazardous activities): Mr. Roman Anatolyevitch Kolodkin (Chairperson), Mr. Pemmaraju Sreenivasa Rao (Special Rapporteur), Mr. João Clemente Baena Soares, Mr. Enrique Candioti, Mr. Choung Il Chee, Mr. Riad Daoudi, Ms. Paula Escarameia, Mr. Giorgio Gaja, Mr. Martti Koskenniemi, Mr. William Mansfield, Mr. Michael Matheson, Mr. Chusei Yamada and Ms. Hanqin Xue (*ex officio*).

(*c*) Reservations to treaties: Mr. Roman Anatolyevitch Kolodkin (Chairperson), Mr. Alain Pellet (Special Rapporteur), Ms. Paula Escarameia, Mr. Salifou Fomba, Mr. Giorgio Gaja, Mr. Zdzislaw Galicki, Mr. Michael Matheson, Mr. Chusei Yamada and Ms. Hanqin Xue (*ex officio*).

(*d*) Responsibility of international organizations: Mr. Roman Anatolyevitch Kolodkin (Chairperson), Mr. Giorgio Gaja (Special Rapporteur), Mr. Constantin Economides, Ms. Paula Escarameia, Mr. William Mansfield, Mr. Michael Matheson, Mr. Djamchid Momtaz, Mr. Eduardo Valencia-Ospina, Mr. Chusei Yamada and Ms. Hanqin Xue (*ex officio*).

(*e*) Shared natural resources: Mr. Roman Anatolyevitch Kolodkin (Chairperson), Mr. Chusei Yamada (Special Rapporteur), Mr. Enrique Candioti, Mr. Pedro Comissário Afonso, Mr. Riad Daoudi, Ms. Paula Escarameia, Mr. Salifou Fomba, Mr. Giorgio Gaja, Mr. Zdzislaw Galicki, Mr. William Mansfield, Mr. Michael Matheson, Mr. Guillaume Pambou-Tchivounda and Ms. Hanqin Xue (*ex officio*).

8. The Drafting Committee held a total of 28 meetings on the five topics indicated above.

D. Working Groups

9. At its 2868th, 2877th and 2888th meetings on 2 and 17 May and 5 July 2006 respectively, the Commission also re-established the following Working Groups and Study Group:

(*a*) Working Group on shared natural resources: Mr. Enrique Candioti (Chairperson), Mr. Chusei Yamada (Special Rapporteur), Mr. João Clemente Baena Soares, Mr. Pedro Comissário Afonso, Mr. Riad Daoudi, Ms. Paula Escarameia, Mr. Salifou Fomba, Mr. Giorgio Gaja, Mr. Zdzislaw Galicki, Mr. Peter Kabatsi, Mr. William Mansfield, Mr. Michael Matheson, Mr. Didier Opertti Badan, Mr. Pemmaraju Sreenivasa Rao and Ms. Hanqin Xue (*ex officio*).

(*b*) Study Group on fragmentation of international law: difficulties arising from the diversification and expansion of international law (open-ended)

Chairperson: Mr. Martti Koskenniemi

(*c*) Working Group on unilateral acts of States (open-ended)

Chairperson: Mr. Alain Pellet

10. The Working Group on the long-term programme of work was re-established and was composed of the following members: Mr. Alain Pellet (Chairperson), Mr. João Clemente Baena Soares, Mr. Zdzislaw Galicki, Mr. Maurice Kamto, Mr. Martti Koskenniemi and Ms. Hanqin Xue (*ex officio*).

E. Secretariat

11. Mr. Nicolas Michel, Under-Secretary-General, United Nations Legal Counsel, represented the Secretary-General. Mr. Václav Mikulka, Director of the Codification Division of the Office of Legal Affairs, acted as Secretary to the Commission and, in the absence of the United Nations Legal Counsel, represented the Secretary-General. Ms. Mahnoush H. Arsanjani, Deputy Director of the Codification Division, acted as Deputy Secretary to the Commission. Mr. George Korontzis, Principal Legal Officer, served as Principal Assistant Secretary. Mr. Trevor Chimimba, Senior Legal Officer, served as Senior Assistant Secretary. Mr. Arnold Pronto, Legal Officer, and Mr. Michele Ameri and Mr. Gionata Buzzini, Associate Legal Officers, served as Assistant Secretaries to the Commission.

F. Agenda

12. At its 2867th meeting, the Commission adopted an agenda for its fifty-eighth session consisting of the following items:

1. Organization of work of the session.
2. Diplomatic protection.
3. International liability for injurious consequences arising out of acts not prohibited by international law (International liability in case of loss from transboundary harm arising out of hazardous activities).
4. Responsibility of international organizations.
5. Shared natural resources.
6. Unilateral acts of States.
7. Reservations to treaties.
8. Expulsion of aliens.
9. Effects of armed conflicts on treaties.
10. The obligation to extradite or prosecute (*aut dedere aut judicare*).
11. Fragmentation of international law: difficulties arising from the diversification and expansion of international law.
12. Programme, procedures and working methods of the Commission and its documentation.
13. Cooperation with other bodies.
14. Date and place of the fifty-ninth session.
15. Other business.

Chapter II

SUMMARY OF THE WORK OF THE COMMISSION AT ITS FIFTY-EIGHTH SESSION

13. Concerning the topic "Diplomatic protection", the Commission considered the seventh report of the Special Rapporteur (A/CN.4/567). The Commission subsequently completed the second reading of the topic. The Commission decided, in accordance with article 23 of its Statute, to recommend to the General Assembly the elaboration of a convention on the basis of the draft articles on diplomatic protection (see chapter IV).

14. With regard to the topic "International liability for injurious consequences arising out of acts not prohibited by international law (International liability in case of loss from transboundary harm arising out of hazardous activities)", the Commission considered the third report of the Special Rapporteur (A/CN.4/566). The Commission subsequently completed the second reading of the topic. The Commission decided, in accordance with article 23 of its Statute, to recommend that the General Assembly endorse the draft principles by a resolution and urge States to take national and international action to implement them (see chapter V).

15. Concerning the topic "Shared natural resources", the Commission established a Working Group on transboundary groundwaters to complete the consideration of the draft articles submitted by the Special Rapporteur in his third report;[3] referred 19 revised draft articles to the Drafting Committee; and subsequently adopted on first reading a set of draft articles on the law of transboundary aquifers, together with commentaries (see chapter VI).

16. As regards the topic "Responsibility of international organizations", the Commission considered the fourth report of the Special Rapporteur (A/CN.4/564 and Add.1–2) and adopted 14 draft articles together with commentaries dealing with circumstances precluding wrongfulness and with the responsibility of a State in connection with the act of an international organization (see chapter VII).

17. Concerning the topic "Reservations to treaties", the Commission considered the second part of the Special Rapporteur's tenth report[4] and referred to the Drafting Committee 16 draft guidelines dealing with the definition of the object and purpose of the treaty and the determination of the validity of reservations. The Commission also adopted five draft guidelines dealing with validity of reservations, together with commentaries. In addition, the Commission reconsidered two draft guidelines dealing with the scope of definitions and the procedure in case of manifestly invalid reservations which were previously adopted, in the light of new terminology (see chapter VIII).

18. With regard to the topic "Unilateral acts of States", the Commission considered the ninth report of the Special Rapporteur (A/CN.4/569 and Add.1) which contained 11 draft principles and reconstituted the Working Group on unilateral acts with the mandate to elaborate conclusions and principles on the topic. The Commission adopted a set of 10 guiding principles together with commentaries relating to unilateral declarations of States capable of creating legal obligations, and commended the guiding principles to the attention of the General Assembly (see chapter IX).

19. As regards the topic "Effects of armed conflicts on treaties", the Commission considered the second report of the Special Rapporteur (A/CN.4/570) (see chapter X).

20. Concerning the topic "The obligation to extradite or prosecute (*aut dedere aut judicare*)", the Commission considered the preliminary report of the Special Rapporteur (A/CN.4/571) (see chapter XI).

21. As regards the topic "Fragmentation of international law: difficulties arising from the diversification and expansion of international law", the Commission considered the report of the Study Group (A/CN.4/L.682 and Corr.1 and Add.1) and took note of its 42 conclusions (see chapter XII), which it commended to the attention of the General Assembly. The report and its conclusions were prepared on the basis of an analytical study finalized by the Chairperson of the Study Group, which summarized and analysed the phenomenon of fragmentation taking account of studies prepared by various members of the Study Group, as well as discussion within the Study Group itself. The Commission requested that the analytical study be made available on its website and be published in its *Yearbook*.

22. The Commission established a Planning Group to consider its programme, procedures and working methods (see chapter XIII, section B.2). The Commission reiterated its view that an *a priori* limitation cannot be placed on the length of its documentation; it recommended that the Codification Division prepare the seventh edition of "Work of the International Law Commission", and also decided to include in its long-term programme of work the following topics: "Immunity of State officials from foreign criminal jurisdiction", "Jurisdictional immunity of international organizations", "Protection of persons in the event of disasters", "Protection of personal data in the transborder flow of information" and "Extraterritorial jurisdiction" (see chapter XIII, section B.1).

23. The Commission continued traditional exchanges of information with the International Court of Justice,

[3] *Yearbook ... 2005*, vol. II (Part One), document A/CN.4/551 and Add.1.

[4] *Ibid.*, document A/CN.4/558 and Add 1–2.

the Asian–African Legal Consultative Organization, the European Committee on Legal Cooperation and the Committee of Legal Advisers on Public International Law of the Council of Europe, and the Inter-American Juridical Committee. Members of the Commission also held informal meetings with other bodies and associations on matters of mutual interest (see chapter XIII, section D).

24. A training seminar was held with 25 participants of different nationalities (see chapter XIII, section F).

25. The Commission decided that its next session be held at the United Nations Office in Geneva in two parts, from 7 May to 8 June 2007 and 9 July to 10 August 2007 (see chapter XIII, section C).

Chapter III

SPECIFIC ISSUES ON WHICH COMMENTS WOULD BE OF PARTICULAR INTEREST TO THE COMMISSION

A. Shared natural resources

26. In view of its completion on first reading of the draft articles on the law of transboundary aquifers, the Commission would welcome from Governments:

(*a*) their comments and observations on all aspects of the draft articles;

(*b*) their comments and observations on the commentaries to the draft articles;

(*c*) their views on the final form of the draft articles.

B. Responsibility of international organizations

27. The Commission would welcome comments and observations from Governments and international organizations on draft articles 17 to 30, in particular on those relating to responsibility in case of provision of competence to an international organization (draft article 28) and to responsibility of a State member of an international organization for the internationally wrongful act of that organization (draft article 29).

28. The Commission would also welcome views from Governments and international organizations on the two following questions, due to be addressed in the next report:

(*a*) Do members of an international organization that are not responsible for an internationally wrongful act of that organization have an obligation to provide compensation to the injured party, should the organization not be in a position to do so?

(*b*) According to draft article 41, paragraph 1, on responsibility of States for internationally wrongful acts approved by the Commission at its fifty-third session,[5] when a State commits a serious breach of an obligation under a peremptory norm of general international law, the other States are under an obligation to cooperate to bring the breach to an end through lawful means. Should an international organization commit a similar breach, are States and also other international organizations under an obligation to cooperate to bring the breach to an end?

C. Reservations to treaties

29. The Commission recommended that the Secretariat, in consultation with the Special Rapporteur on reservations to treaties, organize a meeting during the fifty-ninth session of the Commission with United Nations experts in the field of human rights, including representatives of monitoring bodies, in order to discuss issues relating to reservations to human rights treaties. In that perspective, the Commission would appreciate receiving the views of Governments on adjustments that they would consider it necessary or useful to introduce in the "Preliminary conclusions of the International Law Commission on reservations to normative multilateral treaties including human rights treaties", adopted by the Commission at its forty-ninth session.[6]

D. The obligation to extradite or prosecute (*aut dedere aut judicare*)

30. The Commission would welcome any information that Governments may wish to provide concerning their legislation and practice with regard to this topic, particularly more contemporary ones. If possible, such information should concern:

(*a*) international treaties by which a State is bound, containing the obligation to extradite or prosecute, and reservations made by that State to limit the application of this obligation;

(*b*) domestic legal regulations adopted and applied by a State, including constitutional provisions and penal codes or codes of criminal procedures, concerning the obligation to extradite or prosecute (*aut dedere aut judicare*);

(*c*) judicial practice of a State reflecting the application of the obligation *aut dedere aut judicare*;

(*d*) crimes or offences to which the principle of the obligation *aut dedere aut judicare* is applied in the legislation or practice of a State.

31. The Commission would also welcome any further information that Governments may consider relevant to the topic.

E. Other decisions and conclusions of the Commission

32. With regard to the long-term programme of work, the Commission would welcome the views of Governments on the following (para. 33).

[5] *Yearbook ... 2001*, vol. II (Part Two) and corrigendum, p. 113.

[6] *Yearbook ... 1997*, vol. II (Part Two), pp. 56–57, para. 157.

33. In 1978, the Commission adopted draft articles on most-favoured-nation clauses.[7] In view of the circumstances at the time, the General Assembly took no action with respect to this draft, which clearly is out of date in many aspects today. Some members of the Commission believe that the topic should not be reopened in the Commission at this time, in that the basic policy differences that caused the General Assembly to take no action on the Commission's draft articles have not yet been resolved, and should first be dealt with in international forums that have the necessary technical expertise and policy mandate. Other members consider that, given the changes in the international situation and the continued importance of the most-favoured-nation clause in contemporary treaties, in particular in the fields of trade law and international investments, the time has come to undertake further work on the question and therefore to include the topic in the Commission's long-term programme of work.

[7] *Yearbook ... 1978*, vol. II (Part Two), pp. 16–73, para. 74.

Chapter IV

DIPLOMATIC PROTECTION

A. Introduction

34. At its forty-seventh session (1995), the Commission endorsed the recommendation of the Working Group on the long-term programme of work in favour of the topic, and decided, subject to the approval of the General Assembly, to include it on its agenda.[8] At its forty-eighth session (1996), the Commission identified "Diplomatic protection" as one of three topics appropriate for codification and progressive development.[9] The General Assembly, in its resolution 51/160 of 16 December 1996, subsequently invited the Commission further to examine the topic and to indicate its scope and content in the light of the comments and observations made during the debate in the Sixth Committee and any written comments that Governments might wish to make.[10]

35. At its 2510th meeting, on 11 July 1997, the Commission appointed Mr. Mohamed Bennouna Special Rapporteur for the topic.[11]

36. The General Assembly, in resolution 52/156 of 15 December 1997, endorsed the decision of the Commission to include in its agenda the topic "Diplomatic protection".

37. At its fiftieth session (1998), the Commission had before it the preliminary report of the Special Rapporteur.[12]

38. At its fifty-first session (1999), the Commission appointed Mr. Christopher John Robert Dugard, Special Rapporteur for the topic,[13] after Mr. Bennouna was elected a judge of the International Tribunal for the Former Yugoslavia.

39. The Special Rapporteur subsequently submitted five reports[14] from the fifty-second (2000) to fifty-sixth sessions (2004) of the Commission. At its fifty-sixth session, in 2004, the Commission adopted on first reading a set of 19 draft articles on diplomatic protection together with commentaries.[15] At the same session, the Commission decided, in accordance with draft articles 16 and 21 of its Statute, to transmit the draft articles, through the Secretary-General, to Governments for comments and observations, with the request that such comments and observations be submitted to the Secretary-General by 1 January 2006.[16]

40. At its fifty-seventh session, in 2005, the Commission had before it the sixth report of the Special Rapporteur, dealing with the clean hands doctrine.[17]

B. Consideration of the topic at the present session

41. At the present session, the Commission had before it comments and observations received from Governments on the draft articles adopted on first reading in 2004 (A/CN.4/561 and Add.1–2),[18] as well as the seventh report of the Special Rapporteur (A/CN.4/567), containing proposals for the consideration of draft articles 1 to 19 on second reading, as well as a proposal for an additional draft article, in light of the comments and observations received from Governments. The Commission considered the report of the Special Rapporteur at its 2867th to 2871st meetings, held from 1 to 5 May 2006.

---

[8] *Yearbook ... 1995*, vol. II (Part Two), p. 110, para. 501. The General Assembly, in resolution 50/45 of 11 December 1995, noted the Commission's suggestion to include the topic on its agenda.

[9] *Yearbook ... 1996*, vol. II (Part Two), document A/51/10, p. 97–98, para. 248 and annex II, addendum 1, p. 137.

[10] See A/51/358 and Add.1. Pursuant to General Assembly resolution 51/160, the Commission established a Working Group on the topic at its forty-ninth session (*Yearbook ... 1997*, vol. II (Part Two), p. 60, para. 169). The Working Group submitted a report at the same session, which was endorsed by the Commission (*ibid.*, para. 171). The Working Group proposed an outline for consideration of the topic, which the Commission recommended be used as the basis for the submission of a preliminary report by the Special Rapporteur (*ibid.*, pp. 62–63, paras. 189–190).

[11] *Yearbook ... 1997*, vol. II (Part Two), p. 63, para. 190.

[12] *Yearbook ... 1998*, vol. II (Part One), document A/CN.4/484, p. 309. At the same session, the Commission established an open-ended Working Group to consider possible conclusions that might be drawn on the basis of the discussion on the approach to the topic (see the conclusions of the Working Group, *ibid.*, vol. II (Part Two), p. 49, para. 108).

[13] *Yearbook ... 1999*, vol. II (Part Two), document A/54/10, p. 17, para. 19.

[14] Preliminary report: *Yearbook ... 2000*, vol. II (Part One), document A/CN.4/506 and Add.1 (draft articles 1–9); second report: *Yearbook ... 2001*, vol. II (Part One), document A/CN.4/514 (draft articles 10–13); third report: *Yearbook ... 2002*, vol. II (Part One), document A/CN.4/523 and Add.1 (draft articles 14–16); fourth report: *Yearbook ... 2003*, vol. II (Part One), document A/CN.4/530 and Add.1 (draft articles 17–22); and fifth report: *Yearbook ... 2004*, vol. II (Part One), document A/CN.4/538 (draft articles 23–27). During this period, the Commission established three informal consultations: on draft articles 1, 3 and 6 (at its fifty-second session, in 2000) (see *Yearbook ... 2000*, vol. II (Part Two), pp. 85–86, para. 495)), on draft article 9 (at its fifty-third session, in 2001) (see *Yearbook ... 2001*, vol. II (Part Two) and corrigendum, p. 196, para. 166) and on the question of the diplomatic protection of crews as well as that of corporations and shareholders (at its fifty-fourth session, in 2002) (see *Yearbook ... 2002*, vol. II (Part Two), p. 50, para. 113). The Commission further established a Working Group at its fifty-fifth session, in 2003, to consider draft article 17, paragraph (2) (see *Yearbook ... 2003*, vol. II (Part Two), p. 27, paras. 90–92).

[15] *Yearbook ... 2004*, vol. II (Part Two), pp. 18–44, paras. 59–60.

[16] *Ibid.*, p. 18, para. 57.

[17] *Yearbook ... 2005*, vol. II (Part One), document A/CN.4/546. The Commission further considered several other issues related to the draft articles adopted on first reading in 2004 (*ibid.*, vol, II (Part Two), paras. 237–241).

[18] A set of comments and observations were also submitted by Kuwait on 1 August 2006. The Commission did not have the opportunity to consider these comments and observations as they were received after the adoption of the draft articles on second reading. Those comments and observations are contained in A/CN.4/575.

42. At its 2871st meeting, the Commission instructed the Drafting Committee to commence the second reading of the draft articles taking into account the comments of Governments, the proposals of the Special Rapporteur and the debate in the plenary on the Special Rapporteur's seventh report. The Commission further decided to refer to the Drafting Committee the Special Rapporteur's proposal for an additional draft article.

43. The Commission considered the report of the Drafting Committee (A/CN.4/L.684 and Corr.1–2) at its 2881st meeting, held on 30 May 2006, and adopted the entire set of draft articles on diplomatic protection, on second reading, at the same meeting.

44. At its 2906th to 2909th meetings, held on 4, 7 and 8 August 2006, the Commission adopted the commentaries to the aforementioned draft articles.

45. In accordance with its Statute, the Commission submitted the draft articles to the General Assembly, together with the recommendation set out below.

C. Recommendation of the Commission

46. At its 2909th meeting, the Commission decided in accordance with article 23 of its Statute, to recommend to the General Assembly the elaboration of a convention on the basis of the draft articles on diplomatic protection.

D. Tribute to the Special Rapporteur

47. Also at its 2909th meeting, the Commission, after adopting the draft articles on diplomatic protection, adopted the following resolution by acclamation:

The International Law Commission,

Having adopted the draft articles on diplomatic protection,

Expresses to the Special Rapporteur, Mr. Christopher John Robert Dugard, its deep appreciation and warm congratulations for the outstanding contribution he has made to the preparation of the draft articles through his tireless efforts and devoted work, and for the results achieved in the elaboration of draft articles on diplomatic protection.

48. The Commission also expressed its deep appreciation to the previous Special Rapporteur, Mr. Mohammed Bennouna, for his valuable contribution to the work on the topic.

E. Text of the draft articles on diplomatic protection

1. Text of the draft articles

49. The text of the draft articles adopted by the Commission at its fifty-eighth session is reproduced below.

DIPLOMATIC PROTECTION

PART ONE

GENERAL PROVISIONS

Article 1. Definition and scope

For the purposes of the present draft articles, diplomatic protection consists of the invocation by a State, through diplomatic action or other means of peaceful settlement, of the responsibility of another State for an injury caused by an internationally wrongful act of that State to a natural or legal person that is a national of the former State with a view to the implementation of such responsibility.

Article 2. Right to exercise diplomatic protection

A State has the right to exercise diplomatic protection in accordance with the present draft articles.

PART TWO

NATIONALITY

CHAPTER I

GENERAL PRINCIPLES

Article 3. Protection by the State of nationality

1. The State entitled to exercise diplomatic protection is the State of nationality.

2. Notwithstanding paragraph 1, diplomatic protection may be exercised by a State in respect of a person that is not its national in accordance with draft article 8.

CHAPTER II

NATURAL PERSONS

Article 4. State of nationality of a natural person

For the purposes of the diplomatic protection of a natural person, a State of nationality means a State whose nationality that person has acquired, in accordance with the law of that State, by birth, descent, naturalization, succession of States or in any other manner, not inconsistent with international law.

Article 5. Continuous nationality of a natural person

1. A State is entitled to exercise diplomatic protection in respect of a person who was a national of that State continuously from the date of injury to the date of the official presentation of the claim. Continuity is presumed if that nationality existed at both these dates.

2. Notwithstanding paragraph 1, a State may exercise diplomatic protection in respect of a person who is its national at the date of the official presentation of the claim but was not a national at the date of injury, provided that the person had the nationality of a predecessor State or lost his or her previous nationality and acquired, for a reason unrelated to the bringing of the claim, the nationality of the former State in a manner not inconsistent with international law.

3. Diplomatic protection shall not be exercised by the present State of nationality in respect of a person against a former State of nationality of that person for an injury caused when that person was a national of the former State of nationality and not of the present State of nationality.

4. A State is no longer entitled to exercise diplomatic protection in respect of a person who acquires the nationality of the State against which the claim is brought after the date of the official presentation of the claim.

Article 6. Multiple nationality and claim against a third State

1. Any State of which a dual or multiple national is a national may exercise diplomatic protection in respect of that national against a State of which that person is not a national.

2. Two or more States of nationality may jointly exercise diplomatic protection in respect of a dual or multiple national.

Article 7. Multiple nationality and claim against a State of nationality

A State of nationality may not exercise diplomatic protection in respect of a person against a State of which that person is also a national unless the nationality of the former State is predominant, both at the date of injury and at the date of the official presentation of the claim.

Article 8. Stateless persons and refugees

1. A State may exercise diplomatic protection in respect of a stateless person who, at the date of injury and at the date of the official presentation of the claim, is lawfully and habitually resident in that State.

2. A State may exercise diplomatic protection in respect of a person who is recognized as a refugee by that State, in accordance with internationally accepted standards, when that person, at the date of injury and at the date of the official presentation of the claim, is lawfully and habitually resident in that State.

3. Paragraph 2 does not apply in respect of an injury caused by an internationally wrongful act of the State of nationality of the refugee.

Chapter III

LEGAL PERSONS

Article 9. State of nationality of a corporation

For the purposes of the diplomatic protection of a corporation, the State of nationality means the State under whose law the corporation was incorporated. However, when the corporation is controlled by nationals of another State or States and has no substantial business activities in the State of incorporation, and the seat of management and the financial control of the corporation are both located in another State, that State shall be regarded as the State of nationality.

Article 10. Continuous nationality of a corporation

1. A State is entitled to exercise diplomatic protection in respect of a corporation that was a national of that State, or its predecessor State, continuously from the date of injury to the date of the official presentation of the claim. Continuity is presumed if that nationality existed at both these dates.

2. A State is no longer entitled to exercise diplomatic protection in respect of a corporation that acquires the nationality of the State against which the claim is brought after the presentation of the claim.

3. Notwithstanding paragraph 1, a State continues to be entitled to exercise diplomatic protection in respect of a corporation which was its national at the date of injury and which, as the result of the injury, has ceased to exist according to the law of the State of incorporation.

Article 11. Protection of shareholders

A State of nationality of shareholders in a corporation shall not be entitled to exercise diplomatic protection in respect of such shareholders in the case of an injury to the corporation unless:

(*a*) The corporation has ceased to exist according to the law of the State of incorporation for a reason unrelated to the injury; or

(*b*) The corporation had, at the date of injury, the nationality of the State alleged to be responsible for causing the injury, and incorporation in that State was required by it as a precondition for doing business there.

Article 12. Direct injury to shareholders

To the extent that an internationally wrongful act of a State causes direct injury to the rights of shareholders as such, as distinct from those of the corporation itself, the State of nationality of any such shareholders is entitled to exercise diplomatic protection in respect of its nationals.

Article 13. Other legal persons

The principles contained in this chapter shall be applicable, as appropriate, to the diplomatic protection of legal persons other than corporations.

Part Three

LOCAL REMEDIES

Article 14. Exhaustion of local remedies

1. A State may not present an international claim in respect of an injury to a national or other person referred to in draft article 8 before the injured person has, subject to draft article 15, exhausted all local remedies.

2. "Local remedies" means legal remedies which are open to an injured person before the judicial or administrative courts or bodies, whether ordinary or special, of the State alleged to be responsible for causing the injury.

3. Local remedies shall be exhausted where an international claim, or request for a declaratory judgement related to the claim, is brought preponderantly on the basis of an injury to a national or other person referred to in draft article 8.

Article 15. Exceptions to the local remedies rule

Local remedies do not need to be exhausted where:

(*a*) there are no reasonably available local remedies to provide effective redress, or the local remedies provide no reasonable possibility of such redress;

(*b*) there is undue delay in the remedial process which is attributable to the State alleged to be responsible;

(*c*) there was no relevant connection between the injured person and the State alleged to be responsible at the date of injury;

(*d*) the injured person is manifestly precluded from pursuing local remedies; or

(*e*) the State alleged to be responsible has waived the requirement that local remedies be exhausted.

Part Four

MISCELLANEOUS PROVISIONS

Article 16. Actions or procedures other than diplomatic protection

The rights of States, natural persons, legal persons or other entities to resort under international law to actions or procedures other than diplomatic protection to secure redress for injury suffered as a result of an internationally wrongful act, are not affected by the present draft articles.

Article 17. Special rules of international law

The present draft articles do not apply to the extent that they are inconsistent with special rules of international law, such as treaty provisions for the protection of investments.

Article 18. Protection of ships' crews

The right of the State of nationality of the members of the crew of a ship to exercise diplomatic protection is not affected by the right of the State of nationality of a ship to seek redress on behalf of such crew members, irrespective of their nationality, when they have been injured in connection with an injury to the vessel resulting from an internationally wrongful act.

Article 19. Recommended practice

A State entitled to exercise diplomatic protection according to the present draft articles, should:

(*a*) give due consideration to the possibility of exercising diplomatic protection, especially when a significant injury has occurred;

(*b*) take into account, wherever feasible, the views of injured persons with regard to resort to diplomatic protection and the reparation to be sought; and

(*c*) transfer to the injured person any compensation obtained for the injury from the responsible State subject to any reasonable deductions.

2. Text of the draft articles with commentaries thereto

50. The text of the draft articles with commentaries thereto adopted by the Commission at its fifty-eighth session are reproduced below.

DIPLOMATIC PROTECTION

(1) The drafting of articles on diplomatic protection was originally seen as belonging to the study on State responsibility. Indeed, the first Special Rapporteur on State responsibility, Mr. F. V. García-Amador, included a number of draft articles on this subject in his reports presented from 1956 to 1961.[19] The subsequent codification of State responsibility paid little attention to diplomatic protection and the final draft articles on this subject expressly state that the two topics central to diplomatic protection—nationality of claims and the exhaustion of local remedies—would be dealt with more extensively by the Commission in a separate undertaking.[20] Nevertheless, there is a close connection between the articles on responsibility of States for internationally wrongful acts and the present draft articles. Many of the principles contained in the articles on responsibility of States for internationally wrongful acts are relevant to diplomatic protection and are therefore not repeated in the present draft articles. This applies in particular to the provisions dealing with the legal consequences of an internationally wrongful act. A State responsible for injuring a foreign national is obliged to cease the wrongful conduct and to make full reparation for the injury caused by the internationally wrongful act. This reparation may take the form of restitution, compensation or satisfaction, either singly or in combination. All these matters are dealt with in the articles on responsibility of States for internationally wrongful acts. [21]

(2) Diplomatic protection belongs to the subject of "Treatment of aliens". No attempt is made, however, to deal with the primary rules on this subject—that is, the rules governing the treatment of the person and property of aliens, breach of which gives rise to responsibility to the State of nationality of the injured person. Instead, the present draft articles are confined to secondary rules only: the rules that relate to the conditions that must be met for the bringing of a claim for diplomatic protection. By and large this means rules governing the admissibility of claims. Article 44 of the articles on responsibility of States for internationally wrongful acts provides:

The responsibility of a State may not be invoked if:

(*a*) the claim is not brought in accordance with any applicable rule relating to the nationality of claims;

(*b*) The claim is one to which the rule of exhaustion of local remedies applies and any available and effective local remedy has not been exhausted.[22]

The present draft articles give content to this provision by elaborating on the rules relating to the nationality of claims and the exhaustion of local remedies.

(3) The present draft articles do not deal with the protection of an agent by an international organization, generally described as "functional protection". Although there are similarities between functional protection and diplomatic protection, there are also important differences. Diplomatic protection is traditionally a mechanism designed to secure reparation for injury to the national of a State premised largely on the principle that an injury to a national is an injury to the State itself. Functional protection, on the other hand, is an institution for promoting the efficient functioning of an international organization by ensuring respect for its agents and their independence. Differences of this kind have led the Commission to conclude that protection of an agent by an international organization does not belong in a set of draft articles on diplomatic protection. The question whether a State may exercise diplomatic protection in respect of a national who is an agent of an international organization was answered by the ICJ in the *Reparation for Injuries* case: "In such a case, there is no rule of law which assigns priority to the one or to the other, or which compels either the State or the Organization to refrain from bringing an international claim. The Court sees no reason why the parties concerned should not find solutions inspired by goodwill and common sense".[23]

Part One

GENERAL PROVISIONS

Article 1. Definition and scope

For the purposes of the present draft articles, diplomatic protection consists of the invocation by a State, through diplomatic action or other means of peaceful settlement, of the responsibility of another State for an injury caused by an internationally wrongful act of that State to a natural or legal person that is a national of the former State with a view to the implementation of such responsibility.

Commentary

(1) Draft article 1 makes no attempt to provide a complete and comprehensive definition of diplomatic protection. Instead it describes the salient features of diplomatic protection in the sense in which the term is used in the present draft articles.

---

[19] Preliminary report: *Yearbook ... 1956*, vol. II, document A/CN.4/96, pp. 173–231; second report: *Yearbook ... 1957*, vol. II, document A/CN.4/106, pp. 104–130; third report: *Yearbook ... 1958*, vol. II, document A/CN.4/111, pp. 47–73; fourth report: *Yearbook ... 1959*, vol. II, document A/CN.4/119, pp. 1–36: fifth report: *Yearbook ... 1960*, vol. II, document A/CN.4/125, pp. 41–68; and sixth report: *Yearbook ... 1961*, vol. II, document A/CN.4/134 and Add.1, pp. 1–54.

[20] *Yearbook ... 2001*, vol. II (Part Two) and corrigendum, p. 121 (commentary to article 44, footnotes 683 and 687).

[21] Articles 28, 30, 31 and 34–37 (*ibid.*, pp. 87–94 and 95–107). Much of the commentary on compensation (art. 36) is devoted to a consideration of the principles applicable to claims concerning diplomatic protection.

[22] *Yearbook ... 2001*, vol. II (Part Two) and corrigendum, p. 29, para. 76.

[23] *Reparation for Injuries Suffered in the Service of the United Nations, Advisory Opinion, I.C.J. Reports 1949*, p. 174 at pp. 185–186.

(2) Under international law, a State is responsible for injury to an alien caused by its wrongful act or omission. Diplomatic protection is the procedure employed by the State of nationality of the injured persons to secure protection of that person and to obtain reparation for the internationally wrongful act inflicted. The present draft articles are concerned only with the rules governing the circumstances in which diplomatic protection may be exercised and the conditions that must be met before it may be exercised. They do not seek to define or describe the internationally wrongful acts that give rise to the responsibility of the State for injury to an alien. The draft articles, like those on the responsibility of States for internationally wrongful acts, maintain the distinction between primary and secondary rules and deal only with the latter.[24]

(3) Diplomatic protection has traditionally been seen as an exclusive State right in the sense that a State exercises diplomatic protection in its own right because an injury to a national is deemed to be an injury to the State itself. This approach has its roots, first in a statement by the Swiss jurist Emmerich de Vattel in 1758 that "[w]hoever ill-treats a citizen indirectly injures the State, which must protect that citizen",[25] and, secondly in a dictum of the PCIJ in 1924 in the *Mavrommatis* case that "[b]y taking up the case of one of its subjects and by resorting to diplomatic action or international judicial proceedings on his behalf, a State is in reality asserting its own right—its right to ensure, in the person of its subjects, respect for the rules of international law".[26] Obviously it is a fiction—and an exaggeration[27]—to say that an injury to a national is an injury to the State itself. Many of the rules of diplomatic protection contradict the correctness of this fiction, notably the rule of continuous nationality which requires a State to prove that the injured national remained its national after the injury itself and up to the date of the presentation of the claim. A State does not "in reality"—to quote *Mavrommatis*—assert its own right only. "In reality", it also asserts the right of its injured national.

(4) In the early years of international law the individual had no place, no rights in the international legal order. Consequently, if a national injured abroad was to be protected, this could be done only by means of a fiction—that an injury to the national was an injury to the State itself. This fiction was, however, no more than a means to an end, the end being the protection of the rights of an injured national. Today the situation has changed dramatically. The individual is the subject of many primary rules of international law, both under custom and treaty, which protect him at home, against his own Government, and abroad, against foreign Governments. This has been recognized by the ICJ in the *LaGrand*[28] and *Avena* cases.[29] This protection is not limited to personal rights. Bilateral investment treaties confer rights and protection on both legal and natural persons in respect of their property rights. The individual has rights under international law but remedies are few. Diplomatic protection conducted by a State at the inter-State level remains an important remedy for the protection of persons whose human rights have been violated abroad.

(5) Draft article 1 is formulated in such a way as to leave open the question whether the State exercising diplomatic protection does so in its own right or that of its national—or both. It views diplomatic protection through the prism of State responsibility and emphasizes that it is a procedure for securing the responsibility of the State for injury to the national flowing from an internationally wrongful act.

(6) Draft article 1 deliberately follows the language of the articles on responsibility of States for internationally wrongful acts.[30] It describes diplomatic protection as the invocation of the responsibility of a State that has committed an internationally wrongful act in respect of a national of another State, by the State of which that person is a national, with a view to implementing responsibility. As a claim brought within the context of State responsibility it is an inter-State claim, although it may result in the assertion of rights enjoyed by the injured national under international law.

(7) As draft article 1 is definitional by nature, it does not cover exceptions. Thus no mention is made of the stateless persons and refugees referred to in draft article 8 in this provision. Draft article 3 does, however, make it clear that diplomatic protection may be exercised in respect of such persons.

(8) Diplomatic protection must be exercised by lawful and peaceful means. Several judicial decisions draw a distinction between "diplomatic action" and "judicial proceedings" when describing the action that may be taken by a State when it resorts to diplomatic protection.[31] Draft article 1 retains this distinction but goes further by subsuming judicial proceedings under "other means of peaceful settlement". "Diplomatic action" covers all the lawful procedures employed by a State to inform another State of its views and concerns, including protest and request for an inquiry or for negotiations aimed at the settlement of disputes. "Other means of peaceful settlement" embraces all forms of lawful dispute settlement, from negotiation, mediation and conciliation, to arbitral and judicial dispute settlement. The use of force, prohibited by Article 2, para-

[24] See *Yearbook ... 2001*, vol. II (Part Two) and corrigendum, p. 31 (general commentary, paras. (1)–(3)).

[25] E. de Vattel, *The Law of Nations or the Principles of Natural Law Applied to the Conduct and to the Affairs of Nations and of Sovereigns* (1758), English translation by C. G. Fenwick, Washington D.C., Carnegie Institution, 1916, vol. III, book II, chap. VI, p. 136.

[26] *Mavrommatis Palestine Concessions, Judgment No. 2, 1924, PCIJ, Series A, No. 2*, p. 12. This dictum was repeated by the PCIJ in *Panevezyś-Saldutiskis Railway, Judgment, 1939, PCIJ, Series A/B, No. 76*, p. 4, at p. 16.

[27] See J. L. Brierly, *The Law of Nations: An Introduction to the International Law of Peace*, 6th edition edited by Sir Humphrey Waldock, Oxford, Clarendon Press, 1963, at pp. 276–277.

[28] *La Grand (Germany* v. *United States of America), Judgment, I.C.J. Reports 2001*, p. 466, at pp. 493–494, paras. 76–77.

[29] *Avena and Other Mexican Nationals (Mexico* v. *United States of America), Judgment of 31 March 2004, I.C.J. Reports 2004*, p. 12, at pp. 35–36, para. 40.

[30] See Chapter I of Part Three entitled "Invocation of the Responsibility of a State" (articles 42–48), *Yearbook ... 2001*, vol. II (Part Two) and corrigendum, pp. 116–128. Part Three itself is entitled "The Implementation of the International Responsibility of a State".

[31] *Mavrommatis Palestine Concessions* (see footnote 26 above); *Panevezyś-Saldutiskis Railway* (*ibid.*); *Nottebohm (Liechtenstein* v. *Guatemala), Second Phase, Judgment of 6 April 1955, I.C.J. Reports 1955*, p. 4, at p. 24.

graph 4, of the Charter of the United Nations, is not a permissible method for the enforcement of the right of diplomatic protection. Diplomatic protection does not include *démarches* or other diplomatic action that do not involve the invocation of the legal responsibility of another State, such as informal requests for corrective action.

(9) Diplomatic protection may be exercised through diplomatic action or other means of peaceful settlement. It differs from consular assistance in that it is conducted by the representatives of the State acting in the interest of the State in terms of a rule of general international law, whereas consular assistance is, in most instances, carried out by consular officers, who represent the interests of the individual, acting in accordance with the Vienna Convention on Consular Relations. Diplomatic protection is essentially remedial and is designed to remedy an internationally wrongful act that has been committed, while consular assistance is largely preventive and mainly aims at preventing the national from being subjected to an internationally wrongful act.

(10) Although it is in theory possible to distinguish between diplomatic protection and consular assistance, in practice this task is difficult. This is illustrated by the requirement of the exhaustion of local remedies. Clearly there is no need to exhaust local remedies in the case of consular assistance, as this assistance takes place before the commission of an internationally wrongful act. Logically, as diplomatic protection arises only after the commission of an internationally wrongful act, it would seem that local remedies must always be exhausted, subject to the exceptions described in draft article 15.

(11) In these circumstances, draft article 1 makes no attempt to distinguish between diplomatic protection and consular assistance. The draft articles prescribe conditions for the exercise of diplomatic protection which are not applicable to consular assistance. This means that the circumstances of each case must be considered in order to decide whether it involves diplomatic protection or consular assistance.

(12) Draft article 1 makes clear the point, already raised in the general commentary,[32] that the present draft articles deal only with the exercise of diplomatic protection by a State and not with the protection afforded to its agent by an international organization.[33]

(13) Diplomatic protection mainly covers the protection of nationals not engaged in official international business on behalf of the State. These officials are protected by other rules of international law and instruments, such as the Vienna Convention on Diplomatic Relations of 1961 and the Vienna Convention on Consular Relations of 1963. Where, however, diplomats or consuls are injured in respect of activities outside their functions, they are covered by the rules relating to diplomatic protection, as, for instance, in the case of the expropriation without compensation of property privately owned by a diplomatic official in the country to which he or she is accredited.

[32] See general commentary above, paragraph (3).

[33] *Reparation for Injuries* (see footnote 23 above).

(14) In most circumstances, it is the link of nationality between the State and the injured person that gives rise to the exercise of diplomatic protection, a matter that is dealt with in draft articles 4 and 9. The term "national" in this article covers both natural and legal persons. Later in the draft articles, a distinction is drawn between the rules governing natural and legal persons, and, where necessary, the two concepts are treated separately.

Article 2. Right to exercise diplomatic protection

A State has the right to exercise diplomatic protection in accordance with the present draft articles.

Commentary

(1) Draft article 2 is founded on the notion that diplomatic protection involves an invocation—at the State level—by a State of the responsibility of another State for an injury caused by an internationally wrongful act of that State to a national of the former State. It recognizes that it is the State that initiates and exercises diplomatic protection, that it is the entity in which the right to bring a claim vests. It is without prejudice to the question of whose rights the State seeks to assert in the process—its own right or the rights of the injured national on whose behalf it acts. Like article 1,[34] it is neutral on this subject.

(2) A State has the right to exercise diplomatic protection on behalf of a national. It is under no duty or obligation to do so. The internal law of a State may oblige a State to extend diplomatic protection to a national, but international law imposes no such obligation. The position was clearly stated by the ICJ in the *Barcelona Traction* case:

> within the limits prescribed by international law, a State may exercise diplomatic protection by whatever means and to whatever extent it thinks fit, for it is its own right that the State is asserting. Should the natural or legal person on whose behalf it is acting consider that their rights are not adequately protected, they have no remedy in international law. All they can do is to resort to municipal law, if means are available, with a view to furthering their cause or obtaining redress. ... The State must be viewed as the sole judge to decide whether its protection will be granted, to what extent it is granted, and when it will cease. It retains in this respect a discretionary power the exercise of which may be determined by considerations of a political or other nature, unrelated to the particular case.[35]

(3) Today there is support in domestic legislation[36] and judicial decisions[37] for the view that there is some obligation, however limited, either under national law or international law, on the State to protect its nationals abroad when they have been subjected to serious

[34] See, above, commentary to article 1, paragraphs (3) to (5).

[35] *Barcelona Traction, Light and Power Company, Limited, Second Phase, Judgment, I.C.J. Reports 1970*, p. 3, at p. 44.

[36] See the preliminary report of the Special Rapporteur on diplomatic protection, *Yearbook ... 2000*, vol. II (Part One), document A/CN.4/506 and Add.1, paras. 80–87.

[37] *Rudolf Hess* case, *ILR*, vol. 90 (1992), p. 387; *Abbasi and Juma* v. *Secretary of State for Foreign and Commonwealth Affairs and Secretary of State for the Home Department, Decision of the Supreme Court of Judicature—Court of Appeal (Civil Division) of 6 November 2002,* ILM, vol. 42 (2003), p. 358; *Kaunda and Others* v. *President of the Republic of South Africa and Others, Constitutional Court Decision of 19 and 20 July 2004 and 4 August 2004, The South African Law Reports 2005*, p. 235 (judgement reproduced in ILM, vol. 44 (January 2005), p. 173).

violation of their human rights. Consequently, draft article 19 declares that a State entitled to exercise diplomatic protection "*should** ... give due consideration to the possibility of exercising diplomatic protection, especially when a significant injury has occurred". The discretionary right of a State to exercise diplomatic protection should therefore be read with draft article 19 which recommends to States that they should exercise that right in appropriate cases.

(4) Draft article 2 deals with the right of the State to exercise diplomatic protection. It makes no attempt to describe the corresponding obligation on the respondent State to consider the assertion of diplomatic protection by a State in accordance with the present articles. This is to be implied, however.

Part Two

NATIONALITY

Chapter I

GENERAL PRINCIPLES

Article 3. Protection by the State of nationality

1. The State entitled to exercise diplomatic protection is the State of nationality.

2. Notwithstanding paragraph 1, diplomatic protection may be exercised by a State in respect of a person that is not its national in accordance with draft article 8.

Commentary

(1) Whereas draft article 2 affirms the discretionary right of the State to exercise diplomatic protection, draft article 3 asserts the principle that it is the State of nationality of the injured person that is entitled, but not obliged, to exercise diplomatic protection on behalf of such a person. The emphasis in this draft article is on the bond of nationality between State and national which entitles the State to exercise diplomatic protection. This bond differs in the cases of natural persons and legal persons. Consequently separate chapters are devoted to these different types of persons.

(2) Paragraph 2 refers to the exception contained in draft article 8 which provides for diplomatic protection in the case of stateless persons and refugees.

Chapter II

NATURAL PERSONS

Article 4. State of nationality of a natural person

For the purposes of the diplomatic protection of a natural person, a State of nationality means a State whose nationality that person has acquired, in accordance with the law of that State, by birth, descent, naturalization, succession of States or in any other manner, not inconsistent with international law.

Commentary

(1) Draft article 4 defines the State of nationality for the purposes of diplomatic protection of natural persons. This definition is premised on two principles: first, that it is for the State of nationality to determine, in accordance with its municipal law, who is to qualify for its nationality; secondly, that there are limits imposed by international law on the grant of nationality. Draft article 4 also provides a non-exhaustive list of connecting factors that usually constitute good grounds for the grant of nationality.

(2) The principle that it is for each State to decide in accordance with its law who are its nationals is backed by both judicial decisions and treaties. In 1923, the PCIJ stated in the *Nationality Decrees Issued in Tunis and Morocco* case that "in the present state of international law, questions of nationality are ... in principle within this reserved domain".[38] This principle was confirmed by article 1 of the Convention on Certain Questions relating to the Conflict of Nationality Laws: "It is for each State to determine under its own law who are its nationals." More recently it has been endorsed by the 1997 European Convention on Nationality (art. 3).

(3) The connecting factors for the conferment of nationality listed in draft article 4 are illustrative and not exhaustive. Nevertheless, they include the connecting factors most commonly employed by States for the grant of nationality: birth (*jus soli*), descent (*jus sanguinis*) and naturalization. Marriage to a national is not included in this list as in most circumstances marriage *per se* is insufficient for the grant of nationality: it requires in addition a period of residence, following which nationality is conferred by naturalization. Where marriage to a national automatically results in the acquisition by a spouse of the nationality of the other spouse, problems may arise in respect of the consistency of such an acquisition of nationality with international law.[39] Nationality may also be acquired as a result of the succession of States.[40]

(4) The connecting factors listed in draft article 4 are those most frequently used by States to establish nationality. In some countries, where there are no clear birth records, it may be difficult to prove nationality. In such cases, residence could provide proof of nationality, although it may not constitute a basis for nationality itself. A State may, however, confer nationality on such persons by means of naturalization.

(5) Draft article 4 does not require a State to prove an effective or genuine link between itself and its national,

---

[38] *Nationality Decrees Issued in Tunis and Morocco (French Zone), Advisory Opinion, P.C.I.J. Reports, Series B, No. 4*, 1923, p. 6, at p. 24.

[39] See, e.g., article 9, paragraph 1 of the Convention on the Elimination of All Forms of Discrimination against Women and article 1 of the Convention on the nationality of married women, which prohibit the acquisition of nationality in such circumstances. See also paragraph (6) of this commentary below.

[40] See the draft articles on nationality of natural persons in relation to the succession of States, *Yearbook ... 1999*, vol. II (Part Two), p. 20, para. 47.

along the lines suggested in the *Nottebohm* case,[41] as an additional factor for the exercise of diplomatic protection, even where the national possesses only one nationality. Despite divergent views as to the interpretation of the case, the Commission took the view that there were certain factors that served to limit *Nottebohm* to the facts of the case in question, particularly the fact that the ties between Mr. Nottebohm and Liechtenstein (the applicant State) were "extremely tenuous"[42] compared with the close ties between Mr. Nottebohm and Guatemala (the respondent State) for a period of over 34 years, which led the ICJ to repeatedly assert that Liechtenstein was "not entitled to extend its protection to Nottebohm *vis-à-vis* Guatemala".[43] This suggests that the Court did not intend to expound a general rule[44] applicable to all States, but only a relative rule according to which a State in Liechtenstein's position was required to show a genuine link between itself and Mr. Nottebohm in order to permit it to claim on his behalf against Guatemala with whom he had extremely close ties. Moreover, it is necessary to be mindful of the fact that if the genuine link requirement proposed by *Nottebohm* was strictly applied, it would exclude millions of persons from the benefit of diplomatic protection. Indeed, in today's world of economic globalization and migration, there are millions of persons who have moved away from their State of nationality and made their lives in States whose nationality they never acquire, or have acquired nationality by birth or descent from States with which they have a tenuous connection.

(6) The final phrase in draft article 4 stresses that the acquisition of nationality must not be inconsistent with international law. Although a State has the right to decide who are its nationals, this right is not absolute. Article 1 of the 1930 Convention on Certain Questions relating to the Conflict of Nationality Laws confirmed this by qualifying the provision that "[i]t is for each State to determine under its own law who are its nationals" with the proviso "[t]his law shall be recognised by other States in so far as it is consistent with international conventions, international custom, and the principles of law generally recognised with regard to nationality".[45] Today, conventions, particularly in the field of human rights, require States to comply with international standards in the granting of nationality.[46] For example, article 9, paragraph 1, of the Convention on the Elimination of All Forms of Discrimination against Women provides that

> States parties shall grant women equal rights with men to acquire, change or retain their nationality. They shall ensure in particular that neither marriage to an alien nor change of nationality by the husband during marriage shall automatically change the nationality of the wife, render her stateless or force upon her the nationality of the husband.[47]

(7) Draft article 4 recognizes that a State against which a claim is made on behalf of an injured foreign national may challenge the nationality of such a person where his or her nationality has been acquired contrary to international law. Draft article 4 requires that nationality should be acquired in a manner "not inconsistent with international law". The double negative emphasizes the fact that the burden of proving that nationality has been acquired in violation of international law is upon the State challenging the nationality of the injured person. That the burden of proof falls upon the State challenging nationality follows from the recognition that the State conferring nationality must be given a "margin of appreciation" in deciding upon the conferment of nationality[48] and that there is a presumption in favour of the validity of a State's conferment of nationality.[49]

(8) Where a person acquires nationality involuntarily in a manner inconsistent with international law, as where a woman automatically acquires the nationality of her husband on marriage, that person should in principle be allowed to be protected diplomatically by her or his former State of nationality.[50] If, however, the acquisition of nationality in such circumstances results in the loss of the individual's former nationality, equitable considerations require that the new State of nationality be entitled to exercise diplomatic protection. This would accord with the ruling of the ICJ in its 1971 opinion on *Namibia*[51] that individual rights should not be affected by an illegal act on the part of the State with which the individual is associated.

---

[41] In the *Nottebohm* case, the ICJ stated: "According to the practice of States, to arbitral and judicial decisions and to the opinions of writers, nationality is a legal bond having as its basis a social fact of attachment, a genuine connection of existence, interests and sentiments, together with the existence of reciprocal rights and duties. It may be said to constitute the juridical expression of the fact that the individual upon whom it is conferred, either directly by the law or as the result of an act of the authorities, is in fact more closely connected with the population of the State conferring nationality than with that of any other State. Conferred by a State, it only entitles that State to exercise protection *vis-à-vis* another State, if it constitutes a translation into juridical terms of the individual's connection which has made him its national" (see footnote 31 above), p. 23.

[42] *Ibid.*, p. 25.

[43] *Ibid.*, p. 26.

[44] This interpretation was placed on the *Nottebohm* case by the Italian–United States Conciliation Commission in the *Flegenheimer* case, *Decision No. 182 of 20 September 1958*, UNRIAA, vol. XIV (Sales No. 65.V.4), p. 327, at p. 376; or *ILR* (1958-I), vol. 25 (1963) , p. 91, at p. 148.

[45] See also article 3, paragraph 2 of the European Convention on Nationality.

[46] This was stressed by the Inter-American Court of Human Rights in its advisory opinion on *Proposed Amendments to the Naturalization Provisions of the Political Constitution of Costa Rica*, in which it held that it was "necessary to reconcile the principle that the conferral of nationality fall[s] within the domestic jurisdiction of [a] State … with the further principle that international law imposes certain limits on the State's power, which limits are linked to the demands imposed by the international system for the protection of human rights" (advisory opinion OC-4/84 of 19 January 1984, Series A, No. 4, para. 38).

[47] See also article 20 of the American Convention on Human Rights: "Pact of San José, Costa Rica"; article 5 (*d*) (iii) of the International Convention on the Elimination of All Forms of Racial Discrimination; and article 1 of the Convention on the nationality of married women.

[48] See the advisory opinion of the Inter-American Court of Human Rights in the *Proposed Amendments to the Naturalization Provisions of the Political Constitution of Costa Rica* (footnote 46 above), paras. 62–63.

[49] See *Oppenheim's International Law*, 9th edition, vol. I, *Peace*, R. Y. Jennings and A. D. Watts (eds.), Harlow, Longman, 1992, p. 856.

[50] See article 2 of the Convention on the nationality of married women.

[51] *Legal Consequences for States of the Continued Presence of South Africa in Namibia (South West Africa) notwithstanding Security Council Resolution 276 (1970), Advisory Opinion, I.C.J. Reports 1971*, p. 16, at p. 56, para. 125.

Article 5. Continuous nationality of a natural person

1. A State is entitled to exercise diplomatic protection in respect of a person who was a national of that State continuously from the date of injury to the date of the official presentation of the claim. Continuity is presumed if that nationality existed at both these dates.

2. Notwithstanding paragraph 1, a State may exercise diplomatic protection in respect of a person who is its national at the date of the official presentation of the claim but was not a national at the date of injury, provided that the person had the nationality of a predecessor State or lost his or her previous nationality and acquired, for a reason unrelated to the bringing of the claim, the nationality of the former State in a manner not inconsistent with international law.

3. Diplomatic protection shall not be exercised by the present State of nationality in respect of a person against a former State of nationality of that person for an injury caused when that person was a national of the former State of nationality and not of the present State of nationality.

4. A State is no longer entitled to exercise diplomatic protection in respect of a person who acquires the nationality of the State against which the claim is brought after the date of the official presentation of the claim.

Commentary

(1) Although the continuous nationality rule is well established,[52] it has been subjected to considerable criticism[53] on the ground that it may produce great hardship in cases in which an individual changes his or her nationality for reasons unrelated to the bringing of a diplomatic claim. Suggestions that it be abandoned have been resisted out of fear that this might be abused and lead to "nationality shopping" for the purpose of diplomatic protection.[54] For this reason, draft article 5 retains the continuous nationality rule but allows exceptions to accommodate cases in which unfairness might otherwise result.

(2) Paragraph 1 asserts the traditional principle that a State is entitled to exercise diplomatic protection in respect of a person who was its national both at the time of the injury and at the date of the official presentation of the claim. State practice and doctrine are unclear on whether the national must retain the nationality of the claimant State between these two dates, largely because in practice this issue seldom arises.[55] For these reasons, the Institute of International Law left open in 1965 the question whether continuity of nationality was required between the two dates.[56] It is, however, incongruous to require that the same nationality be shown both at the date of injury and at the date of the official presentation of the claim without requiring it to continue between these two dates. Thus, in an exercise in progressive development of the law, the rule has been drafted to require that the injured person be a national continuously from the date of the injury to the date of the official presentation of the claim. Given the difficulty of providing evidence of continuity, it is presumed if the same nationality existed at both these dates. This presumption is of course rebuttable.

(3) The first requirement is that the injured national be a national of the claimant State at the date of the injury. The date of the injury need not be a precise date but could extend over a period of time if the injury consists of several acts or a continuing act committed over a period of time.

(4) The second temporal requirement contained in paragraph 1 is the date of the official presentation of the claim. There is some disagreement in judicial opinion over the date until which the continuous nationality of the claim is required. This uncertainty stems largely from the fact that conventions establishing mixed claims commissions have employed different language to identify the date of the claim.[57] The phrase "presentation of the claim" is that most frequently used in treaties, judicial decisions and doctrine to indicate the outer date or *dies ad quem* required for the exercise of diplomatic protection. The word "official" has been added to this formulation to indicate that the date of the presentation of the claim is that on which the first official or formal demand is made by the State exercising diplomatic protection, in contrast to informal diplomatic contacts and enquiries on this subject.

(5) The *dies ad quem* for the exercise of diplomatic protection is the date of the official presentation of the claim. There is, however, support for the view that if the individual should change his nationality between this date and the making of an award or a judgment, he ceases to be a national for the purposes of diplomatic protection.[58] In 2003, in the *Loewen* case, an ICSID arbitral tribunal held that "there must be continuous national identity from the date of the events giving rise to the claim, which date is known as the *dies a quo*, through to the date of the resolution of the claim, which date is known as the

[52] See, for instance, the decision of the United States International Claims Commission 1951–1954 in the *Kren* claim, *ILR* (1953), vol. 20 (1957), pp. 233 *et seq.*, at p. 234.

[53] See the comment of Judge Sir Gerald Fitzmaurice in the *Barcelona Traction* case, *Second Phase, Judgment* (footnote 35 above), at pp. 101–102; see also E. Wyler, *La règle dite de la continuité de la nationalité dans le contentieux international*, Paris, Presses universitaires de France, 1990.

[54] See the statement of Umpire Parker in *Administrative Decision No. V*: "Any other rule would open wide the door for abuses and might result in converting a strong nation into a claim agency in behalf of those who after suffering injuries should assign their claims to its nationals or avail themselves of its naturalization laws for the purpose of procuring its espousal of their claims." (United States–Germany Mixed Claims Commission, *Decision of 31 October 1924*, UNRIAA, vol. VII (Sales No. 1956.V.5), p. 119, at p. 141).

[55] See H. W. Briggs, "La protection diplomatique des individus en droit international: la nationalité des réclamations", *Annuaire de l'Institut de droit international*, vol. 51 (1965), tome I, pp. 5 *et seq.*, at pp. 72–73.

[56] See the Institute's Warsaw session, September 1965, *Annuaire de l'Institut de droit international*, vol. 51 (1965), tome II, pp. 260–262.

[57] See the dictum of Umpire Parker in *Administrative Decision No. V* (footnote 54 above), at p. 143.

[58] See *Oppenheim's International Law* (footnote 49 above), p. 512. See also *Minnie Stevens Eschauzier (Great Britain)* v. *United Mexican States, Decision of 24 June 1931*, UNRIAA, vol. V (Sales No. 1952.V.3), p. 207.

dies ad quem".[59] On the facts, the *Loewen* case dealt with the situation in which the person sought to be protected changed nationality after the presentation of the claim to that of the respondent State, in which circumstances a claim for diplomatic protection can clearly not be upheld, as is made clear in draft article 5, paragraph 4. However, the Commission was not prepared to follow the *Loewen* tribunal in adopting a blanket rule that nationality must be maintained to the date of resolution of the claim.[60] Such a rule could be contrary to the interests of the individual, as many years might pass between the presentation of the claim and its final resolution and it could be unfair to penalize the individual for changing nationality, through marriage or naturalization, during this period. Instead, preference is given to the date of the official presentation of the claim as the *dies ad quem*. This date is significant, as it is the date on which the State of nationality shows its clear intention to exercise diplomatic protection—a fact that was hitherto uncertain. Moreover, it is the date on which the admissibility of the claim must be judged. This determination could not be left to the later date of the resolution of the claim, the making of the award.

(6) The word "claim" in paragraphs 1, 2 and 4 includes both a claim submitted through diplomatic channels and a claim filed before a judicial body. Such a claim may specify the conduct that the responsible State should take in order to cease the wrongful act, if it is continuing, and the form reparation should take. This matter is dealt with more fully in article 43 of the draft articles on the responsibility of States for internationally wrongful acts of 2001 and the commentary thereto.[61]

(7) While the Commission decided that it was necessary to retain the continuous nationality rule, it agreed that there was a need for exceptions to this rule. Paragraph 2 accordingly provides that a State may exercise diplomatic protection in respect of a person who was a national at the date of the official presentation of the claim but not at the time of the injury, provided that three conditions are met: first, the person seeking diplomatic protection had the nationality of a predecessor State or has lost his or her previous nationality; secondly, that person has acquired the nationality of another State for a reason unrelated to the bringing of the claim; and thirdly, the acquisition of the new nationality has taken place in a manner not inconsistent with international law.

(8) Paragraph 2 is concerned with cases in which the injured person has lost his or her previous nationality, either voluntarily or involuntarily. In the case of the succession of States, and, possibly, adoption and marriage when a change of nationality is compulsory, nationality will be lost involuntarily. In the case of other changes of nationality, the element of will is not so clear. For reasons of this kind, paragraph 2 does not require the loss of nationality to be involuntary.

(9) In the case of the succession of States, this paragraph is limited to the question of the continuity of nationality for purposes of diplomatic protection. It makes no attempt to regulate succession to nationality, a subject that is covered by the Commission's draft articles on nationality of natural persons in relation to the succession of States.[62]

(10) As stated above,[63] fear that a person may deliberately change his or her nationality in order to acquire the nationality of a State more willing and able to bring a diplomatic claim on his or her behalf is the basis for the rule of continuous nationality. The second condition contained in paragraph 2 addresses this fear by providing that the person in respect of whom diplomatic protection is exercised must have acquired his or her new nationality for a reason unrelated to the bringing of the claim. This condition is designed to limit exceptions to the continuous nationality rule mainly to cases involving compulsory imposition of nationality, such as those in which the person has acquired a new nationality as a necessary consequence of factors such as marriage, adoption or the succession of States. The exception in paragraph 2 will not apply where the person has acquired a new nationality for commercial reasons connected with the bringing of the claim.

(11) The third condition that must be met for the rule of continuous nationality not to apply is that the new nationality has been acquired in a manner not inconsistent with international law. This condition must be read in conjunction with draft article 4.

(12) Paragraph 3 adds another safeguard against abuse of the lifting of the continuous nationality rule. Diplomatic protection may not be exercised by the new State of nationality against a former State of nationality of the injured person in respect of an injury incurred when that person was a national of the former State of nationality and not the present State of nationality.

(13) Paragraph 4 provides that if a person in respect of whom a claim is brought becomes a national of the respondent State after the presentation of the claim, the applicant State loses its right to proceed with the claim, as in such a case the respondent State would in effect be required to pay compensation to its own national. This was the situation in *Loewen* and a number of other cases[64] in which a change in nationality after presentation of the claim was held to preclude its continuation. In practice, in most cases of this kind, the applicant State will withdraw its claim, despite the fact that, in terms of the fiction proclaimed in *Mavrommatis,* the claim is that of the State and the purpose of the claim is to seek reparation for injury

[59] *The Loewen Group, Inc. and Raymond L. Loewen* v. *United States of America, ICSID Case No. ARB(AF)/98/3, Award of 26 June 2003, ICSID Reports*, vol. 7 (2005), pp. 442 *et seq.*, at p. 485, para. 225.

[60] For criticism of the *Loewen* case, see J. Paulsson, *Denial of Justice in International Law,* New York, Cambridge University Press, 2005, pp. 183–184.

[61] *Yearbook ... 2001*, vol. II (Part Two) and corrigendum, p. 119.

[62] See footnote 40 above.

[63] See above paragraph (1) of the commentary to the present draft article.

[64] *Ebenezer Barstow* case, G. H. Hackworth, *Digest of International Law*, vol. V, Washington D.C., United States Government Printing Office, 1943, p. 805; *Executors of F. Lederer (deceased)* v. *German Government* case, *Recueil des Décisions des Tribunaux Arbitraux Mixtes*, tome III, p. 762; *Hawaiian Claims* case, F. K. Nielsen, *American and British Claims Arbitration*, Washington D.C., Government Printing Office, 1926, p. 30; *Chopin, French and American Claims Commission, 1880–1884*, vol. 60, Records of Claims; *Gribble, Papers relating to the Treaty of Washington*, vol. V (*Report of Robert S. Hale, Esq.*), Washington D.C., Government Printing Office, 1874, p. 14.

caused to itself through the person of its national.[65] The applicant State may likewise decide to withdraw its claim when the injured person becomes a national of a third State after the presentation of the claim. If the injured person has in bad faith retained the nationality of the claimant State until the date of presentation and thereafter acquired the nationality of a third State, equity would require that the claim be terminated, but the burden of proof will be upon the respondent State.

(14) Draft article 5 leaves open the question whether the heirs of an injured national, who dies as a consequence of the injury or thereafter, but before the official presentation of the claim, may be protected by the State of nationality of the injured person if he or she has the nationality of another State. Judicial decisions on this subject, while inconclusive, as most deal with the interpretation of particular treaties, tend to support the position that no claim may be brought by the State of nationality of the deceased person if the heir has the nationality of a third State.[66] Where the heir has the nationality of the respondent State, it is clear that no such claim may be brought.[67] There is some support for the view that where the injured national dies before the official presentation of the claim, the claim may be continued because it has assumed a national character.[68] Although considerations of equity might seem to endorse such a position, it has on occasion been repudiated.[69] The inconclusiveness of the authorities makes it unwise to propose a rule on this subject.

Article 6. Multiple nationality and claim against a third State

1. Any State of which a dual or multiple national is a national may exercise diplomatic protection in respect of that national against a State of which that person is not a national.

2. Two or more States of nationality may jointly exercise diplomatic protection in respect of a dual or multiple national.

Commentary

(1) Dual or multiple nationality is a fact of international life. An individual may acquire more than one nationality as a result of the parallel operation of the principles of *jus soli* and *jus sanguinis* or of the conferment of nationality by naturalization or any other manner as envisaged in draft article 4, which does not result in the renunciation of a prior nationality. Although the laws of some States do not permit their nationals to be nationals of other States, international law does not prohibit dual or multiple nationality; indeed such nationality was given approval by article 3 of the Convention on Certain Questions relating to the Conflict of Nationality Laws, which provides: "a person having two or more nationalities may be regarded as its national by each of the States whose nationality he possesses". It is therefore necessary to address the question of the exercise of diplomatic protection by a State of nationality in respect of a dual or multiple national. Draft article 6 is limited to the exercise of diplomatic protection by one or all of the States of which the injured person is a national against a State of which that person is not a national. The exercise of diplomatic protection by one State of nationality against another State of nationality is covered in draft article 7.

(2) Paragraph 1 allows a State of nationality to exercise diplomatic protection in respect of its national even where that person is a national of one or more other States. Like draft article 4, it does not require a genuine or effective link between the national and the State exercising diplomatic protection.

(3) Although there is support for the requirement of a genuine or effective link between the State of nationality and a dual or multiple national in the case of the exercise of diplomatic protection against a State of which the injured person is not a national, in both arbitral decisions[70] and codification endeavours,[71] the weight of authority does not require such a condition. In the *Salem* case, an arbitral tribunal held that Egypt could not raise the fact that the injured individual had effective Persian nationality against a claim from the United States, another State of nationality. It stated that "the rule of international law [is] that in a case of dual nationality a third power is not entitled to contest the claim of one of the two powers whose national is interested in the case by referring to the nationality of the other power".[72] This rule has been followed in other cases[73] and has more recently been upheld by the

[65] See above commentary to article 1, paragraph (3).

[66] *Eschauzier* claim (see footnote 58 above); *Kren* claim (see footnote 52 above); *Captain W. H. Gleadell (Great Britain* v. *United Mexican States), Decision of 19 November 1929*, UNRIAA, vol. V, p. 44; but see *Straub* claim, *ILR*, vol. 20, p. 228.

[67] *Stevenson* case, UNRIAA, vol. IX (Sales No. 1959.V.5), p. 494; *Bogovic* claim, *ILR*, vol. 21, p. 156; *Executors of F. Lederer* case (see footnote 64 above).

[68] See E. M. Borchard, *The Diplomatic Protection of Citizens Abroad or the Law of International Claims*, New York, The Banks Law Publishing Co., 1922, p. 628; see also the *Straub* claim (footnote 66 above).

[69] *Eschauzier* claim (see footnote 58 above), at p. 209.

[70] See the decision of the Yugoslavian–Hungarian Mixed Arbitral Tribunal in the *de Born* case, case No. 205 of 12 July 1926, *Annual Digest of Public International Law Cases, Years 1925 and 1926*, A. D. McNair and H. Lauterpacht (eds.), London, Longmans, Green and Co., 1929, pp. 277–278.

[71] See article 5 of the Convention on Certain Questions relating to the Conflict of Nationality Laws; article 4 (*b*) of the resolution on "the national character of an international claim presented by a State for injury suffered by an individual" adopted by the Institute of International Law at its Warsaw session in 1965, *Tableau des résolutions adoptées (1957–1991)*, Paris, Pedone, 1992, p. 56, at p. 58 (reproduced in *Yearbook ... 1969*, vol. II, p. 142); paragraph 3 of article 23 of the 1960 Harvard draft convention on the international responsibility of States for injuries to aliens (reproduced in L. B. Sohn and R. R. Baxter, "Responsibility of States for injuries to the economic interests of aliens", AJIL, vol. 55, No. 3 (July 1961), p. 548; and article 21, paragraph 4, of the draft on international responsibility of the State for injuries caused in its territory to the person or property of aliens, included in the third report on international responsibility by Special Rapporteur García Amador, *Yearbook ... 1958*, vol. II, document A/CN.4/111, p. 61.

[72] *Salem (Egypt/United States of America), Award of 8 June 1932*, UNRIAA, vol. II (Sales No. 1949.V.1), p. 1165, at p. 1188.

[73] See the decisions of the Italian–United States Conciliation Commission in the *Mergé* claim, 10 June 1955, UNRIAA, vol. XIV (Sales No. 65.V.4), p. 236, or *ILR* (1955), vol. 22 (1958), p. 443, at p. 456; the *Vereano* claim, 17 May 1957, UNRIAA, vol. XIV, p. 321, or *ILR* (1957), vol. 24 (1961), pp. 464–465; and the *Stankovic* claim, 29 July 1963, *ILR*, vol. 40 (1970), p. 153, at p. 155.

Iran–United States Claims Tribunal.[74] The decision not to require a genuine or effective link in such circumstances accords with reason. Unlike the situation in which one State of nationality claims from another State of nationality in respect of a dual national, there is no conflict over nationality where one State of nationality seeks to protect a dual national against a third State.

(4) In principle, there is no reason why two States of nationality may not jointly exercise a right that attaches to each State of nationality. Paragraph 2 therefore recognizes that two or more States of nationality may jointly exercise diplomatic protection in respect of a dual or multiple national against a State of which that person is not a national. While the responsible State cannot object to such a claim made by two or more States acting simultaneously and in concert, it may raise objections where the claimant States bring separate claims either before the same forum or different forums, or where one State of nationality brings a claim after another State of nationality has already received satisfaction in respect of that claim. Problems may also arise where one State of nationality waives the right to diplomatic protection while another State of nationality continues with its claim. It is difficult to codify rules governing varied situations of this kind. They should be dealt with in accordance with the general principles of law recognized by international and national tribunals governing the satisfaction of joint claims.

Article 7. Multiple nationality and claim against a State of nationality

A State of nationality may not exercise diplomatic protection in respect of a person against a State of which that person is also a national unless the nationality of the former State is predominant, both at the date of injury and at the date of the official presentation of the claim.

Commentary

(1) Draft article 7 deals with the exercise of diplomatic protection by one State of nationality against another State of nationality. Whereas draft article 6, dealing with a claim in respect of a dual or multiple national against a State of which the injured person is not a national, does not require an effective link between claimant State and national, draft article 7 requires the claimant State to show that its nationality is predominant, both at the time of the injury and at the date of the official presentation of the claim.

(2) In the past there was strong support for the rule of non-responsibility according to which one State of nationality might not bring a claim in respect of a dual national against another State of nationality. The Convention on Certain Questions relating to the Conflict of Nationality Laws declares in article 4 that "[a] State may not afford diplomatic protection to one of its nationals against a State whose nationality such person also possesses".[75] Later codification proposals adopted a similar approach[76] and there was also support for this position in arbitral awards.[77] In 1949, in its advisory opinion in the case concerning *Reparation for Injuries*, the ICJ described the practice of States not to protect their nationals against another State of nationality as "the ordinary practice".[78]

(3) Even before 1930 there was, however, support in arbitral decisions for another position, namely that the State of dominant or effective nationality might bring proceedings in respect of a national against another State of nationality.[79] This jurisprudence was relied on by the ICJ in another context in the *Nottebohm* case[80] and was given explicit approval by Italian–United States Conciliation Commission in the *Mergé* claim in 1955. Here the Conciliation Commission stated that:

> The principle, based on the sovereign equality of States, which excludes diplomatic protection in the case of dual nationality, must yield before the principle of effective nationality whenever such nationality is that of the claiming State. But it must not yield when such predominance

[74] See *Dallal* v. *Iran* (1983), *Iran–United States Claims Tribunal Reports*, vol. 3, Cambridge, Grotius, 1984, p. 23.

[75] See also article 16 (*a*) of the 1929 Harvard draft convention on responsibility of States for damage done in their territory to the person or property of foreigners, Supplement to the AJIL, vol. 23, special number (vol. 2) (April 1929), p. 133, at p. 200 (reproduced in *Yearbook ... 1956*, vol. II, document A/CN.4/96, annex 9, p. 229, at p. 230).

[76] See article 23, paragraph 5, of the 1960 Harvard draft convention on the international responsibility of States for injuries to aliens (footnote 71 above); and article 4 (*a*) of the resolution on the national character of an international claim presented by a State for injury suffered by an individual adopted by the Institute of International Law at its Warsaw session in 1965 (*ibid.*).

[77] See the *Executors of R.S.C.A. Alexander* v. *United States* case (1898) (United States–British Claims Commission), J. B. Moore, *History and Digest of the International Arbitrations to Which the United States Has Been a Party*, vol. III, Washington D.C., United States Government Printing Office, 1898, p. 2529; the *Oldenbourg* case (British–Mexican Claims Commission), *Decision No. 11 of 19 December 1929*, UNRIAA, vol. V (Sales No. 1952.V.3), p. 74, or *Decisions and Opinions of the Commissioners, October 5, 1929 to February 15, 1930*, London, HM Stationery Office, 1931, p. 97; the *Honey* case (British–Mexican Claims Commission), *Decision No. 23 of 26 March 1931*, UNRIAA, vol. V, p. 133, or *Further Decisions and Opinions of the Commissioners, Subsequent to February 15, 1930*, London, HM Stationery Office, 1933, p. 13; and the *Adams and Blackmore* case (British–Mexican Claims Commission), *Decision No. 69 of 3 July 1931*, UNRIAA, vol. V, p. 216.

[78] *Reparation for Injuries* (see footnote 23 above), p. 186.

[79] *Drummond* case, 2 Knapp, Privy Council I, p. 295, *The English Reports*, vol. 12, Edinburgh/London, William Green and Sons/Stevens and Sons, 1901, p. 492; the *Mathison, Stevenson* (British–Venezuelan Mixed Claims Commission), *Brignone* and *Miliani* (Italian–Venezuelan Mixed Claims Commission) cases, UNRIAA, vol. IX (Sales No. 59.V.5), pp. 485 and 494, and vol. X (Sales No. 60.V.4), pp. 542 and 584 respectively, or *Venezuelan Arbitrations of 1903*, J. H. Ralston (ed.), Washington D.C., United States Government Printing Office, 1904, pp. 429–438, 438–455, 710–720 and 754–762 respectively; the *Canevaro* case (*Italy* v. *Peru*) (Permanent Court of Arbitration), *Decision of 3 May 1912*, UNRIAA, vol. XI (Sales No. 61.V.4), p. 397, or *The Hague Court Reports*, J. B. Scott (ed.), New York, Oxford University Press, 1916, p. 284; the *Hein* case, case No. 148 (1922) (Anglo–German Mixed Arbitral Tribunal), *Annual Digest of Public International Law Cases 1919 to 1922*, J. F. Williams and H. Lauterpacht (eds.), London, Longmans, Green and Co., 1932, p. 216; the *Blumenthal* case (1923) (French–German Mixed Arbitral Tribunal), *Recueil des décisions des tribunaux arbitraux mixtes institués par les traités de paix*, tome 3, Paris, Sirey, 1924, p. 616; the *de Montfort* case, case No. 206 (1926) (French–German Mixed Arbitral Tribunal), *Annual Digest of Public International Law Cases 1925 to 1926* (footnote 70 above), p. 279; the *Pinson* cases, cases No. 194 and 195 (1928) (French–Mexican Mixed Claims Commission), *ibid.* (1927–1928), pp. 297–301, or UNRIAA, vol. V (Sales No. 1952.V.3), p. 327; and the *Tellech* case (1928) (United States–Austria–Hungary Tripartite Claims Commission), UNRIAA, vol. VI (Sales No. 1955.V.3), pp. 248–250.

[80] *Nottebohm* (footnote 31 above), pp. 22–23. *Nottebohm* was not concerned with dual nationality but the Court found support for its finding that Mr. Nottebohm had no effective link with Liechtenstein in cases dealing with dual nationality. See also the judicial decisions referred to in footnote 79 above.

is not proved, because the first of these two principles is generally recognized and may constitute a criterion of practical application for the elimination of any possible uncertainty.[81]

In its opinion, the Conciliation Commission held that the principle of effective nationality and the concept of dominant nationality were simply two sides of the same coin. The rule thus adopted was applied by the Conciliation Commission in over 50 subsequent cases concerning dual nationals.[82] Relying on these cases, the Iran–United States Claims Tribunal has applied the principle of dominant and effective nationality in a number of cases.[83] Codification proposals have given approval to this approach. In his third report on State responsibility to the Commission, Special Rapporteur García Amador proposed that "[i]n cases of dual or multiple nationality, the right to bring a claim shall be exercisable only by the State with which the alien has the stronger and more genuine legal or other ties".[84] A similar view was advanced by Orrego Vicuña in his report to the sixty-ninth conference of the International Law Association.[85]

(4) Even though the two concepts are different, the authorities use the term "effective" or "dominant" without distinction to describe the required link between the claimant State and its national in situations in which one State of nationality brings a claim against another State of nationality. Draft article 7 does not use either of these words to describe the required link, but instead uses the term "predominant" as it conveys the element of relativity and indicates that the individual has stronger ties with one State rather than another. A tribunal considering this question is required to balance the strengths of competing nationalities and the essence of this exercise is more accurately captured by the term "predominant" when applied to nationality than either "effective" or "dominant". It is moreover the term used by the Italian–United States Conciliation Commission in the *Mergé* claim,[86] which may be seen as the starting point for the development of the present customary rule.

(5) No attempt is made to describe the factors to be taken into account in deciding which nationality is predominant. The authorities indicate that such factors include habitual residence, the amount of time spent in each country of nationality, date of naturalization (i.e., the length of the period spent as a national of the protecting State before the claim arose); place, curricula and language of education; employment and financial interests; place of family life; family ties in each country; participation in social and public life; use of language; taxation, bank account, social security insurance; visits to the other State of nationality; possession and use of passport of the other State; and military service. None of these factors is decisive and the weight attributed to each factor will vary according to the circumstances of each case.

(6) Draft article 7 is framed in negative language: "A State of nationality may *not* exercise diplomatic protection ... *unless*" its nationality is predominant. This is intended to show that the circumstances envisaged by draft article 7 are to be regarded as exceptional. This also makes it clear that the burden of proof is on the claimant State to prove that its nationality is predominant.

(7) The main objection to a claim brought by one State of nationality against another State of nationality is that this might permit a State, with which the individual has established a predominant nationality subsequent to an injury inflicted by the other State of nationality, to bring a claim against that State. This objection is overcome by the requirement that the nationality of the claimant State must be predominant both at the date of the injury and at the date of the official presentation of the claim. Although this requirement echoes the principle affirmed in draft article 5, paragraph 1, on the subject of continuous nationality, it is not necessary in this case to prove continuity of predominant nationality between these two dates. The phrases "at the date of injury" and "at the date of the official presentation of the claim" are explained in the commentary on draft article 5. The exception to the continuous nationality rule contained in draft article 5, paragraph 2, is not applicable here as the injured person contemplated in draft article 7 will not have lost his or her other nationality.

Article 8. Stateless persons and refugees

1. A State may exercise diplomatic protection in respect of a stateless person who, at the date of injury and at the date of the official presentation of the claim, is lawfully and habitually resident in that State.

2. A State may exercise diplomatic protection in respect of a person who is recognized as a refugee by that State, in accordance with internationally accepted standards, when that person, at the date of injury and at the date of the official presentation of the claim, is lawfully and habitually resident in that State.

3. Paragraph 2 does not apply in respect of an injury caused by an internationally wrongful act of the State of nationality of the refugee.

Commentary

(1) The general rule was that a State might exercise diplomatic protection on behalf of its nationals only. In 1931,

---

[81] *Mergé,* UNRIAA (see footnote 73 above), p. 247. See also the *de Leon* case, case Nos. 218 and 227 of 15 May 1962 and 8 April 1963, UNRIAA, vol. XVI (Sales No. E/F.69.V.1), p. 239, at p. 247.

[82] See, for example, the *Spaulding* case (1956), UNRIAA, vol. XIV (Sales No. 65.V.4), p. 292, or *ILR* (1957), vol. 24 (1961), p. 452; the *Zangrilli* case (1956), UNRIAA, vol. XIV, p. 294, or *ILR*, vol. 24, p. 454; the *Cestra* case (1957), UNRIAA, vol. XIV, p. 307, or *ILR*, vol. 24, p. 454; the *Salvoni* case (1957), UNRIAA, vol. XIV, p. 311, or *ILR*, vol. 24, p. 455; the *Ruspoli–Droutzkoy* case (1957), UNRIAA, vol. XIV, p. 314, or *ILR*, vol. 24, p. 457; the *Puccini* case (1957), UNRIAA, vol. XIV, p. 323, or *ILR*, vol. 24, p. 454; the *Turri* case (1960), *ILR*, vol. 30 (1966), p. 371; the *Graniero* case (1959), UNRIAA, vol. XIV, p. 393, or *ILR*, vol. 30, p. 351; the *Ganapini* case (1959), UNRIAA, vol. XIV, p. 400, or *ILR*, vol. 30, p. 366; and the *Di Cicio* case (1962), *ILR*, vol. 40 (1970), p. 148.

[83] See, in particular, *Esphahanian* v. *Bank Tejarat* (1983), *Iran–United States Claims Tribunal Reports*, vol. 2, Cambridge, Grotius, 1984, p. 157, at p. 166; *Case No. A/18 (1984), ibid.*, vol. 5, 1985, p. 251; and *Ataollah Golpira* v. *Government of the Islamic Republic of Iran (1983), ibid.*, vol. 2, 1984, p. 174, or *ILR*, vol. 72, p. 493.

[84] Draft on international responsibility of the State for injuries to aliens (see footnote 71 above) art. 21, para. 4.

[85] "The changing law of nationality of claims", interim report, International Law Association, *Report of the Sixty-ninth Conference*, London, 2000, p. 646, para. 11; confirmed in the final report adopted at the 2006 International Law Association Conference in Toronto (*Report of the Seventy-second Conference*, London, 2006).

[86] See footnote 73 above.

the United States–Mexican General Claims Commission in *Dickson Car Wheel Company* held that a stateless person could not be the beneficiary of diplomatic protection when it stated: "A State … does not commit an international delinquency in inflicting an injury upon an individual lacking nationality, and consequently, no State is empowered to intervene or complain on his behalf either before or after the injury."[87] This dictum no longer reflects the accurate position of international law for both stateless persons and refugees. Contemporary international law reflects a concern for the status of both categories of persons. This is evidenced by such conventions as the Convention on the reduction of statelessness of 1961 and the Convention relating to the Status of Refugees of 1951.

(2) Draft article 8, an exercise in progressive development of the law,[88] departs from the traditional rule that only nationals may benefit from the exercise of diplomatic protection and allows a State to exercise diplomatic protection in respect of a non-national where that person is either a stateless person or a refugee. Although draft article 8 is to be seen within the framework of the rules governing statelessness and refugees, it has made no attempt to pronounce on the status of such persons. It is concerned only with the issue of the exercise of the diplomatic protection of such persons.

(3) Paragraph 1 deals with the diplomatic protection of stateless persons. It gives no definition of stateless persons. Such a definition is, however, to be found in article 1 of the Convention relating to the Status of Stateless Persons, which defines a stateless person as "a person who is not considered as a national by any State under the operation of its law". This definition can no doubt be considered as having acquired a customary nature. A State may exercise diplomatic protection in respect of such a person, regardless of how he or she became stateless, provided that he or she was lawfully and habitually resident in that State both at the time of injury and at the date of the official presentation of the claim. Habitual residence in this context is intended to convey continuous residence.

(4) The requirement of both lawful residence and habitual residence sets a high threshold.[89] Although this threshold is high and leads to a lack of effective protection for some individuals, the combination of lawful residence and habitual residence is justified in the case of an exceptional measure introduced *de lege ferenda*.

(5) The temporal requirements for the bringing of a claim are contained in paragraph 1. The stateless person must be a lawful and habitual resident of the claimant State both at the time of the injury and at the date of the official presentation of the claim.

(6) Paragraph 2 deals with the diplomatic protection of refugees by their State of residence. Diplomatic protection by the State of residence is particularly important in the case of refugees as they are "unable or … unwilling to avail [themselves] of the protection of [the State of nationality]"[90] and, if they do so, run the risk of losing refugee status in the State of residence. Paragraph 2 mirrors the language of paragraph 1. Important differences between stateless persons and refugees, as evidenced by paragraph 3, explain why a separate paragraph has been allocated to each category.

(7) Lawful residence and habitual residence are required as preconditions for the exercise of diplomatic protection of refugees, as with stateless persons,[91] despite the fact that article 28 of the Convention relating to the Status of Refugees sets the lower threshold of "lawfully staying"[92] for contracting States in the issuing of travel documents to refugees. Two factors justify this position: first, the fact that the issue of travel documents, in terms of the Convention, does not in any way entitle the holder to diplomatic protection;[93] and secondly, the necessity to set a high threshold when introducing an exception to a traditional rule, *de lege ferenda*.[94]

(8) The term "refugee" in paragraph 2 is not limited to refugees as defined in the 1951 Convention relating to the Status of Refugees and its 1967 Protocol relating to the Status of Refugees but is intended to cover, in addition, persons who do not strictly conform to this definition. The Commission considered using the term "recognized refugees", which appears in article 6, paragraph 4(*g*) of the 1997 European Convention on Nationality, which would have extended the concept to include refugees recognized by regional instruments, such as the OAU Convention governing the specific aspects of refugee problems in Africa,[95] widely seen as the model for the international protection of refugees,[96] and the Cartagena Declaration on Refugees, approved by the General Assembly of the OAS in 1985.[97] However, the Commission preferred to

[87] *Dickson Car Wheel Company (U.S.A.)* v. *United Mexican States, Decision of July 1931*, UNRIAA, vol. IV (Sales No. 1951.V.1), p. 669, at p. 678.

[88] In *Al Rawi & Others, R (on the Application of)* v. *Secretary of State for Foreign Affairs & Another*, [2006] EWHC 972 (Admin), an English court held that draft article 8 was to be considered *lex ferenda* and "not yet part of international law" (para. 63).

[89] The use of the terms "lawful" and "habitual" with regard to residence is based on the European Convention on Nationality, art. 6, para. 4 (*g*), where they are used in connection with the acquisition of nationality. See also article 21, paragraph 3 (c), of the Harvard draft convention on the international responsibility of States for injuries to aliens (footnote 71 above), which includes for the purpose of protection under this Convention a "stateless person having his habitual residence in that State".

[90] Article 1.A.(2) of the Convention relating to the Status of Refugees.

[91] Habitual residence in this context connotes continuous residence.

[92] The *travaux préparatoires* of the Convention make it clear that "stay" means less than habitual residence.

[93] See paragraph 16 of the schedule to the Convention.

[94] See above paragraph (4) of the commentary to this draft article.

[95] This Convention extends the definition of refugee to include "every person who, owing to external aggression, occupation, foreign domination or events seriously disturbing public order in either part or the whole of his country of origin or nationality, is compelled to leave his place of habitual residence in order to seek refuge in another place outside his country of origin or nationality" (art. I.2).

[96] See the Note on International Protection submitted by the United Nations High Commissioner for Refugees (A/AC.96/830), p. 17, para. 35.

[97] Adopted at the Colloquium on the International Protection of Refugees in Central America, Mexico and Panama: Legal and Humanitarian Problems, held in Cartagena de Indias, Colombia, on 19–22 November 1984; the text of the conclusions of the declaration appears in OEA/Ser.L/V/II.66 doc.10 rev.1. OAS General Assembly, fifteenth regular session (1985), resolution approved by the General Commission held at its fifth session on 7 December 1985.

set no limit to the term in order to allow a State to extend diplomatic protection to any person that it recognized and treated as a refugee.[98] Such recognition must, however, be based on "internationally accepted standards" relating to the recognition of refugees. This term emphasizes that the standards expounded in different conventions and other international instruments are to apply as well as the legal rules contained in the 1951 Convention relating to the Status of Refugees and its 1967 Protocol.

(9) The temporal requirements for the bringing of a claim are repeated in paragraph 2. The refugee must be a lawful and habitual resident of the claimant State both at the time of the injury and at the date of the official presentation of the claim.

(10) Paragraph 3 provides that the State of refuge may not exercise diplomatic protection in respect of a refugee against the State of nationality of the refugee. To have permitted this would have contradicted the basic approach of the present draft articles, according to which nationality is the predominant basis for the exercise of diplomatic protection. The paragraph is also justified on policy grounds. Most refugees have serious complaints about their treatment at the hand of their State of nationality, from which they have fled to avoid persecution. To allow diplomatic protection in such cases would be to open the floodgates for international litigation. Moreover, the fear of demands for such action by refugees might deter States from accepting refugees.

(11) Both paragraphs 1 and 2 provide that a State of refuge "*may* exercise diplomatic protection". This emphasizes the discretionary nature of the right. A State has discretion under international law whether to exercise diplomatic protection in respect of a national.[99] *A fortiori* it has discretion whether to extend such protection to a stateless person or refugee.

(12) Draft article 8 is concerned only with the diplomatic protection of stateless persons and refugees. It is *not* concerned with the conferment of nationality upon such persons. The exercise of diplomatic protection in respect of a stateless person or refugee cannot and should not be seen as giving rise to a legitimate expectation of the conferment of nationality. Draft article 28 of the Convention relating to the Status of Refugees, read with paragraph 15 of its schedule, makes it clear that the issue of a travel document to a refugee does not affect the nationality of the holder. *A fortiori* the exercise of diplomatic protection in respect of a refugee, or a stateless person, should in no way be construed as affecting the nationality of the protected person.

Chapter III

LEGAL PERSONS

Article 9. State of nationality of a corporation

For the purposes of the diplomatic protection of a corporation, the State of nationality means the State under whose law the corporation was incorporated. However, when the corporation is controlled by nationals of another State or States and has no substantial business activities in the State of incorporation, and the seat of management and the financial control of the corporation are both located in another State, that State shall be regarded as the State of nationality.

Commentary

(1) Draft article 9 recognizes that diplomatic protection may be extended to corporations. The first part of the article follows the same formula adopted in draft article 4 on the subject of the diplomatic protection of natural persons. The provision makes it clear that in order to qualify as the State of nationality for the purposes of diplomatic protection of a corporation, certain conditions must be met, as is the case with the diplomatic protection of natural persons.

(2) State practice is largely concerned with the diplomatic protection of corporations, that is, profit-making enterprises with limited liability whose capital is generally represented by shares, and not other legal persons. This explains why the present article, and those that follow, are concerned with the diplomatic protection of corporations and shareholders in corporations. Draft article 13 is devoted to the position of legal persons other than corporations.

(3) As with natural persons, the granting of nationality to a corporation is "within [the] reserved domain" of a State.[100] As the ICJ stated in the *Barcelona Traction* case:

> international law has had to recognize the corporate entity as an institution created by States in a domain essentially within their domestic jurisdiction. This in turn requires that, whenever legal issues arise concerning the rights of States with regard to the treatment of companies and shareholders, as to which rights international law has not established its own rules, it has to refer to the relevant rules of municipal law.[101]

Although international law has no rules of its own for the creation, management and dissolution of a corporation or for the rights of shareholders and their relationship with the corporation, and must consequently turn to municipal law for guidance on this subject, it is for international law to determine the circumstances in which a State may exercise diplomatic protection on behalf of a corporation or its shareholders. This matter was addressed by the ICJ in *Barcelona Traction* when it stated that international law "attributes the right of diplomatic protection of a corporate entity to the State under the laws of which it is incorporated and in whose territory it has its registered office".[102] Here the Court set two conditions for the acquisition of nationality by a corporation for the purposes of diplomatic protection: incorporation and the presence of the registered office of the company in the State of incorporation. As the laws of most States require a company incorporated under its laws to maintain a registered office in its territory, even if this is a mere fiction, incorporation is the most important criterion for the purposes of diplomatic

[98] For instance, it may be possible for a State to exercise diplomatic protection on behalf of a person granted political asylum in terms of the 1954 Convention on territorial asylum.

[99] See draft articles 2 and 19 and the commentaries thereto.

[100] See the *Nationality Decrees Issued in Tunis and Morocco* case (footnote 38 above).

[101] *Barcelona Traction, Second Phase, Judgment* (see footnote 35 above), at pp. 33–34, para. 38.

[102] *Ibid.*, p. 42, para. 70.

protection. The Court in *Barcelona Traction* was not satisfied, however, with incorporation as the sole criterion for the exercise of diplomatic protection. Although it did not reiterate the requirement of a "genuine connection" as applied in the *Nottebohm* case,[103] and acknowledged that "in the particular field of the diplomatic protection of corporate entities, no absolute test of the 'genuine connection' has found general acceptance",[104] it suggested that in addition to incorporation and a registered office, there was a need for some "close and permanent connection" between the State exercising diplomatic protection and the corporation.[105] On the facts of this case, the Court found such a connection in the incorporation of the company in Canada for over 50 years, the maintenance of its registered office, accounts and share register there, the holding of board meetings there for many years, its listing in the records of the Canadian tax authorities and the general recognition by other States of the Canadian nationality of the company.[106] All of this meant, said the Court, that "Barcelona Traction's links with Canada are thus manifold".[107] In *Barcelona Traction* the Court was not confronted with a situation in which a company was incorporated in one State but had a "close and permanent connection" with another State. One can only speculate what the Court might have decided in such a situation. Draft article 9 does, however, provide for such cases.

(4) Draft article 9 accepts the basic premise of *Barcelona Traction* that it is incorporation that confers nationality on a corporation for the purposes of diplomatic protection. However, it provides an exception in a particular situation where there is no other significant link or connection between the State of incorporation and the corporation itself, and where certain significant connections exist with another State, in which case that other State is to be regarded as the State of nationality for the purpose of diplomatic protection. Policy and fairness dictate such a solution. It is wrong to place the sole and exclusive right to exercise diplomatic protection in a State with which the corporation has the most tenuous connection, as in practice such a State will seldom be prepared to protect that corporation.

(5) Draft article 9 provides that, in the first instance, the State in which a corporation is incorporated is the State of nationality entitled to exercise diplomatic protection. When, however, the circumstances indicate that the corporation has a closer connection with another State, a State in which the seat of management and financial control are situated, that State shall be regarded as the State of nationality with the right to exercise diplomatic protection. Nevertheless, certain conditions must be fulfilled before this occurs. First, the corporation must be controlled by nationals of another State. Secondly, it must have no substantial business activities in the State of incorporation. Thirdly, both the seat of management and the financial control of the corporation must be located in another State. Only where these conditions are cumulatively fulfilled does the State in which the corporation has its seat of management and in which it is financially controlled qualify as the State of nationality for the purposes of diplomatic protection.

(6) In *Barcelona Traction*, the ICJ warned that the granting of the right of diplomatic protection to the States of nationality of shareholders might result in a multiplicity of actions which "could create an atmosphere of confusion and insecurity in international economic relations".[108] The same confusion might result from the granting of the right to exercise diplomatic protection to several States with which a corporation enjoys a link or connection. Draft article 9 does not allow such multiple actions. The State of nationality with the right to exercise diplomatic protection is *either* the State of incorporation *or*, if the required conditions are met, the State of the seat of management and financial control of the corporation. If the seat of management and the place of financial control are located in different States, the State of incorporation remains the State entitled to exercise diplomatic protection.

Article 10. Continuous nationality of a corporation

1. A State is entitled to exercise diplomatic protection in respect of a corporation that was a national of that State, or its predecessor State, continuously from the date of injury to the date of the official presentation of the claim. Continuity is presumed if that nationality existed at both these dates.

2. A State is no longer entitled to exercise diplomatic protection in respect of a corporation that acquires the nationality of the State against which the claim is brought after the presentation of the claim.

3. Notwithstanding paragraph 1, a State continues to be entitled to exercise diplomatic protection in respect of a corporation which was its national at the date of injury and which, as the result of the injury, has ceased to exist according to the law of the State of incorporation.

Commentary

(1) The general principles relating to the requirement of continuous nationality are discussed in the commentary to draft article 5. In practice, problems of continuous nationality arise less in the case of corporations than with natural persons. Whereas natural persons change nationality easily as a result of naturalization, marriage or adoption, and State succession, corporations generally change nationality only by being re-formed or reincorporated in another State, in which case the corporation assumes a new personality, thereby breaking the continuity of nationality of the corporation.[109] The most frequent instance in which

[103] *Ibid.* For the *Nottebohm* case, see footnote 31 above.

[104] *Barcelona Traction, Second Phase, Judgment* (see footnote 35 above), p. 42, para. 70.

[105] *Ibid.*, para. 71.

[106] *Ibid.*, pp. 42–44, paras. 71–76.

[107] *Ibid.*, p. 42, para. 71.

[108] *Ibid.*, p. 49, para. 96.

[109] See the *Orinoco Steamship Company Case*, American–Venezuelan Mixed Claims Commission, constituted under the Protocol of 17 February 1903, UNRIAA, vol. IX, p. 180. Here a company incorporated in the United Kingdom transferred its claim against the Government of Venezuela to a successor company incorporated in the United States. As the treaty establishing the Commission permitted the United States to bring a claim on behalf of its national in such circumstances, the claim was allowed. However, Umpire Barge made it clear that, but for the treaty, the claim would not have been allowed (*ibid.*, at p. 192). See also the *Loewen* case (footnote 59 above), at pp. 484–485, para. 220.

a corporation may change nationality without changing legal personality is in the case of State succession.

(2) Paragraph 1 asserts the traditional principle that a State is entitled to exercise diplomatic protection in respect of a corporation that was its national both at the time of the injury and at the date of the official presentation of the claim. It also requires continuity of nationality between the date of the injury and the date of the official presentation of the claim. These requirements, which apply to natural persons as well, are examined in the commentary to draft article 5. The date of the official presentation of the claim is preferred to that of the date of the award, for reasons explained in the commentary to draft article 5. An exception is made, however, in paragraph 2 to cover cases in which the corporation acquires the nationality of the State against which the claim is brought after the presentation of the claim.

(3) The requirement of continuity of nationality is met where a corporation undergoes a change of nationality as a result of the succession of States.[110] In effect, this is an exception to the continuity of nationality rule. This matter is covered by the reference to "predecessor State" in paragraph 1.

(4) The word "claim" in paragraph 1 includes both a claim submitted through diplomatic channels and a claim filed before a judicial body. Such a claim may specify the conduct that the responsible State should take in order to cease the wrongful act, if it is continuing, and the form reparation should take.[111]

(5) In terms of paragraph 2, a State is not entitled to exercise diplomatic protection in respect of a corporation that acquires the nationality of the State against which the claim is brought after the presentation of the claim. This paragraph is designed to cater for the type of situation that arose in the *Loewen* case[112] in which a corporation ceased to exist in the State in which the claim was initiated (Canada) and was reorganized in the respondent State (the United States). This matter is further considered in the commentary to draft article 5.[113]

(6) Difficulties arise in respect of the exercise of diplomatic protection of a corporation that has ceased to exist according to the law of the State in which it was incorporated and of which it was a national. If one takes the position that the State of nationality of such a corporation may not bring a claim as the corporation no longer exists at the time of presentation of the claim, then no State may exercise diplomatic protection in respect of an injury to the corporation. A State could not avail itself of the nationality of the shareholders in order to bring such a claim, as it could not show that it had the necessary interest at the time the injury occurred to the corporation. This matter troubled several judges in the *Barcelona Traction* case[114] and it has troubled certain courts, arbitral tribunals[115] and scholars.[116] Paragraph 3 adopts a pragmatic approach and allows the State of nationality of a corporation to exercise diplomatic protection in respect of an injury suffered by the corporation when it was its national and has ceased to exist—and therefore ceased to be its national—as a result of the injury. In order to qualify, the claimant State must prove that it was because of the injury in respect of which the claim is brought that the corporation has ceased to exist. Paragraph 3 must be read in conjunction with draft article 11, paragraph (*a*), which makes it clear that the State of nationality of shareholders will not be entitled to exercise diplomatic protection in respect of an injury to a corporation that led to its demise.

Article 11. Protection of shareholders

A State of nationality of shareholders in a corporation shall not be entitled to exercise diplomatic protection in respect of such shareholders in the case of an injury to the corporation unless:

(*a*) the corporation has ceased to exist according to the law of the State of incorporation for a reason unrelated to the injury; or

(*b*) the corporation had, at the date of injury, the nationality of the State alleged to be responsible for causing the injury, and incorporation in that State was required by it as a precondition for doing business there.

Commentary

(1) The most fundamental principle of the diplomatic protection of corporations is that a corporation is to be protected by the State of nationality of the corporation and *not* by the State or States of nationality of the shareholders in a corporation. This principle was strongly reaffirmed by the ICJ in the *Barcelona Traction* case. In this case, the Court emphasized at the outset that it was concerned only with the question of the diplomatic protection of shareholders in "a limited liability company whose capital is

---

[110] See further, on this subject, the *Panevezys-Saldutiskis Railway* case (footnote 26 above), at p. 18. See also fourth report of Special Rapporteur Václav Mikulka on nationality in relation to the succession of States, which highlights the difficulties surrounding the nationality of legal persons in relation to the succession of States, *Yearbook ... 1998*, vol. II (Part One), document A/CN.4/489, p. 301.

[111] See further, article 43 of the draft articles on the responsibility of States for internationally wrongful acts and the commentary thereto, *Yearbook ... 2001*, vol. II (Part Two) and corrigendum, pp. 119–120.

[112] *Loewen* (see footnote 59 above), at para. 220.

[113] Paras. (5) and (13).

[114] Judges Jessup (see footnote 35 above, at p. 193), Gross (*ibid.*, at p. 277) and Fitzmaurice (*ibid.*, at pp. 101–102) and Judge *ad hoc* Riphagen (*ibid.*, at p. 345).

[115] See the *Kunhardt & Co.* case (opinions in the American–Venezuelan Mixed Claims Commission, constituted under the Protocol of 17 February 1903), UNRIAA, vol. IX, p. 171, and particularly the dissenting opinion of the Venezuelan Commissioner, Mr. Paúl, at p. 180; see also *F. W. Flack, on behalf of the Estate of the Late D. L. Flack (Great Britain)* v. *United Mexican States, Decision No. 10 of 6 December 1929, ibid.*, vol. V, p. 61, at p. 63.

[116] See L. Caflisch, *La protection des sociétés commerciales et des intérêts indirects en droit international public*, The Hague, Martinus Nijhoff, 1969, pp. 206–207; W. E. Beckett, "Diplomatic claims in respect of injuries to companies", in *Transactions of the Grotus Society*, vol. 17, London, Sweet and Maxwell, 1932, pp. 175 *et seq.*, at p. 191; and E. Wyler, *La règle dite de la continuité de la nationalité dans le contentieux international*, Paris, Presses universitaires de France, 1990, pp. 197–202.

represented by shares".[117] Such companies are characterized by a clear distinction between company and shareholders.[118] Whenever a shareholder's interests are harmed by an injury to the company, it is to the company that the shareholder must look to take action, for "although two separate entities may have suffered from the same wrong, it is only one entity whose rights have been infringed".[119] Only where the act complained of is aimed at the direct rights of the shareholders does a shareholder have an independent right of action.[120] Such principles governing the distinction between company and shareholders, said the Court, are derived from municipal law and not international law.[121]

(2) In reaching its decision that the State of incorporation of a company and not the State(s) of nationality of the shareholders in the company is the appropriate State to exercise diplomatic protection in the event of injury to a company, the Court in *Barcelona Traction* was guided by a number of policy considerations. First, when shareholders invest in a corporation doing business abroad they undertake risks, including the risk that the State of nationality of the corporation may, in the exercise of its discretion, decline to exercise diplomatic protection on their behalf.[122] Secondly, if the State of nationality of shareholders is permitted to exercise diplomatic protection, this might lead to a multiplicity of claims by different States, as large corporations frequently comprise shareholders of many nationalities.[123] In this respect, the Court indicated that if the shareholder's State of nationality was empowered to act on his behalf there was no reason why every individual shareholder should not enjoy such a right.[124] Thirdly, the Court was reluctant to apply by way of analogy rules relating to dual nationality to corporations and shareholders, and to allow the States of nationality of both to exercise diplomatic protection.[125]

(3) The Court in *Barcelona Traction* accepted that the State(s) of nationality of shareholders might exercise diplomatic protection on their behalf in two situations: first, where the company had ceased to exist in its place of incorporation[126]—which was not the case with the *Barcelona Traction*; second, where the State of incorporation was itself responsible for inflicting injury on the company and the foreign shareholders' sole means of protection on the international level was through their State(s) of nationality[127]—which was not the case with *Barcelona Traction*. These two exceptions, which were not thoroughly examined by the Court in *Barcelona Traction* because they were not relevant to the case, are recognized in paragraphs (*a*) and (*b*) of draft article 11. As the shareholders in a company may be nationals of different States, several States of nationality may be able to exercise diplomatic protection in terms of these exceptions. In practice, however, States will, and should, coordinate their claims and make sure that States whose nationals hold the bulk of the share capital are involved as claimants.

(4) Draft article 11 is restricted to the interests of shareholders in a corporation, as judicial decisions on this subject, including *Barcelona Traction*, have mainly addressed the question of shareholders. There is no clear authority on the right of the State of nationality to protect investors other than shareholders, such as debenture holders, nominees and trustees. In principle, however, there would seem to be no good reason why the State of nationality should not protect such persons.[128]

(5) Draft article 11, paragraph (*a*) requires that the corporation shall have "ceased to exist" before the State of nationality of the shareholders shall be entitled to intervene on their behalf. Before the *Barcelona Traction* case, the weight of authority favoured a less stringent test, one that permitted intervention on behalf of shareholders when the company was "practically defunct".[129] The Court in *Barcelona Traction*, however, set a higher threshold for determining the demise of a company. The "paralysis" or "precarious financial situation" of a company was dismissed as inadequate.[130] The test of "practically defunct" was likewise rejected as one "which lacks all legal precision".[131] Only the "company's status in law" was considered relevant. The Court stated: "Only in the event of the legal demise of the company are the shareholders deprived of the possibility of a remedy available through the company; it is only if they became deprived of all such possibility that an independent right of action for them and their Government could arise."[132] Subsequent support has been given to this test by the European Court of Human Rights.[133]

(6) The Court in *Barcelona Traction* did not expressly state that the company must have ceased to exist in *the place of incorporation* as a precondition to shareholders' intervention. Nevertheless, it seems clear in the context of the proceedings before it that the Court intended that the company should have ceased to exist in the State of incorporation and not in the State in which the company was injured. The Court was prepared to accept that the

[117] *Barcelona Traction, Second Phase, Judgment* (see footnote 35 above), p. 34, para. 40.

[118] *Ibid.*, para. 41.

[119] *Ibid.*, p. 35, para. 44.

[120] *Ibid.*, p. 36, para. 47.

[121] *Ibid.*, p. 37, para. 50.

[122] *Ibid.*, p. 35, para. 43; p. 46, paras. 86–87; and p. 50, para. 99.

[123] *Ibid.*, pp. 48–49, paras. 94–96.

[124] *Ibid.*, pp. 48–49, paras. 94–95.

[125] *Ibid.*, p. 38, para. 53; and p. 50, para. 98.

[126] *Ibid.*, pp. 40–41, paras. 65–68.

[127] *Ibid.*, p. 48, para. 92.

[128] This is the approach adopted by the United Kingdom. See the comments and observations received from Governments on the draft articles adopted by the Commission on first reading, *Yearbook ... 2005*, vol. II (Part One), document A/CN.4/561 and Add.1–2, annex (United Kingdom of Great Britain and Northern Ireland: Rules Applying to International Claims).

[129] *Delagoa Bay Railway Co.* case, J. B. Moore, *Digest of International Law*, vol. VI, Washington D.C., United States Government Printing Office, 1906, p. 648; *El Triunfo* claim, *ibid.*, p. 649; *Baasch & Römer* case, UNRIAA, vol. X (Sales No. 1960.V.4), p. 713, at p. 723.

[130] See *Barcelona Traction, Second Phase, Judgment* (footnote 35 above), pp. 40–41, paras. 65–66.

[131] *Ibid.*, p. 41, para. 66.

[132] *Ibid.*; see also the separate opinions of Judges Padilla Nervo (*ibid.*, p. 256) and Ammoun (*ibid.*, pp. 319–320).

[133] See *Agrotexim and others* v. *Greece, Decision of 24 October 1995*, European Court of Human Rights, *Series A*, No. 330-A, p. 25, para. 68.

company was destroyed in Spain[134] but emphasized that this did not affect its continued existence in Canada, the State of incorporation: "In the present case, *Barcelona Traction* is in receivership in the country of incorporation. Far from implying the demise of the entity or of its rights, this much rather denotes that those rights are preserved for so long as no liquidation has ensued. Though in receivership, the company continues to exist."[135] A company is "born" in the State of incorporation when it is formed or incorporated there. Conversely, it "dies" when it is wound up in its State of incorporation, the State which gave it existence. It therefore seems logical that the question whether a company has ceased to exist, and is no longer able to function as a corporate entity, must be determined by the law of the State in which it is incorporated.

(7) The final phrase "for a reason unrelated to the injury" aims to ensure that the State of nationality of the shareholders will not be permitted to bring proceedings in respect of the injury to the corporation that is the cause of the corporation's demise. This, according to draft article 10, is the continuing right of the State of nationality of the corporation. The State of nationality of the shareholders will therefore only be able to exercise diplomatic protection in respect of shareholders who have suffered as a result of injuries sustained by the corporation unrelated to the injury that might have given rise to the demise of the corporation. The purpose of this qualification is to limit the circumstances in which the State of nationality of the shareholders may intervene on behalf of such shareholders for injury to the corporation.

(8) Draft article 11, paragraph (*b*), gives effect to the exception allowing the State of nationality of the shareholders in a corporation to exercise diplomatic protection on their behalf where the State of incorporation is itself responsible for inflicting injury on the corporation. The exception is limited to cases where incorporation was required by the State inflicting the injury on the corporation as a precondition for doing business there.

(9) There is support for such an exception in State practice, arbitral awards[136] and doctrine. Significantly, the strongest support for intervention on the part of the State of nationality of the shareholders comes from three claims in which the injured corporation had been *compelled* to incorporate in the wrongdoing State: *Delagoa Bay Railway*, *Mexican Eagle* and *"Salvador Commercial Company" et al. ("El Triunfo Company")*. While there is no suggestion in the language of these claims that intervention is to be limited to such circumstances, there is no doubt that it is in such cases that intervention is most needed. As the Government of the United Kingdom replied to the Mexican argument in *Mexican Eagle* that a State might not intervene on behalf of its shareholders in a Mexican company:

> If the doctrine were admitted that a Government can first make the operation of foreign interests in its territories depend upon their incorporation under local law, and then plead such incorporation as the justification for rejecting foreign diplomatic intervention, it is clear that the means would never be wanting whereby foreign Governments could be prevented from exercising their undoubted right under international law to protect the commercial interests of their nationals abroad.[137]

(10) In *Barcelona Traction*, Spain, the respondent State, was not the State of nationality of the injured company. Consequently, the exception under discussion was not before the ICJ. Nevertheless, the Court did make passing reference to this exception:

> It is quite true that it has been maintained that, for reasons of equity, a State should be able, in certain cases, to take up the protection of its nationals, shareholders in a company which has been the victim of a violation of international law. Thus a theory has been developed to the effect that the State of the shareholders has a right of diplomatic protection when the State whose responsibility is invoked is the national State of the company. Whatever the validity of this theory may be, it is certainly not applicable to the present case, since Spain is not the national State of *Barcelona Traction*.[138]

Judges Fitzmaurice,[139] Tanaka[140] and Jessup[141] expressed full support in their separate opinions in *Barcelona Traction* for the right of the State of nationality of the shareholders to intervene when the company was injured by the State of incorporation.[142] While both Fitzmaurice[143] and Jessup[144] conceded that the need for such a rule was particularly strong where incorporation was required as a precondition for doing business in the State of incorporation, neither was prepared to limit the rule to such circumstances. Judges Padilla Nervo,[145] Morelli[146] and Ammoun,[147] on the other hand, were vigorously opposed to the exception.

(11) Developments relating to the proposed exception in the post-*Barcelona Traction* period have occurred mainly in the context of treaties. Nevertheless, they do indicate support for the notion that the shareholders of a company may intervene against the State of incorporation of the company when it has been responsible for causing

---

[134] See *Barcelona Traction, Second Phase, Judgment* (footnote 35 above), p. 40, para. 65. See also the separate opinions of Judges Fitzmaurice (*ibid.*, p. 75) and Jessup (*ibid.*, p. 194).

[135] *Ibid.*, p. 41, para. 67.

[136] See *Delagoa Bay Railway Company* (footnote 129 above); *Mexican Eagle (El Aguila)*, M. M. Whiteman, *Digest of International Law*, vol. 8 (1967), pp. 1272–1274; *Romano-Americano*, G. H. Hackworth, *op cit.* (footnote 64 above), vol. V, p. 841; *"Salvador Commercial Company" et al. ("El Triunfo Company"), Award of 8 May 1902*, UNRIAA, vol. XV (Sales No. 1966.V.3), p. 455, at p. 467; and *The Deutsche Amerikanische Petroleum Gesellschaft Oil Tankers, Award of 5 August 1926, ibid.*, vol. II (Sales. No. 1949.V.1), p. 777, at p. 790. For a comprehensive examination of the authorities, see Caflisch, *op. cit* (footnote 116 above) and J. M. Jones, "Claims on behalf of nationals who are shareholders in foreign companies", *BYBIL*, vol. 26 (1949), p. 225. See also E. Jiménez de Aréchaga, "International responsibility", in Max Sørensen (ed.), *Manual of Public International Law*, London, Macmillan, 1968, pp. 531 *et seq.*, at pp. 580–581.

[137] *Whiteman, op. cit* (footnote 136 above), pp. 1273–1274.

[138] *Barcelona Traction, Second Phase, Judgment* (footnote 35 above), p. 48, para. 92.

[139] *Ibid.*, pp. 72–75.

[140] *Ibid.*, p. 134.

[141] *Ibid.*, pp. 191–193.

[142] Judge Wellington Koo likewise supported this position in the *Case concerning the Barcelona Traction, Light and Power Company Limited, Preliminary Objections, I.C.J. Reports 1964*, p. 6, at p. 58, para. 20.

[143] *Barcelona Traction, Second Phase, Judgment* (footnote 35 above), p. 73, paras. 15–16.

[144] *Ibid.*, pp. 191–192.

[145] *Ibid.*, pp. 257–259.

[146] *Ibid.*, pp. 240–241.

[147] *Ibid.*, p. 318.

injury to the company.[148] In the *ELSI* case,[149] a Chamber of the ICJ allowed the United States to bring a claim against Italy in respect of damages suffered by an Italian company whose shares were wholly owned by two American companies. The Court avoided pronouncing on the compatibility of its finding with that of *Barcelona Traction* or on the proposed exception left open in *Barcelona Traction*, despite the fact that Italy objected that the company whose rights were alleged to have been violated was incorporated in Italy and that the United States sought to protect the rights of shareholders in the company.[150] This silence might be explained on the ground that the Chamber was not concerned with the evaluation of customary international law but with the interpretation of a bilateral Treaty of Friendship, Commerce and Navigation[151] which provided for the protection of United States shareholders abroad. On the other hand, the proposed exception was clearly before the Chamber.[152] It is thus possible to infer support for the exception in favour of the right of the State of shareholders in a corporation to intervene against the State of incorporation when it is responsible for causing injury to the corporation.[153]

(12) Before *Barcelona Traction*, there was support for the proposed exception, but opinions were divided over whether, or to what extent, State practice and arbitral decisions recognized it. Although arbitral decisions affirmed the principle contained in the exception, these decisions were often based on special agreements between States granting a right to shareholders to claim compensation and, as a consequence, were not necessarily indicative of a general rule of customary international law.[154] The *obiter dictum* in *Barcelona Traction* and the separate opinions of Judges Fitzmaurice, Jessup and Tanaka have undoubtedly added to the weight of authority in favour of the exception. Subsequent developments, albeit in the context of treaty interpretation, have confirmed this trend.[155] In these circumstances it would be possible to sustain a general exception on the basis of judicial opinion. However, draft article 11, paragraph (*b*), does not go this far. Instead it limits the exception to what has been described as a "Calvo corporation", a corporation whose incorporation, like the "Calvo clause",[156] is designed to protect it from the rules of international law relating to diplomatic protection. It limits the exception to the situation in which the corporation had, *at the date of the injury* (a further restrictive feature), the nationality of the State alleged to be responsible for causing the injury and incorporation in that State was required by it as a precondition for doing business there. It is not necessary that the law of that State require incorporation. Other forms of compulsion might also result in a corporation being "required" to incorporate in that State.

Article 12. Direct injury to shareholders

To the extent that an internationally wrongful act of a State causes direct injury to the rights of shareholders as such, as distinct from those of the corporation itself, the State of nationality of any such shareholders is entitled to exercise diplomatic protection in respect of its nationals.

Commentary

(1) That shareholders qualify for diplomatic protection when their own rights are affected was recognized by the ICJ in *Barcelona Traction* when it stated:

> an act directed against and infringing only the company's rights does not involve responsibility towards the shareholders, even if their interests are affected. … The situation is different if the act complained of is aimed at the direct rights of the shareholder as such. It is well known that there are rights which municipal law confers upon the latter distinct from those of the company, including the right to any declared dividend, the right to attend and vote at general meetings, the right to share in the residual assets of the company on liquidation. Whenever one of his direct rights is infringed, the shareholder has an independent right of action.[157]

The Court was not, however, called upon to consider this matter any further because Belgium made it clear that it did not base its claim on an infringement of the direct rights of the shareholders.

(2) The issue of the protection of the direct rights of shareholders came before the Chamber of the ICJ in the *ELSI* case.[158] However, in that case, the rights in question, such as the rights of the shareholders to organize, control and manage the company, were to be found in the Treaty of Friendship, Commerce and Navigation[159] that the Chamber was called on to interpret and the Chamber failed to expound on the rules of customary international law on

---

[148] See *SEDCO Inc.* v. *National Iranian Oil Company and the Islamic Republic of Iran, Case No. 129 of 24 October 1985, ILR*, vol. 84 (1991), pp. 484 and 496 (interpreting article VII(2) of the Algiers Claims Settlement Declaration); and *Liberian Eastern Timber Corporation (LETCO)* v. *The Government of the Republic of Liberia,* ILM, vol. 26 (1987), pp. 647 and 652–654 (interpreting article 25 of the Convention on the settlement of investment disputes between States and nationals of other States).

[149] *Elettronica Sicula S.p.A. (ELSI), Judgment, I.C.J. Reports 1989*, p. 15.

[150] *Ibid.*, pp. 64 (para. 106) and 79 (para. 132).

[151] Signed at Rome on 2 February 1948 (United Nations, *Treaty Series*, vol. 79, No. 1040, p. 171).

[152] This is clear from an exchange of opinions in the *ELSI* case (see footnote 149 above) between Judges Oda (pp. 87–88) and Schwebel (p. 94) on the subject.

[153] This view is expressed by Yoram Dinstein in "Diplomatic protection of companies under international law", in K. Wellens (ed.), *International Law: Theory and Practice—Essays in Honour of Eric Suy*, The Hague, Martinus Nijhoff, 1998, pp. 505 *et seq.*, at p. 512.

[154] See the submission to this effect by the United States on subparagraph (*b*) of draft article 11 in the comments and observations received from Governments on the draft articles adopted by the Commission on first reading, document A/CN.4/561 and Add.1–2 (footnote 128 above).

[155] According to the United Kingdom's 1985 Rules Applying to International Claims, "[w]here a [United Kingdom] national has an interest, as a shareholder or otherwise, in a company incorporated in another State and of which it is therefore a national, and that State injures the company, [Her Majesty's Government] may intervene to protect the interests of that [United Kingdom] national" (Rule VI), reprinted in *International and Comparative Law Quarterly*, vol. 37 (1988), p. 1007 and reproduced in annex to the comments and observations received from Governments on the draft articles adopted by the Commission on first reading, document A/CN.4/561 and Add.1–2 (see footnote 128 above).

[156] Named after the distinguished Argentine jurist Carlos Calvo (1824–1906). See *Yearbook ... 1956*, vol. II, document A/CN.4/96, pp. 206–208.

[157] *Barcelona Traction, Second Phase, Judgment* (footnote 35 above), p. 36, paras. 46–47.

[158] See footnote 149 above.

[159] See footnote 151 above.

this subject. In *Agrotexim*,[160] the European Court of Human Rights, like the International Court of Justice in *Barcelona Traction*, acknowledged the right of shareholders to protection in respect of the direct violation of their rights, but held that *in casu* no such violation had occurred.[161]

(3) Draft article 12 makes no attempt to provide an exhaustive list of the rights of shareholders as distinct from those of the corporation itself. In *Barcelona Traction*, the ICJ mentioned the most obvious rights of shareholders—the right to a declared dividend, the right to attend and vote at general meetings and the right to share in the residual assets of the company on liquidation—but made it clear that this list is not exhaustive. This means that it is left to courts to determine, on the facts of individual cases, the limits of such rights. Care will, however, have to be taken to draw clear lines between shareholders' rights and corporate rights, particularly in respect of the right to participate in the management of corporations. That draft article 12 is to be interpreted restrictively is emphasized by the phrases "the rights of the shareholders as such" and rights "as distinct from those of the corporation itself".

(4) Draft article 12 does not specify the legal order that must determine which rights belong to the shareholder as distinct from the corporation. In most cases, this is a matter to be decided by the municipal law of the State of incorporation. Where the company is incorporated in the wrongdoing State, however, there may be a case for the invocation of general principles of company law in order to ensure that the rights of foreign shareholders are not subjected to discriminatory treatment.[162]

Article 13. Other legal persons

The principles contained in this chapter shall be applicable, as appropriate, to the diplomatic protection of legal persons other than corporations.

Commentary

(1) The provisions of this chapter have hitherto focused on a particular species of legal person, the corporation. There are two explanations for this. First, corporations, unlike other legal persons, have certain common, uniform features: they are profit-making enterprises whose capital is generally represented by shares, in which there is a firm distinction between the separate entity of the corporation and the shareholders, with limited liability attaching to the latter. Secondly, it is mainly the corporation, unlike the public enterprise, the university, the municipality, the foundation and other such legal persons, that engages in foreign trade and investment and whose activities fuel not only the engines of international economic life but also the machinery of international dispute settlement. Diplomatic protection in respect of legal persons is mainly about the protection of foreign investment. This is why the corporation is the legal person that occupies centre stage in the field of diplomatic protection and why the present set of draft articles do—and should—concern themselves largely with this entity.

(2) In the ordinary sense of the word, a "person" is a human being. In the legal sense, however, a "person" is any being, object, association or institution which the law endows with the capacity of acquiring rights and incurring duties. A legal system may confer legal personality on whatever object or association it pleases. There is no consistency or uniformity among legal systems in the conferment of legal personality.

(3) There is jurisprudential debate about the nature of legal personality and, in particular, about the manner in which a legal person comes into being. The fiction theory maintains that no legal person can come into being without a formal act of incorporation by the State. This means that a body other than a natural person may obtain the privileges of personality by an act of State, which by a fiction of law equates it to a natural person, subject to such limitations as the law may impose. According to the realist theory, on the other hand, corporate existence is a reality and does not depend on State recognition. If an association or body acts in fact as a separate legal entity, it becomes a legal person, with all its attributes, without requiring grant of legal personality by the State. Whatever the merits of the realist theory, it is clear that, to exist, a legal person must have some recognition by law, that is, by some municipal law system. This has been stressed by both the European Court of Justice[163] and the ICJ.[164]

(4) Given the fact that legal persons are the creatures of municipal law, it follows that there are today a wide range of legal persons with different characteristics, including corporations, public enterprises, universities, schools, foundations, churches, municipalities, non-profit-making associations, non-governmental organizations (NGOs) and even partnerships (in some countries). The impossibility of finding common, uniform features in all these legal persons provides one explanation for the fact that writers on both public and private international law largely confine their consideration of legal persons in the context of international law to the corporation. Despite this, regard must be had for legal persons other than corporations in the context of diplomatic protection. The case law of the PCIJ shows that a commune[165] (municipality) or university[166] may in certain circumstances qualify as

[160] *Agrotexim and others* v. *Greece* (see footnote 133 above).

[161] *Ibid.*, p. 23, para. 62.

[162] In his separate opinion in *ELSI*, Judge Oda spoke of "the general principles of law concerning companies" in the context of shareholders' rights (see footnote 149 above), pp. 87–88.

[163] *The Queen* v. *H. M. Treasury and Commissioners of Inland Revenue*, ex parte *Daily Mail and General Trust plc, Case 81/87, Judgment of the Court of 27 September 1988*, European Court of Justice, *European Court Reports 1988*, p. 5483, at para. 19.

[164] *Barcelona Traction, Second Phase, Judgment* (footnote 35 above), pp. 33–34, para. 38.

[165] In *Certain German Interests in Polish Upper Silesia*, the PCIJ held that the commune of Ratibor fell within the category of "German national" within the meaning of the German–Polish Convention concerning Upper Silesia (*Merits, Judgment No. 7, 1926, P.C.I.J. Reports, Series A, No. 7*, p. 19, at pp. 73–75). The Convention was signed in Geneva on 15 May 1922 (see G. Kaeckenbeeck, *The International Experiment of Upper Silesia*, London, Oxford University Press, 1942, p. 572).

[166] In the statement from the case *Appeal from a Judgment of the Hungaro/Czechoslovak Mixed Arbitral Tribunal (The Peter Pázmány University)*, the PCIJ held that the Peter Pázmány University was a Hungarian national in terms of article 250 of the Treaty of Peace between the Allied and Associated Powers and Hungary (Treaty of Trianon) and therefore was entitled to the restitution of property belonging to it (*Judgment, 1933, P.C.I.J. Reports, Series A/B, No. 61*, p. 208, at pp. 227–232).

a legal person and as a national of a State. There is no reason why such legal persons should not qualify for diplomatic protection if injured abroad, provided that they are autonomous entities not forming part of the apparatus of the protecting State.[167] Non-profit-making foundations, comprising assets set aside by a donor or testator for a charitable purpose, constitute legal persons without members. Today many foundations fund projects abroad to promote health, welfare, women's rights, human rights and the environment in developing countries. Should such a legal person be subjected to an internationally wrongful act by the host State, it is probable that it would be granted diplomatic protection by the State under whose laws it has been created. NGOs engaged in causes abroad would appear to fall into the same category as foundations.[168]

(5) The diversity of goals and structures in legal persons other than corporations makes it impossible to draft separate and distinct provisions to cover the diplomatic protection of different kinds of legal persons. The wisest, and only realistic, course is to draft a provision that extends the principles of diplomatic protection adopted for corporations to other legal persons—subject to the changes necessary to take account of the different features of each legal person. The proposed provision seeks to achieve this. It provides that the principles governing the State of nationality of corporations and the application of the principle of continuous nationality to corporations, contained in the present chapter, will apply, "as appropriate", to the diplomatic protection of legal persons other than corporations. This will require the necessary competent authorities or courts to examine the nature and functions of the legal person in question in order to decide whether it would be "appropriate" to apply any of the provisions of the present chapter to it. Most legal persons other than corporations do not have shareholders, so only draft articles 9 and 10 may appropriately be applied to them. If, however, such a legal person does have shareholders, draft articles 11 and 12 may also be applied to it.[169]

Part Three

LOCAL REMEDIES

Article 14. Exhaustion of local remedies

1. A State may not present an international claim in respect of an injury to a national or other person referred to in draft article 8 before the injured person has, subject to draft article 15, exhausted all local remedies.

2. "Local remedies" means legal remedies which are open to the injured person before the judicial or administrative courts or bodies, whether ordinary or special, of the State alleged to be responsible for causing the injury.

3. Local remedies shall be exhausted where an international claim, or request for a declaratory judgement related to the claim, is brought preponderantly on the basis of an injury to a national or other person referred to in draft article 8.

Commentary

(1) Draft article 14 seeks to codify the rule of customary international law requiring the exhaustion of local remedies as a prerequisite for the exercise of diplomatic protection. This rule was recognized by the ICJ in the *Interhandel* case as "a well-established rule of customary international law"[170] and by a Chamber of the ICJ in the *ELSI* case as "an important principle of customary international law".[171] The exhaustion of local remedies rule ensures that "the State where the violation occurred should have an opportunity to redress it by its own means, within the framework of its own domestic system".[172] The Commission has previously considered the exhaustion of local remedies in the context of its work on State responsibility and concluded that it is a "principle of general international law" supported by judicial decisions, State practice, treaties and the writings of jurists.[173]

(2) Both natural and legal persons are required to exhaust local remedies. A foreign company financed partly or mainly by public capital is also required to exhaust local remedies. Non-nationals of the State exercising protection, entitled to diplomatic protection in the exceptional circumstances provided for in draft article 8, are also required to exhaust local remedies.

(3) The phrase "all local remedies" must be read subject to draft article 15 which describes the exceptional circumstances in which local remedies need not be exhausted.

(4) The remedies available to an alien that must be exhausted before diplomatic protection can be exercised will, inevitably, vary from State to State. No codification can therefore succeed in providing an absolute rule governing all situations. Paragraph 2 seeks to describe, in broad terms, the main kind of legal remedies that must be exhausted.[174] In the first instance it is clear that the foreign

[167] As diplomatic protection is a process reserved for the protection of natural or legal persons not forming part of the State, it follows that in most instances the municipality, as a local branch of government, and the university, funded and, in the final resort, controlled by the State, will not qualify for diplomatic protection, although it may be protected by other rules dealing with the problem of State organs. Private universities would, however, qualify for diplomatic protection, as would private schools, if they enjoyed legal personality under municipal law.

[168] See further K. Doehring, "Diplomatic protection of non-governmental organizations", in M. Rama-Montaldo (ed.), *El derecho internacional en un mundo en transformación: liber amicorum en homenaje al professor Eduardo Jiménez de Aréchaga*, Montevideo, Fundación Cultura Universitaria, 1994, pp. 571–580.

[169] This would apply to the limited liability company known in civil law countries which is a hybrid between a corporation and a partnership.

[170] *Interhandel, Preliminary Objections, Judgment, I.C.J. Reports 1959*, p. 6, at p. 27.

[171] *ELSI* (see footnote 149 above), p. 42, para. 50.

[172] *Interhandel* (see footnote 170 above), at p. 27.

[173] See article 22 of the draft articles on State responsibility provisionally adopted by the Commission on first reading, *Yearbook ... 1996*, vol. II (Part Two), chap. III, sect. D.1 (draft article 22 was approved by the Commission at its twenty-ninth session and the text and the corresponding commentary are in *Yearbook ... 1977*, vol. II (Part Two), chap. II, sect. B, pp. 30–50); and article 44 of the draft articles on State responsibility for internationally wrongful acts adopted by the Commission at its fifty-third session, *Yearbook... 2001*, vol. II (Part Two) and corrigendum, p. 120; the commentary to this article is on pp. 120–121.

[174] In the *Ambatielos Claim*, the arbitral tribunal declared that "[i]t is the whole system of legal protection, as provided by municipal law, which must have been put to the test" (*Judgment of 6 March 1956,*

national must exhaust all the available judicial remedies provided for in the municipal law of the respondent State. If the municipal law in question permits an appeal in the circumstances of the case to the highest court, such an appeal must be brought in order to secure a final decision in the matter. Even if there is no appeal as of right to a higher court, but such a court has discretion to grant leave to appeal, the foreign national must still apply for leave to appeal to that court.[175] Courts in this connection include both ordinary and special courts since "the crucial question is not the ordinary or extraordinary character of a legal remedy but whether it gives the possibility of an effective and sufficient means of redress".[176]

(5) Administrative remedies must also be exhausted. The injured alien is, however, only required to exhaust such remedies which may result in a binding decision. He is not required to approach the executive for relief in the exercise of its discretionary powers. Local remedies do not include remedies whose "purpose is to obtain a favour and not to vindicate a right"[177] nor do they include remedies of grace[178] unless they constitute an essential prerequisite for the admissibility of subsequent contentious proceedings. Requests for clemency and resort to an ombudsman generally fall into this category.[179]

(6) In order to satisfactorily lay the foundation for an international claim on the ground that local remedies have been exhausted, the foreign litigant must raise the basic arguments he intends to raise in international proceedings in the municipal proceedings. In the *ELSI* case, the Chamber of the ICJ stated that "for an international claim to be admissible, it is sufficient if the essence of the claim has been brought before the competent tribunals and pursued as far as permitted by local law and procedures, and without success".[180] This test is preferable to the stricter test enunciated in the *Finnish Ships Arbitration* that "all the contentions of fact and propositions of law which are brought forward by the claimant Government ... must have been investigated and adjudicated upon by the municipal Courts".[181]

(7) The claimant State must therefore produce the evidence available to it to support the essence of its claim in the process of exhausting local remedies.[182] The international remedy afforded by diplomatic protection cannot be used to overcome faulty preparation or presentation of the claim at the municipal level.[183]

(8) Draft article 14 does not take cognizance of the "Calvo clause",[184] a device employed mainly by Latin American States in the late nineteenth century and early twentieth century to confine an alien to local remedies by compelling him to waive recourse to international remedies in respect of disputes arising out of a contract entered into with the host State. The validity of such a clause has been vigorously disputed by capital-exporting States[185] on the ground that the alien has no right, in accordance with the rule in *Mavrommatis*,[186] to waive a right that belongs to the State and not its national. Despite this, the "Calvo clause" was viewed as a regional custom in Latin America and formed part of the national identity of many States. The "Calvo clause" is difficult to reconcile with international law if it is to be interpreted as a complete waiver of recourse to international protection in respect of an action by the host State constituting an internationally wrongful act (such as denial of justice) or where the injury to the alien was of direct concern to the State of nationality of the alien.[187] The objection to the validity of the "Calvo clause" in respect of general international law are certainly less convincing if one accepts that the right protected within the framework of diplomatic protection are those of the individual protected and not those of the protecting State.[188]

(9) Paragraph 3 provides that the exhaustion of local remedies rule applies only to cases in which the claimant State has been injured "indirectly", that is, through its national. It does not apply where the claimant State is directly injured by the wrongful act of another State, as here the State has a distinct reason of its own for bringing an international claim.[189]

(10) In practice it is difficult to decide whether the claim is "direct" or "indirect" where it is "mixed", in the sense that it contains elements of both injury to the State and injury to the nationals of the State. Many disputes before the ICJ have presented the phenomenon of the mixed claim. In the *United States Diplomatic and Consular Staff in Tehran* case,[190] there was a direct violation on the part of the Islamic Republic of Iran of the duty it owed to the United States of America to protect its diplomats

UNRIAA, vol. XII (Sales No. 63.V.3), p. 120). See further on this subject, C. F. Amerasinghe, *Local Remedies in International Law*, 2nd ed., Cambridge University Press, 2004, pp. 182–192.

[175] This would include the *certiorari* process before the United States Supreme Court.

[176] *B. Schouw Nielsen* v. *Denmark, Application No. 343/57, Decision of 2 September 1959*, European Commission and European Court of Human Rights, *Yearbook of the European Convention on Human Rights 1958–1959*, p. 438, referring to the consideration of the Institute of International Law in its resolution of 1954 (*Annuaire de l'Institut de droit international*, vol. 46 (1956), p. 364). See also *Lawless* v. *Ireland, Application No. 332/57, Decision of 30 August 1958*, European Commission and European Court of Human Rights, *Yearbook of the European Convention on Human Rights 1958–1959*, pp. 308 *et seq.*, at pp. 318–322.

[177] *De Becker* v. *Belgium, Application No. 214/56, Decision of 9 June 1958*, European Commission and European Court of Human Rights, *Yearbook of the European Convention on Human Rights 1958–1959*, p. 238.

[178] See *Claim of Finnish shipowners against Great Britain in respect of the use of certain Finnish vessels during the war ("Finnish Ships Arbitration")*, Award of 9 May 1934, UNRIAA, vol. III (Sales No. 1949.V.2), p. 1479.

[179] See *Avena* (footnote 29 above), at pp. 63–66, paras. 135–143.

[180] *ELSI* (see footnote 149 above), at p. 46, para. 59.

[181] *Finnish Ships Arbitration* (see footnote 178 above), at p. 1502.

[182] See the *Ambatielos Claim* (footnote 174 above).

[183] See D. P. O'Connell, *International Law*, vol. 2, 2nd ed., London, Stevens, 1970, p. 1059.

[184] See footnote 156 above.

[185] See generally D. R. Shea, *The Calvo Clause: A Problem of Inter-American and International Law and Diplomacy*, Minneapolis, University of Minnesota Press, 1955.

[186] See footnote 26 above.

[187] *North American Dredging Company of Texas (U.S.A.)* v. *United Mexican States*, UNRIAA, vol. IV, p. 26.

[188] See above paragraph (5) of commentary to draft article 1.

[189] See generally on this subject, C. F. Amerasinghe, *Local Remedies in International Law* (footnote 174 above), pp. 145–168.

[190] *United States Diplomatic and Consular Staff in Tehran, Judgment, I.C.J. Reports 1980*, p. 3.

and consuls, but at the same time there was injury to the person of the nationals (diplomats and consuls) held hostage; and in the *Interhandel* case,[191] there were claims brought by Switzerland relating to a direct wrong to itself arising out of breach of a treaty and to an indirect wrong resulting from an injury to a national corporation. In the *United States Diplomatic and Consular Staff in Tehran* case, the Court treated the claim as a direct violation of international law; and in the *Interhandel* case, the Court found that the claim was preponderantly indirect and that *Interhandel* had failed to exhaust local remedies. In the *Arrest Warrant of 11 August 2000* case there was a direct injury to the Democratic Republic of the Congo and its national (the Foreign Minister), but the Court held that the claim was not brought within the context of the protection of a national so it was not necessary for the Democratic Republic of the Congo to exhaust local remedies.[192] In the *Avena* case, Mexico sought to protect its nationals on death row in the United States through the medium of the Vienna Convention on Consular Relations, arguing that it had "itself suffered, directly and through its nationals" as a result of the United States' failure to grant consular access to its nationals under article 36, paragraph 1 of the Convention. The Court upheld this argument because of the "interdependence of the rights of the State and of individual rights".[193]

(11) In the case of a mixed claim, it is incumbent upon the tribunal to examine the different elements of the claim and to decide whether the direct or the indirect element is preponderant. In the *ELSI* case, a Chamber of the ICJ rejected the argument of the United States that part of its claim was premised on the violation of a treaty and that it was therefore unnecessary to exhaust local remedies, holding that "the Chamber has no doubt that the matter which colours and pervades the United States claim as a whole, is the alleged damage to Raytheon and Machlett [United States corporations]".[194] Closely related to the preponderance test is the *sine qua non* or "but for" test, which asks whether the claim comprising elements of both direct and indirect injury would have been brought were it not for the claim on behalf of the injured national. If this question is answered negatively, the claim is an indirect one and local remedies must be exhausted. There is, however, little to distinguish the preponderance test from the "but for" test. If a claim is preponderantly based on injury to a national, this is evidence of the fact that the claim would not have been brought but for the injury to the national. In these circumstances only one test is provided for in paragraph 3, that of preponderance.

(12) Other "tests" invoked to establish whether the claim is direct or indirect are not so much tests as factors that must be considered in deciding whether the claim is preponderantly weighted in favour of a direct or an indirect claim or whether the claim would not have been brought but for the injury to the national. The principal factors to be considered in making this assessment are the subject of the dispute, the nature of the claim and the remedy claimed. Thus where the subject of the dispute is a Government official,[195] diplomatic official[196] or State property[197] the claim will normally be direct, and where the State seeks monetary relief on behalf of its national as a private individual the claim will be indirect.

(13) Paragraph 3 makes it clear that local remedies are to be exhausted not only in respect of an international claim, but also in respect of a request for a declaratory judgment brought preponderantly on the basis of an injury to a national. Although there is support for the view that where a State makes no claim for damages for an injured national, but simply requests a decision on the interpretation and application of a treaty, there is no need for local remedies to be exhausted,[198] there are cases in which States have been required to exhaust local remedies where they have sought a declaratory judgment relating to the interpretation and application of a treaty alleged to have been violated by the respondent State in the course of, or incidental to, its unlawful treatment of a national.[199]

(14) Draft article 14 requires that the injured person must himself have exhausted all local remedies. This does not preclude the possibility that the exhaustion of local remedies may result from the fact that another person has submitted the substance of the same claim before a court of the respondent State.[200]

Article 15. Exceptions to the local remedies rule

Local remedies do not need to be exhausted where:

(*a*) there are no reasonably available local remedies to provide effective redress, or the local remedies provide no reasonable possibility of such redress;

(*b*) there is undue delay in the remedial process which is attributable to the State alleged to be responsible;

(*c*) there was no relevant connection between the injured person and the State alleged to be responsible at the date of injury;

(*d*) the injured person is manifestly precluded from pursuing local remedies; or

(*e*) the State alleged to be responsible has waived the requirement that local remedies be exhausted.

---

191 See footnote 170 above.

192 *Arrest Warrant of 11 April 2000 (Democratic Republic of Congo v. Belgium), Judgment, I.C.J. Reports 2002*, p. 3, at pp. 17–18, para. 40.

193 *Avena* (see footnote 29 above), pp. 35–36, para. 40.

194 *ELSI* (see footnote 149 above), at p. 43, para. 52. See also *Interhandel* (footnote 170 above), at p. 28.

195 See *Arrest Warrant of 11 August 2000, I.C.J. Reports 2000* (footnote 192 above), para. 40.

196 See the *United States Diplomatic and Consular Staff in Tehran* case (footnote 190 above).

197 The *Corfu Channel* case, *Merits, Judgment, I.C.J. Reports 1949*, p. 4.

198 See *Air Service Agreement of 27 March 1946 between the United States of America and France, Decision of 9 December 1978*, UNRIAA, vol. XVIII (Sales No. E/F.80.V.7), p. 417; *Applicability of the Obligation to Arbitrate under Section 21 of the United Nations Headquarters Agreement of 26 June 1947, Advisory Opinion, I.C.J. Reports 1988*, p. 12, at p. 29, para. 41.

199 See *Interhandel* (footnote 170 above), at pp. 28–29; and *ELSI* (footnote 149 above), at p. 43.

200 See *ELSI* (footnote 149 above), at p. 46, para. 59.

Commentary

(1) Draft article 15 deals with the exceptions to the exhaustion of local remedies rule. Paragraphs (*a*) and (*b*), which cover circumstances in which local courts offer no prospect of redress, and paragraphs (*c*) and (*d*), which deal with circumstances which make it unfair or unreasonable that an injured alien should be required to exhaust local remedies as a precondition for the bringing of a claim, are clear exceptions to the exhaustion of local remedies rule. Paragraph (*e*) deals with a different situation—that which arises where the respondent State has waived compliance with the local remedies rule.

Paragraph (*a*)

(2) Paragraph (*a*) deals with the exception to the exhaustion of local remedies rule sometimes described, in broad terms, as the "futility" or "ineffectiveness" exception. Three options require consideration for the formulation of a rule describing the circumstances in which local remedies need not be exhausted because of failures in the administration of justice:

(i) the local remedies are obviously futile;

(ii) the local remedies offer no reasonable prospect of success;

(iii) the local remedies provide no reasonable possibility of effective redress.

All three of these options enjoy some support among the authorities.

(3) The "obvious futility" test, expounded by Arbitrator Bagge in the *Finnish Ships Arbitration*,[201] sets too high a threshold. On the other hand, the test of "no reasonable prospect of success", accepted by the European Commission of Human Rights in several decisions,[202] is too generous to the claimant. This leaves the third option, which avoids the stringent language of "obvious futility" but nevertheless imposes a heavy burden on the claimant by requiring that he prove that in the circumstances of the case, and having regard to the legal system of the respondent State, there is no reasonable possibility of effective redress offered by the local remedies. This test has its origin in a separate opinion of Sir Hersch Lauterpacht in the *Certain Norwegian Loans* case[203] and is supported by the writings of jurists.[204] The test, however, fails to include the element of availability of local remedies which was endorsed by the Commission in its articles on responsibility of States for internationally wrongful acts[205] and is sometimes considered as a component of this rule by courts[206] and writers.[207] For this reason the test in paragraph (*a*) is expanded to require that there are no "reasonably available local remedies" to provide effective redress or that the local remedies provide no reasonable possibility of such redress. In this form, the test is supported by judicial decisions which have held that local remedies need not be exhausted where: the local court has no jurisdiction over the dispute in question;[208] the national legislation justifying the acts of which the alien complains will not be reviewed by local courts;[209] the local courts are notoriously lacking in independence;[210] there is a consistent and well-established line of precedents adverse to the alien;[211] the local courts do not have the competence to grant an appropriate and adequate remedy to the alien;[212] or the respondent State does not have an adequate system of judicial protection.[213]

---

[201] *Finnish Ships Arbitration* (see footnote 178 above), p. 1504.

[202] See *Retimag S.A.* v. *Federal Republic of Germany, Application No. 712/60, Decision of 16 December 1961,* European Commission and European Court of Human Rights, *Yearbook of the European Convention on Human Rights 1961*, pp. 385 *et seq.*, at p. 400; *X, Y and Z* v. *the United Kingdom, Application Nos. 8022/77 and 8027/77, Decision of 8 December 1979, European Commission of Human Rights, Decisions and Reports*, vol. 18, pp. 66 *et seq.*, at p. 74. See also the commentary to article 22 of the draft articles on State responsibility adopted by the Commission at its twenty-ninth session (footnote 173 above), p. 50, para. (60).

[203] *Certain Norwegian Loans, Judgment, I.C.J. Reports 1957*, p. 9, at p. 39.

[204] See G. Fitzmaurice, "Hersch Lauterpacht—the scholar as judge", BYBIL, vol. 37 (1961), pp. 1 *et seq.*, at pp. 60–61; and M. Herdegen, "Diplomatischer Schutz und die Erschöpfung von Rechtsbehelfen", in G. Ress and T. Stein (eds.), *Der diplomatische Schutz im Völker- und Europarecht: Aktuelle Probleme und Entwicklungstendenzen* (1996), pp. 63 *et seq.*, at p. 70.

[205] Article 44 requires local remedies to be "available and effective" (*Yearbook ... 2001*, vol. II (Part Two) and corrigendum, p. 120).

[206] In *Loewen* (see footnote 59 above), the tribunal stated that the exhaustion of local remedies rule obliges the injured person "to exhaust remedies which are effective and adequate and are reasonably available" to him (para. 168).

[207] See C. F. Amerasinghe, *Local Remedies in International Law* (footnote 174 above), pp. 181–182, 203–204.

[208] See *Panevezys-Saldutiskis Railway* (footnote 26 above), at p. 18; *Arbitration under Article 181 of the Treaty of Neuilly*, AJIL, vol. 28 (1934), p. 760, at p. 789; *Claim of Rosa Gelbtrunk, Award of 2 May 1902*, and the *"El Triunfo Company"* (footnote 136 above), at pp. 463–466 and pp. 467–479 respectively; *The Lottie May Incident* (arbitration between Honduras and the United Kingdom), *Arbitral Award of 18 April 1899*, UNRIAA, vol. XV, p. 23, at p. 31; Judge Lauterpacht's separate opinion in the *Certain Norwegian Loans* case (footnote 203 above), pp. 39–40; and the *Finnish Ships Arbitration* (see footnote 178 above), p. 1535.

[209] See *Arbitration under Article 181 of the Treaty of Neuilly* (footnote above). See also *Affaire des Forêts du Rhodope central (fond), Decision of 29 March 1933*, UNRIAA, vol. III (Sales No. 1949.V.2), p. 1405; the *Ambatielos Claim* (footnote 174 above), p. 119; and the *Interhandel* case (footnote 170 above), p. 28.

[210] See *Robert E. Brown (United States)* v. *Great Britain, Arbitral Award of 23 November 1923, UNRIAA*, vol. VI (Sales No. 1955.V.3), p. 120; and *Velásquez Rodríguez* v. *Honduras, Judgement of 29 July 1988,* Inter-American Court of Human Rights, *Series C, No. 4* (see also ILM, vol. 28 (1989), pp. 291 *et seq.*, at pp. 304–309).

[211] See *Panevezys-Saldutiskis Railway* case (footnote 26 above); *S.S. "Lisman", Award of 5 October 1937*, UNRIAA, vol. III, p. 1767, at p. 1773; *S.S. "Seguranca", Award of 27 September 1939, ibid.*, p. 1861, at p. 1868; *Finnish Ships Arbitration* (see footnote 178 above), p. 1495; *X.* v. *Federal Republic of Germany, Application No. 27/55, Decision of 31 May 1956, European Commission of Human Rights, Documents and Decisions, 1955–1956–1957*, p. 138; *X* v. *Federal Republic of Germany, Application No. 352/58, Decision of 4 September 1958,* European Commission and European Court of Human Rights, *Yearbook of the European Convention on Human Rights, 1958–1959*, p. 342, at p. 344; and *X.* v. *Austria, Application No. 514/59, Decision of 5 January 1960, Yearbook of the European Convention on Human Rights, 1960*, p. 196, at p. 202.

[212] See *Finnish Ships Arbitration* (see footnote 178 above), pp. 1496–1497; *Velásquez Rodríguez* (see footnote 210 above); *Yağci and Sargin* v. *Turkey, Judgment of 8 June 1995, European Court of Human Rights, Series A: Judgments and Decisions*, vol. 319, p. 3, at p. 17, para. 42; and *Hornsby* v. *Greece, Judgment of 19 March 1997, ibid., Reports of Judgments and Decisions, 1997-II*, No. 33, p. 495, at p. 509, para. 37.

[213] See *Mushikiwabo and Others* v. *Barayagwiza, Decision of 9 April 1996, ILR*, vol. 107 (1997), pp. 457 *et seq.*, at p. 460. During the military dictatorship in Chile, the Inter-American Commission on Human Rights resolved that the irregularities inherent in legal proceedings under military justice obviated the need to exhaust local remedies (see resolution No. 01a/88 of 12 September 1988, case 9755: Chile, *Annual Report of the Inter-American Commission on Human Rights, 1987–1988*, OEA/Ser.L/V/II.74 document 10 rev.1, p. 136).

(4) In order to meet the requirements of paragraph (*a*), it is not sufficient for the injured person to show that the possibility of success is low or that further appeals are difficult or costly. The test is not whether a successful outcome is likely or possible, but whether the municipal system of the respondent State is reasonably capable of providing effective relief. This must be determined in the context of the local law and the prevailing circumstances. This is a question to be decided by the competent international tribunal charged with the task of examining the question whether local remedies have been exhausted. The decision on this matter must be made on the assumption that the claim is meritorious.[214]

Paragraph (*b*)

(5) That the requirement of exhaustion of local remedies may be dispensed with in cases in which the respondent State is responsible for an unreasonable delay in allowing a local remedy to be implemented is confirmed by codification attempts,[215] human rights instruments and practice,[216] judicial decisions[217] and scholarly opinion. It is difficult to give an objective content or meaning to "undue delay", or to attempt to prescribe a fixed time limit within which local remedies are to be implemented. Each case must be judged on its own facts. As the British–Mexican Claims Commission stated in the *El Oro Mining* case: "The Commission will not attempt to lay down with precision just within what period a tribunal may be expected to render judgment. This will depend upon several circumstances, foremost amongst them upon the volume of the work involved by a thorough examination of the case, in other words, upon the magnitude of the latter."[218]

(6) Paragraph (*b*) makes it clear that the delay in the remedial process is attributable to the State alleged to be responsible for an injury to an alien. The phrase "remedial process" is preferred to that of "local remedies" as it is meant to cover the entire process by which local remedies are invoked and implemented and through which local remedies are channelled.

[214] See *Finnish Ships Arbitration* (footnote 178 above), at p. 1504; and the *Ambatielos Claim* (footnote 174 above), at pp. 119–120.

[215] See the discussion of early codification attempts by F. V. García Amador, Special Rapporteur, in his preliminary report on State responsibility, *Yearbook ... 1956*, vol. II , document A/CN.4/96, pp. 173–231, at pp. 223–225; and article 19, paragraph 2, of the draft convention on the international responsibility of States for injuries to aliens, prepared in 1960 by the Harvard Law School, in Sohn and Baxter, *loc. cit.* (see footnote 71 above), at p. 577.

[216] International Covenant on Civil and Political Rights (art. 41, para. 1 (*c*)); American Convention on Human Rights: "Pact of San José, Costa Rica" (art. 46, para. 2 (c)); *Weinberger* v. *Uruguay, Communication No. 28/1978*, Human Rights Committee, *Selected Decisions under the Optional Protocol* (second to sixteenth sessions) (United Nations publication, Sales No. E.84.XIV.2), vol. 1, p. 57, at p. 59; *Las Palmeras, Preliminary Objections, Judgment of 4 February 2000*, Inter-American Court of Human Rights, *Series C: Decisions and Judgments*, No. 67, p. 64, para. 38; and *Erdoğan* v. *Turkey, Application No. 19807/92, Decision of 16 January 1996*, European Commission of Human Rights, *Decisions and Reports*, vol. 84–A, pp. 5 *et seq.*, at p. 15.

[217] See *El Oro Mining and Railway Company (Litd.) (Great Britain)* v. *United Mexican States, Decision No. 55 of 18 June 1931*, UNRIAA, vol. V (Sales No. 1952.V.3), p. 191, at p. 198; and the *Case concerning the Administration of the Prince von Pless, Order of 4 February 1933, P.C.I.J., Series A/B, No. 52*, p. 11, at p. 16.

[218] See footnote 217 above.

Paragraph (*c*)

(7) The exception to the exhaustion of local remedies rule contained in draft article 15, paragraph (*a*), to the effect that local remedies do not need to be exhausted where they are not reasonably available or "provide no reasonable possibility of effective redress", does not cover situations where local remedies are available and might offer the reasonable possibility of effective redress but it would be unreasonable or cause great hardship to the injured alien to exhaust local remedies. For instance, even where effective local remedies exist, it would be unreasonable and unfair to require an injured person to exhaust local remedies where his property has suffered environmental harm caused by pollution, radioactive fallout or a fallen space object emanating from a State in which his property is not situated, or where he is on board an aircraft that is shot down while flying over another State's territory. In such cases it has been suggested that local remedies need not be exhausted because of the absence of a voluntary link or territorial connection between the injured individual and the respondent State.

(8) There is support in the literature for the proposition that in all cases in which the exhaustion of local remedies has been required, there has been some link between the injured individual and the respondent State, such as voluntary physical presence, residence, ownership of property or a contractual relationship with the respondent State.[219] Proponents of this view maintain that the nature of diplomatic protection and the local remedies rule has undergone major changes in recent times. Whereas the early history of diplomatic protection was characterized by situations in which a foreign national resident and doing business in a foreign State was injured by the action of that State and could therefore be expected to exhaust local remedies in accordance with the philosophy that the national going abroad should normally be obliged to accept the local law as he finds it, including the means afforded for the redress of wrong, an individual may today be injured by the act of a foreign State outside its territory or by some act within its territory in circumstances in which the individual has no connection with the territory. Examples of this are afforded by transboundary environmental harm (for example, the explosion at the Chernobyl nuclear plant near Kiev in the Ukraine in 1986, which caused radioactive fallout as far away as Japan and Scandinavia) and the shooting down of an aircraft that has accidentally strayed into a State's airspace (as illustrated by the *Aerial Incident of 27 July 1955* case, in which Bulgaria shot down an El Al flight that had accidentally entered its airspace).[220] The basis for such a voluntary link or territorial connection rule is the assumption of risk by the alien in a foreign State. It is only where the alien has subjected himself voluntarily to the jurisdiction of the respondent State that he would be expected to exhaust local remedies.

[219] See C. F. Amerasinghe, *Local Remedies in International Law* (footnote 174 above), at p. 169; and T. Meron, "The incidence of the rule of exhaustion of local remedies", BYBIL, *1959*, vol. 35, pp. 83 *et seq.*, at p. 94.

[220] *Case Concerning the Aerial Incident of 27 July 1955 (Israel* v. *Bulgaria), Preliminary Objections, Judgment of 26 May 1959, I.C.J. Reports 1959*, p. 127.

(9) Neither judicial authority nor State practice provide clear guidance on the existence of such an exception to the exhaustion of local remedies rule. While there are tentative dicta in support of the existence of such an exception in the *Interhandel*[221] and *Salem*[222] cases, in other cases[223] tribunals have upheld the applicability of the local remedies rule despite the absence of a voluntary link between the injured alien and the respondent State. In both the *Norwegian Loans* case[224] and the *Aerial Incident of 27 July 1955* case,[225] arguments in favour of the voluntary link requirement were forcefully advanced, but in neither case did the ICJ make a decision on this matter. In *Trail Smelter*,[226] involving transboundary pollution in which there was no voluntary link or territorial connection, there was no insistence by Canada on the exhaustion of local remedies. This case and others[227], in which local remedies were dispensed with where there was no voluntary link, have been interpreted as lending support to the requirements of voluntary submission to jurisdiction as a precondition for the application of the local remedies rule. The failure to insist on the application of the local remedies rule in these cases can be explained, however, on the basis that they provide examples of direct injury, in which local remedies do not need to be exhausted, or on the basis that the arbitration agreement in question did not require local remedies to be exhausted.

(10) Paragraph (*c*) does not use the term "voluntary link" to describe this exception, as this emphasizes the subjective intention of the injured individual rather than the absence of an objectively determinable connection between the individual and the host State. In practice, it would be difficult to prove such a subjective criterion. Hence paragraph (*c*) requires the existence of a "relevant connection" between the injured alien and the host State and not a voluntary link. This connection must be "relevant" in the sense that it must relate in some way to the injury suffered. A tribunal will be required to examine not only the question whether the injured individual was present, resided or did business in the territory of the host State but whether, in the circumstances, the individual, by his conduct, had assumed the risk that if he suffered an injury it would be subject to adjudication in the host State. The word "relevant" best allows a tribunal to consider the essential elements governing the relationship between the injured alien and the host State in the context of the injury in order to determine whether there had been an assumption of risk on the part of the injured alien. There must be no "relevant connection" between the injured individual and the respondent State at the date of the injury.

Paragraph (*d*)

(11) Paragraph (*d*) is designed to give a tribunal the power to dispense with the requirement of exhaustion of local remedies where, in all the circumstances of the case, it would be manifestly unreasonable to expect compliance with the rule. This paragraph, which is an exercise in progressive development, must be narrowly construed, with the burden of proof on the injured person to show not merely that there are serious obstacles and difficulties in the way of exhausting local remedies, but that he is "manifestly" precluded from pursuing such remedies. No attempt is made to provide a comprehensive list of factors that might qualify for this exception. Circumstances that may manifestly preclude the exhaustion of local remedies possibly include the situation in which the injured person is prevented by the respondent State from entering its territory, either by law or by threats to his or her personal safety, and thereby denying him or her the opportunity to bring proceedings in local courts, or where criminal syndicates in the respondent State obstruct him or her from bringing such proceedings. Although the injured person is expected to bear the costs of legal proceedings before the courts of the respondent State, there may be circumstances in which such costs are prohibitively high and "manifestly preclude" compliance with the exhaustion of local remedies rule.[228]

Paragraph (*e*)

(12) A State may be prepared to waive the requirement that local remedies be exhausted. As the purpose of the rule is to protect the interests of the State accused of mistreating an alien, it follows that a State may waive this protection itself. The Inter-American Court of Human Rights has stated:

> In cases of this type, under the generally recognized principles of international law and international practice, the rule which requires the prior exhaustion of domestic remedies is designed for the benefit of the State, for that rule seeks to excuse the State from having to respond to charges before an international body for acts which have been imputed to it before it has had the opportunity to remedy them by internal means. The requirement is thus considered a means of defence and, as such, waivable, even tacitly.[229]

(13) Waiver of local remedies may take many different forms. It may appear in a bilateral or multilateral treaty entered into before or after the dispute arises; it may appear in a contract between the alien and the respondent State; it may be express or implied; or it may be inferred from the conduct of the respondent State in circumstances in which it can be described as estoppel or forfeiture.

---

[221] Here the ICJ stated: "it has been considered necessary that the *State where the violation occurred** should have an opportunity to redress it by its own means" (see footnote 170 above), at p. 27.

[222] In the *Salem* case, an arbitral tribunal declared that "[a]s a rule, a foreigner must acknowledge as applicable to himself the kind of justice instituted in the country in which he did choose his residence" (see footnote 72 above), at p. 1202.

[223] *Finnish Ships Arbitration* (see footnote 178 above) and the *Ambatielos Claim* (see footnote 174 above).

[224] *Case of Certain Norwegian Loans (France* v. *Norway), Oral Pleadings of France, I.C.J. Pleadings 1957*, vol. I, p. 408.

[225] *Case concerning the Aerial Incident of 27 July 1955 (Israel* v. *Bulgaria), Preliminary Objections, Oral Pleadings of Israel, I.C.J. Pleadings 1959*, pp. 531–532.

[226] *Trail Smelter*, UNRIAA, vol. III (Sales No. 1949.V.2), p. 1905.

[227] *Case of the "Virginius"* , reported in J. B. Moore, *A Digest of International Law*, vol. 2, Washington D.C., United States Government Printing Office, 1906, p. 895, at p. 903; and the *Jessie* case, reported in AJIL, vol. 16 (1922), pp. 114–116.

[228] On the implications of costs for the exhaustion of local remedies, see *Loewen* (footnote 59 above), at para. 166.

[229] *Viviana Gallardo* et al., *Decision of 13 November 1981, No. G 101/81*, Inter-American Court of Human Rights, *Series A: Judgments and Opinions*, para. 26 (see also *ILR*, vol. 67 (1984), p. 587). See also *ELSI* (footnote 149 above), p. 42, para. 50; and the *De Wilde, Ooms* and *Versyp* cases (*"Vagrancy Cases"*), *Judgment of 18 June 1971*, European Court of Human Rights, *Series A: Judgments and Decisions*, p. 12 (see also *ILR*, vol. 56 (1980), p. 337, at p. 370, para. 55).

(14) An express waiver may be included in an *ad hoc* arbitration agreement concluded to resolve an already existing dispute or in a general treaty providing that disputes arising in the future are to be settled by arbitration or some other form of international dispute settlement. It may also be included in a contract between a State and an alien. There is a general agreement that an express waiver of the local remedies is valid. Waivers are a common feature of contemporary State practice and many arbitration agreements contain waiver clauses. Probably the best-known example is to be found in article 26 of the Convention on the settlement of investment disputes between States and nationals of other States, which provides:

> Consent of the parties to arbitration under this Convention shall, unless otherwise stated, be deemed consent to such arbitration to the exclusion of any other remedy. A Contracting State may require the exhaustion of local administrative or judicial remedies as a condition of its consent to arbitration under this Convention.

It is generally agreed that express waivers, whether contained in an agreement between States or in a contract between State and alien, are irrevocable, even if the contract is governed by the law of the host State.[230]

(15) Waiver of local remedies must not be readily implied. In the *ELSI* case, a Chamber of the ICJ stated in this connection that it was "unable to accept that an important principle of customary international law should be held to have been tacitly dispensed with, in the absence of any words making clear an intention to do so".[231]

(16) Where, however, the intention of the parties to waive the local remedies is clear, effect must be given to this intention. Both judicial decisions[232] and the writings of jurists[233]support such a conclusion. No general rule can be laid down as to when an intention to waive local remedies may be implied. Each case must be determined in the light of the language of the instrument and the circumstances of its adoption. Where the respondent State has agreed to submit disputes to arbitration that may arise in future with the applicant State, there is support for the view that such an agreement "does not involve the abandonment of the claim to exhaust all local remedies in cases in which one of the Contracting Parties espouses the claim of its national".[234] That there is a strong presumption against implied or tacit waiver in such a case was confirmed by the Chamber of the ICJ in the *ELSI* case.[235] A waiver of local remedies may be more easily implied from an arbitration agreement entered into after the dispute in question has arisen. In such a case, it may be contended that such a waiver may be implied if the respondent State entered into an arbitration agreement with the applicant State covering disputes relating to the treatment of nationals after the injury to the national who is the subject of the dispute and the agreement is silent on the retention of the local remedies rule.

(17) Although there is support for the proposition that the conduct of the respondent State during international proceedings may result in that State being estopped from requiring that local remedies be exhausted,[236] paragraph (*e*) does not refer to estoppel in its formulation of the rule governing waiver on account of the uncertainty surrounding the doctrine of estoppel in international law. It is wiser to allow conduct from which a waiver of local remedies might be inferred to be treated as implied waiver.

Part Four

MISCELLANEOUS PROVISIONS

Article 16. Actions or procedures other than diplomatic protection

The rights of States, natural persons, legal persons or other entities to resort under international law to actions or procedures other than diplomatic protection to secure redress for injury suffered as a result of an internationally wrongful act, are not affected by the present draft articles.

Commentary

(1) The customary international law rules on diplomatic protection and the rules governing the protection of human rights are complementary. The present draft articles are therefore not intended to exclude or to trump the rights of States, including both the State of nationality and States other than the State of nationality of an injured individual, to protect the individual under either customary international law or a multilateral or bilateral human rights treaty or other treaty. They are also not intended to interfere with the rights of natural and legal persons or other entities involved in the protection of human rights to resort under international law to actions or procedures other than diplomatic protection to secure redress for injury suffered as a result of an internationally wrongful act.

(2) A State may protect a non-national against the State of nationality of an injured individual or a third State in inter-State proceedings under the International Covenant on Civil and Political Rights (art. 41), the International Convention on the Elimination of All Forms of Racial Discrimination (art. 11), the Convention against Torture and Other Cruel, Inhuman or Degrading Treatment or Punishment (art. 21), the European Convention on Human Rights (art. 24), the American Convention on Human Rights: "Pact of San

[230] See *Viviana Gallardo* et al. (footnote 229 above) and the *De Wilde, Ooms* and *Versyp* cases (*"Vagrancy Cases"*) (*ibid.*).

[231] *ELSI* (see footnote 149 above), at p. 42, para. 50.

[232] See, for example, *Steiner and Gross* v. *Polish State, Case No. 322 (30 March 1928), Annual Digest of Public International Law Cases: Years 1927 and 1928,* A. D. McNair and H. Lauterpacht (eds.), London, Longmans, Green and Co., 1931, p. 472; and *American International Group, Inc.* v. *The Islamic Republic of Iran, Award No. 93-2-3 of 19 December 1983, Iran–United States Claims Tribunal Reports*, vol. 4, Cambridge, Grotius, 1985, p. 96.

[233] See, for example, S. M. Schwebel, *International Arbitration: Three Salient Problems*, Cambridge, Grotius Publishers, 1987, pp. 117–121.

[234] F. A. Mann, "State contracts and international arbitration", BYBIL, *1967*, vol. 42, p. 32.

[235] See footnote 149 above. In the *Panevezys-Saldutiskis Railway* case (see footnote 26 above), the PCIJ held that acceptance of the optional clause under Article 36, paragraph 2, of the Statute of the Court did not constitute implied waiver of the local remedies rule (as had been argued by Judge van Eysinga in his dissenting opinion, *ibid.*, pp. 35–36).

[236] See the *ELSI* case (footnote 149 above), p. 44, para. 54; *United States–United Kingdom Arbitration concerning Heathrow Airport User Charges, Award of 30 November 1992, ILR*, vol. 102 (1996), pp. 216 *et seq.*, at p. 285, para. 6.33; and the *Foti and Others Case, Merits, Judgement of 10 December 1982, ibid.*, vol. 71 (1986), pp. 366 *et seq.*, at p. 380, para. 46.

José, Costa Rica" (art. 45), and the African Charter on Human and Peoples' Rights (arts. 47–54). The same conventions allow a State to protect its own nationals in inter-State proceedings. Moreover, customary international law allows States to protect the rights of non-nationals by protest, negotiation and, if a jurisdictional instrument so permits, legal proceedings. The view taken by the ICJ in the 1966 *South West Africa* cases[237] that a State may not bring legal proceedings to protect the rights of non-nationals has to be qualified in the light of the articles on responsibility of States for internationally wrongful acts.[238] Article 48, paragraph 1(*b*) of the articles on responsibility of States for internationally wrongful acts permits a State other than the injured State to invoke the responsibility of another State if the obligation breached is owed to the international community as a whole,[239] without complying with the requirements for the exercise of diplomatic protection.[240]

(3) The individual is also endowed with rights and remedies to protect him- or herself against the injuring State, whether the individual's State of nationality or another State, in terms of international human rights conventions. This is most frequently achieved by the right to petition an international human rights monitoring body.[241]

(4) Individual rights under international law may also arise outside the framework of human rights. In the *LaGrand* case, the ICJ held that article 36 of the Vienna Convention on Consular Relations "creates individual rights, which, by virtue of Article I of the Optional Protocol, may be invoked in this Court by the national State of the detained person",[242] and in the *Avena* case the Court further observed "that violations of the rights of the individual under Article 36 may entail a violation of the rights of the sending State, and that violations of the rights of the latter may entail a violation of the rights of the individual".[243] A saving clause was inserted in the draft articles on responsibility of States for internationally wrongful acts—article 33—to take account of this development in international law.[244]

(5) The actions or procedures referred to in draft article 16 include those available under both universal and regional human rights treaties as well as any other relevant treaty. Draft article 16 does not, however, deal with domestic remedies.

(6) The right to assert remedies other than diplomatic protection to secure redress for injury suffered as a result of an internationally wrongful act will normally vest in a State or a natural or legal person, with the term "legal person" including both corporations and other legal persons of the kind contemplated in draft article 13. However, there may be "other legal entities" not enjoying legal personality that may be endowed with the right to bring claims for injuries suffered as a result of an internationally wrongful act. Loosely-formed victims' associations provide an example of such an "other entity" which have on occasion been given standing before international bodies charged with the enforcement of human rights. Intergovernmental bodies may also in certain circumstances belong to this category; so too may national liberation movements.

(7) Draft article 16 makes it clear that the present draft articles are without prejudice to the rights that States, natural and legal persons or other entities may have to secure redress for injury suffered as a result of an internationally wrongful act by procedures other than diplomatic protection. Where, however, a State resorts to such procedures it does not necessarily abandon its right to exercise diplomatic protection in respect of a person if that person should be a national or person referred to in draft article 8.

Article 17. Special rules of international law

The present draft articles do not apply to the extent that they are inconsistent with special rules of international law, such as treaty provisions for the protection of investments.

Commentary

(1) Some treaties, particularly those dealing with the protection of foreign investment, contain special rules on the settlement of disputes which exclude or depart substantially from the rules governing diplomatic protection. Such treaties abandon or relax the conditions relating to the exercise of diplomatic protection, particularly the rules relating to the nationality of claims and the exhaustion of local remedies. Bilateral investment treaties (BITs) and the multilateral Convention on the settlement of investment disputes between States and nationals of other States are the primary examples of such treaties.

(2) Today foreign investment is largely regulated and protected by BITs.[245] The number of BITs has grown considerably in recent years and it is today estimated that there are nearly 2,000 such agreements in existence. An important feature of the BIT is its procedure for the settlement of investment disputes. Some BITs provide for the direct settlement of the investment dispute between the investor and the host State, before either an *ad hoc* tribunal or a tribunal

[237] *South West Africa, Second Phase, Judgment, I.C.J. Reports 1966*, p. 6.

[238] *Yearbook ... 2001*, vol. II (Part Two) and corrigendum, p. 127 (commentary to article 48, footnote 725).

[239] See further the separate opinion of Judge Simma in *Armed Activities on the Territory of the Congo (Democratic Republic of Congo v. Uganda), Judgment, I.C.J. Reports 2005*, p. 168, at pp. 347–350, paras. 35–41.

[240] Article 48, paragraph 1(*b*) is not subject to article 44 of the draft articles on responsibility of States for internationally wrongful acts, which requires a State invoking the responsibility of another State to comply with the rules relating to the nationality of claims and to exhaust local remedies. Nor is it subject to the present draft articles (cf. E. Milano, "Diplomatic protection and human rights before the International Court of Justice: re-fashioning tradition?", *Netherlands Yearbook of International Law*, vol. 35 (2004), pp. 85 *et seq.*, at pp. 103–108).

[241] See, for example, the Optional Protocol to the International Covenant on Civil and Political Rights; article 14 of the International Convention on the Elimination of All Forms of Racial Discrimination; article 22 of the Convention against Torture and Other Cruel, Inhuman or Degrading Treatment or Punishment; and the Optional Protocol to the Convention on the Elimination of All Forms of Discrimination against Women.

[242] *La Grand* (see footnote 28 above), at p. 494, para. 77.

[243] *Avena* (see footnote 29 above), at p. 36, para. 40.

[244] Paragraph 2 of this article reads: "This Part is without prejudice to any right, arising from the international responsibility of a State, which may accrue directly to any person or entity other than a State" (*Yearbook ... 2001*, vol. II (Part Two) and corrigendum, para. 76).

[245] This was acknowledged by the ICJ in *Barcelona Traction, Second Phase, Judgment* (see footnote 35 above), at p. 47, para. 90.

established by ICSID under the Convention on the settlement of investment disputes between States and nationals of other States. Other BITs provide for the settlement of investment disputes by means of arbitration between the State of nationality of the investor (corporation or shareholder) and the host State over the interpretation or application of the relevant provision of the BIT. The dispute settlement procedures provided for in BITs and the Convention on the settlement of investment disputes between States and nationals of other States offer greater advantages to the foreign investor than the customary international law system of diplomatic protection, as they give the investor direct access to international arbitration, avoid the political uncertainty inherent in the discretionary nature of diplomatic protection and dispense with the conditions for the exercise of diplomatic protection.[246]

(3) Draft article 17 makes it clear that the present draft articles do not apply to the alternative special regime for the protection of foreign investors provided for in bilateral and multilateral investment treaties. The provision is formulated so that the draft articles do not apply "*to the extent that*" they are inconsistent with the provisions of a BIT. To the extent that the draft articles remain consistent with the BIT in question, they continue to apply.

(4) Draft article 17 refers to "treaty provisions" rather than to "treaties", as treaties other than those specifically designed for the protection of investments may regulate the protection of investments, such as treaties of friendship, commerce and navigation.

Article 18. Protection of ships' crews

The right of the State of nationality of the members of the crew of a ship to exercise diplomatic protection is not affected by the right of the State of nationality of a ship to seek redress on behalf of such crew members, irrespective of their nationality, when they have been injured in connection with an injury to the vessel resulting from an internationally wrongful act.

Commentary

(1) The purpose of draft article 18 is to affirm the right of the State or States of nationality of a ship's crew to exercise diplomatic protection on their behalf, while at the same time acknowledging that the State of nationality of the ship also has a right to seek redress on their behalf, irrespective of their nationality, when they have been injured in the course of an injury to a vessel resulting from an internationally wrongful act. It has become necessary to affirm the right of the State of nationality to exercise diplomatic protection on behalf of the members of a ship's crew in order to preclude any suggestion that this right has been replaced by that of the State of nationality of the ship. At the same time, it is necessary to recognize the right of the State of nationality of the ship to seek redress in respect of the members of the ship's crew. Although this cannot be characterized as diplomatic protection in the absence of the bond of nationality between the flag State of a ship and the members of a ship's crew, there is nevertheless a close resemblance between this type of protection and diplomatic protection.

(2) There is support in the practice of States, in judicial decisions and in the writings of publicists,[247] for the position that the State of nationality of a ship (the flag State) may seek redress for members of the crew of the ship who do not have its nationality. There are also policy considerations in favour of such an approach.

(3) The early practice of the United States, in particular, lends support to such a custom. Under American law, foreign seamen were traditionally entitled to the protection of the United States while serving on American vessels. The American view was that once a seaman enlisted on a ship, the only relevant nationality was that of the flag State.[248] This unique status of foreigners serving on American vessels was traditionally reaffirmed in diplomatic communications and consular regulations of the United States.[249] Doubts have, however, been raised, including by the United States,[250] as to whether this practice provides evidence of a customary rule.[251]

(4) International arbitral awards are inconclusive on the right of a State to extend protection to non-national seamen, but tend to lean in favour of such a right rather than against it. In the *McCready* case, the umpire, Sir Edward Thornton, held that "seamen serving in the naval or mercantile marine under a flag not their own are entitled, for the duration of that service, to the protection of the flag under which they serve".[252] In the "*I'm Alone*" case,[253] which arose from the sinking of a Canadian vessel by a United States coast guard ship, the Government of Canada successfully claimed compensation on behalf of three non-national crew members, asserting that where a claim was on behalf of a vessel, members of the crew were to be deemed, for the purposes of the claim, to be of the same nationality as the vessel. In the *Reparation for Injuries* advisory opinion two judges, in their separate opinions, accepted the right of a State to exercise protection on behalf of alien crew members.[254]

---

[246] Article 27, paragraph (1) of the Convention on the settlement of investment disputes between States and nationals of other States provides: "No Contracting State shall give diplomatic protection, or bring an international claim, in respect of a dispute which one of its nationals and another Contracting State shall have consented to submit or shall have submitted to arbitration under this Convention, unless such other Contracting State shall have failed to abide by and comply with the award rendered in such dispute."

[247] See H. Myers, *The Nationality of Ships*, The Hague, Martinus Nijhoff, 1967, pp. 90–107; R. Dolzer, "Diplomatic protection of foreign nationals", in R. Bernhardt (ed.), *Encyclopedia of Public International Law*, vol. 1, Amsterdam, Elsevier, 1992, p. 1067; and I. Brownlie, *Principles of Public International Law*, 6th ed., Oxford University Press, 2003, p. 460.

[248] See the *Ross* case, *United States Reports*, vol. 140 (1911), p. 453.

[249] See Hackworth, *op. cit.* (footnote 64 above), vol. III, p. 418, and vol. IV, pp. 883–884.

[250] Communication dated 20 May 2003 to the International Law Commission (on file with the Codification Division of the Office of Legal Affairs of the United Nations).

[251] See A. Watts, "The protection of alien seamen", *International and Comparative Law Quarterly*, vol. 7 (1958), p. 691.

[252] *McCready (U.S.* v. *Mexico)*, J. B. Moore, *International Arbitrations*, vol. 3, p. 2536.

[253] *S. S. "I'm Alone" (Canada* v. *United States),* UNRIAA, vol. III, p. 1609.

[254] *Reparation for Injuries* (see footnote 23 above), at pp. 202–203 (Judge Hackworth) and pp. 206–207 (Judge Badawi Pasha).

(5) In 1999, ITLOS handed down its decision in the *"Saiga"* case[255] which provides support for the right of the flag State to seek redress for non-national crew members. The dispute in this case arose out of the arrest and detention of the *"Saiga"* by Guinea, while it was supplying oil to fishing vessels off the coast of Guinea. The *"Saiga"* was registered in St. Vincent and the Grenadines ("St. Vincent") and its master and crew were Ukrainian nationals. There were also three Senegalese workers on board at the time of the arrest. Following the arrest, Guinea detained the ship and crew. In proceedings before ITLOS, Guinea objected to the admissibility of St. Vincent's claim, *inter alia*, on the ground that the injured crew members were not nationals of St. Vincent. The Tribunal dismissed these challenges to the admissibility of the claim and held that Guinea had violated the rights of St. Vincent by arresting and detaining the ship and its crew. It ordered Guinea to pay compensation to St. Vincent for damages to the *"Saiga"* and for injury to the crew.

(6) Although ITLOS treated the dispute mainly as one of direct injury to St. Vincent,[256] the Tribunal's reasoning suggests that it also saw the matter as a case involving the protection of the crew something akin to, but different from, diplomatic protection. Guinea clearly objected to the admissibility of the claim in respect of the crew on the ground that it constituted a claim for diplomatic protection in respect of non-nationals of St. Vincent.[257] St. Vincent, equally clearly, insisted that it had the right to protect the crew of a ship flying its flag "irrespective of their nationality".[258] In dismissing Guinea's objection, ITLOS stated that the United Nations Convention on the Law of the Sea in a number of relevant provisions, including article 292, drew no distinction between nationals and non-nationals of the flag State.[259] It stressed that "the ship, every thing on it, and every person involved or interested in its operations are treated as an entity linked to the flag State. The nationalities of these persons are not relevant".[260]

(7) There are cogent policy reasons for allowing the flag State to seek redress for the ship's crew. This was recognized by ITLOS in *"Saiga"* when it called attention to "the transient and multinational composition of ships' crews" and stated that large ships "could have a crew comprising persons of several nationalities. If each person sustaining damage were obliged to look for protection from the State of which such a person is a national, undue hardship would ensue".[261] Practical considerations relating to the bringing of claims should not be overlooked. It is much easier and more efficient for one State to seek redress on behalf of all crew members than to require the States of nationality of all crew members to bring separate claims on behalf of their nationals.

(8) Support for the right of the flag State to seek redress for the ship's crew is substantial and justified. It cannot, however, be categorized as diplomatic protection, nor should it be seen as having replaced diplomatic protection. Both diplomatic protection by the State of nationality and the right of the flag State to seek redress for the crew should be recognized, without priority being accorded to either. Ships' crews are often exposed to hardships emanating from the flag State, in the form of poor working conditions, or from third States, in the event of the ship being arrested. In these circumstances, they should receive the maximum protection that international law can offer.

(9) The right of the flag State to seek redress for the ship's crew is not limited to redress for injuries sustained during or in the course of an injury to the vessel, but extends also to injuries sustained in connection with an injury to the vessel resulting from an internationally wrongful act that is as a consequence of the injury to the vessel. Thus such a right would arise where members of the ship's crew are illegally arrested and detained after the illegal arrest of the ship itself.

Article 19. Recommended practice

A State entitled to exercise diplomatic protection according to the present draft articles, should:

(*a*) give due consideration to the possibility of exercising diplomatic protection, especially when a significant injury has occurred;

(*b*) take into account, wherever feasible, the views of injured persons with regard to resort to diplomatic protection and the reparation to be sought; and

(*c*) transfer to the injured person any compensation obtained for the injury from the responsible State subject to any reasonable deductions.

Commentary

(1) There are certain practices on the part of States in the field of diplomatic protection which have not yet acquired the status of customary rules and which are not susceptible to transformation into rules of law in the exercise of progressive development of the law. Nevertheless they are desirable practices, constituting necessary features of diplomatic protection that add strength to diplomatic protection as a means for the protection of human rights and foreign investment. These practices are recommended to States for their consideration in the exercise of diplomatic protection in draft article 19, which recommends that States "should" follow certain practices. The use of recommendatory, and not prescriptive, language of this kind is not unknown to treaties, although it cannot be described as a common feature of treaties.[262]

[255] *The M/V "Saiga" (No. 2)* case *(Saint Vincent and the Grenadines* v. *Guinea), Judgment, ITLOS Reports 1999*, vol. 3, p. 10.

[256] *Ibid.*, pp. 45–46, para. 98.

[257] *Ibid.*, p. 47, para. 103.

[258] *Ibid.*, para. 104.

[259] *Ibid.*, pp. 47–48, para. 105.

[260] *Ibid.*, p. 48, para. 106.

[261] *Ibid.*, para. 107.

[262] Article 36, paragraph 3 of the Charter of the United Nations, for instance, provides that in recommending appropriate procedures for the settlement of disputes, "the Security Council *should** also take into consideration that legal disputes *should** as a general rule be referred by the parties to the International Court of Justice in accordance with the provisions of the Statute of the Court". The Geneva Conventions on the Law of the Sea also employ the term "should" rather than "shall". Article 3 of the 1958 Geneva Convention on the High Seas provides that "[i]n order to enjoy freedom of the seas on equal terms with coastal States, States having no sea-coast *should** have free access to the sea". See, too, articles 27, 28, 43 and 123 of the 1982 United Nations Convention on the Law of the Sea.

(2) Paragraph (*a*) recommends to States that they should give consideration to the possibility of exercising diplomatic protection on behalf of a national who suffers significant injury. The protection of human beings by means of international law is today one of the principal goals of the international legal order, as was reaffirmed by resolution 60/1 on the 2005 World Summit Outcome adopted by the General Assembly on 16 September 2005.[263] This protection may be achieved by many means, including consular protection, resort to international human rights treaties mechanisms, criminal prosecution or action by the Security Council or other international bodies—and diplomatic protection. Which procedure or remedy is most likely to achieve the goal of effective protection will, inevitably, depend on the circumstances of each case. When the protection of foreign nationals is in issue, diplomatic protection is an obvious remedy to which States should give serious consideration. After all, it is the remedy with the longest history and has a proven record of effectiveness. Draft article 19 (*a*) serves as a reminder to States that they should consider the possibility of resorting to this remedial procedure.

(3) A State is not obliged under international law to exercise diplomatic protection on behalf of a national who has been injured as a result of an internationally wrongful act attributable to another State. The discretionary nature of the State's right to exercise diplomatic protection is affirmed by draft article 2 of the present draft articles and has been asserted by the ICJ[264] and national courts,[265] as shown in the commentary to draft article 2. Despite this, there is growing support for the view that there is some obligation, however imperfect, on States, either under international law or national law, to protect their nationals abroad when they are subjected to significant human rights violations. The constitutions of many States recognize the right of the individual to receive diplomatic protection for injuries suffered abroad,[266] which must carry with it the corresponding duty of the State to exercise protection. Moreover, a number of national court decisions indicate that although a State has a discretion whether to exercise diplomatic protection or not, there is an obligation on that State, subject to judicial review, to do something to assist its nationals, which may include an obligation to give due consideration to the possibility of exercising diplomatic protection.[267] In *Kaunda,* the Constitutional Court of South Africa stated that:

> There may thus be a duty on government, consistent with its obligations under international law, to take action to protect one of its citizens against a gross abuse of international human rights norms. A request to government for assistance in such circumstances where the evidence is clear would be difficult, and in extreme cases possibly impossible to refuse. It is unlikely that such a request would ever be refused by government, but if it were, the decision would be justiciable and a court would order the government to take appropriate action.[268]

In these circumstances, it is possible to seriously suggest that international law already recognizes the existence of some obligation on the part of a State to consider the possibility of exercising diplomatic protection on behalf of a national who has suffered a significant injury abroad. If customary international law has not yet reached this stage of development, then draft article 19 (*a*) must be seen as an exercise in progressive development.

(4) Paragraph (*b*) provides that a State "should", in the exercise of diplomatic protection, "take into account, wherever feasible, the views of injured persons with regard to resort to diplomatic protection and the reparation to be sought". In practice, States exercising diplomatic protection do have regard to the moral and material consequences of an injury to an alien in assessing the damages to be claimed.[269] In order to do this it is obviously necessary to consult with the injured person. This is also the case with the decision whether to demand satisfaction, restitution or compensation by way of reparation. This has led some scholars to contend that the admonition contained in draft article 19 (*b*) is already a rule of customary international law.[270] If it is not, draft article 19 (*b*) must also be seen as an exercise in progressive development.

(5) Paragraph (*c*) provides that States should transfer any compensation received from the responsible State in respect of an injury to a national to the injured national. This recommendation is designed to encourage the widespread perception that States have absolute discretion in such matters and are under no obligation to transfer moneys received for a claim based on diplomatic protection to the injured national. This perception has its roots in the *Mavrommatis* rule and a number of judicial pronouncements. In terms of the *Mavrommatis* dictum, a State asserts its own right in exercising diplomatic protection and becomes the "sole claimant".[271] Consequently, logic dictates that no restraints be placed on the State, in the interests of the individual, in the settlement of the claim or the payment of any compensation received. That the State has "complete freedom of action" in its exercise of diplomatic protection is confirmed by the *Barcelona Traction* case.[272] Despite the fact that the logic of *Mavrommatis* is undermined by the practice of calculating the amount of damages claimed on the basis of the injury suffered by the individual,[273] which is claimed to be a rule of

---

[263] Paragraphs 119–120 and 138–140.

[264] *Barcelona Traction, Second Phase, Judgment* (footnote 35 above), at p. 44.

[265] See, for example, *Abbasi and Juma* v. *Secretary of State for Foreign and Commonwealth Affairs and Secretary of State for the Home Department* (footnote 37 above) and *Kaunda and Others* v. *President of the Republic of South Africa and Others* (*ibid.*).

[266] See the preliminary report of the Special Rapporteur on diplomatic protection (footnote 36 above).

[267] *Rudolf Hess* case (footnote 37 above), at pp. 392 and 396; and *Abbasi and Juma* v. *Secretary of State for Foreign and Commonwealth Affairs and Secretary of State for the Home Department* (*ibid.*), paras. 69, 79–80, 82–83 and 107–108. See generally A. Vermeer-Künzli, "Restricting discretion: judicial review of diplomatic protection", *Nordic Journal of International Law*, vol. 75 (2006), p. 279.

[268] *Kaunda and Others* v. *President of the Republic of South Africa and Others* (see footnote 37 above), para. 69.

[269] *Case Concerning the Factory at Chorzów, Merits, Judgment No. 13 of 13 September 1928, PCIJ, Series A, No. 17*, at p. 28; see also the separate opinion of Judge Morelli in *Barcelona Traction, Second Phase, Judgment* (footnote 35 above) p. 223.

[270] See B. Bollecker-Stern, *Le préjudice dans la théorie de la responsabilité internationale*, Paris, Pedone, 1973, at p. 98; and L. Dubouis, "La distinction entre le droit de l'État réclamant et le droit au ressortissant dans la protection diplomatique", *Revue critique de droit international privé* (October–December 1978), pp. 615 *et seq.*, at p. 624.

[271] *Mavrommatis Palestine Concessions* (footnote 26 above), at p. 12.

[272] *Barcelona Traction, Second Phase, Judgment* (footnote 35 above), at p. 44, para. 79.

[273] See *Chorzów Factory* (footnote 269 above), at p. 28.

customary international law,[274] the view persists that the State has absolute discretion in the disposal of compensation received. This is illustrated by the dictum of Umpire Parker in the United States–German Mixed Claims Commission in *Administrative Decision No. V*:

> In exercising such control [the nation] is governed not only by the interest of the particular claimant but by the larger interests of the whole people of the nation and must exercise an untrammeled discretion in determining when and how the claim will be presented and pressed, or withdrawn or compromised, and the private owner will be bound by the action taken. *Even if payment is made to the espousing nation in pursuance of an award, it has complete control over the fund so paid to and held by it and may, to prevent fraud, correct a mistake, or protect the national honor, at its election return the fund to the nation paying it or otherwise dispose of it**.[275]

Similar statements are to be found in a number of English judicial decisions,[276] which are seen by some to be an accurate statement of international law.[277]

(6) It is by no means clear that State practice accords with the above view. On the one hand, States agree to lump sum settlements in respect of multiple individual claims, which in practice result in individual claims receiving considerably less than was claimed.[278] On the other hand, some States have enacted legislation to ensure that compensation awards are fairly distributed to individual claimants. Moreover, there is clear evidence that in practice States do pay moneys received in diplomatic claims to their injured nationals. In *Administrative Decision No. V*, Umpire Parker stated:

> But where a demand is made on behalf of a designated national, and an award and payment is made on that specific demand, the fund so paid is not a national fund in the sense that the title vests in the nation receiving it entirely free from any obligation to account to the private claimant, on whose behalf the claim was asserted and paid and who is the real owner thereof. Broad and misleading statements susceptible of this construction are found in cases where lump-sum awards and payments have been made to the demanding nation covering numerous claims put forward by it and where the tribunal making the award did not undertake to adjudicate each claim or to allocate any specified amount to any designated claim. It is not believed that any case can be cited in which an award has been made by an international tribunal in favor of the demanding nation on behalf of its designated national in which the nation receiving payment of such award has, in the absence of fraud or mistake, hesitated to account to the national designated, or those claiming under him, for the full amount of the award received. So far as the United States is concerned it would seem that the Congress has treated funds paid the nation in satisfaction of specific claims as held "in trust for citizens of the United States or others".[279]

That this is the practice of States is confirmed by scholars.[280] Further evidence of the erosion of the State's discretion is to be found in the decisions of arbitral tribunals which prescribe how the award is to be divided.[281] Moreover, in 1994, the European Court of Human Rights decided in *Beaumartin*[282] that an international agreement making provision for compensation could give rise to an enforceable right on the part of the injured persons to compensation.

(7) Paragraph (*c*) acknowledges that it would not be inappropriate for a State to make reasonable deductions from the compensation transferred to injured persons. The most obvious justification for such deductions would be to recoup the costs of State efforts to obtain compensation for its nationals, or to recover the cost of goods or services provided by the State to them.

(8) Although there is some support for curtailing the absolute right of the State to withhold payment of compensation received to the injured national in national legislation, judicial decisions and doctrine, this probably does not constitute a settled practice. Nor is there any sense of obligation on the part of States to limit their freedom of disposal of compensation awards. On the other hand, public policy, equity and respect for human rights support the curtailment of the State's discretion in the disbursement of compensation. It is against this background that draft article 19, paragraph (*c*), has been adopted. While it is an exercise in progressive development, it is supported by State practice and equity.

---

[274] See Bollecker-Stern, *op. cit.* (footnote 270 above) and Dubouis, *loc. cit.* (*ibid.*).

[275] *Administrative Decision No. V, Decision of 31 October 1924*, UNRIAA, vol. VII (Sales No. 1956.V.5), p. 119, at p. 152.

[276] *Civilian War Claimants Association* v. *R.*, United Kingdom, House of Lords, *The Law Reports of the Incorporated Council of Law Reporting 1932*, p. 14; *Lonrho Exports Ltd.* v. *Export Credits Guarantee Department, The All England Law Reports 1996*, vol. 4, p. 673, at p. 687.

[277] *Restatement of the Law Third, Restatement of the Law, The Foreign Relations Law of the United States*, vol. 2, St. Paul (Minnesota), American Law Institute Publishers, 1987, pp. 348–349; *Distribution of the Aslop Award by the Secretary of State (1912)*, Opinion of J. Reuben Clark, Department of State (cited in G. H. Hackworth, *Digest of International Law*, vol. 5, p. 766); and Bollecker-Stern, *op. cit.* (footnote 270 above), p. 108.

[278] See W. K. Geck, "Diplomatic protection", in R. Bernhardt (ed.), *op. cit.* (footnote 247 above), at p. 1058; D. J. Bederman, "Interim report on 'Lump sum agreements and diplomatic protection'", International Law Association, *Report of the Seventieth Conference, New Delhi, 2–6 April 2002*, London, 2002, p. 230; R. B. Lillich, "The United States–Hungarian Claims Agreement of 1973", AJIL, vol. 69 (1975), p. 534; and R. B Lillich and B. H. Weston, *International Claims: Their Settlement by Lump Sum Agreements*, Charlottesville, University Press of Virginia, 1975.

[279] *Administrative Decision No. V* (see footnote 275 above).

[280] Geck, *loc. cit.* (footnote 278 above), at p. 1057; F. V. García-Amador, L. B. Sohn and R. R. Baxter, *Recent Codification of the Law of State Responsibility for Injuries to Aliens*, Dobbs Ferry (New York), Oceana Publications, 1974, p. 151.

[281] See B. Bollecker-Stern, *op. cit.* (footnote 270 above), p. 109.

[282] *Beaumartin* v. *France, Case No. 15287/89, Judgement of 24 November 1994*, European Court of Human Rights, *Series A: Judgments and Decisions*, vol. 296-B .

Chapter V

INTERNATIONAL LIABILITY FOR INJURIOUS CONSEQUENCES ARISING OUT OF ACTS NOT PROHIBITED BY INTERNATIONAL LAW (INTERNATIONAL LIABILITY IN CASE OF LOSS FROM TRANSBOUNDARY HARM ARISING OUT OF HAZARDOUS ACTIVITIES)

A. Introduction

51. The Commission, at its thirtieth session (1978), included the topic "International liability for injurious consequences arising out of acts not prohibited by international law" in its programme of work and appointed Mr. Robert Q. Quentin-Baxter Special Rapporteur.[283]

52. From the thirty-second (1980) to the thirty-sixth (1984) sessions, the Commission received and considered five reports from the Special Rapporteur. In the fifth report, five draft articles were proposed by the Special Rapporteur but no decision was made to refer them to the Drafting Committee.[284]

53. The Commission, at its thirty-seventh session (1985), appointed Mr. Julio Barboza, Special Rapporteur for the topic, and from its thirty-seventh (1985) to forty-eighth (1996) sessions it received and considered 12 reports from the Special Rapporteur.[285] During this period, the Commission also established two working groups, one in 1992 to consider general issues relating to the scope, the approach to be taken and the possible direction of the future work on the topic,[286] and the other in 1996 to review the topic in all its aspects in the light of the reports of the Special Rapporteur and the discussions held, over the years, in the Commission, and to make recommendations to the Commission. The report of the latter working group provided a complete picture of the topic relating to the principle of prevention and that of liability for compensation or other relief, presenting articles and commentaries thereto.[287]

54. At its forty-ninth (1997) session, the Commission, on the basis of recommendations of the Working Group on international liability for injurious consequences arising out of activities not prohibited by international law established to consider how the Commission should proceed with its work on this topic,[288] decided to deal first with the issue of prevention under the subtitle "Prevention of transboundary damage from hazardous activities" and appointed Mr. Pemmaraju Sreenivasa Rao Special Rapporteur for the topic.[289] From its fiftieth (1998) to its fifty-second (2000) sessions, the Commission received and considered three reports from the Special Rapporteur.[290]

[283] At that session, the Commission established a working group to consider, in a preliminary manner, the scope and nature of the topic. For the report of the Working Group, see *Yearbook ... 1978*, vol. II (Part Two), pp. 150–152.

[284] For the five reports of the Special Rapporteur, see preliminary report: *Yearbook ... 1980*, vol. II (Part One), document A/CN.4/334 and Add.1–2, p. 247; second report: *Yearbook ... 1981*, vol. II (Part One), document A/CN.4/346 and Add.1–2, p. 103; third report: *Yearbook ... 1982*, vol. II (Part One), document A/CN.4/360, p. 51; fourth report: *Yearbook ... 1983*, vol. II (Part One), document A/CN.4/373, p. 201; and fifth report: *Yearbook ... 1984*, vol. II (Part One), document A/CN.4/383 and Add.1, p. 155. These reports sought to develop a conceptual basis and schematic outline for the topic and contained proposals for five draft articles. The schematic outline was set out in the Special Rapporteur's third report (1982). In 1984, the Commission also had before it the replies to a questionnaire addressed in 1983 by the Legal Counsel of the United Nations to 16 selected international organizations to ascertain whether, amongst other matters, obligations which States owe to each other and discharge as members of international organizations may, to that extent, fulfil or replace some of the procedures referred to in the schematic outline, *Yearbook ... 1984*, vol. II (Part One), document A/CN.4/378, p. 129, and a study prepared by the Secretariat entitled "Survey of State practice relevant to international liability for injurious consequences arising out of acts not prohibited by international law", *Yearbook ... 1985*, vol. II (Part One), addendum, document A/CN.4/384, p. 1. See also the survey of "Liability regimes relevant to the topic 'International liability for injurious consequences arising out of acts not prohibited by international law'", *Yearbook ... 1995*, vol. II (Part One), document A/CN.4/471, p. 61.

[285] For the 12 reports of the Special Rapporteur, see preliminary report: *Yearbook ... 1985*, vol. II (Part One), document A/CN.4/394, p. 97; second report: *Yearbook ... 1986*, vol. II (Part One), document A/CN.4/402, p. 145; third report: *Yearbook ... 1987*, vol. II (Part One), document A/CN.4/405, p. 47; fourth report: *Yearbook ... 1988*, vol. II (Part One), document A/CN.4/413, p. 251; fifth report: *Yearbook ... 1989*, vol. II (Part One), document A/CN.4/423, p. 131; sixth report: *Yearbook ... 1990*, vol. II (Part One), document A/CN.4/428 and Add.1, p. 83; seventh report: *Yearbook ... 1991*, vol. II (Part One), document A/CN.4/437, p. 71; eighth report: *Yearbook ... 1992*, vol. II (Part One), document A/CN.4/443, p. 59; ninth report: *Yearbook ... 1993*, vol. II (Part One), document A/CN.4/450, p. 187; tenth report: *Yearbook ... 1994*, vol. II (Part One), document A/CN.4/459, p. 129; eleventh report: *Yearbook ... 1995*, vol. II (Part One), document A/CN.4/468, p. 51; and twelfth report: *Yearbook ... 1996*, vol. II (Part One), document A/CN.4/475 and Add.1, p. 29.

[286] See *Yearbook ... 1992*, vol. II (Part Two), document A/47/10, p. 51, paras. 341–343. On the basis of the recommendation of the working group, the Commission, at its 2282nd meeting, on 8 July 1992, decided to continue the work on this topic in stages: first completing work on prevention of transboundary harm, and subsequently proceeding with remedial measures. The Commission decided, in view of the ambiguity in the title of the topic, to continue with the working hypothesis that the topic dealt with "activities" and to defer any formal change of the title. For the detailed recommendation of the Commission see *ibid.*, paras. 344–349. See also *Yearbook ... 1995*, vol. II (Part Two), chap. V.

[287] *Yearbook ... 1996*, vol. II (Part Two), Annex I, p. 100.

[288] *Yearbook ... 1997*, vol. II (Part Two), p. 59, paras. 162–165.

[289] *Ibid.*, para. 168. The General Assembly took note of this decision in paragraph 7 of its resolution 52/156 of 15 December 1997.

[290] For the three reports of the Special Rapporteur, see preliminary report: *Yearbook ... 1998*, vol. II (Part One), document A/CN.4/487 and Add.1, p. 175; second report: *Yearbook ... 1999*, vol II (Part One), document A/CN.4/501, p. 111; and third report: *Yearbook ... 2000*, vol. II (Part One), document A/CN.4/510, p. 113. The Commission also had before it comments and observations from Governments: *Yearbook ... 2000*, vol. II (Part One), A/CN.4/509, p. 127; and *Yearbook ... 2001*, vol. II (Part One), document A/CN.4/516 (received in 2001), p. 169.

55. At its fiftieth session (1998), the Commission adopted on first reading a set of 17 draft articles on prevention of transboundary harm from hazardous activities[291] and at its fifty-third session (2001), it adopted the final text of a draft preamble and a set of 19 draft articles on prevention of transboundary harm from hazardous activities,[292] thus concluding its work on the first part of the topic. Furthermore, the Commission recommended to the General Assembly the elaboration of a convention on the basis of the draft articles.[293]

56. At its fifty-fourth session (2002), the Commission resumed its consideration of the second part of the topic and, upon the recommendation of the Working Group on international liability for injurious consequences arising out of activities not prohibited by international law established to consider the conceptual outline of the topic,[294] appointed Mr. Pemmaraju Sreenivasa Rao Special Rapporteur for the topic under the subtitle "International liability in the case of loss from transboundary harm arising out of hazardous activities".[295]

57. Between the fifty-fifth (2003) and the fifty-sixth (2004) sessions, the Commission received and considered two reports of the Special Rapporteur.[296] During this period, the Commission also established two working groups, one in 2003 to assist the Special Rapporteur in considering the future orientation of the topic in the light of his report and the debate in the Commission, and the other in 2004 to examine the proposals submitted by the Special Rapporteur, taking into account the debate in the Commission, with a view to recommending draft principles ripe for referral to the Drafting Committee, while also continuing discussions on other issues, including the form that work on the topic should take. At its 2815th meeting, on 9 July 2004, the Commission received the oral report of the Chairperson of the Working Group and decided to refer eight draft principles proposed by the Working Group to the Drafting Committee with a request to also prepare a text of a preamble.

58. Also at the fifty-sixth session (2004), the Commission completed on first reading a set of eight draft principles on the allocation of loss in the case of transboundary harm arising out of hazardous activities[297] and decided, in accordance with articles 16 and 21 of its Statute, to transmit the draft principles, through the Secretary-General, to Governments for comments and observations, with the request that such comments and observations be submitted to the Secretary-General by 1 January 2006.

[291] *Yearbook ... 1998*, vol. II (Part Two), pp. 20–21, para. 52.

[292] *Yearbook ... 2001*, vol. II (Part Two) and corrigendum, pp. 146–148, para. 97.

[293] *Ibid.*, para. 94.

[294] The General Assembly, in operative paragraph 3 of resolution 56/82 of 12 December 2001, requested the Commission to resume its consideration of the liability aspects of the topic, bearing in mind the interrelationship between prevention and liability, and taking into account the developments in international law and comments by Governments.

[295] *Yearbook ... 2002*, vol. II (Part Two), p. 90, para. 441. The report of the Working Group set out some initial understandings on the topic "International liability for injurious consequences arising out of acts not prohibited by international law (International liability in case of loss from transboundary harm arising out of hazardous activities)" and presented views on its scope and the approaches to be pursued (*ibid.*, pp. 90–92, paras. 442–457).

[296] For the two reports of the Special Rapporteur on the legal regime for allocation of loss in case of transboundary harm arising out of hazardous activities, see first report: *Yearbook ... 2003*, vol. II (Part One), document A/CN.4/531; and second report: *Yearbook ... 2004*, vol. II (Part One), document A/CN.4/540.

[297] *Yearbook ... 2004*, vol. II (Part Two), para. 175.

B. Consideration of the topic at the present session

59. At the present session, the Commission had before it the third report of the Special Rapporteur on the legal regime for allocation of loss in case of transboundary harm arising out of hazardous activities (A/CN.4/566). The Commission also had before it comments and observations received from Governments (A/CN.4/562 and Add.1). The Commission considered the report at its 2872nd to 2875th meetings, on 9, 10, 11 and 12 May 2006, and at the last meeting decided to refer the draft principles adopted in 2004, on first reading, to the Drafting Committee for a second reading taking into account the views expressed in the Commission and comments and observations received from Governments.

60. At its 2882nd meeting, on 2 June 2006, the Commission received and considered the report of the Drafting Committee (A/CN.4/L.686 and Corr.1) and adopted on second reading the text of the preamble and a set of eight draft principles on the allocation of loss in the case of transboundary harm arising out of hazardous activities.

61. At its 2909th and 2910th meetings, on 8 August 2006, the Commission adopted the commentaries to the aforementioned draft principles.

62. In accordance with its Statute, the Commission submits the draft preamble and the draft principles to the General Assembly, together with a recommendation set out below.

C. Recommendation of the Commission

63. At its 2910th meeting on 8 August 2006, the Commission recalled that at its forty-ninth session (1997) it decided to consider the topic in two parts,[298] and that at its fifty-third session (2001) it completed the first part[299] and recommended to the General Assembly the elaboration of a convention on the basis of the draft articles on prevention of transboundary harm from hazardous activities.[300] The Commission's recommendation was based on its view that, taking into account the existing State practice, the first part of the topic lent itself to codification and progressive development through a convention. The adoption by the Commission of the draft principles on the allocation of loss in the case of transboundary harm arising out of hazardous activities completes the second part, thus concluding work on the topic "International liability for injurious consequences arising out of acts not prohibited by international law". In accordance with article 23 of its Statute the Commission recommends, for this second part, that the General Assembly endorse the draft principles by a resolution and urge States to take national and international action to implement them.

[298] *Yearbook ... 1997*, vol. II (Part Two), p. 59, para. 165.

[299] *Yearbook ... 2001*, vol. II (Part Two) and corrigendum, p. 145, para. 91.

[300] *Ibid.*, p. 145, and para. 94 and p. 146, para. 97.

D. Tribute to the Special Rapporteur

64. At its 2910th meeting, on 8 August 2006, the Commission, following the adoption of the text of the preamble and the draft principles on the allocation of loss in the case of transboundary harm arising out of hazardous activities, adopted the following resolution by acclamation:

The International Law Commission,

Having adopted the draft preamble and draft principles on the allocation of loss in the case of transboundary harm arising out of hazardous activities,

Expresses to the Special Rapporteur, Mr. Pemmaraju Sreenivasa Rao, its deep appreciation and warm congratulations for the outstanding contribution he has made to the preparation of the draft preamble and draft principles through his tireless efforts and devoted work, and for the results achieved in the elaboration of the draft preamble and draft principles on the allocation of loss in the case of transboundary harm arising out of hazardous activities.

65. The Commission also expressed its deep appreciation to the previous Special Rapporteurs, Mr. Robert Q. Quentin-Baxter and Mr. Julio Barboza, for their outstanding contribution to the work on the topic.

E. Text of the draft principles on the allocation of loss in the case of transboundary harm arising out of hazardous activities

1. Text of the draft principles

66. The text of the draft principles adopted by the Commission at its fifty-eighth session is reproduced below.

DRAFT PRINCIPLES ON THE ALLOCATION OF LOSS IN THE CASE OF TRANSBOUNDARY HARM ARISING OUT OF HAZARDOUS ACTIVITIES

The General Assembly,

Reaffirming **Principles 13 and 16 of the Rio Declaration on Environment and Development,**

Recalling **the draft articles on the prevention of transboundary harm from hazardous activities,**

Aware **that incidents involving hazardous activities may occur despite compliance by the relevant State with its obligations concerning prevention of transboundary harm from hazardous activities,**

Noting **that as a result of such incidents other States and/or their nationals may suffer harm and serious loss,**

Emphasizing **that appropriate and effective measures should be in place to ensure that those natural and legal persons, including States, that incur harm and loss as a result of such incidents are able to obtain prompt and adequate compensation,**

Concerned **that prompt and effective response measures should be taken to minimize the harm and loss which may result from such incidents,**

Noting **that States are responsible for infringements of their obligations of prevention under international law,**

Recalling **the significance of existing international agreements covering specific categories of hazardous activities and stressing the importance of the conclusion of further such agreements,**

Desiring **to contribute to the development of international law in this field,**

…

Principle 1. Scope of application

The present draft principles apply to transboundary damage caused by hazardous activities not prohibited by international law.

Principle 2. Use of terms

For the purposes of the present draft principles:

(*a*) "damage" means significant damage caused to persons, property or the environment; and includes:

(i) loss of life or personal injury;

(ii) loss of, or damage to, property, including property which forms part of the cultural heritage;

(iii) loss or damage by impairment of the environment;

(iv) the costs of reasonable measures of reinstatement of the property, or environment, including natural resources;

(v) the costs of reasonable response measures;

(*b*) "environment" includes natural resources, both abiotic and biotic, such as air, water, soil, fauna and flora and the interaction between the same factors, and the characteristic aspects of the landscape;

(*c*) "hazardous activity" means an activity which involves a risk of causing significant harm;

(*d*) "State of origin" means the State in the territory or otherwise under the jurisdiction or control of which the hazardous activity is carried out;

(*e*) "transboundary damage" means damage caused to persons, property or the environment in the territory or in other places under the jurisdiction or control of a State other than the State of origin;

(*f*) "victim" means any natural or legal person or State that suffers damage;

(*g*) "operator" means any person in command or control of the activity at the time the incident causing transboundary damage occurs.

Principle 3. Purposes

The purposes of the present draft principles are:

(*a*) to ensure prompt and adequate compensation to victims of transboundary damage; and

(*b*) to preserve and protect the environment in the event of transboundary damage, especially with respect to mitigation of damage to the environment and its restoration or reinstatement.

Principle 4. Prompt and adequate compensation

1. Each State should take all necessary measures to ensure that prompt and adequate compensation is available for victims of transboundary damage caused by hazardous activities located within its territory or otherwise under its jurisdiction or control.

2. These measures should include the imposition of liability on the operator or, where appropriate, other person or entity. Such liability should not require proof of fault. Any conditions, limitations or exceptions to such liability shall be consistent with draft principle 3.

3. These measures should also include the requirement on the operator or, where appropriate, other person or entity, to establish and maintain financial security such as insurance, bonds or other financial guarantees to cover claims of compensation.

4. In appropriate cases, these measures should include the requirement for the establishment of industry-wide funds at the national level.

5. In the event that the measures under the preceding paragraphs are insufficient to provide adequate compensation, the State of origin should also ensure that additional financial resources are made available.

Principle 5. Response measures

Upon the occurrence of an incident involving a hazardous activity which results or is likely to result in transboundary damage:

(*a*) the State of origin shall promptly notify all States affected or likely to be affected of the incident and the possible effects of the transboundary damage;

(*b*) the State of origin, with the appropriate involvement of the operator, shall ensure that appropriate response measures are taken and should, for this purpose, rely upon the best available scientific data and technology;

(*c*) the State of origin, as appropriate, should also consult with and seek the cooperation of all States affected or likely to be affected to mitigate the effects of transboundary damage and if possible eliminate them;

(*d*) the States affected or likely to be affected by the transboundary damage shall take all feasible measures to mitigate and if possible to eliminate the effects of such damage;

(*e*) the States concerned should, where appropriate, seek the assistance of competent international organizations and other States on mutually acceptable terms and conditions.

Principle 6. International and domestic remedies

1. States shall provide their domestic judicial and administrative bodies with the necessary jurisdiction and competence and ensure that these bodies have prompt, adequate and effective remedies available in the event of transboundary damage caused by hazardous activities located within their territory or otherwise under their jurisdiction or control.

2. Victims of transboundary damage should have access to remedies in the State of origin that are no less prompt, adequate and effective than those available to victims that suffer damage, from the same incident, within the territory of that State.

3. Paragraphs 1 and 2 are without prejudice to the right of the victims to seek remedies other than those available in the State of origin.

4. States may provide for recourse to international claims settlement procedures that are expeditious and involve minimal expenses.

5. States should guarantee appropriate access to information relevant for the pursuance of remedies, including claims for compensation.

Principle 7. Development of specific international regimes

1. Where, in respect of particular categories of hazardous activities, specific global, regional or bilateral agreements would provide effective arrangements concerning compensation, response measures and international and domestic remedies, all efforts should be made to conclude such specific agreements.

2. Such agreements should, as appropriate, include arrangements for industry and/or State funds to provide supplementary compensation in the event that the financial resources of the operator, including financial security measures, are insufficient to cover the damage suffered as a result of an incident. Any such funds may be designed to supplement or replace national industry-based funds.

Principle 8. Implementation

1. Each State should adopt the necessary legislative, regulatory and administrative measures to implement the present draft principles.

2. The present draft principles and the measures adopted to implement them shall be applied without any discrimination such as that based on nationality, domicile or residence.

3. States should cooperate with each other to implement the present draft principles.

2. Text of the draft principles and commentaries thereto

67. The text of the draft principles with commentaries thereto adopted by the Commission at its fifty-eighth session, are reproduced below.

DRAFT PRINCIPLES ON THE ALLOCATION OF LOSS IN THE CASE OF TRANSBOUNDARY HARM ARISING OUT OF HAZARDOUS ACTIVITIES

General commentary

(1) The background to these draft principles, together with the underlying approach, is outlined in the preamble. It places the draft principles in the context of the relevant provisions of the Rio Declaration on Environment and Development ("Rio Declaration")[301] but then specifically recalls the draft articles on the prevention of transboundary harm from hazardous activities, approved by the Commisison at its fifty-third session, in 2001.[302]

(2) It briefly provides the essential background that, even if the relevant State fully complies with its prevention obligations, under international law, accidents or other incidents may nonetheless occur and have transboundary consequences that cause harm and serious loss to other States and their nationals.

(3) It is important, as the preamble records, that those who suffer harm or loss as a result of such incidents involving hazardous activities are not left to carry those losses and are able to obtain prompt and adequate compensation. These draft principles establish the means by which this may be accomplished.

(4) As the preamble notes, the necessary arrangements for compensation may be provided under international agreements covering specific hazardous activities, and the draft principles encourage the development of such agreements at the international, regional or bilateral level as appropriate.

(5) The draft principles are therefore intended to contribute to the process of development of international law in this field, both by providing appropriate guidance to States in respect of hazardous activities not covered by specific agreements, and by indicating the matters that should be dealt with in such agreements.

(6) The preamble also makes the point that States are responsible under international law for infringement of their prevention obligations. The draft principles are

[301] *Report of the United Nations Conference on Environment and Development, Rio de Janeiro, 3–14 June 1992* (United Nations publication, Sales No. E.93.I.8 and corrigenda), vol. I: *Resolutions adopted by the Conference*, resolution 1, Annex I.

[302] See footnote 292 above.

therefore without prejudice to the rules relating to State responsibility and any claim that may lie under those rules in the event of a breach of the obligations of prevention.

(7) In preparing the draft principles, the Commission has proceeded on the basis of a number of basic understandings. In the first place, there is a general understanding that (*a*) the regime should be general and residual in character; and that (*b*) such a regime should be without prejudice to the relevant rules of State responsibility adopted by the Commission in 2001.[303] Secondly, there is an understanding that the scope of the liability aspects should be the same as the scope of the draft articles on prevention of transboundary harm from hazardous activities, which the Commission also adopted in 2001.[304] In particular, to trigger the regime governing transboundary damage, the same threshold, "significant", that is made applicable in the case of transboundary harm is employed. The Commission also carefully considered the desirability of examining the issues concerning global commons. After observing that the issues associated with that topic are different and had their own particular features, the Commission came to the conclusion that they require a separate treatment.[305] Thirdly, the work has proceeded on the basis of certain policy considerations: (*a*) that while the activities contemplated for coverage under the present topic are essential for economic development and beneficial to society, the regime must provide for prompt and adequate compensation for the innocent victims in the event that such activities give rise to transboundary damage; and (*b*) that contingency plans and response measures should be in place over and above those contemplated in the draft articles on prevention.

(8) Fourthly, the various existing models of liability and compensation have confirmed that State liability is accepted essentially in the case of outer space activities. Liability for activities falling within the scope of the present draft principles primarily attaches to the operator, and such liability would be without the requirement of proof of fault, and may be limited or subject to conditions, limitations and exceptions. However, it is equally recognized that such liability need not always be placed on the operator of a hazardous or a risk-bearing activity and other entities could equally be designated by agreement or by law. The important point is that the person or entity concerned is functionally in command or control or directs or exercises overall supervision and hence, as the beneficiary of the activity, may be held liable.

(9) Fifthly, it may be noted that provision is made for supplementary funding in many schemes of allocation of loss, and such funding in the present case would be particularly important if the concept of limited liability is adopted. The basic understanding is to adopt a scheme of allocation of loss, spreading the loss among multiple actors, including, as appropriate, the State. In view of the general and residual character, it is not considered necessary to predetermine the share for the different actors or to precisely identify the role to be assigned to the State. At the same time, it is recognized that the State has, under international law, duties of prevention, and these entail certain minimum standards of due diligence.[306] States are obliged, in accordance with such duties, to allow hazardous activities with a risk of significant transboundary harm only upon prior authorization, utilizing environmental and transboundary impact assessments and monitoring those impacts as appropriate. The attachment of primary liability on the operator, in other words, does not in any way absolve the State from discharging its own duties of prevention under international law.

(10) Sixthly, while there is broad understanding on the basic elements to be incorporated in the regime governing the scheme of allocation of loss in case of damage arising from hazardous activities, it is understood that in most cases the substantive or applicable law to resolve compensation claims may involve other aspects such as civil liability or criminal liability or both, and would depend on a number of variables. Principles of civil law, common law or private international law governing choice of forums as well as the applicable law may come into focus depending upon the context and the jurisdiction involved. Accordingly, the proposed scheme is not only general and residuary but is also flexible and without any prejudice to the claims that might arise or to questions of the applicable law and procedures.

(11) As the draft principles are general and residuary in character they are cast as a non-binding declaration of draft principles. The different characteristics of particular hazardous activities may require the adoption of different approaches with regard to specific arrangements. In addition, the choices or approaches adopted may vary under different legal systems. Further, the choices and approaches adopted and their implementation may also be influenced by different stages of economic development of the countries concerned.

(12) On balance, the Commission has concluded that recommended draft principles would have the advantage of not requiring a harmonization of national laws and legal systems, which is fraught with difficulties. Moreover, it is felt that the goal of widespread acceptance of the substantive provisions is more likely to be met if the outcome is cast as principles. In their essential parts, they provide that victims that suffer the damage should be compensated promptly and adequately, and that environmental damage, relating to which States may pursue claims, be mitigated through prompt response measures and, to the extent possible, be restored or reinstated.

(13) The commentaries are organized as containing an explanation of the scope and context of each draft principle, as well as an analysis of relevant trends and possible options available to assist States in the adoption

[303] For the text and commentaries of the articles on responsibility of States for internationally wrongful acts, *Yearbook ... 2001*, vol. II (Part Two) and corrigendum, para. 77.

[304] *Ibid.*, para. 98.

[305] See *Yearbook ... 2002*, vol. II (Part Two), para. 447.

[306] Birnie and Boyle have observed in respect of the draft articles on prevention that "there is ample authority in treaties, case law and state practice for regarding these provisions of the Commission's draft convention [on the prevention of transboundary harm] as codification of existing international law. They represent the minimum standard required of states when managing transboundary risks and giving effect to Principle 2 of the Rio Declaration" (P. W. Birnie and A. E. Boyle, *International Law and the Environment*, 2nd ed., Oxford University Press, 2002, p. 113).

of appropriate national measures of implementation and in the elaboration of specific international regimes. The focus of the Commission was on the formulation of the substance of the draft principles as a coherent set of standards of conduct and practice. It did not attempt to identify the current status of the various aspects of the draft principles in customary international law, and the way in which the draft principles are formulated is not intended to affect that question.

Preamble

The General Assembly,

***Reaffirming* Principles 13 and 16 of the Rio Declaration on Environment and Development,**

***Recalling* the draft articles on the prevention of transboundary harm from hazardous activities,[307]**

***Aware* that incidents involving hazardous activities may occur despite compliance by the relevant State with its obligations concerning prevention of transboundary harm from hazardous activities,**

***Noting* that as a result of such incidents other States and/or their nationals may suffer harm and serious loss,**

***Emphasizing* that appropriate and effective measures should be in place to ensure that those natural and legal persons, including States, that incur harm and loss as a result of such incidents are able to obtain prompt and adequate compensation,**

***Concerned* that prompt and effective response measures should be taken to minimize the harm and loss which may result from such incidents,**

***Noting* that States are responsible for infringements of their obligations of prevention under international law,**

***Recalling* the significance of existing international agreements covering specific categories of hazardous activities and stressing the importance of the conclusion of further such agreements,**

***Desiring* to contribute to the development of international law in this field,**

...

Commentary

(1) In the past, the Commission has generally presented to the General Assembly sets of draft articles without a draft preamble, leaving its elaboration to States. However, there have also been precedents during which the Commission has submitted a draft preamble. This was the case with respect to the draft convention on the elimination of future statelessness and the draft convention on the reduction of future statelessness,[308] and the draft articles on the nationality of natural persons in relation to the succession of States,[309] as well as with respect to the draft articles on prevention.[310] Since the Commission would be presenting a draft declaration of principles, a preamble is considered all the more pertinent.

(2) As noted in the introduction, the *first* preambular paragraph commences with a reference to Principles 13 and 16 of the Rio Declaration.[311] The need to develop national law regarding liability and compensation for the victims of pollution and other environmental damage is stressed in Principle 13 of that Declaration, which reiterates Principle 22 of the Declaration of the United Nations Conference on the Human Environment ("Stockholm Declaration").[312] Principle 16 of the Rio Declaration addresses the promotion of internalization of environmental costs, taking into account the "polluter pays" principle. The Commission considers the "polluter pays" principle as an essential component in underpinning the present draft principles to ensure that victims that suffer harm as a result of an incident involving a hazardous activity are able to obtain prompt and adequate compensation.

(3) The *second* preambular paragraph is self-explanatory. It links the present draft principles to the draft articles on prevention. The *third*, *fourth*, *fifth* and *sixth* preambular paragraphs seek to provide the essential rationale for the present draft principles.

(4) The *seventh* preambular paragraph stresses that these draft principles do not affect the responsibility that a State may incur as a result of infringement of its obligations of prevention under international law; it seeks to keep claims arising from implementation of that regime from the scope of application of these draft principles.

(5) The *eighth* preambular paragraph recognizes the existence of specific international agreements for various categories of hazardous activities and the importance of concluding further such agreements, while the *last* preambular paragraph captures the desire to contribute to the process of development of international law in this field.

Principle 1. Scope of application

The present draft principles apply to transboundary damage caused by hazardous activities not prohibited by international law.

Commentary

(1) The "scope of application" provision is drafted to contextualize the draft principles and to reflect the understanding that the present draft principles would have the same scope of application as the 2001 draft articles on

[307] *Yearbook ... 2001*, vol. II (Part Two) and corrigendum, pp. 146 *et seq.*, para. 97.

[308] *Yearbook ... 1954*, vol. II, document A/2693, p. 140.

[309] *Yearbook ... 1999*, vol. II (Part Two), document A/54/10, p. 20 *et seq.*, para. 47.

[310] See footnote 292 above.

[311] See footnote 301 above.

[312] *Report of the United Nations Conference on the Human Environment, Stockholm, 5–16 June 1972* (United Nations publication, Sales No. E.73.II.A.14), part one, chap. I.

prevention of transboundary harm from hazardous activities.[313] The interrelated nature of the concepts of "prevention" and "liability" needs no particular emphasis in the context of the work of the Commission.[314] This provision identifies that the focus of the present draft principles is transboundary damage. The notion of "transboundary damage", like the notion of "transboundary harm", focuses on damage caused in the jurisdiction of one State by activities situated in another State.

(2) In the first instance, hazardous activities coming within the scope of the present draft principles are those not prohibited by international law and involve the "risk of causing significant transboundary harm through their physical consequences". Different types of activities could be envisaged under this category. As the title of the draft principles indicates, any hazardous or by implication any ultrahazardous activity, which involves, at a minimum, a risk of causing significant transboundary harm, is covered. These are activities that have a high probability of causing significant transboundary harm or a low probability of causing disastrous transboundary harm. The combined effect of the probability of occurrence of an accident and the magnitude of its injurious impact separates such activities from any other activities.[315]

(3) Following the same approach adopted in the case of the draft articles on prevention, the Commission opted to dispense with the specification of a list of activities. Such specification of a list of activities is not without problems and functionally it is not considered essential. Any such list of activities is likely to be under-inclusive and might quickly need review in the light of ever-evolving technological developments. Further, except for certain ultrahazardous activities which are mostly the subject of special regulation, e.g., in the nuclear field or in the context of activities in outer space, the risk that flows from an activity is primarily a function of the particular application, the specific context and the manner of operation. It is felt that it is difficult to capture these elements in a generic list. However, the activities coming within the scope of the present principles are the same as those that are subject to the requirement of prior authorization under the draft articles on prevention. Moreover, it is always open to States to specify activities coming within the scope of the present principles through multilateral, regional or bilateral arrangements[316] or to do so in their national legislation.

(4) The phrase "transboundary damage caused by hazardous activities not prohibited by international law" has a similar import as the phrase "activities not prohibited by international law which involve a risk of causing significant transboundary harm through their physical consequences" in article 1 of the draft articles on prevention. It has a particular meaning, which is well understood as containing four elements, namely (*a*) such activities are not prohibited by international law; (*b*) such activities involve a risk of causing significant harm; (*c*) such harm must be transboundary; and (*d*) the transboundary harm must be caused by such activities through their physical consequences.[317]

(5) Like the draft articles on prevention, the activities coming within the scope of the present principles have an element of human causation and are qualified as "activities not prohibited by international law". This particular phrase has been adopted essentially to distinguish the present principles from the operation of the rules governing State responsibility. The Commission recognized the importance, not only of questions of responsibility for internationally wrongful acts, but also questions concerning the obligation to make good any harmful consequences arising out of certain activities, especially those which, because of their nature, present certain risks. However, in view of the entirely different basis of liability for risk and the different nature of the rules governing it, as well as its content and the forms it may assume, the Commission decided to address the two subjects separately.[318] That is, for the purpose of the principles, the focus is on the consequences of the activity and not on the lawfulness of the activity itself.

(6) The present draft principles, like the draft articles on prevention, are concerned with primary rules. Accordingly, the non-fulfilment of the duty of prevention prescribed by the draft articles on prevention could engage State responsibility without necessarily giving rise to the implication that the activity itself is prohibited.[319] In such

[313] See footnote 292 above.

[314] See the recommendation of the Working Group on international liability for injurious consequences arising out of acts not prohibited by international law established by the Commission at its fifty-fourth session, in 2002, *Yearbook ... 2002*, vol. II (Part Two), p. 91, paras. 447–448.

[315] See *Yearbook ... 2001*, vol. II (Part Two) and corrigendum, p. 152 (paragraph (1) of the commentary to article 2 of the draft articles on prevention).

[316] For example, various liability regimes deal with the type of activities which come under their scope: the Convention on the Protection of the Marine Environment of the Baltic Sea Area; the Convention on the Transboundary Effects of Industrial Accidents; Annex I to the Protocol on Civil Liability and Compensation for Damage caused by the Transboundary Effects of Industrial Accidents on Transboundary Waters; and Annex II to the Convention on Civil Liability for Damage resulting from Activities Dangerous to the Environment, where activities such as the installations or sites for the partial or complete disposal of solid, liquid or gaseous wastes by incineration on land or at sea, and installations or sites for thermal degradation of solid, gaseous or liquid wastes under reduced oxygen supply, have been identified as dangerous activities; this Convention also has a list of dangerous substances in Annex I. See also Directive 2004/35/CE of the European Parliament and of the Council of 21 April 2004 on environmental liability with regard to the prevention and remedying of environmental damage, *Official Journal of the European Union*, No. L 143, 30 April 2004, p. 56.

[317] See *Yearbook ... 2001*, vol. II (Part Two) and corrigendum, pp. 149–151 (commentary to article 1 of the draft articles on prevention).

[318] *Yearbook ... 1973*, vol. II, document A/9010/Rev.1, p. 169, para. 38.

[319] See *Yearbook ... 2001*, vol. II (Part Two) and corrigendum, p. 150 (paragraph (6) of the commentary to article 1). See also M. B. Akehurst, "International liability for injurious consequences arising out of acts not prohibited by international law", *Netherlands Yearbook of International Law*, vol. 16 (1985), pp. 3–16; A. E. Boyle, "State responsibility and international liability for injurious consequences of acts not prohibited by international law: a necessary distinction?", *International and Comparative Law Quarterly*, vol. 39 (1990), pp. 1–26; K. Zemanek, "State responsibility and liability", in W. Lang, H. Neuhold and K. Zemanek (eds.), *Environmental Protection and International Law*, London, Graham and Trotman/Martinus Nijhoff, 1991, p. 197; the second report on international liability for injurious consequences arising out of acts not prohibited by international law (prevention of transboundary harm from hazardous activities) by Special Rapporteur Pemmaraju Sreenivasa Rao, *Yearbook ... 1999*, vol. II (Part One), document A/CN.4/501, paras. 35–37; J. Barboza, "La responsabilité 'causale' à la Commission du droit international", *Annuaire français de droit international*, vol. 34 (1988), pp. 513–522; Ph. Cahier, "Le problème de la responsabilité pour risque en droit international", in *International Relations in a Changing World*, Leyden, Sijthoff, 1977, pp. 409–434;

a case, State responsibility could be invoked to implement not only the obligations of the State itself but also the civil responsibility or duty of the operator.[320] Indeed, this is well understood throughout the work on draft articles on prevention.[321]

(7) It is recognized that harm could occur despite implementation of the duties of prevention. Transboundary harm could occur for several other reasons not involving State responsibility. For instance, there could be situations where the preventive measures were followed but actually proved inadequate, or where the particular risk that caused transboundary harm could not be identified at the time of initial authorization and hence appropriate preventive measures were not envisaged.[322] In other words, transboundary harm could occur accidentally or it may take place in circumstances not originally anticipated. Further, harm could occur because of gradually accumulated adverse effects over a period of time. This distinction ought to be borne in mind for purposes of compensation. Because of problems of establishing a causal link between the hazardous activity and the damage incurred, claims in the latter case are not commonplace.[323]

(8) For the purpose of the present draft principles it is assumed that duties of due diligence under the obligations of prevention have been fulfilled. Accordingly, the focus of the present draft principles is on damage caused despite the fulfilment of such duties.

(9) The second criterion, implicit in the present provision on scope of application, is that activities covered by these principles are those that originally carried a "risk" of causing significant transboundary harm. As noted in paragraph (2) above, this risk element encompasses activities with a low probability of causing disastrous transboundary harm or a high probability of causing significant transboundary harm.[324]

(10) The third criterion is that the activities must involve "transboundary" harm. Thus, three concepts are embraced by the (extra)territorial element. The term "transboundary" harm comprises questions of "territory", "jurisdiction" and "control".[325] The activities must be conducted in the territory or otherwise in places within the jurisdiction or control of one State and have an impact in the territory or places within the jurisdiction or control of another State.

(11) It should be noted that the draft principles are concerned with "transboundary damage caused" by hazardous activities. In the present context, the reference to the broader concept of transboundary harm has been retained where the reference is only to the risk of harm and not to the subsequent phase where harm has actually occurred. The term "damage" is employed to refer to the latter phase. The notion of "transboundary damage" is introduced to denote specificity to the harm which occurred. The term also has the advantage of familiarity. It is the usual term used in liability regimes.[326] The word "transboundary"

C. G. Caubet, "Le droit international en quête d'une responsabilité pour les dommages résultant d'activités qu'il n'interdit pas", *Annuaire français de droit international*, vol. 29 (1983), pp. 99–120; D. Lévy, "La responsabilité pour omission et la responsabilité pour risque en droit international public", *Revue générale de droit international public*, vol. 32, No. 1 (1961), pp. 744–764; and P. Šturma, "La responsabilité en dehors de l'illicite en droit international économique", *Polish Yearbook of International Law*, vol. 20 (1993), pp. 91–112.

[320] See P.-M. Dupuy, *La responsabilité internationale des États pour les dommages d'origine technologique et industrielle*, Paris, Pedone, 1977; I. Brownlie, *System of the Law of Nations: State Responsibility, Part I*, Oxford, Clarendon Press, 1983, p. 50; A. Rosas, "State responsibility and liability under civil liability regimes", in O. Bring and S. Mahmoudi (eds.), *Current International Law Issues: Nordic Perspectives (Essays in honour of Jerzy Sztucki)*, Dordrecht, Martinus Nijhoff, 1994, p. 161; and F. Bitar, *Les mouvements transfrontaliers de déchets dangereux selon la Convention de Bâle. Étude des régimes de responsabilité*, Paris, Pedone, 1997, pp. 79–138. However, different standards of liability, burden of proof and remedies apply to State responsibility and liability. See also P.-M. Dupuy, "Où en est le droit international de l'environnement à la fin du siècle?", *Revue générale de droit international public*, vol. 101, No. 4 (1997), pp. 873–903; T. A. Berwick, "Responsibility and liability for environmental damage: a roadmap for international environmental regimes", *Georgetown International Environmental Law Review*, vol. 10, No. 2 (1998), pp. 257–267; and P.-M. Dupuy, "À propos des mésaventures de la responsabilité internationale des États dans ses rapports avec la protection internationale de l'environnement", in M. Prieur and C. Lambrechts (eds.), *Les hommes et l'environnement: quels droits pour le vingt et unième siècle? Études en hommage à Alexandre Kiss*, Paris, Frison-Roche, 1998, pp. 269–282.

[321] See *Yearbook ... 2002*, vol. II (Part Two), p. 90, para. 443.

[322] *Ibid.*, para. 444.

[323] See P. Wetterstein, "A proprietary or possessory interest: A *conditio sine qua non* for claiming damages for environmental impairment?", in P. Wetterstein (ed.), *Harm to the Environment: the Right to Compensation and Assessment of Damage*, Oxford, Clarendon Press, 1997, pp. 29–54, at p. 30. See also H. Xue, *Transboundary Damage in International Law*, Cambridge University Press, 2003, pp. 19–105 and 113–182.

[324] See *Yearbook ... 2001*, vol. II (Part Two) and corrigendum, p. 152 (paragraph (1) of the commentary to draft article 2).

[325] *Ibid.*, pp. 150–151 (paras. (7)–(12) of the commentary to draft article 1).

[326] "Damage" is defined in: article 2, paragraph 2 (*c*) of the Basel Protocol on Liability and Compensation for Damage Resulting from Transboundary Movements of Hazardous Wastes and their Disposal; article 2, paragraph 2 (*d*) of the Protocol on Civil Liability and Compensation for Damage caused by the Transboundary Effects of Industrial Accidents on Transboundary Waters; article 2, paragraph 7 of the Convention on Civil Liability for Damage resulting from Activities Dangerous to the Environment; article 1, paragraph 6 of the International Convention on Liability and Compensation for Damage in Connection with the Carriage of Hazardous and Noxious Substances by Sea (HNS Convention); and article 1, paragraph 10 of the Convention on Civil Liability for Damage caused during Carriage of Dangerous Goods by Road, Rail and Inland Navigation Vessels (CRTD). See also article 2, paragraph 2 of the 2004 European Parliament and the Council Directive 2004/35/CE on environmental liability with regard to prevention and remedying of environmental damage (footnote 316 above); and article I (*a*) of the Convention on the international liability for damage caused by space objects.

"Pollution damage" is defined in: article 1, paragraph 6 of the International Convention on Civil Liability for Oil Pollution Damage; article 1, paragraph 6 of the Convention as amended by the Protocol to amend the International Convention on Civil Liability for Oil Pollution Damage (see also P. W. Birnie and A. E. Boyle, *Basic Documents on International Law and the Environment*, Oxford, Clarendon Press, 1995, pp. 91–106); article 1, paragraph 9 of the International Convention on Civil Liability for Bunker Oil Pollution Damage; and article 1, paragraph 6 of the International Convention on Civil Liability for Oil Pollution Damage resulting from the Exploration for and Exploitation of Seabed Mineral Resources.

For definition of "nuclear damage", see article I, paragraph 1 (*k*) of the Vienna Convention on civil liability for nuclear damage; article I, paragraph 1 (*k*) of the Convention as amended by article 2 of the Protocol to amend the Vienna Convention on civil liability for nuclear damage; article 1 of the Convention on Supplementary Compensation for Nuclear Damage; article I.B.vii) of the Protocol to amend the Convention on Third Party Liability in the field of Nuclear Energy of 29 July 1960, as amended by the Additional Protocol of 28 January 1964 and by the Protocol of 16 November 1982.

(*Continued on next page.*)

qualifies "damage" to stress the transboundary orientation of the scope of the present principles.

(12) Another important consideration which delimits the scope of application is that transboundary harm caused by State policies in trade, monetary, socio-economic or similar fields is excluded from the scope of the present principles.[327] Thus, significant transboundary harm must have been caused by the "physical consequences" of activities in question.

Principle 2. Use of terms

For the purposes of the present draft principles:

(*a*) "damage" means significant damage caused to persons, property or the environment; and includes:

(i) loss of life or personal injury;

(ii) loss of, or damage to, property, including property which forms part of the cultural heritage;

(iii) loss or damage by impairment of the environment;

(iv) the costs of reasonable measures of reinstatement of the property, or environment, including natural resources;

(v) the costs of reasonable response measures;

(*b*) "environment" includes: natural resources, both abiotic and biotic, such as air, water, soil, fauna and flora and the interaction between the same factors; and the characteristic aspects of the landscape;

(*c*) "hazardous activity" means an activity which involves a risk of causing significant harm;

(*d*) "State of origin" means the State in the territory or otherwise under the jurisdiction or control of which the hazardous activity is carried out;

(*e*) "transboundary damage" means damage caused to persons, property or the environment in the territory or in other places under the jurisdiction or control of a State other than the State of origin;

(*f*) "victim" means any natural or legal person or State that suffers damage;

(*g*) "operator" means any person in command or control of the activity at the time the incident causing transboundary damage occurs.

Commentary

(1) The present "Use of terms" seeks to define and set out the meaning of the terms or concepts used in the present draft principles. The definition of "damage" is crucial for the purposes of the present draft principles. The elements of damage are identified in part to set out the basis of claims for damage. Before identifying the elements of damage, it is important to note that damage, to be eligible for compensation, should reach a certain threshold. For example, the *Trail Smelter* award addressed an injury by fumes, when the case is of "serious consequences" and the injury is established by clear and convincing evidence.[328] The *Lake Lanoux* award made reference to serious injury.[329] A number of conventions have also referred to "significant", "serious" or "substantial" harm or damage as the threshold for giving rise to legal claims.[330] "Significant" has also been used in other legal instruments and domestic law.[331] The threshold is designed to prevent frivolous or vexatious claims.

(*Footnote 326 continued.*)

See also article 1, paragraph 15 of the Convention on the Regulation of Antarctic Mineral Resource Activities (CRAMRA), which defines damage to the Antarctic environment or dependent or associated ecosystems; and the Convention on the Law of the Non-Navigational Uses of International Watercourses which seeks in article 7 to "prevent the causing of significant harm". Article 2 (*b*) of Annex VI to the Protocol on Environmental Protection to the Antarctic Treaty on Liability Arising From Environmental Emergencies defines "environmental emergency" as "any accidental event that ... results in, or imminently threatens to result in, any significant and harmful impact on the Antarctic environment".

[327] See *Yearbook ... 2001*, vol. II (Part Two) and corrigendum, p. 151 (paragraphs (16)–(17) of the commentary to article 1 of the draft articles on prevention).

[328] *Trail Smelter* (see footnote 226 above), at p. 1965.

[329] *Lake Lanoux Arbitration (France* v. *Spain)*, UNRIAA, vol. XII (Sales No. 1963.V.3), p. 281.

[330] See, for example, article 4, paragraph 2 of the Convention on the Regulation of Antarctic Mineral Resource Activities (CRAMRA); paragraphs 1 and 2 of article 2 of the Convention on Environmental Impact Assessment in a Transboundary Context; article 1 (*d*) of the Convention on the Transboundary Effects of Industrial Accidents; and article 7 of the Convention on the Law of the Non-Navigational Uses of International Watercourses. See also P. N. Okowa, *State Responsibility for Transboundary Air Pollution in International Law*, Oxford University Press, 2000, p. 176; and R. Lefeber, *Transboundary Environmental Interference and the Origin of State Liability* , The Hague, Kluwer Law International, 1996, pp. 86–89, who notes the felt need for a threshold and examines the rationale for and the possible ways of explaining the meaning of the threshold of "significant harm". See also J. G. Lammers, *Pollution of International Watercourses: a Search for Substantive Rules and Principles of Law*, The Hague, Martinus Nijhoff Publishers, 1984, pp. 346–347; and R. Wolfrum, "Purposes and principles of international environmental law", *German Yearbook of International Law*, vol. 33 (1990), pp. 308–330, at p. 311. As a general rule, noting the importance of a threshold of damage for triggering claims for restoration and compensation, while considering environmental damage, it is suggested that "the more the effects deviate from the state that would be regarded as being sustainable and the less foreseeable and limited the consequential losses are, the closer the effects come to the threshold of significance". This is to be determined against a "baseline condition", which States generally define or should define (R. Wolfrum, Ch. Langenfeld and P. Minnerop, *Environmental Liability in International Law: Towards a Coherent Conception*, Berlin, Erich Schmidt Verlag, 2005, p. 501).

[331] See, for example, article 5 of the draft convention on industrial and agricultural uses of international rivers and lakes, prepared by the Inter-American Juridical Committee in 1965 (Organization of American States, *Ríos y lagos internacionales (utilización para fines agrícolas e industriales)*, 4th ed. rev. (OEA/Ser.1/VI, CIJ-75 Rev.2), Washington D.C., 1971, p. 132; Guidelines on responsibility and liability regarding transboundary water pollution, elaborated by the United Nations Economic Commission for Europe in 1990 (ENVWA/R.45, annex); article X of the Helsinki Rules on the Uses of the Waters of International Rivers (International Law Association, *Report of the Fifty-second Conference, Helsinki, 1966*, London, 1967, p. 496); article 16 of the Berlin Rules on Equitable Use and Sustainable Development of Waters (*ibid., Report of the Seventy-First Conference, Berlin, 16–21 August 2004*, London, 2004, p. 334); paragraphs 1 and 2 of General Assembly resolution 2995 (XXVII) of 15 December 1972 concerning cooperation between States in the field of the environment; paragraph 6 of the annex to OECD Council recommendation C(74)224 of 14 November 1974 on principles concerning transfrontier pollution (OECD, *OECD*

(2) The term "significant" is understood to refer to something more than "detectable" but need not be at the level of "serious" or "substantial".[332] The harm must lead to a real detrimental effect on matters such as, for example, human health, industry, property, environment or agriculture in other States. Such detrimental effects must be susceptible of being measured by factual and objective standards. The ecological unity of the planet does not correspond to political boundaries. In carrying out lawful activities within their own territories, States have impacts on each other. These mutual impacts, so long as they have not reached the level of "significant", are considered tolerable and do not fall within the scope of the present draft principles.

(3) The determination of "significant damage" involves both factual and objective criteria, and a value determination. The latter is dependent on the circumstances of a particular case and the period in which it is made. For instance, a deprivation which is considered significant in one region may not necessarily be so in another. A certain deprivation at a particular time might not be considered "significant" because scientific knowledge or human appreciation at that specific time might have considered such deprivation tolerable. However, that view might later change and the same deprivation might then be considered "significant damage". For instance, the sensitivity of the international community to air and water pollution levels has been constantly changing.

(4) Paragraph (*a*) defines "damage" as significant damage caused to persons, property or the environment. Subparagraphs (i) and (ii) cover personal injury and property damage, including some aspects of consequential economic loss, as well as property, which forms part of the national cultural heritage, which may be State property.

(5) Damage does not occur in isolation or in a vacuum. It occurs to somebody or something; it may be to a person or property. In subparagraph (i), damage to persons includes loss of life or personal injury. There are examples in domestic law[333] and treaty practice.[334] Even those liability regimes that exclude application of injury to persons recognize that other rules would apply.[335] Those regimes that are silent on the matter do not seem to entirely exclude the possible submission of a claim under this heading of damage.[336]

(6) In subparagraph (ii) damage to property includes loss of or damage to property. Property includes movable and immovable property. There are examples in domestic law[337] and in treaty practice.[338] Some liability regimes exclude claims concerning damage to property of the person liable on the policy consideration which seeks to deny a tortfeasor the opportunity to benefit from one's own wrongs. Article 2, paragraph 2 (*c*) (ii) of the Basel Protocol on Liability and Compensation for Damage Resulting from Transboundary Movements of Hazardous Wastes and their Disposal, article 2, paragraph 7(*b*) of the Convention on Civil Liability for Damage resulting from Activities Dangerous to the Environment and article 2, paragraph 2 (*d*) (ii) of the Protocol on Civil Liability and Compensation for Damage caused by the Transboundary Effects of Industrial Accidents on Transboundary Waters contain provisions to this effect.

(7) Traditionally, proprietary rights have been more closely related to the private rights of the individual rather than rights of the public. An individual would face

and the Environment, Paris, 1986, p. 142, reprinted in ILM, vol. 14, No. 1 (January 1975), p. 246); the Memorandum of Intent constituting an agreement concerning transboundary air pollution, between the Government of the United States and the Government of Canada, of 5 August 1980 (United Nations, *Treaty Series*, vol. 1274, No. 21009, p. 235); and article 7 of the Agreement between Mexico and the United States of America on co-operation for the protection and improvement of the environment in the border area, signed on 14 August 1983 (*ibid.*, vol. 1352, No. 22805, p. 71, reproduced in ILM, vol. 22, No. 5 (September 1983), p. 1025). The United States has also used the word "significant" in its domestic law dealing with environmental issues. See American Law Institute, *Restatement of the Law Third, The Foreign Relations Law of the United States*, vol. 2, St. Paul (Minnesota), American Law Institute Publishers, 1987, pp. 111–112.

[332] See *Yearbook ...2001*, vol. II (Part Two) and corrigendum, p. 152 (paragraphs (4)–(5) of the commentary to article 2 of the draft articles on prevention).

[333] Germany's Environmental Liability Act, for example, covers anyone who suffers death or personal injury. Finland's Act on Compensation for Environmental Damage, the Swedish Environmental Code, and Denmark's Act on Compensation for Environmental Damage all cover personal injury. See generally P. Wetterstein, "Environmental damage in the legal systems of the Nordic countries and Germany", in M. Bowman and A. Boyle (eds.), *Environmental Damage in International Law and Comparative Law: Problems of Definition and Valuation*, Oxford University Press, 2002, pp. 223–242.

[334] Some liability regimes provide as follows: article I, paragraph 1 (*k*) of the Vienna Convention on civil liability for nuclear damage defines nuclear damage to include "(i) loss of life, any personal injury or any loss of, or damage to, property …"; article I, paragraph 1(*k*) of the Protocol to amend the Vienna Convention on civil liability for nuclear damage also refers to "(i) loss of life or personal injury; (ii) loss of or damage to property"; article I.B.vii) of the Protocol to amend the Convention on Third Party Liability in the field of Nuclear Energy of 29 July 1960, as amended by the Additional Protocol of 28 January 1964 and by the Protocol of 16 November 1982, defines nuclear damage to include "1. loss of life or personal injury …; 2. loss of or damage to property …"; the Convention on Civil Liability for Damage caused during Carriage of Dangerous Goods by Road, Rail and Inland Navigation Vessels (CRTD) defines the concept of "damage" in paragraph 10 of article 1 as "(a) loss of life or personal injury ...; (b) loss of or damage to property ..."; the Basel Protocol on Liability and Compensation for Damage Resulting from Transboundary Movements of Hazardous Wastes and their Disposal defines "damage", in article 2, paragraph 2 (*c*), as: "(i) Loss of life or personal injury; (ii) Loss of or damage to property other than property held by the person liable in accordance with the present Protocol"; the Protocol on Civil Liability and Compensation for Damage caused by the Transboundary Effects of Industrial Accidents on Transboundary Waters defines damage in article 2 paragraph 2 (*d*), as: "(i) Loss of life or personal injury; (ii) Loss of, or damage to, property other than property held by the person liable in accordance with the Protocol"; and the Convention on Civil Liability for Damage resulting from Activities Dangerous to the Environment defines damage in article 2, paragraph 7 as: "a. loss of life or personal injury; b. loss or damage to property other than to the installation itself or property held under the control of the operator, at the site of the dangerous activity".

[335] Directive 2004/35/CE of the European Parliament and of the Council on environmental liability with regard to the prevention and remedying of environmental damage (see footnote 316 above) does not apply to cases of personal injury, to damage to private property or to any economic loss and does not affect any rights regarding such types of damages.

[336] Pollution damage is defined in article 1, paragraph 6 of the International Convention on Civil Liability for Oil Pollution Damage and in article 2, paragraph 3 of the 1992 Protocol to amend the International Convention on Civil Liability for Oil Pollution Damage.

[337] For example, Finland's Act on Compensation for Environmental Damage covers damage to property, chapter 32 of the Swedish Environmental Code also provides for compensation for damage to property and Denmark's Act on Compensation for Environmental Damage covers damage to property.

[338] See the examples in footnote 334 above.

no difficulty to pursue a claim concerning his personal or proprietary rights. These are claims concerning possessory or proprietary interests which are involved in loss of life or personal injury or loss of or damage to property. Furthermore, tort law has also tended to cover damage that may relate to economic losses. In this connection, a distinction is often made between consequential and pure economic losses.[339]

(8) For the purposes of the present draft principles, consequential economic losses are covered under subparagraphs (i) and (ii). Such losses are the result of a loss of life or personal injury or damage to property. These would include loss of earnings due to personal injury. Such damage is supported in treaty practice[340] and under domestic law although different approaches are followed, including in respect of compensation for loss of income.[341] Other economic loss may arise that is not linked to personal injury or damage to property. In the absence of a specific legal provision for claims covering loss of income, it would be reasonable to expect that if an incident involving a hazardous activity directly causes loss of income, efforts would be made to ensure the victim is not left uncompensated.

(9) Subparagraph (ii) also covers property which forms part of cultural heritage. State property may be included in the national cultural heritage. It embraces a wide range of aspects, including monuments, buildings and sites, while natural heritage denotes natural features and sites and geological and physical formations. Their value cannot easily be quantifiable in monetary terms but lies in their historical, artistic, scientific, aesthetic, ethnological or anthropological importance or in their conservation or natural beauty. The 1972 Convention for the protection of world cultural and natural heritage has a comprehensive definition of "cultural heritage".[342] Not all civil liability regimes include aspects concerning cultural heritage under this head. For example, the Convention on Civil Liability for Damage resulting from Activities Dangerous to the Environment includes in its definition of "environment", property which forms part of the cultural heritage and, to that extent, cultural heritage may also be embraced by the broader definition of "environment".[343]

(10) Respecting and safeguarding cultural property are primary considerations in times of peace as they are in times of armed conflict. This principle is asserted in the Convention for the Protection of Cultural Property in the Event of Armed Conflict. Moreover, international humanitarian law prohibits commission of hostilities directed against historical monuments and works of art which constitute the cultural heritage of peoples.[344]

(11) Subparagraphs (iii) to (v) deal with claims that are usually associated with damage to the environment. They may all be treated as parts of one whole concept. Together, they constitute the essential elements inclusive in a definition of damage to the environment. These subparagraphs are concerned with questions concerning damage to the

[339] See B. Sandvik and S. Suikkari, "Harm and reparation in international treaty regimes: an overview", in P. Wetterstein (ed.), *op. cit.* (footnote 323 above), p. 57. See generally E. H. P. Brans, *Liability for Damage to Public Natural Resources: Standing, Damage and Damage Assessment*, The Hague, Kluwer Law International, 2001, pp. 9–63. See also the eleventh report on international liability for injurious consequences arising out of acts not prohibited by international law of Special Rapporteur Julio Barboza (footnote 285 above).

[340] See, for example, article I (1) (*k*) of the Vienna Convention on civil liability for nuclear damage as modified by article 2, paragraph 2 of the Protocol to amend the Convention, which defines "nuclear damage" as including "each of the following to the extent determined by the law of the competent court– (iii) economic loss arising from loss or damage referred to in sub-paragraph (i) or (ii), insofar as not included in those sub-paragraphs, if incurred by a person entitled to claim in respect of such loss or damage; … (vii) any other economic loss, other than any caused by the impairment of the environment, if permitted by the general law on civil liability of the competent court …". See also article 1 (*f*) of the Convention on Supplementary Compensation for Nuclear Damage, which covers each of the following to the extent determined by the law of the competent court: "(iii) economic loss arising from loss or damage referred to in sub-paragraph (i) or (ii), insofar as not included in those sub-paragraphs, if incurred by a person entitled to claim in respect of such loss or damage; … (vii) any other economic loss, other than any caused by the impairment of the environment, if permitted by the general law on civil liability of the competent court". Article I.B.vii) of the Protocol to amend the Convention on Third Party Liability in the field of Nuclear Energy of 29 July 1960, as amended by the Additional Protocol of 28 January 1964 and by the Protocol of 16 November 1982, defines "nuclear damage" as including "each of the following to the extent determined by the law of the competent court, (3) economic loss arising from loss or damage referred to in sub-paragraph 1 or 2 above insofar as not included in those sub-paragraphs, if incurred by a person entitled to claim in respect of such loss or damage".

[341] For example, under subsection 2702 (*b*) of the United States Oil Pollution Act any person may recover damages for injury to, or economic losses resulting from, the destruction of real or personal property which shall be recoverable by a claimant who owns or leases such property. The subsection also provides that any person may recover "damages equal to the *loss of profits or impairment of earning capacity** due to the injury, destruction, or loss of real property, personal property …" (*United States Code 2000 Edition containing the general and permanent laws of the United States, in force on January 2, 2001*, vol. 18, Washington D.C., United States Government Printing Office, 2001, p. 694). Similarly, section 252 of the German Civil Code provides that any loss of profit is to be compensated.

[342] Article 1 defines "cultural heritage" for purposes of the Convention as:

"—monuments: architectural works, works of monumental sculpture and painting, elements or structures of an archaeological nature, inscriptions, cave dwellings and combinations of features, which are of outstanding universal value from the point of view of history, art or science;

—groups of buildings: groups of separate or connected buildings which, because of their architecture, their homogeneity or their place in the landscape, are of outstanding universal value from the point of view of history, art or science;

—sites: works of man or the combined works of nature and of man, and areas including archaeological sites which are of outstanding universal value from the historical, aesthetic, ethnological or anthropological point of view."

See also the definition of "cultural property" in article 1 of the Convention for the Protection of Cultural Property in the Event of Armed Conflict, which essentially covers movable and immovable property of great importance to the cultural heritage of peoples. See also the Convention on the means of prohibiting and preventing the illicit import, export and transfer of ownership of cultural property; and the Convention for the Safeguarding of the Intangible Cultural Heritage.

[343] See also article 1, paragraph 2 of the Convention on the Protection and Use of Transboundary Watercourses and International Lakes.

[344] See article 53 of the Protocol additional to the Geneva Conventions of 12 August 1949, and relating to the protection of victims of international armed conflicts and article 16 of the Protocol additional to the Geneva Conventions of 12 August 1949, and relating to the protection of victims of non-international armed conflicts. See also the Hague Conventions respecting the Laws and Customs of War on Land, particularly Convention IV (articles 27 and 56 of the Regulations concerning the Laws and Customs of War on Land, in annex to Conventions II and IV of 1899 and 1907) and Convention IX concerning Bombardment by Naval Forces in Time of War (article 5).

environment *per se*. This is damage caused by the hazardous activity to the environment itself with or without simultaneously causing damage to persons or property, and hence is independent of any damage to such persons and property. The broader reference to claims concerning the environment incorporated in subparagraphs (iii)–(v) thus not only builds upon trends that have already become prominent as part of recently concluded international liability regimes,[345] but opens up possibilities for further developments of the law for the protection of the environment *per se*.[346]

(12) An oil spill off a seacoast may immediately lead to lost business for the tourism and fishing industry within the precincts of the incident. Such claims have led to claims of pure economic loss in the past without much success. However, some liability regimes now recognize this head of compensable damage.[347] Article 2 (*d*) (iii) of the Protocol on Civil Liability and Compensation for Damage caused by the Transboundary Effects of Industrial Accidents on Transboundary Waters and article 2, paragraph 2 (*d*) (iii) of the Basel Protocol on Liability and Compensation for Damage Resulting from Transboundary Movements of Hazardous Wastes and their Disposal cover loss of income directly deriving from an economic interest in any use of the environment, incurred as a result of impairment of the environment, taking into account savings and costs.[348] In the case of the Protocol on Civil Liability and Compensation for Damage caused by the Transboundary Effects of Industrial Accidents on Transboundary Waters, such interest should be a "legally protected interest". Examples also exist at the domestic level.[349]

(13) Subparagraph (iii) relates to the form that damage to the environment would take. This would include "loss or damage by impairment". Impairment includes injury to, modification, alteration, deterioration, destruction or loss. This entails diminution of quality, value or excellence in an injurious fashion. Claims concerning loss of income directly deriving from an economic interest in any use of the environment, incurred as a result of impairment of the environment, may fall under this heading.

(14) In other instances of damage to the environment *per se*, it is not easy to establish standing. Some aspects of the environment do not belong to anyone, and are generally considered to be common property (*res communis omnium*) not open to private possession, as opposed

[345] For an analysis of these developments, see L. de la Fayette, "The concept of environmental damage in international liability regimes", in Bowman and Boyle (eds.), *op. cit.* (footnote 333 above) pp. 149–189. See also Brans, *op. cit.* (footnote 339 above), chap. 7, concerning international civil liability for damage to natural resources.

[346] Italian law, for example, appears to go further in recognizing damage to the environment *per se* and Italy is also a signatory to the Convention on Civil Liability for Damage resulting from Activities Dangerous to the Environment. In the *Patmos* case, Italy lodged a claim for 5,000 million lire before the court of Messina, Italy, for ecological damage caused to its territorial waters as a result of 1,000 tonnes of oil spilled into the sea following a collision between the Greek oil tanker Patmos and the Spanish tanker Castillo de Monte Aragon on 21 March 1985. While the lower Court rejected its claim, the higher Court on appeal upheld its claim in *Patmos II*. According to the Court,

> "although the notion of environmental damage cannot be grasped by resorting to any mathematical or accounting method, it can be evaluated in the light of the economic relevance that the destruction, deterioration, or alteration of the environment has *per se* and for the community, which benefits from environmental resources and, in particular, from marine resources in a variety of ways (food, health, tourism, research, biological studies)" (A Bianchi, "Harm to the environment in Italian practice: the interaction of international law and domestic law", in P. Wetterstein (ed.), *op. cit.* (see footnote 323 above), p. 116).

Noting that these benefits are the object of protection of the State, it was held that the State can claim, as a trustee of the community, compensation for the diminished economic value of the environment. The Court also observed that the loss involved not being assignable any market value, compensation can only be provided on the basis of an equitable appraisal. The Court, after rejecting the report received from experts on the quantification of damages, which attempted to quantify the damage on the basis of the nekton (fish) which the biomass could have produced had it not been polluted, resorted to an equitable appraisal and awarded 2,100 million lire. Incidentally, this award fell within the limits of liability of the owner, as set by the IOPC Fund, and was not appealed or contested, see generally Bianchi, *loc. cit.* (above), pp. 113–129, at p. 103. See also M. C. Maffei, "The compensation for ecological damage in the '*Patmos*' case", in F. Francioni and T. Scovazzi (eds.), *International Responsibility for Environmental Harm*, London, Graham and Trotman, 1991.

[347] See Wetterstein, "A proprietary or possessory interest ... ", *loc. cit.* (footnote 323 above), p. 37. On the need to limit the concept of "directly related" "pure economic loss" with a view not to open floodgates or enter "damages lottery" encouraging indeterminate liability which will then be a disincentive to get proper insurance or economic perspective, see L. Bergkamp, *Liability and Environment: Private and Public Law Aspects of Civil Liability for Environmental Harm in an International Context*, The Hague, Kluwer, 2001, pp. 346–350. It is also suggested that such an unlimited approach may limit "the acceptance of the definition of damage and thus, it has to be solved on the national level" (Wolfrum, Langenfeld and Minnerop, *op. cit.* (footnote 330 above) p. 503).

Directive 2004/35/CE of the European Parliament and of the Council covers environmental damage in article 2 (see footnote 316 above).

[348] See also article 1, paragraph 1 (*k*) of the Vienna Convention on civil liability for nuclear damage as modified by article 2, paragraph 2 of the Protocol to amend the Convention, which states that nuclear damage includes each of the following damages "to the extent determined by the law of the competent court: ... (v) loss of income deriving from an economic interest in any use or enjoyment of the environment, incurred as a result of a significant impairment of that environment, and insofar as not included in sub-paragraph (ii)". See also the Convention on Supplementary Compensation for Nuclear Damage, article 1 (*f*): "(v) loss of income deriving from an economic interest in any use or enjoyment of the environment, incurred as a result of a significant impairment of that environment, and insofar as not included in subparagraph (ii)". Article I.B.vii) of the Protocol to amend the Convention on Third Party Liability in the field of Nuclear Energy of 29 July 1960, as amended by the Additional Protocol of 28 January 1964 and by the Protocol of 16 November 1982 defines nuclear damage as "each of the following to the extent determined by the law of the competent court: ... 5. loss of income deriving from a direct economic interest in any use or enjoyment of the environment, incurred as a result of a significant impairment of that environment, and insofar as not included in subparagraph 2". See also, for example, article 2, paragraph 7 *d* of the Convention on Civil Liability for Damage resulting from Activities Dangerous to the Environment; the Convention on the Transboundary Effects of Industrial Accidents (article 1 (*c*)); the Convention on the Protection and Use of Transboundary Watercourses and International Lakes (articles 1–2); the Convention on the Regulation of Antarctic Mineral Resource Activities (CRAMRA) (article 8, paragraph 2 (*a*), (*b*) and (*d*)); and the Convention on Civil Liability for Damage caused during Carriage of Dangerous Goods by Road, Rail and Inland Navigation Vessels (CRTD) (article 10 (*c*)).

[349] Subsection 2702 (*b*) of the United States Oil Pollution Act provides that any person may recover "[d]amages equal to the *loss of profits or impairment of earning capacity** due to the injury, destruction, or loss of ... natural resources" (see footnote 341 above). Finland's Act on Compensation for Environmental Damage includes pure economic loss, except where such losses are insignificant. Chapter 32 of the Swedish Environmental Code also provides for pure economic loss. Pure economic loss not caused by criminal behaviour is compensable only to the extent that it is significant. Denmark's Act on Compensation for Environmental Damage covers economic loss and reasonable costs for preventive measures or for the restoration of the environment. See generally Wetterstein, "Environmental damage in the legal systems ... ", *loc. cit.* (footnote 333 above), pp. 222–242.

to *res nullius*, that is, property not belonging to anyone but open to private possession. A person does not have an individual right to such common property and would not ordinarily have standing to pursue a claim in respect of damage to such property.[350] Moreover, it is not always easy to appreciate who may suffer loss of ecological or aesthetic values or be injured as a consequence for purposes of establishing a claim. States instead may hold such property in trust, and usually public authorities and more recently, public interest groups, have been given standing to pursue claims.[351]

(15) It may be noted that the references to "costs of reasonable measures of reinstatement" in subparagraph (iv) and reasonable costs of clean-up associated with the "costs of reasonable response measures" in subparagraph (v) are recent concepts. These elements of damage have gained recognition because, as noted by one commentator, "there is a clear shift towards a greater focus on damage to the environment *per se*, rather than primarily on damage to persons and to property".[352] Subparagraph (iv) includes in the concept of damage an element of the type of compensation that is available, namely reasonable costs of measures of reinstatement. Recent treaty practice[353] and domestic law[354] has tended to acknowledge the importance of such measures, but has left it to domestic law to indicate who may be entitled to take such measures. Such measures have been described as any reasonable measures aiming to assess, reinstate or restore damaged or destroyed components of the environment or where this is not possible, to introduce, where appropriate, the equivalent of these components into the environment.[355]

(16) The reference to "reasonable" is intended to indicate that the costs of such measures should not be excessively disproportionate to the usefulness resulting from the measure. In the *Zoe Colocotroni case*, the United States First Circuit Court of Appeals stated:

> [Recoverable costs are costs] reasonably to be incurred ... to restore or rehabilitate the environment in the affected area to its pre-existing condition, or as close thereto as is possible without grossly disproportionate expenditures. The focus in determining such a remedy should be [on] the steps a reasonable and prudent sovereign or agency would take to mitigate the harm done by the pollution, with attention to such factors as technical feasibility, harmful side effects, compatibility with or duplication of such regeneration as is naturally to be expected, and the extent to which efforts beyond a certain point would become either redundant or disproportionately expensive.[356]

(17) Subparagraph (v) includes costs of reasonable response measures in the concept of damage as an element of available compensation. Recent treaty practice has tended to acknowledge the importance of such measures, but has left it to domestic law to indicate who may be entitled to take such measures.[357] Such measures include

---

[350] In *Burgess* v. *M/V Tamano*, the court noted that "[i]t is also uncontroverted that the right to finish or to harvest clams … is not the private right of any individual, but is a public right held by the State 'in trust for the common benefit of the people'" (opinion of 27 July 1973, United States District Court, Maine, *Federal Supplement*, vol. 370 (1973), p. 247).

[351] Under the United States Comprehensive Environmental Response, Compensation and Liability Act of 1980 (CERCLA), United States Code Annotated, title 42, chapter 103, sections 9601 *et seq.*; the Clean Water Act of 1977, *ibid.*, title 33, chapter 26, section 1251; the Oil Pollution Act of 1990 (see footnote 341 above), sections 2701 *et seq.*, the United States "Congress empowered government agencies with management jurisdiction over natural resources to act as trustees to assess and recover damages ... [t]he public trust is defined broadly to encompass 'natural resources' ... belonging to, managed by, held in trust by, appertaining to or otherwise controlled by Federal, state or local governments or Indian tribes".

[352] De la Fayette, *loc. cit.* (footnote 345 above), at pp. 166–167.

[353] See, for example, article 1, paragraph 1 (*k*) (iv) of the Vienna Convention on civil liability for nuclear damage as modified by article 2, paragraph 2 of the Protocol to amend the Convention: "the costs of measures of reinstatement of impaired environment, unless such impairment is insignificant, if such measures are actually taken or to be taken, and insofar as not included in sub-paragraph (ii)"; and article I.B.vii of the Protocol to amend the Convention on Third Party Liability in the field of Nuclear Energy of 29 July 1960, as amended by the Additional Protocol of 28 January 1964 and by the Protocol of 16 November 1982: "the costs of measures of reinstatement of impaired environment, unless such impairment is insignificant, if such measures are actually taken or to be taken, and insofar as not included in sub-paragraph 2". Article 1, paragraph 6 of the International Convention on Civil Liability for Oil Pollution Damage refers to "impairment of the environment other than loss of profit from such impairment", and specifies that compensation for such impairment "shall be limited to costs of reasonable measures of reinstatement actually undertaken or to be undertaken". See also article 2, paragraph 2 (*c*) (iv) and (*d*) of the Basel Protocol on Liability and Compensation for Damage Resulting from Transboundary Movements of Hazardous Wastes and their Disposal; articles 2, 7 (*c*) and 8 of the Convention on Civil Liability for Damage resulting from Activities Dangerous to the Environment; and article 2, paragraph 2 (*d*) (iv) and (*g*) of the Protocol on Civil Liability and Compensation for Damage caused by the Transboundary Effects of Industrial Accidents on Transboundary Waters.

[354] German law allows for reimbursement of reasonable costs of reinstatement and restoration of environmental damage through making good the loss suffered by individuals but that may also involve restoring the environment to its *status quo*. Section 16 of Germany's Environmental Liability Act and section 32 of the German Genetic Engineering Act provide that in the event of impairment of a natural complex, section 251 (2) of the German Civil Code is to be applied with the proviso that the expenses of restoring the *status quo* shall not be deemed unreasonable merely because it exceeds the value of the object concerned. See Wolfrum, Langenfeld and Minnerop, *op. cit.* (footnote 330 above), pp. 223–303 ("Part 5: Environmental liability law in Germany (Grote/Renke)"), at p. 278.

[355] It may be noted that in the context of the work of the UNCC, a recent decision sanctioned compensation in respect of three projects: for loss of rangeland and habitats, Jordan received $160 million; for shoreline preserves, Kuwait got $8 million; and Saudi Arabia was awarded $46 million by way of replacing ecological services that were irreversibly lost in the wake of the 1991 Gulf War. See the report and recommendations made by the Panel of Commissioners concerning the fifth instalment of "F4" claims (S/AC.26/2005/10), technical annexes I–III, See also P. H. Sand, "Compensation for environmental damage from the 1991 Gulf War", *Environmental Policy and Law*, vol. 35, No. 6 (December 2005), pp. 244–249, at p. 247.

[356] *Commonwealth of Puerto Rico,* et al. v. *Zoe Colocotroni*, et al., 628 F.2d, p. 652, United States Court of Appeals, First Circuit, 1980, cited in C. de la Rue, "Environmental damage assessment", in R. P. Kröner (ed.), *Transnational Environmental Liability and Insurance*, London, Graham and Trotman, 1993, p. 72.

[357] See, for example, article I, paragraph 1 (*k*) (vi) of the Vienna Convention on civil liability for nuclear damage as modified by article 2, paragraph 2 of the Protocol to amend the Convention: "the costs of preventive measures, and further loss or damage caused by such measures"; the Convention on Supplementary Compensation for Nuclear Damage, article 1 (*f*) (vi): "the costs of preventive measures, and further loss or damage caused by such measures"; and the Protocol to amend the Convention on Third Party Liability in the field of Nuclear Energy of 29 July 1960, as amended by the Additional Protocol of 28 January 1964 and by the Protocol of 16 November 1982, article I.B.vii): "the costs of preventive measures, and further loss or damage caused by such measures, in the case of subparagraphs 1 to 5 above, to the extent that the loss or damage arises out of or results from ionising radiation emitted by any source of radiation inside a nuclear installation, or emitted from nuclear fuel or radioactive products or waste". Article 1, paragraph 6 of the 1992 Protocol to amend the International Convention on Civil Liability for Oil Pollution Damage refers to costs of preventive measures and further loss or damage caused by preventive measures.

any reasonable measures taken by any person including public authorities, following the occurrence of the transboundary damage, to prevent, minimize or mitigate possible loss or damage or to arrange for environmental clean-up. The response measures must be reasonable.

(18) Recent trends are also encouraging in allowing compensation for loss of "non-use value" of the environment. There is some support for this claim from the Commission itself when it adopted its draft articles on State responsibility for internationally wrongful acts, even though it is admitted that such damage is difficult to quantify.[358] The recent decisions of the United Nations Compensation Commission (UNCC) in opting for a broad interpretation of the term "environmental damage" is a pointer of developments to come. In the case of the "F4" category of environmental and public health claims, the F4 Panel of the UNCC allowed claims for compensation for damage to natural resources without commercial value (so-called "pure" environmental damage) and also claims where there was only a temporary loss of resource use during the period prior to full restoration.[359]

(19) Paragraph (*b*) defines "environment". Environment could be defined in different ways for different purposes and it is appropriate to bear in mind that there is no universally accepted definition. It is considered useful, however, to offer a working definition for the purposes of the present draft principles. It helps to put into perspective the scope of the remedial action required in respect of environmental damage.[360]

(20) "Environment" could be defined in a restricted way, limiting it exclusively to natural resources, such as air, soil, water, fauna and flora, and their interaction. A broader definition could embrace environmental values also. The Commission has opted to include in the definition the latter, also encompassing non-service values such as aesthetic aspects of the landscape.[361] This includes the enjoyment of nature because of its natural beauty and its recreational attributes and opportunities associated with it. This broader approach is justified by the general and residual character of the present draft principles.[362]

(21) Moreover, the Commission in taking such a holistic approach is, in the words of the ICJ in the *Gabčíkovo–Nagymaros Project* case:

> mindful that, in the field of environmental protection, vigilance and prevention are required on account of the often irreversible character of damage to the environment and of the limitations inherent in the very mechanism of reparation of this type of damage.[363]

(22) Furthermore, a broader definition would attenuate any limitation imposed by the remedial responses acceptable in the various liability regimes and as reflected in commentary in respect of subparagraphs (iv) and (v) above.

(23) Thus, the reference in paragraph (*b*) to "natural resources … and the interaction" of its factors embraces the idea of a restricted concept of environment within a protected ecosystem,[364] while the reference to "the characteristic aspects of the landscape" denotes an acknowledgement of a broader concept of environment.[365] The

---

See also article 2, paragraph 2 (*c*) (v) and (*d*) of the Basel Protocol on Liability and Compensation for Damage Resulting from Transboundary Movements of Hazardous Wastes and their Disposal; article 2, paragraphs 7 (*d*) and 9 of the Convention on Civil Liability for Damage resulting from Activities Dangerous to the Environment; and article 2, paragraph 2 (*d*) (v) and (*h*) of the Protocol on Civil Liability and Compensation for Damage caused by the Transboundary Effects of Industrial Accidents on Transboundary Waters. Article 2 (*f*) of Annex VI to the Protocol on Environmental Protection to the Antarctic Treaty on Liability Arising From Environmental Emergencies defines response action as "reasonable measures taken after an environmental emergency has occurred to avoid, minimise or contain the impact of that environmental emergency, which to that end may include clean-up in appropriate circumstances, and includes determining the extent of that emergency and its impact".

[358] "[E]nvironmental damage will often extend beyond that which can be readily quantified in terms of clean-up costs and property devaluation. Damage to such environmental values (biodiversity, amenity, etc.—sometimes referred to as 'non-use values') is, as a matter of principle, no less real and compensable than damage to property, though it may be difficult to quantify" (*Yearbook ... 2001*, vol. II (Part Two) and corrigendum, p. 101 (para. (15) of the commentary to article 36)).

[359] See the report and recommendations made by the Panel of Commissioners concerning the fifth instalment of "F4" claims (footnote 355 above). See also Sand, "Compensation for environmental damage …", *loc. cit.* (*ibid.*), p. 247. Elaborated in five instalment reports, the awards recommended by the F4 Panel and approved without change by the Governing Council amount to $5.26 billion, "the largest … in the history of international environmental law" (Sand, "Compensation for environmental damage…", *loc. cit.* (*ibid.*), p. 245). See also the *Guidelines for the Follow-up Programme for Environmental Awards* of the UNCC (*ibid.*), pp. 276–281.

[360] See the Communication from the Commission to the Council and Parliament and the Economic and Social Committee: Green Paper on remedying environmental damage, COM (93) 47 final, of 14 May 1993, p. 10.

[361] For a philosophical analysis underpinning a regime for damage to biodiversity, see M. Bowman, "Biodiversity, intrinsic value and the definition and valuation of environmental harm", in Bowman and Boyle (eds.), *op. cit.* (footnote 333 above), pp. 41–61. Article 2 of the Convention for the protection of the world cultural and natural heritage defines "natural heritage" as "natural features consisting of physical and biological formations or groups of such formations, which are of outstanding universal value from the aesthetic or scientific point of view; geological and physiographical formations and precisely delineated areas which constitute the habitat of threatened species of animals and plants of outstanding universal value from the point of view of science or conservation; natural sites or precisely delineated natural areas of outstanding universal value from the point of view of science, conservation or natural beauty".

[362] For a concise discussion of the differing approaches on the definition of environmental damage, see Ph. Sands, *Principles of International Environmental Law*, 2nd ed., Cambridge University Press, 2003, pp. 876–878.

[363] *Gabčíkovo–Nagymaros Project (Hungary/Slovakia), Judgment, I.C.J. Reports 1997*, p. 7, at p. 78, para. 140. The Court in this connection also alluded to the need to keep in view the inter-generational and intra-generational interests and the contemporary demand to promote the concept of sustainable development.

[364] Under article 2 of the Convention on Biological Diversity, "'[e]cosystem' means a dynamic complex of plant, animal and micro-organism communities and their non-living environment interacting as a functional unit". Under article 1, paragraph 15 of the Convention on the Regulation of Antarctic Mineral Resource Activities (CRAMRA),

> "'[d]amage to the Antarctic environment or dependent or associated ecosystems' means any impact on the living or non-living components of that environment or those ecosystems, including harm to atmospheric, marine or terrestrial life, beyond that which is negligible or which has been assessed and judged to be acceptable pursuant to this Convention".

[365] Article 2, paragraph 10 of the Convention on Civil Liability for Damage resulting from Activities Dangerous to the Environment contains a non-exhaustive list of components of the environment which includes: "natural resources both abiotic and biotic, such as air, water, soil, fauna and flora and the interaction between the same factors; property which forms part of the cultural heritage; and the characteristic

(*Continued on next page.*)

definition of "natural resources" covers living and non-living natural resources, including their ecosystems.

(24) Paragraph (*c*) defines "hazardous activity" by reference to any activity which has a risk of causing transboundary harm. It is understood that such risk of harm should be through its physical consequences, thereby excluding such impacts as may be caused by trade, monetary, socio-economic or fiscal policies. The commentary concerning the scope of application of these draft principles above has explained the meaning and significance of the terms involved.

(25) Paragraph (*d*) defines the State of origin. This means the State in the territory or otherwise under jurisdiction or control of which the hazardous activity is carried out. The term "territory", "jurisdiction", or "control" is understood in the same way as in the draft articles on prevention.[366] Other terms are also used for the purpose of the present principles. They include, as defined under the draft articles on prevention, the "State likely to be affected" (a State on whose territory or in other places under whose jurisdiction or control there is the risk of significant transboundary harm) and there may be more than one such State likely to be affected in relation to any given situation of transboundary damage. The draft principles also use the term "States concerned" (the State of origin, any State affected and any State likely to be affected). "State affected" is not defined by the draft articles on prevention. For the purposes of the present draft principles it would be the States in whose territory, or in places under jurisdiction or control of which, damage occurs as a result of an incident concerning a hazardous activity in the State of origin. More than one State may be so affected. These terms have not been defined in the "Use of terms" for reasons of balance and economy.

(26) Paragraph (*e*) defines "transboundary damage". It refers to damage occurring in one State because of an accident or incident involving a hazardous activity with effect in another State. This concept is based on the well-accepted notions of territory, jurisdiction or control by a State. In that sense, it refers to damage caused in the territory or in other places outside the territory but under the jurisdiction or control of a State other than the State in the territory or otherwise under the jurisdiction or control of which the hazardous activities are carried out. It does not matter whether or not the States in question share a common border. This definition includes, for example, activities conducted under the jurisdiction or control of a State such as on its ships or platforms on the high seas, with effects on the territory of another State or in places under its jurisdiction or control. However, it goes without stating that some other possibilities could also be involved, which may not be readily contemplated.

(27) The definition is intended to clearly identify and distinguish a State under whose jurisdiction or control an activity covered by these principles is conducted, from a State which has suffered the injurious impact.

(28) As is often the case with incidents falling within the scope of the present draft principles, there may be victims both within the State of origin and within the other States where damage is suffered. In the disbursement of compensation, particularly in terms of the funds expected to be made available to victims as envisaged in draft principle 4 below, some funds may also be made available for damage suffered in the State of origin. Article XI of the Convention on Supplementary Compensation for Nuclear Damage envisages such a system.

(29) Paragraph (*f*) defines "victim". The definition includes natural and legal persons, and includes the State as custodian of public property.[367] This definition is linked to and may be deduced from the definition of damage in paragraph (*a*) which includes damage to persons, property or the environment.[368] A person who suffers personal injury or damage or loss of property would be a victim for the purposes of the draft principles. A group of persons or a municipality ("*commune*") could also be a victim. In the *People of Enewetek* case, the Marshall Islands Nuclear Claims Tribunal, established under the 1987 Marshall Islands Nuclear Claims Tribunal Act, considered questions of compensation in respect of the people of Enewetek for past and future loss of use of the Enewetak Atoll; for restoration of Enewetak to a safe and productive state; and for the hardships suffered by the people of Enewetak as a result of their relocation attendant to their loss of use occasioned by the nuclear tests conducted on the atoll.[369] In the *Amoco Cadiz* litigation, following the Amoco Cadiz supertanker disaster off Brittany, the French administrative *départements* of Côtes du Nord and Finistère and numerous "*communes*", and various French individuals, businesses and associations sued the owner of the Amoco Cadiz, and its parent company in the United States. The claims involved lost business. The French

(*Footnote 365 continued.*)

aspects of the landscape"; article 1 (*c*) of the Convention on the Transboundary Effects of Industrial Accidents refers to the adverse consequences of industrial accidents on "(i) [h]uman beings, flora and fauna; (ii) [s]oil, water, air and landscape; (iii) [t]he interaction between the factors in (i) and (ii); (iv) [m]aterial assets and cultural heritage, including historical monuments"; article 1, paragraph 2 of the Convention on the Protection and Use of Transboundary Watercourses and International Lakes says that "effects on the environment include effects on human health and safety, flora, fauna, soil, air, water, climate, landscape and historical monuments or other physical structures or the interaction among these factors; they also include effects on the cultural heritage or socio-economic conditions resulting from alterations to those factors".

[366] *Yearbook ... 2001*, vol. II (Part Two) and corrigendum, pp. 150–151 (paras. (7)–(10) of the commentary to draft article 1).

[367] On the contribution of Edith Brown Weiss to the development of the concept of "stewardship" or "trusteeship" as striking "a deep chord with Islamic, Judeo-Christian, African, and other traditions", and for the view that "[s]ome forms of public trusteeships are incorporated in most legal systems" including the United Kingdom and India, see R. Mushkat, *International Environmental Law and Asian Values: Legal Norms and Cultural Influences*, Vancouver, UBC Press, 2004, p. 18. See also J. Razzaque, *Public Interest Environmental Litigation in India, Pakistan and Bangladesh*, The Hague, Kluwer Law International, 2004, p. 424, for the role of public trust doctrine in Bangladesh, India and Pakistan.

[368] In respect of international criminal law, see the Declaration of Basic Principles of Justice for Victims of Crime and Abuse of Power, General Assembly resolution 40/34 of 29 November 1985. See also the Rome Statute of the International Criminal Court (article 79).

[369] *In the Matter of the People of Enewetak*, ILM, vol. 39, No. 5 (September 2000), pp. 1214 *et seq*. In December 1947, the population of Enewetak was moved from Enewetak Atoll to Ujelang Atoll. At the time of the move, the acreage of the Enewetek Atoll was 1,919.49 acres. Upon their return on 1 October 1980, 43 tests of atomic devices had been conducted, at which time 815.33 acres were returned for use, another 949.8 acres were not available for use and an additional 154.36 acres had been vaporized (*ibid.*, p. 1214).

Government itself laid claims for recovery of pollution damages and clean-up costs.[370]

(30) The definition of "victim" is thus linked to the question of standing. Some liability regimes, such as the Convention on Civil Liability for Damage resulting from Activities Dangerous to the Environment and the Directive 2004/35/CE of the European Parliament and of the Council on environmental liability with regard to the prevention and remedying of environmental damage, provide standing for NGOs.[371] The 1998 Convention on Access to Information, Public Participation in Decision-making and Access to Justice in Environmental Matters also gives standing to NGOs to act on behalf of public environmental interests. Victims may also be those designated under national laws to act as public trustees to safeguard those resources and hence may have the legal standing to sue. The concept of "public trust" in many jurisdictions provides proper standing to different designated persons to lay claims for restoration and clean-up in case of any transboundary damage.[372] For example, under the United States Oil Pollution Act, such a right is given to the United States Government, a state, an Indian tribe and a foreign Government. Under the United States Comprehensive Environmental Response, Compensation and Liability Act of 1980 (CERCLA), as amended in 1986 by the Superfund Amendments and Reauthorization Act, *locus standi* has been given only to the federal Government, authorized representatives of states, as trustees of natural resources, or by designated trustees of Indian tribes. In some other jurisdictions, public authorities have been given a similar right of recourse. Thus, Norwegian law provides standing to private organizations and societies to claim restoration costs. In France, some environmental associations have been given the right to claim compensation in criminal cases involving violation of certain environmental statutes. The Supreme Court of India has entertained petitions from individuals or groups of individuals under its well-developed public interest litigation cases or class action suits to protect the environment from damage and has awarded compensation to victims of industrial and chemical pollution.[373]

(31) Paragraph (*g*) defines "operator". There is no general definition of "operator" under international law, although the term is employed in domestic law[374] and in treaty practice. In the latter, the nuclear damage regimes impose liability on the operator.[375] The definition of "operator" would vary, however, depending upon the nature of the activity. The channelling of liability onto one single entity, whether owner or operator, is the hallmark of strict liability regimes. Thus, some person other than the operator may be specifically identified as liable depending on the interests involved in respect of a particular hazardous activity. For example, at the 1969 Conference leading to the adoption of the 1969 International Convention on Civil Liability for Pollution Damage, the possibility existed of imposing liability on the shipowner or the cargo owner or both.[376] Under an agreed compromise, the shipowner was made strictly liable.[377]

(32) The draft principles envisage the definition of "operator" in functional terms and it is based on a factual determination as to who has use, control and direction of the object at the relevant time. Such a definition

---

[370] See *In the Matter of: Oil Spill by the Amoco Cadiz off the coast of France on March 16, 1978*, United States Court of Appeals for the Seventh Circuit, 954 F.2d 1279. See also M. C. Maffei, *loc. cit.* (footnote 346 above), p. 381.

[371] See article 18 of the Convention on Civil Liability for Damage resulting from Activities Dangerous to the Environment and article 12 of Directive 2004/35/CE of the European Parliament and of the Council on environmental liability with regard to the prevention and remedying of environmental damage (footnote 316 above).

[372] P. Wetterstein, "A proprietary or possessory interest ...", *loc. cit.* (footnote 323 above), pp. 50–51.

[373] See Law Commission of India, *One Hundred Eighty Sixth Report on Proposal to Constitute Environmental Courts*, September 2003, p. 31 (available at http://lawcommissionofindia.nic.in/reports.htm). Articles 32 and 226 of the Indian Constitution provide for writ jurisdiction of the Supreme Court and the High Courts of India in this regard. The Courts have also used article 21 of the Indian Constitution and expanded the meaning of "life" to include the "right to a healthy environment". See also Razzaque, *op. cit.* (footnote 367 above), pp. 314–315, 429 and 443, where the author refers to arguments that the liberal standing provided before the courts of Bangladesh, India and Pakistan to bring environmental causes of action have led to the immobility and inefficiency in administration as well as the clogging of cases before the courts. This contribution is noteworthy for the overall assessment of progress made and reforms needed in the subcontinent to promote protection of the environment.

[374] For domestic law, see, for example, the 1990 Oil Pollution Act (footnote 341 above), in which the following individuals may be held liable: (*a*) a responsible party such as the owner or operator of a vessel, onshore and offshore facility, deepwater port and pipeline; (*b*) the "guarantor", the "person other than the responsible party, who provides evidence of financial responsibility for a responsible party"; and (*c*) third parties (individuals other than those mentioned in the first two categories, their agents or employees or their independent contractors, whose conduct is the sole cause of injury). See also the United States Comprehensive Environmental Response, Compensation and Liability Act (CERCLA) (footnote 351 above).

[375] See, for example, the Convention on third party liability in the field of nuclear energy and the Protocol to amend the Convention on Third Party Liability in the field of Nuclear Energy of 29 July 1960, as amended by the Additional Protocol of 28 January 1964 and by the Protocol of 16 November 1982: "'operator' in relation to a nuclear installation means to the person designated or recognised by the competent public authority as the operator of that installation" (common article 1 (vi)). See also the Vienna Convention on civil liability for nuclear damage (operator) (article IV); the Protocol to amend the Vienna Convention on civil liability for nuclear damage ("operator") (article 1 (*c*)); and the Convention on the Liability of Operators of Nuclear Ships ("operator of nuclear ships") (article II).

[376] See *Official Records of the International Legal Conference on Marine Pollution Damage, 1969*, Inter-Governmental Maritime Consultative Organization, 1973 (LEG/CONF/C.2/SR.2–13), cited in D. W. Abecassis and R. L. Jarashow, *Oil Pollution from Ships: International, United Kingdom and United States Law and Practice*, 2nd ed., London, Stevens and Sons, 1985, p. 253. Some regimes that attach liability to the shipowner are the 1992 Protocol to amend the International Convention on Civil Liability for Pollution Damage (art. III, para. 1); the International Convention on Civil Liability for Bunker Oil Pollution Damage (art. 3); and the 1996 International Convention on Liability and Compensation for Damage in Connection with the Carriage of Hazardous and Noxious Substances by Sea (HNS Convention) (art. 7, para. 1).

[377] See also the Convention on Civil Liability for Damage caused during Carriage of Dangerous Goods by Road, Rail and Inland Navigation Vessels (CRTD), which defines "carrier" with respect to inland navigation vessels as "the person who at the time of the incident controls the use of the vehicle on board which the dangerous goods are carried" (art. 1, para. 8); the International Convention on Civil Liability for Oil Pollution Damage resulting from Exploration for and Exploitation of Seabed Mineral Resources defines the operator of a continental shelf installation to include, in the absence of a designation by a Contracting Party, "the person who is in overall control of the activities carried on at the installation" (art. 1, para. 3); and under the EU Directive 2004/35/CE of the European Parliament and of the Council on environmental liability with regard to the prevention and remedying of environmental damage (footnote 316 above), which attaches liability to the operator, the term "operator" includes any natural or legal, private or public person who operates or controls the occupational activity.

is generally in conformity with notions prevailing in civil law.[378] More generally, while no basic definition of "operator" has been developed, "recognition has been gained for the notion that by operator is meant one in actual, legal or economic control of the polluting activity".[379]

(33) The term "command" connotes an ability to use or control some instrumentality. Thus it may include the person making use of an aircraft at the time of the damage, or the owner of the aircraft if he retained the rights of navigation.[380] It should be clear, however, that the term "operator" would not include employees who work or are in control of the activity at the relevant time.[381] The term "control" denotes power or authority to manage, direct, regulate, administer or oversee.[382] This could cover the person to whom decisive power over the technical functioning of an activity has been delegated, including the holder of a permit or authorization for such an activity or the person registering or notifying such an activity.[383] It may also include a parent company or other related entity, whether corporate or not, particularly if that entity has actual control of the operation.[384] An operator may be a public or private entity. It is envisaged that a State could be an operator for purposes of the present definition.

(34) The phrase "at the time of the incident" is intended to establish a connection between the operator and the transboundary harm. The looser and less concrete the link between the incident in question and the property claimed to have been damaged, the less certain the right to get compensation.

[378] See E. Reid, "Liability for dangerous activities: a comparative analysis", *International and Comparative Law Quarterly*, vol. 48 (October 1999), pp. 731–756, at p. 755.

[379] M.-L. Larsson, *The Law of Environmental Damage: Liability and Reparation*, The Hague, Kluwer Law International, 1999, p. 401.

[380] See the Convention on damage caused by foreign aircraft to third parties on the surface (article 12).

[381] See article 2 (*c*) of Annex VI to the Protocol on Environmental Protection to the Antarctic Treaty on Liability Arising From Environmental Emergencies: "'operator' means any natural or juridical person, whether governmental or non-governmental, which organises activities to be carried out in the Antarctic Treaty area. An operator does not include a natural person who is an employee, contractor, subcontractor, or agent of, or who is in the service of, a natural or juridical person, whether governmental or non-governmental, which organises activities to be carried out in the Antarctic Treaty area, and does not include a juridical person that is a contractor or subcontractor acting on behalf of a State operator".

[382] The definition of "ship owner" in the International Convention on Civil Liability for Bunker Oil Pollution is broad. It includes "the registered owner, bareboat charterer, manager and operator of the ship" (art. 1, para. 3).

[383] See Directive 2004/35/CE of the European Parliament and of the Council on environmental liability with regard to the prevention and remedying of environmental damage (footnote 316 above), article 2, para. 6.

[384] Under article 8 of the Convention on the Regulation of Antarctic Mineral Resource Activities (CRAMRA), the primary liability lies with the *operator*, which is defined in article 1, paragraph 11 as "a Party; or an agency or instrumentality of a Party; or a juridical person established under the law of a Party; or a joint venture consisting exclusively of any combination of the foregoing". Pursuant to section 16.1 of the Standard clauses for exploration contract annexed to the Regulations on the Prospecting and Exploration for Polymetallic Nodules in the Area adopted by the International Seabed Authority on 13 July 2000, the *contractor* is "liable for the actual amount of any damage, including damage to the marine environment, arising out of its wrongful acts or omissions, and those of its employees, subcontractors, agents and all persons engaged in working or acting for them" (ISBA/6/A/18, Annex 4, Clause 16).

Principle 3. Purposes

The purposes of the present draft principles are:

(*a*) to ensure prompt and adequate compensation to victims of transboundary damage; and

(*b*) to preserve and protect the environment in the event of transboundary damage, especially with respect to mitigation of damage to the environment and its restoration or reinstatement.

Commentary

(1) The two-fold purpose of the present draft principles is to ensure protection to victims suffering damage from transboundary harm and to preserve and protect the environment *per se* as common resource of the community.

(2) The purpose of ensuring protection to victims suffering damage from transboundary harm has been an essential element from the inception of the study of the topic by the Commission. In his schematic outline, Robert Q. Quentin-Baxter focused on the need to protect victims, which required "measures of prevention that as far as possible avoid a risk of loss or injury and, in so far as that is not possible, measures of reparation", so that "an innocent victim should not be left to bear his loss or injury".[385] The former consideration is already addressed by the draft articles on prevention.[386]

(3) The notion of prompt and adequate compensation in paragraph (*a*) reflects the understanding and the desire that victims of transboundary damage should not have to wait long in order to be compensated. The importance of ensuring prompt and adequate compensation to victims of transboundary damage has its underlying premise in the *Trail Smelter* arbitration[387] and the *Corfu Channel* case,[388] as further elaborated and encapsulated in principle 21 of the Stockholm Declaration, namely:

> States have, in accordance with the Charter of the United Nations and the principles of international law, the sovereign right to exploit their own resources pursuant to their own environmental policies, and the responsibility to ensure that activities within their jurisdiction or control do not cause damage to the environment of other States or of areas beyond the limits of national jurisdiction.[389]

(4) The notion of liability and compensation for victims is also reflected in principle 22 of the Stockholm Declaration, wherein a common conviction is expressed that:

[385] *Yearbook ... 1982,* vol. II (Part One), document A/CN.4/360, p. 63, para. 53 (schematic outline, section 5, paras. 2–3).

[386] See footnote 292 above.

[387] "[U]nder the principles of international law, ... no State has the right to use or permit the use of its territory in such a manner as to cause injury by fumes in or to the territory of another or the properties or persons therein, when the case is of serious consequences and the injury is established by clear and convincing evidence" (*Trail Smelter* (see footnote 226 above), p. 1965).

[388] In this case, the Court stated that it was "every State's obligation not to allow knowingly its territory to be used for acts contrary to the rights of other States" (*Corfu Channel* (see footnote 197 above), at p. 22).

[389] See footnote 312 above.

States shall co-operate to develop further the international law regarding liability and compensation for the victims of pollution and other environmental damage caused by activities within the jurisdiction or control of such States to areas beyond their jurisdiction.[390]

(5) This is further addressed more broadly in principle 13 of the Rio Declaration:

States shall develop national law regarding liability and compensation for the victims of pollution and other environmental damage. States shall also cooperate in an expeditious and more determined manner to develop further international law regarding liability and compensation for adverse effects of environmental damage caused by activities within their jurisdiction or control to areas beyond their jurisdiction.[391]

While the principles in these Declarations are not intended to give rise to legally binding obligations, they demonstrate aspirations and preferences of the international community.[392]

(6) Paragraph (*b*) gives a prominent place to the protection and preservation of the environment and to the associated obligations to mitigate the damage and to restore or reinstate the same to its original condition to the extent possible. Thus, it emphasizes the more recent concern of the international community to recognize protection of the environment *per se* as a value by itself without having to be seen only in the context of damage to persons and property. It reflects the policy to preserve the environment as a valuable resource not only for the benefit of the present generation but also for future generations. In view of its novelty and the common interest in its protection, it is important to emphasize that damage to environment *per se* could constitute damage subject to prompt and adequate compensation, which includes reimbursement of reasonable costs of response and restoration or reinstatement measures undertaken.

(7) The aim is not to restore or return the environment to its original state but to enable it to maintain its permanent functions. In the process it is not expected that expenditures disproportionate to the results desired would be incurred and such costs should be reasonable. Where restoration or reinstatement of the environment is not possible, it is reasonable to introduce the equivalent of those components into the environment.[393]

(8) In general terms, as noted above in the commentary on the "Use of terms" with respect to subparagraphs (iii)–(v), the earlier reluctance to accept liability for damage to environment *per se*, without linking such damage to damage to persons or property[394] is gradually disappearing.[395] In the case of damage to natural resources or the environment, there is a right of compensation or reimbursement for costs incurred by way of reasonable preventive, restoration or reinstatement measures. This is further limited in the case of some conventions to measures *actually* undertaken, excluding loss of profit from the impairment of the environment.[396]

(9) The State or any other public agency which steps in to undertake response or restoration measures may recover the costs later for such operations from the operator. For example, such is the case under the United States Comprehensive Environmental Response, Compensation and Liability Act of 1980 (CERCLA). The Statute establishes the Superfund with tax dollars to be replenished by the costs recovered from liable parties, to pay for clean-ups

---

[390] *Idem.*

[391] See footnote 301 above.

[392] Birnie and Boyle note that "[t]hese principles all reflect more recent developments in international law and state practice; their present status as principles of general international law is more questionable, but the evidence of consensus support provided by the Rio Declaration is an important indication of their emerging legal significance" (Birnie and Boyle, *International Law ...*, *op. cit.* (footnote 306 above), at p. 105).

[393] For an analysis of the definition of "environment" and the compensable elements of damage to the environment, see the eleventh report on international liability for injurious consequences arising out of acts not prohibited by international law of the Special Rapporteur Julio Barboza (footnote 285 above), at p. 57, para. 28. For an interesting account of the problem of damage, definition of harm, damage, adverse effects and damage valuation, see M. A. Fitzmaurice, "International protection of the environment", *Collected Courses of the Hague Academy of International Law, 2001*, vol. 293 (2002), pp. 9 *et seq.*, at pp. 225–233.

[394] For contrasting results, see *Blue Circle Industries plc* v. *Ministry of Defence, The All England Law Reports 1998*, vol. 3, p. 385, and *Merlin and another* v. *British Nuclear Fuels plc, The All England Law Reports 1990*, vol. 3, p. 711.

[395] For difficulties involved in claims concerning ecological damage and prospects, see the *Patmos* and *Haven* cases. See generally A. Bianchi, "Harm to the environment in Italian practice: the interaction of international law and domestic law", in P. Wetterstein (ed.), *op. cit.* (footnote 323 above), p. 103, at 113–129. See also Maffei, *loc. cit.* (footnote 346 above), p. 381, at pp. 383–390; and D. Ong, "The relationship between environmental damage and pollution: marine oil pollution laws in Malaysia and Singapore", in M. Bowman and A. Boyle (eds.), *op. cit.* (footnote 333 above), p. 191, at 201–204. See also Sands, *op. cit.* (footnote 362 above), at pp. 918–922. See also the 1979 *Antonio Gramsci* incident and the 1987 *Antonio Gramsci* incident (IOPC Fund, *Report on the Activities of the International Oil Pollution Compensation Fund during 1980; ibid., Annual Report 1989*, p. 26; and *ibid., Annual Report 1990*, p. 27). See also, generally, W. Chao, *Pollution from the Carriage of Oil by Sea: Liability and Compensation*, London, Kluwer, 1996, pp. 361–366: the IOPC Fund resolution No. 3 of 17 October 1980 did not allow the court to assess compensation to be paid by the Fund "on the basis of an abstract quantification of damage calculated in accordance with theoretical models" (FUND/A/ES.1/13, Annex I). In the *Amoco Cadiz* case (see footnote 370 above), the Northern District Court of Illinois ordered Amoco Oil Corporation to pay $85.2 million in fines—$45 million for the costs of the spill and $39 million in interest. It denied compensation for non-economic damage. It thus dismissed claims concerning lost image and ecological damage. The Court noted: "it is true that the commune was unable for a time to provide clean beaches for the use of its citizens, and that it could not maintain the normal peace, quiet, and freedom from the dense traffic which would have been the normal condition of the commune absent the cleanup efforts", but concluded that the "loss of enjoyment claim by the communes is not a claim maintainable under French law" (Maffei, *loc. cit.* (footnote 346 above), p. 393). Concerning lost image, the Court observed that the plaintiffs' claim was compensable in measurable damage, to the extent that it could be demonstrated that this loss of image resulted in specific consequential harm to the *commune* by virtue of tourists and visitors who might otherwise have come staying away. Yet this is precisely the subject matter of the individual claims for damages by hotels, restaurants, campgrounds, and other businesses within the *communes*. As regards ecological damage, the Court dealt with problems of evaluating "the species killed in the intertidal zone by the oil spill" and observed that "this claimed damage is subject to the principle of *res nullius* and is not compensable for lack of standing of any person or entity to claim therefor" (*ibid.*, at pp. 393–394). See also *In the Matter of the People of Enewetak* (footnote 369 above), before the Marshall Islands Nuclear Claims Tribunal. The Tribunal had an opportunity to consider whether restoration was an appropriate remedy for loss incurred by the people of the Enewetak Atoll arising from nuclear tests conducted by the United States. It awarded clean-up and rehabilitation costs as follows: $22 million for soil removal; $15.5 million for potassium treatment; $31.5 million for soil disposal (causeway); $10 million for clean-up of plutonium; $4.51 million for surveys; and $17.7 million for soil rehabilitation and revegetation (pp. 1222–1223).

[396] See generally the commentary to draft principle 2 above.

if necessary. The United States Environmental Agency operates the Superfund and has the broad powers to investigate contamination, select appropriate remedial actions and either order liable parties to perform the clean-up or do the work itself and recover its costs.[397]

(10) In addition to the present purposes, the draft principles serve or imply the serving of other objectives, including: (*a*) providing incentives to the operator and other relevant persons or entities to prevent transboundary damage from hazardous activities; (*b*) resolving disputes among States concerning transboundary damage in a peaceful manner that promotes friendly relations among States; (*c*) preserving and promoting the viability of economic activities that are important to the welfare of States and peoples; and (*d*) providing compensation in a manner that is predictable, equitable, expeditious and cost-effective. Wherever possible, the draft principles should be interpreted and applied so as to further all these objectives.[398]

(11) In particular, the principle of ensuring "prompt and adequate" compensation by the operator should be perceived from the perspective of achieving "cost internalization", which constituted the core, in its origins, of the "polluter pays" principle. It is a principle that argues for internalizing the true economic costs of pollution control, clean-up and protection measures within the costs of the operation of the activity itself. It thus attempted to ensure that Governments did not distort the costs of international trade and investment by subsidizing these environmental costs. This policy was endorsed in the policy of OECD and the European Union. The contexts in which the principle was endorsed have envisaged their own variations in its implementation.

(12) In one sense, the "polluter pays" principle seeks to provide an incentive for the operator and other relevant persons or entities to prevent a hazardous activity from causing transboundary damage. The principle is referred to in a number of international instruments. It appears in very general terms as principle 16 of the Rio Declaration:

> National authorities should endeavour to promote the internalization of environmental costs and the use of economic instruments, taking into account the approach that the polluter should, in principle, bear the cost of pollution, with due regard to the public interest and without distorting international trade and investment.[399]

(13) In treaty practice, the principle has formed the basis for the construction of liability regimes on the basis of strict liability. This is the case with the Convention on Civil Liability for Damage resulting from Activities Dangerous to the Environment, which in the preamble has "regard to the desirability of providing for strict liability in this field taking into account the 'Polluter Pays' Principle". The Protocol on Civil Liability and Compensation for Damage caused by the Transboundary Effects of Industrial Accidents on Transboundary Waters, in its preamble, refers to the "polluter pays" principle as "a general principle of international environmental law, accepted also by the parties to" the Convention on the Protection and Use of Transboundary Watercourses and International Lakes and the Convention on the Transboundary Effects of Industrial Accidents.[400] National jurisdictions have also placed reliance on it as playing a remedial and compensatory function.[401]

---

[397] For an analysis of CERCLA, see W. D. Brighton and D. F. Askman, "The role of the government trustees in recovering compensation for injury to natural resources", in P. Wetterstein (ed.), *op. cit.* (footnote 323 above), pp. 177–206, at pp. 183–184.

[398] See also Bergkamp, *op. cit.* (footnote 347 above), p. 70, footnote 19, who has identified seven functions relevant to a liability regime, namely compensation, distribution of losses, allocation of risks, punishment, corrective justice, vindication or satisfaction, and deterrence and prevention.

[399] See footnote 301 above.

[400] It also finds reference, for example, in the International Convention on oil pollution preparedness, response and cooperation; the Convention for the protection of the marine environment of the North-East Atlantic (OSPAR Convention); the Convention on the Protection of the Marine Environment of the Baltic Sea Area; the Convention on the protection of the Black Sea against pollution; the Convention on the Protection and Use of Transboundary Watercourses and International Lakes; the Convention on the Transboundary Effects of Industrial Accidents; the Convention on Civil Liability for Damage resulting from Activities Dangerous to the Environment; and Directive 2004/35/CE of the European Parliament and of the Council on environmental liability with regard to the prevention and remedying of environmental damage (see footnote 316 above).

[401] In its report on the implementation of Agenda 21, the United Nations notes:

> "Progress has been made in incorporating the principles contained in the Rio Declaration ... —including ... the polluter pays principle ...—in a variety of international and national legal instruments. While some progress has been made in implementing United Nations Conference on Environment and Development commitments through a variety of international legal instruments, much remains to be done to embody the Rio principles more firmly in law and practice."

(*Official Records of the General Assembly, Nineteenth Special Session, Supplement No. 2* (A/S-19/33), para. 14)

However, the "polluter pays" principle has been endorsed or is being endorsed in different national jurisdictions. The Supreme Court of India, in *Vellore Citizens' Welfare Forum* v. *Union of India and others* (see *All India Reporter, 1996*, vol. 83, p. 2715), noted that the precautionary principle, the "polluter pays" principle and the new burden of proof, supported by articles 21, 47, 48A, and 51A (*g*) of the Constitution of India, have become "part of the environmental law of the country" (Law Commission of India, *One Hundred Eighty Sixth Report on Proposal to Constitute Environmental Courts* (see footnote 373 above), p. 36). Access to justice, particularly in environmental matters, is an essential facet of article 21 of the Constitution of India. Australia and New Zealand already have environmental courts. Multiple provincial statutes of Canada regarding liability for environmental damage and subsequent remediation recognize the principle. In Spain, the courts have relied on the principle *cuius est commodum, eius est incommodum*—that is, the person who derives a benefit from an activity must also pay for resulting damage—to impose liability on persons for damage caused by mines, waste, damage as a result of loss of water, and toxic gas. In Japan, with regard to pollution caused by mining activities and marine pollution, the polluter pays to clean up the contamination to the commons and to restore the victim's property to its pre-damage state. The French legal system has endorsed in various forms the "polluter pays" principle. In *Époux Vullion* v. *Société immobilière Vernet-Saint Christophe et autres*, France's *Cour de cassation* held that "the owner's right to enjoy his property in the most absolute manner not prohibited by law or regulation is subject to his obligation not to cause damage to the property of anyone else which exceeds the normal incommodities of neighbourhood" (*Juris-Classeur périodique (La semaine juridique)*, 1971, II.16781. See the English translation by the Institute for Transnational Law of the School of Law of the University of Texas at Austin, available at www.utexas.edu/law/academics/centers/transnational). Sweden's Environmental Code of 1998, which came into force on 1 January 1999, makes the party who is liable for pollution to pay, to a reasonable extent, for investigations of possible pollution, clean-up and mitigation of damage. The test of reasonableness is determined with reference to (*a*) the length of time elapsed since the pollution occurred, (*b*) environmental risk involved and (*c*) the operator's contribution. Ireland enacted statutes to integrate, into domestic law, intentional treaties imposing strict liability for oil and hazardous waste spills by ships. Irish Courts have already begun to rely upon the "polluter pays" principle. In Brazil, strict liability is becoming a standard for damage caused by activities which are hazardous

(14) The principle has its limitations. It has thus been noted:

> The extent to which civil liability makes the polluter pay for environmental damage depends on a variety of factors. If liability is based on negligence, not only does this have to be proved, but harm which is neither reasonably foreseeable nor reasonably avoidable will not be compensated and the victim or the taxpayer, not the polluter, will bear the loss. Strict liability is a better approximation of the 'polluter pays' principle, but not if limited in amount, as in internationally agreed schemes involving oil tankers or nuclear installations. Moreover, a narrow definition of damage may exclude environmental losses which cannot be easily quantified in monetary terms, such as wildlife, or which affect the quality of the environment without causing actual physical damage.[402]

(15) Moreover, it has been asserted that the principle "cannot be treated as a rigid rule of universal application, nor are the means used to implement it going to be the same in all cases".[403] Thus, a "great deal of flexibility will be inevitable, taking full account of differences in the nature of the risk and the economic feasibility of full internalization of environmental costs in industries whose capacity to bear them will vary".[404] Some commentators doubt "whether [the 'polluter pays' principle] has achieved the status of a generally applicable rule of customary international law, except perhaps in relation to states in the [European Community], the UNECE, and the OECD".[405]

(16) The aspect of promptness and adequacy of compensation is related to the question of measurement of compensation. General international law does not specify "principles, criteria or methods for determining *a priori* how reparation is to be made for the injury caused by a wrongful act or omission".[406] Reparation under international law is a consequence of a breach of a primary obligation. The general obligation to make full reparation is restated in article 31 of the draft articles on responsibility of States for internationally wrongful acts.[407] The content of this obligation was detailed by the PCIJ in the *Chorzów Factory* case, when it stated *obiter dicta*:

> The essential principle contained in the actual notion of an illegal act—a principle which seems to be established by international practice and in particular by the decisions of arbitral tribunals—is that reparation must, as far as possible, wipe out all the consequences of the illegal act and reestablish the situation which would, in all probability, have existed if that act had not been committed. Restitution in kind, or, if this is not possible, payment of a sum corresponding to the value which a restitution in kind would bear; the award, if need be, of damages for loss sustained which is not covered by restitution in kind or payment in place of it—such are the principles which should serve to determine the amount of compensation due for an act contrary to international law.[408]

(17) The *Chorzów Factory* standard applies in respect of internationally wrongful acts, which are not covered by the present draft principles. It is useful, however, in appreciating the limits and the parallels that ought to be drawn in respect of activities covered by the present draft principles. There are questions about principles on the basis of which compensation could be awarded: Should compensation be awarded only in respect of the actual loss suffered by the victim to the extent it can be quantified? Or should compensation go beyond that and reflect the paying capacity of the operator? Two guiding principles seem relevant. The first is that damages awarded should not have a punitive function.[409] The second is

---

or those that harm or have a risk of causing harm to the environment. Intent need not be proved. Under South Africa's National Environmental Management Act of 1998, strict liability is imposed on operators who may cause, have caused or are causing significant pollution or degradation of environmental harm. Singapore provides strict liability for criminal offences. It imposes obligations of clean-up on polluters without the need for any intentional or negligent behaviour. See also the survey, prepared by the Secretariat, of liability regimes relevant to the topic of international liability for injurious consequences arising out of acts not prohibited by international law (international liability in case of loss from transboundary harm arising out of hazardous activities), *Yearbook ... 2004*, vol. II (Part One), document A/CN.4/543, paras. 272–286.

[402] Birnie and Boyle, *International Law* ..., *op. cit.* (footnote 306 above), pp. 93–94.

[403] *Ibid.*, pp. 94–95. See also the survey prepared by the Secretariat of liability regimes (footnote 401 above), chapter II.

[404] P. W. Birnie and A. E. Boyle, *International Law ..., op. cit.* (footnote 306 above), p. 95. The authors noted that "reference to 'public interest' in Principle 16 [of the Rio Declaration] leaves ample room for exceptions .... As adopted at Rio, the 'polluter pays' principle is neither absolute nor obligatory" (p. 93). They also noted that in the case of East European nuclear installations, "Western European Governments, who represent one large group of potential victims ... have funded the work needed to improve safety standards" (p. 94).

[405] Sands, *op. cit.* (footnote 362 above), p. 280, an illustration of the flexible way in which this principle is applied in the context of OECD and the European Union. Rüdiger Wolfrum, notes that "[a]lthough the International Convention on Oil Pollution Preparedness, Response and Co-operation, 1990 and the Convention on the Transboundary Effects of Industrial Accidents both refer in their Preambles to the polluter-pays principle as being a 'general principle of international environmental law', such view is not sustained in light of the United States' practice and also in light of the uncertainties about its scope and consequences" (R. Wolfrum, "International environmental law: purposes, principles and means of ensuring compliance", in F. L. Morrison and R. Wolfrum (eds.), *International, Regional, and National Environmental Law*, The Hague, Kluwer Law International, 2000, p. 19). See generally N. de Sadeleer, *Environmental Principles: from Political Slogans to Legal Rules*, Oxford University Press, 2002, pp. 21–60.

In the arbitration between France and the Netherlands, concerning the application of the 1976 Convention on the protection of the Rhine against pollution by chlorides and the 1991 Additional Protocol to the Convention on the protection of the Rhine against pollution by chlorides, the Arbitral Tribunal was requested to consider the "polluter pays" principle in its interpretation of the Convention, although it was not expressly referred to therein. The Tribunal in its 2004 award concluded that, despite its importance in treaty law, the "polluter pays" principle is not a part of general international law, and was therefore not pertinent to its interpretation of the Convention. The Tribunal, stated, in relevant part: "The Tribunal notes that the Netherlands has referred to the 'polluter pays' principle in support of its claim. ... The Tribunal observes that this principle features in several international instruments, bilateral as well as multilateral, and that it operates at various levels of effectiveness. Without denying its importance in treaty law, the Tribunal does not view this principle as being a part of general international law" (*Case concerning the audit of accounts between the Netherlands and France in application of the Protocol of 25 September 1991 Additional to the Convention for the Protection of the Rhine from Pollution by Chlorides of 3 December 1976, Arbitral award of 12 March 2004*, UNRIAA, vol. XXV (Sales No. E/F.05.V.5), p. 312, paras. 102–103). The text of the award is also available at www.pca-cpa.org.

[406] F. V. García-Amador, L. B. Sohn and R. R. Baxter (eds.), *Recent Codification of the Law of State Responsibility for Injury to Aliens* (see footnote 280 above), p. 89. See also A. Boyle, "Reparation for environmental damage in international law: some preliminary problems", in Bowman and Boyle, *Environmental Damage ... op. cit.* (footnote 333 above), pp. 17–26. See also the eleventh report on international liability for injurious consequences arising out of acts not prohibited by international law of the Special Rapporteur Julio Barboza (footnote 285 above).

[407] *Yearbook ... 2001*, vol. II (Part Two) and corrigendum, pp. 91–94 (art. 31 and its commentary).

[408] *Chorzów Factory* (see footnote 269 above), at p. 47.

[409] See B. Graefrath, "Responsibility and damages caused: relationship between responsibility and damages", *Recueil des cours: Collected courses of the Hague Academy of International Law, 1984-II*, vol. 185 (1985), pp. 9–150, at pp. 100–102. See also the draft articles on State responsibility for internationally wrongful acts, *Yearbook ... 2001*, vol. II (Part Two) and corrigendum, pp. 98–105 (article 36 and its commentary).

that the victim can only be compensated for the loss suffered but cannot expect to financially gain from the harm caused.[410] While keeping in view these two basic principles, the point can still be made that equity, as well as the "polluter pays" principle, demands that the operator should not be allowed to seek out safe havens to engage in risk-bearing hazardous activities without expecting to pay for damage caused, so as to provide an incentive to exert utmost care and due diligence to prevent damage in the first instance.[411]

(18) Some general principles concerning payment of compensation have evolved over a period of time and were endorsed by the ICJ and other international tribunals. These may be briefly noted:[412] (*a*) financially assessable damage, that is, damage quantifiable in monetary terms, is compensable; (*b*) this includes damage suffered by the State to its property or personnel or in respect of expenditures reasonably incurred to remedy or mitigate damage, as well as damage suffered by natural or legal persons, both nationals and those who are resident and suffered injury on its territory; (*c*) the particular circumstances of the case, the content of the obligation breached, the assessment of reasonableness of measures undertaken by parties in respect of the damage caused, and finally, consideration of equity and mutual accommodation. These factors will determine the terms or heads against which precise sums of compensation would be payable. Accordingly, the following guidelines on the basis of awards rendered by international courts and tribunals may be noted:[413] compensation is payable in respect of personal injury, for directly associated material loss such as loss of earnings and earning capacity, medical expenses including costs for achieving full rehabilitation; compensation is also payable for non-material damage suffered as, for example, for "loss of loved ones, pain and suffering as well as the affront to sensibilities associated with an intrusion on the person, home or private life".[414]

(19) In respect of damage to property, the loss is usually assessed against capital value, loss of profits and incidental expenses. In this context, different valuation techniques and concepts like assessment of "fair market value", "net book value", "liquidation or dissolution value" and "discounted cash flow" factoring elements of risk and probability have been used. On these and other issues associated with quantification of compensation there is ample material, particularly in the context of injury caused to aliens and their property through nationalization of their companies or property.[415]

(20) The principles developed in the context of disputes concerning foreign investment may not automatically be extended to apply to the issues of compensation in the field of transboundary damage. There may be difficult questions regarding claims eligible for compensation, such as economic loss, pain and suffering, permanent disability, loss of amenities or of consortium, and the evaluation of the injury. Similarly, damage to property which could be repaired or replaced could be compensated on the basis of the value of the repair or replacement. It is difficult to compensate damage caused to objects of historical or cultural value, except on the basis of arbitrary evaluation made on a case-by-case basis. Further, the looser and less concrete the link between the incident in question with the property claimed to have been damaged, the less certain the right to receive compensation. The commentary to draft principle 2 reveals the extent to which some of these problems have been overcome.

Principle 4. Prompt and adequate compensation

1. Each State should take all necessary measures to ensure that prompt and adequate compensation is available for victims of transboundary damage caused by hazardous activities located within its territory or otherwise under its jurisdiction or control.

2. These measures should include the imposition of liability on the operator or, where appropriate, other person or entity. Such liability should not require proof of fault. Any conditions, limitations or exceptions to such liability shall be consistent with draft principle 3.

3. These measures should also include the requirement on the operator or, where appropriate, other person or entity, to establish and maintain financial security such as insurance, bonds or other financial guarantees to cover claims of compensation.

4. In appropriate cases, these measures should include the requirement for the establishment of industry-wide funds at the national level.

5. In the event that the measures under the preceding paragraphs are insufficient to provide adequate compensation, the State of origin should also ensure that additional financial resources are made available.

Commentary

(1) This draft principle reflects an important role that is envisaged for the State of origin in fashioning a workable system for compliance with the principle of "prompt and adequate compensation". The reference to "[e]ach State" in the present context is to the State

[410] For the principles stated in the "*Lusitania*" case, UNRIAA, vol. VII, p. 32, and the *Chorzów Factory* case (see footnote 269 above) on the function of compensation, see *Yearbook ... 2001*, vol. II (Part Two) and corrigendum, pp. 98–105 (article 36 and its commentary).

[411] The Supreme Court of India in the *M. C. Mehta v. Union of India* (the Oleum gas leak case) stressed the point that the "larger and more prosperous the enterprise, the greater must be the amount of compensation payable by it for the harm caused on account of an accident in the carrying on of the hazardous or inherently dangerous activity by the enterprise" (Law Commission of India, *One Hundred Eighty Sixth Report on Proposal to Constitute Environmental Courts* (see footnote 373 above), p. 31).

[412] See the draft articles on State responsibility for internationally wrongful acts, *Yearbook ... 2001*, vol. II (Part Two) and corrigendum, pp. 98–105 (article 36 and its commentary and the cases cited therein).

[413] *Ibid.*

[414] *Ibid.*, p. 101 (para. (16) of the commentary to article 36). See also V. S. Mishra, "Emerging right to compensation in Indian environmental law", *Delhi Law Review*, vol. 23 (2001), pp. 58–79.

[415] See R. D. Bishop, J. Crawford and W. M. Reisman, *Foreign Investment Disputes: Cases, Materials and Commentary*, The Hague, Kluwer Law International, 2005, pp. 1331–1372 (on methods for valuing losses). See also C. F. Amerasinghe, "Issues of compensation for the taking of alien property in the light of recent cases and practice", *International and Comparative Law Quarterly*, vol. 41 (1992), pp. 22–65.

of origin. The principle contains four interrelated elements: (*a*) the State should ensure prompt and adequate compensation and for this purpose should put in place an appropriate liability regime; (*b*) any such liability regime may place primary liability on the operator, and should not require the proof of fault; (*c*) any conditions, limitations or exceptions that may be placed on such liability should not defeat the purpose of the principle of prompt and adequate compensation; and (*d*) various forms of securities, insurance and industry-wide funding are the means to provide sufficient financial guarantees for compensation. The five paragraphs of draft principle 4 express these four elements.

(2) It should be recalled that the assumption under the present draft principles is that the State of origin would have performed fully all its obligations concerning prevention of transboundary harm from hazardous activities under international law. Without prejudice to other claims that may be made under international law, the responsibility of the State for damage in the context of present principles is therefore not contemplated.

(3) Thus paragraph 1 focuses on the principle that States should ensure payment of adequate and prompt compensation. The State itself is not necessarily obliged to pay such compensation. The principle, in its present form, responds to and reflects a growing demand and consensus in the international community: as part of arrangements for permitting hazardous activities within its jurisdiction and control, it is widely expected that States would make sure that adequate mechanisms are also available to respond to claims for compensation in case of any damage.

(4) The emphasis in paragraph 1 is on all "necessary measures" and each State is given sufficient flexibility to achieve the objective of ensuring prompt and adequate compensation. This is highlighted without prejudice to any *ex gratia* payments to be made or contingency and relief measures that States or other responsible entities may otherwise consider extending to the victims.

(5) As noted in the commentary concerning the "Purposes" of the present draft principles, the need to develop liability regimes in an international context has been recognized and finds expression, for example, in Principle 22 of the 1972 Stockholm Declaration and Principle 13 of the 1992 Rio Declaration.[416]

(6) The basic principle that a State should ensure payment of prompt and adequate compensation for hazardous activities could be traced back as early as the *Trail Smelter* arbitration,[417] a case in which clear and convincing evidence was available for the serious consequence and injury caused to property within one State by the iron ore smelter in another. Since then, numerous treaties, some important decisions and the extensive national law and practice which have evolved have given considerable weight to claims for compensation in respect of transfrontier pollution and damage. Some commentators regard this as a customary law obligation.[418]

(7) The standard of promptness and adequacy in paragraph 1 is a standard that also finds support in the *Trail Smelter* arbitration.[419] The notion of "promptness" refers to the procedures that would govern access to justice, and that would influence the time and duration for the rendering of decisions on compensation payable in a given case. This is also a necessary criterion to be emphasized in view of the fact that litigation in domestic courts involving claims of compensation could be costly and protracted over several years, as it was in the *Amoco Cadiz* case, which took 13 years.[420] To render access to justice more widespread, efficient and prompt, suggestions have been

[416] See above, footnotes 312 and 301, respectively. See also the Malmö Ministerial Declaration, adopted by the Governing Council of UNEP at its sixth special session, *Official Records of the General Assembly, Fifty-fifth Session, Supplement No. 25* (A/55/25), Annex I, decision SS.VI/1 of 31 May 2000; the Programme for the Development and Periodic Review of Environmental Law for the First Decade of the Twenty-First Century (Montevideo Programme III), adopted by the UNEP Governing Council at its twenty-first special session, UNEP-E-GC21, decision 21/23 of 9 February 2001; and the Plan of Implementation of the World Summit on Sustainable Development, A/CONF.199/20, resolution 2 of 4 September 2002, Annex.

[417] See footnote 226 above.

[418] For a mention of different sources as a basis for arriving at this conclusion, see P.-T. Stoll, "Transboundary pollution", in Morrison and Wolfrum (eds.), *op. cit.* (footnote 405 above), pp. 169–200, at pp. 169–174. Stoll notes:

> "It must be recalled, however, that the prohibition principle is based on sovereign right of states to their territory. There is no evidence that it is necessary to refer to a specific entitlement based on a single component in raising a complaint about transboundary pollution. One can thus conclude that the prohibition of transboundary pollution is based on the state interest in the environmental integrity of its territory. Treaty law reflects this notion. ... Sovereignty, while creating a right to the environmental integrity of a territory or area at one hand, at the other hand is the very basis of states' responsibility for the pollution which originates within their territory" (*ibid.*, pp. 174–175)

In addition, it is also suggested that principles of abuse of rights and good neighbourhood have provided a basis for the prohibition against transboundary harm. See J. G. Lammers, "Centre for Studies and Research (1985). The present state of research carried out by the English-speaking Section of the Centre for Studies and Research", *Transfrontier Pollution and International Law*, The Hague, Kluwer Law International, 1986, p. 89–133, at p. 100.

[419] See footnote 226 above. See also Principle 10 of the Rio Declaration (footnote 301 above); article 235, paragraph 2 of the United Nations Convention on the Law of the Sea; article 2, paragraph 1 of the 1996 Helsinki articles on international watercourses (K. W. Cuperus and A. E. Boyle, "Articles on private law remedies for transboundary damage in international watercourses", in International Law Association, *Report of the Sixty-seventh Conference, Helsinki, 12–17 August 1996*, London, 1996, pp. 403 *et seq.*) and human rights law precedents. See also A. E. Boyle, "Globalising environmental liability: the interplay of national and international law", *Journal of Environmental Law*, vol. 17, No. 1 (2005), pp. 3–26, at p. 18.

[420] See footnote 370 above. See also E. Fontaine, "The French experience: '*Tanio*' and '*Amoco Cadiz*' incidents compared", in C. M. de la Rue (ed.), *Liability for Damage to the Marine Environment*, London, Lloyd's of London Press, 1993, pp. 101–108, at p. 105. Similarly, in the case of the Bhopal gas tragedy, it was stated that by the time the case first reached the Supreme Court of India on the issue whether interim relief assessed against Union Carbide on behalf of victims was appropriate, litigation had been underway in India for more than five years without even reaching the commencement of pretrial discovery, see K. F. McCallion and H. R. Sharma, "International resolution of environmental disputes and the Bhopal catastrophe", in The International Bureau of the Permanent Court of Arbitration (ed.), *International Investments and Protection of the Environment*, The Hague, Kluwer Law International, 2001, pp. 239–270, at p. 249. It is also stated that *Trail Smelter* arbitration took about 14 years to adjudicate upon the claims of private parties. See P. McNamara, *The Availability of Civil Remedies to Protect Persons and Property from Transfrontier Pollution Injury*, Frankfurt, Alfred Metzner Verlag, 1981, p. 70.

made to establish special national or international environmental courts.[421]

(8) On the other hand, the notion of "adequacy" of compensation refers to any number of issues.[422] For example, a lump sum amount of compensation agreed upon as a result of negotiations between the operator or the State of origin and the victims or other concerned States following the consolidation of claims of all the victims of harm may be regarded as adequate compensation. So would compensation awarded by a court as a result of the litigation entertained in its jurisdiction, subject to confirmation by superior courts wherever necessary. It is *ipso facto* adequate as long as the due process requirements are met. As long as compensation given is not arbitrary and grossly disproportionate to the damage actually suffered, even if it is less than full, it can be regarded as adequate. In other words, adequacy is not intended to denote "sufficiency".

(9) The phrase "its territory or otherwise under its jurisdiction or control" has the same meaning as the terms used in paragraph 1 (*a*) of article 6 of the draft articles on prevention.[423]

(10) Paragraph 2 spells out the first important measure that may be taken by each State, namely the imposition of liability on the operator or, where appropriate, other person or entity. The draft principles envisage the definition of "operator" in functional terms, based on the factual determination as to who has the use, control and direction of the object at the relevant time. It is worth stressing that liability in case of significant damage is generally channelled[424] to the operator of the installation. There are, however, other possibilities that exist. In the case of ships, it is channelled to the owner, not the operator. This means that charterers—who may be the actual operators—are not liable under the 1992 Protocol to amend the International Convention on Civil Liability for Oil Pollution Damage. In other cases, liability is channelled through more than one entity. Under the Basel Protocol on Liability and Compensation for Damage Resulting from Transboundary Movements of Hazardous Wastes and their Disposal, waste generators, exporters, importers and disposers are all potentially liable at different stages in the transit of waste. The real underlying principle is not that "operators" are always liable, but that the party with the most effective control of the risk at the time of the accident or with the ability to provide compensation is made primarily liable.

(11) Operator's liability has gained ground for several reasons and principally on the belief that one who created high risks seeking economic benefit must bear the burden of any adverse consequences of controlling the activity.[425] The imposition of the primary liability on the operator is widely accepted in international treaty regimes and in national law and practice.[426]

(12) The second sentence of paragraph 2 provides that such liability should not require proof of fault. Various designations are used to describe contemporary doctrine imposing strict liability, among them: "liability without fault" (*responsabilité sans faute*); "negligence without fault" (*négligence sans faute*), "presumed responsibility" (*responsabilité présumée*), "fault *per se*" (*négligence objective*), "objective liability" (*responsabilité objective*) or "risk liability" (*responsabilité pour risque créé*).[427] The phrase "[s]uch liability should not require proof of fault" seeks to capture this broad spectrum of designations.

(13) Hazardous and ultrahazardous activities, the subject of the present draft principles, involve complex operations and carry with them certain inherent risks of causing significant harm. In such matters, it is widely recognized that it would be unjust and inappropriate to make the claimant shoulder a heavy burden of proof of fault or negligence in respect of highly complex technological activities whose risks and operation the concerned industry closely guards as secret. Strict liability is recognized in many jurisdictions when assigning liability for inherently dangerous or hazardous activities.[428] The case for strict liability for ultrahazardous or abnormally dangerous activities was held to be the most appropriate technique, both under common and civil law, to enable victims of dangerous and ultrahazardous activities to recover compensation without having to establish proof of fault on the basis of what is often detailed

[421] See A. Rest, "Need for an international court for the environment? Underdeveloped legal protection for the individual in transnational litigation", *Environmental Policy and Law*, vol. 24, No. 4 (June 1994), pp. 173–187. For the view that the establishment of an international environmental court may not be a proper answer to the "need to enhance the rule of law through access to justice and the representation of community interests", see E. Hey, "Reflections on an international environmental court", in The International Bureau of the Permanent Court of Arbitration (ed.), *International Investments ... op. cit.* (footnote 420 above), pp. 271–301, at p. 299–300. At the national level, the Law Commission of India made a very persuasive case for the establishment of national environmental courts in India (see Law Commission of India, *One Hundred Eighty Sixth Report on Proposal to Constitute Environmental Courts* (footnote 373 above)). Australia and New Zealand already have environmental courts. Available at: http://lawcommissionofindia.nic.in/reports.htm.

[422] For an exhaustive enumeration of the implementation of the principle of prompt, adequate and effective compensation in practice, see Lefeber, *op. cit.* (footnote 330 above), pp. 229–312.

[423] *Yearbook ... 2001*, vol. II (Part Two) and corrigendum, p. 156. See also draft article 1 and the commentary thereto, especially paragraphs (7)–(12) (*ibid.*, pp. 149–151).

[424] According to Goldie, the nuclear liability conventions initiated the new trend of channelling liability back to the operator "no matter how long the chain of causation, nor how novel the intervening factors (other than a very limited number of exculpatory ones)" (L. F. E. Goldie, "Concepts of strict and absolute liability and the ranking of liability in terms of relative exposure to risk", *Netherlands Yearbook of International Law*, vol. 16 (see footnote 319 above), p. 196). On this point see also L. F. E. Goldie, "Liability for damage and the progressive development of international law", *The International and Comparative Law Quarterly*, vol. 14 (1965), pp. 1189 *et seq.*, at pp. 1215–1218.

[425] For an interesting account of economic, political and strategic factors influencing the choices made in channelling liability, see G. Doeker and T. Gehring, "Private or international liability for transnational environmental damage—the precedent of conventional liability regimes", *Journal of Environmental Law*, vol. 2, No. 1 (1990), pp. 1–16, at p. 7.

[426] See the survey prepared by the Secretariat of liability regimes (footnote 401 above), paras. 340–386.

[427] See F. F. Stone, "Liability for damage caused by things", in A. Tunc (ed.), *International Encyclopedia of Comparative Law*, vol. XI (Torts), part I, The Hague, Martinus Nijhoff, 1983, chapter 5, p. 3, paragraph 1.

[428] See the survey prepared by the Secretariat of liability regimes (footnote 401 above), paras. 29–260. The Supreme Court of India, in *M. C. Mehta v. Union of India* (see footnote 411 above), held that in the case of hazardous activities, exceptions which could be pleaded to avoid absolute or strict liability, like that the damage is not foreseeable, and that the use involved is a natural one, are not available.

technical evidence,[429] which, in turn, would require on the part of victims a complete understanding of the complicated and complex operation or activity. The case for strict liability is strengthened when the risk has been introduced unilaterally by the defendant.[430]

(14) In the case of damage arising from hazardous activities, it is fair to designate strict liability of the operator at the international level.[431] Strict liability has been adopted as the basis of liability in several instruments, and among the recently negotiated instruments it is provided for in article 4 of the Protocol on Civil Liability and Compensation for Damage caused by the Transboundary Effects of Industrial Accidents on Transboundary Waters, article 4 of the Basel Protocol on Liability and Compensation for Damage Resulting from Transboundary Movements of Hazardous Wastes and their Disposal and article 8 of the Convention on Civil Liability for Damage resulting from Activities Dangerous to the Environment.

(15) In the case of activities which are not dangerous but still carry the risk of causing significant harm, there perhaps is a better case for liability to be linked to fault or negligence. In addition, since profits associated with the risky activity provide a motivation for industry in undertaking such activity, strict liability regimes are generally assumed to provide incentives for better management of the risk involved. However, this is an assumption which may not always hold up. As these activities have been accepted only because of their social utility and indispensability for economic growth, States may consider at the opportune time reviewing their indispensability by exploring more environmentally sound alternatives which are also less hazardous.

(16) Strict liability may alleviate the burden that victims may otherwise have in proving fault of the operator, but it does not eliminate the difficulties involved in establishing the necessary causal connection of the damage to the source of the activity. The principle of causation is linked to questions of foreseeability and proximity or direct loss. Courts in different jurisdictions have applied the principles and notions of proximate cause, adequate causation, foreseeability and remoteness of the damage. This is a highly discretionary and unpredictable branch of law. Different jurisdictions have applied these concepts with different results. It may be mentioned that the test of proximity seems to have been gradually eased in modern tort law. Developments have moved from strict *condicio sine qua non* theory over the foreseeability ("adequacy") test to a less stringent causation test requiring only the "reasonable imputation" of damage. Further, the foreseeability test could become less and less important with the progress being made in the fields of medicine, biology, biochemistry, statistics and other relevant fields. Given these reasons, such tests have not been included in a more general analytical model on loss allocation.[432]

(17) The point worth bearing in mind is that in transforming the concept of strict liability from a domestic, national context—where it is well-established but with all the differences associated with its invocation and application in different jurisdictions—into an international standard, its elements should be carefully defined, while keeping its basic objective in view, that is, to make the person liable without any proof of fault for having created a risk by engaging in a dangerous or hazardous activity. Such a definition is necessary not only to capture the most positive elements of the concept of strict liability as they are obtained in different jurisdictions, making the international standard widely acceptable, but would also ensure the standard adopted truly serves the cause of the victims exposed to dangerous activities, thus facilitating prompt and effective remedies.

(18) This task can be approached in different ways.[433] For example, it could be done by adopting a proper definition of damage as has been done in the case of the "Use of terms", which defines "damage" as damage to person, property and the environment. It could also be done by designating strict liability as the standard for invoking liability, while also specifying that it is meant to include all damage foreseeable in its most generalized form and that knowledge of the extent of the potential danger is not a prerequisite of liability. Further, it may be clarified as part of the application of the rule that it is sufficient if the use posed a risk of harm to the others and, accordingly, that it is not open to the operator to plead exemption from liability on the ground that the use involved is a natural one.

(19) The third sentence of paragraph 2 recognizes that it is part of the practice for States borne out in domestic and treaty practice to subject liability to certain conditions, limitations or exceptions. However, it must be ensured that such conditions, limitations or exceptions do not fundamentally alter the purpose of providing for prompt and adequate compensation. The point has thus been emphasized that any such conditions, limitations or exceptions shall be consistent with the purposes of the present draft principles.

(20) It is common to associate the concept of strict liability with the concept of limited liability. Limited liability has several policy objectives. It is justified as a matter of convenience to encourage the operator to continue to be engaged in such a hazardous but socially and economically beneficial activity. Strict liability is also aimed at securing reasonable insurance coverage for the activity.

---

[429] See Reid, *loc. cit.* (footnote 378 above), p. 756. See also the survey prepared by the Secretariat of liability regimes (footnote 401 above), para. 23.

[430] See the survey prepared by the Secretariat of liability regimes, *ibid.*

[431] The Commission's Working Group on international liability for injurious consequences arising out of activities not prohibited by international law exhibited hesitation in 1996 in designating damage arising from all activities covered within the scope of the draft principles subject to the regime of strict liability. It may be recalled that the Commission noted that the concepts of strict and absolute liability which "are familiar in the domestic law in many States and in relation to certain [that is, ultrahazardous] activities in international law … have not been fully developed in international law, in respect to a large group of activities such as those covered by article 1" (*Yearbook ... 1996*, vol. II (Part Two), Annex I, p. 128 (para. (1) of the general commentary to chapter III). In arriving at this conclusion, the Working Group had the benefit of the survey prepared by the Secretariat of liability regimes relevant to the topic of international liability for injurious consequences arising out of acts not prohibited by international law (see footnote 284 above).

[432] See Wetterstein, "A proprietary or possessory interest …", *loc. cit.* (footnote 323 above), at p. 40.

[433] See the observations of Reid, *loc. cit.* (footnote 378 above), pp. 741–743.

Further, if liability has to be strict, that is, if liability has to be established without a strict burden of proof for the claimants, limited liability may be regarded as a reasonable *quid pro quo*. Although none of the propositions are self-evident truths, they are widely regarded as relevant.[434]

(21) It is arguable that a scheme of limited liability is unsatisfactory, as it is not capable of providing sufficient incentive to the operator to take stricter measures of prevention. If the limits are set too low, it could even become a licence to pollute or cause injury to others and externalize the real costs of the operator. Secondly, it may not be able to meet all the legitimate demands and claims of innocent victims for reparation in case of injury. For this reason, it is important to set limits of financial liability at a sufficiently high level, keeping in view the magnitude of the risk of the activity and the reasonable possibility for insurance to cover a significant portion of the risk involved.

(22) Article 9 of the Protocol on Civil Liability and Compensation for Damage caused by the Transboundary Effects of Industrial Accidents on Transboundary Waters and article 12 of the Basel Protocol on Liability and Compensation for Damage Resulting from Transboundary Movements of Hazardous Wastes and their Disposal provide for strict but limited liability. In contrast, article 6, paragraph 1 and article 7, paragraph 1 of the Convention on Civil Liability for Damage resulting from Activities Dangerous to the Environment provide for strict liability without any provision for limiting liability. Where limits are imposed on the financial liability of operator, generally such limits do not affect any interest or costs awarded by the competent court. Moreover, limits of liability are subject to review on a regular basis.

(23) Financial limits are well known in the case of regimes governing oil pollution at sea and nuclear incidents. For example, under the 1992 Protocol to amend the International Convention on Civil Liability for Oil Pollution Damage, the shipowner's maximum limit of liability is 59.7 million Special Drawing Rights (SDRs) (art. 6); thereafter the IOPC is liable to compensate for further damage up to a total of 135 million SDRs (including the amounts received from the owner), or in the case of damage resulting from natural phenomena, 200 million SDRs.[435] Similarly, the Protocol to amend the Vienna Convention on civil liability for nuclear damage also prescribed appropriate limits for an operator's liability.[436]

(24) Most liability regimes exclude limited liability in case of fault. The operator is made liable for the damage caused or contributed to by his or her wrongful intentional, reckless or negligent acts or omissions. Specific provisions to this extent are available for example in article 5 of the Basel Protocol on Liability and Compensation for Damage Resulting from Transboundary Movements of Hazardous Wastes and their Disposal and article 5 of the Protocol on Civil Liability and Compensation for Damage caused by the Transboundary Effects of Industrial Accidents on Transboundary Waters. In the case of operations involving highly complicated chemical or industrial processes or technology, fault liability could pose a serious burden of proof for the victims. Their rights could nevertheless be better safeguarded in several ways. For example, the burden of proof could be reversed, requiring the operator to prove that no negligence or intentional wrongful conduct was involved. Liberal inferences may be drawn from the inherently dangerous activity. Statutory obligations could be imposed upon the operator to give access to the victims or the public to the information concerning the operations.

(25) One advantage of a strict but limited liability from the perspective of the victim is that the person concerned need not prove negligence and would also know precisely whom to sue. In cases where harm is caused by more than one activity and could not reasonably be traced to any one of them or cannot be separated with a sufficient degree of certainty, jurisdictions have tended to make provision for joint and several liability.[437] Existing international instruments also provide for that kind of liability.[438]

(26) If, however, the person who has suffered damage has by his or her own fault caused the damage or

[434] See R. R. Churchill, "Facilitating (transnational) civil liability litigation for environmental damage by means of treaties: progress, problems, and prospects", *Yearbook of International Environmental Law*, vol. 12 (2001), pp. 3–41, at pp. 35–37.

[435] See article V, paragraph 1 of the 1969 International Convention on Civil Liability for Oil Pollution Damage as amended by the 1992 Protocol, article 4 of the International Convention on the establishment of an international fund for compensation for oil pollution damage, and article 6 of the Protocol of 1992 to amend the International Convention on the establishment of an international fund for compensation for oil pollution damage. Following the sinking of the *Erika* off the French coast in December 1999, the maximum limit was raised to 89.77 million SDRs, effective 1 November 2003. Under the 2000 amendments to the Protocol of 1992 to amend the International Convention on the establishment of an international fund for compensation for oil pollution damage, that would enter into force in November 2003, the amounts were raised from 135 million SDRs to 203 million SDRs. If three States contributing to the Fund receive more than 600 million tons of oil per annum, the maximum amount is raised to 300,740,000 SDRs, from 200 million SDRs. See also Sands, *op. cit.* (footnote 362 above), pp. 915–917.

[436] The installation State is required to assure that the operator is liable for any one incident for not less than 300 million SDRs or for a transition period of 10 years, a transitional amount of 150 million SDRs is to be assured, in addition by the installation State itself. The Convention on Supplementary Compensation for Nuclear Damage provides an additional sum, which may exceed $1 billion (see articles III and IV).

[437] On joint and several liability, see Bergkamp, *op. cit.* (footnote 347 above), pp. 298–306.

[438] For examples of treaty practice, see for example article IV of the International Convention on Civil Liability for Oil Pollution Damage; article 4 of the 1992 Protocol to amend the International Convention on Civil Liability for Oil Pollution Damage; article 8 of the International Convention on Liability and Compensation for Damage in Connection with the Carriage of Hazardous and Noxious Substances by Sea (HNS Convention); article 5 of the International Convention on Civil Liability for Bunker Oil Pollution Damage; article 4 of the Basel Protocol on Liability and Compensation for Damage Resulting from Transboundary Movements of Hazardous Wastes and their Disposal; article 4 of the Protocol on Civil Liability and Compensation for Damage caused by the Transboundary Effects of Industrial Accidents on Transboundary Waters; and article 11 of the Convention on Civil Liability for Damage resulting from Activities Dangerous to the Environment. See also article VII of the Convention on the Liability of Operators of Nuclear Ships; article 2 of the Protocol to amend the Vienna Convention on civil liability for nuclear damage; article II of the Vienna Convention on civil liability for nuclear damage; article 3 of the Convention on third party liability in the field of nuclear energy; and article 3 of the Protocol to amend the Convention on Third Party Liability in the field of Nuclear Energy of 29 July 1960, as amended by the Additional Protocol of 28 January 1964 and by the Protocol of 16 November 1982.

contributed to it, compensation may be denied or reduced having regard to all the circumstances.

(27) It is also usual for liability regimes and domestic law providing for strict liability to specify a limited set of fairly uniform exceptions to the liability of the operator. A typical illustration of the exceptions to liability can be found in articles 8 and 9 of the Convention on Civil Liability for Damage resulting from Activities Dangerous to the Environment, article 3 of the Basel Protocol on Liability and Compensation for Damage Resulting from Transboundary Movements of Hazardous Wastes and their Disposal or article 4 of the Protocol on Civil Liability and Compensation for Damage caused by the Transboundary Effects of Industrial Accidents on Transboundary Waters. Liability is excepted if, despite taking all appropriate measures, the damage was (*a*) the result of an act of armed conflict, hostilities, civil war or insurrection; (*b*) the result of a natural phenomenon of exceptional, inevitable, unforeseeable and irresistible character; (*c*) wholly the result of compliance with a compulsory measure of a public authority in the State of injury; or (*d*) wholly the result of the wrongful intentional conduct of a third party.[439]

(28) Paragraph 3 provides that the "measures" envisaged under paragraph 1 should include imposition of a requirement on the operator or, where appropriate, other person or entity, to establish and maintain financial security such as insurance, bonds or other financial guarantees to cover claims of compensation. The objective here is to ensure that the operator has sufficient funds at his disposal to enable him to meet claims of compensation, in the event of an accident or incident. It is understood that availability of insurance and other financial securities for hazardous operations depends upon many factors and mostly on the ability of the operator to identify the "risk" involved as precisely as possible. The assessment of "risk" for this purpose should not only consider the risk inherent in the activity to cause damage but also the statistical probability of the type and number of claims to which such damage might give rise as well as the number of claimants that may be involved.

(29) In the case of activities with a risk of causing significant transboundary harm, the insurance coverage would have to provide for the "foreign loss event" in addition to the "domestic loss event". The modern dynamics of law governing causation multiplies the factors that the operator in the first instance—and the insurers ultimately—would have to take into account while assessing the "risk" that needed to be covered. In this connection, the liberal tests that are invoked to establish a causal link, widening the reach of the tests of "proximate cause" and "foreseeability" and even replacing the same with a broader "general capability" test, are at issue.[440]

(30) Despite these difficulties, it is encouraging that insurance coverage is increasingly being made available for damage to persons, property or the environment due to oil spills and other hazardous activities.[441] This is mainly because of the growing recognition on the part of the industry, consumers and Governments that the products and services that the hazardous industry is able to provide are worthy of protection in the public interest. In order to maintain these products and services, the losses that such activities generate must be widely allocated and shared. Insurance and financial institutions are indispensable actors in any such scheme of allocation. These are institutions with expertise to manage risk and their profitability lies in pooling financial resources and wisely investing in risk-bearing activities.[442] However, it is inevitable that premiums for insurance coverage of the hazardous activities will grow in direct proportion to the range and magnitude of the risk that is sought to be covered. The increase in the premium costs is also directly related to the growing trend to designate an operator's liability as strict. Further, the trend to raise the limits of liability to

[439] Under paragraphs 2 and 3 of article III of the International Convention on Civil Liability for Oil Pollution Damage as amended by the 1992 Protocol, *war, hostilities, civil war, insurrection or natural phenomena of an exceptional, inevitable and irresistible character* are elements providing exoneration from liability for the owner, independently of negligence on the part of the claimant. See also article III of the International Convention on Civil Liability for Oil Pollution Damage; article 3 of the International Convention on Civil Liability for Bunker Oil Pollution Damage; and article 7 of the International Convention on Liability and Compensation for Damage in Connection with the Carriage of Hazardous and Noxious Substances by Sea (HNS Convention). Article 3 of the International Convention on Civil Liability for Oil Pollution Damage resulting from the Exploration for and Exploitation of Seabed Mineral Resources provides similar language in respect of the *operator of an installation*. See also article 3 of the Convention on Civil Liability for Damage caused during Carriage of Dangerous Goods by Road, Rail and Inland Navigation Vessels (CRTD).

Exemptions are also referred to in article 6 of the Protocol to amend the Vienna Convention on civil liability for nuclear damage: under this Convention, no liability shall attach to an operator if he proves that the nuclear damage is directly due to an act of armed conflict, civil war or insurrection. See also article IV, paragraph 3 of the Vienna Convention on civil liability for nuclear damage; article 9 of Protocol to amend the Convention on Third Party Liability in the field of Nuclear Energy of 29 July 1960, as amended by the Additional Protocol of 28 January 1964 and by the Protocol of 16 November 1982; article 3, paragraph 5 of the annex to the Convention on Supplementary Compensation for Nuclear Damage; and article 4, paragraph 1 of Directive 2004/35/CE of the European Parliament and of the Council on environmental liability with regard to the prevention and remedying of environmental damage (footnote 316 above). The Directive also does not apply to activities whose main purpose is to serve national defence or international security. In accordance with article 4, paragraph 6, it also does not apply to activities whose sole purpose is to protect from natural disasters. Terrorist acts are included in the most recent liability instrument: article 8, paragraph 1 of Annex VI to the Protocol on Environmental Protection to the Antarctic Treaty on Liability Arising From Environmental Emergencies provides that "[a]n operator shall not be liable pursuant to Article 6 if it proves that the environmental emergency was caused by: (*a*) an act or omission necessary to protect human life or safety; (*b*) an event constituting in the circumstances of Antarctica a natural disaster of an exceptional character, which could not have been reasonably foreseen, either generally or in the particular case, provided all reasonable preventative measures have been taken that are designed to reduce the risk of environmental emergencies and their potential adverse impact; (*c*) an act of terrorism; or (*d*) an act of belligerency against the activities of the operator". For examples of domestic law, see the survey prepared by the Secretariat of liability regimes (footnote 401 above), paras. 434–476.

[440] H.-D. Sellschopp, "Multiple tort feasors/combined polluter theories, causality and assumption of proof/statistical proof, technical insurance aspects" in Kröner (ed.), *op. cit.* (footnote 356 above), pp. 51–57, at pp. 52–53.

[441] See Ch. S. Donovan and E. M. Miller, "Limited insurability of unlimited liability: serial claims, aggregates and alternatives: the American view", in Kröner (ed.), *op. cit.* (footnote 356 above), pp. 129–158; and W. Pfennigstorf, "Limited insurability of unlimited liability: serial claims, aggregates and alternatives: the Continental view", *ibid.*, pp. 159–165.

[442] See A. J. E. Fitzsimmons, "Non-marine environmental liability: the use of insurance pools and the European dimension", *ibid.*, pp. 166–173, at pp. 166–167.

higher and higher levels, even if the operator's liability is capped, is also a factor in the rising costs of premiums.

(31) The State concerned may establish minimum limits for financial securities for such purposes, taking into consideration the availability of capital resources through banks or other financial agencies. Even insurance schemes may require a certain minimum financial solvency from the operator to extend their coverage. Under most of the liability schemes, the operator is obliged to obtain insurance and such other suitable financial securities.[443] This may be particularly necessary to take advantage of the limited financial liability scheme, where it is available. However, in view of the diversity of legal systems and differences in economic conditions, some flexibility for States in requiring and arranging suitable financial and security guarantees may be envisaged.[444] An effective insurance system may also require wide participation by potentially interested States.[445]

(32) The importance of such mechanisms cannot be overemphasized. It has been noted that "financial assurance is beneficial for all stakeholders: for public authorities and the public in general, it is one of the most effective, if not the only, way of ensuring that restoration actually takes place in line with the polluter-pays principle; for industry operators, it provides a way of spreading risks and managing uncertainties; for the insurance industry, it is a sizeable market".[446] Such insurance coverage should also be available for clean-up costs.[447]

(33) Insurance coverage is available in some jurisdictions, such as Europe and the United States. The experience gained in such markets can be quickly transferred to other markets as the insurance industry is increasingly global. Article 14 of Directive 2004/35/CE of the European Parliament and of the Council on environmental liability with regard to the prevention and remedying of environmental damage,[448] for example, provides that member States shall take measures to encourage the development of security instruments and markets by the appropriate security, economic and financial operators, including financial mechanisms in case of insolvency, with the aim of enabling operators to use financial guarantees to cover their responsibilities under the Directive.

(34) One of the consequences of ensuring the availability of insurance and financial security is that a claim for compensation may be allowed as one option under domestic law directly against any person providing financial security coverage. However, such a person may be given the right to require the operator to be joined in the proceedings. Such a person is also entitled to invoke the defences to which the operator would otherwise be entitled under the law. Article 11, paragraph 3 of the Protocol on Civil Liability and Compensation for Damage caused by the Transboundary Effects of Industrial Accidents on Transboundary Waters and article 14, paragraph 4 of the Basel Protocol on Liability and Compensation for Damage Resulting from Transboundary Movements of Hazardous Wastes and their Disposal provide for such possibilities. However, both Protocols allow States to make a declaration, if they wish, not allowing for such direct action.

(35) Paragraphs 4 and 5 refer to the other equally important measures that the State should focus upon. This is about establishing supplementary funds at the national level. Of course, this does not preclude the assumption of these responsibilities at a subordinate level of government in the case of a State with a federal system. Available schemes of allocation of loss envisage some sort of supplementary funding to meet claims of compensation in case the funds at the disposal of the operator are not adequate to compensate victims. Most liability regimes concerning dangerous activities provide for additional funding sources to meet the claims of damage, and particularly to meet the costs of response and restoration measures that are essential to contain the damage and restore value to affected natural resources and public amenities.

(36) Additional sources of funding could be created out of different accounts. One account could be out of public funds, as part of the national budget. In other words, the State could share in the allocation of loss created by the damage, as has happened in the case of the nuclear energy operations. Another account could be a common pool of funds created by contributions either from operators of the same category of dangerous activities or from entities for whose direct benefit the dangerous or hazardous activity is carried out. This is the case with management of risks associated with transport of oil by sea. However, in the case of hazardous activities which are very special, supplementary funds may have to be developed through some form of taxation on consumers of the products and services the industry generates and supports. This may be particularly necessary if the pool of operators and directly interested consumers is very small and not connected by any common economic or strategic interest.

---

[443] For treaty practice, see, for example, article III of the Convention on the Liability of Operators of Nuclear Ships; article 7 of the Protocol to amend the Vienna Convention on civil liability for nuclear damage; article VII of the Vienna Convention on civil liability for nuclear damage; article 10 of the Convention on third party liability in the field of nuclear energy; and article 10 of the Protocol to amend the Convention on Third Party Liability in the field of Nuclear Energy of 29 July 1960, as amended by the Additional Protocol of 28 January 1964 and by the Protocol of 16 November 1982. See also article V of the International Convention on Civil Liability for Oil Pollution Damage as amended by the 1992 Protocol; article 12 of the International Convention on Liability and Compensation for Damage in Connection with the Carriage of Hazardous and Noxious Substances by Sea (HNS Convention); article 7 of the International Convention on Civil Liability for Bunker Oil Pollution Damage; article 14 of the Basel Protocol on Liability and Compensation for Damage Resulting from Transboundary Movements of Hazardous Wastes and their Disposal; article 11 of the Protocol on Civil Liability and Compensation for Damage caused by the Transboundary Effects of Industrial Accidents on Transboundary Waters; and article 12 of the Convention on Civil Liability for Damage resulting from Activities Dangerous to the Environment.

[444] See, for example, the statement by China, *Official Records of the General Assembly, Fifty-eighth Session, Sixth Committee, 19th meeting* (A/C.6/58/SR.19), para. 43.

[445] See, for example, the statement by Italy, *ibid., 17th meeting* (A/C.6/58/SR.17), para. 28.

[446] Proposal for a directive of the European Parliament and of the Council on environmental liability with regard to the prevention and remedying of environmental damage, of 23 January 2002 (COM (2002) 17 final).

[447] *Ibid.*

[448] See footnote 316 above.

(37) Paragraph 4 deals with industry funding and provides that in appropriate cases, these measures should include the requirement for the establishment of industry funds at the national level. The words "these measures" reflects the fact that the State has the option of achieving the objective of setting up of industry-wide funding in a variety of ways, depending upon the particular circumstances.

(38) Paragraph 5 provides that in the event the measures mentioned in the preceding paragraphs are insufficient to provide adequate compensation, the State of origin should also ensure that additional financial resources are made available. While it does not directly require the State of origin to set up government funds to guarantee prompt and adequate compensation, it provides that the State of origin should ensure that sufficient financial resources are available in case of damage arising from a hazardous operation situated within its territory or in areas under its jurisdiction.

(39) Paragraphs 3, 4 and 5 are framed as guidelines to encourage States to adopt best practices. The freedom of States to choose one option or the other in accordance with its particular circumstances and conditions is the central theme of the present draft principle. This will, however, require vigilance on the part of the State of origin to continuously review its domestic law to ensure that its regulations are kept up to date with the development of technology and industry practices at home and elsewhere.

Principle 5. Response measures

Upon the occurrence of an incident involving a hazardous activity which results or is likely to result in transboundary damage:

(*a*) the State of origin shall promptly notify all States affected or likely to be affected of the incident and the possible effects of the transboundary damage;

(*b*) the State of origin, with the appropriate involvement of the operator, shall ensure that appropriate response measures are taken and should, for this purpose, rely upon the best available scientific data and technology;

(*c*) the State of origin, as appropriate, should also consult with and seek the cooperation of all States affected or likely to be affected to mitigate the effects of transboundary damage and if possible eliminate them;

(*d*) the States affected or likely to be affected by the transboundary damage shall take all feasible measures to mitigate and if possible to eliminate the effects of such damage;

(*e*) the States concerned should, where appropriate, seek the assistance of competent international organizations and other States on mutually acceptable terms and conditions.

Commentary

(1) Draft principle 5 deals with the situation arising after the occurrence of transboundary damage from both legal and practical perspectives. As soon as an incident involving a hazardous activity results or is likely to result in transboundary damage, with or without simultaneous damage within the territory of the State of origin, the State of origin is called upon to do several things. First, it is expected to obtain from the operator the full facts available about the incident, and most importantly about the dangers the damage poses to the population, their property and the environment in the immediate vicinity. Second, it is expected to ensure that appropriate measures are taken within the means and contingency preparedness at its disposal to mitigate the effects of damage and if possible to eliminate them. Such response measures should include not only clean-up and restoration measures within the jurisdiction of the State of origin but also extend to contain the geographical range of the damage to prevent it from becoming transboundary damage, if it has already not become so. Third, the State of origin is duty-bound to inform all States affected or likely to be affected. The notification must contain all necessary information about the nature of the damage, its likely effects on persons, property and the environment, and the possible precautions that need to be taken to protect them from its ill-effects or to contain, mitigate or eliminate the damage altogether.

(2) Paragraph (*a*), which deals with prompt notification, is an obligation of due diligence imposed upon the State of origin.[449] The notification obligation has to be performed as soon as is practicable. It shall contain all relevant information that is available to the State of origin. In some instances it may not be immediately possible for the State of origin to ascertain the full set of relevant facts and to gather information about the nature of damage and remedial action that can and should be taken.

(3) Paragraph (*b*) requires the State to take appropriate response measures and provides that it should rely upon the best available means and technology. The State of origin is expected to perform due diligence both at the stage of authorization of hazardous activities[450] and in

[449] See Ph. N. Okowa, "Procedural obligations in international environmental agreements", BYBIL, *1996*, vol. 67 (1997), pp. 275–336, at p. 330, where it is observed that the existence in general international law of the duty to warn States at risk in emergency situations has received the "endorsement of the International Court in the *Corfu Channel* case and in the *Nicaragua case*". It is a duty that is the subject of the 1986 Convention on early notification of a nuclear accident, which "confirms an established position at customary law" (*ibid.*, at p. 332).

[450] Closely associated with the duty of prior authorization is the duty to conduct an environmental impact statement (EIA). See Xue, *op. cit.* (footnote 323 above), at p. 166. Phoebe Okowa notes at least five types of ancillary duties associated with the obligation to conduct an EIA. One of them is that the nature of the activity as well as its likely consequences must be clearly articulated and communicated to the States likely to be affected. However, she notes that with the exception of a few conventions, it is widely provided that the State proposing the activity is the sole determinant of the likelihood or seriousness of adverse impact. None of the treaties under consideration permit third States to propose additional or different assessments if they are dissatisfied with those put forward by the State of origin. See Okowa, *loc. cit.* (footnote 449 above), at pp. 282–285, and on the content of an EIA, *ibid.*, at p. 282, footnote 25, and p. 286.

monitoring the activities in progress after authorization and extending into the phase when damage might actually materialize, in spite of best efforts to prevent it. In the *Gabčíkovo–Nagymaros Project* case, the ICJ noted the need for continuous monitoring of hazardous activities as a result of the "awareness of the vulnerability of the environment and the recognition that environmental risks have to be assessed on a continuous basis".[451]

(4) Further, the State concerned should be ever-vigilant and ready to prevent the damage as far as possible, and when damage does occur, ready to mitigate the effects of damage with the best available technology.[452] The role of the State envisaged under the present draft principle is thus complementary to the role assigned to it under articles 16 and 17 of the draft articles on prevention, which deal with requirements of "emergency preparedness" and "notification of emergency".[453]

(5) The present draft principle should be distinguished, however, and goes beyond the provisions of articles 16 and 17 of the draft articles on prevention. States should develop, by way of response measures, necessary contingency preparedness, and employ the best means at their disposal once the emergency arises, consistent with the contemporary knowledge of risks and technical, technological and financial means available to manage them. The present draft principle deals with the need to take necessary response action within the State of origin after the occurrence of an incident resulting in damage, but if possible before it acquires the character of transboundary damage. In this process, the States concerned should seek if necessary assistance from competent international organizations and other States as provided in subparagraph (*e*).

(6) The requirement in paragraph (*b*) is directly connected to the application of the precautionary approach.[454] As with the application of the precautionary approach in any particular field, this allows some flexibility and is expected to be performed keeping in view all social and economic costs and benefits.[455] Indeed, the principle that States should ensure that activities within their jurisdiction and control do not give rise to transboundary harm cannot be overemphasized. By the same token, the importance of response action once an accident or incident has occurred and triggers significant damage cannot be overstated. In fact, such measures are necessary to contain the damage from spreading, and should be taken immediately. This is done in most cases without wasting any time identifying the responsible person or the cause or fault that triggered the event. Paragraph (*b*) assigns to the State of origin the responsibility of determining how such measures should be taken and by whom, which includes the appropriate involvement of the operator. The State would have the option of securing a reimbursement of costs of reasonable response measures.

(7) It is common for the authorities of the State to take action immediately and evacuate affected people to places of safety and provide immediate emergency medical and other relief. It is for this reason that the principle recognizes the important role that the State plays and should play in taking necessary measures as soon as the emergency arises, given its role in securing public welfare and protecting the public interest at all times.

(8) Any measure that the State takes in responding to the emergency created by the hazardous activity does not and should not, however, relegate the operator to a secondary or residuary role. The operator has a primary responsibility for maintaining emergency preparedness and operationalizing any such measures as soon as an incident occurs. The operator can and should give the State all the assistance it needs to discharge its responsibilities. Particularly, the operator is in the best position to indicate the details of the accident, its nature, the time of its occurrence and its exact location and the possible measures that parties likely to be affected could take to minimize the consequences of the damage.[456] Accordingly, the possibility of an operator, including a transnational corporation, being first to react is not intended to be precluded. In case the operator is unable to take the necessary response action, the State of origin shall make arrangements to take such action.[457] In this process it can seek necessary and available help from other States or competent international organizations.

(9) Paragraph (*c*) provides that the State of origin, in its own interest and even as a matter of duty born out of "elementary considerations of humanity",[458] should consult

---

[451] *Gabčíkovo–Nagymaros Project* (see footnote 363 above), para. 112.

[452] *Ibid.*, at para. 140. The Court stated that it "is mindful that, in the field of environmental protection, vigilance and prevention are required on account of the often irreversible character of damage to the environment and of the limitations inherent in the very mechanism of reparation of this type of damage".

[453] For the text and commentaries of articles 16 and 17 of the draft articles on prevention, see *Yearbook ... 2001*, vol. II (Part Two) and corrigendum, pp. 168–169. For the view that the treaty obligations to maintain contingency plans and respond to pollution emergencies must be seen as part of State's duty of due diligence in controlling sources of known environmental harm, see Birnie and Boyle, *International Law ..., op. cit.* (footnote 306 above), p. 137. The authors also note that "it is legitimate to view the *Corfu Channel* case as authority for a customary obligation to give warning of known environmental hazards" (p. 136).

[454] On the requirement of best available technology, Rüdiger Wolfrum noted that it is closely associated with the precautionary principle. See R. Wolfrum, *loc. cit.* (footnote 405 above), at p. 15. It is also suggested that "[t]he term 'available' suggests that states are responsible for applying only those technological advances that have already been marketed, as opposed to every new development in pollution control" (Stoll, *loc. cit.* (footnote 418 above), p. 182).

[455] See "Guidelines for Applying the Precautionary Principle—Biodiversity Conservation and NRM Management" (joint initiative of Fauna and Flora International and the World Conservation Union (IUCN)), *Environmental Policy and Law*, vol. 35/6 (2005), pp. 274–275, at p. 275.

[456] States are required to notify such details in case of nuclear incidents. See article 2 of the Convention on early notification of a nuclear accident. They must also give, through the IAEA, the States likely to be affected other necessary information to minimize the radiological consequences. See Sands, *op. cit.* (footnote 362 above), at pp. 845–846.

[457] Under articles 5 and 6 of the Directive 2004/35/CE of the European Parliament and of the Council, competent authorities, to be designated under article 11, may require the operator to take necessary preventive or restoration measures or take such measures themselves, if the operator does not take them or cannot be found (see footnote 316 above).

[458] See *Corfu Channel* (footnote 197 above), p. 22. For reference to the particular concept as part of "obligations ... based ... on certain general and well-recognized principles" (*ibid.*), as distinguished from the traditional sources of international law enumerated in Article 38 of the Statute of the International Court of Justice, see B. Simma, "From bilateralism to community interest in international law", *Recueil des cours: Collected courses of the Hague Academy of International Law 1994-VI*, vol. 250 (1997), pp. 220 *et seq.*, at pp. 291–292.

the States affected or likely to be affected to determine the best possible response action to prevent or mitigate transboundary damage.[459] Consultations are usually triggered upon request. It is considered that the qualification "as appropriate" is sufficiently flexible to accommodate necessary consultation among concerned States and to engage them in all possible modes of cooperation, depending upon the circumstances of each case. The readiness of States to cooperate may not be uniform; it depends on their location and the degree to which they feel obligated to cooperate, as well as their preparedness and capacity.

(10) Paragraph (*d*), on the other hand, requires States affected or likely to be affected to extend to the State of origin their full cooperation. Once notified, the States affected also are under a duty to take all appropriate and reasonable measures to mitigate the damage to which they are exposed.[460] These States should take such response measures as are within their power in areas under their jurisdiction or control to help prevent or mitigate such transboundary damage. They may also seek such assistance as is available from the competent international organizations and other States as envisaged in paragraph (*e*). Such response action is essential not only in the public interest but also to enable the appropriate authorities and courts to treat the subsequent claims for compensation and reimbursement of costs incurred for response measures taken as reasonable.[461]

(11) Paragraph (*e*) is self-explanatory and is modelled on article 28 of the 1997 Convention on the Law of the Non-Navigational Uses of International Watercourses (hereinafter the "1997 Watercourses Convention"). It is expected that arrangements for assistance between States or competent international organizations and the States concerned would be on the basis of mutually agreed terms and conditions. Such arrangements may be conditioned by the priorities of assistance of the receiving State, the constitutional provisions and mandates of the competent international organizations, and financial and other arrangements concerning local hospitality or immunities and privileges. Any such arrangements should not be based on purely commercial terms and should be consistent with the elementary considerations of humanity and the importance of rendering humanitarian assistance to victims in distress.

Principle 6. International and domestic remedies

1. States shall provide their domestic judicial and administrative bodies with the necessary jurisdiction and competence and ensure that these bodies have prompt, adequate and effective remedies available in the event of transboundary damage caused by hazardous activities located within their territory or otherwise under their jurisdiction or control.

2. Victims of transboundary damage should have access to remedies in the State of origin that are no less prompt, adequate and effective than those available to victims that suffer damage, from the same incident, within the territory of that State.

3. Paragraphs 1 and 2 are without prejudice to the right of the victims to seek remedies other than those available in the State of origin.

4. States may provide for recourse to international claims settlement procedures that are expeditious and involve minimal expenses.

5. States should guarantee appropriate access to information relevant for the pursuance of remedies, including claims for compensation.

Commentary

(1) Draft principle 6 indicates some broad measures necessary to operationalize and implement the objective set forth in draft principle 4. In one sense, draft principles 4 and 6 together encompass the substantive and procedural measures reflected in the expectation that the State of origin and other States concerned would provide minimum standards without which it would be difficult or impossible to implement the requirement to provide effective remedies, including the opportunity to seek payment of prompt and adequate compensation to victims of transboundary damage.[462] The substantive minimum requirements such as channelling of liability; designating liability without proof of fault; specifying minimum conditions, limitations or exceptions for such liability; and establishing arrangements for financial

[459] On the duty of States to notify and consult with each other with a view to take appropriate actions to mitigate damage, see Principle 18 of the Rio Declaration (footnote 301 above); the Convention on the Transboundary Effects of Industrial Accidents; the Convention on Biological Diversity; and the Cartagena Protocol on Biosafety to the Convention on Biological Diversity as well as the treaties in the field of nuclear accidents and the Convention on early notification of a nuclear accident. See also Sands, *op. cit.* (footnote 362 above), pp. 841–847.

[460] In the *Gabčíkovo–Nagymaros Project* case (see footnote 363 above), in defense of "Variant C" that it implemented on the river Danube appropriating nearly 80 to 90 per cent water of the river Danube, in the face of Hungary's refusal to abide by the terms of the Treaty concerning the construction and operation of the Gabčikovo–Nagymaros system of locks concluded between Czechoslovakia and Hungary (signed at Budapest on 16 September 1977, United Nations, *Treaty Series*, vol. 1109, No. 17134, p. 235), Slovakia argued that "[i]t is a general principle of international law that a party injured by the non-performance of another contract party must seek to mitigate the damage he has sustained" (p. 55, para. 80). The Court, referring to this principle, noted that "[i]t would follow from such a principle that an injured State which has failed to take the necessary measures to limit the damage sustained would not be entitled to claim compensation for that damage which could have been avoided" (*ibid.*). The Court observed that "[w]hile this principle might thus provide a basis for the calculation of damages, it could not, on the other hand, justify an otherwise wrongful act" (*ibid.*). It is a different matter that the Court found the implementation of Variant C as a wrongful act and hence did not go further to examine the principle of the duty of the affected States to mitigate the effects of damage to which they are exposed. The very willingness of the Court to consider any failure in this regard as an important factor in the computation of damages to which those States would eventually be entitled amounts to an important recognition under general international law of the duty imposed on States affected by transboundary harm to mitigate the damage to the best extent they can.

[461] In general, on the criterion of reasonableness in computing costs admissible for recovery, see Wetterstein, "A proprietory or possessory interest ...", *loc. cit.* (footnote 323 above), pp. 47–50.

[462] René Lefeber perceptively noted that the purpose of minimum standards, in the context of developing a legal regime addressing transboundary damage, is to facilitate victims obtaining prompt (timely), adequate (quantitatively) and effective (qualitative) compensation. It has procedural and substantive sides. See Lefeber, *op. cit.* (footnote 330 above), pp. 234–236.

guarantees or securities to cover liability are addressed within the framework of draft principle 4. On the other hand, draft principle 6 deals with the procedural minimum standards. They include equal or non-discriminatory access to justice, availability of effective legal remedies, and recognition and enforcement of foreign judicial and arbitral decisions. Draft principle 6 also addresses the need to provide recourse to international procedures for claim settlements that are expeditious and less costly.

(2) Paragraphs 1, 2 and 3 focus on domestic procedures and the development and confirmation of the principle of equal or non-discriminatory access. The 1974 Convention on the protection of the environment between Denmark, Finland, Norway and Sweden is one of the most advanced forms of international cooperation available among States recognizing the right to equal access to justice. This was of course possible because the environmental standards are largely the same among the Nordic countries. Article 3 of the Convention provides equal right of access to persons who have been or may be affected by an environmental harmful activity in another State. The right of equal access to courts or administrative agencies of that State is provided "to the same extent and on the same terms as a legal entity of the State in which the activity is being carried on". The transboundary applicant is allowed to raise questions concerning the permissibility of the activity, appeal against the decisions of the Court or the administrative authority and seek measures necessary to prevent damage. Similarly, the transboundary victim could seek compensation for damage caused on terms no less favourable than the terms under which compensation is available in the State of origin.[463]

(3) The principle of equal access goes beyond the requirement that States meet a minimum standard of effectiveness in the availability of remedies for transboundary claimants by providing for access to information, and helping appropriate cooperation between the relevant courts and national authorities across national boundaries. This principle is also reflected in Principle 10 of the Rio Declaration[464] and in Principle 23 of the World Charter for Nature.[465] It is also increasingly recognized in national constitutional law regarding protection of the environment.[466]

(4) Paragraph 1 sets forth the obligation to provide domestic judicial and administrative bodies with the necessary jurisdiction and competence to be able to entertain claims concerning transboundary harm, as well as effective remedies. It stresses the importance of removing hurdles in order to ensure participation in administrative hearings and judicial proceedings. Once the transboundary damage occurs, transboundary victims should be provided equal access to administrative or quasi-judicial and/or judicial bodies charged with jurisdiction to deal with claims for compensation. As already described in the commentary to draft principle 4, this may be satisfied by providing access to domestic courts in accordance with due process or by negotiation with victims or States concerned.

(5) Paragraph 2 emphasizes the importance of the principle of non-discrimination in the determination of claims concerning hazardous activities.[467] This principle provides that the State of origin should ensure no less prompt, adequate and effective remedies to victims of transboundary damage than those that are available to victims within its territory for similar damage. The principle of non-discrimination could thus be seen to be referring to both procedural and substantive requirements. In terms of its procedural aspects, it means that the State of origin should grant access to justice to the residents of the affected State on the same basis as it does for its own nationals or residents. This is an aspect which is gaining increasing acceptance in State practice.[468]

(6) The substantive aspect of the principle, on the other hand, raises more difficult issues concerning its precise content and lacks similar consensus.[469] On the face of it, as long as the same substantive level of remedies are available to the nationals as are provided to the transboundary victims, the requirements of the principle appear to

[463] For comment on the Convention, see S. C. McCaffrey, "*Private remedies for transfrontier environmental disturbances", IUCN Environmental Policy and Law Paper, No. 8* (1975), pp. 85–87. The main contribution of the Convention is the creation of a Special Administrative Agency to supervise the transboundary nuisances in each State party for more intensive intergovernmental consultation and cooperation. The Agency is given standing before the courts and administrative bodies of other contracting States. The Convention does not apply to pending causes, however. It does not have an express provision for waiver of State immunity. It is also silent on the question of the proper applicable law for the determination of liability and calculation of indemnities, although it is assumed that the proper law for the purposes will be the law of the place where the injury is sustained. In contrast, the OECD recommended to its members a more gradual implementation of flexible bilateral or multilateral accords on measures for the facilitation at the procedural level of transnational pollution abatement litigation. See McNamara, *op. cit.* (footnote 420 above), pp. 146–147.

[464] See footnote 301 above.

[465] General Assembly resolution 37/7 of 28 October 1982, annex.

[466] See Cuperus and Boyle, *loc. cit.* (footnote 419 above), p. 407.

[467] It may be recalled that article 16 of the draft articles on prevention provides for a similar obligation for States in respect of the phase of prevention during which they are required to manage the risk with all due diligence (*Yearbook ... 2001*, vol. II (Part Two) and corrigendum, p. 168–169). A similar provision covering the phase where injury actually occurred, despite all best efforts to prevent damage, can be found in article 32 of the 1997 Watercourses Convention.

[468] See A. Kiss and D. Shelton, *International Environmental Law*, Ardsley (New York), Transnational Publishers, 2004, pp. 201–203; and Birnie and Boyle, *International Law ..., op. cit.* (footnote 306 above), pp. 269–270. According to the procedural aspect of non-discrimination, some requirements of the procedural laws of the State of origin should be removed; among them are, as Cuperus and Boyle note, the "security for costs from foreign plaintiffs, the denial of legal aid to such plaintiffs, and the rule found in various forms in certain jurisdictions that deny jurisdiction over actions involving foreign land" (Cuperus and Boyle, *loc . cit.* (footnote 419 above), p. 408).

[469] Birnie and Boyle note that insofar as it is possible to review State practice on such a disparate topic as equal access, it is not easy to point to any clear picture (Birnie and Boyle, *International Law..., op. cit.* (footnote 306 above), pp. 271–274). On the limitations of the non-discrimination rule, *ibid.*, pp. 274–275. Also see Xue, *op. cit.* (footnote 323 above), pp. 106–107. See also Kiss and Shelton, *op. cit.* (footnote 468 above), pp. 201–203; Birnie and Boyle, *International Law..., op. cit.* (footnote 306 above) pp. 269–270; and P.-M. Dupuy, "La contribution du principe de non -discrimination à l'élaboration du droit international de l'environnement", *Revue québécoise de droit international*, vol. 7, No. 2 (1991–1992), p. 135. For the view that the principle of non-discrimination has become a principle of general international law, see H. Smets, "Le principe de non-discrimination en matière de protection de l'environnement", *Revue européenne de droit de l'environnement*, No. 1 (2000), at p. 3.

have been met. However, the problem arises if nationals themselves are not provided with the minimum substantive standards, in which case the principle of non-discrimination would not guarantee any such minimum standards to foreign victims involved in the transboundary damage. A number of States are in the process of developing minimum substantive standards as part of their national law and procedures.

(7) Paragraph 3 provides a "without prejudice" clause. It should be noted that paragraphs 1 and 2 do not alleviate problems concerning choice of law or choice of forum, which, given the diversity and lack of any consensus among States, may be a significant obstacle to the delivery of prompt, adequate and effective judicial recourse and remedies to victims,[470] particularly if they are poor and not assisted by expert counsel in the field. States could move matters forward by promoting the harmonization of laws and by agreeing to extend such access and remedies.

(8) It may be noted with respect to choice of forum that instead of the law of the domicile[471] of the operator, the claimant may seek recourse to a forum which he or she deems most appropriate to pursue the claim. This may be the forum of the State where an act or omission causing injury took place or where the damage arose.[472] It has been asserted that the provision of such a choice is considered to be based on "a trend now firmly established in both international Conventions on international jurisdiction and in national systems".[473] Under the Convention concerning judicial competence and the execution of decisions in civil and commercial matters, signed at Brussels in 1968, remedies may be made available only in the jurisdiction of a party where: (*a*) the act or omission causing injury took place; (*b*) the damage was suffered; (*c*) the operator has his domicile or her habitual residence; or (*d*) the operator has his or her principal place of business. Article 19 of the Convention on Civil Liability for Damage resulting from Activities Dangerous to the Environment, article 17 of the Basel Protocol on Liability and Compensation for Damage Resulting from Transboundary Movements of Hazardous Wastes and their Disposal, and article 13 of the Protocol on Civil Liability and Compensation for Damage caused by the Transboundary Effects of Industrial Accidents on Transboundary Waters provide for similar choice of forum.

(9) In the matter of choice of law, State practice is not uniform: different jurisdictions have adopted either the law that is most favourable to the victim or the law of the place which has the most significant relationship with the event and the parties.[474]

(10) Paragraph 4 highlights a different aspect in the process of ensuring the existence of remedies for victims of transboundary harm. It is intended to bring more specificity to the nature of the procedures that may be involved other than domestic procedures. It refers to "international claims settlement procedures". Several procedures could be envisaged. For example, States could, in the case of transboundary damage, negotiate and agree on the quantum of compensation payable or even make payment *ex gratia*.[475] These may include mixed claims commissions and negotiations for lump sum payments. The international component does not preclude possibilities whereby a State of origin may make a contribution to the State affected to disburse compensation through a national claims procedure established by the affected State. Such negotiations need not, unless otherwise desired, bar negotiations between the State of origin and the private injured parties, and such parties and the person responsible for the activity causing significant damage. A lump sum compensation could be agreed either as a result of a trial or an out-of-court settlement.[476] Victims could immediately

[470] See Cuperus and Boyle, *loc. cit.* (footnote 419 above), pp. 403–411, at p. 406. See also Lefeber, *op. cit.* (footnote 330 above), pp. 264–266, on the divergence of State practice in matters of deciding on the choice of forum and applicable law.

[471] This is based on the principle *actor sequitur forum rei*, a principle that promotes the policy that the defendant is best able to defend himself or itself in the courts of the State in which he or it is domiciled. This is justified on the ground that the force of a judgment is directed against the defendant. However, while the domicile of the natural person is left to be determined by the law of each State, the case of the nationality of the legal persons or the corporations is less settled. The Convention concerning judicial competence and the execution of decisions in civil and commercial matters, signed at Brussels in 1968, and the Convention on jurisdiction and the enforcement of judgments in civil and commercial matters, signed at Lugano in 1988, "leave the determination of the domicile to the law that is determined by the law of conflict of laws as administered by the courts of the State where the claim is filed" (C. von Bar, "Environmental damage in private international law", *Recueil des cours: Collected courses of the Hague Academy of International Law 1997*, vol. 268 (1997), p. 336).

[472] See the second report on transnational enforcement of environmental law (by Christophe Bernasconi and Gerrit Betlem), International Law Association, *Report of the Seventy-First Conference* (footnote 331 above), pp. 896–938, at p. 900. A defence against this ground of jurisdiction is admissible, however, if it can be established that damage in the State, not being the State of origin, is not foreseeable.

[473] *Ibid.*, p. 899.

[474] The "most favourable law principle" is adopted in several jurisdictions in Europe, Tunisia and the Bolivarian Republic of Venezuela. However, United States law appears to favour the law of the place which has the "most significant relationship" with the event and the parties, *ibid.*, pp. 911–915.

[475] In the case of damage caused to fishermen, nationals of Japan, due to nuclear tests conducted by the United States of America in 1954 near the Marshall Islands, the latter paid to Japan US$ 2 million (see *Department of State Bulletin* (Washington D.C.), vol. 32, No. 812 (January 1955), pp. 90–91). For a similar payment of Can$ 3 million by way of compensation by the Union of Soviet Socialist Republics to Canada following the crash of the Cosmos 954 in January 1978, see ILM, vol. 18 (1979), p. 907. Sands notes that, although several European States paid compensation to their nationals for damage suffered due to the Chernobyl nuclear accident, they did not attempt to make formal claims for compensation, even while they reserved their right to do so (Sands, *op. cit.* (footnote 362 above), pp. 886–889). The State may agree to pay *ex gratia* directly to the victims, e.g. the United States Government agreed to pay to Iranian victims of the shooting of the Iranian Airbus 655 by the USS "Vincennes". States may also conclude treaties setting up international claims commission to settle compensation claims as between private parties. See Lefeber, *op. cit.* (footnote 330 above), p. 238, footnote 21. Mention may also be made of the draft articles 21 and 22 adopted by the Working Group established by the Commisison in 1996 on international liability for injurious consequences arising out of activities not prohibited by international law and included in its report to the Commission. Draft article 21 recommended that the State of origin and the affected States should negotiate at the request of either party on the nature and extent of compensation and other relief. Draft article 22 referred to several factors that States may wish to consider for arriving at the most equitable quantum of compensation (see *Yearbook ... 1996*, vol. II (Part Two), annex I, at pp. 130–132).

[476] In connection with the Bhopal gas leak disaster, the Government of India attempted to consolidate the claims of the victims. It sought to seek compensation by approaching the United States court first, but the action failed on grounds of *forum non conveniens*. The matter was

(*Continued on next page.*)

be given reasonable compensation on a provisional basis, pending a decision on the admissibility of the claim and the award of compensation. National courts, claims commissions or joint claims commissions established for this purpose could examine the claims and settle the final payments of compensation.[477]

(11) The United Nations Compensation Commission[478] and the Iran–United States Claims Tribunal[479] may offer themselves as useful models for some of the procedures envisaged under paragraph 4.

(12) The Commission is aware of the practical difficulties, such as expenses and the delays involved, in pursuing claims in a transnational context or on an international plane. There is justification in the criticism, applicable to some cases but not all, that civil law remedies requiring victims to pursue their claims in foreign national judicial and other forums may be "very complex, costly and ultimately devoid of a guarantee of success".[480] The reference to procedures that are expeditious and involving minimal expenses is intended to respond to this aspect of the matter and reflect the desire not to overburden the victim with an excessively lengthy procedure which may act as a disincentive. There have been several incidents of damage in recent years involving settlement of claims for compensation.[481] Some of them are settled out of court. Others have been settled by recourse to civil liability regimes. The conclusion from the experience of different cases is that both States and concerned entities representing the victims must get involved to settle claims out of court or the victims must be given equal or non-discriminatory right of access to civil law remedies.[482]

(13) Paragraph 5 addresses access to information. This is an important matter without which the principle of equal access envisaged in paragraphs 1, 2 and 3 for victims of transboundary damage cannot be realized expeditiously or without great expense. Paragraph 5 may equally be applicable in respect of the international procedures contemplated in paragraph 4. States should collect and maintain the information as part of the performance of their duties of due diligence and make it available to those that seek it.[483] Elements of information include: the precise nature of the risk; the standards of safety required; the financial basis of the activity; provisions concerning the insurance or financial guarantees the operator is required to maintain; applicable laws and regulations; and institutions designated to deal with complaints, including complaints about non-compliance with the required safety standards and the redress of grievances.

(14) Access to information is an evolving principle. Even in countries with some advanced forms of governance and modern elements of administrative law, development of the concept and making it a legally enforceable

(*Footnote 476 continued.*)

then litigated before the Supreme Court of India. The Bhopal Gas Leak Disaster (Processing of Claims) Act, 1985 provided the basis for the consolidation of claims. The Supreme Court of India, in the *Union Carbide Corporation* v. *Union of India and others* case, gave an order settling the quantum of compensation to be paid in a lump sum. It provided for Union Carbide to pay a lump sum of US$ 470 million to the Union of India in full settlement of all claims, rights and liabilities related to and arising out of the Bhopal gas disaster (see *All India Reporter 1990*, vol. 77, pp. 273 *et seq.*). The original claim of the Government of India was over US$ 1 billion.

[477] For the April 2002 award of US$ 324,949,311 to the people of Enewetak in respect of damages to the land arising out of nuclear programmes carried out by the United States between 1946–1958, see *In the Matter of the People of Enewetak* (footnote 369 above).

[478] On the procedure adopted by the United Nations Claims Commission, see M. Kazazi, "Environmental damage in the practice of the United Nations Compensation Commission", in Bowman and Boyle (eds.), *op. cit.* (footnote 333 above), pp. 111–131.

[479] The rules of procedure of the Iran–United States Claims Tribunal are available at www.iusct.org.

[480] Lefeber, *op. cit.* (footnote 330), p. 259 and footnote 104.

[481] In the explosion of the Ixtoc I oil well in June 1979 in the Bay of Campeche off the coast of Mexico, the oil rig was owned by a United States company, controlled by a Mexican State-owned company and operated by a privately-owned Mexican drilling company. The incident involved US$ 12.5 million in clean-up costs and an estimated US$ 400 million loss for the fishing and tourism industry. The case was settled out of court between the United States Government and the United States company without going into questions of formal liability. The settlement included US$ 2 million paid to the United States Government and US$ 2.14 million towards losses suffered by fishermen, tourist resorts and others affected by the oil spill. See in this respect Lefeber, *op cit.* (footnote 330 above), pp. 239–240. See also ILM, vol. 22 (1983) p. 580. In the Cherry Point oil spill, the Canada and Atlantic Richfield Oil Refinery, a corporation of the United States, settled claims out of court, in respect of an oil spill caused by a Liberian tanker while unloading oil at Cherry Point (Washington State) in United States waters, causing oil pollution to the beaches of the Canadian West coast. See in this respect Lefeber, p. 249. See also *The Canadian Yearbook of International Law*, vol. XI (1973), tome 11, p. 333. In the Sandoz case, the water used to extinguish fire that broke out at the Sandoz Chemical Corporation on 1 November 1986 polluted the River Rhine, and caused significant harm downstream in France, Germany and the Netherlands. Economic harm had to be compensated. This involved clean-up costs and other response measures including monitoring and restoration costs. Pure economic loss was also involved as a result of loss caused to the freshwater fishing industry. The settlement of claims took place at the private level. More than 1,000 claims were settled for a total of 36 million German marks. Most of the compensation was paid to States, but some private parties also received compensation. See in this respect Lefeber, pp. 251–252. In the Bhopal gas leak case, the claim was settled out of court between the Union Carbide Corporation, the United States and the Government of India for US$ 470 million, while the initial claim for compensation was much more than that. See in this respect Lefeber, pp. 252–254. In the *Mines de Potasse d'Alsace* case, a French company polluted the River Rhine with chlorides through discharge of waste salts. Such discharge was considered a normal operation. But the high salinity of the river was a matter of concern downstream to potable water companies, industry and market gardeners, which traditionally used the water for their commerce. The Governments concerned, France, Germany, the Netherlands and Switzerland, negotiated an agreement to reduce the chloride pollution in 1976 at Bonn (Convention on the protection of the Rhine against pollution by chlorides) which came into force only in 1985 and did not last. Another Protocol was concluded in 1991 (Additional Protocol to the Convention on the protection of the Rhine against pollution by chlorides). Still the problem of high salinity continued. As the Government of the Netherlands was not willing to bring a claim against the Government of France, some victims launched private litigation in the courts of the Netherlands in 1974. The litigation continued until 1988 when the case was settled out of court, just before the Supreme Court of the Netherlands ruled in favour of the plaintiffs. The settlement was around US$ 2 million in favour of the cooperatives of market gardeners. The claims of the potable water industry did not succeed in the French court on the ground that there was no sufficient causal link between the discharge of waste salts and the corrosion damage for which the water industry sought compensation. See in this respect Lefeber, pp. 254–258. See also the survey prepared by the Secretariat of liability regimes (footnote 401 above), paras. 399–433.

[482] See Lefeber, *op. cit.* (footnote 330 above), p. 260.

[483] For example, Section 4 of the Right to Information Act, 2005 of India obligates all public authorities to collect and maintain, if possible in computerized form, all records duly catalogued and indexed in a manner and the form which facilitates the right to information under the Act. For the text of Act 22 of 2005, see http://indiacode.nic.in.

right, in all its varied dimensions, is taking time.[484] Such a right of access is contained in several instruments.[485]

(15) The reference to "appropriate" access in paragraph 5 is intended to indicate that in certain circumstances access to information or disclosure of information may be denied. It is, however, important that even in such circumstances information is made readily available concerning the applicable exceptions, the grounds for refusal, procedures for review and the charges applicable, if any. Where feasible, such information should be accessible free of charge or at minimal expense.

(16) Also implicated in the present draft principles is the question of the recognition and enforcement of foreign judgments and arbitral awards. Such recognition and enforcement would be essential to ensure the effects of decisions rendered in jurisdictions in which the defendant did not have enough assets, so that victims could recover compensation in other jurisdictions where such assets are available. Most States subject the recognition and enforcement of foreign judgments and arbitral awards to specific conditions prescribed in their law or enforce them in accordance with their international treaty obligations. Generally, fraud, the lack of a fair trial, public policy and irreconcilability with the earlier decisions could be pleaded as grounds to deny recognition and enforcement of foreign judgments and arbitral awards. Other conditions may apply or other possibilities may exist.[486]

Principle 7. Development of specific international regimes

1. Where, in respect of particular categories of hazardous activities, specific global, regional or bilateral agreements would provide effective arrangements concerning compensation, response measures and international and domestic remedies, all efforts should be made to conclude such specific agreements.

2. Such agreements should, as appropriate, include arrangements for industry and/or State funds to provide supplementary compensation in the event that the financial resources of the operator, including financial security measures, are insufficient to cover the damage suffered as a result of an incident. Any such funds may be designed to supplement or replace national industry-based funds.

Commentary

(1) Draft principle 7 corresponds to the set of provisions contained in draft principle 4, except that they are intended to operate at international level. It builds upon Principle 22 of the Stockholm Declaration and Principle 13 of the Rio Declaration.[487] Paragraph 1 encourages States to conclude specific global, regional or bilateral agreements where such approaches would provide the most effective arrangements in the areas which the present principles are concerned with: (*a*) compensation; (*b*) response measures; and (*c*) redress and remedies.

(2) Paragraph 2 encourages States, as appropriate, to include in such arrangements various financial security schemes, whether through industry funds or State funds, in order to make sure that there is supplementary funding for victims of transboundary damage. It points to the need for States to enter into specific arrangements and tailor them to the particular circumstances of individual hazardous activities. It also recognizes that there are several variables in the regime concerning liability for transboundary damage that are best left to the discretion of individual States or their national laws or practice to select or choose, given their own particular needs, political realities and stages of economic development. Arrangements concluded on a regional basis with respect to a specific category of hazardous activities are likely to be more fruitful and durable in protecting the interest of their citizens, the environment and natural resources on which they are dependent.

(3) It may also be recalled that from the very inception of the topic, the Commission proceeded on the assumption that its primary aim was "to promote the construction of regimes to regulate without recourse to prohibition, the conduct of any particular activity which is perceived to entail actual or potential dangers of a substantial nature and to have transnational effects".[488]

---

[484] The Scandinavian countries, the countries of the European Union and the United States have progressed along the route to establish the right of access to information, but much remains to be achieved even in the context of those countries, and even more so in other jurisdictions. See in this respect *Secrecy and Liberty: National Security, Freedom of Expression and Access to Information*, S. Coliver, P. Hoffman, J. Fitzpatrick and S. Bowen (eds.), The Hague, Kluwer Law International, 1999 (International Studies in Human Rights, vol. 58); and U. Öberg, "EU citizens' right to know: the improbable adoption of a European Freedom of Information Act", in A. Dashwood and A. Ward (eds.), *Cambridge Yearbook of European Legal Studies*, vol. 2 (1999), pp. 303–328. "Right to know" laws have been enacted in Canada and in at least 25 states in the United States. For information on these and other initiatives and analysis of the right of access to information, see P. H. Sand, "Information disclosure as an instrument of environmental governance", *Zeitschrift für ausländisches öffentliches Recht und Völkerrecht—Heidelberg Journal of International Law*, vol. 63 (2003), pp. 487–502. On the availability of the right to information in the context of access to environmental justice in New Zealand, see P. Salmon, "Access to environmental justice", *New Zealand Journal of Environmental Law*, vol. 2 (1998), pp. 1–23, at pp. 9–11. The World Bank is also implementing procedures to promote public disclosure of operational information concerning the projects it supports worldwide. See in this respect I. F. I. Shihata, *The World Bank Inspection Panel*, New York, Oxford University Press, 1994.

[485] See the 1998 Convention on Access to Information, Public Participation in Decision-making and Access to Justice in Environmental Matters, 1998, which has been in force since 30 October 2001; the Convention for the protection of the marine environment of the North-East Atlantic (OSPAR Convention) (article 9); the Convention on Civil Liability for Damage resulting from Activities Dangerous to the Environment (articles 15 and 16), the 1995 UNECE Guidelines on Access to Environmental Information and Public Participation in Environmental Decision-making ("Sofia Guidelines") (articles 4 and 5), ECE/CEP/24; and Directive 2003/4/EC of the European Parliament and of the Council of 28 January 2003 on public access to environmental information, *Official Journal of the European Union*, No. L 41, 14 February 2003, p. 26. See also the survey prepared by the Secretariat of liability regimes (footnote 401 above), paras. 287–336.

[486] For example, the United States District Court which dismissed the Indian claims for compensation in the Bhopal case on grounds of *forum non conveniens* and referred the plaintiffs to courts in India, stipulated that judgments rendered in India could be enforced in the United States. See Lefeber, *op. cit.* (footnote 330 above), pp. 267–268.

[487] See above, footnotes 312 and 301, respectively.

[488] Preliminary report on international liability for injurious consequences arising out of acts not prohibited by international law, by Mr. Robert Q. Quentin-Baxter, Special Rapporteur, *Yearbook ... 1980*, vol. II (Part One), document A/CN.4/334 and Add.1–2, p. 250, para. 9.

Principle 8. Implementation

1. Each State should adopt the necessary legislative, regulatory and administrative measures to implement the present draft principles.

2. The present draft principles and the measures adopted to implement them shall be applied without any discrimination such as that based on nationality, domicile or residence.

3. States should cooperate with each other to implement the present draft principles.

Commentary

(1) Paragraph 1 restates what is implied in the other draft principles, namely, that each State should adopt legislative, regulatory and administrative measures for the implementation of these draft principles. It intends to highlight the significance of national implementation through domestic legislation of international standards or obligations agreed to by States parties to international arrangements and agreements.

(2) Paragraph 2 emphasizes that these draft principles and any implementing provisions shall be applied without any discrimination on any grounds prohibited by international law. The emphasis on "any" is intended to denote that discrimination on any such ground is not valid. The references to nationality, domicile or residence are only illustrative. For example, discrimination on the basis of race, gender, religion or belief would obviously be precluded as well.

(3) Paragraph 3 is a general hortatory clause, which provides that States should cooperate with each other to implement the present draft principles. It is modelled on article 8 of the Protocol on Civil Liability and Compensation for Damage caused by the Transboundary Effects of Industrial Accidents on Transboundary Waters. The importance of implementation mechanisms cannot be overemphasized. From the perspective of general and conventional international law, it operates at the international plane essentially as between States and it requires implementation at the national level through specific domestic constitutional and other legislative techniques. It is important that States enact suitable domestic legislation to implement these principles, lest victims of transboundary damage be left without adequate recourse.

Chapter VI

SHARED NATURAL RESOURCES

A. Introduction

68. The Commission, at its fifty-fourth session (2002), decided to include the topic "Shared natural resources" in its programme of work and appointed Mr. Chusei Yamada as Special Rapporteur.[489] A working group was also established to assist the Special Rapporteur in sketching out the general orientation of the topic in the light of the syllabus prepared in 2000.[490] The Special Rapporteur indicated his intention to deal with confined transboundary groundwaters, oil and gas in the context of the topic and proposed a step-by-step approach beginning with groundwaters.[491]

69. From its fifty-fifth (2003) to fifty-seventh (2005) sessions, the Commission received and considered three reports from the Special Rapporteur.[492] During this period, the Commission established two working groups, one in 2004, chaired by the Special Rapporteur, to assist in furthering the Commission's consideration of the topic and the other, in 2005, chaired by Mr. Enrique Candioti, to review and revise the 25 draft articles on the law of transboundary aquifers proposed by the Special Rapporteur in his third report, taking into account the debate in the Commission. The 2005 Working Group did not complete its work.

B. Consideration of the topic at the present session

70. At the present session, the Commission decided, at its 2868th meeting, on 2 May 2006, to reconvene the Working Group on shared natural resources, chaired by Mr. Enrique Candioti. The Working Group held five meetings and completed the review and revision of the draft articles submitted by the Special Rapporteur in his third report. At the 2878th meeting of the Commission, on 18 May 2006, the Chairperson of the Working Group submitted the report of the Working Group containing in its annex 19 revised draft articles.

71. The Commission, at its 2878th and 2879th meetings, on 18 and 19 May 2006, considered the report of the Working Group, and at the latter meeting decided to refer the 19 draft articles to the Drafting Committee.

72. The Commission considered the report of the Drafting Committee at its 2885th meeting, on 9 June 2006, and adopted on first reading draft articles on the law of transboundary aquifers consisting of 19 draft articles and at its 2903rd, 2905th and 2906th meetings on 2, 3 and 4 August 2006, adopted the commentaries thereto.

73. At its 2903rd meeting, on 2 August 2006, the Commission decided, in accordance with articles 16 to 21 of its Statute, to transmit the draft articles (see section C below), through the Secretary-General, to Governments for comments and observations, with the request that such comments and observations be submitted to the Secretary-General by 1 January 2008.

74. At its 2906th meeting, on 4 August 2006, the Commission expressed its deep appreciation for the outstanding contribution that the Special Rapporteur, Mr. Chusei Yamada, had made to the treatment of the topic through his scholarly research and vast experience, thus enabling the Commission to bring to a successful conclusion its first reading of the draft articles on the law of transboundary aquifers. It also acknowledged the untiring efforts and contribution of the Working Group on shared natural resources under the Chairpersonship of Mr. Enrique Candioti, as well as the various briefings during the development of the topic by experts on groundwaters from UNESCO, FAO, UNECE and the IAH.

C. Text of the draft articles on the law of transboundary aquifers adopted by the Commission on first reading

1. Text of the draft articles

75. The text of the draft articles adopted by the Commission on first reading is reproduced below.

Part I

INTRODUCTION

Article 1. Scope

The present draft articles apply to:

(*a*) utilization of transboundary aquifers and aquifer systems;

(*b*) other activities that have or are likely to have an impact upon those aquifers and aquifer systems; and

(*c*) measures for the protection, preservation and management of those aquifers and aquifer systems.

Article 2. Use of terms

For the purposes of the present draft articles:

(*a*) "aquifer" means a permeable water-bearing underground geological formation underlain by a less permeable layer and the water contained in the saturated zone of the formation;

(*b*) "aquifer system" means a series of two or more aquifers that are hydraulically connected;

[489] *Yearbook ... 2002*, vol. II (Part Two), p. 100, paras. 518–519. The General Assembly, in paragraph 2 of resolution 57/21 of 19 November 2002, took note of the Commission's decision to include the topic "Shared natural resources" in its programme of work.

[490] *Yearbook ... 2000*, vol. II (Part Two), annex, p. 141–142.

[491] *Yearbook ... 2002*, vol. II (Part Two), pp. 100–102, para. 520.

[492] Preliminary report: *Yearbook ... 2003*, vol. II (Part One), document A/CN.4/533 and Add.1; second report: *Yearbook ... 2004*, vol. II (Part One), document A/CN.4/539 and Add.1; and third report: *Yearbook ... 2005*, vol. II (Part One), document A/CN.4/551 and Add.1.

(*c*) "transboundary aquifer" or "transboundary aquifer system" means, respectively, an aquifer or aquifer system, parts of which are situated in different States;

(*d*) "aquifer State" means a State in whose territory any part of a transboundary aquifer or aquifer system is situated;

(*e*) "recharging aquifer" means an aquifer that receives a non-negligible amount of contemporary water recharge;

(*f*) "recharge zone" means the zone which contributes water to an aquifer, consisting of the catchment area of rainfall water and the area where such water flows to an aquifer by runoff on the ground and infiltration through soil;

(*g*) "discharge zone" means the zone where water originating from an aquifer flows to its outlets, such as a watercourse, a lake, an oasis, a wetland or an ocean.

Part II

GENERAL PRINCIPLES

Article 3. Sovereignty of aquifer States

Each aquifer State has sovereignty over the portion of a transboundary aquifer or aquifer system located within its territory. It shall exercise its sovereignty in accordance with the present draft articles.

Article 4. Equitable and reasonable utilization

Aquifer States shall utilize a transboundary aquifer or aquifer system according to the principle of equitable and reasonable utilization, as follows:

(*a*) they shall utilize the transboundary aquifer or aquifer system in a manner that is consistent with the equitable and reasonable accrual of benefits therefrom to the aquifer States concerned;

(*b*) they shall aim at maximizing the long-term benefits derived from the use of water contained therein;

(*c*) they shall establish individually or jointly an overall utilization plan, taking into account present and future needs of, and alternative water sources for, the aquifer States; and

(*d*) they shall not utilize a recharging transboundary aquifer or aquifer system at a level that would prevent continuance of its effective functioning.

Article 5. Factors relevant to equitable and reasonable utilization

1. Utilization of a transboundary aquifer or aquifer system in an equitable and reasonable manner within the meaning of draft article 4 requires taking into account all relevant factors, including:

(*a*) the population dependent on the aquifer or aquifer system in each aquifer State;

(*b*) the social, economic and other needs, present and future, of the aquifer States concerned;

(*c*) the natural characteristics of the aquifer or aquifer system;

(*d*) the contribution to the formation and recharge of the aquifer or aquifer system;

(*e*) the existing and potential utilization of the aquifer or aquifer system;

(*f*) the effects of the utilization of the aquifer or aquifer system in one aquifer State on other aquifer States concerned;

(*g*) the availability of alternatives to a particular existing and planned utilization of the aquifer or aquifer system;

(*h*) the development, protection and conservation of the aquifer or aquifer system and the costs of measures to be taken to that effect;

(*i*) the role of the aquifer or aquifer system in the related ecosystem.

2. The weight to be given to each factor is to be determined by its importance with regard to a specific transboundary aquifer or aquifer system in comparison with that of other relevant factors. In determining what is equitable and reasonable utilization, all relevant factors are to be considered together and a conclusion reached on the basis of all the factors. However, in weighing different utilizations of a transboundary aquifer or aquifer system, special regard shall be given to vital human needs.

Article 6. Obligation not to cause significant harm to other aquifer States

1. Aquifer States shall, in utilizing a transboundary aquifer or aquifer system in their territories, take all appropriate measures to prevent the causing of significant harm to other aquifer States.

2. Aquifer States shall, in undertaking activities other than utilization of a transboundary aquifer or aquifer system that have, or are likely to have, an impact on that transboundary aquifer or aquifer system, take all appropriate measures to prevent the causing of significant harm through that aquifer or aquifer system to other aquifer States.

3. Where significant harm nevertheless is caused to another aquifer State, the aquifer States whose activities cause such harm shall take, in consultation with the affected State, all appropriate measures to eliminate or mitigate such harm, having due regard for the provisions of draft articles 4 and 5.

Article 7. General obligation to cooperate

1. Aquifer States shall cooperate on the basis of sovereign equality, territorial integrity, sustainable development, mutual benefit and good faith in order to attain equitable and reasonable utilization and appropriate protection of their transboundary aquifer or aquifer system.

2. For the purpose of paragraph 1, aquifer States should establish joint mechanisms of cooperation.

Article 8. Regular exchange of data and information

1. Pursuant to draft article 7, aquifer States shall, on a regular basis, exchange readily available data and information on the condition of the transboundary aquifer or aquifer system, in particular of a geological, hydrogeological, hydrological, meteorological and ecological nature and related to the hydrochemistry of the aquifer or aquifer system, as well as related forecasts.

2. Where knowledge about the nature and extent of some transboundary aquifer or aquifer systems is inadequate, aquifer States concerned shall employ their best efforts to collect and generate more complete data and information relating to such aquifer or aquifer systems, taking into account current practices and standards. They shall take such action individually or jointly and, where appropriate, together with or through international organizations.

3. If an aquifer State is requested by another aquifer State to provide data and information relating to the aquifer or aquifer systems that are not readily available, it shall employ its best efforts to comply with the request. The requested State may condition its compliance upon payment by the requesting State of the reasonable costs of collecting and, where appropriate, processing such data or information.

4. Aquifer States shall, where appropriate, employ their best efforts to collect and process data and information in a manner that facilitates their utilization by the other aquifer States to which such data and information are communicated.

Part III

PROTECTION, PRESERVATION AND MANAGEMENT

Article 9. Protection and preservation of ecosystems

Aquifer States shall take all appropriate measures to protect and preserve ecosystems within, or dependent upon, their transboundary aquifers or aquifer systems, including measures to ensure that the quality and quantity of water retained in the aquifer or aquifer system, as well as that released in its discharge zones, are sufficient to protect and preserve such ecosystems.

Article 10. Recharge and discharge zones

1. Aquifer States shall identify recharge and discharge zones of their transboundary aquifer or aquifer system and, within these zones, shall take special measures to minimize detrimental impacts on the recharge and discharge processes.

2. All States in whose territory a recharge or discharge zone is located, in whole or in part, and which are not aquifer States with regard to that aquifer or aquifer system, shall cooperate with the aquifer States to protect the aquifer or aquifer system.

Article 11. Prevention, reduction and control of pollution

Aquifer States shall, individually and, where appropriate, jointly, prevent, reduce and control pollution of their transboundary aquifer or aquifer system, including through the recharge process, that may cause significant harm to other aquifer States. In view of uncertainty about the nature and extent of transboundary aquifers or aquifer systems and of their vulnerability to pollution, aquifer States shall take a precautionary approach.

Article 12. Monitoring

1. Aquifer States shall monitor their transboundary aquifer or aquifer system. They shall, wherever possible, carry out these monitoring activities jointly with other aquifer States concerned and, where appropriate, in collaboration with the competent international organizations. Where, however, monitoring activities are not carried out jointly, the aquifer States shall exchange the monitored data among themselves.

2. Aquifer States shall use agreed or harmonized standards and methodology for monitoring their transboundary aquifer or aquifer system. They should identify key parameters that they will monitor based on an agreed conceptual model of the aquifer or aquifer system. These parameters should include parameters on the condition of the aquifer or aquifer system as listed in draft article 8, paragraph 1, and also on the utilization of the aquifer and aquifer system.

Article 13. Management

Aquifer States shall establish and implement plans for the proper management of their transboundary aquifer or aquifer system in accordance with the provisions of the present draft articles. They shall, at the request by any of them, enter into consultations concerning the management of the transboundary aquifer or aquifer system. A joint management mechanism shall be established, wherever appropriate.

PART IV

ACTIVITIES AFFECTING OTHER STATES

Article 14. Planned activities

1. When a State has reasonable grounds for believing that a particular planned activity in its territory may affect a transboundary aquifer or aquifer system and thereby may have a significant adverse effect upon another State, it shall, as far as practicable, assess the possible effects of such activity.

2. Before a State implements or permits the implementation of planned activities which may affect a transboundary aquifer or aquifer system and thereby may have a significant adverse effect upon another State, it shall provide that State with timely notification thereof. Such notification shall be accompanied by available technical data and information, including any environmental impact assessment, in order to enable the notified State to evaluate the possible effects of the planned activities.

3. If the notifying and the notified States disagree on the possible effect of the planned activities, they shall enter into consultations and, if necessary, negotiations with a view to arriving at an equitable resolution of the situation. They may utilize an independent fact-finding body to make an impartial assessment of the effect of the planned activities.

PART V

MISCELLANEOUS PROVISIONS

Article 15. Scientific and technical cooperation with developing States

States shall, directly or through competent international organizations, promote scientific, educational, technical and other cooperation with developing States for the protection and management of transboundary aquifers or aquifer systems. Such cooperation shall include, *inter alia*:

(*a*) training of their scientific and technical personnel;

(*b*) facilitating their participation in relevant international programmes;

(*c*) supplying them with necessary equipment and facilities;

(*d*) enhancing their capacity to manufacture such equipment;

(*e*) providing advice on and developing facilities for research, monitoring, educational and other programmes;

(*f*) providing advice on and developing facilities for minimizing the detrimental effects of major activities affecting transboundary aquifers or aquifer systems;

(*g*) preparing environmental impact assessments.

Article 16. Emergency situations

1. For the purpose of the present draft article, "emergency" means a situation, resulting suddenly from natural causes or from human conduct, that poses an imminent threat of causing serious harm to aquifer States or other States.

2. Where an emergency affects a transboundary aquifer or aquifer system and thereby poses an imminent threat to States, the following shall apply:

(*a*) the State within whose territory the emergency originates shall:

(i) without delay and by the most expeditious means available, notify other potentially affected States and competent international organizations of the emergency;

(ii) in cooperation with potentially affected States and, where appropriate, competent international organizations, immediately take all practicable measures necessitated by the circumstances to prevent, mitigate and eliminate any harmful effect of the emergency;

(*b*) States shall provide scientific, technical, logistical and other cooperation to other States experiencing an emergency. Cooperation may include coordination of international emergency actions and communications, making available trained emergency response personnel, emergency response equipments and supplies, scientific and technical expertise and humanitarian assistance.

3. Where an emergency poses a threat to vital human needs, aquifer States, notwithstanding draft articles 4 and 6, may take measures that are strictly necessary to meet such needs.

Article 17. Protection in time of armed conflict

Transboundary aquifers or aquifer systems and related installations, facilities and other works shall enjoy the protection accorded by the principles and rules of international law applicable in international and non-international armed conflicts and shall not be used in violation of those principles and rules.

Article 18. Data and information concerning national defence or security

Nothing in the present draft articles obliges a State to provide data or information the confidentiality of which is essential to its national defence or security. Nevertheless, that State shall cooperate in good faith with other States with a view to providing as much information as possible under the circumstances.

Article 19. Bilateral and regional agreements and arrangements

For the purpose of managing a particular transboundary aquifer or aquifer system, aquifer States are encouraged to enter into a bilateral or regional agreement or arrangement among themselves. Such agreement or arrangement may be entered into with respect to an entire aquifer or aquifer system or any part thereof or a particular project, programme or utilization except insofar as the agreement or arrangement adversely affects, to a significant extent, the utilization, by one or more other aquifer States of the water in that aquifer or aquifer system, without their express consent.

2. Text of the draft articles with commentaries thereto

76. The text of the draft articles on the law of transboundary aquifers with commentaries thereto as adopted by the Commission on first reading at its fifty-eighth session, is reproduced below.

THE LAW OF TRANSBOUNDARY AQUIFERS

General commentary

(1) At its fifty-fourth session (2002), the International Law Commission decided on the inclusion in the programme of work of the Commission of the topic entitled "Shared natural resources". It was generally understood that this topic included groundwaters, oil and natural gas, although some preferred to include also such resources as migratory birds and animals on one hand, and others preferred to limit it so as to deal solely with groundwaters on the other.

(2) The Special Rapporteur of the topic considered that it would be appropriate to begin with the consideration of groundwaters as the follow-up of the Commission's previous work on the codification of the law of surface waters[493] and also that it would complicate the work if the Commission was to deal with three different resources simultaneously. Accordingly, he decided to focus on transboundary groundwaters for the time being and at least during the first reading of the draft articles. This approach has generally been endorsed. He is nevertheless aware of some common characteristics among these three different resources, in particular between non-renewable groundwaters contained in non-recharging aquifers on one hand, and oil and natural gas on the other. While he is also aware of dissimilarities among these resources, he recognizes that the work on transboundary groundwaters could affect any future codification work by the Commission on oil and natural gas. Moreover, the Commission might also wish to take into account some relevant elements of the existing regulations and State practice on oil and natural gas before finalizing its work on transboundary groundwaters. He therefore proposed to consider this aspect during the second reading of the draft articles. One member held the view that the decision would have to be taken whether to proceed further with respect to oil and natural gas when that second reading is completed.

(3) The first reading text is provisionally presented in the form of draft articles. Consistent with the practice of the Commission, the term "draft articles" has been used without prejudice as to the final form of the product, whether it should be a convention or otherwise. The question of the final form that the draft articles should take is of course a matter that is of relevance to the formulation of the text of draft articles, and should be addressed in due course, while focus has been on the substance at this stage. The Commission took the view that it was still premature to reach a conclusion on the question of final form in light of the differing views expressed by States in the Sixth Committee. The draft articles presented thus do not include provisions on dispute settlement, final clauses and any article which might prejudice the issue of final form. If a decision is taken to proceed with a convention, other changes would likely be necessary on second reading, including specifying the relationship of the convention to other agreements and arrangements, and relations with non-parties.

(4) The Commission considered the question of whether it would be necessary to structure the draft articles in such a way as to have obligations that will apply to all States generally, obligations of aquifer States *vis-à-vis* other aquifer States and obligations of aquifer States *vis-à-vis* non-aquifer States. It was decided that, in order to be effective, some draft articles would have to impose obligations on States which do not share the transboundary aquifer in question and in certain cases give rights to the latter States towards the States of that aquifer. In reaching these conclusions, the Commission stressed the need to protect the transboundary aquifer or aquifer system.

(5) The draft articles rely to a large extent on the 1997 Watercourses Convention. Some argue that there exist differences between surface waters and groundwaters. Others contend that the Convention was a failure because it has not attracted the ratifications necessary for it to come into force. There are, of course, differences between these two resources. However, there are many more similarities between them, in particular in the way of managing these resources. It is true that the Convention has not yet come into force.[494] However, it is a framework convention reflecting a certain authority. The ICJ recognized such authority when it referred to the 1997 Watercourses Convention in its judgment in the *Gabčíkovo–Nagymaros Project* case.[495] Many substantive provisions of the 2000 Revised Protocol on Shared Watercourses in the Southern African Development Community (SADC) reproduce almost word for word the provisions of the 1997 Watercourses Convention, and they are being implemented.[496] The Convention thus offers a useful basis for codification of provisions related to transboundary groundwaters.

(6) There are also abundant treaties and other legal documents which provide useful inputs to the current work.

[493] 1997 Watercourses Convention.

[494] Article 36, paragraph 1 reads as follows: "The present Convention shall enter into force on the ninetieth day following the date of deposit of the thirty-fifth instrument of ratification, acceptance, approval or accession". As at 6 August 2006, 14 States had become parties. They are Finland, Hungary, Iraq, Jordan, Lebanon, the Libyan Arab Jamahiriya, Namibia, the Netherlands, Norway, Portugal, Qatar, South Africa, Sweden and the Syrian Arab Republic.

[495] *Gabčíkovo–Nagymaros Project* (see footnote 363 above), para. 85.

[496] Entry into force: 22 September 2003. Parties and/or signatories: Angola, Botswana, Congo, Lesotho, Malawi, Mauritius, Mozambique, Namibia, Seychelles, South Africa, Swaziland, United Republic of Tanzania, Zambia, Zimbabwe.

Those instruments are compiled by FAO in association with UNESCO,[497] and relevant parts are reproduced in the addendum to the third report of the Special Rapporteur.[498] It has been ascertained that almost all States with land borders also have transboundary groundwaters with their neighbours. Accordingly, most States have a stake in one way or another in the topic. Substantial State practice is emerging. In addition to the valuable contributions from various States, the UNESCO International Hydrological Program (IHP) has, since 2003, provided scientific and technical advice to the Special Rapporteur and the Commission on the issues related to hydrogeology, inviting, coordinating and supporting the contributions of international experts, international and national institutions, including centres on groundwater resources, the IAH, FAO, the United Nations Environment Programme/Global Environmental Fund (UNEP/GEF), the Organization of American States (OAS), IUCN, the International Groundwater Resources Assessment Centre (IGRAC) and UNECE, to which the Special Rapporteur and the Commission are sincerely grateful.

Part I

INTRODUCTION

Article 1. Scope

The present draft articles apply to:

(*a*) utilization of transboundary aquifers and aquifer systems;

(*b*) other activities that have or are likely to have an impact upon those aquifers and aquifer systems; and

(*c*) measures for the protection, preservation and management of those aquifers and aquifer systems.

Commentary

(1) Draft article 1 provides the scope to which the present draft articles apply. The term "groundwaters" has been consistently used in the Commission and in the United Nations General Assembly. While it is perfectly appropriate to commonly denote a body of underground waters that constitutes a unitary whole and could be extracted for human use as "groundwaters", for the purposes of the present draft articles the technical term "aquifer" is opted for, as the term is more scientifically precise and leaves no ambiguity for both lawyers and groundwater scientists and administrators. An aquifer is often hydraulically connected to one or more other aquifers. In such a case, these aquifers must be treated as a single system for proper management as there is hydraulic consistency between them. This series of two or more aquifers is termed an "aquifer system". In the draft articles, "an aquifer" and "an aquifer system" are always used together.

(2) The mandate given to the Commission is to codify the law on "shared natural resources". Accordingly, the present draft articles will apply only to transboundary aquifers. Domestic aquifers are excluded from the scope. If the domestic aquifers are connected to international watercourses as defined in the 1997 Watercourses Convention, they will be governed by that Convention and not by the present draft articles. On the other hand, all transboundary aquifers will be governed by the present draft articles, regardless of whether they are hydraulically connected or not to international watercourses. Those transboundary aquifers that are hydraulically connected to international watercourses will be governed by the 1997 Watercourses Convention in accordance with its article 2 (*a*) and also by the present draft articles. The dual application of the provisions of these two legal regimes to such aquifers would not in principle cause any problem, as these legal regimes would not be expected to be in conflict with each other. Were there conflicts between them, it would become necessary to address such situation. However, in order not to prejudge the final form of the draft articles, the relationship between the 1997 Watercourses Convention and the present draft articles is not dealt with for the moment.

(3) Draft article 1 specifies, in subparagraphs (*a*) to (*c*), three different categories of activities which must be covered by the draft articles. The activities regulated by article 1 of the 1997 Watercourses Convention are (*a*) the uses of the resources and (*b*) measures of protection, preservation and management related to the uses of those resources. They are substantially reproduced in paragraphs (*a*) and (*c*) of this draft article.

(4) In subparagraph (*a*), the term "utilization" instead of "uses" was adopted, as "utilization" would include also the mode of uses. It is noted that the 1997 Watercourses Convention adopts the phrase "international watercourses and of their waters" to indicate that the articles apply both to the watercourse itself (channel or system of surface waters and groundwaters) and to its waters, to the extent that there may be any difference between the two. Such a consideration is not necessary in this paragraph because the definition of an "aquifer" in draft article 2 makes it clear that an aquifer consists of both geological formation and waters contained therein.

(5) In subparagraph (*c*), "measures for the protection, ..." was considered more appropriate than "measures of protection, ..." in the comparable provision of the 1997 Watercourses Convention, and also the phrase "related to the uses of" found in the Convention was deleted to widen the scope of the present draft articles. The "measures" are meant to embrace not only those to be taken to deal with degradation of aquifers but also the various forms of cooperation, whether or not institutionalized, concerning the utilization, development, conservation and management of transboundary aquifers.

(6) In addition to these two categories of activities, subparagraph (*b*) provides an additional category of "other activities that have or are likely to have an impact upon those aquifers and aquifer systems". In the case of aquifers, it would be necessary to regulate activities other than utilization of aquifers in order to properly manage them. Such activities are those that are carried out above or

[497] S. Burchi and K. Mechlem, *Groundwater in International Law: Compilation of Treaties and Other Legal Instruments*, Rome, FAO/UNESCO, 2005.

[498] See footnote 492 above.

around aquifers and cause some adverse effects on them. For example, farming utilizing chemical fertilizers and pesticides may pollute waters in the aquifer. Construction of subways may destroy geological formations or impair the recharge or discharge process. There must, of course, be a causal link between the activities and their effects. The term "impact" is often used to express such adverse or negative effects in the field of the environment, for instance "impact assessment".

(7) "Impact" is broader than the concept of "harm" or "damage", which is more specific. In and of itself, the term "impact" does not relate to either a positive or a negative effect. However, the term "impact" may be understood to have a negative connotation if the context in which it is used is negative, as in the case of subparagraph (*b*). Accordingly, in the context of subparagraph (*b*), "impact" relates to a forceful, strong or otherwise substantial adverse effect, while the threshold of such an effect is not defined here. The determination of the threshold is left to later substantive draft articles such as draft articles 6 and 10. Impact upon aquifers would include deterioration of water quality, reduction of water quantity and adverse changes of the functioning of the aquifer. The assessment of whether an "impact" occurred, as well as the type of impact and the extent of the impact, must be based on measurements prepared prior to the impact and then compared to measurements after the impact. The measurements prepared prior to the impact provide a baseline or reference level that can be used to compare against subsequent measurements.

Article 2. Use of terms

For the purposes of the present draft articles:

(*a*) "aquifer" means a permeable water-bearing underground geological formation underlain by a less permeable layer and the water contained in the saturated zone of the formation;

(*b*) "aquifer system" means a series of two or more aquifers that are hydraulically connected;

(*c*) "transboundary aquifer" or "transboundary aquifer system" means, respectively, an aquifer or aquifer system, parts of which are situated in different States;

(*d*) "aquifer State" means a State in whose territory any part of a transboundary aquifer or aquifer system is situated;

(*e*) "recharging aquifer" means an aquifer that receives a non-negligible amount of contemporary water recharge;

(*f*) "recharge zone" means the zone which contributes water to an aquifer, consisting of the catchment area of rainfall water and the area where such water flows to an aquifer by runoff on the ground and infiltration through soil;

(*g*) "discharge zone" means the zone where water originating from an aquifer flows to its outlets, such as a watercourse, a lake, an oasis, a wetland or an ocean.

Commentary

(1) There are various definitions of "aquifer" and "groundwaters" in existing treaties and other international legal documents[499] but they are not precise enough for the purposes of the present draft articles. The definition of an aquifer in subparagraph (*a*) offers the precise description of the two elements of which an aquifer consists. One element is the underground geological formation which functions as a container for waters. The other element is the waters stored therein which are extractable.

(2) Oil and natural gas are stored also in similar geological formations. The term "water-bearing" has been employed to distinguish coverage of the draft articles from oil and natural gas. "Water-bearing" is not used here in the sense of "capable of bearing waters". It is used to indicate that the formation is currently bearing waters. The water-bearing formation includes both saturated and unsaturated parts of the formation. In other words, "water-bearing" is a wider concept than "saturated". The reference to "underground" is meant to indicate that aquifers are found on the subsurface. A "geological formation" consists of naturally occurring materials, either consolidated or unconsolidated, such as rock, gravel and sand. All the aquifers are underlain by less permeable layers which serve, so to speak, as the bottom of the container. Some aquifers are also upper-lain by less permeable layers. The waters stored in such aquifers are termed as

[499] Article 2, paragraph 11 of Directive 2000/60/EC of the European Parliament and of the Council of 23 October 2000 establishing a framework for Community action in the field of water policy: "'Aquifer' means a subsurface layer or layers of rock or other geological strata of sufficient porosity and permeability to allow either a significant flow of groundwater or the abstraction of significant quantities of groundwater" (*Official Journal of the European Union*, No. L 327, 22 December 2000, p. 6).

UNCC, report and recommendations made by the Panel of Commissioners concerning the third instalment of "F4" claims: "aquifer: Natural water-bearing geological formation found below the surface of the earth" (S/AC.26/2003/31, glossary).

Article 1, paragraph 1 of the Bellagio "Model Agreement Concerning the Use of Transboundary Groundwaters" of 1989: "'Aquifer' means a subsurface water bearing geologic formation from which significant quantities of water may be extracted" (Burchi and Mechlem, *op. cit.* (footnote 497 above), p. 537).

Article 3, paragraph 2 of the International Law Association's Berlin Rules on Water Resources of 2004: "'Aquifer' means a subsurface layer or layers of geological strata of sufficient porosity and permeability to allow either a flow of or the withdrawal of usable quantities of groundwater" (*Report of the Seventy-First Conference* (see footnote 331 above), p. 9).

Article 1, paragraph 2 (*a*) of Council Directive 80/68/EEC of 17 December 1979 on the protection of groundwater against pollution caused by certain dangerous substances (*Official Journal*, No. L 20, 26 January 1980, p. 43); article 2 (*a*) of Council Directive 91/676/EEC of 12 December 1991 concerning the protection of waters against pollution caused by nitrates from agricultural sources (*Official Journal*, No. L 375, 31 December 1991, p. 6); article 2, paragraph 3 of the Protocol on Water and Health to the 1992 Convention on the Protection and Use of Transboundary Watercourses and International Lakes; and article 2, paragraph 2 of Directive 2000/60/EC of the European Parliament and of the Council of 23 October 2000 establishing a framework for Community action in the field of water policy: "'groundwater' means all water which is below the surface of the ground in the saturation zone and in direct contact with the ground or subsoil".

Article 3, paragraph 11 of the International Law Association's Berlin Rules on Water Resources : "'Groundwater' means water beneath the surface of the ground located in a saturated zone and in direct contact with the ground or soil".

"confined" groundwaters as they are pressurized by more than atmospheric pressure.

(3) The definition of the waters in an aquifer is limited to those stored in the saturated zone of the geological formation, as only those waters are extractable. The waters located above the saturated zone of the geological formation, like the waters located underground outside an aquifer, are kept in pores and mixed with air and in the form of vapour and cannot be extracted. They are like shale oil. It is, of course, theoretically possible to separate such waters from air and soil but it is not technically or economically possible to do so at present. The question was raised whether the draft articles should also apply to the formations containing only minimal amounts of waters. While it is obvious that States are not concerned with an aquifer that has no significance to them, it would not be possible to define an absolute criterion for that.

(4) An "aquifer system" consists of two or more aquifers that are hydraulically connected to each other. These aquifers could be of the same geological formations, but could also be of different geological formations. Aquifers could be hydraulically connected vertically and horizontally as well. "Hydraulically connected" refers to a physical relationship between two or more aquifers whereby an aquifer is capable of transmitting some quantity of water to the other aquifers and *vice versa*. The quantity of waters that is capable of being transmitted is important since an insignificant or *de minimis* quantity of waters may not translate to a true hydraulic connection. The standard for determining whether a quantity is significant is directly related to the potential of the transmitting aquifer to have an effect on the quantity and quality of waters in the receiving aquifers. It would not be possible to formulate general and absolute criteria for such an effect. A judgment has to be made in each specific case on whether those aquifers should be treated as a system for the proper management of the aquifers.

(5) Subparagraph (*c*) defines the terms "transboundary aquifer" and "transboundary aquifer system" which are used in draft article 1 on the scope and in many other draft articles. The focus in this paragraph is on the adjective "transboundary". The paragraph provides that, in order to be regarded as a "transboundary" aquifer or aquifer system, parts of the aquifer or aquifer system in question must be situated in different States. Whether parts of an aquifer or aquifer system are situated in different States depends on physical factors. In the case of surface waters, the existence of such factors can be easily established by simple observation of rivers and lakes. In the case of groundwaters, the determination of the existence of transboundary aquifers under the jurisdiction of a particular State requires more sophisticated methods, relying on drilling and scientific technology such as isotope tracing to define the outer limit of the aquifers.

(6) Subparagraph (*d*) defines the term an "aquifer State", which is used throughout the draft articles. Once the existence of a part of a transboundary aquifer or aquifer system is established in the territory under the jurisdiction of a particular State in accordance with the methods referred to in paragraph (5) above, that State is an aquifer State for the purposes of the draft articles.

(7) The definition of "recharging aquifer" in subparagraph (*e*) is needed because different rules would apply to a "recharging aquifer" and a "non-recharging aquifer". Waters in a recharging aquifer are renewable resources, while those in a non-recharging aquifer are non-renewable resources. For the purposes of management of aquifers, "non-recharging" aquifers are those aquifers that receive "negligible" water recharge "contemporarily". The term "negligible" refers to the transmission of some quantity of waters. The measurement of whether the quantity is "negligible" should be assessed with reference to the specific characteristics of the receiving aquifer, including the volume of waters in the receiving aquifer, the volume of waters discharged from the receiving aquifer (naturally and artificially), the volume of waters that recharges the receiving aquifer and the rate at which the recharge occurs.

(8) The term "contemporary" should be understood for convenience as a timespan of approximately 100 years, 50 years in the past and 50 years in the future. The scientists generally classify those aquifers located in an arid zone where an annual rainfall is less than 200 mm as non-recharging aquifers. It is possible to ascertain whether a particular aquifer has been receiving water recharge during the period of approximately the last 50 years by using radioactive tracers. These tracers are cesium and tritium from nuclear weapons tests with a peak of injection at 1963/1964 and krypton from the continuous emission of the nuclear industry from mid-1950s. They have been floating in the atmosphere for the last 50 years and can be detected in the aquifer that has received recharge from rainfall during that period.

(9) The definitions of "recharge zone" and "discharge zone" in subparagraphs (*f*) and (*g*) are needed for the application of draft article 10. Those zones exist for a recharging aquifer and are located outside the aquifer, although they are hydraulically connected to the latter. A recharge zone contributes water to an aquifer and includes the zone where the rainfall water directly infiltrates the ground, the zone of surface runoff which eventually infiltrates the ground and the underground unsaturated zone of infiltration. The discharge zone is the area through which water from the aquifer flows to its outlet, which may be a river, a lake, an ocean, an oasis or a wetland. Such outlets are not part of the discharge zone itself.

PART II

GENERAL PRINCIPLES

Article 3. Sovereignty of aquifer States

Each aquifer State has sovereignty over the portion of a transboundary aquifer or aquifer system located within its territory. It shall exercise its sovereignty in accordance with the present draft articles.

Commentary

(1) The need to have an explicit reference in the form of a draft article on the sovereignty of States over the natural resources within their territories was advocated by many States, particularly by those aquifer States that are of the

opinion that water resources belong to the States in which they are located and are subject to the exclusive sovereignty of those States. They also pointed out that groundwaters must be regarded as belonging to the States where they are located, along the lines of oil and gas. Reference was made, in that regard, to General Assembly resolution 1803 (XVII) of 14 December 1962, entitled "Permanent sovereignty over natural resources". Some thought that it would be enough to have a reference to it in the preamble, while others considered that such reference would be undesirable for the proper management of aquifers.

(2) Many treaties, other legal instruments and non-legally binding instruments refer to sovereignty of States over natural resources located within their territory.[500] There are basically two types of formulation in State practice with regard to this issue. One type is the positive formulation. Some have limiting conditions to the exercise of this sovereign right. An example is "States have, in accordance with the Charter of the United Nations and the principles of international law, a sovereign right to exploit their own resources pursuant to their environmental and developmental policies, and the responsibility to ensure that activities within their jurisdiction or control do not cause damage to the environment of other States or of areas beyond the limits of their national jurisdiction".[501] The other type is the saving or disclaimer clause such as: "Nothing in this Convention shall affect the sovereign right of States to exploit, develop and manage their own natural resources".[502]

(3) Draft article 3 adopts the positive type and represents an appropriately balanced text. The two sentences in the draft article are necessary in order to maintain such a balance. In essence, each aquifer State has sovereignty over the transboundary aquifer or aquifer system to the extent located within its territory. It is understood also that the present draft articles do not cover all limits imposed by international law on the exercise of sovereignty. Accordingly, the draft articles will have to be interpreted and applied against the background of general international law.

Article 4. Equitable and reasonable utilization

Aquifer States shall utilize a transboundary aquifer or aquifer system according to the principle of equitable and reasonable utilization, as follows:

(*a*) they shall utilize the transboundary aquifer or aquifer system in a manner that is consistent with the equitable and reasonable accrual of benefits therefrom to the aquifer States concerned;

(*b*) they shall aim at maximizing the long-term benefits derived from the use of water contained therein;

(*c*) they shall establish individually or jointly an overall utilization plan, taking into account present and future needs of, and alternative water sources for, the aquifer States; and

(*d*) they shall not utilize a recharging transboundary aquifer or aquifer system at a level that would prevent continuance of its effective functioning.

Commentary

(1) Transboundary aquifers are shared natural resources. Utilization of the aquifer can be divided into two categories, as the aquifer consists of the geological formation and the water contained in it. The use of the water is most common and the water is mainly used for drinking and other human life support, such as sanitation, irrigation and industry. The utilization of the geological formation is rather rare. A typical example is the artificial recharge being undertaken in the Franco–Swiss Genevese Aquifer system where the waters from the River Arve are used for such recharge. The functioning of the aquifer treats the waters with less cost than building a water treatment installation and also produces high quality water.

(2) The basic principle applicable to the utilization of shared natural resources is the equitable and reasonable utilization of the resources. It is embodied in many legal regimes such as water-related treaties and high seas fishery conventions. While the concept of equitable utilization

[500] (*a*) Treaties referring to the concept within their preambles: the Vienna Convention for the Protection of the Ozone Layer (1985); the 1991 Agreement on air quality between Canada and the United States (United Nations, *Treaty Series*, vol. 1852, No. 31532, p. 79, reproduced in ILM, vol. 30 (1991), p. 678); the United Nations Framework Convention of Climate Change (1992); the Convention on Biological Diversity (1992); the Convention to combat desertification in those countries experiencing serious drought and/or desertification, particularly in Africa (1994); and the Convention on the sustainable management of Lake Tanganyika (2003).

(*b*) Treaties referring to the concept within their provisions: the Vienna Convention on succession of States in respect of treaties (1978); the African Charter on Human and Peoples' Rights (1981); the United Nations Convention on the Law of the Sea (1982); the Convention for the Protection of the Natural Resources and Environment of the South Pacific Region (1986); the Agreement for the Implementation of the Provisions of the United Nations Convention on the Law of the Sea of 10 December 1982 relating to the Conservation and Management of Straddling Fish Stocks and Highly Migratory Fish Stocks (1995); the Protocol on Water and Health to the 1992 Convention on the Protection and Use of Transboundary Watercourses and International Lakes (1999); and the African Convention on the Conservation of Nature and Natural Resources (2003).

(*c*) Non-binding international instruments referring to the concept: the draft articles on prevention of transboundary harm from hazardous activities, adopted by the Commission at its fifty-third session, in 2001 (see footnote 292 above); "Concerted action for economic development of economically less developed countries" (General Assembly resolution 1515 (XV) of 15 December 1960); "Permanent sovereignty over natural resources" (General Assembly resolution 1803 (XVII) of 14 December 1962); the Stockholm Declaration (1972) (see footnote 312 above); the Charter of Economic Rights and Duties of States (General Assembly resolution 3281 (XXIX) of 12 December 1974); the Declaration on the Right to Development (General Assembly resolution 41/128 of 4 December 1986); and the Rio Declaration (1992) (see footnote 301 above).

(*d*) Other related treaties: the ASEAN Agreement on the Conservation of Nature and Natural Resources (1985, not in force).

[Treaties referring to the concept of peoples' right over natural resources.]

The International Covenant on Economic, Social and Cultural Rights (1966); the International Covenant on Civil and Political Rights (1966); and the African Charter on Human and Peoples' Rights (1981).

[501] African Convention on the Conservation of Nature and Natural Resources (2003), preamble.

[502] Convention for the Protection of the Natural Resources and Environment of the South Pacific Region (1986), art. 4, para. 6.

and that of reasonable utilization are different, they are closely interrelated and often combined in various legal regimes.[503] The *chapeau* of draft article 4 sets out this principle and the subparagraphs elaborate the meaning of the principle.

(3) Subparagraph (*a*) explains that equitable and reasonable utilization of the transboundary aquifer should result in an equitable allocation of benefits to be derived from such utilization among States sharing the aquifer. It is understood that "equitable" is not co-terminus with "equal".

(4) Subparagraphs (*b*) to (*d*) mainly concern reasonable utilization. In various legal regimes concerning renewable natural resources, "reasonable utilization" is often defined as "sustainable utilization" or "optimum utilization". There is a well-established scientific definition of this doctrine. It is to take measures on the best scientific evidence available to maintain at, or to restore to, the level of the resources which produces the maximum sustainable yield.[504] In plain language, it requires measures to keep the resources in perpetuity. The 1997 Watercourses Convention dealt with renewable waters which receive substantial recharge. Therefore, sustainable utilization was fully applicable. In the case of aquifers, the situation is completely different. Waters in non-recharging aquifers are not renewable. Any exploitation of such resources leads to depletion. While waters in recharging aquifers are renewable, the quantity of recharge water is usually extremely small compared to the large quantity of water stored in the aquifer over thousands of years. To limit exploitation of water to the quantity of recharge would be tantamount to prohibiting the utilization of even recharging aquifers.

(5) Subparagraphs (*b*) and (*c*) apply to both renewable and non-renewable resources of the aquifer (recharging and non-recharging). It is not appropriate to explicitly state the concept of "sustainability" in the case of an aquifer. Instead, the concept of "maximizing the long-term benefits" is adopted. The phrase "maximizing the long-term benefits" refers to the act of maintaining certain benefits over a long period of time, it being understood that utilization cannot be maintained indefinitely. Wasteful utilization must be avoided and the benefits could better be shared among generations. The provisions, however, do not refer to an obligation of maintaining the groundwater resource or the volume of water in the aquifer at or over some minimum level. Rather, it reflects a conscious decision-making process that determines what constitutes a benefit, what benefits are desirable, how many benefits should be enjoyed and the time period over which benefits should be enjoyed. Such decisions are entirely for the aquifer States concerned to make. In order to maximize long-term benefits, it is a prerequisite to have an overall utilization plan. Therefore, States are required to establish a suitable plan, preferably jointly with the other States concerned on the basis of an agreed lifespan of the aquifer. However, the phrase "individually or jointly" has been added to signify the importance of having a prior overall plan, while at the same time stressing that such a plan need not necessarily emanate from a joint endeavour by the aquifer States concerned. In some circumstances, a controlled and planned depletion could be considered.

(6) For a recharging aquifer, it is desirable to plan a much longer period of utilization than in the case of a non-recharging aquifer. However, it is not necessary to limit the level of utilization to the level of recharge. Subparagraph (*d*) provides that any utilization of such an aquifer should not destroy permanently its capacity to function as an aquifer.

(7) Paragraph 2 of the comparable article 5 of the 1997 Watercourses Convention provides another principle for equitable and reasonable participation[505] by watercourse States which includes both the right to utilize the watercourse and the duty to cooperate in the protection and development thereof. It is not included here, as it serves as an underlying basis for the provisions concerning international cooperation to be formulated in later draft articles.[506]

Article 5. Factors relevant to equitable and reasonable utilization

1. Utilization of a transboundary aquifer or aquifer system in an equitable and reasonable manner within the meaning of draft article 4 requires taking into account all relevant factors, including:

(*a*) the population dependent on the aquifer or aquifer system in each aquifer State;

(*b*) the social, economic and other needs, present and future, of the aquifer States concerned;

(*c*) the natural characteristics of the aquifer or aquifer system;

(*d*) the contribution to the formation and recharge of the aquifer or aquifer system;

(*e*) the existing and potential utilization of the aquifer or aquifer system;

(*f*) the effects of the utilization of the aquifer or aquifer system in one aquifer State on other aquifer States concerned;

(*g*) the availability of alternatives to a particular existing and planned utilization of the aquifer or aquifer system;

(*h*) the development, protection and conservation of the aquifer or aquifer system and the costs of measures to be taken to that effect;

(*i*) the role of the aquifer or aquifer system in the related ecosystem.

[503] See, for example, the 1997 Watercourses Convention, article 5, paragraph 1.

[504] See United Nations Convention on the Law of the Sea, article 119.

[505] See paragraphs (5) and (6) of the commentary to article 5 of the draft articles on the law of the non-navigational uses of international watercourses, *Yearbook ... 1994*, vol. II (Part Two), p. 97.

[506] Draft articles 7–18.

2. The weight to be given to each factor is to be determined by its importance with regard to a specific transboundary aquifer or aquifer system in comparison with that of other relevant factors. In determining what is equitable and reasonable utilization, all relevant factors are to be considered together and a conclusion reached on the basis of all the factors. However, in weighing different utilizations of a transboundary aquifer or aquifer system, special regard shall be given to vital human needs.

Commentary

(1) Draft article 5 lists the factors to be taken into account in determining equitable and reasonable utilization as provided for in draft article 4. "Factors" include "circumstances", and they will be considered in the context of the circumstances surrounding each case. It is a non-exhaustive list and is not based on any particular order of priority. The rules of equitable and reasonable utilization are necessarily general and flexible, and require for their proper application that aquifer States take into account concrete factors and circumstances of the resources as well as of the need of the aquifer States concerned. What is an equitable and reasonable utilization in a specific case will depend on a weighing of all relevant factors and circumstances. This draft article is almost a literal reproduction of article 6 of the 1997 Watercourses Convention.

(2) In subparagraph (*c*), "natural characteristics" is used instead of listing factors of a natural character of aquifers. The reason for this is that factors of a natural character should be taken into account, not one by one, but as the characteristics of aquifers. "Natural characteristics" refers to the physical characteristics that define and distinguish a particular aquifer. If a system approach is followed, one can separate the natural characteristics into three categories: input variables, output variables and system variables. Input variables are related to groundwater recharge from precipitation, rivers and lakes. Output variables are related to groundwater discharge to springs and rivers. System variables relate to aquifer conductivity (permeability) and storability which describe the state of the system. They are groundwater-level distribution and water characteristics such as temperature, hardness, pH (acidity and alkalinity), electro-conductivity and total dissolved solids. Together, the three categories of variables describe aquifer characteristics in terms of quantity, quality and dynamics. In effect, these characteristics are identical to those identified in paragraph 1 of draft article 8, on regular exchange of data and information.

(3) Subparagraph (*g*) relates to whether there are available alternatives to a particular planned or existing utilization of an aquifer. In practice, an alternative would take the form of another source of water supply and the overriding factors would be comparable feasibility, practicability and cost-effectiveness in comparison with the planned or existing utilization of the aquifer. For each of the alternatives a cost/benefits analysis needs to be performed. Besides feasibility and sustainability, the viability of alternatives plays an important role in the analysis. For example, a sustainable alternative could be considered as preferable in terms of aquifer recharge and discharge ratio, but less viable than a controlled depletion alternative.

(4) Subparagraphs (*d*) and (*i*) are factors additional to those listed in the 1997 Watercourses Convention. The contribution to the formation and recharge of the aquifer or aquifer system in subparagraph (*d*) means the comparative size of the aquifer in each aquifer State and the comparative importance of the recharge process in each State where the recharge zone is located. The role of the aquifer in the related ecosystem in subparagraph (*i*) is a necessarily relevant factor, in particular for reasonable utilization. The "role" signifies the variety of purposive functions that an aquifer has in a related ecosystem. This may be a relevant consideration in particular in an arid region. There exist different meanings attached to the term "ecosystem" within the scientific community. The term "related ecosystem" must be considered in conjunction with "ecosystems" in draft article 9. It refers to an ecosystem that is dependent on aquifers or on groundwaters stored in aquifers. Such an ecosystem may exist within aquifers, such as in karstic aquifers, and be dependent on the functioning of aquifers for its own survival. A related ecosystem may also exist outside aquifers and be dependent on aquifers for a certain volume or quality of groundwaters for its existence. For instance, in some lakes an ecosystem is dependent on aquifers. Lakes may have a complex groundwater flow system associated with them. Some lakes receive groundwater inflow throughout their entire bed. Some have seepage loss to aquifers throughout their entire bed. Others receive groundwater inflow through part of their bed and have seepage loss to aquifers through other parts. Lowering of lake water levels as a result of groundwater pumping can affect the ecosystems supported by the lake. The reduction of groundwater discharge to the lake significantly affects the input of dissolved chemicals which can be the principal source to the lake, even in cases where such discharge is a small component of the lake's water budget, and may result in altering key constituents of the lake, such as nutrients and dissolved oxygen.

(5) The text of the first two sentences of paragraph 2 was formulated during the final negotiating stage of the 1997 Watercourses Convention. It clarifies that all relevant factors are to be considered together and the conclusion must be reached on the basis of all of them. It remains, however, that the weight to be accorded to individual factors, as well as their relevance, will vary with the circumstances. Special consideration should be given to drinking waters and other essentials for human needs. The reference in the last sentence of paragraph 2 that "special regard shall be given to vital human needs" seeks to accommodate these considerations. The different kinds of utilization of water in an aquifer may be numerous, especially in arid and semi-arid regions where the aquifer is the only source of water. They are for drinking, agriculture, industry, human domestic needs and support for the terrestrial and aquatic ecosystem. When a conflict arises between different kinds of utilization, it should be resolved in accordance with the principle of equitable utilization. In such determination, special regard shall be given to the requirement of "vital human needs". During the elaboration of the 1997 Watercourses Convention, the Chairperson of the Working Group of the Whole took note of the following statement of understanding pertaining to "vital human needs": "In determining 'vital human needs', special attention is to be paid to providing sufficient water to sustain human life, including both drinking water and water required for

production of food in order to prevent starvation."[507] This statement seems to be more precise and narrower than other definitions.[508]

Article 6. Obligation not to cause significant harm to other aquifer States

1. Aquifer States shall, in utilizing a transboundary aquifer or aquifer system in their territories, take all appropriate measures to prevent the causing of significant harm to other aquifer States.

2. Aquifer States shall, in undertaking activities other than utilization of a transboundary aquifer or aquifer system that have, or are likely to have, an impact on that transboundary aquifer or aquifer system, take all appropriate measures to prevent the causing of significant harm through that aquifer or aquifer system to other aquifer States.

3. Where significant harm nevertheless is caused to another aquifer State, the aquifer States whose activities cause such harm shall take, in consultation with the affected State, all appropriate measures to eliminate or mitigate such harm, having due regard for the provisions of draft articles 4 and 5.

Commentary

(1) Draft article 6 deals with another basic obligation of aquifer States not to cause harm to other aquifer States. It addresses questions of significant harm arising from utilization and significant harm from activities other than utilization as contemplated in draft article 1, as well as questions of elimination and mitigation of significant harm occurring despite due diligence efforts to prevent such harm.

(2) *Sic utere tuo ut alienum non laedas* (use your own property so as not to injure that of another) is the established principle of international liability. The obligation contained in this draft article is that of "[taking] all appropriate measures". It is in substance the same as the obligation of "due diligence". The change from "due diligence" to "to take all appropriate measures" took place during the last negotiating stage of the 1997 Watercourses Convention. It is an obligation of conduct and not an obligation of result. An aquifer State has breached this obligation only when it has intentionally or negligently caused the event that must be prevented or has intentionally or negligently not prevented others in its territory from causing that event or has abstained from abating it. In the case of paragraph 1, it is implicit that the harm is caused to other States through transboundary aquifers. In the case of paragraph 2, it is expressly made clear that the draft article applies only to the harm that is caused to other States "through that aquifer or aquifer system".

(3) The debate continues whether the threshold of "significant harm" is appropriate for such fragile natural resources as aquifers. The view has been expressed widely that a lower threshold than "significant" harm is required for aquifers that are more fragile and, once polluted, take longer to clean than surface rivers. The Commission considered this question of the threshold extensively in its previous codification works on the 1997 Watercourses Convention and "Prevention of transboundary harm from hazardous activities" within the framework of the topic of "International liability for injurious consequences arising out of acts not prohibited by international law" and had established a position on the threshold of "significant harm".

(4) During the elaboration of the draft convention on the law of non-navigational uses of international watercourses, the Chairperson of the Working Group of the Whole took note of the statements of understanding to the texts of the Convention. On the term "significant", the following understanding was recorded: the term "significant" is not used in this article or elsewhere in the present Convention in the sense of "substantial". What is to be avoided are localized agreements, or agreements concerning a particular project, programme or use, that have a significant adverse effect upon third watercourse States. While such an effect must be capable of being established by objective evidence and not be trivial in nature, it needs not rise to the level of being substantial.[509] The threshold of "significant harm" is a flexible and relative concept and can serve as an appropriate threshold also for aquifers. Even when an aquifer is contaminated by a small amount of pollutant, the harm it may suffer could be evaluated as significant if the contamination has long-lasting effects, while the contamination of a watercourse by the same amount of pollutant might not be evaluated as significant.

(5) This draft article is intended to cover activities undertaken in a State's own territory. The scenario where an aquifer State would cause harm to another State through an aquifer by engaging in activities outside its territory is considered unlikely, but is not excluded.

(6) Paragraph 3 deals with the eventuality of significant harm even if all appropriate measures are taken. The reference to "activities" in paragraph 3 covers both utilization and "activities other utilization" in paragraphs 1 and 2. That eventuality is possible because activities have a risk of causing harm and such risk cannot be eliminated. The reference to the question of compensation found in the corresponding article of the 1997 Watercourses Convention is not included. The Commission decided not to address in these draft articles the issue of compensation in circumstances where harm resulted despite efforts to prevent such harm. The issue is covered by other rules of international law, including the draft principles on liability, and does not require specialized treatment with respect to transboundary aquifers.

Article 7. General obligation to cooperate

1. Aquifer States shall cooperate on the basis of sovereign equality, territorial integrity, sustainable

[507] A/51/869, para. 8.

[508] "'Vital human needs' means waters used for immediate human survival, including drinking, cooking, and sanitary needs, as well as water needed for the immediate sustenance of a household" (see article 3, paragraph 20 of the International Law Association's Berlin Rules on Water Resources, *Report of the Seventy-First Conference* (footnote 331 above)).

[509] See A/51/869.

development, mutual benefit and good faith in order to attain equitable and reasonable utilization and appropriate protection of their transboundary aquifer or aquifer system.

2. For the purpose of paragraph 1, aquifer States should establish joint mechanisms of cooperation.

Commentary

(1) Draft article 7 sets out the principle of a general obligation of aquifer States to cooperate with each other and contemplates procedures for such cooperation. Cooperation among aquifer States is a prerequisite for the fulfilment of the obligations throughout the draft articles. The importance of the obligation to cooperate is indicated in Principle 24 of the 1972 Stockholm Declaration.[510] The importance of such an obligation for the present subject is confirmed by the Mar del Plata Action Plan adopted by the United Nations Water Conference in 1977[511] and Chapter 18 of Agenda 21 on the Protection of the Quality and Supply of Freshwater Resources: Application of Integrated Approaches to the Development, Management and Use of Water Resources, of the 1992 United Nations Conference on Environment and Development.[512] A wide variety of international instruments on surface waters and groundwater issues call for cooperation between parties with regard to the protection, preservation and management of transboundary aquifers.[513]

(2) Paragraph 1 provides for the basis and objectives of cooperation and reproduces more or less the text of article 8 of the 1997 Watercourses Convention. To some members of the Commission, the question remains as to whether the principles of "sovereign equality" and "territorial integrity" could better be reflected elsewhere in the draft articles rather than in the context of the cooperation provision. The principle of "sustainable development" has been included as a general principle that ought to be taken into account in addition to the text of the 1997 Watercourses Convention. The term "sustainable development" denotes the general principle of sustainable development and should be distinguished from the concept of "sustainable utilization".[514]

(3) Paragraph 2 envisages the establishment of "joint mechanisms for cooperation" which refers to a mutually agreeable means of decision-making among aquifer States. In practical terms, it means a commission, an authority or other institution established by the aquifer States concerned to achieve a specified purpose. The competence of such a body would be for the aquifer States concerned to determine. The objectives in creating such a mechanism is to cooperate in decision-making, coordinate activities and avert, to the extent possible, disputes among aquifer States.

(4) Europe has a long tradition of international river commissions such as the International Commission for the Protection of the Rhine, the International Meuse Commission and the Danube Commission. Within these commissions or in close cooperation with them, bilateral cross-border commissions such as the Permanent Dutch–German Boundary Waters Commission operate. The existing commissions deal primarily with surface water issues. The European Union water framework Directive 2000/60/EC[515] is implemented mainly through commissions for delineation and monitoring. In the future, these commissions will become responsible for transboundary aquifer management as well.[516] In other parts of the world, it is also expected that comparable regional organizations play a role in promoting establishment of similar joint mechanisms.[517] It is also noted that there are many cases of joint mechanisms established by local governments along the border.[518]

Article 8. Regular exchange of data and information

1. Pursuant to draft article 7, aquifer States shall, on a regular basis, exchange readily available data and information on the condition of the transboundary aquifer or aquifer system, in particular of a geological, hydrogeological, hydrological, meteorological and ecological nature and related to the hydrochemistry of the aquifer or aquifer system, as well as related forecasts.

2. Where knowledge about the nature and extent of some transboundary aquifer or aquifer systems is inadequate, aquifer States concerned shall employ their best efforts to collect and generate more complete data and information relating to such aquifer or aquifer systems, taking into account current practices and standards. They shall take such action individually or jointly and, where appropriate, together with or through international organizations.

---

[510] See footnote 312 above.

[511] See *Report of the United Nations Water Conference, Mar del Plata, 14–25 March 1977* (United Nations publication, Sales No. E.77.II.A.12), Part One, p. 51 (recommendation 85).

[512] *Report of the United Nations Conference on Environment and Development, Rio de Janeiro, 3–14 June 1992* (see footnote 301 above).

[513] ASEAN Agreement on the Conservation of Nature and Natural Resources (1985), Convention on the Protection and Use of Transboundary Watercourses and International Lakes (1992), Protocol on Water and Health to the 1992 Convention on the Protection and Use of Transboundary Watercourses and International Lakes (1999), Convention on cooperation for the protection and sustainable use of the river Danube (1994), Convention for the Protection of the Rhine (1999), African Convention on the Conservation of Nature and Natural Resources (2003), Framework Convention on the Protection and Sustainable Development of the Carpathians (2003), Convention on the sustainable management of Lake Tanganyika (2003), and Protocol for Sustainable Development of Lake Victoria Basin (2003).

[514] See above, paragraph (4) of the commentary to draft article 4.

[515] See footnote 499 above.

[516] The European Union water framework Directive requires member States to establish a management plan. See also guidelines 2 and 8 of the Guidelines on Monitoring and Assessment of Transboundary Groundwaters of the UNECE, Institute for Inland Water Management and Waste Water Treatment, *UN/ECE Task Force on Monitoring & Assessment under the Convention on the Protection and Use of Transboundary Watercourses and International Lakes (Helsinki, 1992)—Working programme 1996/1999.*

[517] African Union: paragraph 3 of article VII (Water) of the African Convention on the Conservation of Nature and Natural Resources, and SADC: article 5 (Institutional framework for implementation) of the Revised Protocol on Shared Watercourses in the Southern African Development Community.

[518] Franco–Swiss Commission on the Genevese Aquifer established by the Canton of Geneva and the Prefect of Haute-Savoie, and Memorandum of Agreement Related to Referral of Water Right Applications (10 October 1996)—Appendix to British Columbia/Washington Memorandum of Understanding (12 April 1996), Burchi and Mechlem, *op. cit.* (footnote 497 above), p. 230.

3. If an aquifer State is requested by another aquifer State to provide data and information relating to the aquifer or aquifer systems that are not readily available, it shall employ its best efforts to comply with the request. The requested State may condition its compliance upon payment by the requesting State of the reasonable costs of collecting and, where appropriate, processing such data or information.

4. Aquifer States shall, where appropriate, employ their best efforts to collect and process data and information in a manner that facilitates their utilization by the other aquifer States to which such data and information are communicated.

Commentary

(1) Regular exchange of data and information is the first step for cooperation among aquifer States. The text of article 9 of the 1997 Watercourses Convention has been adjusted to meet the special characteristics of aquifers. In particular, paragraph 2 is additionally formulated in view of the insufficient status of scientific findings of some aquifers. There are several stages for the exchange of data and information throughout the draft articles. Data and information in this draft article are limited to those concerning the conditions of aquifers. They include not only raw statistics but also the results of research and analysis. Data and information concerning monitoring, utilization of aquifers, other activities affecting aquifers and their impact on aquifers are dealt with in later draft articles, including draft articles 12, 13 and 14.

(2) Draft article 8 sets out the general and minimum requirements for the exchange between aquifer States of the data and information necessary to ensure the equitable and reasonable utilization of transboundary aquifers. Aquifer States require data and information concerning the condition of the aquifer in order to apply draft article 5, which calls for aquifer States to take into account "all relevant factors" and circumstances in implementing the obligation of equitable and reasonable utilization laid down in draft article 4. The rules contained in draft article 8 are residual. They apply in the absence of a specially agreed regulation of the subject and they do not prejudice the regulation set out by an arrangement concluded among the States concerned for a specific transboundary aquifer. In fact, the need is clear for aquifer States to conclude such agreements among themselves in order to provide, *inter alia*, for the collection and exchange of data and information in the light of the characteristics of the transboundary aquifer concerned.

(3) The requirement of paragraph 1 that data and information be exchanged on a regular basis is designed to ensure that aquifer States will have the facts necessary to enable them to comply with their obligations under draft articles 4, 5 and 6. In requiring the "regular" exchange of data and information, paragraph 1 provides for an ongoing and systematic process, as distinct from the *ad hoc* provision of such information as concerning planned activities envisaged in draft article 14. Paragraph 1 requires that aquifer States exchange data and information that are "readily available". This expression is used to indicate that, as a matter of general legal duty, an aquifer State is under an obligation to provide only such data and information as is readily at its disposal, for example, that it has already collected for its own use or is easily accessible. In a specific case, whether data and information are "readily" available would depend upon an objective evaluation of such factors as the efforts and costs which their provision would entail, taking into account the human, technical, financial and other relevant resources of the requested aquifer State. The term "readily", as used in paragraphs 1 and 3, is thus a term of art having a meaning corresponding roughly to the expression "in the light of all the relevant circumstances" or to the word "feasible", rather than, for example, "rationally" or "logically". The importance of the exchange of data and information is indicated in a wide variety of agreements.[519]

(4) The phrase in paragraph 1 "in particular of geological, hydrogeological, hydrological, meteorological and ecological nature and related to the hydrochemistry of the aquifer or aquifer system" relate to the data and information that define and distinguish characteristics of the aquifer. "Geology" describes the age, composition and structure of the aquifer matrix. "Hydrogeology" describes the ability of the aquifer to store, transmit and discharge groundwaters. "Hydrology" describes elements other than groundwater of the water cycle, primarily effective precipitation and surface water that are important for aquifer recharge, the aquifer regime, storage and discharge. Effective precipitation is the part of precipitation which enters aquifers. In other words, it is total precipitation minus evaporation, surface runoff and vegetation. "Meteorology" provides data on precipitation, temperature and humidity which is necessary to calculate evaporation. "Ecology" provides data on plants, necessary to calculate plants' transpiration. "Hydrochemistry" yields data on chemical composition of the water necessary to define water quality. Aquifer States are required by paragraph 1 to exchange not only data and information on the present condition of the aquifer, but also related forecasts. The forecasts envisaged would relate to such matters as weather patterns and their possible effects upon water levels and flow; the amount of recharge and discharge; foreseeable ice conditions; possible long-term effects of present utilization; and the condition or movement of living resources. The requirement in paragraph 1 applies even in the relatively rare instances in which an aquifer State is not utilizing, or has no plan of utilizing, the transboundary aquifer.

[519] Convention on the Protection and Use of Transboundary Watercourses and International Lakes (1992), Programme for the Development of a Regional Strategy for the utilisation of the Nubian Sandstone Aquifer System (2000), Framework Convention on the Protection and Sustainable Development of the Carpathians (2003), African Convention on the Conservation of Nature and Natural Resources (2003), Convention on cooperation for the protection and sustainable use of the river Danube (1994), Tripartite Interim Agreement Between the Republic of Mozambique, the Republic of South Africa and the Kingdom of Swaziland for Co-operation on the Protection and Sustainable Utilisation of the Water Resources of the Incomati and Maputo Watercourses (2002), Framework Agreement on the Sava River Basin (2002), Convention on the sustainable management of Lake Tanganyika (2003), Protocol for Sustainable Development of Lake Victoria Basin (2003), Protocol amending the 1978 Agreement between the United States of America and Canada on Great Lakes water quality, as amended in 1983 (signed at Toledo on 18 November 1987, United Nations, *Treaty Series*, vol. 2185, No. 18177, p. 504), and Agreement on cooperation for the protection and sustainable use of the waters of the Spanish–Portuguese hydrographic basins (signed at Albufeira on 30 November 1998, *ibid.*, vol. 2099, No. 36496, p. 314).

(5) Paragraph 2 requires aquifer States to pay due regard to the uncertainties of transboundary aquifers. One of the difficulties in realizing effective international cooperation in the present subject is the uncertainty of scientific knowledge about transboundary aquifers. The aquifer States are required to cooperate with each other or with relevant international organizations in order to collect new data and information and make such data and information available to other aquifer States. The concept of "generation" of data involves the processing of raw data into usable information. UNESCO-IHP compiles reliable global data and information, including aquifer locations and characteristics, and makes them available to the scientific and management community of aquifers.

(6) Paragraph 3 concerns requests for data or information that are not readily available in the State from which they are sought. In such cases, the State in question is to employ its "best efforts" to comply with the request. It is to act in good faith and in a spirit of cooperation in endeavouring to provide the data or information sought by the requesting aquifer State. In the absence of agreement to the contrary, aquifer States are not required to process the data and information to be exchanged. Under paragraph 3 of draft article 8, however, they are to employ their best efforts to comply with the request. The requested State may condition its compliance with the request on payment by the requesting State of the reasonable costs of collecting and, where appropriate, processing the data. The expression "where appropriate" is used in order to provide a measure of flexibility, which is necessary for several reasons. In some cases, it may not be necessary to process data and information in order to render it usable by another State. In other cases, such processing may be necessary in order to ensure that the material is usable by other States, but this may entail undue burdens for the State providing the material.

(7) For data and information to be of practical value to aquifer States, they must be in a form which allows them to be easily usable. Paragraph 4 therefore requires aquifer States to use "their best efforts to collect and process data and information in a manner that facilitates their utilization" by the other aquifer State.

Part III

PROTECTION, PRESERVATION AND MANAGEMENT

Article 9. Protection and preservation of ecosystems

Aquifer States shall take all appropriate measures to protect and preserve ecosystems within, or dependent upon, their transboundary aquifers or aquifer systems, including measures to ensure that the quality and quantity of water retained in the aquifer or aquifer system, as well as that released in its discharge zones, are sufficient to protect and preserve such ecosystems.

Commentary

(1) Draft article 9 introduces Part III by laying down a general obligation to protect and preserve the ecosystems within a transboundary aquifer and also the outside ecosystems dependent on the aquifer by ensuring adequate quality and sufficient quantity of discharge water. Like article 192 of the United Nations Convention on the Law of the Sea and article 20 of the 1997 Watercourses Convention, draft article 9 contains obligations of both protection and preservation. These obligations relate to the "ecosystems" within and outside transboundary aquifers.

(2) The term "ecosystem" is explained in paragraph (4) of the commentary to draft article 5. "Ecosystem" refers generally to an ecological unit consisting of living and non-living components that are interdependent and function as a community. "In ecosystems, everything depends on everything else and nothing is really wasted."[520] An external impact affecting one component of an ecosystem may cause reactions among other components and may disturb the equilibrium of the entire ecosystem. Such an "external impact" or interference may impair or destroy the ability of an ecosystem to function as a life-support system. Human interferences may irreversibly disturb the equilibrium of freshwater ecosystems, in particular, rendering them incapable of supporting human and other forms of life. Interactions between freshwater ecosystems on the one hand and human activities on the other are becoming more complex and incompatible as socio-economic development proceeds. The obligation to protect and preserve the ecosystems within and outside transboundary aquifers addresses this problem, which is already acute in some parts of the world and which is likely to become so elsewhere. There are certain differences in the modalities of the protection and preservation of the ecosystem within aquifers and those of the protection and preservation of the outside ecosystems dependent on the aquifers. The quality and quantity of the discharge water exert great influence on the outside ecosystems.

(3) The obligation to "protect" the ecosystems requires the aquifer States to shield the ecosystems from harm or damage. The obligation to "preserve" the ecosystems applies in particular to freshwater ecosystems that are in a pristine or unspoiled condition. It requires that these ecosystems be treated in such a way as to maintain, as much as possible, their natural state. Together, protection and preservation of aquatic ecosystems help to ensure their continued viability as life-support systems.

(4) The obligation of States to take "all appropriate measures" is limited to the protection of relevant ecosystems. This allows States greater flexibility in the implementation of their responsibilities under this provision. It was noted, in particular, that there may be instances in which changing an ecosystem in some appreciable way may be justified by other considerations, including the planned usage of the aquifer in accordance with the draft articles.

(5) There are ample precedents for the obligation contained in draft article 9 in the practices of States and the work of international organizations. The ASEAN Agreement on the Conservation of Nature and Natural Resources (1985) provides for the obligation of conservation of species and ecosystems and conservation of ecological processes. The Convention on the Protection and Use

[520] ENVWA/WP.3/R.7/Rev.1, para. 9.

of Transboundary Watercourses and International Lakes (1992) sets out the obligation to "ensure conservation and, where necessary, restoration of ecosystems" (art. 2). The Protocol on Water and Health to the 1992 Convention on the Protection and Use of Transboundary Watercourses and International Lakes (1999) provides for the obligation to "take all appropriate measures for the purpose of ensuring … [e]ffective protection of water resources used as sources of drinking water, and their related water ecosystems, from pollution from other causes" (art. 4). The Tripartite Interim Agreement Between the Republic of Mozambique, the Republic of South Africa and the Kingdom of Swaziland for Co-operation on the Protection and Sustainable Utilisation of the Water Resources of the Incomati and Maputo Watercourses (2002) provides that "[t]he Parties shall, individually and, where appropriate, jointly, take all measures to protect and preserve the ecosystems of the Incomati and Maputo watercourses" (art. 6). The Protocol for Sustainable Development of Lake Victoria Basin (2003) provides for the obligation to "take all appropriate measures, individually or jointly and where appropriate with participation of all stakeholders to protect, conserve and where necessary rehabilitate the Basin and its ecosystems".

Article 10. Recharge and discharge zones

1. Aquifer States shall identify recharge and discharge zones of their transboundary aquifer or aquifer system and, within these zones, shall take special measures to minimize detrimental impacts on the recharge and discharge processes.

2. All States in whose territory a recharge or discharge zone is located, in whole or in part, and which are not aquifer States with regard to that aquifer or aquifer system, shall cooperate with the aquifer States to protect the aquifer or aquifer system.

Commentary

(1) Groundwater experts explain the importance of the measures to be taken for the protection and preservation of recharge and discharge zones in order to ensure the proper functioning of an aquifer. Disrupting or blocking recharge or discharge processes by, for example, constructing a concrete barrier in these zones would seriously and adversely affect the aquifer. Recharge or discharge zones are outside the aquifer in accordance with the definition of "aquifer" in subparagraph (*a*) of draft article 2 and accordingly this separate draft article is required to regulate such zones. Paragraph 1 provides for the obligations of aquifer States with regard to the protection of recharge and discharge zones of their transboundary aquifers. There are two phases for implementing such obligations. The first is the obligation to identify the recharge or discharge zones of their transboundary aquifers and the second is to take special measures to protect such zones for the purposes of the sound functioning of the aquifers.

(2) As far as the identification of recharge and discharge zones are concerned, those zones must be hydraulically connected to the aquifer directly. Once the recharge and discharge zones are identified and as far as they are located in the territories of the aquifer States concerned, those States are under the obligation to take special measures to minimize detrimental impacts on the recharge and discharge processes. Such measures play a pivotal role for the protection and preservation of the aquifer. It is noted that it is vitally important to take all measures in recharge zones to prevent pollutants from entering the aquifer. However, the obligation to protect the recharge zone from polluting the aquifers is dealt with in the context of draft article 11, which deals specifically with pollution.

(3) Paragraph 2 deals with the case that recharge or discharge zones of a particular transboundary aquifer are located in a State other than the aquifer States that share the transboundary aquifer in question. Considering the importance of the recharge and discharge mechanisms for the proper functioning of aquifers, it was decided to include an obligation on all States in whose territory a recharge or discharge zone is located to cooperate with aquifer States to protect the aquifer. It should be recalled, in this regard, that aquifer States are themselves covered by the general duty to cooperate in draft article 7.

Article 11. Prevention, reduction and control of pollution

Aquifer States shall, individually and, where appropriate, jointly, prevent, reduce and control pollution of their transboundary aquifer or aquifer system, including through the recharge process, that may cause significant harm to other aquifer States. In view of uncertainty about the nature and extent of transboundary aquifers or aquifer systems and of their vulnerability to pollution, aquifer States shall take a precautionary approach.

Commentary

(1) Draft article 11 sets forth the general obligation of aquifer States to prevent, reduce and control pollution of their transboundary aquifer that may cause significant harm to other aquifer States. The harm is that caused to other aquifer States through the transboundary aquifer and the aquifer-related environment. The problem dealt with here is essentially the quality of the water contained in the aquifer. This provision is a specific application of the general principles contained in draft articles 4 and 6.

(2) Some transboundary aquifers are already polluted to varying degrees, while others are not. In view of this state of affairs, draft article 11 employs the formula "prevent, reduce and control" in relation to the pollution. This expression is used in the 1982 United Nations Convention on the Law of the Sea in connection with marine pollution and in the 1997 Watercourses Convention. With respect to both the marine environment and international watercourses, the situation is similar. The obligation to "prevent" relates to new pollution, while the obligations to "reduce" and "control" relate to existing pollution. As with the obligation to "protect" ecosystems under draft article 9, the obligation to "prevent … pollution … that may cause significant harm" includes the duty to exercise due diligence to prevent the threat of such harm. This obligation is expressed by the words "may cause". The requirement that aquifer States "reduce and control" existing pollution reflects the practice of States.

A requirement that existing pollution causing such harm be abated immediately could, in some cases, result in undue hardship, especially where the detriment to an aquifer State of origin was grossly disproportionate to the benefit that would accrue to an aquifer State experiencing the harm. On the other hand, failure of the aquifer State of origin to exercise due diligence in reducing the pollution to acceptable levels would entitle the affected State to claim that the State of origin had breached its obligation to do so. As stated in paragraph (2) of the commentary to draft article 10, a specific reference to the recharge process was added to this draft article.

(3) This draft article requires that the measures in question be taken "individually or jointly". The obligation to take joint action derives from certain general obligations contained in draft article 7, in particular, in its paragraph 2.

(4) The obligations of prevention, reduction and control all apply to pollution "that may cause significant harm to other aquifer States". Pollution below that threshold would not fall within the present article but, depending upon the circumstances, might be covered by draft article 9.

(5) The last sentence of the present article obligates aquifer States to take a precautionary approach in view of uncertainty about the nature and extent of some transboundary aquifers or aquifer systems and of their vulnerability to pollution. Groundwater experts emphasize how fragile a transboundary aquifer or aquifer system is. They also emphasize that once a transboundary aquifer or aquifer system is polluted, it is very difficult to remove the pollutant and that the pollution could be irreversible in many cases. Considering such fragilities and scientific uncertainties of a transboundary aquifer or aquifer system, a precautionary approach is required.

(6) Some members of the Commission strongly suggested that an independent draft article should be formulated on the basis of the "precautionary principle". There are differing views as to whether the "precautionary principle" has been established as customary international law. It is true that there are several regional treaties or conventions in which the "precautionary principle" is expressly mentioned.[521] As far as universal treaties or conventions are concerned, different expressions such as "precautionary approach" and "precautionary measures" are used.[522] The majority of the members of the Commission considered that it would be better to avoid the conceptual and difficult discussions concerning the expression of "precautionary principle". The less disputed expression of "precautionary approach" could satisfy the basic necessity of introducing the special consideration of scientific uncertainties and vulnerability of aquifers. Of course, such a minimum requirement is residual and is without prejudice to the conventions with regard to a specific transboundary aquifer or aquifer system to be concluded by the aquifer States concerned to embody the precautionary principle.

Article 12. Monitoring

1. Aquifer States shall monitor their transboundary aquifer or aquifer system. They shall, wherever possible, carry out these monitoring activities jointly with other aquifer States concerned and, where appropriate, in collaboration with the competent international organizations. Where, however, monitoring activities are not carried out jointly, the aquifer States shall exchange the monitored data among themselves.

2. Aquifer States shall use agreed or harmonized standards and methodology for monitoring their transboundary aquifer or aquifer system. They should identify key parameters that they will monitor based on an agreed conceptual model of the aquifer or aquifer system. These parameters should include parameters on the condition of the aquifer or aquifer system as listed in draft article 8, paragraph 1, and also on the utilization of the aquifer and aquifer system.

Commentary

(1) Most groundwater experts (scientists and administrators) emphasize that monitoring is indispensable for the proper management of a transboundary aquifer. In practice, monitoring is usually initiated individually by the State concerned, and also in many cases by local government, and develops later into a joint effort with the neighbouring States concerned. However, experts agree that ultimate and ideal monitoring is joint monitoring based on the agreed conceptual model of the aquifer.

(2) Accordingly, paragraph 1 sets out the obligation of aquifer States to monitor their transboundary aquifer. It requires aquifer States to monitor, wherever possible, jointly with other aquifer States concerned. It also recognizes the case where such joint monitoring has not been implemented and sets out the obligation of aquifer States to monitor individually and share the results of monitoring with other aquifer States concerned. The general obligation of international cooperation is provided in draft article 7. There are several stages in the obligation

---

[521] The Convention for the protection of the marine environment of the North-East Atlantic (OSPAR Convention, 1992), the Convention on the Protection of the Marine Environment of the Baltic Sea Area (1992), the Convention for the Protection of the Marine Environment and the Coastal Region of the Mediterranean (1995), the Convention on the Protection and Use of Transboundary Watercourses and International Lakes (1992), the Treaty establishing the European Economic Community (1957), the Bamako Convention on the Ban of the Import into Africa and the Control of Transboundary Movement and Management of Hazardous Wastes within Africa (1991), the Protocol on Water and Health to the 1992 Convention on the Protection and Use of Transboundary Watercourses and International Lakes (1999), the Framework Convention on the Protection and Sustainable Development of the Carpathians (2003), the Convention on cooperation for the protection and sustainable use of the river Danube (1994), the Convention on the Protection of the Rhine (1999), the Convention on the sustainable management of Lake Tanganyika (2003), and the Protocol for Sustainable Development of Lake Victoria Basin (2003).

[522] For example, the 1996 Protocol to the 1972 Convention on the Prevention of Marine Pollution by Dumping of Wastes and Other Matter and the Agreement for the Implementation of the Provisions of the United Nations Convention on the Law of the Sea of 10 December 1982 relating to the Conservation and Management of Straddling Fish Stocks and Highly Migratory Fish Stocks (1995) use the expression "precautionary approach". The United Nations Framework Convention on Climate Change (1992) provides for the obligation to take "precautionary measures".

of international cooperation including regular exchange of data and information, monitoring, management and planned activities. Draft article 12 elaborates one of such stages of international cooperation.

(3) The importance of monitoring is widely recognized in many international instruments, for example, the 1989 Charter on Ground-Water Management[523] and the Guidelines on Monitoring and Assessment of Groundwaters of 2000,[524] both prepared by UNECE, the 1992 Convention on the Protection and Use of Transboundary Watercourses and International Lakes and the African Convention on the Conservation of Nature and Natural Resources.

(4) Draft article 12 is also related to draft article 8 on regular exchange of data and information. For the implementation of the obligation of regular exchange of data and information, effective monitoring is required. However, the data and information required by draft article 8 is limited to those concerning the condition of the aquifer. As stipulated in paragraph 2, monitoring needs to cover not only the conditions of the aquifer but also utilization of the aquifer such as withdrawal and artificial recharge of water.

(5) The purposes of monitoring are: (*a*) to clarify the conditions and utilization of a specific transboundary aquifer in order to take effective measures for its protection, preservation and management; and (*b*) to carry out regular surveillance of it in order to acquire information about any change or damage at an early stage. Effective monitoring through international cooperation will also contribute to further development of scientific knowledge about transboundary aquifers.

(6) There are various international instruments for the joint monitoring of a specific transboundary aquifer. An example is the Programme for the Development of a Regional Strategy for the utilisation of the Nubian Sandstone Aquifer System established in 2000. One of the agreements for the execution of this programme is the Terms of Reference for the Monitoring and Exchange of Groundwater Information. The 2003 Framework Convention on the Protection and Sustainable Development of the Carpathians provides for the obligation to pursue the policies aiming at joint or complementary monitoring programmes, including the systematic monitoring of the state of the environment. The 1994 Convention on cooperation for the protection and sustainable use of the river Danube provides for not only an obligation to harmonize individual monitoring but also an obligation to elaborate and implement joint programmes for monitoring the riverine conditions in the Danube catchment area concerning water quality and quantity, sediments and riverine ecosystem. The European Union water framework Directive 2000/60/EC sets out that "Member States shall ensure the establishment of programmes for the monitoring of water status in order to establish a coherent and comprehensive overview of water status within each river basin district" (art. 8).[525]

(7) As far as the aquifer States can agree to establish such a joint mechanism, it is the most effective approach. However, there are many cases where the aquifer States concerned have not yet initiated any consultation or have not yet reached any agreement to establish a joint mechanism. Even in such cases, they are at least under an obligation to conduct individual monitoring and share the results with the other aquifer States concerned. The 2003 African Convention on the Conservation of Nature and Natural Resources sets out the obligation of each party to monitor the status of their natural resources as well as the impact of development activities and project upon such resources. The 2002 Tripartite Interim Agreement Between the Republic of Mozambique, the Republic of South Africa and the Kingdom of Swaziland for Co-operation on the Protection and Sustainable Utilisation of the Water Resources of the Incomati and Maputo Watercourses sets out the obligation of each party to establish comparable monitoring systems, methods and procedures and implement a regular monitoring programme, including biological and chemical aspects for the Incomati and Maputo watercourses and report, at the intervals established by the Tripartite Permanent Technical Committee, on the status and trends of the associated aquatic, marine and riparian ecosystems in relation to the water quality of the said watercourses. The 2002 Framework Agreement on the Sava River Basin provides for the obligation of the parties to agree to establish a methodology of permanent monitoring of implementation of the Agreement and activities based upon it. The 2003 Convention on the sustainable management of Lake Tanganyika includes the obligation of monitoring in the provision for the prevention and control of pollution. The 2003 Protocol for Sustainable Development of Lake Victoria Basin provides for the obligation of monitoring undertaken by individual States in a standardized and harmonized manner.

(8) Paragraph 2 provides the essential elements of the obligation of aquifer States to realize effective monitoring, i.e. the agreement or harmonization of the standard and the methodology for monitoring. Without such agreement or harmonization, collected data would not be useful. Before a State can use data collected by other States, it must first understand when, where, what, why and how such data were collected. With these "metadata" (data about data), the State can independently assess the quality of those datasets and, if they meet their minimum data standards, the State can proceed with harmonizing available data and interpreting the consolidated database. In the case of the Franco–Swiss Commission on the Genevese Aquifer, the two sides started with each other's data standard and, with time and practice, reached a level of harmonization such that their data are comparable. The aquifer States should also agree on the conceptual model of the specific aquifer in order to be able to select key parameters which they will monitor. There are two kinds of conceptual models. One is the physical matrix and the other is the hydro-dynamic model. The aquifer States can agree on a model at the beginning and then change it as they gain better knowledge of the aquifer as a result of

[523] Adopted by UNECE in 1989. See *Charter on Ground-Water Management* (United Nations publication, Sales No. E.89.II.E.21), document E/ECE/1197-ECE/ENVWA/12.

[524] Drafted by the UNECE Task Force on Monitoring & Assessment under the Convention on the Protection and Use of Transboundary Watercourses and International Lakes and endorsed by the parties to the Convention in March 2000 (see footnote 516 above).

[525] See footnote 499 above.

monitoring. Key parameters to be monitored include the condition of the aquifer and the utilization of the aquifer as noted in paragraph (4) of the present commentary. The data on the condition of the aquifer relate to extent, geometry, flow path, hydrostatic pressure distribution, quantities of flow, hydrochemistry, etc., and are equivalent to those fields listed in paragraph 1 of draft article 8.

(9) While the general obligations are couched in mandatory language, the modalities for achieving compliance with the main obligations remain recommendatory, in order to facilitate compliance by States. It is also noted that the aquifers to be monitored are ones that are being utilized.

Article 13. Management

Aquifer States shall establish and implement plans for the proper management of their transboundary aquifer or aquifer system in accordance with the provisions of the present draft articles. They shall, at the request by any of them, enter into consultations concerning the management of the transboundary aquifer or aquifer system. A joint management mechanism shall be established, wherever appropriate.

Commentary

(1) Draft article 13 sets out the obligation of the aquifer States to establish and implement plans for the proper management of their transboundary aquifer. In view of the sovereignty over the aquifer located in the State's territory and the need for cooperation among aquifer States, two kinds of obligations are introduced in the present draft article: first, the obligation of each aquifer State to establish its own plan with regard to its aquifer and to implement it, and second, the obligation to enter into consultation with other aquifer States concerned at the request of any of the latter States.

(2) Paragraph 2 of article 24 of the 1997 Watercourses Convention provides that "'management' refers, in particular, to: (*a*) Planning the sustainable development of an international watercourse and providing for the implementation of any plans adopted; and (*b*) Otherwise promoting the rational and optimal utilization, protection and control of the watercourse". Exactly the same definition is accepted in the 2000 Revised Protocol on Shared Watercourses in the Southern African Development Community. This protocol entered into force in 2003. Such a definition can be used in the present subject *mutatis mutandis*.

(3) The rules in relation to the management of transboundary aquifers are provided in Part II. The obligations to utilize them in an equitable and reasonable manner, not to cause harm to other States and to cooperate with other aquifer States are the basis of the proper management of transboundary aquifers. The term "management" encompasses the measures to be taken for the maximization of the long-term benefits derived from the utilization of aquifers. It also includes the protection and preservation of transboundary aquifers.

(4) The first sentence of this draft article states an obligation for each aquifer State to establish plans with regard to its aquifer and to implement them for the proper management of the aquifer, taking into due consideration the rights of the other aquifer States concerned. The second sentence requires that State to enter into consultations concerning the management of the transboundary aquifer, if any other aquifer State should so request. The last sentence mandates that a joint management mechanism be established wherever appropriate. The Commission felt that the strengthening of this obligation was particularly important in the light of the value placed by groundwater experts on the joint management of transboundary aquifers. It was also recognized that, in practice, it may not always be possible to establish such a mechanism. The outcome of the consultations is left in the hands of the States concerned. States have established numerous joint commissions, many of which are charged with management. In particular, the modes of cooperation with regard to a specific transboundary aquifer are undertaken in less formal means, such as by holding regular meetings between the appropriate agencies or the representatives of the States concerned. Most of the transboundary aquifers in Europe are rather small and are managed often on the transfrontier level or by local municipalities. Such cooperation between local authorities should be encouraged. Thus the present draft article refers to a joint management "mechanism" rather than an organization in order to provide for such less formal means of joint management.

(5) The Convention on the Protection and Use of Transboundary Watercourses and International Lakes provides for the obligation of the management of the water resources "so that the needs of the present generation are met without compromising the ability of future generations to meet their own needs" (art. 2). The 1999 Protocol on Water and Health to the 1992 Convention on the Protection and Use of Transboundary Watercourses and International Lakes further clarifies the elements to be considered for the purpose of water management. The Framework Convention on the Protection and Sustainable Development of the Carpathians sets out the obligation of "river basin management" (art. 4). The African Convention on the Conservation of Nature and Natural Resources provides for the obligation to "manage their water resources so as to maintain them at the highest possible quantitative and qualitative levels" (art. VII).

(6) There are some examples in which a regional institution or mechanism is established for the purpose of the management of a specific transboundary aquifer. The 2000 Revised Protocol on Shared Watercourses in the Southern African Development Community "seeks to: … promote and facilitate the establishment of shared watercourse agreements and Shared Watercourse Institutions for the management of shared watercourses" (art. 2). The 2002 Framework Agreement on the Sava River Basin provides for the obligation to "cooperate … to achieve [the e]stablishment of sustainable water management" (art. 2). It also sets out the obligation "to develop joint and/or integrated Plan on the management of the water resources of the Sava River Basin" (art. 12). The Convention on the sustainable management of Lake Tanganyika sets out the obligation of the management of the natural resources of Lake Tanganyika and establishes the Lake Tanganyika Authority. One of the functions of this Authority is to advance and represent the common

interest of the contracting States in matters concerning the management of Lake Tanganyika and its Basin. The 2003 Protocol for Sustainable Development of Lake Victoria Basin provides for the obligations of parties and the Commission established by this Protocol with regard to the management plans for the conservation and the sustainable utilization of the resources of the Basin.

Part IV

ACTIVITIES AFFECTING OTHER STATES

Article 14. Planned activities

1. When a State has reasonable grounds for believing that a particular planned activity in its territory may affect a transboundary aquifer or aquifer system and thereby may have a significant adverse effect upon another State, it shall, as far as practicable, assess the possible effects of such activity.

2. Before a State implements or permits the implementation of planned activities which may affect a transboundary aquifer or aquifer system and thereby may have a significant adverse effect upon another State, it shall provide that State with timely notification thereof. Such notification shall be accompanied by available technical data and information, including any environmental impact assessment, in order to enable the notified State to evaluate the possible effects of the planned activities.

3. If the notifying and the notified States disagree on the possible effect of the planned activities, they shall enter into consultations and, if necessary, negotiations with a view to arriving at an equitable resolution of the situation. They may utilize an independent fact-finding body to make an impartial assessment of the effect of the planned activities.

Commentary

(1) The 1997 Watercourses Convention has nine articles on planned measures which may have a significant adverse effect upon other watercourse States. They set out detailed procedures to be followed by the States concerned. In the case of international watercourses, there have been a number of large development projects and related disputes among the States concerned, and detailed procedures to avoid disputes and mitigate such disputes were required. In the case of transboundary aquifers, detailed procedures for dealing with planned activities have not yet been developed and it seems to be the general preference to have simpler procedural requirements which could be provided only in one draft article. Draft article 14 has a broader scope in that it applies to any State that has reasonable grounds for believing that a planned activity in its territory could affect a transboundary aquifer or aquifer system and thereby cause a significant adverse effect on another State, whether it is an aquifer State or not. Thus, the provision does not apply only to aquifer States.

(2) The activities to be regulated in this draft article could be carried out either by States, their subsidiary organs or private enterprises. In order to fulfil the obligations under this draft article in Part IV on activities affecting other States, States must know in advance all the planning of such activities and therefore must establish the domestic legal regime which requires the authorization by the States of such activities.

(3) Paragraph 1 sets out the minimum obligation of a State to undertake prior assessment of the potential effect of the planned activity. Planned activities include not only utilization of transboundary aquifers, but also other activities that have or are likely to have an impact upon those aquifers. Such an obligation should be distinguished from the general obligations in Part III concerning protection, preservation and management, in the sense that it is closely related to the planning of activities. In addition to the measures to be taken under Part III, an aquifer State is under the obligation to undertake assessment of any adverse effects of a planned activity on the transboundary aquifers. This obligation is a minimum requirement in two senses. First, a State is required to assess the potential effects of the planned activity only when it has reasonable grounds for anticipating the probability of adverse effects. Second, the State is not under this obligation if the assessment is not practicable.

(4) The obligation of the assessment by a State that is planning a particular activity is provided in a wide variety of treaties and conventions. For example, the 1985 ASEAN Agreement on the Conservation of Nature and Natural Resources sets forth the obligation to "endeavour ... to make environmental impact assessment before engaging in any activity that may create a risk of significantly affecting the environment or the natural resources of another Contracting Party or the environment or natural resources beyond national jurisdiction" (art. 20). The 2003 African Convention on the Conservation of Nature and Natural Resources provides for the obligation to "ensure that policies, plans, programmes, strategies, projects and activities likely to affect natural resources, ecosystems and the environment in general are the subject of adequate impact assessment at the earliest possible stage" (art. XIV). The 1998 Agreement on cooperation for the protection and sustainable use of the waters of the Spanish–Portuguese hydrographic basins provides that "[t]he Parties shall adopt the necessary provisions to ensure that projects and activities covered by this Agreement which, owing to their nature, size and location, must be subjected to transborder impact assessment are so assessed before they are approved" (art. 9).[526]

(5) The importance of the environmental impact assessment is also indicated in the instruments prepared by the United Nations. For example, the 1989 Charter on Ground-Water Management prepared by UNECE provides that "[a]ll projects in any economic sector expected to affect aquifers adversely should be subject to an assessment procedure aiming at evaluating the project's possible impact on the water régime and/or the quality of ground-water resources, with particular attention to the important role ground water plays in the ecological system" (art. XIV).[527] Chapter 18 of Agenda 21 (1992), entitled "Protection of the Quality and Supply of Freshwater Resources: Application of Integrated Approaches to the

---

[526] See footnote 519 above.

[527] See footnote 523 above.

Development, Management and Use of Water Resources", suggests that all States could implement "mandatory environmental impact assessment of all major water resource development projects potentially impairing water quality and aquatic ecosystems".[528]

(6) The results from the assessment contribute to the sound planning of the activity. They also constitute the basis for the further procedures in paragraphs 2 and 3. Those paragraphs establish a procedural framework designed to avoid disputes relating to planned activities. When the assessment of the potential effects of a planned activity conducted in accordance with paragraph 1 indicates that such activity would cause an adverse effect on the transboundary aquifers and that it may have a significant adverse effect on other States, the original State is obliged under paragraph 2 to notify the States concerned of its finding. Such notification is to be accompanied by available technical data and information, including environmental impact assessment, and is to provide the potentially affected States with the necessary information to make their own evaluation of the possible effects of the planned activity.

(7) If the notified States are satisfied with the information and the assessment provided by the notifying States, they have the common ground to deal with the planned activity. On the other hand, if they disagree on the assessment of the effects of the planned activity, they have an obligation to endeavour to arrive at an equitable resolution of the situation in accordance with paragraph 3. The precondition to such resolution would be for the States concerned to have a common understanding of the possible effects. To that end, an independent fact-finding mechanism would play an important role in providing a scientific and impartial assessment of the effect of the planned activity. Article 33 of the 1997 Watercourses Convention provides for a compulsory recourse to such fact-finding. It seems that there exists no evidence as yet for such an obligation in relation to groundwaters. Accordingly, an optional reference to such a fact-finding mechanism is adopted.

(8) The procedure provided for in this draft article is triggered by the criterion that the planned activity may have "a significant adverse effect" upon other States. This threshold is lower than that of "significant harm" under draft article 6.

Part V

MISCELLANEOUS PROVISIONS

Article 15. Scientific and technical cooperation with developing States

States shall, directly or through competent international organizations, promote scientific, educational, technical and other cooperation with developing States for the protection and management of transboundary aquifers or aquifer systems. Such cooperation shall include, *inter alia*:

(*a*) training of their scientific and technical personnel;

(*b*) facilitating their participation in relevant international programmes;

(*c*) supplying them with necessary equipment and facilities;

(*d*) enhancing their capacity to manufacture such equipment;

(*e*) providing advice on and developing facilities for research, monitoring, educational and other programmes;

(*f*) providing advice on and developing facilities for minimizing the detrimental effects of major activities affecting transboundary aquifers or aquifer systems;

(*g*) preparing environmental impact assessments.

Commentary

(1) Draft article 15 deals with the scientific and technical cooperation with developing States. It should be highlighted that the term "cooperation" was preferred to the term "assistance" in this draft article. The term "cooperation" better represents the two-sided process necessary to foster sustainable growth in developing States. Under the first sentence of this provision, States are required to promote scientific, technical and other cooperation. The types of cooperation listed in the second sentence represent some of the various options available to States to fulfil the obligation set forth in the first sentence. States will not be required to engage in each of the types of cooperation listed, but will be allowed to choose their means of cooperation.

(2) The science of groundwaters, hydrogeology, is rapidly developing. Such new and rapidly developing scientific knowledge is mainly owned by developed States and is not yet fully shared by many developing States. Scientific and technical cooperation with developing States has been provided through the competent international organizations. UNESCO-IHP plays a central role in this field and is the global intergovernmental scientific programme of the United Nations system which can respond to specific national and regional needs and demands. The regional arrangements are also developing successfully due to wide ranges of assistance rendered by the competent international organizations. It would be appropriate to provide for the obligation of individual States to promote scientific and technical cooperation.

(3) The obligation under this draft article is one of the modalities of cooperation among States and its roots are to be found in article 202 (Scientific and technical assistance to developing States) of the 1982 United Nations Convention on the Law of the Sea. The Stockholm Declaration[529] indicates the importance of technological assistance as a supplement to the domestic effort of the

[528] *Report of the United Nations Conference on Environment and Development, Rio de Janeiro, 3–14 June 1992* (see footnote 301 above), para. 40.

[529] See footnote 312 above.

development and the special consideration of developing States for the purpose of development and environmental protection (Principles 9 and 12). The Rio Declaration[530] suggests the common but differentiated responsibilities in Principle 7. Principle 9 of this Declaration provides that "States should cooperate to strengthen endogenous capacity-building for sustainable development by improving scientific understanding through exchanges of scientific and technological knowledge, and by enhancing the development, adaptation, diffusion and transfer of technologies, including new and innovative technologies".

(4) The cooperation under this draft article mainly focuses on scientific, educational and technical cooperation. The expression "other cooperation" covers other possible modes of cooperation, for example, procedural or legal assistance to establish appropriate programmes or systems. This list follows the one provided in article 202 of the United Nations Convention on the Law of the Sea. It would be appropriate to place the emphasis upon cooperation for the education and training of the scientific and technical personnel and for the capacity-building of developing States concerning the measures for protection, monitoring or impact assessment. Such cooperation will contribute to the development of mutual cooperation among developing States in the future. The list is not exhaustive.

(5) The elements of cooperation stipulated in this draft article are also mentioned in several conventions and treaties. The Convention on the Protection and Use of Transboundary Watercourses and International Lakes provides for the obligation of mutual assistance. The Protocol on Water and Health to the 1992 Convention on the Protection and Use of Transboundary Watercourses and International Lakes emphasizes the importance of the "education and training of the professional and technical staff who are needed for managing water resources and for operating systems of water supply and sanitation" and of the "updating and improvement of their knowledge and skills" (art. 9). Article 14 of this Protocol enumerates the aspects in which international support for national action is required as follows:

> (*a*) [p]reparation of water-management plans in transboundary, national and/or local contexts and of schemes for improving water supply and sanitation; (*b*) [i]mproved formulation of projects, especially infrastructure projects, in pursuance of such plans and schemes, in order to facilitate access to sources of finance; (*c*) [e]ffective execution of such projects; (*d*) [e]stablishment of systems for surveillance and early-warning systems, contingency plans and response capacities in relation to water-related disease; (*e*) [p]reparation of legislation needed to support the implementation of this Protocol; (*f*) [e]ducation and training of key professional and technical staff; (*g*) [r]esearch into, and development of, cost-effective means and techniques for preventing, controlling and reducing water-related disease; (*h*) [o]peration of effective networks to monitor and assess the provision and quality of water-related services, and development of integrated information systems and databases; (*i*) [a]chievement of quality assurance for monitoring activities, including inter-laboratory comparability.

It is also noted that the 1994 Convention to combat desertification in those countries experiencing serious drought and/or desertification, particularly in Africa, provides a specific article regarding the obligations of developed country parties in article 6. It enumerates such obligations and one of them is to "promote and facilitate access by affected country Parties, particularly affected developing country Parties, to appropriate technology, knowledge and know-how".

(6) The obligation of mutual cooperation is also provided in regional conventions. One of the examples is the 2003 African Convention on the Conservation of Nature and Natural Resources, which sets out the obligation to "encourage and strengthen cooperation for the development and use, as well as access to and transfer of, environmentally sound technologies on mutually agreed terms", and, to this effect, to "adopt legislative and regulatory measures which provide for, *inter alia*, economic incentives for the development, importation, transfer and utilization of environmentally sound technologies in the private and public sectors" (art. XIX).

(7) The importance of the scientific and technical assistance is also mentioned in other non-binding declarations. The Mar del Plata Action Plan adopted by the United Nations Water Conference in 1977 points out the lack of sufficient scientific knowledge about water resources. With regard to groundwater, it recommends that the countries should:

> (i) Offer assistance for the establishment or strengthening of observational networks for recording quantitative and qualitative characteristics of ground-water resources;
>
> (ii) Offer assistance for the establishment of ground-water data banks and for reviewing the studies, locating gaps and formulating programmes of future investigations and prospection;
>
> (iii) Offer help, including personnel and equipment, to make available the use of advanced techniques, such as geophysical methods, nuclear techniques, mathematical models etc.[531]

(8) Chapter 18 of Agenda 21 adopted by the United Nations Conference on Environment and Development (1992) points out that one of the four principal objectives to be pursued is "[t]o identify and strengthen or develop, as required, in particular in developing countries, the appropriate institutional, legal and financial mechanisms to ensure that water policy and its implementation are a catalyst for sustainable social progress and economic growth".[532] It also suggests that:

> [a]ll States, according to their capacity and available resources, and through bilateral or multilateral cooperation, including the United Nations and other relevant organizations as appropriate, could implement the following activities to improve integrated water resources management: … Development and strengthening, as appropriate, of cooperation, including mechanisms where appropriate, at all levels concerned, namely: … (iv) At the global level, improved delineation of responsibilities, division of labour and coordination of international organizations and programmes, including facilitating discussions and sharing of experiences in areas related to water resources management.[533]

It also points out that one of the three objectives to be pursued concurrently to integrate water-quality elements into

---

[530] See footnote 301 above.

[531] See footnote 511 above.

[532] *Report of the United Nations Conference on Environment and Development, Rio de Janeiro, 3–14 June 1992* (see footnote 301 above), para. 9 d.

[533] *Ibid.*, para. 12.

water resource management is "human resources development, a key to capacity-building and a prerequisite for implementing water-quality management".[534] The Plan of Implementation of the World Summit on Sustainable Development (2002) also mentions technical assistance (chap. IV, para. 25).[535]

Article 16. Emergency situations

1. For the purpose of the present draft article, "emergency" means a situation, resulting suddenly from natural causes or from human conduct, that poses an imminent threat of causing serious harm to aquifer States or other States.

2. Where an emergency affects a transboundary aquifer or aquifer system and thereby poses an imminent threat to States, the following shall apply:

(*a*) The State within whose territory the emergency originates shall:

(i) without delay and by the most expeditious means available, notify other potentially affected States and competent international organizations of the emergency;

(ii) in cooperation with potentially affected States and, where appropriate, competent international organizations, immediately take all practicable measures necessitated by the circumstances to prevent, mitigate and eliminate any harmful effect of the emergency;

(*b*) States shall provide scientific, technical, logistical and other cooperation to other States experiencing an emergency. Cooperation may include coordination of international emergency actions and communications, making available trained emergency response personnel, emergency response equipments and supplies, scientific and technical expertise and humanitarian assistance.

3. Where an emergency poses a threat to vital human needs, aquifer States, notwithstanding draft articles 4 and 6, may take measures that are strictly necessary to meet such needs.

Commentary

(1) Draft article 16 deals with the obligations of States in responding to actual emergency situations that are related to transboundary aquifers. It is to be contrasted with draft article 11 which deals with the prevention and mitigation of conditions that may be harmful to aquifer States. The 1997 Watercourses Convention contains a similar provision in article 28. In the case of aquifers, emergencies might not be as numerous and destructive as in the case of watercourses. However, it would be desirable to insert an article on this issue in view of the devastating tsunami disaster along the coast of the Indian Ocean, which resulted from a great earthquake that occurred off Banda Aceh, Indonesia, in December 2004. Although no definite studies have yet been published, a great number of aquifers must have been negatively affected. Owing to the destruction of the discharge processes, salinization of aquifers might have occurred. In consultation with groundwater experts, this draft article was prepared to address such situations.

(2) Paragraph 1 gives the definition of "emergency". The commentary to paragraph 1 of article 28 of the 1997 Watercourses Convention explains that the definition of "emergency" contains a number of important elements, and includes several examples that are provided for purposes of illustration. As defined, an "emergency" must cause, or pose an imminent threat of causing, "serious harm" to other States. The seriousness of the harm involved, together with the suddenness of the emergency's occurrence, justifies the measures required by the draft article. The expression "other States" refers to both aquifer and non-aquifer States that might be affected by an emergency. These would usually be the States in whose territories either aquifers or the recharge or discharge zones are located. The situation constituting an emergency must arise "suddenly". However, the provision covers the case where the "emergency" can be expected by weather forecast.

(3) As the emergency situation would pose "an imminent threat of causing serious harm", the State in whose territory the emergency originates is obligated under paragraph 2, subparagraph (*a*) (i) to notify, "without delay and by the most expeditious means available", other potentially affected States and competent international organizations of the emergency. A similar obligation is contained, for example, in the 1986 Convention on early notification of a nuclear accident, the 1982 United Nations Convention on the Law of the Sea and a number of agreements concerning transboundary aquifers. "Without delay" means immediately upon learning of the emergency, and the phrase "by the most expeditious means available" means that the most rapid means of communication that is accessible is to be utilized. The States to be notified are not confined to aquifer States, since non-aquifer States may also be affected by an emergency. The subparagraph also calls for the notification of "competent international organizations". Such an organization would have to be competent to participate in responding to the emergency by virtue of its constituent instrument. Most frequently, such an organization would be one established by the aquifer States to deal, *inter alia*, with emergencies. Finally, the situation may result either "from natural causes or from human conduct". While there may well be no liability on the part of a State for the harmful effects in another State of an emergency originating in the former and resulting entirely from natural causes, the obligations under paragraph 2, subparagraphs (*a*) and (*b*) would nonetheless apply to such an emergency.

(4) Paragraph 2, subparagraph (*a*) (ii) requires that a State within whose territory an emergency originated "immediately take all practicable measures … to prevent, mitigate and eliminate any harmful effect of the emergency". The effective action to counteract most emergencies resulting from human conduct is that to be

[534] *Ibid.*, para. 38 *c*.

[535] See footnote 416 above.

taken where the industrial accident, vessel grounding or other incident occurs. However, the paragraph requires only that all "practicable" measures be taken, meaning those that are feasible, workable and reasonable. Further, only such measures as are "necessitated by the circumstances" need to be taken, meaning those that are warranted by the factual situation of the emergency and its possible effect upon other States. Like paragraph 2, subparagraph (*a*) (i), paragraph 2, subparagraph (*a*) (ii) foresees the possibility that there will be a competent international organization, such as a joint commission, with which the States may cooperate in taking the requisite measures. And finally, cooperation with potentially affected States (again including non-aquifer States) is also provided for. Such cooperation may be especially appropriate in the case of contiguous aquifers or aquifer systems or where a potentially affected State is in a position to render cooperation in the territory of the aquifer State where the emergency originated.

(5) The obligation of immediate notification to other States of any natural disasters or other emergencies that are likely to produce sudden harmful effects on the environment of those States is suggested in Principle 18 of the Rio Declaration.[536] Several regional conventions provide for the obligation of notification without delay to the potentially affected States, regional commission or agency and other competent organizations. They are, for example, the 2000 Revised Protocol on Shared Watercourses in the Southern African Development Community, the 2002 Tripartite Interim Agreement Between the Republic of Mozambique, the Republic of South Africa and the Kingdom of Swaziland for Co-operation on the Protection and Sustainable Utilisation of the Water Resources of the Incomati and Maputo Watercourses, the 2003 Convention on the sustainable management of Lake Tanganyika and the 2003 Protocol for Sustainable Development of Lake Victoria Basin. The 2003 African Convention on the Conservation of Nature and Natural Resources sets out the right of the State party to be provided with all relevant available data by the other party in whose territory environmental emergency or natural disaster occurs and is likely to affect the natural resources of the former State.

(6) Some of the conventions have established mechanisms or systems for the early notification of emergency situations. The Convention on the Protection and Use of Transboundary Watercourses and International Lakes provides that "[t]he Riparian Parties shall without delay inform each other about any critical situation that may have transboundary impact" (art. 14) and provides for the obligation to set up, where appropriate, and to operate coordinated or joint communication, warning and alarm systems. The 1994 Convention on cooperation for the protection and sustainable use of the river Danube establishes "coordinated or joint communication, warning and alarm systems" (art. 16) and provides for the obligation to consult on ways and means of harmonizing domestic communication, warning and alarm systems and emergency plans. The 1998 Agreement on cooperation for the protection and sustainable use of the waters of the Spanish–Portuguese hydrographic basins[537] provides for the obligation of the parties to establish or improve joint or coordinated communication systems to transmit early warning or emergency information.

(7) Paragraph 2, subparagraph (*b*) sets out the obligation of assistance by all States regardless of whether they are experiencing in any way the serious harm arising from an emergency. Groundwater scientists and administrators are unanimous in recognizing the need for joint efforts by all States to cope effectively with an emergency. Assistance required would relate to coordination of emergency actions and communication, providing trained emergency response personnel, response equipments and supplies, and extending scientific and technical expertise and humanitarian assistance.

(8) UNESCO-IHP has the project entitled "Groundwater for Emergency Situations". The aim of the project is to consider natural and man-induced catastrophic events that could adversely influence human health and life and to identify in advance potential safe, low vulnerability groundwater resources which could temporarily replace damaged supply systems. Secure drinking water for endangered populations is one of the highest priorities during and immediately after disasters.

(9) Paragraph 3 provides for exceptions to the obligations under draft articles 4 and 6 in an emergency. Aquifer States may temporarily derogate from the obligations under those draft articles where water is critical for the population to alleviate an emergency situation. Although the 1997 Watercourses Convention does not contain such a clause in the case of aquifers, special account should be taken in an emergency situation of vital human needs. For example, in the case of natural disasters, such as earthquakes or floods, an aquifer State must immediately satisfy its population's need for drinking water. In the case of watercourses, States could meet such a requirement without derogation from the obligations, as the recharge of the water to the watercourses would likely be sufficient. However, in the case of the aquifers, the States concerned would not be able to do so, as there would be no recharge or little recharge. Accordingly, States must be entitled to exploit the aquifer temporarily without fulfilling their obligations under draft articles 4 and 6. However, the present article deals only with the temporary derogation. There might be cases where States would not be able to fulfil the obligations in other draft articles also in an emergency. In such a case, States could invoke such circumstances precluding wrongfulness in general international law, such as *force majeure*, distress or necessity.

Article 17. Protection in time of armed conflict

Transboundary aquifers or aquifer systems and related installations, facilities and other works shall enjoy the protection accorded by the principles and rules of international law applicable in international and non-international armed conflicts and shall not be used in violation of those principles and rules.

---

[536] See footnote 301 above.

[537] See footnote 519 above.

Commentary

(1) Draft article 17 concerns the protection to be accorded to transboundary aquifers and related installations in time of armed conflict. The 1997 Watercourses Convention contains an article regarding the same subject and the basic idea of the present article is the same. This draft article, which is without prejudice to existing law, does not lay down any new rule. It simply serves as a reminder that the principles and rules of international law applicable in international and internal armed conflict contain important provisions concerning water resources and related works. These provisions fall generally into two categories: those concerning the protection of water resources and related works, and those dealing with the utilization of such water resources and works. Since detailed regulation of this subject matter would be beyond the scope of a framework instrument, draft article 17 does no more than to refer to each of these categories of principles and rules.

(2) Draft article 17 is not addressed only to aquifer States, in view of the fact that transboundary aquifers and related works may be utilized or attacked in time of armed conflict by non-aquifer States as well. The draft article's principal function is to serve as a reminder to all States of the applicability of the law of armed conflict to transboundary aquifers.

(3) The obligation of the aquifer States to protect and utilize transboundary aquifers and related works in accordance with the present draft articles should remain in effect even in times of armed conflict. Warfare may, however, affect transboundary aquifers as well as the protection and utilization thereof by aquifer States. In such cases, draft article 17 makes it clear that the rules and principles governing armed conflict apply, including various provisions of conventions on international humanitarian law to the extent that the States in question are bound by them. For example, the poisoning of water supplies is prohibited by the Hague Convention 1907 (IV) respecting the Laws and Customs of War on Land and article 54 of the 1977 Protocol additional to the Geneva Conventions of 12 August 1949, and relating to the protection of victims of international armed conflicts (Protocol I), while article 56 of that Protocol protects dams, dikes and other works from attacks that "may cause the release of dangerous forces and consequent severe losses among the civilian population". Similar protections apply in non-international armed conflicts under articles 14 and 15 of the Protocol additional to the Geneva Conventions of 12 August 1949, and relating to the protection of victims of non-international armed conflicts (Protocol II). Also relevant to the protection of water resources in time of armed conflict is the provision of Protocol I that "[c]are shall be taken in warfare to protect the natural environment against widespread, long-term and severe damage" (art. 55). In cases not covered by a specific rule, certain fundamental protections are afforded by the "Martens clause". That clause, which was originally inserted in the Preamble of the Hague Conventions respecting the Laws and Customs of War on Land of 1899 and 1907 and has subsequently been included in a number of conventions and protocols, now has the status of general international law. In essence, it provides that even in cases not covered by specific international agreements, civilians and combatants remain under the protection and authority of the principles of international law derived from established custom, the principles of humanity and the dictates of public conscience. Paragraph 2 of draft article 5 of the present draft articles provides that in reconciling a conflict between utilizations of transboundary aquifers, special attention is to be paid to the requirement of vital human needs.

Article 18. Data and information concerning national defence or security

Nothing in the present draft articles obliges a State to provide data or information the confidentiality of which is essential to its national defence or security. Nevertheless, that State shall cooperate in good faith with other States with a view to providing as much information as possible under the circumstances.

Commentary

(1) Draft article 18 creates a very narrow exception to the requirement of draft articles requiring provision of information. The same rule is provided in the 1997 Watercourses Convention. States cannot realistically be expected to agree to the release of information that is vital to their national defence or security. At the same time, however, an aquifer State that may experience adverse effects of planned measures should not be left entirely without information concerning those possible effects. Draft article 18 therefore requires the State withholding information to "cooperate in good faith with other States with a view to providing as much information as possible under the circumstances". The "circumstances" referred to are those that led to the withholding of the data or information. The obligation to provide "as much information as possible" could be fulfilled in many cases by furnishing a general description of the manner in which the measures would alter the condition of the aquifer or affect other States. The draft article is thus intended to achieve a balance between the legitimate needs of the States concerned: the need for the confidentiality of sensitive information, on one hand, and the need for information pertaining to possible adverse effects of planned measures, on the other. As always, the exception created by draft article 18 is without prejudice to the obligations of the planning State under draft articles 4 and 6.

(2) The inclusion of this draft article was one of the most contentious issues discussed in the Commission. Some members were of the view that such a provision could lend itself to abuse and had difficulty imagining a situation where national security issues should take precedence over the other provisions of the draft articles. They were of the view that such an article should not be included. It was also stressed that article 31 of the 1997 Watercourses Convention limited the discretion of the State for exemption to a much higher extent. It requires the data and information to be vital (and not essential) to its national defence and security. Other members expressed the view that such protection was of utmost importance to States and would be called for by the Sixth Committee. They argued that, in many circumstances, the draft articles required States to share more information than

was strictly necessary for the protection of the aquifer and aquifer system. Moreover, they were of the view that the protection of information vital to national security would not unduly interfere with the functioning of the other provisions of the draft articles.

(3) It is also noted that a suggestion was made to add the protection of industrial secrets and intellectual property to the text of the draft article, in line with article 14 of the draft articles on prevention of transboundary harm from hazardous activities.[538] However, some members considered that it was unclear whether such a protection was necessary or helpful in the case of transboundary aquifers and expressed concern that such an exemption might be too broad in the groundwater context. In any event, the existence of intellectual property could be one of the factors to be considered in determining what data is readily available under draft article 8.

Article 19. Bilateral and regional agreements and arrangements

For the purpose of managing a particular transboundary aquifer or aquifer system, aquifer States are encouraged to enter into a bilateral or regional agreement or arrangement among themselves. Such agreement or arrangement may be entered into with respect to an entire aquifer or aquifer system or any part thereof or a particular project, programme or utilization except insofar as the agreement or arrangement adversely affects, to a significant extent, the utilization, by one or more other aquifer States of the water in that aquifer or aquifer system, without their express consent.

Commentary

(1) The importance of bilateral or regional agreements and arrangements that take due account of the historical, political, social and economic characteristics of the region and of the specific transboundary aquifer must be stressed. The first sentence calls upon the aquifer States to cooperate among themselves and encourages them to enter into bilateral or regional agreements or arrangements for the purpose of managing the particular transboundary aquifer. The concept of reserving the matter to the group of aquifer States concerned with the particular aquifer is based on the principles that are set forth in the United Nations Convention on the Law of the Sea.[539] It also corresponds to the "watercourse agreements" provided for in article 3 of the 1997 Watercourses Convention. In the case of surface watercourses, numerous bilateral and regional agreements have been concluded. However, in the case of groundwater, such international collective measures are still in an embryonic stage and the framework for cooperation remains to be properly developed. Therefore, the term "arrangement" has been added in this paragraph This paragraph also provides that the States concerned should have equal opportunity to participate in such agreements or arrangements.

(2) Such agreements or arrangements may be entered into with respect to an entire aquifer or aquifer system or any part thereof or a particular project, programme or utilization. When an agreement or arrangement is for the entire aquifer or aquifer system, all the aquifer States sharing the same aquifer or aquifer system are most likely to be involved except for some rare cases. On the other hand, when an agreement or arrangement is for any part of the aquifer or aquifer system or for a particular project, only a few of the aquifer States sharing the same aquifer would be involved. In any event, the second sentence obligates the aquifer States not to enter into an agreement or arrangement which would adversely affect the position of the excluded aquifer States without their express consent. It does not mean to give a veto power to those other States.

[538] *Yearbook ... 2001*, vol. II (Part Two) and corrigendum, pp. 166–167.

[539] United Nations Convention on the Law of the Sea, article 118 (Co-operation of States in the conservation and management of living resources) and article 197 (Co-operation on a global or regional basis).

Chapter VII

RESPONSIBILITY OF INTERNATIONAL ORGANIZATIONS

A. Introduction

77. At its fifty-second session (2000), the Commission decided to include the topic "Responsibility of international organizations" in its long-term programme of work.[540] The General Assembly, in paragraph 8 of its resolution 55/152 of 12 December 2000, took note of the Commission's decision with regard to the long-term programme of work, and of the syllabus for the new topic annexed to the Commission's 2000 report to the General Assembly on the work of its fifty-second session. The General Assembly, in paragraph 8 of its resolution 56/82 of 12 December 2001, requested the Commission to begin its work on the topic "Responsibility of international organizations".

78. At its fifty-fourth session, in 2002, the Commission decided to include the topic in its programme of work and appointed Mr. Giorgio Gaja as Special Rapporteur for the topic.[541] At the same session, the Commission established a working group on the topic.[542] The Working Group in its report[543] briefly considered the scope of the topic, the relations between the new project and the draft articles on responsibility of States for internationally wrongful acts adopted by the Commission at its fifty-third session,[544] questions of attribution, issues relating to the responsibility of member States for conduct that is attributed to an international organization, and questions relating to the content of international responsibility, implementation of responsibility and settlement of disputes. At the end of its fifty-fourth session, the Commission adopted the report of the Working Group.[545]

79. From its fifty-fifth (2003) to its fifty seventh (2005) sessions, the Commission had received and considered three reports from the Special Rapporteur,[546] and provisionally adopted draft articles 1 to 16 [15].[547]

[540] *Yearbook ... 2000*, vol. II (Part Two), p. 131, para. 729.

[541] *Yearbook ... 2002*, vol. II (Part Two), p. 93, paras. 461–463.

[542] *Ibid.*, para. 462.

[543] *Ibid.*, pp. 93–96, paras. 465–488.

[544] *Yearbook ... 2001*, vol. II (Part Two) and corrigendum, p. 26, para. 76.

[545] *Yearbook ... 2002*, vol. II (Part Two), p. 93, para. 464.

[546] Preliminary report: *Yearbook ... 2003*, vol. II (Part One), document A/CN.4/532; second report: *Yearbook ... 2004*, vol. II (Part One), document A/CN.4/541; and third report: *Yearbook ... 2005*, vol. II (Part One), document A/CN.4/553.

[547] Draft articles 1 to 3 were adopted at the fifty-fifth session (*Yearbook ... 2003*, vol. II (Part Two), p. 18, para. 49), draft articles 4 to 7 at the fifty-sixth session (*Yearbook ... 2004*, vol. II (Part Two), p. 46, para. 69) and draft articles 8 to 16 [15] at the fifty-seventh session (*Yearbook ... 2005*, vol. II (Part Two), para. 203).

B. Consideration of the topic at the present session

80. At the present session, the Commission had before it the fourth report of the Special Rapporteur (A/CN.4/564 and Add.1–2), as well as written comments received so far from international organizations and from governments.[548]

81. The fourth report of the Special Rapporteur, like the previous reports, followed the general pattern of the articles on responsibility of States for internationally wrongful acts.

82. The fourth report contained 13 draft articles. Eight draft articles corresponded to those contained in Chapter V of the articles on responsibility of States for internationally wrongful acts, under the heading "Circumstances precluding wrongfulness". Five draft articles dealt with the responsibility of a State in connection with the wrongful act of an international organization.

83. The Special Rapporteur presented the eight draft articles relating to circumstances precluding wrongfulness, namely, draft articles 17 to 24: article 17 (Consent),[549] article 18 (Self-defence),[550] article 19 (Countermeasures),[551]

[548] Following the recommendations of the Commission (*Yearbook ... 2002*, vol. II (Part Two), pp. 93–96, paras. 464–488, and *Yearbook ... 2003*, vol. II (Part Two), p. 18, para. 52), the Secretariat, on annual basis, has been circulating the relevant chapter, included in the Commission's report to the General Assembly on the work at its session, to international organizations asking for their comments and for any relevant materials which they could provide to the Commission. For comments from Governments and international organizations, see *Yearbook ... 2004*, vol. II (Part One), documents A/CN.4/545 and A/CN.4/547, and *Yearbook ... 2005*, vol. II (Part One), document A/CN.4/556. See also document A/CN.4/568 and Add.1 (reproduced in *Yearbook ... 2006*, vol. II (Part One)).

[549] Draft article 17 reads as follows:

"*Article 17. Consent*

"Valid consent by a State or an international organization to the commission of a given act by another international organization precludes the wrongfulness of that act in relation to that State or the former organization to the extent that the act remains within the limits of that consent."

[550] Draft article 18 reads as follows:

"*Article 18. Self-defence*

"The wrongfulness of an act of an international organization is precluded if the act constitutes a lawful measure of self-defence taken in conformity with the Charter of the United Nations."

[551] Draft article 19 reads as follows:

"*Article 19. Countermeasures*

"Alternative A

"[...]

"Alternative B

"The wrongfulness of an act of an international organization not in conformity with an international obligation towards another international organization [or a State] is precluded if and to the extent that the act constitutes a lawful countermeasure taken against the latter organization [or the State]."

article 20 (*Force majeure*),[552] article 21 (Distress),[553] article 22 (Necessity),[554] article 23 (Compliance with peremptory norms),[555] and article 24 (Consequences of invoking a circumstance precluding wrongfulness).[556]

84. Draft articles 17 to 24 are closely modelled on the corresponding articles on responsibility of States for internationally wrongful acts, namely, draft articles 20 to 27.[557] In the view of the Special Rapporteur, the principles contained in the chapter on circumstances precluding wrongfulness were equally applicable to international organizations, although in some cases they needed to be adjusted to fit the particular nature of international organizations. Although the available practice with regard to circumstances precluding wrongfulness was limited, clear parallels could be drawn between States and international organizations in this regard. Thus, there was no reason for departing from the general approach taken in the context of States. However, this did not signify that the provisions would apply the same way in the case of international organizations.

85. The Special Rapporteur also presented draft articles relating to the responsibility of a State in connection with the wrongful act of an international organization, namely, draft articles 25 to 29: article 25 (Aid or assistance by a State in the commission of an internationally wrongful act by an international organization),[558] article 26 (Direction and control exercised by a State over the commission of an internationally wrongful act by an international organization),[559] article 27 (Coercion of an international organization by a State),[560] article 28 (Use by a State that is a member of an international organization of the separate personality of that organization),[561] and article 29 (Responsibility of a State

---

[552] Draft article 20 reads as follows:

"*Article 20.* Force majeure

"1. The wrongfulness of an act of an international organization not in conformity with an international obligation of that organization is precluded if the act is due to *force majeure*, that is, the occurrence of an irresistible force or of an unforeseen event, beyond the control of the organization, making it materially impossible in the circumstances to perform the obligation.

"2. Paragraph 1 does not apply if:

"(*a*) The situation of *force majeure* is due, either alone or in combination with other factors, to the conduct of the organization invoking it; or

"(*b*) The organization has assumed the risk of that situation occurring."

[553] Draft article 21 reads as follows:

"*Article 21. Distress*

"1. The wrongfulness of an act of an international organization not in conformity with an international obligation of that organization is precluded if the author of the act in question has no other reasonable way, in a situation of distress, of saving the author's life or the lives of other persons entrusted to the author's care.

"2. Paragraph 1 does not apply if:

"(*a*) The situation of distress is due, either alone or in combination with other factors, to the conduct of the organization invoking it; or

"(*b*) The act in question is likely to create a comparable or greater peril."

[554] Draft article 22 reads as follows:

"*Article 22. Necessity*

"1. Necessity may not be invoked by an international organization as a ground for precluding the wrongfulness of an act not in conformity with an international obligation of that organization unless the act:

"(*a*) Is the only means for the organization to safeguard against a grave and imminent peril an essential interest that the organization has the function to protect; and

"(*b*) Does not seriously impair an essential interest of the State or States towards which the obligation exists, or of the international community as a whole.

"2. In any case, necessity may not be invoked by an international organization as a ground for precluding wrongfulness if:

"(*a*) The international obligation in question excludes the possibility of invoking necessity; or

"(*b*) The organization has contributed to the situation of necessity."

[555] Draft article 23 reads as follows:

"*Article 23. Compliance with peremptory norms*

"Nothing in this chapter precludes the wrongfulness of any act of an international organization which is not in conformity with an obligation arising under a peremptory norm of general international law."

[556] Draft article 24 reads as follows:

"*Article 24. Consequences of invoking a circumstance precluding wrongfulness*

"The invocation of a circumstance precluding wrongfulness in accordance with this chapter is without prejudice to:

"(*a*) Compliance with the obligation in question, if and to the extent that the circumstance precluding wrongfulness no longer exists;

"(*b*) The question of compensation for any material loss caused by the act in question."

[557] *Yearbook ... 2001*, vol. II (Part Two) and corrigendum, pp. 72–86.

[558] Draft article 25 reads as follows:

"*Article 25. Aid or assistance by a State in the commission of an internationally wrongful act by an international organization*

"A State which aids or assists an international organization in the commission of an internationally wrongful act by the latter is internationally responsible for doing so if:

"(*a*) That State does so with knowledge of the circumstances of the internationally wrongful act; and

"(*b*) The act would be internationally wrongful if committed by that State."

[559] Draft article 26 reads as follows:

"*Article 26. Direction and control exercised by a State over the commission of an internationally wrongful act by an international organization*

"A State which directs and controls an international organization in the commission of an internationally wrongful act by the latter is internationally responsible for that act if:

"(*a*) That State does so with knowledge of the circumstances of the internationally wrongful act; and

"(*b*) The act would be internationally wrongful if committed by that State."

[560] Draft article 27 reads as follows:

"*Article 27. Coercion of an international organization by a State*

"A State which coerces an international organization to commit an act is internationally responsible for that act if:

"(*a*) The act would, but for the coercion, be an internationally wrongful act of that international organization; and

"(*b*) That State does so with knowledge of the circumstances of the act."

[561] Draft article 28 reads as follows:

"*Article 28. Use by a State that is a member of an international organization of the separate personality of that organization*

"1. A State that is a member of an international organization incurs international responsibility if:

"(*a*) It avoids compliance with an international obligation relating to certain functions by transferring those functions to that organization; and

"(*b*) The organization commits an act that, if taken by that State, would have implied non-compliance with that obligation.

"2. Paragraph 1 applies whether or not the act in question is internationally wrongful for the international organization."

that is a member of an international organization for the internationally wrongful act of that organization).[562]

86. In presenting these articles, the Special Rapporteur stated that Chapter IV of Part One of the articles on responsibility of States for internationally wrongful acts deals with aid or assistance, direction or control and coercion by one State in the commission of the wrongful act by another State. That chapter does not address the question of such relationships between a State and an international organization. Draft articles 25 to 27 cover that gap and they largely correspond to draft articles 16 to 18 of responsibility of States for internationally wrongful acts.[563] Draft articles 28 and 29 are unique to this topic and have no equivalent in the articles on State responsibility.

87. The Commission considered the fourth report of the Special Rapporteur at its 2876th to 2879th and 2891st to 2895th meetings, from 16 to 19 May and from 11 to 14 and 18 July 2006 respectively. At its 2879th meeting, on 19 May 2006, and its 2895th meeting, on 18 July 2006, the Commission referred draft articles 17 to 24 and 25 to 29 to the Drafting Committee.

88. The Commission considered and adopted the report of the Drafting Committee on draft articles 17 to 24 at its 2884th meeting, on 8 June 2006, and draft articles 25 to 30 at its 2902nd meeting on 28 July 2006 (see section C.1 below).

89. At its 2910th meeting on 8 August 2006, the Commission adopted the commentaries to the aforementioned draft articles (see section C.2 below).

C. Text of the draft articles on responsibility of international organizations provisionally adopted so far by the Commission

1. Text of the draft articles

90. The text of the draft articles provisionally adopted so far by the Commission is reproduced below.

RESPONSIBILITY OF INTERNATIONAL ORGANIZATIONS

Part One

THE INTERNATIONALLY WRONGFUL ACT OF AN INTERNATIONAL ORGANIZATION

Chapter I

INTRODUCTION

Article 1.[564] *Scope of the present draft articles*

1. The present draft articles apply to the international responsibility of an international organization for an act that is wrongful under international law.

2. The present draft articles also apply to the international responsibility of a State for the internationally wrongful act of an international organization.

Article 2.[565] *Use of terms*

For the purposes of the present draft articles, the term "international organization" refers to an organization established by a treaty or other instrument governed by international law and possessing its own international legal personality. International organizations may include as members, in addition to States, other entities.

Article 3.[566] *General principles*

1. Every internationally wrongful act of an international organization entails the international responsibility of the international organization.

2. There is an internationally wrongful act of an international organization when conduct consisting of an action or omission:

(*a*) is attributable to the international organization under international law; and

(*b*) constitutes a breach of an international obligation of that international organization.

Chapter II[567]

ATTRIBUTION OF CONDUCT TO AN INTERNATIONAL ORGANIZATION

Article 4.[568] *General rule on attribution of conduct to an international organization*

1. The conduct of an organ or agent of an international organization in the performance of functions of that organ or agent shall be considered as an act of that organization under international law whatever position the organ or agent holds in respect of the organization.

2. For the purposes of paragraph 1, the term "agent" includes officials and other persons or entities through whom the organization acts.[569]

3. Rules of the organization shall apply to the determination of the functions of its organs and agents.

4. For the purpose of the present draft article, "rules of the organization" means, in particular: the constituent instruments; decisions, resolutions and other acts taken by the organization in accordance with those instruments; and established practice of the organization.[570]

Article 5.[571] *Conduct of organs or agents placed at the disposal of an international organization by a State or another international organization*

The conduct of an organ of a State or an organ or agent of an international organization that is placed at the disposal of another international organization shall be considered under international law an act of the latter organization if the organization exercises effective control over that conduct.

---

[562] Draft article 29 reads as follows:

"*Article 29. Responsibility of a State that is a member of an international organization for the internationally wrongful act of that organization*

"Except as provided in the preceding articles of this chapter, a State that is a member of an international organization is not responsible for an internationally wrongful act of that organization unless:

"(*a*) It has accepted with regard to the injured third party that it could be held responsible; or

"(*b*) It has led the injured third party to rely on its responsibility."

[563] *Yearbook ... 2001*, vol. II (Part Two) and corrigendum, pp. 65–70.

[564] For the commentary to this article, see *Yearbook ... 2003*, vol. II (Part Two), chapter IV, section C.2, para. 54.

[565] *Ibid.*

[566] *Ibid.*

[567] For the commentary to this chapter, see *Yearbook ... 2004*, vol. II (Part Two), chapter V, section C.2, para. 72.

[568] For the commentary to this article, see *ibid.*

[569] The location of paragraph 2 may be reconsidered at a later stage with a view to eventually placing all definitions of terms in article 2.

[570] The location of paragraph 4 may be reconsidered at a later stage with a view to eventually placing all definitions of terms in article 2.

[571] For the commentary to this article, see *Yearbook ... 2004*, vol. II (Part Two), chapter V, section C.2, para. 72.

Article 6.[572] *Excess of authority or contravention of instructions*

The conduct of an organ or an agent of an international organization shall be considered an act of that organization under international law if the organ or agent acts in that capacity, even though the conduct exceeds the authority of that organ or agent or contravenes instructions.

Article 7.[573] *Conduct acknowledged and adopted by an international organization as its own*

Conduct which is not attributable to an international organization under the preceding draft articles shall nevertheless be considered an act of that international organization under international law if and to the extent that the organization acknowledges and adopts the conduct in question as its own.

CHAPTER III[574]

BREACH OF AN INTERNATIONAL OBLIGATION

Article 8.[575] *Existence of a breach of an international obligation*

1. There is a breach of an international obligation by an international organization when an act of that international organization is not in conformity with what is required of it by that obligation, regardless of its origin and character.

2. Paragraph 1 also applies to the breach of an obligation under international law established by a rule of the international organization.

Article 9.[576] *International obligation in force for an international organization*

An act of an international organization does not constitute a breach of an international obligation unless the international organization is bound by the obligation in question at the time the act occurs.

Article 10.[577] *Extension in time of the breach of an international obligation*

1. The breach of an international obligation by an act of an international organization not having a continuing character occurs at the moment when the act is performed, even if its effects continue.

2. The breach of an international obligation by an act of an international organization having a continuing character extends over the entire period during which the act continues and remains not in conformity with the international obligation.

3. The breach of an international obligation requiring an international organization to prevent a given event occurs when the event occurs and extends over the entire period during which the event continues and remains not in conformity with that obligation.

Article 11.[578] *Breach consisting of a composite act*

1. The breach of an international obligation by an international organization through a series of actions and omissions defined in aggregate as wrongful, occurs when the action or omission occurs which, taken with the other actions or omissions, is sufficient to constitute the wrongful act.

2. In such a case, the breach extends over the entire period starting with the first of the actions or omissions of the series and lasts for as long as these actions or omissions are repeated and remain not in conformity with the international obligation.

CHAPTER IV[579]

RESPONSIBILITY OF AN INTERNATIONAL ORGANIZATION IN CONNECTION WITH THE ACT OF A STATE OR ANOTHER INTERNATIONAL ORGANIZATION

Article 12.[580] *Aid or assistance in the commission of an internationally wrongful act*

An international organization which aids or assists a State or another international organization in the commission of an internationally wrongful act by the State or the latter organization is internationally responsible for doing so if:

(*a*) that organization does so with knowledge of the circumstances of the internationally wrongful act; and

(*b*) the act would be internationally wrongful if committed by that organization.

Article 13.[581] *Direction and control exercised over the commission of an internationally wrongful act*

An international organization which directs and controls a State or another international organization in the commission of an internationally wrongful act by the State or the latter organization is internationally responsible for that act if:

(*a*) that organization does so with knowledge of the circumstances of the internationally wrongful act; and

(*b*) the act would be internationally wrongful if committed by that organization.

Article 14.[582] *Coercion of a State or another international organization*

An international organization which coerces a State or another international organization to commit an act is internationally responsible for that act if:

(*a*) the act would, but for the coercion, be an internationally wrongful act of the coerced State or international organization; and

(*b*) the coercing international organization does so with knowledge of the circumstances of the act.

Article 15 [16].[583] *Decisions, recommendations and authorizations addressed to member States and international organizations*

1. An international organization incurs international responsibility if it adopts a decision binding a member State or international organization to commit an act that would be internationally wrongful if committed by the former organization and would circumvent an international obligation of the former organization.

2. An international organization incurs international responsibility if:

(*a*) it authorizes a member State or international organization to commit an act that would be internationally wrongful if committed by the former organization and would circumvent an international obligation of the former organization, or recommends that a member State or international organization commit such an act; and

(*b*) that State or international organization commits the act in question in reliance on that authorization or recommendation.

3. Paragraphs 1 and 2 apply whether or not the act in question is internationally wrongful for the member State or international organization to which the decision, authorization or recommendation is directed.

---

[572] *Ibid.*

[573] *Ibid.*

[574] For the commentary to this chapter, see *Yearbook ... 2005,* vol. II (Part Two), chapter VI, section C.2, para. 206.

[575] For the commentary to this article, see *ibid.*

[576] *Ibid.*

[577] *Ibid.*

[578] *Ibid.*

[579] For the commentary to this chapter, see *ibid.*

[580] For the commentary to this article, see *ibid.*

[581] *Ibid.*

[582] *Ibid.*

[583] *Ibid.* The square bracket refers to the corresponding article in the third report of the Special Rapporteur, *Yearbook ... 2005*, vol. II (Part One), document A/CN.4/553.

Article 16 [15].[584] *Effect of this chapter*

This chapter is without prejudice to the international responsibility of the State or international organization which commits the act in question, or of any other State or international organization.

Chapter V[585]

CIRCUMSTANCES PRECLUDING WRONGFULNESS

Article 17.[586] *Consent*

Valid consent by a State or an international organization to the commission of a given act by another international organization precludes the wrongfulness of that act in relation to that State or the former organization to the extent that the act remains within the limits of that consent.

Article 18.[587] *Self-defence*

The wrongfulness of an act of an international organization is precluded if the act constitutes a lawful measure of self-defence taken in conformity with the principles of international law embodied in the Charter of the United Nations.

Article 19.[588] *Countermeasures*

...*[589]

Article 20.[590] Force majeure

1. The wrongfulness of an act of an international organization not in conformity with an international obligation of that organization is precluded if the act is due to *force majeure*, that is, the occurrence of an irresistible force or of an unforeseen event, beyond the control of the organization, making it materially impossible in the circumstances to perform the obligation.

2. Paragraph 1 does not apply if:

(*a*) the situation of *force majeure* is due, either alone or in combination with other factors, to the conduct of the organization invoking it; or

(*b*) the organization has assumed the risk of that situation occurring.

Article 21.[591] *Distress*

1. The wrongfulness of an act of an international organization not in conformity with an international obligation of that organization is precluded if the author of the act in question has no other reasonable way, in a situation of distress, of saving the author's life or the lives of other persons entrusted to the author's care.

2. Paragraph 1 does not apply if:

(*a*) the situation of distress is due, either alone or in combination with other factors, to the conduct of the organization invoking it; or

(*b*) the act in question is likely to create a comparable or greater peril.

Article 22.[592] *Necessity*

1. Necessity may not be invoked by an international organization as a ground for precluding the wrongfulness of an act not in conformity with an international obligation of that organization unless the act:

(*a*) is the only means for the organization to safeguard against a grave and imminent peril an essential interest of the international community as a whole when the organization has, in accordance with international law, the function to protect that interest; and

(*b*) does not seriously impair an essential interest of the State or States towards which the obligation exists, or of the international community as a whole.

2. In any case, necessity may not be invoked by an international organization as a ground for precluding wrongfulness if:

(*a*) the international obligation in question excludes the possibility of invoking necessity; or

(*b*) the organization has contributed to the situation of necessity.

Article 23.[593] *Compliance with peremptory norms*

Nothing in this chapter precludes the wrongfulness of any act of an international organization which is not in conformity with an obligation arising under a peremptory norm of general international law.

Article 24.[594] *Consequences of invoking a circumstance precluding wrongfulness*

The invocation of a circumstance precluding wrongfulness in accordance with this chapter is without prejudice to:

(*a*) compliance with the obligation in question, if and to the extent that the circumstance precluding wrongfulness no longer exists;

(*b*) the question of compensation for any material loss caused by the act in question.

Chapter (x)[595]

RESPONSIBILITY OF A STATE IN CONNECTION WITH THE ACT OF AN INTERNATIONAL ORGANIZATION

Article 25.[596] *Aid or assistance by a State in the commission of an internationally wrongful act by an international organization*

A State which aids or assists an international organization in the commission of an internationally wrongful act by the latter is internationally responsible for doing so if:

(*a*) that State does so with knowledge of the circumstances of the internationally wrongful act; and

(*b*) the act would be internationally wrongful if committed by that State.

Article 26.[597] *Direction and control exercised by a State over the commission of an internationally wrongful act by an international organization*

A State which directs and controls an international organization in the commission of an internationally wrongful act by the latter is internationally responsible for that act if:

(*a*) that State does so with knowledge of the circumstances of the internationally wrongful act; and

---

[584] For the commentary, see *ibid.*

[585] For the commentary to this chapter, see section C.2 below.

[586] For the commentary to this article, see section C.2 below.

[587] *Ibid.*

[588] *Ibid.*

[589] Draft article 19 concerns countermeasures by an international organization in respect of an internationally wrongful act of another international organization or a State as circumstances precluding wrongfulness. The text of this draft article will be drafted at a later stage, when the issues relating to countermeasures by an international organization are examined in the context of the implementation of the responsibility of an international organization.

[590] For the commentary to this article, see section C.2 below.

[591] *Ibid.*

[592] *Ibid.*

[593] *Ibid.*

[594] *Ibid.*

[595] The location of this chapter will be determined at a later stage.

[596] For the commentary to this article, see section C.2 below.

[597] *Ibid.*

(*b*) the act would be internationally wrongful if committed by that State.

Article 27.[598] *Coercion of an international organization by a State*

A State which coerces an international organization to commit an act is internationally responsible for that act if:

(*a*) the act would, but for the coercion, be an internationally wrongful act of that international organization; and

(*b*) that State does so with knowledge of the circumstances of the act.

Article 28.[599] *International responsibility in case of provision of competence to an international organization*

1. A State member of an international organization incurs international responsibility if it circumvents one of its international obligations by providing the organization with competence in relation to that obligation, and the organization commits an act that, if committed by that State, would have constituted a breach of that obligation.

2. Paragraph 1 applies whether or not the act in question is internationally wrongful for the international organization.

Article 29.[600] *Responsibility of a State member of an international organization for the internationally wrongful act of that organization*

1. Without prejudice to draft articles 25 to 28, a State member of an international organization is responsible for an internationally wrongful act of that organization if:

(*a*) it has accepted responsibility for that act; or

(*b*) it has led the injured party to rely on its responsibility.

2. The international responsibility of a State which is entailed in accordance with paragraph 1 is presumed to be subsidiary.

Article 30.[601] *Effect of this chapter*

This chapter is without prejudice to the international responsibility, under other provisions of these draft articles, of the international organization which commits the act in question, or of any other international organization.

2. Text of the draft articles with commentaries thereto adopted by the Commission at its fifty-eighth session

91. The text of the draft articles together with commentaries thereto provisionally adopted by the Commission at its fifty-eighth session is produced below.

Chapter V

CIRCUMSTANCES PRECLUDING WRONGFULNESS

General commentary

(1) Under the heading "Circumstances precluding wrongfulness", draft articles 20 to 27 on responsibility of States for internationally wrongful acts[602] consider a series of circumstances that are different in nature but are brought together by their common effect. This is to preclude wrongfulness of conduct that would otherwise be in breach of an international obligation. As the commentary to the introduction to the relevant chapter explains,[603] these circumstances apply to any internationally wrongful act, whatever the source of the obligation; they do not annul or terminate the obligation, but provide a justification or excuse for non-performance.

(2) Also with regard to circumstances precluding wrongfulness, available practice relating to international organizations is limited. Moreover, certain circumstances are unlikely to occur in relation to some, or even most, international organizations. However, there would be little reason for holding that circumstances precluding wrongfulness of conduct of States could not be relevant also for international organizations: that, for instance, only States could invoke *force majeure*. This does not imply that there should be a presumption that conditions under which an organization may invoke a certain circumstance precluding wrongfulness are the same as those applicable to States.

Article 17. Consent

Valid consent by a State or an international organization to the commission of a given act by another international organization precludes the wrongfulness of that act in relation to that State or the former organization to the extent that the act remains within the limits of that consent.

Commentary

(1) This text corresponds to draft article 20 on responsibility of States for internationally wrongful acts.[604] As the commentary explains,[605] this article "reflects the basic international law principle of consent". It concerns "consent in relation to a particular situation or a particular course of conduct", as distinguished from "consent in relation to the underlying obligation itself".[606]

(2) Like States, international organizations perform several functions which would give rise to international responsibility were they not consented to by a State or another international organization. What is generally relevant is consent by the State on whose territory the organization's conduct takes place. Also with regard to international organizations, consent could affect the underlying obligation, or concern only a particular situation or a particular course of conduct.

(3) As an example of consent that renders a specific conduct on the part of an international organization lawful, one could give that of a State allowing an investigation to be carried out on its territory by a commission of inquiry set up by the United Nations Security Council.[607]

---

598 *Ibid.*

599 *Ibid.*

600 *Ibid.*

601 *Ibid.*

602 *Yearbook ... 2001*, vol. II (Part Two) and corrigendum, pp. 72–86.

603 *Ibid.*, p. 71, para. (2).

604 *Ibid.*, p. 72. See also the related commentary, pp. 72–74.

605 *Ibid.*, p. 72, para. (1).

606 *Ibid.*, pp. 72–73, para. (2) of the commentary.

607 For the requirement of consent, see para. 6 of the Declaration on Fact-finding by the United Nations in the Field of the Maintenance of International Peace and Security annexed to General Assembly resolution 46/59 of 9 December 1991.

Another example is consent by a State to the verification of the electoral process by an international organization.[608] A further, and specific, example is consent to the deployment of the Aceh Monitoring Mission in Indonesia, following an invitation addressed in July 2005 by the Government of Indonesia to the European Union and seven contributing States.[609]

(4) Consent dispensing with the performance of an obligation in a particular case must be "valid". This term refers to matters "addressed by international law rules outside the framework of State responsibility",[610] such as whether the agent or person who gave the consent was authorized to do so on behalf of the State or international organization, or whether the consent was vitiated by coercion or some other factor. The requirement that consent does not affect compliance with peremptory norms is stated in draft article 23. This is a general provision covering all the circumstances precluding wrongfulness.

(5) Draft article 17 is based on article 20 on of the draft articles on responsibility of States for internationally wrongful acts. The only textual changes consist in the addition of a reference to an "international organization" with regard to the entity giving consent and the replacement of the term "State" with "international organization" with regard to the entity to which consent is given.

Article 18. Self-defence

The wrongfulness of an act of an international organization is precluded if the act constitutes a lawful measure of self-defence taken in conformity with the principles of international law embodied in the Charter of the United Nations.

Commentary

(1) According to the commentary to the corresponding article (article 21) of the draft articles on responsibility of States for internationally wrongful acts, that article considers "self-defence as an exception to the prohibition against the use of force".[611] The reference in that article to the "lawful" character of the measure of self-defence is explained as follows:

> the term "lawful" implies that the action taken respects those obligations of total restraint applicable in international armed conflict, as well as compliance with the requirements of proportionality and of necessity inherent in the notion of self-defence. Article 21 simply reflects the basic principle for the purposes of chapter V, leaving questions of the extent and application of self-defence to the applicable primary rules referred to in the Charter.[612]

(2) For reasons of coherency, the concept of self-defence which has thus been elaborated with regard to States should be used also with regard to international organizations, although it is likely to be relevant only for a small number of organizations, such as those administering a territory or deploying an armed force.

(3) In the practice relating to United Nations forces, the term "self-defence" has often been used in a wider sense, with regard to situations other than those contemplated in Article 51 of the Charter of the United Nations. References to "self-defence" have been made also in relation to the "defence of the mission".[613] For instance, in relation to the United Nations Protection Force (UNPROFOR), a memorandum of the Legal Bureau of the Canadian Department of Foreign Affairs and International Trade held that "'[s]elf defence' could very well include the defence of the safe areas and the civilian population in those areas."[614] While these references to "self-defence" confirm that self-defence represents a circumstance precluding wrongfulness of conduct by an international organization, the term is given a meaning that encompasses cases which go well beyond those in which a State or an international organization responds to an armed attack by a State. In any event, the question of the extent to which United Nations forces are entitled to resort to force depends on the primary rules concerning the scope of the mission and need not be discussed here.

(4) Also, the conditions under which an international organization may resort to force in response to an armed attack by a State pertain to the primary rules and need not be examined in the present context. One of those questions relates to the invocability of collective self-defence on the part of an international organization when one of its member States has become the object of an armed attack and the international organization is given the power to act in collective self-defence.[615]

(5) With regard to article 21 of the draft articles on responsibility of States for internationally wrongful acts concerning self-defence, what is required in the present context is only to state that measures of self-defence should be regarded as lawful. In view of the fact that international organizations are not members of the United Nations, the reference to the Charter of the United Nations has been replaced here with that to "principles of international law embodied in the Charter of the United Nations". This wording already appears, for similar reasons, in article 52 of the Vienna Convention on the Law of Treaties (hereinafter "1969 Vienna Convention"), concerning invalidity of treaties because of coercion, and in the corresponding article of the Vienna Convention on the

[608] With regard to the role of consent in relation to the function of verifying an electoral process, see the report of the Secretary-General on enhancing the effectiveness of the principle of periodic and genuine elections (A/49/675), para. 16.

[609] A reference to the invitation by the Government of Indonesia may be found in the preambular paragraph of the European Union Council Joint Action 2005/643/CFSP of 9 September 2005, *Official Journal of the European Union*, No. L 234, 10 September 2005, p. 13.

[610] *Yearbook ... 2001*, vol. II (Part Two) and corrigendum, p. 73 (para. (4) of the commentary to article 20 of the draft articles on responsibility of States for internationally wrongful acts).

[611] *Ibid.*, p. 74, para. (1).

[612] *Ibid.*, p. 75, para. (6) of the commentary to article 21.

[613] As was noted by the High-Level Panel on Threats, Challenges and Change, "the right to use force in self-defence ... is widely understood to extend to the 'defence of the mission'" (report of the High-level Panel on Threats, Challenges and Change, *A More Secure World: Our Shared Responsibility*, document A/59/565 and Corr.1, para. 213).

[614] *The Canadian Yearbook of International Law*, vol. 34 (1996), p. 389.

[615] A positive answer is implied in article 25 (*a*) of the Protocol relating to the Mechanism for Conflict Prevention, Management, Resolution, Peace-keeping and Security, adopted on 10 December 1999 by the member States of ECOWAS, which provides for the application of the "Mechanism" "in cases of aggression or conflict in any Member State or threat thereof".

Law of Treaties between States and International Organizations or between International Organizations (hereinafter "1986 Vienna Convention"). The only other change with regard to the text of article 21 of the draft articles on responsibility of States for internationally wrongful acts concerns the replacement of the term "State" with "international organization".

Article 19. *Countermeasures*

...[616]

Article 20. Force majeure

1. The wrongfulness of an act of an international organization not in conformity with an international obligation of that organization is precluded if the act is due to *force majeure*, that is, the occurrence of an irresistible force or of an unforeseen event, beyond the control of the organization, making it materially impossible in the circumstances to perform the obligation.

2. Paragraph 1 does not apply if:

(*a*) the situation of *force majeure* is due, either alone or in combination with other factors, to the conduct of the organization invoking it; or

(*b*) the organization has assumed the risk of that situation occurring.

Commentary

(1) With regard to States, *force majeure* had been defined in article 23 of the draft articles on responsibility of States for internationally wrongful acts as "an irresistible force or ... an unforeseen event ... beyond the control of the State ... which makes it materially impossible in the circumstances to perform the obligation".[617] This circumstance precluding wrongfulness does not apply when the situation is due to the conduct of the State invoking it or the State has assumed the risk of that situation occurring.

(2) There is nothing in the differences between States and international organizations that would justify the conclusion that *force majeure* is not equally relevant for international organizations or that other conditions should apply.

(3) One may find a few instances of practice concerning *force majeure*. Certain agreements concluded by international organizations provide examples to that effect. For instance, article XII, paragraph 6, of the Executing Agency Agreement of 1992 between the United Nations Development Programme (UNDP) and the World Health Organization (WHO) stated that:

> [i]n the event of *force majeure* or other similar conditions or events which prevent the successful execution of a Project by the Executing Agency, the Executing Agency shall promptly notify the UNDP of such occurrence and may, in consultation with the UNDP, withdraw from execution of the Project. In case of such withdrawal, and unless the Parties agree otherwise, the Executing Agency shall be reimbursed the actual costs incurred up to the effective date of the withdrawal.[618]

Although this paragraph concerns withdrawal from the Agreement, it implicitly considers that non-compliance with an obligation under the Agreement because of *force majeure* does not constitute a breach of the Agreement.

(4) *Force majeure* has been invoked by international organizations in order to exclude wrongfulness of conduct in proceedings before international administrative tribunals.[619] In Judgement No. 24, *Fernando Hernández de Agüero* v. *Secretary General of the Organization of American States*, the Administrative Tribunal of the Organization of American States rejected the plea of *force majeure*, which had been made in order to justify termination of an official's contract:

> The Tribunal considers that in the present case there is no *force majeure* that would have made it impossible for the General Secretariat to fulfill the fixed-term contract, since it is much-explored law that by *force majeure* is meant an irresistible happening of nature.[620]

Although the Tribunal rejected the plea, it clearly recognized the invocability of *force majeure*.

(5) A similar approach was taken by the Administrative Tribunal of the International Labour Organization (ILO) in its Judgment No. 664, in the *Barthl* case. The Tribunal found that *force majeure* was relevant to an employment contract and said: "*Force majeure* is an unforeseeable occurrence, beyond the control and independent of the will of the parties, which unavoidably frustrates their common intent".[621] It is immaterial that in the case at hand *force majeure* had been invoked by the employee against the international organization instead of by the organization.

(6) The text of draft article 20 differs from that of article 23 of the draft articles on responsibility of States for

---

[616] See footnote 589 above.

[617] *Yearbook ... 2001* , vol. II (Part Two) and corrigendum, p. 76. See also the related commentary, at pp. 76–78.

[618] Signed at New York on 17 September 1992 and at Geneva on 19 October 1992, United Nations, *Treaty Series*, vol. 1691, No. 1066, p. 325, at p. 331.

[619] These cases related to the application of the rules of the organization concerned. The question whether those rules pertain to international law has been discussed in the commentary to draft article 8 (*Yearbook ... 2005*, vol. II (Part Two), pp. 42–43, para. 206).

[620] *Fernando Hernández de Agüero* v. *Secretary General of the Organization of American States, Judgment No. 24 of 16 November 1976*, para. 3 (OAS, *Sentencias del Tribunal Administrativo, Nos. 1–56 (1971–1980)*, p. 282). The text is also available at http://www.oas.org (decisions of the Administrative Tribunal). In a letter to the United Nations Legal Counsel dated 8 January 2003, the OAS noted that:

"The majority of claims presented to the OAS Administrative Tribunal allege violations of the OAS General Standards, other resolutions of the OAS General Assembly, violations of rules promulgated by the Secretary General pursuant to his authority under the OAS Charter, and violations of rules established by the Tribunal itself in its jurisprudence. Those standards and rules, having been adopted by duly constituted international authorities, all constitute international law. Thus, the complaints claiming violations of those norms and rules may be characterized as alleging violations of international law (comments and observations received from international organizations on responsibility of international organizations, *Yearbook ... 2004*, vol. II (Part One), document A/CN.4/545, under the heading "Practice regarding claims filed against an international organization for violations of international law. Organization of American States").

[621] *Barthl* case, judgement of 19 June 1985, para. 3. The Registry's translation from the original French is available at www.ilo.org /public /english/tribunal (decisions of the Administrative Tribunal).

internationally wrongful acts only because the term “State” has been replaced once with the term “international organization” and four times with the term “organization”.

Article 21. Distress

1. The wrongfulness of an act of an international organization not in conformity with an international obligation of that organization is precluded if the author of the act in question has no other reasonable way, in a situation of distress, of saving the author’s life or the lives of other persons entrusted to the author’s care.

2. Paragraph 1 does not apply if:

(*a*) the situation of distress is due, either alone or in combination with other factors, to the conduct of the organization invoking it; or

(*b*) the act in question is likely to create a comparable or greater peril.

Commentary

(1) Article 24 of the draft articles on responsibility of States for internationally wrongful acts includes distress among the circumstances precluding wrongfulness of an act and describes this circumstance as the case in which “the author of the act in question has no other reasonable way, in a situation of distress, of saving the author’s life or the lives of other persons entrusted to the author’s care”.[622] The commentary gives the example from practice of a British military ship entering Icelandic territorial waters for seeking shelter during a heavy storm,[623] and notes that, “[a]lthough historically practice has focused on cases involving ships and aircraft, article 24 is not limited to such cases”.[624]

(2) Similar situations could occur, though more rarely, with regard to an organ or agent of an international organization. Notwithstanding the absence of known cases of practice in which an international organization invoked distress, the same rule should apply both to States and to international organizations.

(3) As with regard to States, the line between cases of distress and those which may be considered as pertaining to necessity[625] is not always obvious. The commentary to article 24 of the draft articles on responsibility of States for internationally wrongful acts notes that “general cases of emergencies ... are more a matter of necessity than distress”.[626]

(4) Article 24 of the draft articles on responsibility of States for internationally wrongful acts only applies when the situation of distress is not due to the conduct of the State invoking distress and the act in question is not likely to create a comparable greater peril. These conditions appear to be equally applicable to international organizations.

[622] *Yearbook ... 2001*, vol. II (Part Two) and corrigendum, p. 78.

[623] *Ibid.*, p. 79, para. (3).

[624] *Ibid.*, para. (4).

[625] Necessity is considered in the following draft article.

[626] *Yearbook ... 2001*, vol. II (Part Two) and corrigendum, p. 80, para. (7).

(5) Draft article 21 is textually identical to the corresponding article on State responsibility, with the only changes due to the replacement of the term “State” once with the term “international organization” and twice with the term “organization”.

Article 22. Necessity

1. Necessity may not be invoked by an international organization as a ground for precluding the wrongfulness of an act not in conformity with an international obligation of that organization unless the act:

(*a*) is the only means for the organization to safeguard against a grave and imminent peril an essential interest of the international community as a whole when the organization has, in accordance with international law, the function to protect that interest; and

(*b*) does not seriously impair an essential interest of the State or States towards which the obligation exists, or of the international community as a whole.

2. In any case, necessity may not be invoked by an international organization as a ground for precluding wrongfulness if:

(*a*) the international obligation in question excludes the possibility of invoking necessity; or

(*b*) the organization has contributed to the situation of necessity.

Commentary

(1) Conditions for the invocability of necessity by States have been listed in article 25 of the draft articles on responsibility of States for internationally wrongful acts.[627] In brief, the relevant conditions are as follows: the State’s conduct should be the only means to safeguard an essential interest against a grave and imminent peril; the conduct in question should not impair an essential interest of the State or the States towards which the obligation exists, or of the international community as a whole; the international obligation in question does not exclude the possibility of invoking necessity; the State invoking necessity has not contributed to the situation of necessity.

(2) With regard to international organizations, practice reflecting the invocation of necessity is scarce. One case in which necessity was held to be invocable is Judgement No. 2183 of the ILO Administrative Tribunal in the *T. D.-N.* v. *CERN* case. This case concerned access to the electronic account of an employee who was on leave. The Tribunal said that:

> in the event that access to an e-mail account becomes necessary for reasons of urgency or because of the prolonged absence of the account holder, it must be possible for organizations to open the account using appropriate technical safeguards. That state of necessity, justifying access to data which may be confidential, must be assessed with the utmost care.[628]

[627] *Ibid.* See also the related commentary, pp. 80–84.

[628] *T. D.-N.* v. *CERN*, Judgement of 3 February 2003, para. 19. The Registry’s translation from the original French is available at www.ilo.org (decisions of the Administrative Tribunal).

(3) Even if practice is scarce, as was noted by INTERPOL: "necessity does not pertain to those areas of international law that, by their very nature, are patently inapplicable to international organizations".[629] The invocability of necessity by international organizations was also advocated in written statements by the Commission of the European Union,[630] the International Monetary Fund,[631] the World Intellectual Property Organization[632] and the World Bank.[633]

(4) While the conditions set by article 25 of the draft articles on responsibility of States for internationally wrongful acts are applicable also with regard to international organizations, the scarcity of specific practice and the considerable risk that invocability of necessity entails for compliance with international obligations suggest that, as a matter of policy, necessity should not be invocable by international organizations as widely as by States. This could be achieved by limiting the essential interests which may be protected by the invocation of necessity to those of the international community as a whole, to the extent that the organization has, in accordance with international law, the function to protect them. This solution may be regarded as an attempt to reach a compromise between two opposite positions with regard to necessity which appeared in the debates in the Sixth Committee[634] and also in the Commission: the view of those who favour placing international organizations on the same level as States, and the opinion of those who would totally rule out the invocability of necessity by international organizations. According to some members of the Commission, although subparagraph (1) (*a*) only refers to the interests of the international community as a whole, an organization should nevertheless be entitled to invoke necessity for protecting an essential interest of its member States.

[629] Letter dated 9 February 2005 from the General Counsel of INTERPOL to the Secretary of the International Law Commission (see the comments and observations received from international organizations on responsibility of international organizations, *Yearbook ... 2005*, vol. II (Part One), document A/CN.4/556 (under the heading "Necessity as a circumstance to preclude wrongfulness")).

[630] Letter dated 18 March 2005 from the European Commission to the Legal Counsel of the United Nations (*ibid.*).

[631] Letter dated 1 April 2005 from the International Monetary Fund to the Legal Counsel of the United Nations (*ibid.*).

[632] Letter dated 19 January 2005 from the Legal Counsel of the World Intellectual Property Organization to the Legal Counsel of the United Nations (*ibid.*).

[633] Letter dated 31 January 2006 from the Senior Vice President and General Counsel of the World Bank to the Secretary of the International Law Commission (see the comments and observations received from international organizations on responsibility of international organizations, *Yearbook ... 2006*, vol. II (Part One), document A/CN.4/568 and Add.1 (under the heading "Circumstances precluding wrongfulness—necessity. World Bank")).

[634] Statements clearly in favour of the invocability of necessity by international organizations were made by France, *Official Records of the General Assembly, Fifty-ninth Session, Sixth Committee, Summary record of the 22nd meeting* (A/C.6/59/SR.22), para. 12; Austria, *ibid.*, para. 23; Denmark, speaking also on behalf of Finland, Iceland, Norway and Sweden, *ibid.*, para. 65; Belgium, *ibid.*, para. 76; the Russian Federation, *ibid., 23rd meeting* (A/C.6/59/SR.23), para. 23; and Cuba, *ibid.*, para. 25. A tentatively favourable position was taken also by Spain, *ibid., 22nd meeting* (A/C.6/59/SR.22), para. 49. The contrary view was expressed in statements by Germany, *ibid., 21st meeting* (A/C.6/59/SR.21), para. 22; China, *ibid.*, para. 42; Poland, *ibid., 22nd meeting* (A/C.6/59/SR.22), para. 2; Belarus, *ibid.*, para. 45; and Greece, *ibid., 23rd meeting* (A/C.6/59/SR.23), para. 43. Tentatively negative positions were taken by Singapore, *ibid., 22nd meeting* (A/C.6/59/SR.22), para. 57; and New Zealand, *ibid., 23rd meeting* (A/C.6/59/SR.23), para. 10.

(5) There is no contradiction between the reference in subparagraph (1) (*a*) to the protection of an essential interest of the international community and the condition in subparagraph (1) (*b*) that the conduct in question should not impair an essential interest of the international community. The interests in question are not necessarily the same.

(6) In view of the solution adopted for subparagraph (1) (*a*), which does not allow the invocation of necessity for the protection of the essential interests of an international organization unless they coincide with those of the international community, the essential interests of international organizations have not been added in subparagraph (1) (*b*) to those that should not be seriously impaired.

(7) Apart from the change in subparagraph (1) (*a*), the text reproduces article 25 of the draft articles on responsibility of States for internationally wrongful acts, with the replacement of the term "State" with the terms "international organization" or "organization" in the *chapeau* of both paragraphs.

Article 23. Compliance with peremptory norms

Nothing in this chapter precludes the wrongfulness of any act of an international organization which is not in conformity with an obligation arising under a peremptory norm of general international law.

Commentary

(1) Chapter V of Part One of the draft articles on responsibility of States for internationally wrongful acts contains a "without prejudice" provision which applies to all the circumstances precluding wrongfulness considered in that chapter. The purpose of this provision—article 26—is to state that an act, which would otherwise not be considered wrongful, would be so held if it was "not in conformity with an obligation arising under a peremptory norm of general international law".[635]

(2) The commentary to article 26 of the draft articles on responsibility of States for internationally wrongful acts, provides that "peremptory norms that are clearly accepted and recognized include the prohibitions of aggression, genocide, slavery, racial discrimination, crimes against humanity and torture, and the right to self-determination".[636] In its judgment in the *Armed Activities on the Territory of the Congo* case, the ICJ found that the prohibition of genocide "assuredly" was a peremptory norm.[637]

(3) Since peremptory norms also bind international organizations, it is clear that, like States, international organizations could not invoke a circumstance precluding wrongfulness in the case of non-compliance with an obligation arising under a peremptory norm. Thus, there is the need for a "without prejudice" provision matching the one applicable to States.

[635] *Yearbook ... 2001* , vol. II (Part Two) and corrigendum, p. 85. See also the related commentary, pp. 84–85.

[636] *Ibid.*, p. 85, para. (5).

[637] *Armed Activities on the Territory of the Congo (New Application: 2002) (Democratic Republic of the Congo* v. *Rwanda), Jurisdiction and Admissibility, Judgment, I.C.J. Reports 2006*, p. 6, at p. 32, para. 64. The text of the judgment is also available at www.icj-cij.org.

(4) The present article reproduces the text of article 26 of the draft articles on responsibility of States for internationally wrongful acts with the only replacement of the term "State" with "international organization".

Article 24. Consequences of invoking a circumstance precluding wrongfulness

The invocation of a circumstance precluding wrongfulness in accordance with this chapter is without prejudice to:

(*a*) compliance with the obligation in question, if and to the extent that the circumstance precluding wrongfulness no longer exists;

(*b*) the question of compensation for any material loss caused by the act in question.

Commentary

(1) Article 27 of the draft articles on responsibility of States for internationally wrongful acts makes two points.[638] The first point is that a circumstance precludes wrongfulness only if and to the extent that the circumstance exists. While the wording appears to emphasize the element of time,[639] it is clear that a circumstance may preclude wrongfulness only insofar as it covers a particular situation. Beyond the reach of the circumstance, wrongfulness of the act is not affected.

(2) The second point is that the question of compensation is left unprejudiced. It would be difficult to set a general rule concerning compensation for losses caused by an act that would be wrongful, but for the presence of a certain circumstance.

(3) Since the position of international organizations does not differ from that of States with regard to both matters covered by article 27 of the draft articles on responsibility of States for internationally wrongful acts, and no change in the wording is required in the present context, draft article 24 is identical to the corresponding draft article on responsibility of States for internationally wrongful acts.

CHAPTER (X)[640]

RESPONSIBILITY OF A STATE IN CONNECTION WITH THE ACT OF AN INTERNATIONAL ORGANIZATION

General commentary

(1) In accordance with draft article 1, paragraph 2[641] of these draft articles (above), the present chapter is intended to fill a gap that was deliberately left in the articles on responsibility of States for internationally wrongful acts. As stated in article 57 of the draft articles on responsibility of States for internationally wrongful acts, these articles are "without prejudice to any question of the responsibility of … any State for the conduct of an international organization".[642]

(2) Not all the questions that may affect the responsibility of a State in connection with the act of an international organization are examined in the present draft articles. For instance, questions relating to attribution of conduct to a State are covered only in the draft articles on responsibility of States for internationally wrongful acts. Thus, if an issue arises as to whether certain conduct is to be attributed to a State or to an international organization or to both, the present draft articles will provide criteria for ascertaining whether conduct is to be attributed to the international organization, while the draft articles on State responsibility for internationally wrongful acts will regulate attribution of conduct to the State.

(3) The present chapter assumes that there exists conduct attributable to an international organization. In most cases, it also assumes that that conduct is internationally wrongful. However, exceptions are provided for the cases envisaged in draft articles 27 and 28, which deal respectively with coercion of an international organization by a State and with international responsibility in case of provision of competence to an international organization.

(4) According to draft articles 28 and 29, the State that incurs responsibility in connection with the act of an international organization is necessarily a member of that organization. In the cases envisaged in draft articles 25, 26 and 27, the responsible State may or may not be a member.

(5) The present chapter does not address the question of responsibility that may arise for entities other than States that are also members of an international organization. Chapter IV of Part One of the present draft already considers the responsibility that an international organization may incur when it aids or assists or directs and controls in the commission of an internationally wrongful act of another international organization of which the former organization is a member. The same chapter also deals with coercion by an international organization that is a member of the coerced organization. Following draft articles 28 and 29, which consider further cases of responsibility of States as members of an international organization, additional provisions would have to be introduced in Chapter IV in order to deal with parallel situations concerning international organizations as members of other international organizations. Questions relating to the responsibility of entities, other than States or international organizations, that are also members of international organizations fall beyond the scope of the present draft.

(6) The position of the present chapter within the structure of the draft still needs to be determined. For this reason the chapter is provisionally called "Chapter (x)". Should the current position be retained, it could constitute a separate part or the final chapter of Part One. In the latter case, Part One would have to be given a more appropriate heading.

---

[638] *Yearbook ... 2001*, vol. II (Part Two) and corrigendum, p. 85. See also the related commentary, pp. 85–86.

[639] This temporal element may have been emphasized because the ICJ had said in the *Gabčíkovo–Nagymaros Project* case (see footnote 363 above) that "[a]s soon as the state of necessity ceases to exist, the duty to comply with treaty obligations revives" (p. 63, para. 101).

[640] The location of the chapter will be determined at a later stage.

[641] See the commentary to this article adopted by the Commission at its fifty-fifth session in *Yearbook ... 2003*, vol. II (Part Two), pp. 18–19.

[642] *Yearbook ... 2001*, vol. II (Part Two) and corrigendum, p. 141.

Article 25. Aid or assistance by a State in the commission of an internationally wrongful act by an international organization

A State which aids or assists an international organization in the commission of an internationally wrongful act by the latter is internationally responsible for doing so if:

(*a*) that State does so with knowledge of the circumstances of the internationally wrongful act; and

(*b*) the act would be internationally wrongful if committed by that State.

Commentary

(1) Draft article 25 addresses a situation parallel to the one covered in draft article 12 (above), which concerns aid or assistance by an international organization in the commission of an internationally wrongful act by another international organization.[643] Both draft articles closely follow the text of draft article 16 on responsibility of States for internationally wrongful acts.[644]

(2) A State aiding or assisting an international organization in the commission of an internationally wrongful act may or may not be a member of that organization. Should the State be a member, the influence that may amount to aid or assistance could not simply consist in participation in the decision-making process of the organization according to the pertinent rules of the organization. However, it cannot be totally ruled out that aid or assistance could result from conduct taken by the State within the framework of the organization. This could entail some difficulties in ascertaining whether aid or assistance has taken place in borderline cases. The factual context such as the size of membership and the nature of the involvement will probably be decisive.

(3) Aid or assistance by a State could constitute a breach of an obligation that the State has acquired under a primary norm. For example, a nuclear State party to the Treaty on the Non-Proliferation of Nuclear Weapons would have to refrain from assisting a non-nuclear State in the acquisition of nuclear weapons, and the same would seem to apply to assistance given to an international organization of which some non-nuclear States are members. In that case, international responsibility that may arise for the State would have to be determined in accordance with the draft articles on responsibility of States for internationally wrongful acts.

(4) Draft article 25 sets under (*a*) and (*b*) the conditions for international responsibility to arise for the aiding or assisting State. The draft article uses the same wording as article 16 of the draft articles on responsibility of States for internationally wrongful acts, because it would be hard to find reasons for applying a different rule when the aided or assisted entity is an international organization rather than a State. It is to be noted that no distinction is made with regard to the temporal relation between the conduct of the State and the internationally wrongful act of the international organization.

(5) The heading of draft article 16 on responsibility of States for internationally wrongful acts has been slightly adapted, by introducing the words "by a State", in order to distinguish the heading of the present draft article from that of draft article 12.

Article 26. Direction and control exercised by a State over the commission of an internationally wrongful act by an international organization

A State which directs and controls an international organization in the commission of an internationally wrongful act by the latter is internationally responsible for that act if:

(*a*) that State does so with knowledge of the circumstances of the internationally wrongful act; and

(*b*) the act would be internationally wrongful if committed by that State.

Commentary

(1) While draft article 13 (above) relates to direction and control exercised by an international organization in the commission of an internationally wrongful act by another international organization,[645] draft article 26 considers the case in which direction and control are exercised by a State. Both draft articles closely follow the text of article 17 of the draft articles on responsibility of States for internationally wrongful acts.[646]

(2) The State directing and controlling an international organization in the commission of an internationally wrongful act may or may not be a member of that organization. As in the case of aid or assistance, which is considered in draft article 25 and the related commentary, a distinction has to be made between participation by a member State in the decision-making process of the organization according to its pertinent rules, and direction and control which would trigger the application of the present draft article. Since the latter conduct could take place within the framework of the organization, in borderline cases one would face the same problems that have been referred to in the commentary on the previous draft article.

(3) Draft article 26 sets under (*a*) and (*b*) the conditions for the responsibility of the State to arise with the same wording that is used in article 17 of the draft articles on responsibility of States for internationally wrongful acts. There are no reasons for making a distinction between the case in which a State directs and controls another State in the commission of an internationally wrongful act and the case in which the State similarly directs and controls an international organization.

[643] See the commentary on this article adopted by the Commission at its fifty-seventh session in *Yearbook ... 2005*, vol. II (Part Two), p. 45, para. 206.

[644] *Yearbook ... 2001*, vol. II (Part Two) and corrigendum, p. 65.

[645] See the commentary on this article adopted by the Commission at its fifty-seventh session in *Yearbook ... 2005*, vol. II (Part Two), p. 46, para. 206.

[646] *Yearbook ... 2001*, vol. II (Part Two) and corrigendum, pp. 67–68.

(4) With regard to article 17 of the draft articles on responsibility of States for internationally wrongful acts, the heading of the present draft article has been slightly adapted, by adding the words "by a State", in order to distinguish it from the heading of draft article 13.

Article 27. Coercion of an international organization by a State

A State which coerces an international organization to commit an act is internationally responsible for that act if:

(*a*) the act would, but for the coercion, be an internationally wrongful act of that international organization; and

(*b*) that State does so with knowledge of the circumstances of the act.

Commentary

(1) Draft article 14 (above) deals with coercion by an international organization in the commission of what would be, but for the coercion, a wrongful act of another international organization.[647] The present draft article concerns coercion by a State in a similar situation. Both draft articles closely follow article 18 of the draft articles on responsibility of States for internationally wrongful acts.[648]

(2) The State coercing an international organization may or may not be a member of that organization. Should the State be a member, a distinction that is similar to the one that was made with regard to the previous two draft articles has to be made between participation in the decision-making process of the organization according to its pertinent rules, on the one hand, and coercion, on the other hand.

(3) The conditions that draft article 27 sets for international responsibility to arise are identical to those that are listed in article 18 of the draft articles on responsibility of States for internationally wrongful acts. Also with regard to coercion, there is no reason to provide a different rule from that which applies in the relations between States.

(4) The heading of the present draft article slightly adapts that of article 18 of the draft articles on responsibility of States for internationally wrongful acts by introducing the words "by a State", this in order to distinguish it from the heading of draft article 14.

Article 28. International responsibility in case of provision of competence to an international organization

1. A State member of an international organization incurs international responsibility if it circumvents one of its international obligations by providing the organization with competence in relation to that obligation, and the organization commits an act that, if committed by that State, would have constituted a breach of that obligation.

2. Paragraph 1 applies whether or not the act in question is internationally wrongful for the international organization.

Commentary

(1) Draft article 28 concerns a situation which is to a certain extent analogous to those considered in draft article 15 (above).[649] According to that draft article, an international organization incurs international responsibility when it circumvents one of its international obligations by adopting a decision binding a member State or international organization to commit an act that would be internationally wrongful if committed by the former organization. Draft article 15 also considers circumvention through authorizations or recommendations given to member States or international organizations. The present draft article concerns circumvention by a State of one of its international obligations when it avails itself of the separate legal personality of an international organization of which it is a member.

(2) As the commentary to draft article 15 explains, the existence of a specific intention of circumvention is not required and responsibility cannot be avoided by showing the absence of an intention to circumvent the international obligation.[650] The use of the term "circumvention" is meant to exclude that international responsibility arises when the act of the international organization, which would constitute a breach of an international obligation if taken by the State, has to be regarded as an unwitting result of providing the international organization with competence. On the other hand, the term "circumvention" does not refer only to cases in which the member State may be said to be abusing its rights.[651]

(3) The jurisprudence of the European Court of Human Rights provides a few examples of States being held responsible when they have provided competence to an international organization and have failed to ensure compliance with their obligations under the European Convention on Human Rights. In *Waite and Kennedy v. Germany*, the Court examined the question as to whether the right of access to justice had been unduly impaired by a State that granted immunity to the European Space Agency, of which it was a member, in relation to claims concerning employment. The Court said that:

> where States establish international organisations in order to pursue or strengthen their cooperation in certain fields of activities, and where they attribute to these organisations certain competences and accord

[647] See the commentary on this article adopted by the Commission at its fifty-seventh session in *Yearbook ... 2005*, vol. II (Part Two), pp. 46–47, para. 206.

[648] *Yearbook ... 2001*, vol. II (Part Two) and corrigendum, p. 69.

[649] See the commentary on this article adopted by the Commission at its fifty-seventh session in *Yearbook ... 2005*, vol. II (Part Two), para. 206.

[650] *Ibid.* (para. (4) of the commentary).

[651] In article 5 (*b*) of a resolution adopted in 1995 at Lisbon on the "Legal Consequences for Member States of the Non-fulfilment by International Organizations of their Obligations towards Third Parties", the Institute of International Law stated: "In particular circumstances, members of an international organization may be liable for its obligations in accordance with a relevant general principle of law, such as ... the abuse of rights" (*Yearbook of the Institute of International Law*, vol. 66–II (1996), p. 449).

them immunities, there may be implications as to protection of fundamental rights. It would be incompatible with the purpose and object of the Convention, however, if the Contracting States were thereby absolved from their responsibility under the Convention in relation to the field of activity covered by such attribution.[652]

(4) In *Bosphorus Hava Yollari Turizm ve Ticaret Anonim Şirketi* v. *Ireland*, the Court took a similar approach with regard to a State measure implementing a regulation of the European Community. The Court said that a State could not free itself from its obligations under the European Convention on Human Rights by transferring functions to an international organization, because:

[a]bsolving Contracting States completely from their [European Convention on Human Rights] responsibility in the areas covered by such a transfer would be incompatible with the purpose and object of the Convention; the guarantees of the Convention could be limited or excluded at will, thereby depriving it of its peremptory character and undermining the practical and effective nature of its safeguards … . The State is considered to retain Convention liability in respect of treaty commitments subsequent to the entry into force of the Convention.[653]

(5) According to the present draft article, two elements are required for international responsibility to arise. The first one is that the State provides the international organization with competence in relation to the international obligation that is circumvented. This could occur through the transfer of State functions to an organization of integration. However, the cases covered are not so limited. Moreover, an international organization could be established in order to exercise functions that States may not have. What is relevant for the purposes of international responsibility to arise according to the present draft article, is that the international obligation covers the area in which the international organization is provided with competence. The obligation may specifically relate to that area or be more general, as in the case of obligations under treaties for the protection of human rights.

(6) The second condition for international responsibility to arise is that the international organization commits an act that, if committed by the State, would have constituted a breach of that obligation. The fact that the organization is not bound by the obligation is not sufficient for international responsibility to arise. An act that would constitute a breach of the obligation has to be committed. On the other hand, there is no requirement that the State cause the international organization to commit the act in question.

(7) Paragraph 2 explains that draft article 28 does not require the act to be internationally wrongful for the international organization concerned. Circumvention is more likely to occur when the international organization is not bound by the international obligation. However, the sheer existence of an international obligation for the organization does not necessarily exempt the State from international responsibility.

(8) Should the act of the international organization be wrongful and the act be caused by the member State, there could be an overlap between the cases covered in draft article 28 and those considered in the three previous articles. This would occur when the conditions set by one of these articles are fulfilled. However, such an overlap would not be problematic, because it would only imply the existence of a plurality of bases for holding the State responsible.

Article 29. Responsibility of a State member of an international organization for the internationally wrongful act of that organization

1. Without prejudice to draft articles 25 to 28, a State member of an international organization is responsible for an internationally wrongful act of that organization if:

(*a*) it has accepted responsibility for that act; or

(*b*) it has led the injured party to rely on its responsibility.

2. The international responsibility of a State which is entailed in accordance with paragraph 1 is presumed to be subsidiary.

Commentary

(1) The saving clause with reference to draft articles 25 to 28 at the beginning of paragraph 1 of the present draft article intends to make it clear that a State member of an international organization may be held responsible also in accordance with the previous draft articles. Therefore, draft article 29 envisages two additional cases in which member States incur responsibility. Member States may furthermore be responsible according to the articles on responsibility of States for internationally wrongful acts,[654] but this need not be the object of a saving clause since it is beyond the scope of the present draft.

---

[652] *Waite and Kennedy* v. *Germany, Application no. 26083/94, Judgement of 18 February 1999*, Grand Chamber, European Court of Human Rights, *Reports of Judgments and Decisions 1999-I*, p. 393, at p. 410, para. 67. The Court concluded that "the essence of [the applicants'] 'right to a court'" under the Convention had not been impaired (p. 412, para. 73). After examining the dictum in *Waite and Kennedy* v. *Germany* reproduced above, Ian Brownlie noted that, "[w]hilst the context is that of human rights, the principle invoked would seem to be general in its application" (I. Brownlie, "The responsibility of States for the acts of international organizations", in M. Ragazzi (ed.), *International Responsibility Today: Essays in Memory of Oscar Schachter*, Leiden/Boston, Martinus Nijhoff, 2005, p. 361). Views similar to those of the European Court of Human Rights were expressed by Antonietta Di Blasé in "Sulla responsabilità internazionale per attività dell'ONU", *Rivista di diritto internazionale*, vol. 57 (1974), p. 250, at pp. 275–276; Moshe Hirsch in *The Responsibility of International Organizations toward Third Parties*, Dordrecht/Boston/London, Martinus Nijhoff, 1995, p. 179; Karl Zemanek, in *Yearbook of the Institute of International Law*, vol. 66-I (1995), p. 329; Philippe Sands in *Bowett's Law of International Institutions*, P. Sands and P. Klein (eds.), London, Sweet and Maxwell, 2001, p. 524; and Dan Sarooshi in *International Organizations and their Exercise of Sovereign Powers*, Oxford University Press, 2005, p. 64.

[653] *Bosphorus Hava Yollari Turizm ve Ticaret Anonim Şirketi* v. *Ireland, Application no. 45036/98, Decision of 30 June 2005*, Grand Chamber, European Court of Human Rights, *Reports of Judgments and Decisions 2005-VI*, para. 154. The Court found that the defendant State had not incurred responsibility because the relevant fundamental rights were protected within the European Community "in a manner which can be considered at least equivalent to that for which the Convention provides" (para. 155).

[654] This would apply to the case envisaged by the Institute of International Law in article 5 (*c*) (ii) of its resolution on the "Legal Consequences for Member States of the Non-fulfilment by International Organizations of their Obligations toward Third Parties": the case that "the international organization has acted as the agent of the State, in law or in fact" (*Yearbook of the Institute of International Law*, vol. 66–II (1996), p. 449).

(2) Consistently with the approach generally taken by the present draft as well as by the articles on responsibility of States for internationally wrongful acts, the present draft article positively identifies those cases in which a State incurs responsibility and does not say when responsibility is not deemed to arise. Although some members did not agree, the Commission found that it would be inappropriate to include in the draft a provision stating a residual, and negative, rule for those cases in which, according to the draft, responsibility does not arise for a State in connection with the act of an international organization. It is clear, however, that such a conclusion is implied and that membership does not as such entail for member States international responsibility when the organization commits an internationally wrongful act.

(3) The view that member States cannot generally be regarded as internationally responsible for the internationally wrongful acts of the organization has been defended by several States in contentious cases. The Government of Germany recalled in a written comment that it had:

> advocated the principle of separate responsibility before the European Commission of Human Rights (*M. & Co.*), the European Court of Human Rights (*Senator Lines*) and the International Court of Justice (*Legality of Use of Force*) and [had] rejected responsibility for reason of membership for measures taken by the European Community, NATO and the United Nations.[655]

(4) A similar view was taken by the majority opinions in the British courts in the litigation concerning the International Tin Council (ITC), albeit incidentally in disputes concerning private contracts. The clearest expressions were given by Lord Kerr in the Court of Appeal and by Lord Templeman. Lord Kerr said that he could not:

> find any basis for concluding that it has been shown that there is any rule of international law, binding upon the member States of the I.T.C., whereby they can be held liable—let alone jointly and severally—in any national court to the creditors of the I.T.C. for the debts of the I.T.C. resulting from contracts concluded by the I.T.C. in its own name.[656]

In the House of Lords, with regard to an alleged rule of international law imposing on "States members of an international organization, joint and several liability for the default of the organization in the payment of its debts unless the treaty which establishes the international organization clearly disclaims any liability on the part of the members", Lord Templeman found that:

> [n]o plausible evidence was produced of the existence of such a rule of international law before or at the time of I.T.A.6 [the Sixth International Tin Agreement] in 1982 or thereafter.[657]

(5) Although doctrine is divided on the question of responsibility of States when an international organization of which they are members commits an internationally wrongful act, it is noteworthy that the Institute of International Law adopted in 1995 a resolution in which it took the position that:

> [s]ave as specified in article 5, there is no general rule of international law whereby States members are, due solely to their membership, liable concurrently or subsidiarily, for the obligations of an international organization of which they are members.[658]

(6) The view that member States are not in general responsible does not rule out that there are certain cases, other than those considered in the previous draft articles, in which a State would be responsible for the internationally wrongful act of the organization. The least controversial case is that of acceptance of international responsibility by the States concerned. This case is stated in subparagraph (*a*). No qualification is given to acceptance. This is intended to mean that acceptance may be expressly stated or implied and may occur either before or after the time when responsibility arises for the organization.

(7) In his opinion in the judgment of the Court of Appeal concerning the International Tin Council, Lord Ralph Gibson referred to acceptance of responsibility in the "constituent document".[659] One can certainly envisage that acceptance results from the constituent instrument of the international organization or from other rules of the organization. However, member States would then incur international responsibility towards a third party only if their acceptance produced legal effects in their relations to the third party.[660] It could well be that member States only bind themselves towards the organization or agree to provide the necessary financial resources as an internal matter.[661]

(8) Paragraph 1 envisages a second case of responsibility of member States: when the conduct of member States has given the third party reason to rely on the responsibility of member States, for instance, that they would stand in

---

[655] Comments and observations received from international organizations on responsibility of international organizations, *Yearbook ... 2005*, vol. II (Part One), document A/CN.4/556 (under the heading "Practice relating to responsibility of international organizations. Germany").

[656] *Maclaine Watson & Co. Ltd.* v. *Department of Trade and Industry; J.H. Rayner (Mincing Lane) Ltd.* v. *Department of Trade and Industry and Others, Judgment of 27 April 1988*, ILR, vol. 80, p. 109.

[657] *Australia & New Zealand Banking Group Ltd., et al.* v. *Australia and 23 Others*; *Amalgamated Metal Trading Ltd. and Others* v. *Department of Trade and Industry and Others*; *Maclaine Watson & Co. Ltd.* v. *Department of Trade and Industry*; *Maclaine Watson & Co. Ltd.* v. *International Tin Council, Judgment of 26 October 1989*, ILM, vol. 29 (1990), p. 675.

[658] Article 6 (*a*). Article 5 reads as follows: "(*a*) The question of the liability of the members of an international organization for its obligations is determined by reference to the Rules of the organization; (*b*) In particular circumstances, members of an international organization may be liable for its obligations in accordance with a relevant general principle of law, such as acquiescence or the abuse of rights; (*c*) In addition, a member State may incur liability to a third party (i) through undertakings by the State, or (ii) if the international organization has acted as the agent of the State, in law or in fact" (*Yearbook of the Institute of International Law*, vol. 66–II (1996), p. 449).

[659] *Maclaine Watson & Co. Ltd.* v. *Department of Trade and Industry; J.H. Rayner (Mincing Lane) Ltd.* v. *Department of Trade and Industry and Others* (see footnote 656 above), p. 172.

[660] The conditions set by article 36 of the 1969 Vienna Convention would then apply.

[661] For instance, article 300, paragraph 7, of the Treaty establishing the European Community reads as follows: "Agreements concluded under the conditions set out in this Article shall be binding on the institutions of the Community and on Member States". The European Court of Justice pointed out that this provision does not imply that member States are bound towards non-member States and may as a consequence incur responsibility towards them under international law. See *French Republic* v. *Commission of the European Communities, Case C-327/91, Judgment of 9 August 1994, Reports of Cases before the Court of Justice and the Court of First Instance, 1994-8*, p. I–3641, at p. I–3674, para. 25.

if the responsible organization did not have the necessary funds for making reparation.[662]

(9) An example of responsibility of member States based on reliance engendered by the conduct of member States was provided by the second arbitral award in the dispute concerning Westland Helicopters. The panel found that the special circumstances of the case invited "the trust of third parties contracting with the Organization as to its ability to cope with its commitments because of the constant support of the member States".[663]

(10) Reliance is not necessarily based on an implied acceptance. It may also reasonably arise from circumstances which cannot be taken as an expression of an intention of the member States to bind themselves. Among the factors that have been suggested as relevant is the small size of membership,[664] although this factor, together with all the pertinent factors, would have to be considered globally. There is clearly no presumption that a third party should be able to rely on the responsibility of member States.

(11) Subparagraph (*b*) uses the term "injured party". In the context of international responsibility, this injured party would in most cases be another State or another international organization. However, it could also be a subject of international law other than a State or an international organization. While Part One of the draft articles on responsibility of States for internationally wrongful acts considers the breach of any obligation that a State may have under international law, Part Two, which concerns the content of international responsibility, only deals with relations between States, but contains in article 33 of these draft articles a saving clause concerning the rights that may arise for "any person or entity other than a State".[665] Similarly, subparagraph (*b*) is intended to cover any State, international organization, person or entity with regard to whom a member State may incur international responsibility.

(12) According to subparagraphs (*a*) and (*b*), international responsibility arises only for those member States who accepted that responsibility or whose conduct induced reliance. Even when acceptance of responsibility results from the constituent instrument of the organization, this could provide for the responsibility only of certain member States.

(13) Paragraph 2 considers the nature of the responsibility that is entailed in accordance with paragraph 1. Acceptance of responsibility by a State could relate either to subsidiary or to joint and several responsibility. The same applies to responsibility based on reliance. As a general rule, one could only state a rebuttable presumption. Also, in view of the limited nature of the cases in which responsibility arises according to the present draft article, it is reasonable to presume that, when member States accept responsibility, only subsidiary responsibility, which has a supplementary character, is intended.[666]

Article 30. Effect of this chapter

This chapter is without prejudice to international responsibility, under other provisions of these draft articles, of the international organization which commits the act in question, or of any other international organization.

Commentary

(1) The present draft article finds a parallel in draft article 16 [15] (above), according to which the chapter on responsibility of an international organization in connection with the act of a State or another international organization is "without prejudice to the international responsibility of the State or international organization which commits the act in question, or of any other State or international organization".

(2) Draft article 30 is a saving clause relating to the whole chapter. It corresponds to article 19 of the draft articles on responsibility of States for internationally wrongful acts.[667] The purpose of that provision, which concerns only relations between States, is first to clarify that the responsibility of the State aiding or assisting, or directing and controlling another State in the commission of an internationally wrongful act is without prejudice to the responsibility that the State committing the act may incur. Moreover, as the commentary on article 19 of the draft articles on responsibility of States explains, the article is also intended to make it clear "that the provisions of [the chapter] are without prejudice to any other basis for establishing the responsibility of the assisting, directing or coercing State under any rule of international law defining particular conduct as wrongful" and to preserve the responsibility of any other State "to whom the internationally wrongful conduct might also be attributable under other provisions of the articles".[668]

---

[662] Amerasinghe held, on the basis of "policy reasons", that "the presumption of nonliability could be displaced by evidence that members (some or all of them) or the organization, with the approval of members, gave creditors reason to assume that members (some or all of them) would accept concurrent or secondary liability even without an express or implied intention to that effect in the constituent instrument" (C. F. Amerasinghe, "Liability to third parties of member States of international organizations: practice, principle and juridical precedent", AJIL, vol. 85 (1991), p. 280. Pierre Klein also considered that conduct of member States may imply that they provide a guarantee for the respect of obligations arising for the organization (see P. Klein, *La responsabilité des organisations internationales dans les ordres juridiques internes et en droit des gens*, Bruxelles, Bruylant/Editions de l'Université, 1998, pp. 509–510).

[663] *Westland Helicopters Ltd.* v. *Arab Organization for Industrialization, Award of 21 July 1991*, para. 56, cited by Rosalyn Higgins in "The legal consequences for member states of non-fulfilment by international organizations of their obligations toward third parties: provisional report", *Yearbook of the Institute of International Law*, vol. 66–I (1995), pp. 393–394.

[664] See in this respect the comment made by Belarus, *Official Records of the General Assembly, Sixtieth Session, Sixth Committee, Summary record of the 12th meeting* (A/C.6/60/SR.12) and corrigendum, para. 52.

[665] *Yearbook ... 2001*, vol. II (Part Two) and corrigendum, p. 94.

[666] In the opinion referred to above, in the judgment of 27 April 1988, *Maclaine Watson & Co. Ltd.* v. *Department of Trade and Industry*; *J.H. Rayner (Mincing Lane) Ltd.* v. *Department of Trade and Industry and Others* (see footnote 656 above), Lord Ralph Gibson held that, in case of acceptance of responsibility, "direct secondary liability has been assumed by the members" (p. 172).

[667] *Yearbook ... 2001*, vol. II (Part Two) and corrigendum, p. 70.

[668] *Ibid.*, pp. 70–71, paras. (2)–(3).

(3) There appears to be less need for an analogous "without prejudice" provision in a chapter concerning responsibility of States which is included in a draft on responsibility of international organizations. It is hardly necessary to save responsibility that may arise for States according to articles on responsibility of States for internationally wrongful acts and not according to the present draft. On the contrary, a "without prejudice" provision analogous to that of article 19 of the draft articles on responsibility of States for internationally wrongful acts would have some use if it concerned international organizations. The omission in the chapter of a provision analogous to draft article 19 could have raised doubts. Moreover, at least in the case of a State aiding or assisting or directing and controlling an international organization in the commission of an internationally wrongful act, there is some use in saying that the responsibility of the State is without prejudice to the responsibility of the international organization that commits the act.

(4) In the present draft article the references to the term "State" in article 19 of the draft articles on responsibility of States for internationally wrongful acts have been replaced by references to the term "international organization".

Chapter VIII

RESERVATIONS TO TREATIES

A. Introduction

92. The General Assembly, in its resolution 48/31 of 9 December 1993, endorsed the decision of the International Law Commission to include in its agenda the topic "The law and practice relating to reservations to treaties".

93. At its forty-sixth session (1994), the Commission appointed Mr. Alain Pellet, Special Rapporteur for the topic.[669]

94. At its forty-seventh session (1995), the Commission received and discussed the first report of the Special Rapporteur.[670]

95. Following that discussion, the Special Rapporteur summarized the conclusions he had drawn from the Commission's consideration of the topic; they related to the title of the topic, which should now read "Reservations to treaties"; the form of the results of the study, which should be a guide to practice in respect of reservations; the flexible way in which the Commission's work on the topic should be carried out; and the consensus in the Commission that there should be no change in the relevant provisions of the 1969 Vienna Convention, the Vienna Convention on succession of States in respect of treaties (hereinafter "1978 Vienna Convention") and the 1986 Vienna Convention.[671] In the view of the Commission, those conclusions constituted the results of the preliminary study requested by the General Assembly in resolutions 48/31 of 9 December 1993 and 49/51 of 9 December 1994. As far as the Guide to Practice was concerned, it would take the form of draft guidelines with commentaries, which would be of assistance for the practice of States and international organizations; these guidelines would, if necessary, be accompanied by model clauses.

96. Also at its forty-seventh session, the Commission, in accordance with its earlier practice,[672] authorized the Special Rapporteur to prepare a detailed questionnaire on reservations to treaties, to ascertain the practice of, and problems encountered by, States and international organizations, particularly those which were depositaries of multilateral conventions.[673] The questionnaire was sent to the addressees by the Secretariat. In its resolution 50/45 of 11 December 1995, the General Assembly took note of the Commission's conclusions, inviting it to continue its work along the lines indicated in its report and also inviting States to answer the questionnaire.[674]

97. At its forty-eighth session (1996), the Commission had before it the Special Rapporteur's second report on the topic.[675] The Special Rapporteur had annexed to his report a draft resolution of the International Law Commission on reservations to multilateral normative treaties, including human rights treaties, which was addressed to the General Assembly for the purpose of drawing attention to and clarifying the legal aspects of the matter.[676]

98. At its forty-ninth session (1997), the Commission adopted preliminary conclusions on reservations to normative multilateral treaties, including human rights treaties.[677]

99. In its resolution 52/156 of 15 December 1997, the General Assembly took note of the Commission's preliminary conclusions and of its invitation to all treaty bodies set up by normative multilateral treaties that might wish to do so to provide, in writing, their comments and observations on the conclusions, while drawing the attention of Governments to the importance for the International Law Commission of having their views on the preliminary conclusions.

100. From its fiftieth session (1998) to its fifty-seventh session (2005) the Commission considered eight more reports[678] by the Special Rapporteur and provisionally adopted 71 draft guidelines and the commentaries thereto.

B. Consideration of the topic at the present session

101. At the current session, the Commission had before it the second part of the tenth report of the Special Rapporteur (A/CN.4/558 and Add.1–2) on validity of reservations and the concept of the object and purpose of the

---

[669] See *Yearbook ... 1994*, vol. II (Part Two), p. 179, para. 381.

[670] *Yearbook ... 1995*, vol. II (Part One), document A/CN.4/470.

[671] *Ibid.*, vol. II (Part Two), p. 108, para. 487.

[672] See *Yearbook ... 1993*, vol. II (Part Two), p. 83, para. 286.

[673] See *Yearbook ... 1995*, vol. II (Part Two), p. 108, para. 489. The questionnaires sent to Member States and international organizations are reproduced in *Yearbook ... 1996*, vol. II (Part One), document A/CN.4/477 and Add.1, Annexes II and III.

[674] As of 31 July 2003, 33 States and 25 international organizations had answered the questionnaire.

[675] *Yearbook ... 1996*, vol. II (Part One), documents A/CN.4/477 and Add.1 and A/CN.4/478.

[676] *Ibid.*, vol. II (Part Two), p. 83, para. 136 and footnote 238.

[677] See footnote 6 above.

[678] Third report: *Yearbook ... 1998*, vol. II (Part One), document A/CN.4/491 and Add.1–6; fourth report: *Yearbook ... 1999*, vol. II (Part One), documents A/CN.4/499 and A/CN.4/478/Rev.1; fifth report: *Yearbook ... 2000*, vol. II (Part One), document A/CN.4/508 and Add.1–4; sixth report: *Yearbook ... 2001*, vol. II (Part One), document A/CN.4/518 and Add.1–3; seventh report: *Yearbook ... 2002*, vol. II (Part One), document A/CN.4/526 and Add.1–3; eighth report: *Yearbook ... 2003*, vol. II (Part One), document A/CN.4/535 and Add.1; ninth report: *Yearbook ... 2004*, vol. II (Part One), document A/CN.4/544; and tenth report: *Yearbook ... 2005*, vol. II (Part One), document A/CN.4/558 and Add.1–2. See a detailed historical presentation of the third to fifth reports in *Yearbook ... 2004*, vol. II (Part Two), pp. 97–98, paras. 257–269.

treaty.[679] In this regard the Special Rapporteur, after the debate that took place during the fifty-seventh session (2005), had also prepared a note (A/CN.4/572) relating to draft guideline 3.1.5 (Definition of the object and purpose of the treaty) and presenting a new version of this guideline including two alternative texts.[680] The Special Rapporteur also submitted his eleventh report (A/CN.4/574) and the Commission decided to consider it at its fifty-ninth session (2007).

102. The Commission considered the second part of the tenth report of the Special Rapporteur at its 2888th to 2891st meetings, held on 5, 6, 7 and 11 July 2006.

103. At its 2891st meeting, the Commission decided to refer draft guidelines 3.1.5 to 3.1.13, 3.2, 3.2.1 to 3.2.4, 3.3 and 3.3.1 to the Drafting Committee.

104. At its 2883rd meeting, on 6 June 2006, the Commission considered and provisionally adopted draft guidelines 3.1 (Permissible reservations), 3.1.1 (Reservations expressly prohibited by the treaty), 3.1.2 (Definition of specified reservations), 3.1.3 (Permissibility of reservations not prohibited by the treaty) and 3.1.4 (Permissibility of specified reservations) to the Drafting Committee. Moreover, the Commission provisionally adopted draft guidelines 1.6 (Scope of definitions) and 2.1.8 [2.1.7 *bis*] (Procedure in case of manifestly invalid reservations) as redrafted.

105. Those draft guidelines had already been sent to the Drafting Committee at the Commission's fifty-seventh session (2005).

106. At its 2911th and 2912th meetings, held on 9 and 10 August 2006, the Commission adopted the commentaries relating to the aforementioned draft guidelines.

107. The text of the draft guidelines and the commentaries thereto are reproduced in section C.2 below.

1. Introduction by the Special Rapporteur of the second part of his tenth report

108. The Special Rapporteur recalled that, for lack of time, one portion of his tenth report could not be considered in depth during the previous Commission session and the final part concerning the validity of reservations had not been considered at all. In the light of the criticisms of the definition of the object and purpose of the treaty that had been voiced during the debate at the fifty-seventh session, the Special Rapporteur had formulated a new definition of the object and purpose of the treaty (A/CN.4/572).[681] For the new definition he offered two alternatives, not very different in their general meaning, although he preferred the first alternative. In the second addendum to his tenth report, the Special Rapporteur had tried to give a pragmatic answer to two important and difficult questions: who was competent to assess the validity of reservations and what were the consequences of an invalid reservation.

109. With regard to draft guideline 3.2,[682] the Special Rapporteur said that it followed from articles 20, 21 and 23 of the 1969 and 1986 Vienna Conventions that any contracting State or international organization could assess the validity of the reservations formulated with respect to a treaty. In that regard the term "State" meant the entire State apparatus, including, as applicable, the domestic courts. Such an assessment could also be made by the courts of the reserving State, although the Special Rapporteur was aware of only a single case in which a domestic court had declared a reservation formulated by the State invalid.[683] In order to take that possibility into account, the wording of the first bullet point of draft guideline 3.2 should be changed by deleting the word "other" before "contracting States" and before "contracting organizations". The dispute settlement bodies and the treaty implementation monitoring bodies could also rule on the validity of reservations, but it should be noted that the category of treaty monitoring bodies was relatively a new one and had not become well developed until after the adoption of the 1969 Vienna Convention.

110. The considerations that had led the Commission to adopt in 1997 preliminary conclusions on reservations to normative multilateral treaties including human rights treaties[684] were still relevant. The third bullet point of draft guideline 3.2 reflected practice and corresponded to paragraph 5 of the preliminary conclusions.

111. Draft guideline 3.2.1[685] spelled out that idea, at the same time indicating that, in so doing, monitoring bodies could go no further than their general mandate authorized.

---

[679] Reproduced in *Yearbook ... 2005*, vol. II (Part One).

[680] Reproduced in *Yearbook ... 2006*, vol. II (Part One).

[681] Alternative 1:

"3.1.5 *Definition of the object and purpose of the treaty*

"For the purpose of assessing the validity of reservations, the object and purpose of the treaty means the essential rules, rights and obligations indispensable to the general architecture of the treaty, which constitute the *raison d'être* thereof and whose modification or exclusion could seriously disturb the balance of the treaty."

Alternative 2:

"3.1.5 *Incompatibility of a reservation with the object and purpose of the treaty*

"A reservation shall be incompatible with the object and purpose of the treaty if it has a serious impact on the essential rules, rights or obligations indispensable to the general architecture of the treaty, thereby depriving it of its *raison d'être*."

[682] "3.2 *Competence to assess the validity of reservations*

"The following are competent to rule on the validity of reservations to a treaty formulated by a State or an international organization:

"(*a*) the other contracting States [including, as applicable, their domestic courts] or other contracting organizations;

"(*b*) dispute settlement bodies that may be competent to interpret or apply the treaty; and

"(*c*) treaty implementation monitoring bodies that may be established by the treaty."

[683] See the decision of the Swiss Federal Supreme Court of 17 December 1992 in the case of *F. v. R. and the Council of State of Thurgau Canton, Journal des tribunaux* (1995), pp. 523.

[684] See footnote 6 above.

[685] "3.2.1 *Competence of the monitoring bodies established by the treaty*

"Where a treaty establishes a body to monitor application of the treaty, that body shall be competent, for the purpose of discharging the functions entrusted to it, to assess the validity of reservations formulated by a State or an international organization.

"The findings made by such a body in the exercise of this competence shall have the same legal force as that deriving from the performance of its general monitoring role."

If they had decision-making power, they could also decide as to the validity of reservations, and their decisions in that regard would be binding on States parties; otherwise, they could only make recommendations. That was also in keeping with paragraph 8 of the preliminary conclusions.

112. Draft guideline 3.2.2[686] echoed paragraph 7 of the preliminary conclusions in the form of a recommendation and was very much in keeping with the pedagogic spirit of the Guide to Practice, as was draft guideline 3.2.3,[687] which reminded States and international organizations that they should give effect to the decisions of the treaty monitoring bodies (if they had decision-making power) or take account of their recommendations in good faith.

113. Draft guideline 3.2.4,[688] corresponding to paragraph 6 of the preliminary conclusions adopted in 1997, recalled that, when there were several mechanisms for assessing the validity of reservations, they were not mutually exclusive but supportive.

114. The last section of the tenth report deals with the consequences of the invalidity of a reservation, a matter that constituted one of the most serious gaps on the topic in the 1969 and 1986 Vienna Conventions, which were silent on that point, whether deliberately or otherwise.

115. Despite the positions taken by certain authors, who draw a distinction between subparagraphs (*a*) and (*b*) of article 19 of the Vienna Conventions, on the one hand, and subparagraph (*c*) on the other, the Special Rapporteur was of the view that all the three subparagraphs had the same function (a view supported by the *travaux préparatoires*, practice and case law). The unity of article 19, which was confirmed by article 21, paragraph 1, of the Vienna Conventions, was expressed in draft guideline 3.3.[689]

116. The Special Rapporteur then sought to respond to some of the questions to which a response could be given at that stage. Draft guideline 3.3.1[690] explained that the formulation of an invalid reservation posed problems of validity, not of the responsibility of its author. Hence, draft guideline 3.3.2[691] expressed the idea that a reservation that did not fulfil the conditions for validity set forth in article 19 of the Vienna Conventions was null and void.

117. Draft guideline 3.3.3[692] expressed the idea that the other contracting parties, acting unilaterally, could not remedy the nullity of a reservation that did not meet the criteria of article 19. Otherwise, the unity of the treaty regime would be broken up, which would be incompatible with the principle of good faith.

118. The Special Rapporteur was of the view that what the contracting parties could not do unilaterally they might do collectively, provided they did it expressly, which would amount to an amendment of the treaty. If all parties formally accepted a reservation that was *a priori* invalid, they could be considered to be amending the treaty by unanimous agreement, as article 39 of the Vienna Conventions allowed. That idea was expressed in draft guideline 3.3.4.[693]

2. Summary of the debate

119. With regard to draft guideline 3.1.5, in the new version proposed by the Special Rapporteur, it was pointed out that the notion of "the balance of the treaty" was not necessarily applicable to all treaties, particularly those relating to human rights. The object and purpose of a treaty consisted in the objective underlying the essential rules, rights and obligations, rather than within those rules, rights and obligations themselves.

120. According to another point of view, the reference to "essential rules, rights and obligations" in the new version was a better way to describe the *raison d'être* of a treaty.

---

[686] "3.2.2 *Clauses specifying the competence of monitoring bodies to assess the validity of reservations*

"States or international organizations should insert, in treaties establishing bodies to monitor their application, clauses specifying the nature and, where appropriate, the limits of the competence of such bodies to assess the validity of reservations. Protocols to existing treaties could be adopted to the same ends."

[687] "3.2.3 *Cooperation of States and international organizations with monitoring bodies*

"States and international organizations that have formulated reservations to a treaty establishing a body to monitor its application are required to cooperate with that body and take fully into account that body's assessment of the validity of the reservations that they have formulated. When the body in question is vested with decision-making power, the author of the reservation is bound to give effect to the decision of that body [provided that it is acting within the limits of its competence]."

[688] "3.2.4 *Plurality of bodies competent to assess the validity of reservations*

"When the treaty establishes a body to monitor its application, the competence of that body neither excludes nor affects in any other way the competence of other contracting States or other contracting international organizations to assess the validity of reservations to a treaty formulated by a State or an international organization, nor that of such dispute settlement bodies as may be competent to interpret or apply the treaty."

[689] "3.3 *Consequences of the non-validity of a reservation*

"A reservation formulated in spite of the express or implicit prohibition arising from the provisions of the treaty or from its incompatibility with the object and purpose of the treaty is not valid, without there being any need to distinguish between these two grounds for invalidity."

[690] "3.3.1 *Non-validity of reservations and responsibility*

"The formulation of an invalid reservation produces its effects within the framework of the law of treaties. It shall not, in itself, engage the responsibility of the State or international organization which has formulated it."

[691] "3.3.2 *Nullity of invalid reservations*

"A reservation that does not fulfil the conditions for validity laid down in guideline 3.1 is null and void."

[692] "3.3.3 *Effect of unilateral acceptance of an invalid reservation*

"Acceptance of a reservation by a contracting State or by a contracting international organization shall not change the nullity of the reservation."

[693] "3.3.4 *Effect of collective acceptance of an invalid reservation*

"A reservation that is explicitly or implicitly prohibited by the treaty or which is incompatible with its object and its purpose, may be formulated by a State or an international organization if none of the other contracting parties object to it after having been expressly consulted by the depositary.

"During such consultation, the depositary shall draw the attention of the signatory States and international organizations and of the contracting States and international organizations and, where appropriate, the competent organ of the international organization concerned, to the nature of the legal problems raised by the reservation."

121. The view was also expressed that the revised version of the draft guideline introduced terms that were difficult to understand and interpret and were extremely subjective. The earlier version accompanied by commentary would be a more appropriate way to clarify the notion of object and purpose. It was also pointed out that the phrase "has a serious impact" appeared to make the scope of the draft guideline very restrictive. It was noted that a reservation, without necessarily compromising the *raison d'être* of the treaty, might nonetheless compromise an essential part of it and thus be incompatible with its object and purpose.

122. The view was also expressed that when a treaty prohibited all reservations, it did not necessarily mean that all the provisions of the treaty constituted its *raison d'être*, and, conversely, when a treaty allowed specific reservations it did not necessarily mean that the particular provisions that might be the subject of reservations were not essential. The political context in which the treaty had been concluded should also be taken into account.

123. With regard to draft guideline 3.1.6, it was pointed out that the reference to "the articles that determine [the] basic structure" of the treaty gave the impression that the object and purpose of a treaty was to be found in certain provisions of the treaty, which was not necessarily the case. The reference to subsequent practice could be deleted, since the intention of the parties at the time the treaty was concluded was the essential consideration. The view was also expressed that the reference to the "subsequent practice of the parties" should be deleted both for the sake of consistency with previous decisions of the Commission and for the sake of the stability of treaty relations. However, another view held that the reference to subsequent practice should be retained and was an essential element of interpretation according to article 31 of the 1969 and 1986 Vienna Conventions.

124. With regard to draft guideline 3.1.7, it was observed that even vague, general reservations were not necessarily incompatible with the object and purpose of the treaty, since they might affect matters of lesser importance.

125. Several members voiced support for draft guideline 3.1.8.

126. With regard to draft guideline 3.1.9, the view was expressed that it might be possible to formulate a reservation to some aspect of a treaty provision setting forth a rule of *jus cogens* that did not actually contradict the *jus cogens* rule itself.

127. With regard to draft guideline 3.1.10, it was observed that a reservation might be made to a provision relating to non-derogable rights, provided the reservation was not incompatible with the object and purpose of the treaty as a whole.

128. Several members expressed support for draft guidelines 3.1.11, 3.1.12 and 3.1.13.

129. The view was expressed that another category of reservations deserved mention, namely, reservations to provisions relating to the implementation of the treaty through domestic legislation.

130. With regard to draft guideline 3.2, it was stressed that the competence of treaty monitoring bodies was not automatic unless provided for by the treaty. It was also suggested that the text should refer to "monitoring bodies that may be established within the framework of the treaty" rather than "by the treaty" in order to include bodies established subsequently, such as the Committee on Economic, Social and Cultural Rights. The question was raised whether monitoring bodies with quasi-judicial functions could rule on the legality of reservations formulated by States even if such a power was not expressly foreseen in the treaty.

131. The view was expressed that the draft guideline departed from positive treaty law and the practice of States in conferring competence on monitoring bodies to rule on (rather than simply to assess) the validity of reservations. Others held the contrary view.

132. Some members thought that draft guidelines 3.2.1 and 3.2.2 should state that the monitoring bodies were competent to the extent provided by the treaty. The point was also made that the monitoring bodies did not take account of the positions adopted by the contracting States, an issue that was at the heart of the problem of the competence of such bodies to assess the validity of reservations.

133. Among the dispute settlement bodies, judicial bodies deserved special mention, since their decisions produced effects quite different from those produced by the decisions of other organs.

134. The point was made that national authorities other than courts might have occasion, within their sphere of competence, to consider the validity of some reservations formulated by other States.

135. It was observed that the reference to protocols might entail the risk of encouraging their use in order to limit or criticize the competence of monitoring bodies.

136. It was also pointed out that draft guideline 3.2.4 did not answer certain questions that might arise, such as what would happen if the various competent bodies did not agree on their assessment of the reservation, or its validity.

137. It was noted that the Commission had decided not to mention implicit prohibition, so that the term should be deleted from draft guideline 3.3.

138. With regard to draft guideline 3.3.1, the view was expressed that the Commission should refrain from stating a position on whether the international responsibility of a State or international organization that had formulated an invalid reservation was or was not engaged. It was stated that such an assertion does not appear to be compatible with the law of State responsibility and might even have the effect of encouraging States to formulate invalid reservations in the belief that their responsibility would not be engaged.

139. With regard to draft guidelines 3.3.2, 3.3.3 and 3.3.4, it was observed that they raised questions that it would be premature to decide at the current stage. They should be given further consideration before being referred to the Drafting Committee.

140. It was observed that an invalid reservation could not be null and void, because such a reservation could produce effects in certain situations.

141. Several members expressed doubts about draft guidelines 3.3.3 and 3.3.4, noting contradictions and ambiguities, and were not in agreement with the role of arbitrator in the matter of reservations that the guidelines appeared to confer on the depositary.

142. It was even questioned whether the Commission should take up the matter of the consequences of the invalidity of reservations, which, perhaps wisely, had not been addressed in the 1969 and 1986 Vienna Conventions. Perhaps that gap should not be filled; the regime that allowed States to decide on the validity of reservations and to draw the consequences already existed, and there was no reason to change it.

143. It was observed, with reference to article 20 of the Vienna Conventions concerning acceptance of reservations and objections to reservations, that there was no indication in the Vienna Conventions that the article was meant to apply to invalid reservations as well. In practice, States relied on article 20 when objecting to reservations that they considered incompatible with the object and purpose of the treaty, yet still maintained contractual relations between themselves and the State that had made the reservation. The Guide to Practice should take account of that practice and give guidance to States if the practice was thought to be incompatible with the Vienna regime.

3. Special Rapporteur's concluding remarks

144. Summing up the discussion, the Special Rapporteur noted that the rich debate had afforded him insights into different points of view on the major issues and produced some interesting comments that contributed constructively to the work of the Commission.

145. With regard to draft guidelines 3.1.5 and 3.1.6, he had noted that the participants in the debate had thought that they formed a whole defining the concept of the object and purpose of a treaty. The three versions of draft guideline 3.1.5 proposed in 2005[694] and 2006 (A/CN.4/572, paras. 7–8) could serve as a basis for a possible definition, bearing in mind, of course, the element of subjectivity inherent in the concept.

146. Since contracting States might have differing opinions on what was essential in a treaty, he was convinced that an effort should be made to identify the point of equilibrium, which he had expressed in the idea of "the general architecture" or "the balance of the treaty". He had noted, however, that the idea had not commanded general support and that the phrase "rules, rights and obligations" had been preferred to the phrase "essential conditions" of the treaty.

147. He was alive to the argument that the "*raison d'être*" of a treaty might be difficult to identify, since a treaty could have more than one *raison d'être*, if it had more than one objective or if the parties had different expectations. On the other hand, he did not think that the word "seriously" should be deleted from the phrase "could seriously disturb". Since a reservation by definition affected the integrity of a treaty, it was logical to suppose that only a serious impact was capable of threatening the object and purpose of the treaty.

148. With regard to draft guideline 3.1.6, he was doubtful about the wisdom of including a reference to the subsequent practice of the parties, although a majority of the members had been in favour of it. It was true that a treaty evolved over time, but it should be recalled that the reservation was generally formulated at the beginning of a treaty's life when practice still had little relevance. Moreover, he was not sure that the object and purpose of a treaty could evolve over time.

149. The Special Rapporteur noted that draft guidelines 3.1.7 to 3.1.13 and the pragmatic approach they represented had generally met with support. He was not sure that he had grasped how the additional category of reservations that a member had proposed, namely reservations to provisions relating to the implementation of treaties through domestic legislation, differed from those set out in draft guideline 3.1.11; however, he was not opposed to having the Drafting Committee consider whether to add a draft guideline on that point. He was persuaded by the argument put forward by several members that the vague and general nature of a reservation could cause it to be invalid, but for reasons other than incompatibility with the object and purpose of the treaty.

150. On draft guideline 3.1.9, several members had echoed the doubts that he himself had expressed at the previous session. He agreed that the draft guideline was grounded in article 53 of the 1969 Vienna Convention, rather than in article 19 (*c*).

151. He was not insensitive to the concern of some members that reservations to provisions relating to non-derogable rights should constitute the exception and should be strictly limited; however, that concern could be dealt with by rewording draft guideline 3.1.10 and did not call into question the underlying principle.

152. The Special Rapporteur had noted with satisfaction that no member had disputed the principle that States or international organizations had competence to assess the validity of reservations. He had listened with interest to the comments of several members on the relation between that principle and article 20 of the Vienna Convention, but he felt it would be more appropriate to take up the point when the Commission considered the effects of acceptance of and objections to reservations.

153. As to the competence of dispute settlement bodies or treaty implementation monitoring bodies to assess the validity of reservations, he recalled that he had simply taken note of practice without "conferring" (or refusing to confer) powers on such bodies, which, in his view, did not have greater competence in that area than they had in general.

[694] Tenth report on reservations to treaties, *Yearbook ... 2005*, vol. II (Part One), document A/CN.4/4/558 and Add.1–2.

154. He pointed out that all the draft guidelines on that point were in keeping with the preliminary conclusions on reservations to normative multilateral treaties, including human rights treaties adopted by the Commission in 1997. He would also like to repeat his proposal to delete the word "other" in both places from the phrase "The other contacting States … or other contracting organizations" in draft guideline 3.2, in order to accommodate the point that domestic courts might have occasion to assess the validity of reservations formulated by their own State.

155. The Drafting Committee might consider the possibility of supplementing draft guideline 3.2.4 with another specifying that monitoring bodies should take into account the assessment by contracting States of the validity of reservations.

156. With regard to draft guideline 3.3.1, he was convinced that an invalid reservation did not violate the treaty to which it referred and did not engage the responsibility of its author; if the reservation was invalid, it was null and void.

157. In conclusion, the Special Rapporteur said that it would be preferable to defer a decision on draft guidelines 3.3.2, 3.3.3 and 3.3.4 until the Commission could consider the effect of objections to and acceptance of reservations.

C. Text of the draft guidelines on reservations to treaties provisionally adopted so far by the Commission

1. Text of the draft guidelines

158. The text of the draft guidelines provisionally adopted so far by the Commission is reproduced below.[695]

RESERVATIONS TO TREATIES

Guide to practice

Explanatory note

Some draft guidelines in the present Guide to Practice are accompanied by model clauses. The adoption of these model clauses may have advantages in specific circumstances. The user should refer to the commentaries for an assessment of the circumstances appropriate for the use of a particular model clause.

1. ***Definitions***

1.1 ***Definition of reservations***

"Reservation" means a unilateral statement, however phrased or named, made by a State or an international organization when signing, ratifying, formally confirming, accepting, approving or acceding to a treaty or by a State when making a notification of succession to a treaty, whereby the State or organization purports to exclude or to modify the legal effect of certain provisions of the treaty in their application to that State or to that international organization.

1.1.1 [1.1.4][696] ***Object of reservations***

A reservation purports to exclude or modify the legal effect of certain provisions of a treaty or of the treaty as a whole with respect to certain specific aspects in their application to the State or to the international organization which formulates the reservation.

1.1.2 ***Instances in which reservations may be formulated***

Instances in which a reservation may be formulated under guideline 1.1 include all the means of expressing consent to be bound by a treaty mentioned in article 11 of the Vienna Convention on the Law of Treaties and the Vienna Convention on the Law of Treaties between States and International Organizations or between International Organizations.

1.1.3 [1.1.8] ***Reservations having territorial scope***

A unilateral statement by which a State purports to exclude the application of a treaty or some of its provisions to a territory to which that treaty would be applicable in the absence of such a statement constitutes a reservation.

1.1.4 [1.1.3] ***Reservations formulated when notifying territorial application***

A unilateral statement by which a State purports to exclude or to modify the legal effect of certain provisions of a treaty in relation to a territory in respect of which it makes a notification of the territorial application of the treaty constitutes a reservation.

1.1.5 [1.1.6] ***Statements purporting to limit the obligations of their author***

A unilateral statement formulated by a State or an international organization at the time when that State or that organization expresses its consent to be bound by a treaty by which its author purports to limit the obligations imposed on it by the treaty constitutes a reservation.

1.1.6 ***Statements purporting to discharge an obligation by equivalent means***

A unilateral statement formulated by a State or an international organization when that State or that organization expresses its consent to be bound by a treaty by which that State or that organization purports to discharge an obligation pursuant to the treaty in a manner different from but equivalent to that imposed by the treaty constitutes a reservation.

1.1.7 [1.1.1] ***Reservations formulated jointly***

The joint formulation of a reservation by several States or international organizations does not affect the unilateral nature of that reservation.

1.1.8 ***Reservations made under exclusionary clauses***

A unilateral statement made by a State or an international organization when that State or organization expresses its consent to be bound by a treaty, in accordance with a clause expressly authorizing the parties or some of them to exclude or to modify the legal effect of certain provisions of the treaty in their application to those parties, constitutes a reservation.

---

[695] See the commentary to guidelines 1.1, 1.1.2, 1.1.3 [1.1.8], 1.1.4 [1.1.3] and 1.1.7 [1.1.1] in *Yearbook ... 1998*, vol. II (Part Two), pp. 99–107; the commentary to guidelines 1.1.1 [1.1.4], 1.1.5 [1.1.6], 1.1.6, 1.2, 1.2.1 [1.2.4], 1.2.2 [1.2.1], 1.3, 1.3.1, 1.3.2 [1.2.2], 1.3.3 [1.2.3], 1.4, 1.4.1 [1.1.5], 1.4.2 [1.1.6], 1.4.3 [1.1.7], 1.4.4 [1.2.5], 1.4.5 [1.2.6], 1.5, 1.5.1 [1.1.9], 1.5.2 [1.2.7], 1.5.3 [1.2.8] and 1.6 in *Yearbook ... 1999*, vol. II (Part Two), pp. 93–126; the commentary to guidelines 1.1.8, 1.4.6 [1.4.6, 1.4.7], 1.4.7 [1.4.8], 1.7, 1.7.1 [1.7.1, 1.7.2, 1.7.3, 1.7.4] and 1.7.2 [1.7.5] in *Yearbook ... 2000*, vol. II (Part Two), pp. 108–123; the commentary to guidelines 2.2.1, 2.2.2 [2.2.3], 2.2.3 [2.2.4], 2.3.1, 2.3.2, 2.3.3, 2.3.4, 2.4.3, 2.4.4 [2.4.5], 2.4.5 [2.4.4], 2.4.6 [2.4.7] and 2.4.7 [2.4.8] in *Yearbook ... 2001*, vol. II (Part Two) and corrigendum, pp. 180–195; the commentary to guidelines 2.1.1, 2.1.2, 2.1.3, 2.1.4 [2.1.3 *bis*, 2.1.4], 2.1.5, 2.1.6 [2.1.6, 2.1.8], 2.1.7, 2.1.8 [2.1.7 *bis*], 2.4, 2.4.1, 2.4.2 [2.4.1 *bis*] and 2.4.7 [2.4.2, 2.4.9] in *Yearbook ... 2002*, vol. II (Part Two), pp. 28–48; the commentary to the explanatory note and to guidelines 2.5, 2.5.1, 2.5.2, 2.5.3, 2.5.4 [2.5.5], 2.5.5 [2.5.5 *bis*, 2.5.5 *ter*], 2.5.6, 2.5.7 [2.5.7, 2.5.8] and 2.5.8 [2.5.9], to model clauses A, B and C, and to guidelines 2.5.9 [2.5.10], 2.5.10 [2.5.11] and 2.5.11 [2.5.12] in *Yearbook ... 2003*, vol. II (Part Two), pp. 70–92; the commentary to guidelines 2.3.5, 2.4.9, 2.4.10, 2.5.12 and 2.5.13 in *Yearbook ... 2004*, vol. II (Part Two), pp. 106–110; and the commentary to guidelines 2.6, 2.6.1 and 2.6.2 in *Yearbook ... 2005*, vol. II (Part Two). The commentary to guidelines 3, 3.1, 3.1.1, 3.1.2, 3.1.3 and 3.1.4, as well as the commentary to guidelines 1.6 and 2.1.8 [2.1.7 *bis*] in its new version are in section 2 below.

[696] The number between square brackets indicates the number of this draft guideline in the report of the Special Rapporteur or, as the case may be, the original number of a draft guideline in the report of the Special Rapporteur which has been merged with the final draft guideline.

1.2 *Definition of interpretative declarations*

"Interpretative declaration" means a unilateral statement, however phrased or named, made by a State or by an international organization whereby that State or that organization purports to specify or clarify the meaning or scope attributed by the declarant to a treaty or to certain of its provisions.

1.2.1 [1.2.4] *Conditional interpretative declarations*

A unilateral statement formulated by a State or an international organization when signing, ratifying, formally confirming, accepting, approving or acceding to a treaty, or by a State when making a notification of succession to a treaty, whereby the State or international organization subjects its consent to be bound by the treaty to a specific interpretation of the treaty or of certain provisions thereof, shall constitute a conditional interpretative declaration.

1.2.2 [1.2.1] *Interpretative declarations formulated jointly*

The joint formulation of an interpretative declaration by several States or international organizations does not affect the unilateral nature of that interpretative declaration.

1.3 *Distinction between reservations and interpretative declarations*

The character of a unilateral statement as a reservation or an interpretative declaration is determined by the legal effect it purports to produce.

1.3.1 *Method of implementation of the distinction between reservations and interpretative declarations*

To determine whether a unilateral statement formulated by a State or an international organization in respect of a treaty is a reservation or an interpretative declaration, it is appropriate to interpret the statement in good faith in accordance with the ordinary meaning to be given to its terms, in light of the treaty to which it refers. Due regard shall be given to the intention of the State or the international organization concerned at the time the statement was formulated.

1.3.2 [1.2.2] *Phrasing and name*

The phrasing or name given to a unilateral statement provides an indication of the purported legal effect. This is the case in particular when a State or an international organization formulates several unilateral statements in respect of a single treaty and designates some of them as reservations and others as interpretative declarations.

1.3.3 [1.2.3] *Formulation of a unilateral statement when a reservation is prohibited*

When a treaty prohibits reservations to all or certain of its provisions, a unilateral statement formulated in respect thereof by a State or an international organization shall be presumed not to constitute a reservation except when it purports to exclude or modify the legal effect of certain provisions of the treaty or of the treaty as a whole with respect to certain specific aspects in their application to its author.

1.4 *Unilateral statements other than reservations and interpretative declarations*

Unilateral statements formulated in relation to a treaty which are not reservations nor interpretative declarations are outside the scope of the present Guide to Practice.

1.4.1 [1.1.5] *Statements purporting to undertake unilateral commitments*

A unilateral statement formulated by a State or an international organization in relation to a treaty, whereby its author purports to undertake obligations going beyond those imposed on it by the treaty constitutes a unilateral commitment which is outside the scope of the present Guide to Practice.

1.4.2 [1.1.6] *Unilateral statements purporting to add further elements to a treaty*

A unilateral statement whereby a State or an international organization purports to add further elements to a treaty constitutes a proposal to modify the content of the treaty which is outside the scope of the present Guide to Practice.

1.4.3 [1.1.7] *Statements of non-recognition*

A unilateral statement by which a State indicates that its participation in a treaty does not imply recognition of an entity which it does not recognize constitutes a statement of non-recognition which is outside the scope of the present Guide to Practice even if it purports to exclude the application of the treaty between the declaring State and the non-recognized entity.

1.4.4 [1.2.5] *General statements of policy*

A unilateral statement formulated by a State or by an international organization whereby that State or that organization expresses its views on a treaty or on the subject matter covered by the treaty, without purporting to produce a legal effect on the treaty, constitutes a general statement of policy which is outside the scope of the present Guide to Practice.

1.4.5 [1.2.6] *Statements concerning modalities of implementation of a treaty at the internal level*

A unilateral statement formulated by a State or an international organization whereby that State or that organization indicates the manner in which it intends to implement a treaty at the internal level, without purporting as such to affect its rights and obligations towards the other contracting parties, constitutes an informative statement which is outside the scope of the present Guide to Practice.

1.4.6. [1.4.6, 1.4.7] *Unilateral statements made under an optional clause*

1. A unilateral statement made by a State or by an international organization, in accordance with a clause in a treaty expressly authorizing the parties to accept an obligation that is not otherwise imposed by the treaty, is outside the scope of the present Guide to Practice.

2. A restriction or condition contained in such statement does not constitute a reservation within the meaning of the present Guide to Practice.

1.4.7 [1.4.8] *Unilateral statements providing for a choice between the provisions of a treaty*

A unilateral statement made by a State or an international organization, in accordance with a clause in a treaty that expressly requires the parties to choose between two or more provisions of the treaty, is outside the scope of the present Guide to Practice.

1.5 *Unilateral statements in respect of bilateral treaties*

1.5.1 [1.1.9] *"Reservations" to bilateral treaties*

A unilateral statement, however phrased or named, formulated by a State or an international organization after initialling or signature but prior to entry into force of a bilateral treaty, by which that State or that organization purports to obtain from the other party a modification of the provisions of the treaty to which it is subjecting the expression of its final consent to be bound, does not constitute a reservation within the meaning of the present Guide to Practice.

1.5.2 [1.2.7] *Interpretative declarations in respect of bilateral treaties*

Draft guidelines 1.2 and 1.2.1 are applicable to interpretative declarations in respect of multilateral as well as bilateral treaties.

1.5.3 [1.2.8] *Legal effect of acceptance of an interpretative declaration made in respect of bilateral treaty by the other party*

The interpretation resulting from an interpretative declaration made in respect of a bilateral treaty by a State or an international organization party to the treaty and accepted by the other party constitutes the authentic interpretation of that treaty.

1.6 *Scope of definitions*[697]

The definitions of unilateral statements included in the present chapter of the Guide to Practice are without prejudice to the validity and effects of such statements under the rules applicable to them.

1.7 *Alternatives to reservations and interpretative declarations*

1.7.1 [1.7.1, 1.7.2, 1.7.3, 1.7.4] *Alternatives to reservations*

In order to achieve results comparable to those effected by reservations, States or international organizations may also have recourse to alternative procedures, such as:

(*a*) the insertion in the treaty of restrictive clauses purporting to limit its scope or application;

(*b*) the conclusion of an agreement, under a specific provision of a treaty, by which two or more States or international organizations purport to exclude or modify the legal effects of certain provisions of the treaty as between themselves.

1.7.2 [1.7.5] *Alternatives to interpretative declarations*

In order to specify or clarify the meaning or scope of a treaty or certain of its provisions, States or international organizations may also have recourse to procedures other than interpretative declarations, such as:

(*a*) the insertion in the treaty of provisions purporting to interpret the same treaty;

(*b*) the conclusion of a supplementary agreement to the same end.

2. *Procedure*

2.1 *Form and notification of reservations*

2.1.1 *Written form*

A reservation must be formulated in writing.

2.1.2 *Form of formal confirmation*

Formal confirmation of a reservation must be made in writing.

2.1.3 *Formulation of a reservation at the international level*

1. Subject to the customary practices in international organizations which are depositaries of treaties, a person is considered as representing a State or an international organization for the purpose of formulating a reservation if:

(*a*) that person produces appropriate full powers for the purposes of adopting or authenticating the text of the treaty with regard to which the reservation is formulated or expressing the consent of the State or organization to be bound by the treaty; or

(*b*) it appears from practice or other circumstances that it was the intention of the States and international organizations concerned to consider that person as competent for such purposes without having to produce full powers.

2. By virtue of their functions and without having to produce full powers, the following are considered as representing a State for the purpose of formulating a reservation at the international level:

(*a*) Heads of State, Heads of Government and Ministers for Foreign Affairs;

(*b*) representatives accredited by States to an international conference for the purpose of formulating a reservation to a treaty adopted at that conference;

(*c*) representatives accredited by States to an international organization or one of its organs, for the purpose of formulating a reservation to a treaty adopted by that organization or body;

(*d*) heads of permanent missions to an international organization, for the purpose of formulating a reservation to a treaty between the accrediting States and that organization.

2.1.4 [2.1.3 *bis*, 2.1.4] *Absence of consequences at the international level of the violation of internal rules regarding the formulation of reservations*

1. The determination of the competent authority and the procedure to be followed at the internal level for formulating a reservation is a matter for the internal law of each State or relevant rules of each international organization.

2. A State or an international organization may not invoke the fact that a reservation has been formulated in violation of a provision of the internal law of that State or the rules of that organization regarding competence and the procedure for formulating reservations as invalidating the reservation.

2.1.5 *Communication of reservations*

1. A reservation must be communicated in writing to the contracting States and contracting organizations and other States and international organizations entitled to become parties to the treaty.

2. A reservation to a treaty in force which is the constituent instrument of an international organization or to a treaty which creates an organ that has the capacity to accept a reservation must also be communicated to such organization or organ.

2.1.6 [2.1.6, 2.1.8] *Procedure for communication of reservations*

1. Unless otherwise provided in the treaty or agreed by the contracting States and contracting organizations, a communication relating to a reservation to a treaty shall be transmitted:

(*a*) if there is no depositary, directly by the author of the reservation to the contracting States and contracting organizations and other States and international organizations entitled to become parties to the treaty; or

(*b*) if there is a depositary, to the latter, which shall notify the States and organizations for which it is intended as soon as possible.

2. A communication relating to a reservation shall be considered as having been made by the author of the reservation only upon receipt by the State or by the organization to which it was transmitted, or as the case may be, upon its receipt by the depositary.

3. The period during which an objection to a reservation may be raised starts at the date on which a State or an international organization received notification of the reservation.

4. Where a communication relating to a reservation to a treaty is made by electronic mail or by facsimile, it must be confirmed by diplomatic note or depositary notification. In such a case the communication is considered as having been made at the date of the electronic mail or the facsimile.

2.1.7 *Functions of depositaries*

1. The depositary shall examine whether a reservation to a treaty formulated by a State or an international organization is in due and proper form and, if need be, bring the matter to the attention of the State or international organization concerned.

2. In the event of any difference appearing between a State or an international organization and the depositary as to the performance of the latter's functions, the depositary shall bring the question to the attention of:

(*a*) the signatory States and organizations and the contracting States and contracting organizations; or

(*b*) where appropriate, the competent organ of the international organization concerned.

[697] This draft guideline has been reconsidered and modified during the Commission's fifty-eighth session (2006). For the new commentary, see section C.2 below.

2.1.8 [2.1.7 *bis*] *Procedure in case of manifestly invalid reservations*[698]

1. Where, in the opinion of the depositary, a reservation is manifestly invalid, the depositary shall draw the attention of the author of the reservation to what, in the depositary's view, constitutes the grounds for the invalidity of the reservation.

2. If the author of the reservation maintains the reservation, the depositary shall communicate the text of the reservation to the signatory States and international organizations and to the contracting States and international organizations and, where appropriate, the competent organ of the international organization concerned, indicating the nature of legal problems raised by the reservation.

2.2.1 *Formal confirmation of reservations formulated when signing a treaty*

If formulated when signing a treaty subject to ratification, act of formal confirmation, acceptance or approval, a reservation must be formally confirmed by the reserving State or international organization when expressing its consent to be bound by the treaty. In such a case the reservation shall be considered as having been made on the date of its confirmation.

2.2.2 [2.2.3] *Instances of non-requirement of confirmation of reservations formulated when signing a treaty*

A reservation formulated when signing a treaty does not require subsequent confirmation when a State or an international organization expresses by its signature the consent to be bound by the treaty.

2.2.3 [2.2.4] *Reservations formulated upon signature when a treaty expressly so provides*

A reservation formulated when signing a treaty, where the treaty expressly provides that a State or an international organization may make such a reservation at that time, does not require formal confirmation by the reserving State or international organization when expressing its consent to be bound by the treaty.

...[699]

2.3.1 *Late formulation of a reservation*

Unless the treaty provides otherwise, a State or an international organization may not formulate a reservation to a treaty after expressing its consent to be bound by the treaty except if none of the other contracting parties objects to the late formulation of the reservation.

2.3.2 *Acceptance of late formulation of a reservation*

Unless the treaty provides otherwise or the well-established practice followed by the depositary differs, late formulation of a reservation shall be deemed to have been accepted by a contracting party if it has made no objections to such formulation after the expiry of the 12-month period following the date on which notification was received.

2.3.3 *Objection to late formulation of a reservation*

If a contracting party to a treaty objects to late formulation of a reservation, the treaty shall enter into or remain in force in respect of the reserving State or international organization without the reservation being established.

2.3.4 *Subsequent exclusion or modification of the legal effect of a treaty by means other than reservations*

A contracting party to a treaty may not exclude or modify the legal effect of provisions of the treaty by:

(*a*) interpretation of a reservation made earlier; or

(*b*) a unilateral statement made subsequently under an optional clause.

2.3.5 *Widening of the scope of a reservation*

The modification of an existing reservation for the purpose of widening its scope shall be subject to the rules applicable to the late formulation of a reservation. However, if an objection is made to that modification, the initial reservation remains unchanged.

2.4 *Procedure for interpretative declarations*

2.4.1 *Formulation of interpretative declarations*

An interpretative declaration must be formulated by a person who is considered as representing a State or an international organization for the purpose of adopting or authenticating the text of a treaty or expressing the consent of the State or international organization to be bound by a treaty.

[2.4.2 [2.4.1 *bis*] *Formulation of an interpretative declaration at the internal level*

1. The determination of the competent authority and the procedure to be followed at the internal level for formulating an interpretative declaration is a matter for the internal law of each State or relevant rules of each international organization.

2. A State or an international organization may not invoke the fact that an interpretative declaration has been formulated in violation of a provision of the internal law of that State or the rules of that organization regarding competence and the procedure for formulating interpretative declarations as invalidating the declaration.]

2.4.3 *Time at which an interpretative declaration may be formulated*

Without prejudice to the provisions of guidelines 1.2.1, 2.4.6 [2.4.7], and 2.4.7 [2.4.8], an interpretative declaration may be formulated at any time.

2.4.4 [2.4.5] *Non-requirement of confirmation of interpretative declarations made when signing a treaty*

An interpretative declaration made when signing a treaty does not require subsequent confirmation when a State or an international organization expresses its consent to be bound by the treaty.

2.4.5 [2.4.4] *Formal confirmation of conditional interpretative declarations formulated when signing a treaty*

If a conditional interpretative declaration is formulated when signing a treaty subject to ratification, act of formal confirmation, acceptance or approval, it must be formally confirmed by the declaring State or international organization when expressing its consent to be bound by the treaty. In such a case the interpretative declaration shall be considered as having been made on the date of its confirmation.

2.4.6 [2.4.7] *Late formulation of an interpretative declaration*

Where a treaty provides that an interpretative declaration may be made only at specified times, a State or an international organization may not formulate an interpretative declaration concerning that treaty subsequently except if none of the other contracting parties objects to the late formulation of the interpretative declaration.

[2.4.7 [2.4.2, 2.4.9] *Formulation and communication of conditional interpretative declarations*

1. A conditional interpretative declaration must be formulated in writing.

2. Formal confirmation of a conditional interpretative declaration must also be made in writing.

3. A conditional interpretative declaration must be communicated in writing to the contracting States and contracting organizations and other States and international organizations entitled to become parties to the treaty.

---

[698] *Ibid.*

[699] Section 2.3 proposed by the Special Rapporteur deals with the late formulation of reservations.

4. A conditional interpretative declaration regarding a treaty in force which is the constituent instrument of an international organization or a treaty which creates an organ that has the capacity to accept a reservation must also be communicated to such organization or organ.]

2.4.8 ***Late formulation of a conditional interpretative declaration***[700]

A State or an international organization may not formulate a conditional interpretative declaration concerning a treaty after expressing its consent to be bound by the treaty except if none of the other contracting parties objects to the late formulation of the conditional interpretative declaration.

2.4.9 ***Modification of an interpretative declaration***

Unless the treaty provides that an interpretative declaration may be made or modified only at specified times, an interpretative declaration may be modified at any time.

2.4.10 ***Limitation and widening of the scope of a conditional interpretative declaration***

The limitation and the widening of the scope of a conditional interpretative declaration are governed by the rules respectively applicable to the partial withdrawal and the widening of the scope of reservations.

2.5 ***Withdrawal and modification of reservations and interpretative declarations***

2.5.1 ***Withdrawal of reservations***

Unless the treaty otherwise provides, a reservation may be withdrawn at any time and the consent of a State or of an international organization which has accepted the reservation is not required for its withdrawal.

2.5.2 ***Form of withdrawal***

The withdrawal of a reservation must be formulated in writing.

2.5.3 ***Periodic review of the usefulness of reservations***

1. States or international organizations which have made one or more reservations to a treaty should undertake a periodic review of such reservations and consider withdrawing those which no longer serve their purpose.

2. In such a review, States and international organizations should devote special attention to the aim of preserving the integrity of multilateral treaties and, where relevant, give consideration to the usefulness of retaining the reservations, in particular in relation to developments in their internal law since the reservations were formulated.

2.5.4 [2.5.5] ***Formulation of the withdrawal of a reservation at the international level***

1. Subject to the usual practices in international organizations which are depositaries of treaties, a person is competent to withdraw a reservation made on behalf of a State or an international organization if:

(*a*) that person produces appropriate full powers for the purposes of that withdrawal; or

(*b*) it appears from practice or other circumstances that it was the intention of the States and international organizations concerned to consider that person as competent for such purposes without having to produce full powers.

2. By virtue of their functions and without having to produce full powers, the following are competent to withdraw a reservation at the international level on behalf of a State:

(*a*) Heads of State, Heads of Government and Ministers for Foreign Affairs;

(*b*) representatives accredited by States to an international organization or one of its organs, for the purpose of withdrawing a reservation to a treaty adopted by that organization or body;

(*c*) heads of permanent missions to an international organization, for the purpose of withdrawing a reservation to a treaty between the accrediting States and that organization.

2.5.5 [2.5.5 ***bis*****, 2.5.5** ***ter*****]** ***Absence of consequences at the international level of the violation of internal rules regarding the withdrawal of reservations***

1. The determination of the competent body and the procedure to be followed for withdrawing a reservation at the internal level is a matter for the internal law of each State or the relevant rules of each international organization.

2. A State or an international organization may not invoke the fact that a reservation has been withdrawn in violation of a provision of the internal law of that State or the rules of that organization regarding competence and the procedure for the withdrawal of reservations as invalidating the withdrawal.

2.5.6 ***Communication of withdrawal of a reservation***

The procedure for communicating the withdrawal of a reservation follows the rules applicable to the communication of reservations contained in guidelines 2.1.5, 2.1.6 [2.1.6, 2.1.8] and 2.1.7.

2.5.7 [2.5.7, 2.5.8] ***Effect of withdrawal of a reservation***

1. The withdrawal of a reservation entails the application as a whole of the provisions on which the reservation had been made in the relations between the State or international organization which withdraws the reservation and all the other parties, whether they had accepted the reservation or objected to it.

2. The withdrawal of a reservation entails the entry into force of the treaty in the relations between the State or international organization which withdraws the reservation and a State or international organization which had objected to the reservation and opposed the entry into force of the treaty between itself and the reserving State or international organization by reason of that reservation.

2.5.8 [2.5.9] ***Effective date of withdrawal of a reservation***

Unless the treaty otherwise provides, or it is otherwise agreed, the withdrawal of a reservation becomes operative in relation to a contracting State or a contracting organization only when notice of it has been received by that State or that organization.

Model clauses

A. ***Deferment of the effective date of the withdrawal of a reservation***

A contracting party which has made a reservation to this treaty may withdraw it by means of notification addressed to [the depositary]. The withdrawal shall take effect on the expiration of a period of X [months] [days] after the date of receipt of the notification by [the depositary].

B. ***Earlier effective date of withdrawal of a reservation***

A contracting party which has made a reservation to this treaty may withdraw it by means of a notification addressed to [the depositary]. The withdrawal shall take effect on the date of receipt of such notification by [the depositary].

C. ***Freedom to set the effective date of withdrawal of a reservation***

A contracting party which has made a reservation to this treaty may withdraw it by means of a notification addressed to [the depositary]. The withdrawal shall take effect on the date set by that State in the notification addressed to [the depositary].

---

[700] This draft guideline (formerly 2.4.7 [2.4.8]) was renumbered as a result of the adoption of new draft guidelines at the fifty-fourth session of the Commission, in 2002.

2.5.9 [2.5.10] *Cases in which a reserving State or international organization may unilaterally set the effective date of withdrawal of a reservation*

The withdrawal of a reservation takes effect on the date set by the withdrawing State or international organization where:

(*a*) that date is later than the date on which the other contracting States or international organizations received notification of it; or

(*b*) the withdrawal does not add to the rights of the withdrawing State or international organization, in relation to the other contracting States or international organizations.

2.5.10 [2.5.11] *Partial withdrawal of a reservation*

1. The partial withdrawal of a reservation limits the legal effect of the reservation and achieves a more complete application of the provisions of the treaty, or of the treaty as a whole, to the withdrawing State or international organization.

2. The partial withdrawal of a reservation is subject to the same formal and procedural rules as a total withdrawal and takes effect on the same conditions.

2.5.11 [2.5.12] *Effect of a partial withdrawal of a reservation*

1. The partial withdrawal of a reservation modifies the legal effect of the reservation to the extent of the new formulation of the reservation. Any objection made to the reservation continues to have effect as long as its author does not withdraw it, insofar as the objection does not apply exclusively to that part of the reservation which has been withdrawn.

2. No objection may be made to the reservation resulting from the partial withdrawal, unless that partial withdrawal has a discriminatory effect.

2.5.12 *Withdrawal of an interpretative declaration*

An interpretative declaration may be withdrawn at any time by the authorities competent for that purpose, following the same procedure applicable to its formulation.

2.5.13 *Withdrawal of a conditional interpretative declaration*

The withdrawal of a conditional interpretative declaration is governed by the rules applying to the withdrawal of reservations.

2.6.1 *Definition of objections to reservations*

"Objection" means a unilateral statement, however phrased or named, made by a State or an international organization in response to a reservation to a treaty formulated by another State or international organization, whereby the former State or organization purports to exclude or to modify the legal effects of the reservation, or to exclude the application of the treaty as a whole, in relations with the reserving State or organization.

2.6.2 *Definition of objections to the late formulation or widening of the scope of a reservation*

"Objection" may also mean a unilateral statement whereby a State or an international organization opposes the late formulation of a reservation or the widening of the scope of a reservation.

3. *Validity of reservations and interpretative declarations*

3.1 *Permissible reservations*

A State or an international organization may, when signing, ratifying, formally confirming, accepting, approving or acceding to a treaty, formulate a reservation unless:

(*a*) the reservation is prohibited by the treaty;

(*b*) the treaty provides that only specified reservations, which do not include the reservation in question, may be made; or

(*c*) in cases not falling under subparagraphs (*a*) and (*b*), the reservation is incompatible with the object and purpose of the treaty.

3.1.1 *Reservations expressly prohibited by the treaty*

A reservation is expressly prohibited by the treaty if it contains a particular provision:

(*a*) prohibiting all reservations;

(*b*) prohibiting reservations to specified provisions and a reservation in question is formulated to one of such provisions; or

(*c*) prohibiting certain categories of reservations and a reservation in question falls within one of such categories.

3.1.2 *Definition of specified reservations*

For the purposes of guideline 3.1, the expression "specified reservations" means reservations that are expressly envisaged in the treaty to certain provisions of the treaty or to the treaty as a whole with respect to certain specific aspects.

3.1.3 *Permissibility of reservations not prohibited by the treaty*

Where the treaty prohibits the formulation of certain reservations, a reservation which is not prohibited by the treaty may be formulated by a State or an international organization only if it is not incompatible with the object and purpose of the treaty.

3.1.4 *Permissibility of specified reservations*

Where the treaty envisages the formulation of specified reservations without defining their content, a reservation may be formulated by a State or an international organization only if it is not incompatible with the object and purpose of the treaty.

2. Text of the draft guidelines and commentaries thereto provisionally adopted by the Commission at its fifty-eighth session

159. The text of the draft guidelines with commentaries thereto adopted by the Commission at its fifty-eighth session are reproduced below.

3. *Validity of reservations and interpretative declarations*

General commentary

(1) The purpose of the third part of the Guide to Practice, following the first part, devoted to definitions, and the second, which deals with the procedure of formulation of reservations and interpretative declarations, is to determine the conditions for the validity of reservations to treaties.

(2) After extensive debate, the Commission decided, despite hesitation on the part of some members, to retain the term "validity of reservations" to describe the intellectual operation consisting in determining whether a unilateral statement made[701] by a State or an international organization and purporting to exclude or modify the legal effect of certain provisions of the treaty[702] in their application to that State or organization was capable of producing the effects attached in principle to the formulation of a reservation.

---

[701] Since the mere formulation of a reservation does not allow it to produce the effects intended by its author, the word "formulated" would have been more appropriate (see below the commentary to draft guideline 3.1, paras. (6) and (7)), but the Vienna Conventions use the word "made" and as a matter of principle the Commission does not wish to revisit the Vienna text.

[702] Or of the treaty as a whole with respect to certain specific aspects (see draft guideline 1.1.1).

(3) Adhering to the definition found in article 2, paragraph 1 (*d*), of the 1969 and 1986 Vienna Conventions, reproduced in draft guideline 1.1 of the Guide to Practice, the Commission accepted that all unilateral statements meeting that definition constituted reservations. But, as the Commission stated very clearly in its commentary on draft guideline 1.6, "[d]efining is not the same as regulating. … [A] reservation may or may not be permissible, but it remains a reservation if it corresponds to the definition established".[703] It went on to say: "Furthermore, the exact determination of the nature of a statement is a precondition for the application of a particular legal regime, in the first place, for the assessment of its permissibility. It is only once a particular instrument has been defined as a reservation ... that a decision can be taken as to whether it is permissible or not, its legal scope can be evaluated and its effect can be determined".[704]

(4) This terminology poses a problem. At an early stage, the Commission opted for the words "permissibility" and "impermissibility" in preference to "validity" and "invalidity" or "non-validity" in order to respond to the concerns expressed by some members of the Commission and some States who considered that the term "validity" cast doubt on the nature of statements that fit the definition of reservations given in article 2, paragraph 1 (*d*), of the Vienna Conventions but do not fulfil the conditions set forth in article 19.[705] Actually, the word "validity" seemed to a majority of the members of the Commission to be quite neutral in that regard. It offered the advantage that it did not prejudge the doctrinal controversy,[706] central to the question of reservations, between the proponents of "permissibility", who hold that "[t]he issue of 'permissibility' is the preliminary issue. It must be resolved by reference to the treaty and is essentially an issue of treaty interpretation; it has nothing to do with the question of whether, as a matter of policy, other Parties find the reservations acceptable or not",[707] and the proponents of "opposability", who hold that "the validity of a reservation depends solely on the acceptance of the reservation by another contracting State" and who therefore view article 19, subparagraph (*c*), of the 1969 Vienna Convention "as a mere doctrinal assertion, which may serve as a basis for guidance to States regarding acceptance of reservations, but no more than that".[708]

(5) Moreover, it was thought that the term "impermissible" ("*illicite*") was not appropriate in any case to characterize reservations that did not fulfil the conditions of form or substance set by the Vienna Conventions. According to a majority of the members of the Commission, "in international law, an internationally wrongful act entails its author's responsibility, and this is plainly not the case of the formulation of reservations which are contrary to the provisions of the treaty to which they relate or incompatible with its object and purpose".[709] Consequently, the Commission, which in 2002 had decided to reserve its position on this matter pending an examination of the effect of such reservations,[710] thought that it would be better to settle that question of terminology without further delay.

(6) It appeared to the Commission:

— In the first place, that the term "permissible" ("*licite*") implied that the formulation of reservations contrary to the provisions of article 19 of the Vienna Conventions would engage the responsibility of the reserving State or international organization, which was certainly not the case;[711] and

— In the second place, that the term "permissible" used in the English text of the draft guidelines adopted to date and their commentaries implied that it was exclusively a question of permissibility and not of opposability, which had the disadvantage of unprofitably prejudging the doctrinal dispute discussed above.[712]

(7) However, the term "permissibility" was retained to denote the substantive validity of reservations that fulfilled the requirements of article 19 of the Vienna Conventions, since, according to the English speakers, the term did not imply taking a position as to the consequences of non-fulfilment of those conditions. That term was rendered in French by the expression "*validité matérielle*".

(8) The third part of the Guide to Practice deals successively with the questions relating to:

— The permissibility of reservations;

— Competence to assess the validity of reservations; and

— The consequences of the invalidity of a reservation.

[703] *Yearbook ... 1999*, vol. II, (Part Two), p. 126, para. (2) of the commentary; see also, below, the commentary to the draft guideline as amended at the fifty-eighth session of the Commission.

[704] *Ibid.*, para. (3) of the commentary. See also the commentary to draft guideline 1.1.1 [1.1.4] in *Yearbook ... 1998*, vol. II (Part Two), p. 101, especially para. (3) of the commentary, and the third report of the Special Rapporteur on reservations to treaties, *ibid.*, vol. II (Part One), document A/CN.4/491 and Add.1–6, p. 250, para. 154, and p. 252, para. 175.

[705] See the statement of the United Kingdom in the Sixth Committee on 2 November 1993, *Official Records of the General Assembly, Forty-eighth Session, Sixth Committee, summary record of the 24th meeting* (A/C.6/48/SR.24), para. 42.

[706] On this doctrinal dispute, see in particular J. K. Koh, "Reservations to multilateral treaties: how international legal doctrine reflects world vision", *Harvard International Law Journal*, vol. 23 (1982–1983), pp. 71–116, *passim*, in particular pp. 75–77; see also C. Redgwell, "Universality or integrity? Some reflections on reservations to general multilateral treaties", BYBIL, vol. 64 (1993), pp. 245–282, at pp. 263–269; and I. Sinclair, *The Vienna Convention on the Law of Treaties*, 2nd ed., Manchester University Press, 1984, p. 81, footnote 78.

[707] D. W. Bowett, "Reservations to non-restricted multilateral treaties", BYBIL, vol. 48 (1976–1977), p. 88.

[708] J. M. Ruda, "Reservations to treaties", *Recueil des cours: Collected courses of the Hague Academy of International Law, 1975–III*, vol. 146 (1977), p. 190.

[709] Commentary to draft guideline 2.1.8 [2.1.7 *bis*] (Procedure in case of manifestly [impermissible] reservations), *Yearbook ... 2002*, vol. II (Part Two), p. 46, para. (7) of the commentary. According to a minority view, the formulation of an impermissible reservation would engage the responsibility of its author. The issue will be discussed in greater detail in the commentary to draft guideline 3.3.1.

[710] See the commentary to draft guideline 2.1.8 [2.1.7 *bis*], *Yearbook ... 2002*, vol. II (Part Two), pp. 45–46; see also draft guideline 2.1.7 (Functions of depositaries) and the commentary thereto, *ibid.*, pp. 42–45.

[711] See above paragraph (5) of the commentary to this draft guideline.

[712] See above paragraph (4) of the commentary to this draft guideline.

A special section will be devoted to the same questions in relation to interpretative declarations.

3.1 *Permissible reservations*

A State or an international organization may, when signing, ratifying, formally confirming, accepting, approving or acceding to a treaty, formulate a reservation unless:

(*a*) the reservation is prohibited by the treaty;

(*b*) the treaty provides that only specified reservations, which do not include the reservation in question, may be made; or

(*c*) in cases not falling under subparagraphs (*a*) and (*b*), the reservation is incompatible with the object and purpose of the treaty.

Commentary

(1) Draft guideline 3.1 faithfully reproduces the wording of article 19 of the 1986 Vienna Convention, which is patterned after the corresponding provision of the 1969 Convention with just two additions, which were needed in order to cover treaties concluded by international organizations.

(2) By providing that, when signing, ratifying, formally confirming, accepting, approving or acceding to a treaty, "[a] State or an international organization may ... formulate a reservation", albeit under certain conditions, this draft guideline sets out "the general principle that the formulation of reservations is permitted".[713] This is an essential element of the "flexible system" stemming from the advisory opinion of the ICJ of 1951 on *Reservations to the Convention on Genocide*,[714] and it is no exaggeration to say that, on this point, it reverses the traditional presumption resulting from the system of unanimity,[715] the stated aim being to facilitate the widest possible participation in treaties and, ultimately, their universality.

(3) In this regard, the text of article 19 finally adopted in 1969 resulted directly from Waldock's proposals and takes the opposite view from the drafts prepared by the Special Rapporteurs on the law of treaties who preceded him, all of whom started from the inverse assumption, expressing in negative or restrictive terms the principle that a reservation might only be formulated (or "made")[716] if certain conditions were met.[717] Waldock,[718] on the other hand, presents the principle as the "power to formulate, that is, to *propose*, a reservation", which a State has "in virtue of its sovereignty".[719]

(4) However, this power is not unlimited:

— In the first place, it is limited in time, since a reservation may only be formulated "when signing, ratifying, formally confirming, accepting, approving or acceding to a treaty";[720]

— In the second place, the formulation of reservations may be incompatible with the object of some treaties, either because they are limited to a small group of States—a situation that is taken into account in article 20, paragraph 2, of the 1969 Vienna Convention,[721] which reverts to the system of unanimity where such instruments are concerned—or, in the case of instruments of universal scope, because the parties intend to make the integrity of the treaty take precedence over its universality or, at any rate, to limit the power of States to formulate reservations; on this issue, as on all others, the Vienna Convention is only intended to be residuary in nature, and there is nothing to prevent the negotiators from inserting in the treaty "reservations clauses" that limit or modify the freedom set out as a principle in article 19.[722]

[713] Commentary to article 18 of the draft articles on the law of treaties, adopted by the Commission on first reading in 1962, *Yearbook ... 1962*, vol. II, p. 180, para. (15); see also the commentary to draft article 16 adopted on second reading, *Yearbook ... 1966*, vol. II, p. 207, para. (17). For the 1986 Vienna Convention, see the commentary to draft article 19 (Formulation of reservations in the case of treaties between several international organizations), adopted by the Commission in 1977, *Yearbook ... 1977*, vol. II (Part Two), p. 106, para. (1), and to draft article 19 *bis* (Formulation of reservations by States and international organizations in the case of treaties between States and one or more international organizations or between international organizations and one or more States), *ibid.*, p. 108, para. (3).

[714] *Reservations to the Convention on the Prevention and Punishment of the Crime of Genocide, Advisory Opinion, I.C.J. Reports 1951*, p. 15.

[715] This concept, which had undoubtedly become the customary norm in the period between the wars (see the joint dissenting opinion of Judges Guerrero, McNair, Read and Hsu Mo, appended to the advisory opinion in *Reservations to the Convention on Genocide* (footnote 714 above), pp. 34–35), significantly restricted the freedom to make reservations: this was possible only if all the other parties to the treaty accepted the reservation, otherwise the author remained outside the treaty. In its comments on article 18 of the draft articles on the law of treaties, adopted by the Commission on first reading in 1962 (see footnote 713 above), Japan proposed reverting to the opposite presumption (see the fourth report of Special Rapporteur Sir Humphrey Waldock on the law of treaties, *Yearbook ... 1965*, vol. II, document A/CN.4/177 and Add.1–2, p. 49).

[716] On this point, see below paragraphs (6) and (7) of the commentary to this draft guidline.

[717] See, for example, draft article 10 (1) of the draft convention on the law of treaties, proposed by J. L. Brierly (*Yearbook ... 1950*, vol. II, document A/CN.4/23, p. 238); the various drafts of article 9 proposed by Special Rapporteur H. Lauterpacht in his preliminary report (*Yearbook ... 1953*, vol. II, document A/CN.4/63, pp. 91–92) and his second report (*Yearbook ... 1954*, vol. II, document A/CN.4/87, p. 131); or draft article 39, paragraph 1, proposed by Special Rapporteur G. G. Fitzmaurice (*Yearbook ... 1956*, vol. II, document A/CN.4/101, p. 115). See also the comments of Pierre-Henri Imbert in *Les réserves aux traités multilatéraux*, Paris, Pedone, 1978, pp. 88–89.

[718] "A State is free, when signing, ratifying, acceding to or accepting a treaty, to formulate a reservation ... unless: ..." (preliminary report on the law of treaties , *Yearbook ... 1962*, vol. II, document A/CN.4/144 and Add.1, article 17, para. 1 (*a*), p. 60).

[719] *Ibid.*, para. (9) of the commentary to article 17, p. 65.

[720] In this regard, see below paragraph (9) of the commentary to this guideline.

[721] "When it appears from the limited number of the negotiating States and the object and purpose of a treaty that the application of the treaty in its entirety between all the parties is an essential condition of the consent of each one to be bound by the treaty, a reservation requires acceptance by all the parties."

[722] With regard to the residuary nature of the Vienna regime, see in particular A. Aust, *Modern Treaty Law and Practice*, Cambridge University Press, 2000, pp. 124–126; J. K. Gamble, Jr., "Reservations to multilateral treaties: a macroscopic view of State practice", AJIL, vol. 74 (1980), pp. 383–391; P.-H. Imbert, *Les réserves aux traités ..., op. cit.* (footnote 717 above), pp. 162–230; A. McNair, *The Law of Treaties*, Oxford, Clarendon Press, 1961, pp. 169–173; J. Polakiewicz, *Treaty-making in the Council of Europe*, Strasbourg, Council of Europe, 1999, pp. 85–90 and 101–104; and R. Riquelme Cortado, *Las reservas a los tratados: Lagunas, formulación y ambigüedades del Régimen de Viena*, Universidad de Murcia, 2004, pp. 89–136.

(5) It is probably excessive to speak of a "right to reservations",[723] even though the 1969 Vienna Convention proceeds from the principle that there is a presumption in favour of their validity. Some members contested the existence of such a presumption. This, moreover, is the significance of the very title of article 19 of the 1969 and 1986 Vienna Conventions (Formulation of reservations),[724] which is confirmed by its *chapeau*: "A State may ... formulate a reservation unless ...". Certainly, by using the verb "may", the introductory clause of article 19 recognizes that States have a right, but it is only the right to "formulate" reservations.[725]

(6) The words "formulate" and "formulation" were carefully chosen. They signify that, while it is up to the State intending to attach a reservation to its expression of consent to be bound to indicate how it means to modify its participation in the treaty,[726] this formulation is not sufficient of itself. The reservation is not "made": it does not produce any effect, merely by virtue of such a statement. For that reason, an amendment by China seeking to replace the words "formulate a reservation" with the words "make reservations"[727] was rejected by the Drafting Committee of the Vienna Conference on the Law of Treaties.[728] As Waldock noted, "there is an inherent ambiguity in saying ... that a State may '*make*' a reservation; for the very question at issue is whether a reservation *formulated* by one State can be held to have been effectively 'made' unless and until it has been assented to by the other interested States".[729] Now, not only is a reservation only "established"[730] if certain procedural conditions—admittedly, not very restrictive ones[731]—are met, but it must also comply with the substantive conditions set forth in the three subparagraphs of article 19 of the Vienna Conventions, as the word "unless" clearly demonstrates.[732]

(7) According to some authors, the terminology used in this provision is not consistent in that regard, since "*[l]orsque le traité autorise certaines réserves (article 19, alinéa* b*), elles n'ont pas besoin d'être acceptées par les autres États ... . Elles sont donc 'faites' dès l'instant de leur 'formulation' par l'État réservataire*" ["when the treaty permits specified reservations (article 19, subparagraph (*b*)), they do not need to be accepted by the other States .... They are thus 'made' from the moment of their formulation by the reserving State"].[733] Now, if subparagraph (*b*) meant to say that such reservations "may be *made*", the *chapeau* of article 19 of the Vienna Conventions would be misleading, for it implies that they, too, are merely "formulated" by their author.[734] But this is an empty argument:[735] subparagraph (*b*) is not about reservations that are established (or made) simply by virtue of being formulated, but rather about reservations that are not permitted by the treaty. As in the situation in subparagraph (*a*), such reservations may not be formulated: in one case (subparagraph (*a*)), the prohibition is explicit; in the other (subparagraph (*b*)), it is implied.

(8) Moreover, the principle of freedom to formulate reservations cannot be separated from the exceptions to the principle. For this reason, the Commission, which in

---

[723] Some members of the Commission, however, spoke in support of the existence of such a right.

[724] Concerning the modification of this title in the context of the Guide to Practice, see below, paragraph (10) of the Commentary to this draft guideline.

[725] See Imbert, *Les réserves aux traités ..., op. cit.* (see footnote 717 above), p. 83; see also P. Reuter, *Introduction au droit des traités*, 3rd ed. revised and augmented by Ph. Cahier, Paris, Presses universitaires de France, 1995, p. 75; or Riquelme Cortado, *op. cit.* (footnote 722 above), p. 84. It may also be noted that a proposal by Briggs to replace the word "free" in Waldock's draft (see footnote 718 above) with the words "legally entitled" (*Yearbook ... 1962*, vol. I, 651st meeting, 25 May 1962, p. 140, para. 22) was not accepted, nor was an amendment along the same lines proposed by the Union of Soviet Socialist Republics at the Vienna Conference (A/CONF.39/C.1/L.115, *Official Records of the United Nations Conference on the Law of Treaties, First and second sessions, Vienna, 26 March–24 May 1968 and 9 April–22 May 1969, Documents of the Conference* (document A/CONF.39/11/Add.2, United Nations publication, Sales No. E.70.V.5), Report of the Committee of the Whole on its work at the first session of the Conference, document A/CONF.39/14, p. 133, para. 175). The current wording ("A State may ... formulate a reservation unless ...") was adopted by the Commission's Drafting Committee (see *Yearbook ... 1962*, vol. I, 663rd meeting, 18 June 1962, p. 221, para. 3), then by the Commission in plenary meeting in 1962 (*ibid.*, vol. II, pp. 175–176, article 18, para. 1). No amendments were made in 1966, other than the replacement of the words "*Tout État*" in the French text with the words "*Un État*" (see *Annuaire de la Commission du droit international 1965*, vol. I, 813th meeting, 29 June 1965, p. 287, para. 1 (text adopted by the Drafting Committee), and *Yearbook ... 1966*, vol. II, p. 202 (article 16 adopted on second reading)).

[726] See D. W. Greig, "Reservations: equity as a balancing factor?", *Australian Year Book of International Law*, vol. 16 (1995), pp. 21 *et seq.*, at p. 22.

[727] A/CONF.39/C.1/L.161, *Official Records of the United Nations Conference on the Law of Treaties, First and second sessions...* (footnote 725 above), p. 134, para. 177.

[728] See *Official Records of the United Nations Conference on the Law of Treaties, First session, Vienna, 26 March–24 May 1968, Summary records of the plenary meetings and of the meetings of the Committee of the Whole* (document A/CONF.39/11, United Nations publication, Sales No. E.68.V.7), Committee of the Whole, 23rd meeting, 11 April 1968, p. 121, para. 2 (explanations by China), and 24th meeting, 16 April 1968, p. 126, para. 13 (statement by the Expert Consultant, Sir Humphrey Waldock).

[729] First report on the law of treaties, *Yearbook ... 1962*, vol. II, document A/CN.4/144 and Add.1, p. 62, para. (1) of the commentary to draft articles 17, 18 and 19.

[730] See paragraph 1 of article 21 of the 1969 and 1986 Vienna Conventions: "A reservation established with regard to another party in accordance with articles 19, 20 and 23 ...".

[731] See articles 20, paragraphs 3–5, article 21, paragraph 1, and article 23 of the Vienna Conventions, and draft guidelines 2.1 to 2.2.3. See also M. Coccia, "Reservations to multilateral treaties on human rights", *California Western International Law Journal*, vol. 15 (1985), at p. 28.

[732] "This article states the general principle that the *formulation* of reservations is permitted except in three cases" (*Yearbook ... 1966*, vol. II, p. 207, commentary to art. 16, para. (17)); the use of the word "*faire*" in the French text of the commentary is open to criticism, but it is probably a translation error, rather than a deliberate choice –*contra*: Imbert, *Les réserves aux traités ..., op. cit.* (footnote 717 above), p. 90. Moreover, the English text of the commentary is correct.

[733] Imbert, *Les réserves aux traités ..., op. cit.* (footnote 717 above), pp. 83–84.

[734] See also Ruda, *loc. cit.* (footnote 708 above), pp. 179–180, as well as the far more restrained criticism by Frank Horn in *Reservations and Interpretative Declarations to Multilateral Treaties*, vol. 5, The Hague, T.M.C. Asser Instituut, Swedish Institute of International Law, Studies in International Law, (1988), pp. 111–112.

[735] One may, however, question the use of the verbs "formulate" and "make" in article 23, para. 2 of the Vienna Conventions; it is not consistent to state, at the end of this provision, that, if a reservation formulated when signing a treaty is confirmed at the time of the expression of consent to be bound, "the reservation shall be considered as having been *made** on the date of its confirmation". In elaborating the Guide to Practice on reservations, the Commission has endeavoured to adopt consistent vocabulary in this regard (the criticisms directed at it by Riquelme Cortado, *op. cit.* (footnote 722 above), p. 85, appear to be based on a translation error in the Spanish text).

general has avoided modifying the wording of the provisions of the Vienna Conventions that it has carried over into the Guide to Practice, decided against elaborating a separate draft guideline dealing only with the principle of the presumption of the validity of reservations.

(9) For the same reason, the Commission chose not to leave out of draft guideline 3.1 a reference to all the different moments (or "cases" or "instances", to reproduce the terminology used at various times in draft guideline 1.1.2),[736] "in which a reservation may be formulated". As discussed above,[737] article 19 of the Vienna Conventions reproduces the temporal limitations included in the definition of reservations in article 2, paragraph 1 (*d*), of the Conventions,[738] and this repetition is no doubt superfluous, as was stressed by Denmark[739] during the consideration of the draft articles on the law of treaties adopted in 1962.[740] However, the Commission did not think it necessary to correct the anomaly when the final draft was adopted in 1966,[741] and the repetition is not a sufficiently serious drawback to merit rewriting the 1969 Vienna Convention, which allowed this drawback to remain.

(10) The repetition also provides a discreet reminder that the validity of reservations does not depend solely on the substantive conditions set forth in article 19 of the Vienna Conventions but is also dependent on conformity with conditions of form and timeliness. However, those formal conditions are dealt with in the second part of the Guide to Practice, so that the third part places more emphasis on the substantive validity, that is, the permissibility of reservations—hence the title of "Permissible reservations" chosen by the Commission for draft guideline 3.1, for which it was not possible to retain the title of article 19 of the Vienna Conventions (Formulation of reservations), already used for draft guideline 2.1.3 (Formulation of a reservation at the international level).[742] In any case, it would tend to put the accent, inappropriately, on the formal conditions for the validity of reservations.

3.1.1 *Reservations expressly prohibited by the treaty*

A reservation is expressly prohibited by the treaty if it contains a particular provision:

(*a*) prohibiting all reservations;

(*b*) prohibiting reservations to specified provisions and a reservation in question is formulated to one of such provisions; or

(*c*) prohibiting certain categories of reservations and a reservation in question falls within one of such categories.

Commentary

(1) According to Paul Reuter, the situations envisaged in subparagraphs (*a*) and (*b*) of article 19 of the 1969 and 1986 Vienna Conventions (reproduced in draft guideline 3.1) constitute very simple cases.[743] However, this does not seem to be so. It is true that these provisions refer to cases where the treaty to which a State or an international organization wishes to make a reservation contains a special clause prohibiting or permitting the formulation of reservations. But, aside from the fact that not all possibilities are explicitly covered,[744] delicate problems can arise regarding the exact scope of a clause prohibiting reservations and the effects of a reservation formulated despite that prohibition.

(2) Draft guideline 3.1.1 is intended to clarify the scope of subparagraph (*a*) of draft guideline 3.1, which does not indicate what is meant by "reservation prohibited by the treaty", while draft guidelines 3.1.2 and 3.1.4 undertake to clarify the meaning and the scope of the expression "specified reservations" contained in subparagraph (*b*).

(3) In draft article 17, paragraph 1 (*a*), which he submitted to the Commission in 1962, Waldock distinguished three situations:

— Reservations "prohibited by the terms of the treaty or excluded by the nature of the treaty or by the established usage of an international organization";[745]

— Reservations not provided for by a clause that restricts the reservations that can be made; or

— Reservations not provided for by a clause that authorizes certain reservations.

What these three cases had in common was that, unlike reservations incompatible with the object and purpose of the treaty,[746] "when a reservation is formulated which is not prohibited by the treaty, the other States are called upon to indicate whether they accept or reject it but, when the reservation is one prohibited by the treaty, they have no need to do so, for they have already expressed their objection to it in the treaty itself".[747]

[736] The commentary to this draft guideline is in *Yearbook ... 1998*, vol. II (Part Two), pp. 103–104.

[737] See above paragraph (4) of the commentary to the present draft guideline.

[738] See draft guidelines 1.1 (Definition of reservations) and 1.1.2 (Cases in which a reservation may be formulated) and the commentary thereto in *Yearbook ... 1998*, vol. II (Part Two), pp. 99–100 and 103–104.

[739] See the fourth report of Special Rapporteur Sir Humphrey Waldock on the law of treaties, *Yearbook ... 1965*, vol. II, document A/CN.4/177 and Add.1–2, p. 46.

[740] *Yearbook ... 1962*, vol. II, pp. 165–186.

[741] *Yearbook ... 1966*, vol. II, pp. 177–274.

[742] The text of this draft guideline and its commentary can be found in *Yearbook ... 2002*, vol. II (Part Two), pp. 31–33.

[743] P. Reuter, "Solidarité et divisibilité des engagements conventionnels", in Y. Dinstein (ed.), *International Law at a Time of Perplexity—Essays in Honour of Shabtai Rosenne*, Dordrecht, Martinus Nijhoff, 1989, p. 625; also reproduced in P. Reuter, *Le développement de l'ordre juridique international—Écrits de droit international*, Paris, Economica, 1995, p. 363.

[744] See below footnote 749 and paragraph (9) of the commentary to draft guideline 3.1.3.

[745] First report of Special Rapporteur Sir Humphrey Waldock on the law of treaties, *Yearbook ... 1962*, vol. II, document A/CN.4/144 and Add.1, art. 17, para 1 (*a*), p. 60.

[746] Situation envisaged in paragraph 2 of draft article 17 included in the first report of Special Rapporteur Sir Humphrey Waldock on the law of treaties (*ibid.*), but in a rather different form than in the current text.

[747] *Ibid.*, p. 65, para. (9) of the commentary to article 17.

(4) Even though it was taken up again, in a slightly different form, by the Commission,[748] this categorization was unnecessarily complicated and, at the rather general level at which the authors of the 1969 Vienna Convention intended to operate, there was no point in drawing a distinction between the first two situations identified by the Special Rapporteur.[749] In draft article 18, paragraph 2, which he proposed in 1965 in the light of the observations by Governments,[750] he limited himself to distinguishing reservations prohibited by the terms of the treaty (or "by the established rules of an international organization"[751]) from those implicitly prohibited as a result of the authorization of specified reservations by the treaty. This distinction is found in a more refined form[752] in article 19, subparagraphs (*a*) and (*b*), of the 1969 Vienna Convention, without any distinction being made as to whether the treaty prohibits, or fully or partially authorizes reservations.[753]

(5) According to Tomuschat, the prohibition in subparagraph (*a*), as it is drafted, should be understood as covering both express prohibitions and implicit prohibitions of reservations.[754] Some justification for this interpretation can be found in the *travaux préparatoires* for this provision:

— In the original wording, proposed by Waldock in 1962,[755] it was specified that the provision concerned reservations that were "prohibited by the terms of the treaty", a clarification that was abandoned in 1965 without explanation by the Special Rapporteur and with little light shed by the discussions in the Commission on this matter;[756]

— In the commentary on draft article 16 adopted by the Commission on second reading in 1966, the Commission in effect seems to place on the same footing "[r]eservations expressly or implicitly prohibited by the provisions of the treaty".[757]

(6) This interpretation, however, is open to discussion. The idea that certain treaties could "by their nature", exclude reservations was discarded by the Commission in 1962, when it rejected the proposal along those lines made by Waldock.[758] Thus, apart from the case of

[748] Draft article 18, para. 1 (*b*), (*c*) and (*d*), *Yearbook ... 1962*, vol. II, pp. 175–176; see also paragraph (15) of the commentary to this article, *ibid.*, p. 180.

[749] On the contrary, during the discussion of the draft, Briggs considered that "the distinction was between the case set out in sub-paragraph (*a*), where all reservations were prohibited, and the case set out in sub-paragraphs (*b*) and (*c*), where only some reservations were either expressly prohibited or impliedly excluded" (*Yearbook ... 1962*, vol. I, 663rd meeting, 18 June 1962, p. 222, para. 12); see also the dissenting opinion of Waldock, *ibid.*, p. 223, para. 32. As the example of article 12 of the 1958 Convention on the Limits of the Continental Shelf indicates (see paragraph (6) of the commentary to draft guideline 3.1.2 above), this comment is highly relevant.

[750] Fourth report of Special Rapporteur Sir Humphrey Waldock on the law of treaties, *Yearbook ... 1965*, vol. II, document A/CN.4/177 and Add.1–2, p. 50.

[751] *Ibid.* Although the principle had not been disputed at the time of the debate in the plenary Commission in 1965, it had been disputed by Lachs in 1962 (see *Yearbook ... 1962*, vol. I, 651st meeting, 25 May 1962, p. 142, para. 53) and had been retained in the text adopted during the first part of the seventeenth session (see *Yearbook ... 1965*, vol. II, pp. 161–162), this indication disappeared without explanation from draft article 16 as finally adopted by the Commission in 1966 following the "final cleanup" by the Drafting Committee (see *Yearbook ... 1966*, vol. I (Part Two), 887th meeting, 11 July 1966, p. 295, para. 91). The deletion of this phrase should be seen in the context of the general safeguards clause concerning constituent instruments of international organizations and treaties adopted within an international organization appearing in article 5 of the Convention and adopted the same day in its final form by the Commission (*ibid.*, p. 294, para. 79). In practice, it is very unusual to allow reservations to be formulated to the constituent instruments of an international organization (see M. H. Mendelson, "Reservations to the constitutions of international organizations", BYBIL, vol. 45 (1971), pp. 137–171). As for treaties concluded within the context of international organizations, the best example of (purported) exclusion of reservations is that of the ILO, whose consistent practice is not to accept the deposit of instruments of ratification of international labour conventions when accompanied by reservations (see the memorandum submitted by the Director of the International Labour Office to the Council of the League of Nations on the admissibility of reservations to general conventions, *Official Journal of the League of Nations*, July 1927, p. 882; the memorandum submitted by the ILO to the ICJ in 1951 in the case concerning *Reservations to the Convention on Genocide, I.C.J. Pleadings, Oral Arguments and Documents*, pp. 227–228; or the statement of Wilfred Jenks, Legal Adviser of the International Labour Office, during the oral pleadings on that case, *Official Records of the United Nations Conference on the Law of Treaties, First session...* (footnote 728 above), seventh meeting, 1 April 1968, p. 37, para. 11). For a discussion and critique of this position, see paragraphs (3)–(5) of the commentary to draft guideline 1.1.8 (Reservations made under exclusionary clauses) of the Guide to Practice, adopted by the Commission at its fifty-second session, *Yearbook ... 2000*, vol. II (Part Two), pp. 109–110.

[752] On the editorial changes made by the Commission, see the debate on draft article 18 (*Yearbook ... 1965*, vol. I, especially the 797th and 798th meetings, 8 and 9 June 1965, pp. 147–163) and the text adopted by the Drafting Committee (*ibid.*, 813th meeting, 29 June 1965, pp. 263–264, para. 1) and the debate on it (*ibid.*, pp. 263–265). The final texts of article 16 (*a*) and (*b*) adopted on second reading by the Commission read as follows: "A State may ... formulate a reservation unless: (*a*) The reservation is prohibited by the treaty; (*b*) The treaty authorizes specified reservations which do not include the reservation in question" (*Yearbook ... 1966*, vol. II, p. 202). See also the commentary to draft guideline 3.1.2 below, in particular paragraph (2).

[753] The "alternative drafts" proposed *de lege ferenda* in 1953 in the first report submitted by Hersch Lauterpacht all refer to treaties that "[do] not ... prohibit or restrict the faculty of making reservations" (*Yearbook ... 1953*, vol. II, document A/CN.4/63, p. 124).

[754] See C. Tomuschat, "Admissibility and legal effects of reservations to multilateral treaties—Comments on arts. 16 and 17 of the ILC's 1966 draft articles on the law of treaties", *Zeitschrift für ausländisches öffentliches Recht und Völkerrecht*, vol. 27 (1967), p. 463, at p. 469.

[755] See above paragraph (3) of the commentary to the present draft guideline.

[756] See, however, the statement by Yasseen in the Commission's discussion at its seventeenth session: "the words 'the terms of' (*expressément*) could be deleted and it could read simply: '[unless] the making of reservations is prohibited by the treaty ...'. For it was enough that the treaty was not silent on the subject; it did not matter whether it referred to reservations implicitly or expressly" (*Yearbook ... 1965*, vol. I, 797th meeting, 8 June 1965, p. 149, para. 19), but he was referring to the 1962 text.

[757] Like, moreover, "those expressly or impliedly authorized" (*Yearbook ... 1966*, vol. II, p. 205, para. (10) of the commentary; see also p. 207, para. (17)). In the same vein, article 19, para. 1 (*a*) of the draft articles on the law of treaties concluded between States and international organizations or between two or more international organizations adopted by the Commission in 1981 places on equal footing cases where reservations are prohibited by treaties and those where it is "otherwise established that the negotiating States and negotiating organizations were agreed that the reservation is prohibited" (*Yearbook ... 1981*, vol. II (Part Two), p. 137).

[758] See above paragraph (4) of the commentary to the present draft guideline. The Special Rapporteur indicated that, in drafting this clause, "what he had had in mind was the Charter of the United Nations, which, by its nature, was not open to reservations" (*Yearbook ... 1962*, vol. I, 651st meeting, 25 May 1962, p. 143, para. 60). This exception is covered by the safeguard clause of article 5 of the 1969 Vienna Convention (see footnote 751 above). The words "nature of the treaty" drew little attention during the discussion (Castrén, however, found the expression imprecise, *ibid.*, 652nd meeting, 28 May 1962, p. 148, para. 28; see also the statement of Verdross, *ibid.*, p. 149, para. 35); it was deleted by the Drafting Committee (*ibid.*, 663rd meeting, 18 June 1962, p. 221, para. 3).

reservations to the constituent instruments of international organizations—which will be covered by one or more specific draft guidelines—it is hard to see what prohibitions could derive "implicitly" from a treaty, except in the cases covered by subparagraphs (*a*) and (*b*)[759] of article 19,[760] and it must be recognized that subparagraph (*a*) concerns only reservations expressly prohibited by the treaty. Moreover, this interpretation appears to be compatible with the relative flexibility that pervades all the provisions of the 1969 Vienna Convention that deal with reservations.

(7) There is no problem—other than determining whether or not the declaration in question constitutes a reservation[761]—if the prohibition is clear and precise, in particular when it is a general prohibition, on the understanding, however, that there are relatively few such examples[762] even if some are famous, such as that in article 1 of the Covenant of the League of Nations: "The original Members of the League shall be those of the Signatories ... as shall accede without reservation to this Covenant."[763] Likewise, article 120 of the 1998 Rome Statute of the International Criminal Court states: "No reservations may be made to this Statute."[764] And similarly, article 26, paragraph 1, of the 1989 Basel Convention on the control of transboundary movements of hazardous wastes and their disposal states: "No reservation or exception may be made to this Convention."[765]

(8) Sometimes, however, the prohibition is more ambiguous. Thus, in accordance with paragraph 14 of the Final Act of the 1961 Geneva conference which adopted the European Convention on International Commercial Arbitration, "the delegations taking part in the negotiation of the European Convention on International Commercial Arbitration declare that their respective countries do not intend to make any reservations to the Convention":[766] not only is it not a categorical prohibition, but this declaration of intention is even made in an instrument separate from the treaty. In a case of this type, it could seem that reservations are not strictly speaking prohibited, but that if a State formulates a reservation, the other parties should, logically, object to it.

(9) More often, the prohibition is partial and relates to one or more specified reservations or one or more categories of reservations. The simplest (but rather rare)

[759] The amendments of Spain (A/CONF.39/C.1/L.147, *Official Records of the United Nations Conference on the Law of Treaties, First and second sessions*...(footnote 725 above), p. 134, para. 177) and of Colombia and the United States (A/CONF.39/C.1/L.126 and Add.1, *ibid.*), aimed at reintroducing the idea of the "nature" of the treaty in subparagraph (*c*), were withdrawn by their authors or rejected by the Drafting Committee (see the reaction of the United States, *Official Records of the United Nations Conference on the Law of Treaties*, Second session, Vienna, 9 April–22 May 1969, *Summary records of the plenary meetings and of the meetings of the Committee of the Whole* (document A/CONF.39/11/Add.1, United Nations publication, Sales No. E.70.V.6), p. 37). During the Commission's discussion of draft guideline 3.1.1, some members stated the view that certain treaties, such as the Charter of the United Nations, by their very nature excluded any reservations. The Commission nonetheless concluded that this idea was consistent with the principle enunciated in subparagraph (*c*) of article 19 of the Vienna Conventions and that, where the Charter was concerned, the requirement of the acceptance of the competent organ of the organization (see article 20, para. 3, of the Vienna Conventions) provided sufficient guarantees.

[760] This is also the final conclusion arrived at by C. Tomuschat, *loc. cit.* (footnote 754 above), p. 471.

[761] See draft guideline 1.3.1 (Method of implementation of the distinction between reservations and interpretive declarations) and its commentary, adopted by the Commission at its fifty-first session, *Yearbook ... 1999*, vol. II (Part Two), pp. 107–109.

[762] Even in the area of human rights (see P.-H. Imbert, "Reservations and human rights conventions", *The Human Rights Review*, vol. VI, No. 1 (1981), pp. 28 *et seq.*, at p. 28, or W. A. Schabas, "Reservations to human rights treaties: time for innovation and reform", *Canadian Yearbook of International Law 1994*, pp. 39 *et seq.*, at p. 46). See, however, for example, the 1956 Supplementary Convention on the Abolition of Slavery, the Slave Trade, and Institutions and Practices Similar to Slavery (article 9), the 1960 Convention against discrimination in education (article 9), Protocol No. 6 to the Convention of 4 November 1950 for the Protection of Human Rights and Fundamental Freedoms, concerning the abolition of the death penalty, of 1983 (article 4), or the 1987 European Convention for the prevention of torture and inhuman or degrading treatment or punishment (article 21), which all prohibit any reservations to their provisions. Reservation clauses in human rights treaties sometimes refer to the provisions of the 1969 Vienna Convention concerning reservations (cf. article 75 of the American Convention on Human Rights: "Pact of San José, Costa Rica")—which conventions containing no reservation clauses do implicitly—or reproduce its provisions (cf. article 28, paragraph 2, of the 1979 Convention on the Elimination of All Forms of Discrimination against Women or article 51, paragraph 2, of the 1989 Convention on the Rights of the Child).

[763] It could be maintained that this rule was set aside when the Council of the League recognized the neutrality of Switzerland (in this respect, see Mendelson, *loc. cit.* (footnote 751 above), pp. 140–141).

[764] However straightforward it may seem, this prohibition is not actually totally devoid of ambiguity: the highly regrettable article 124 of the Statute, which authorizes "a State on becoming a party [to] declare that, for a period of seven years after the entry into force of this Statute for the State concerned, it does not accept the jurisdiction of the Court" with respect to war crimes, constitutes an exception to the rule stated in article 120, for such declarations amount to reservations (see A. Pellet, "Entry into force and amendment of the Statute" in A. Cassese, P. Gaeta and J. R. W. D. Jones (eds.), *The Rome Statute of the International Criminal Court: a Commentary*, vol. I, Oxford University Press, 2002, pp. 145 *et seq.*, at p. 157); see also the European Convention on the service abroad of documents relating to administrative matters, whose article 21 prohibits reservations, while several other provisions authorize certain reservations. For other examples, see S. Spiliopoulou Åkermark, "Reservation clauses in treaties concluded within the Council of Europe", *International and Comparative Law Quarterly*, vol. 48 (July 1999), pp. 493–494; P. Daillier and A. Pellet, *Droit international public (Nguyen Quoc Dinh)*, 7th ed., Paris, Librairie générale de droit et de jurisprudence, 2002, p. 181; Imbert, *Les réserves aux traités ..., op. cit.* (footnote 717 above), pp. 165–166; Horn, *op. cit.* (footnote 734 above), p. 113; Riquelme Cortado, *op. cit.* (footnote 722 above), pp. 105–108; and Schabas, *op. cit.* (footnote 762 above), p. 46.

[765] For a very detailed commentary, see A. Fodella, "The declarations of States parties to the Basel Convention", in P. Ziccardi *et al.* (eds.), *Comunicazioni e Studi*, vol. 22, Milan, Giuffrè, 2002, pp. 111–148; article 26, paragraph 2 of the Convention authorizes States parties to make "declarations or statements, however phrased or named, with a view, *inter alia*, to the harmonization of its laws and regulations with the provisions of this Convention, provided that such declarations or statements do not purport to exclude or to modify the legal effects of the provisions of the Convention in their application to that State". The distinction between the reservations of paragraph 1 and the declarations of paragraph 2 can prove laborious, but this is a problem of definition that does not in any way restrict the prohibition stated in paragraph 1: if a declaration made under paragraph 2 proves to be a reservation, it is prohibited. The combination of articles 309 and 310 of the 1982 United Nations Convention on the Law of the Sea poses the same problems and calls for the same responses (see, in particular, A. Pellet, "Les réserves aux conventions sur le droit de la mer", in *La mer et son droit—Mélanges offerts à Laurent Lucchini et Jean-Pierre Quéneudec*, Paris, Pedone, 2003, pp. 501 *et seq.*, at pp. 505–517; see also the commentary to draft guideline 3.1.2 below, footnote 787).

[766] Final Act of the Special Meeting of Plenipotentiaries for the purpose of negotiating and signing a European Convention on International Commercial Arbitration, United Nations, *Treaty Series*, vol. 484, p. 349. Example given by Imbert, *Les réserves aux traités ..., op. cit.* (footnote 717 above), pp. 166–167.

situation is that of clauses listing the provisions of the treaty to which reservations are not permitted.[767] Examples are article 42 of the 1951 Convention relating to the Status of Refugees[768] and article XIV of the 1972 International Convention for Safe Containers (CSC).

(10) The situation is more complicated where the treaty does not prohibit reservations to specified provisions but excludes certain categories of reservations. An example of this type of clause is provided by article 78, paragraph 3, of the International Sugar Agreement of 1977: "Any Government entitled to become a Party to this Agreement may, on signature, ratification, acceptance, approval or accession, make reservations which do not affect the economic functioning of this Agreement."

(11) The distinction between reservation clauses of this type and those excluding specific reservations was made in Sir Humphrey Waldock's draft in 1962.[769] For their part, the 1969 and 1986 Vienna Conventions do not make such distinctions, and, despite the uncertainty that prevailed in their *travaux préparatoires*, it should certainly be assumed that subparagraph (*a*) of article 19 covers all three situations that a more precise analysis can discern:

— Reservation clauses prohibiting all reservations;

— Reservation clauses prohibiting reservations to specified provisions;

— Lastly, reservation clauses prohibiting certain categories of reservations.

(12) This clarification seems all the more helpful in that the third of these situations poses problems (of interpretation)[770] of the same nature as those arising from the criterion of compatibility with the object and purpose of the treaty, which certain clauses actually reproduce expressly.[771] By indicating that these reservations, prohibited without reference to a specific provision of the treaty, still come under article 19, subparagraph (*a*), of the Vienna Conventions, the Commission seeks from the outset to emphasize the unity of the legal regime applicable to the reservations mentioned in the three subparagraphs of article 19.

[767] This situation is very similar to that in which the treaty specifies the provisions to which reservations are permitted; see paragraph (5) of the commentary to draft guideline 3.1.2, below, and the comments by Briggs with respect to article 17 of the draft articles on the law of treaties presented by the Drafting Committee at the Commission's fourteenth session, *Yearbook ... 1962*, vol. I, 663rd meeting, 18 June 1962, p. 222.

[768] With regard to this provision, Imbert notes that the influence of the advisory opinion of the ICJ on *Reservations to the Convention on Genocide* (see footnote 714 above) adopted two months earlier is very clear, since such a clause effectively protects the provisions which cannot be the object of reservations (*Les réserves aux traités ..., op. cit.* (footnote 717 above), p. 167); see the other examples given, *ibid.*, or in paragraphs (5)–(8) of the commentary to draft guideline 3.1.2 below.

[769] First report on the law of treaties, *Yearbook ... 1962*, vol. II, document A/CN.4/144 and Add.1, p. 60, art. 17, para. 1 (*a*).

[770] "Whether a reservation is permissible under exceptions (*a*) or (*b*) will depend on interpretation of the treaty" (A. Aust, *op. cit.* (footnote 722 above), p. 110).

[771] See the examples given in footnote 762 above. This is a particular example of "categories of prohibited reservations"—in a particularly vague way, it is true.

3.1.2 *Definition of specified reservations*

For the purposes of guideline 3.1, the expression "specified reservations" means reservations that are expressly envisaged in the treaty to certain provisions of the treaty or to the treaty as a whole with respect to certain specific aspects.

Commentary

(1) A cursory reading of article 19, subparagraph (*b*), of the 1969 and 1986 Vienna Conventions might suggest that it represents one side of the coin and subparagraph (*a*) represents the other. The symmetry is far from total, however. To create such symmetry, it would have been necessary to stipulate that reservations other than those expressly provided for in the treaty were prohibited, but that is not the case. Subparagraph (*b*) contains two additional elements which prevent oversimplification. The implicit prohibition of certain reservations arising from this provision, which is considerably more complex than it seems, depends on the fulfilment of three conditions:

(*a*) The treaty's reservation clause must permit the formulation of reservations;

(*b*) the reservations permitted must be "specified"; and

(*c*) it must be specified that "only" those reservations "may be made".[772]

The purpose of draft guideline 3.1.2 is to clarify the meaning of the expression "specified reservations", which is not defined by the 1969 and 1986 Vienna Conventions. This definition could, however, have important consequences for the applicable legal regime, as, among other things, reservations which are not "specified" must pass the test of compatibility with the object and purpose of the treaty.[773]

(2) The origin of article 19, subparagraph (*b*), of the Vienna Conventions can be traced back to paragraph 3 of draft article 37 submitted to the Commission in 1956 by Fitzmaurice: "In those cases where the treaty itself permits certain specific reservations, or a class of reservations, to be made, there is a presumption that any other reservations are excluded and cannot be accepted."[774] Waldock took up that concept again in paragraph 1 (*a*) of draft article 17, which he proposed in 1962[775] and which the Commission used in paragraph 1 (*c*) of draft article 18. That draft article was adopted the same year[776] and, following a number of minor drafting changes, was incorporated into article 16, subparagraph (*b*), of the 1966 draft,[777] then into

[772] On this word, see paragraphs (6)–(7) of the commentary to draft guideline 3.1, above.

[773] See draft guideline 3.1.4 below.

[774] *Yearbook ... 1956*, vol. II, document A/CN.4/101, p. 115; see also p. 127, para. 95.

[775] First report on the law of treaties, *Yearbook ... 1962*, vol. II, document A/CN.4/144 and Add.1, p. 60.

[776] Report of the Commission to the General Assembly, document A/5209, pp. 175–176. See paragraphs (3)–(4) of the commentary to draft guideline 3.1.1, above.

[777] See footnote 752 above.

article 19 of the 1969 Convention. That course of action did not go unchallenged, however, as during the Vienna Conference on the Law of Treaties a number of amendments were submitted with a view to deleting the provision[778] on the pretext that it was too "rigid"[779] or redundant because it duplicated subparagraph (*a*),[780] or that it had not been confirmed by practice;[781] all those amendments were, however, withdrawn or rejected.[782]

(3) The only change to subparagraph (*b*) was made by means of a Polish amendment inserting the word "only" after the word "authorizes", which was accepted by the Drafting Committee of the Vienna Conference on the Law of Treaties "[i]n the interest of greater clarity".[783] This bland description must not obscure the vast practical implications of this specification, which actually reverses the presumption made by the Commission and, in keeping with the Eastern countries' persistent desire to facilitate as much as possible the formulation of reservations, offers the possibility of doing so even when the negotiators have taken the precaution of expressly indicating the provisions in respect of which a reservation is permitted.[784] This amendment does not, however, exempt a reservation which is neither expressly permitted nor implicitly prohibited from the requirement to observe the criterion of compatibility with the object and purpose of the treaty.[785] Such a reservation may also be subject to objections on other grounds. This is why, in the wording of draft guideline 3.1.2, the Commission favoured the word "envisaged" over the word "authorized" to qualify the reservations in question, in contrast to the expression "reservation expressly authorized", as found in article 20, paragraph 1, of the Vienna Conventions.

(4) In practice, the types of clauses permitting reservations are comparable to those containing prohibitive provisions and pose the same kind of difficulties with regard to determining *a contrario* those reservations which may not be formulated:[786]

— Some of them authorize reservations to particular provisions, expressly and restrictively listed either affirmatively or negatively;

— Others authorize specified categories of reservations;

— Lastly, others (few in number) authorize reservations in general.

(5) Article 12, paragraph 1, of the 1958 Convention on the Continental Shelf appears to illustrate the first of those categories: "At the time of signature, ratification or accession, any State may make reservations to articles of the Convention other than to articles 1 to 3 inclusive."[787] As Ian Sinclair noted, "[a]rticle 12 of the 1958 Convention did not provide for *specified reservations*, even though it may have specified articles to which reservations might

---

[778] Amendments by Colombia and the United States (A/CONF.39/C.1/L.126 and Add.1) and the Federal Republic of Germany (A/CONF.39/C.1/L.128), which were specifically designed to delete subparagraph (*b*), and by Ceylon (A/CONF.39/C.1/L.139), France (A/CONF.39/C.1/L.169), Spain (A/CONF.39/C.1/L.147) and the Union of Soviet Socialist Republics (A/CONF.39/C.1/L.115), which proposed major revisions of article 16 (or of articles 16 and 17) that would also have led to the disappearance of that provision (for the text of these amendments, see *Official Records of the United Nations Conference on the Law of Treaties*, First and second sessions… (footnote 725 above), pp. 133–134, paras. 174–177). During the Commission's discussion of the draft, certain members had also taken the view that that provision was unnecessary (see *Yearbook ... 1965*, vol. I, 797th meeting, 8 June 1965, Yasseen, p. 149, para. 18; Tunkin, *ibid.*, p. 150, para. 29; but, for a more nuanced position, see *ibid.*, p. 151, para. 33; or Ruda, p. 154, para. 70).

[779] According to the representatives of Poland and the United States at the twenty-first and twenty-second meetings of the Plenary Committee (10 and 11 April 1968, respectively), *Official Records of the United Nations Conference on the Law of Treaties, First session…* (footnote 728 above), p. 108, para. 8, and p. 118, para. 42); see also the statement made by the representative of the Federal Republic of Germany (*ibid.*, p. 109, para. 23).

[780] See the statement of the representative of Colombia, *ibid.*, p. 113, para. 68.

[781] See the statement of the representative of Sweden, *ibid.*, p. 117, para. 29.

[782] See *Official Records of the United Nations Conference on the Law of Treaties, First and second sessions…* (footnote 725 above), pp. 136–138, paras. 181–188. See also the explanations of the Expert Consultant, Sir Humphrey Waldock, *Official Records of the United Nations Conference on the Law of Treaties, First session…* (footnote 728 above), twenty-fourth meeting, 16 April 1968, p. 126, para. 6, and the results of the votes on those amendments, *ibid.*, twenty-fifth meeting, 16 April 1968, p. 135, paras. 23–25.

[783] A/CONF.39/C.1/L.136, *Official Records of the United Nations Conference on the Law of Treaties,* First and second sessions… (footnote 725 above), p. 134, para. 177 and p. 137, para. 183; see also *Official Records of the United Nations Conference on the Law of Treaties,* First session… (footnote 728 above), Committee of the Whole, 70th meeting, 14 May 1968, p. 415, para. 16. Already in 1965, during the Commission's discussion of draft article 18, subparagraph (*b*), as reviewed by the Drafting Committee, Castrén proposed inserting "only" after "authorizes" in subparagraph (*b*) (*Yearbook ... 1965*, vol. I, 797th meeting, 8 June 1965, p. 149, para. 14, and 813th meeting, 29 June 1965, p. 264, para. 13; see also the similar proposal made by Yasseen, *ibid.*, para. 11), which, in the end, was not accepted following a further review by the Drafting Committee (see *ibid.*, 816th meeting, p. 283, para. 41).

[784] In this repsect, see Horn, *op. cit.* (footnote 734 above), p. 114; L. Lijnzaad, *Reservations to UN-Human Rights Treaties: Ratify and Ruin?*, T.M.C. Asser Instituut, Dordrecht, Martinus Nijhoff, 1995, p. 39; J. Ruda, *loc. cit.* (footnote 708 above), p. 181; or R. Szafarz, "Reservations to multilateral treaties", *Polish Yearbook of International Law*, vol. 3 (1970), pp. 299–300. Such restrictive formulas are not unusual: see, for example, article 17 of the 1961 Convention on the reduction of statelessness ("1. At the time of signature, ratification or accession any State may make a reservation in respect of articles 11, 14 or 15; 2. No other reservations to this Convention shall be admissible") and the other examples given by Riquelme Cortado, *op. cit.* (footnote 722 above), pp. 128–129. On the significance of the reversal of the presumption, see also the statement of Patrick Lipton Robinson during the Commission's discussion of the law and practice relating to reservations to treaties at its forty-seventh session, *Yearbook ... 1995*, vol. I, 2402nd meeting, p. 158, para. 17.

[785] See below draft guideline 3.1.3 and the related commentary, in particular paragraphs (2)–(3).

[786] See above draft guideline 3.1.1 and the related commentary.

[787] Article 309 of the United Nations Convention on the Law of the Sea provides: "No reservations or exceptions may be made to this Convention unless expressly permitted by other articles of this Convention" (on this provision, see Pellet, "Les réserves aux convention…", *loc. cit.* (footnote 765 above), pp. 505–511). A treaty may set a maximum number of reservations or provisions that can be subject to reservations (see, for example, article 25 of the 1967 European Convention on the adoption of children). These provisions may be compared with those authorizing parties to accept certain obligations or to choose between the provisions of a treaty, which are not reservation clauses *stricto sensu* (see draft guidelines 1.4.6. [1.4.6, 1.4.7] and 1.4.7. [1.4.8], and the related commentary, adopted by the Commission at its fifty-second session, *Yearbook ... 2000*, vol. II (Part Two), pp. 112–116).

be made"[788] and neither the scope nor the effects of that authorization are self-evident, as demonstrated by the judgment of the ICJ in the *North Sea Continental Shelf* case[789] and, above all, by the arbitral award given in 1977 in the *English Channel* case.[790]

(6) In that case, the Arbitral Tribunal emphasized that:

> Article 12 [of the 1958 Geneva Convention on the Continental Shelf], by its clear terms, authorised any contracting State, in particular the French Republic, to make its consent to be bound by the Convention subject to reservations to articles other than Articles 1 to 3 inclusive.[791]

However,

> Article 12 cannot be read as committing States to accept in advance any and every reservation to articles other than Articles 1, 2 and 3 ... . Such an interpretation of Article 12 would amount almost to a license to contracting States to write their own treaty and would manifestly go beyond the purpose of the Article. Only if the Article had authorised the making of specific reservations could the parties to the Convention be understood as having accepted a particular reservation in advance. But that is not the case with Article 12, which authorises the making of reservations to articles other than Article 1 to 3 in quite general terms.[792]

(7) The situation is different when the reservation clause defines the categories of permissible reservations. Article 39 of the 1928 General Act of Arbitration (Pacific Settlement of International Disputes) provides an example of this:

> 1. In addition to the power given in the preceding article[793], a Party, in acceding to the present General Act, may make his acceptance conditional upon the reservations exhaustively enumerated in the following paragraph These reservations must be indicated at the time of accession.
>
> 2. These reservations may be such as to exclude from the procedure described in the present Act:
>
> (*a*) Disputes arising out of facts prior to the accession either of the Party making the reservation or of any other Party with whom the said party may have a dispute;
>
> (*b*) Disputes concerning questions which by international law are solely within the domestic jurisdiction of States;
>
> (*c*) Disputes concerning particular cases or clearly specified subject-matters, such as territorial status, or disputes falling within clearly defined categories.

As the ICJ pointed out in its judgment of 1978 in the *Aegean Sea Continental Shelf* case:

> When a multilateral treaty thus provides in advance for the making only of particular, designated categories of reservations, there is clearly a high probability, if not an actual presumption, that reservations made in terms used in the treaty are intended to relate to the corresponding categories in the treaty,

even when States do not "meticulously [follow] the pattern" set out in the reservation clause.[794]

(8) Another particularly famous and widely discussed example[795] of a clause authorizing reservations (which falls under the second category mentioned above)[796] is found in article 57 of the European Convention on Human Rights (article 64 prior to the entry into force of Protocol No. 11 to the Convention for the Protection of Human Rights and Fundamental Freedoms of 4 November 1950, restructuring the control machinery established thereby):

> (1) Any State may, when signing this Convention or when depositing its instrument of ratification, make a reservation in respect of any particular provision of the Convention to the extent that any law then in force in its territory is not in conformity with the provision. Reservations of a general character shall not be permitted under this article.
>
> (2) Any reservation made under this article shall contain a brief statement of the law concerned.

In this instance, the power to formulate reservations is limited by conditions relating to both form and content; in addition to the usual limitations *ratione temporis*,[797] a reservation to the European Convention on Human Rights must:

---

[788] Sinclair, *op. cit.* (footnote 706 above), p. 73. On the distinction between specified and non-specified reservations, see also below paragraphs (11)–(13) of the commentary to the present draft guideline.

[789] *North Sea Continental Shelf, Judgment, I.C.J. Reports 1969*, p. 3, at pp. 38–41.

[790] *Case concerning the delimitation of the continental shelf between the United Kingdom of Great Britain and Northern Ireland, and the French Republic, decision of 30 June 1977*, UNRIAA, vol. XVIII (Sales No. E/F.80.V.7), pp. 32–35, paras. 39–44.

[791] *Ibid.*, p. 32, para. 39.

[792] *Ibid.*, pp. 32–33.

[793] Article 38 provides that parties may accede to only parts of the General Act.

[794] *Aegean Sea Continental Shelf, Judgment of 19 December 1978, I.C.J. Reports 1978*, p. 3, at p. 23, para. 55.

[795] See A. Bonifazi, "La disciplina delle riserve alla Convenzione europea dei diritti dell'uomo", in *Les clauses facultatives de la Convention européenne des droits de l'homme (Minutes of the round table organized in Bari on 17 and 18 December 1973 by the Faculty of Law of the University of Bari)*, Bari, Levante, 1974, pp. 301–319; G. Cohen-Jonathan, *La Convention européenne des droits de l'homme*, Paris, Economica, 1989, pp. 85–94; J. A. Frowein, "Reservations to the European Convention on Human Rights", in F. Matscher and H. Petzold (eds.), *Protecting Human Rights: The European Dimension—Studies in Honour of Gérard J. Wiarda*, Cologne, Carl Heymanns Verlag, 1988, pp. 193–200; P.-H. Imbert, "Reservations to the European Convention on Human Rights before the Strasbourg Commission: the *Temeltasch* case", *International and Comparative Law Quarterly*, vol. 33 (1984), pp. 558–595; Rolf Kühner, "Vorbehalte und auslegende Erklärungen zur Europäischen Menschenrechtskonvention: Die Problematik des Art. 64 MRK am Beispiel der schweizerischen 'auslegenden Erklärung' zu Art. 6 Abs. 3 *lit.*e MRK", *Zeitschrift für ausländisches öffentlisches Recht und Völkerrecht*, vol. 42 (1982), pp. 58–92 (summary in English); S. Marcus-Helmons, "L'article 64 de la Convention de Rome ou les réserves à la Convention européenne des droits de l'homme", *Revue de droit international et de droit comparé*, forty-fifth year, No. 1 (1968), pp. 7–26; M. J. M. Pires, *As reservas à Convenção europeia dos direitos do homem*, Coimbra, Almedina, 1997; R. Sapienza, "Sull'ammissibilità di riserve all'accettazione della competenza della Commissione europea dei diritti dell'uomo", *Rivista di diritto internazionale*, vol. 70, Nos. 3–4 (1987), pp. 641–654; and W. A. Schabas, "Article 64" in L.-E. Pettiti, E. Decaux and P.-H. Imbert (eds.), *La Convention européenne des droits de l'homme: commentaire article par article*, Paris, Economica, 1995, pp. 923–942.

[796] See above paragraph (4) of the commentary to the present draft guideline. For other examples, see Aust, *op. cit.* (footnote 722 above), pp. 109–110; Spiliopoulou Åkermark, *loc. cit.* (footnote 764 above), pp. 495–496; W. W. Bishop, Jr., "Reservations to treaties", *Recueil des cours: Collected courses of the Hague Academy of International Law*, vol. 103, 1961–II, pp. 323–324; or Daillier and Pellet, *op. cit.* (footnote 764 above), p. 181; see also the table of Council of Europe conventions showing clauses falling into each of the first two categories of permissible reservation clauses mentioned above in paragraph (4) of the commentary to the present draft guideline, in Riquelme Cortado, *op. cit.* (footnote 722 above), p. 125, and the other examples of partial authorizations given by this author, pp. 126–129.

[797] See the commentary to draft guideline 3.1, footnote 715 above.

— refer to a particular provision of the Convention;

— be justified by the state of legislation [in the reserving State] at the time that the reservation is formulated;

— not be "couched in terms that are too vague or broad for it to be possible to determine their exact meaning and scope";[798] and

— be accompanied by a brief statement explaining "the scope of the Convention provision whose application a State intends to prevent by means of a reservation".[799]

Assessing whether each of these conditions has been met raises problems. It must surely be considered, however, that the reservations authorized by the European Convention on Human Rights are "specified" within the meaning of article 19 (*b*) of the 1969 and 1986 Vienna Conventions and that only such reservations are valid.

(9) It has been noted that the wording of article 57 of the European Convention on Human Rights is not fundamentally different[800] from that used, for example, in article 26, paragraph 1, of the 1957 European Convention on Extradition: "Any Contracting Party may, when signing this Convention or when depositing its instrument of ratification or accession, make a reservation in respect of any provision or provisions of the Convention", even though the latter could be interpreted as a general authorization. While, however, the type of reservations that can be formulated to the European Convention on Human Rights is "specified", here the authorization is restricted only by the exclusion of "across the board" reservations.[801]

(10) In fact, a general authorization of reservations[802] itself does not necessarily resolve all the problems. It leaves unanswered the question of whether the other parties may still object to reservations[803] and whether these authorized reservations[804] are subject to the test of compatibility with the object and purpose of the treaty.[805] The latter question is addressed by draft guideline 3.1.4,[806] which draws a distinction between specified reservations whose reservation clause defines the content and those which leave the content relatively open.

(11) This distinction is not self-evident. It caused particular controversy following the 1977 arbitration award in the *English Channel* case[807] and divided the Commission, whose members advocated different positions. Some reserving States thought that a reservation was "specified" if the treaty set precise limits within which it could be formulated; those criteria then superseded (but only in that instance) the criterion of the object and purpose.[808] Others pointed out that this occurred very exceptionally, perhaps only in the rare case of "negotiated reservations",[809] and, furthermore, that the Commission had not retained Mr. Rosenne's proposal that the expression "specified reservations", which he considered "unduly narrow", should be replaced by "reservations to specific provisions";[810] accordingly, it would be unrealistic to require the content of specified reservations to be established with precision by the treaty, otherwise subparagraph (*b*) would be rendered meaningless.[811] According to a third view, a compromise was possible between the undoubtedly excessive position that would require the content of the reservations envisaged to be precisely stated in the reservation clause and the position that equated a specified reservation with a "reservation expressly authorized by the treaty",[812] even though article 19, paragraph (*b*), and article 20, paragraph 1, of the Vienna Conventions use different expressions. Consequently, it was suggested that it should be recognized that reservations that were specified within the meaning of article 19, subparagraph (*b*) (and of draft guideline 3.1 (*b*)), must, on the one hand, relate to specific provisions and, on the other, fulfil certain conditions specified in the treaty, but without going so far as to require their content to be predetermined.[813]

---

[798] *Belilos* v. *Switzerland, Judgement of 29 April 1988, Application no. 10328/83*, European Court of Human Rights, *Series A: Judgments and Decisions*, vol. 132, p. 25, para. 55.

[799] *Temeltasch* v. *Switzerland, Application No. 9116/80,* Council of Europe, European Commission of Human Rights, *Decisions and Reports*, vol. 31, 1983, p. 150, para. 90.

[800] Imbert, *Les réserves aux traités ..., op. cit.* (footnote 717 above), p. 186; see also Riquelme Cortado, *op. cit.* (footnote 722 above), p. 122.

[801] Regarding this concept, see draft guideline 1.1.1 [1.1.4] adopted by the Commission at its fifty-first session and the related commentary, *Yearbook ... 1999*, vol. II (Part Two), pp. 93–95.

[802] For another even clearer example, see article 18, paragraph 1, of the 1983 European Convention on the compensation of victims of violent crimes: "Any State may, at the time of signature or when depositing its instrument of ratification, acceptance, approval or accession, declare that it avails itself of one or more reservations."

[803] This is sometimes expressly stated (see, for example, article VII of the 1953 Convention on the Political Rights of Women and the related comments by Riquelme Cortado, *op. cit.* (footnote 722 above), p. 121).

[804] It cannot be reasonably argued that subparagraph (*b*) could include "implicitly authorized" reservations, other than on the grounds that any reservations that are not prohibited are, *a contrario*, authorized, subject to the provisions of subparagraph (*c*).

[805] See the questions raised by Spiliopoulou Åkermark, *loc. cit.* (footnote 764 above), pp. 496–497, or Riquelme Cortado, *op. cit.* (footnote 722 above), p. 124.

[806] See the commentary to this draft guideline below.

[807] See footnote 790 above.

[808] See Bowett, *loc. cit.* (footnote 707 above), pp. 71–72.

[809] On this concept, see paragraph (11) of the commentary to guideline 1.1.8 (Reservations made under exclusionary clauses) adopted by the Commission at its fifty-second sesson, *Yearbook ... 2000*, vol. II (Part Two), p. 111. See also W. P. Gormley, "The modification of multilateral conventions by means of 'negotiated reservations' and other 'alternatives': a comparative study of the ILO and Council of Europe–part one", *Fordham Law Review*, vol. 39 (1970–1971), pp. 59 *et seq.*, at pp. 75–76. See also the annex to the European Convention on Civil Liability for Damage Caused by Motor Vehicles, which accords to Belgium the faculty over a period of three years to make a specific reservation; or article 32, paragraph 1 (*b*), of the 1989 European Convention on Transfrontier Television, which exclusively grants the United Kingdom the ability to formulate a specified reservation (examples provided by Spiliopoulou Åkermark, *loc. cit.* (footnote 764 above), p. 499). The main example given by Bowett to illustrate his theory relates precisely to a "negotiated reservation", *loc. cit.* (footnote 707 above), p. 71.

[810] *Yearbook ... 1965*, vol. I, 813th meeting, 29 June 1965, p. 264, para. 7. Imbert points out, however, that, even though Mr. Rosenne's proposal was not accepted, Sir Humphrey Waldock himself had also drawn this parallel (*ibid.*, p. 265, para. 27); see P.-H. Imbert, "La question des réserves dans la décision arbitrale du 30 juin 1977 relative à la délimitation du plateau continental entre la République française et le Royaume-Uni de Grande-Bretagne et d'Irlande du Nord", *Annuaire français de droit international*, vol. 24 (1978), pp. 29–58, at p. 52.

[811] Imbert, "La question des réserves..." (footnote 810 above), pp. 50–53.

[812] In this respect, see *ibid.*, p. 53.

[813] See the tenth report on reservations to treaties, *Yearbook ... 2005*, vol. II (Part One), document A/CN.4/558 and Add.1–2, para. 49.

(12) The case law was not very helpful in reconciling those opposing views. The arbitral award of 1977 in the *English Channel* case, invoked by the proponents of both arguments, says more about what a specified reservation is not than what it is.[814] Indeed, the result of all this is that the mere fact that a reservation clause authorizes reservations to particular provisions of the treaty is not enough to "specify" these reservations within the meaning of article 19, subparagraph (*b*) of the Vienna Conventions.[815] The Tribunal, however, confined itself to requiring reservations to be "specific",[816] without indicating what the test of that specificity was to be. In addition, during the Vienna Conference on the Law of Treaties, K. Yasseen, Chairperson of the Drafting Committee, assimilated specified reservations to those which were expressly authorized by the treaty[817] with no further clarification.

(13) Accordingly, most members of the Commission held that a reservation should be considered specified if a reservation clause indicated the treaty provisions in respect of which a reservation was possible or, to take into account draft guideline 1.1.1 [1.1.4] on "across the board" reservations,[818] indicated that reservations were possible to the treaty as a whole in certain specific aspects. The divergence between these different points of view should not be overstated, however; while the term "envisaged" reservations, which was preferred to "authorized" reservations, undoubtedly gives more weight to the broad-brush approach favoured by the Commission, at the same time, in draft guideline 3.1.4, the Commission introduced a distinction between specified reservations with defined content and those whose content is not defined, the latter being subject to the test of compatibility with the object and purpose of the treaty.

3.1.3 *Permissibility of reservations not prohibited by the treaty*

Where the treaty prohibits the formulation of certain reservations, a reservation which is not prohibited by the treaty may be formulated by a State or an international organization only if it is not incompatible with the object and purpose of the treaty.

Commentary

(1) Draft guidelines 3.1.3 and 3.1.4 specify the scope of article 19, subparagraphs (*a*) and (*b*), of the Vienna Conventions (the 1986 text of which is repeated in draft guideline 3.1). They make explicit what the Conventions leave implicit: that failing a contrary provision in the treaty—and in particular if the treaty authorizes specified reservations as defined in draft guideline 3.1.2—any reservation must satisfy the basic requirement, set forth in article 19, subparagraph (*c*), of not being incompatible with the object and purpose of the treaty.

(2) This principle is one of the fundamental elements of the flexible system established by the Vienna regime, moderating the "radical relativism"[819] resulting from the pan-American system, which reduces multilateral treaties to a network of bilateral relations,[820] while avoiding the rigidity resulting from the system of unanimity.

(3) The notion of the object and purpose of the treaty,[821] which first appeared in connection with reservations in the 1951 advisory opinion of the ICJ,[822] has become increasingly accepted. It is now the fulcrum between the need to preserve the essence of the treaty and the desire to facilitate accession to multilateral treaties by the greatest possible number of States. There is, however, a major difference between the role of the criterion of compatibility with the object and purpose of the treaty according to the 1951 advisory opinion, on the one hand, and article 19, subparagraph (*c*), of the 1969 Vienna Convention, on the other.[823] In the advisory opinion, the criterion applied equally to the formulation of reservations and to objections: "The object and purpose of the [Convention on the Prevention and Punishment of the Crime of Genocide] thus limit both the freedom of making reservations and that of objecting to them."[824] In the 1969 Vienna Convention, it is restricted to reservations: article 20 does not restrict the ability of other contracting States to formulate objections.

(4) While there is no doubt that this requirement that a reservation must be compatible with the object and purpose of the treaty now represents a rule of customary law which is unchallenged,[825] its content remains vague[826]

[814] See above, paragraph (6) of the commentary to the present draft guideline and footnote 790.

[815] See above, paragraphs (6)–(7) of the commentary to the present draft guideline.

[816] In reality, it is the authorization that must apply to specific or specified reservations—terms which the Tribunal considered to be synonymous, in the *English Channel* case (see footnote 790 above).

[817] See *Official Records of the United Nations Conference on the Law of Treaties, First session*... (footnote 728 above), seventieth meeting, 14 May 1968, p. 416, para. 23.

[818] See *Yearbook ... 1999*, vol. II (Part Two), pp. 93–95.

[819] P. Reuter, *Introduction au droit des traités*, *op. cit.* (footnote 725 above), p. 73, para. 130. This author applies the term to the system adopted by the ICJ in its 1951 advisory opinion on *Reservations to the Convention on the Prevention and Punishment of the Crime of Genocide* (see footnote 714 above); the criticism applies perfectly well, however, to the pan-American system.

[820] On the pan-American system, see the bibliography in Imbert, *Les réserves aux traités ...*, *op. cit.* (footnote 717 above), pp. 485–486. See also, in addition to the description by Imbert himself (*ibid.*, pp. 33–38), M. M. Whiteman, *Digest of International Law*, vol. 14 (1970), pp. 141–144, or Ruda, *loc. cit.* (footnote 708 above), pp. 115–133.

[821] This notion will be defined in draft guideline 3.1.5.

[822] *Reservations to the Convention on the Prevention and Punishment of the Crime of Genocide* (see footnote 714 above), pp. 24 and 26.

[823] See Coccia, *loc. cit.* (footnote 731 above), p. 9; Lijnzaad, *op. cit.* (footnote 784 above), p. 40; M. Rama-Montaldo, "Human rights conventions and reservations to treaties", in *Héctor Gros Espiell* Amicorum Liber*: Human Person and International Law*, vol. II, Brussels, Bruylant, 1997, pp. 1265–1266; or Sinclair, *op. cit.* (footnote 706 above), p. 61.

[824] *Reservations to the Convention on the Prevention and Punishment of the Crime of Genocide* (see footnote 714 above), p. 24.

[825] See the many arguments to that effect given by Riquelme Cortado, *op. cit.* (footnote 722 above), pp. 138–143. See also the preliminary conclusions of the Commission in 1997, in which it reiterated its view that "articles 19 to 23 of the Vienna Conventions on the Law of Treaties of 1969 and of the Vienna Convention on the Law of Treaties between States and Inernational Organizations or between International Organizations of 1986 govern the regime of reservations to treaties and that, in particular, the object and purpose of the treaty is the most important of the criteria for determining the admissibility of reservations" (*Yearbook ... 1997*, vol. II (Part Two), p. 57, first conclusion).

[826] See draft guidelines 3.1.5 to 3.1.13 proposed by the Special Rapporteur in his tenth report on reservations to treaties, *Yearbook ... 2005*, vol. II (Part One), document A/CN.4/558 and Add.1–2.

and there is some uncertainty as to the consequences of incompatibility.[827] Moreover, article 19 of the 1969 Vienna Convention does not dispel the ambiguity as to its scope of application.

(5) The principle set forth in article 19, subparagraph (*c*), whereby a reservation incompatible with the object and purpose of the treaty may not be formulated, is of a subsidiary nature since it applies only in cases not covered in article 20, paragraphs 2 and 3, of the Convention[828] and where the treaty itself does not resolve the reservations issue.

(6) If the treaty does regulate reservations, a number of cases must be distinguished which offer different answers to the question whether the reservations concerned are subject to the test of compatibility with the object and purpose of the treaty. In two of these cases, the answer is clearly negative:

— There is no doubt that a reservation expressly prohibited by the treaty cannot be held to be valid on the pretext that it is compatible with the object and purpose of the treaty;[829]

— The same applies to "specified" reservations that are expressly authorized by the treaty, with a defined content: they are automatically valid without having to be accepted by the other contracting States[830] and they are not subject to the test of compatibility with the object and purpose of the treaty.[831]

In the Commission's view, these obvious truths are not worth mentioning in separate provisions of the Guide to Practice; they follow directly and inevitably from article 19, subparagraph (*c*), of the Vienna Conventions, the text of which is repeated in draft guideline 3.1.

(7) The same is not true of two other cases which arise *a contrario* out of the provisions of article 19, subparagraphs (*a*) and (*b*):

— Those in which a reservation is authorized because it does not fall under the category of prohibited reservations (subparagraph (*a*));

— Those in which a reservation is authorized without being "specified" within the meaning of subparagraph (*b*) as spelt out in draft guideline 3.1.2.

(8) In both these cases, it cannot be presumed that treaty-based authorization to formulate reservations offers States or international organizations *carte blanche* to formulate any reservation they wish, even if it would leave the treaty bereft of substance.

(9) On the subject of implicitly authorized reservations, Sir Humphrey Waldock recognized, in his fourth report on the law of treaties, that "[a] conceivable exception [to the principle of automatic validity of reservations permitted by the treaty] might be where a treaty expressly forbids certain specified reservations and thereby implicitly permits others; for it might not be unreasonable to regard compatibility with the object and purpose as still an implied limitation on the making of other reservations". However, he excluded that eventuality not because this was untrue but because "this may, perhaps, go too far in refining the rules regarding the intentions of the parties, and there is something to be said for keeping the rules in article 18 [which became article 19 of the Convention] as simple as possible".[832] These considerations do not apply to the Guide to Practice, the aim of which is precisely to provide States with coherent answers to all questions they may have in the area of reservations.

(10) This is why draft guideline 3.1.3 stipulates that reservations which are implicitly authorized because they are not formally excluded by the treaty must be compatible with the object and purpose of the treaty. It would be paradoxical, to say the least, if reservations to treaties containing reservations clauses should be allowed more liberally than in the case of treaties which contain no such clauses.[833] Thus the criterion of compatibility with the object and purpose of the treaty applies.

3.1.4 *Permissibility of specified reservations*

Where the treaty envisages the formulation of specified reservations without defining their content, a reservation may be formulated by a State or an international organization only if it is not incompatible with the object and purpose of the treaty.

Commentary

(1) Draft guideline 3.1.3 states that reservations not prohibited by the treaty are still subject to the criterion of compatibility with the object and purpose of the treaty. Draft guideline 3.1.4 does likewise in the case of specified reservations in the sense of draft guideline 3.1.1 where the treaty does not define the content of the reservation: the same problem arises, and the considerations put forward in support of draft guideline 3.1.3 apply *mutatis mutandis*.

---

827 See draft guidelines 3.3 to 3.3.4 proposed by the Special Rapporteur in his tenth report, *ibid.*

828 In the case of treaties with limited participation and the constituent instruments of international organizations. These cases do not constitute instances of implicit prohibitions of formulating reservations; they reintroduce the system of unanimity for particular types of treaties.

829 In its observations on the draft articles on the law of treaties adopted on first reading by the Commission, Canada had suggested that "consideration should be given to extending the criterion of 'compatibility with the object and purpose' equally to reservations made pursuant to express treaty provisions in order not to have different criteria for cases where the treaty is silent on the making of reservations and cases where it permits them" (fourth report of the Special Rapporteur on the law of treaties, *Yearbook ... 1965*, vol. II, document A/CN.4/177 and Add.1–2, p. 46). That proposal, which was not very clear, was not retained by the Commission; cf. the clearer proposals along the same lines by Briggs in *Yearbook ... 1962*, vol. I, 663rd meeting, 18 June 1962, p. 222, paras. 13 and 14, and *Yearbook ... 1965*, vol. I, 813th meeting, 29 June 1965, p. 264, para. 10; or by Ago (*contra*), *ibid.*, para. 16.

830 See paragraph 1 of article 20 of the 1969 Vienna Convention.

831 See above draft guideline 3.1.2 and the commentary thereto.

832 *Yearbook ... 1965*, vol. II, document A/CN.4/177 and Add.1–2, p. 50, para. 4.

833 In that vein, see the statement of Rosenne during the Commission's debate at its seventeenth session, *Yearbook ... 1965*, vol. I, 797th meeting, 8 June 1965, p. 149, para. 10.

(2) The Polish amendment to subparagraph (*b*) of article 19, adopted by the Vienna Conference on the Law of Treaties in 1968, restricted the possibility of implicit prohibition of reservations to treaties which provided that "*only* specified reservations which do not include the reservation in question" may be formulated.[834] But it does not follow that reservations thus authorized may be made at will: the arguments applicable to non-prohibited reservations[835] apply here, and if one accepts the broad definition of specified reservations favoured by the majority of Commission members,[836] a distinction must be drawn between reservations whose content is defined in the treaty itself and those which are permitted in principle but which there is no reason to suppose should be allowed to deprive the treaty of its object or purpose. The latter must be subject to the same general conditions as reservations to treaties which do not contain specific clauses.

(3) The modification made to article 19, subparagraph (*c*) of the 1969 Vienna Convention following the Polish amendment in fact goes in that direction. In the Commission's text, subparagraph (*c*) was drafted as follows: "(*c*) In cases where the treaty contains no provisions regarding reservations, the reservation is incompatible with the object and purpose of the treaty." [837] This was consistent with subparagraph (*b*), which prohibited the formulation of reservations other than those authorized by a reservations clause. Once an authorization was no longer interpreted *a contrario* as automatically excluding other reservations, the formula could not be retained;[838] it was therefore changed to the current wording by the Drafting Committee of the Vienna Conference.[839] The result is, *a contrario*, that if a reservation does not fall within the scope of subparagraph (*b*) (because its content is not specified), it is subject to the test of compatibility with the object and purpose of the treaty.

(4) That was, indeed, the reasoning followed by the arbitral tribunal which settled the *English Channel* dispute in deciding that the mere fact that article 12 of the Convention on the Continental Shelf authorized certain reservations without specifying their content[840] did not necessarily mean that such reservations were automatically valid.[841]

(5) In such cases, the validity of the reservation "cannot be assumed simply on the ground that it is, or purports to be, a reservation to an article to which reservations are permitted".[842] Its validity must be assessed in the light of its compatibility with the object and purpose of the treaty.[843]

(6) *A contrario*, it goes without saying that when the content of a specified reservation is indeed indicated in the reservations clause itself, a reservation consistent with that provision is not subject to the test of compatibility with the object and purpose of the treaty.

1.6 *Scope of definitions*

The definitions of unilateral statements included in the present chapter of the Guide to Practice are without prejudice to the validity and effects of such statements under the rules applicable to them.

Commentary

(1) This draft guideline was provisionally adopted by the Commission at its fiftieth session, in 1998, in a form which referred only to reservations. The related draft commentary indicated that its title and placement in the Guide to Practice would be determined at a later stage and that the Commission would consider the possibility of referring under a single caveat to both reservations and interpretative declarations, which, in the view of some members, posed identical problems.[844] At its fifty-first session, the plenary Commission adopted this approach, deeming it necessary to clarify and specify the scope of the entire set of draft guidelines relating to the definition of all unilateral statements which are envisaged, in order to make their particular object clear.[845]

[834] See above paragraph (3) of the commentary to draft guideline 3.1.2 and footnote 783.

[835] See above paragraph (9) of the commentary to draft guideline 3.1.3.

[836] See above paragraph (13) of the commentary to draft guideline 3.1.2.

[837] *Yearbook ... 1966*, vol. II, p. 202 (art. 16).

[838] Poland had not, however, put forward any amendment to subparagraph (*c*), drawing the consequences from the amendment it had successfully proposed for subparagraph (*b*). An amendment by Viet Nam, however, intended to delete the phrase "in cases where the treaty contains no provisions regarding reservations" (A/CONF.39/C.1/L.125, *Official Records of the United Nations Conference on the Law of Treaties, First and second sessions...* (footnote 725 above), p. 134, para. 177), was rejected by the plenary Commission (*ibid.*, p. 136, para. 182).

[839] Curiously, the reason given by the Chairperson of the Drafting Committee makes no connection between the modifications made to subparagraphs (*b*) and (*c*); Yasseen merely stated that "[s]ome members of the Committee had considered that a treaty might conceivably contain a provision on reservation which did not fall into any of the categories contemplated in paragraphs (*a*) and (*b*)" (*Official Records of the United Nations Conference on the Law of Treaties, First session...* (footnote 728 above), Committee of the Whole, seventieth meeting, 14 May 1968, p. 415, para. 17). Cf. a remark by Briggs in 1965 to the same effect during discussions in the Commission at its seventeenth session, *Yearbook ... 1965*, vol. I, 796th meeting, 4 June 1965, p. 146, para. 37.

[840] See above paragraph (5) of the commentary to draft guideline 3.1.2 and footnote 790.

[841] See the *Case concerning the delimitation of the continental shelf between the United Kingdom of Great Britain and Northern Ireland, and the French Republic* (footnote 790 above), p. 32, para. 39. See also above paragraph (6) of the commentary to draft guideline 3.1.2.

[842] Bowett, *loc. cit.* (footnote 707 above), p. 72. In the same vein, see Ruda, *loc. cit.* (footnote 708 above), p. 182; or G. Teboul, "Remarques sur les réserves aux conventions de codification", *Revue générale de droit international public, vol. 86 (*1982), pp. 691–692. *Contra:* Imbert, "La question des réserves dans la décision arbitrale du 30 juin 1977 ...", *loc. cit.* (footnote 810 above), pp. 50–53; this opinion, very well argued, does not sufficiently take into account the consequences of the modification made to subparagraph (*c*) of article 19 of the 1969 Vienna Convention at the Vienna Conference on the Law of Treaties (see above, paragraph (3) of the commentary to the present draft guideline).

[843] C. Tomuschat gives a pertinent example: "If, for example, a convention on the protection of human rights prohibits in a 'colonial clause' the exception of dependent territories from the territorial scope of the treaty, it would be absurd to suppose that consequently reservations of any kind, including those relating to the most elementary guarantees of individual freedom, are authorised, even if by these restrictions the treaty would be deprived of its very substance" (*loc. cit.* (footnote 754 above), p. 474).

[844] *Yearbook ... 1998*, vol. II (Part Two), pp. 107–108.

[845] See *Yearbook ... 1999*, vol. II (Part Two), p. 126 (paragraph (1) of the commentary to draft guideline 1.6).

(2) As originally worded, draft guideline 1.6 read: "The definitions of unilateral statements included in the present chapter of the Guide to Practice are without prejudice to the *permissibility* and effects of such statements under the rules applicable to them." At the fifty-seventh session, however, some members argued that the word "permissibility" was not appropriate: in international law, an internationally wrongful act entailed its author's responsibility,[846] and that was plainly not the case of the formulation of reservations that did not fulfil the conditions relating to form or substance that the Vienna Conventions imposed on reservations. At its fifty-eighth session, the Commission decided to replace "permissibility" by "validity", a term the majority of members considered more neutral. The commentary to draft guideline 1.6 was amended accordingly.[847]

(3) Defining is not the same as regulating. As "[a] precise statement of the essential nature of a thing",[848] the sole function of a definition is to determine the general category in which a given statement should be classified. However, this classification does not in any way prejudge the validity of the statements in question: a reservation may or may not be permissible, but it remains a reservation if it corresponds to the definition established. *A contrario*, it is not a reservation if it does not meet the criteria set forth in these draft guidelines, but this does not necessarily mean that such statements are valid (or invalid) from the standpoint of other rules of international law. The same is true of interpretative declarations, which might conceivably not be valid either because they would alter the nature of the treaty or because they were not formulated at the required time,[849] etc.[850]

(4) Furthermore, the exact determination of the nature of a statement is a precondition for the application of a particular legal regime, in the first place, for the assessment of its validity. It is only once a particular instrument has been defined as a reservation (or an interpretative declaration, either simple or conditional) that it can be decided whether it is valid, that its legal scope can be evaluated and that its effect can be determined. However, this validity and these effects are not otherwise affected by the definition, which requires only that the relevant rules be applied.

(5) For example, the fact that draft guideline 1.1.2 indicates that a reservation "may be formulated" in all the cases referred to in draft guideline 1.1 and in article 11 of the 1969 and 1986 Vienna Conventions does not mean that such a reservation is necessarily valid; its validity depends upon whether it meets the conditions stipulated in the law on reservations to treaties and, in particular, those stipulated in article 19 of the 1969 and 1986 Vienna Conventions. Similarly, the Commission's confirmation of the well-established practice of "across the board" reservations in draft guideline 1.1.1 [1.1.4] is in no way meant to constitute a decision on the validity of such a reservation in a specific case, which would depend on its contents and context; the sole purpose of the draft is to show that a unilateral statement of such a nature is indeed a reservation and, as such, subject to the legal regime governing reservations.

(6) The "rules applicable" referred to in draft guideline 1.6 are, first of all, the relevant rules in the 1969, 1978 and 1986 Vienna Conventions and, in general, the customary rules applicable to reservations and to interpretative declarations, which this Guide to Practice is intended to codify and develop progressively in accordance with the Commission's mandate, and those relating to other unilateral statements which States and international organizations may formulate in respect of treaties, but which are not covered in the Guide to Practice.

(7) More generally, all the draft guidelines adopted thus far are interdependent and cannot be read and understood in isolation from one another.

2.1.8 [2.1.7 *bis*] *Procedure in case of manifestly invalid reservations*

1. Where, in the opinion of the depositary, a reservation is manifestly invalid, the depositary shall draw the attention of the author of the reservation to what, in the depositary's view, constitutes the grounds for the invalidity of the reservation.

2. If the author of the reservation maintains the reservation, the depositary shall communicate the text of the reservation to the signatory States and international organizations and to the contracting States and international organizations and, where appropriate, the competent organ of the international organization concerned, indicating the nature of legal problems raised by the reservation.

Commentary

(1) During the discussion of draft guideline 2.1.7, some members of the Commission considered that purely and simply applying the rules it established in the case of a reservation that was manifestly "invalid" gave rise to certain difficulties. In particular, they stressed that there was no reason to provide for a detailed examination of the formal validity of the reservation by the depositary, as the first paragraph of draft guideline 2.1.7 did, while precluding him from reacting in the case of a reservation that was manifestly impermissible from a substantive viewpoint (in particular, when the conditions specified in article 19 of the Vienna Conventions were not met).

(2) However, allowing him to intervene in the latter case would constitute a progressive development of international law, which, it had to be acknowledged, departed from the spirit in which the provisions of the Vienna Conventions on the functions of depositaries had been drawn

[846] Cf. article 1 of the draft articles on responsibility of States for internationally wrongful acts, *Yearbook ... 2001*, vol. II (Part Two) and corrigendum, p. 32, and General Assembly resolution 56/83 of 12 December 2001, annex.

[847] And likewise the text of and commentary to draft guideline 2.1.8. For the original wording of the commentary, see *Yearbook ... 1999*, vol. II (Part Two), p. 126.

[848] *The Oxford English Dictionary*, 2nd ed., Oxford, Clarendon Press, 1989.

[849] This problem may very likely arise in connection with conditional interpretative declarations (see draft guideline 1.2.1 [1.2.4]).

[850] The same may obviously be said about unilateral statements which are neither reservations nor interpretative declarations, referred to in section 1.4.

up.[851] That is why, during its fifty-third session, the Commission considered it useful to consult Member States in the Sixth Committee of the General Assembly about whether the depositary could or should "refuse to communicate to States and international organizations concerned a reservation that is manifestly inadmissible, particularly when it is prohibited by a provision of a treaty".[852]

(3) The nuanced responses given to this question by the delegations to the Sixth Committee inspired the wording of draft guideline 2.1.8. Generally speaking, States expressed a preference for the strict alignment of the Guide to Practice with the provisions of the 1969 Vienna Convention concerning the role of the depositary, in particular article 77 thereof. Some of the delegations that spoke stressed that the depositary must demonstrate impartiality and neutrality in the exercise of his functions and should therefore limit himself to transmitting to the parties the reservations that were formulated. However, a number of representatives to the Sixth Committee expressed the view that, when a reservation was manifestly not valid, it was incumbent upon the depositary to refuse to communicate it or at least to first inform the author of the reservation of his position and, if the author maintained the reservation, to communicate it and draw the attention of the other parties to the problem.

(4) Most members of the Commission supported this intermediate solution. They considered that it was not possible to allow any type of censure by the depositary, but that it would be inappropriate to oblige him to communicate the text of a manifestly invalid reservation to the contracting or signatory States and international organizations without previously having drawn the attention of the reserving State or international organization to the defects that, in his opinion, affected it. Nevertheless, it was to be understood that, if the author of the reservation maintained it, the normal procedure would resume and the reservation should be transmitted, with an indication of the nature of the legal problems in question. In point of fact, this amounts to bringing the procedure to be followed in the case of a reservation that is not manifestly valid in terms of substance into line with the procedure to be followed in the case of reservations that present problems of form. According to draft guideline 2.1.7, should there be a difference of opinion regarding such problems, the depositary "shall bring the question to the attention of: (*a*) the signatory States and organizations and the contracting States and contracting organizations; or (*b*) where appropriate, the competent organ of the international organization concerned".

(5) According to some members of the Commission, this procedure should be followed only if the "invalidity" invoked by the depositary is based on subparagraphs (*a*) and (*b*) of article 19 of the 1969 and 1986 Vienna Conventions (a reservation prohibited by the treaty, or not provided for in a treaty that authorizes only certain specific reservations). Other members consider that the only real problem is that of the compatibility of the reservation with the object and purpose of the treaty (subparagraph (*c*) of article 19). The majority considered that this procedure applied to all the subparagraphs and therefore the Commission did not consider it justified to distinguish among the different types of invalidity listed in article 19.

(6) Similarly, despite the contrary opinion of some of its members, the Commission did not consider it useful to confine the exchange of opinions between the author of the reservation and the depositary implied by draft guideline 2.1.7 within strict time limits. The draft does not diverge from draft guideline 2.1.6, paragraph 1 (*b*), under which the depositary must act "as soon as possible". And, in any case, the reserving State or international organization must advise whether it is willing to discuss the matter with the depositary. If it is not, the procedure must follow its course and the reservation must be communicated to the other contracting parties or signatories.

(7) Although the Commission initially used the word "impermissible" to characterize reservations covered by the provisions of article 19 of the Vienna Conventions,[853] some members pointed out that the word was not appropriate in that case: in international law, an internationally wrongful act entails its author's responsibility,[854] but this is plainly not the case with reservations which are contrary to the provisions of the treaty to which they relate or which are incompatible with its object and purpose or which do not respect the stipulations as to form or time limits laid down by the Vienna Conventions. At its fifty-eighth session, the Commission therefore decided to replace the words "permissible", "impermissible", "permissibility" and "impermissibility" by "valid", "invalid", "validity" and "invalidity", and to amend this commentary accordingly.[855]

[851] See paragraphs (9)–(10) of the commentary to draft guideline 2.1.7.

[852] *Yearbook ... 2001*, vol. II (Part Two) and corrigendum, p. 18, para. 25.

[853] For the original version of draft guideline 2.1.8 [2.1.7 *bis*] and the commentary thereto, see *Yearbook ... 2002*, vol. II (Part Two), pp. 45–46.

[854] Cf. draft article 1 of the draft articles on responsibility of States for internationally wrongful acts (footnote 846 above).

[855] The text of and commentary to draft guideline 1.6 have been similarly amended.

Chapter IX

UNILATERAL ACTS OF STATES

A. Introduction

160. In the report of the Commission to the General Assembly on the work of its forty-eighth session (1996), the Commission proposed to the General Assembly that the law of unilateral acts of States should be included as a topic appropriate for the codification and progressive development of international law.[856]

161. The General Assembly, in paragraph 13 of resolution 51/160 of 16 December 1996, *inter alia*, invited the Commission to further examine the topic "Unilateral acts of States" and to indicate its scope and content.

162. At its forty-ninth session (1997), the Commission established an open-ended working group on the topic which reported to the Commission on the admissibility and feasibility of a study on the topic, its possible scope and content and an outline for a study on the topic. At the same session, the Commission considered and endorsed the report of the Working Group.[857]

163. Also at its forty-ninth session, the Commission appointed Mr. Víctor Rodríguez Cedeño, Special Rapporteur on the topic.[858]

164. The General Assembly, in paragraph 8 of its resolution 52/156 of 15 December 1997, endorsed the Commission's decision to include the topic in its work programme.

165. From its fiftieth session (1998) to its fifty-seventh session (2005), the Commission received and considered eight reports from the Special Rapporteur.[859]

166. The Commission also reconvened the Working Group on unilateral acts of States from its fiftieth session (1998) to its fifty-third session (2001) and from its fifty-fifth session (2003) to its fifty-seventh session (2005). The Working Group in its report at the fifty-sixth session (2004) established a grid which would permit it to use uniform analytical tools.[860] Individual members of the Working Group took up a number of studies, which were carried out in accordance with the established grid. These studies were transmitted to the Special Rapporteur for the preparation of his eighth report. The Commission requested the Working Group at the fifty-seventh session (2005) to consider the points on which there was general agreement and which might form the basis for preliminary conclusions or proposals on the topic.

B. Consideration of the topic at the present session

167. At the present session, the Commission had before it the Special Rapporteur's ninth report (A/CN.4/569 and Add.1) which it considered at its 2886th, 2887th and 2888th meetings on 3, 4 and 5 July 2006.

168. The ninth report of the Special Rapporteur comprised two parts. The first part related to the causes of invalidity,[861]

[856] *Yearbook ... 1996*, vol. II (Part Two), document A/51/10, pp. 97–98, para. 248, and Annex II, p. 133.

[857] *Yearbook ... 1997*, vol. II (Part Two), A/52/10, pp. 64–65, paras. 194 and 196–210.

[858] *Ibid.*, pp. 66 and 71, paras. 212 and 234.

[859] First report: *Yearbook ... 1998*, vol. II (Part One), document A/CN.4/486; second report: *Yearbook ... 1999*, vol. II (Part One), document A/CN.4/500 and Add.1; third report: *Yearbook ... 2000*, vol. II (Part One), document A/CN.4/505; fourth report: *Yearbook ... 2001*, vol. II (Part One), document A/CN.4/519; fifth report: *Yearbook ... 2002*, vol. II (Part One), document A/CN.4/525 and Add.1–2; sixth report: *Yearbook ... 2003*, vol. II (Part One), document A/CN.4/534; seventh report: *Yearbook ... 2004*, vol. II (Part One), document A/CN.4/542; and eighth report: *Yearbook ... 2005*, vol. II (Part One), document A/CN.4/557.

[860] The grid included the following elements: date; author/organ; competence of author/organ; form; content; context and circumstances; aim; addressees; reactions of addressees; reactions of third parties; basis; implementation; modification; termination/revocation; legal scope; decision of a judge or an arbitrator; comments; literature, *Yearbook ... 2004*, vol. II (Part Two), p. 96, para. 247 and footnote 516.

[861] "Principle 5.

"*Invalidity of an act formulated by a person not qualified to do so*

"A unilateral act formulated by a person not authorized or qualified to do so may be declared invalid, without prejudice to the possibility that the State from which the act was issued may confirm it in accordance with guiding principle 4."

"Principle 6.

"*Invalidity of a unilateral act that conflicts with a norm of fundamental importance to the domestic law of the State formulating it*

"A State that has formulated a unilateral act may not invoke as grounds for invalidity the fact that the act conflicts with its domestic law, unless it conflicts with a norm of fundamental importance to its domestic law and the contradiction is manifest."

"Principle 7.

"*Invalidity of unilateral acts*

"1. (*a*) A State that is the author of a unilateral act may not invoke error as grounds for declaring the act invalid, unless the act was formulated on the basis of an error of fact or a situation that was assumed by the State to exist at the time when the act was formulated and that fact or that situation formed an essential basis of its consent to be bound by the unilateral act.

"(*b*) The foregoing shall not apply if the author State contributed by its own conduct to the error or if the circumstances were such as to put that State on notice of the possibility of such an error.

"2. Fraud may be invoked as grounds for declaring a unilateral act invalid if the author State was induced to formulate the act by the fraudulent conduct of another State.

"3. Corruption of the representative of the State may be invoked as grounds for declaring a unilateral act invalid if the act was formulated owing to the corruption of the person formulating it.

"4. Coercion of the person who formulated a unilateral act may be invoked as grounds for declaring its invalidity if that person formulated it as a result of acts or threats directed against him or her.

"5. Any unilateral act formulated as a result of the threat or use of force in violation of the principles of international law embodied in the Charter of the United Nations is invalid.

"6. Any unilateral act which at the time of its formulation is contrary to (or conflicts with) a peremptory norm of general international law (*jus cogens*) is invalid."

and termination[862] of unilateral acts. The second part dealt with definition,[863] the capacity of a State to formulate a unilateral act,[864] the competence to formulate unilateral acts on behalf of the State,[865] the subsequent confirmation of an act formulated by a person without authorization,[866] the basis for the binding nature of the unilateral acts,[867] and the interpretation of unilateral acts.[868]

169. On 5 July 2006 the Commission decided to re-establish the open-ended Working Group under the chairpersonship of Mr. Alain Pellet. The Working Group was requested to prepare conclusions of the Commission on the topic "Unilateral acts of States" taking into consideration the various views expressed, the draft guiding principles of the Special Rapporteur and its previous work on the topic.

170. The Commission, at its 2906th meeting on 4 August 2006, considered the report of the Working Group. Following its consideration of the report of the Working Group, the Commission adopted a set of 10 "guiding principles" together with commentaries applicable to unilateral declarations of States capable of creating legal obligations (section D below)[869] and commended the guiding principles to the attention of the General Assembly.

C. Tribute to the Special Rapporteur

171. At its 2913th meeting, on 11 August 2006, the Commission, after adopting the text of the guiding principles, adopted the following resolution by acclamation:

The International Law Commission,

Having adopted the guiding principles applicable to unilateral declarations of States capable of creating legal obligations and commentaries thereto,

Expresses its deep appreciation and warm congratulations to the Special Rapporteur, Mr. Víctor Rodríguez Cedeño, for the outstanding contribution he has made, through his devoted work and tireless efforts, to the preparation of the guiding principles applicable to unilateral declarations of States capable of creating legal obligations and for the results he has achieved in the elaboration of the said principles.

172. The Commission also expressed its deep appreciation to the Working Group on unilateral acts of States under the chairpersonship of Mr. Alain Pellet for its untiring efforts and contribution to the work on the topic.

D. Text of the guiding principles applicable to unilateral declarations of States capable of creating legal obligations adopted by the Commission

Introductory note

173. Having examined the nine reports submitted by the Special Rapporteur and after extensive debates, the Commission believes it necessary to come to some conclusions on a topic, the difficulties and the value of which have both become apparent. Clearly, it is important for States to be in a position to judge with reasonable certainty whether and to what extent their unilateral conduct may legally bind them on the international plane.

174. The Commission is aware, however, that the concept of a unilateral act is not uniform. On the one hand, certain unilateral acts are formulated in the framework and on the basis of an express authorization under international law,[870] whereas others are formulated by States in

---

[862] "Principle 8.

"*Termination of unilateral acts*

"A unilateral act may be terminated or revoked by the formulating State:

"(*a*) If a specific time limit for termination of the act was set at the time of its formulation (or if termination was implicit following the performance of one or more acts);

"(*b*) If the act was subject to a resolutory condition at the time of its formulation;

"(*c*) If the subject matter of the unilateral act has ceased to exist;

"(*d*) If there has been a fundamental change in the circumstances that prompted the formulation of the act (*rebus sic stantibus*) which renders its fulfilment impossible;

"(*e*) If a peremptory norm of international law has emerged following its formulation which conflicts with the act."

[863] "Principle 1.

"*Definition of a unilateral act*

"A unilateral act of a State means a unilateral declaration formulated by a State with the intent of producing certain legal effects under international law."

Addressees of unilateral acts of States

Option A

A unilateral act may be addressed to one or more States, the international community as a whole, one or more international organizations or any other entity subject to international law.

Option B

A unilateral act formulated in accordance with international law will produce legal effects, regardless of whom it was addressed to.

[864] "Principle 2.

"*Capacity of States to formulate unilateral acts*

"Every State possesses capacity to formulate unilateral acts in accordance with international law.

[865] "Principle 3.

"*Competence to formulate unilateral acts on behalf of the State*

"1. By virtue of their office, Heads of State, Heads of Government and Ministers for Foreign Affairs are considered to represent their State and to have the capacity to formulate unilateral acts on its behalf.

"2. In addition to the persons mentioned in the previous paragraph, other persons may be considered able to formulate unilateral acts on behalf of the State if that may be inferred from the practice followed in that regard by the formulating State and from the circumstances in which the act was formulated."

[866] "Principle 4.

"*Subsequent confirmation of an act formulated by a person without authorization (or not qualified to do so)*

"A unilateral act formulated by a person not authorized (or qualified) to act on behalf of the State, in accordance with the previous guiding principles, may be confirmed subsequently by the State either expressly or through conclusive acts from which such confirmation can be clearly inferred."

[867] "Principle 10.

"*Basis for the binding nature of unilateral acts*

"The binding nature of the unilateral acts of States is based on the principle of good faith and the intent to be bound of the State that formulated the act."

[868] "Principle 11.

"*Interpretation of unilateral acts*

"The context in which a unilateral act was formulated by a State, together with the clarity and precision of its terms, shall be given weight in interpreting it."

[869] See the *Nuclear Tests* cases (*Australia* v. *France*) and (*New Zealand* v. *France*), *Judgments of 20 December 1974, I.C.J. Reports 1974*, pp. 253 and 457, at p. 267, para. 43, and p. 472, para. 46.

[870] See the laws establishing the extent of the territorial sea or reservations to treaties, which are unilateral acts closely circumscribed by specific rules of international law.

exercise of their freedom to act on the international plane; in accordance with the Commission's previous decisions, only the latter have been examined by the Commission and its Special Rapporteur.[871] On the other hand, in this second case, there exists a very wide spectrum of conduct covered by the designation "unilateral acts", and the differences among legal cultures partly account for the misunderstandings to which this topic has given rise, as, for some, the concept of a juridical act necessarily implies an express manifestation of a will to be bound on the part of the author State, whereas for others any unilateral conduct by the State producing legal effects on the international plane may be categorized as a unilateral act.

175. As was decided at its fifty-sixth session, in 2004,[872] the Commission and its Special Rapporteur have accorded priority to the study of unilateral acts in the first of these senses, while bearing in mind that a State may be bound by conduct other than formal declarations.

1. Text of the guiding principles

176. The text of the guiding principles adopted by the Commission is reproduced below.

GUIDING PRINCIPLES APPLICABLE TO UNILATERAL DECLARATIONS OF STATES CAPABLE OF CREATING LEGAL OBLIGATIONS

The International Law Commission,

***Noting that* States may find themselves bound by their unilateral behaviour on the international plane,**

***Noting that* behaviours capable of legally binding States may take the form of formal declarations or mere informal conduct including, in certain situations, silence, on which other States may reasonably rely,**

***Noting also that* the question whether a unilateral behaviour by the State binds it in a given situation depends on the circumstances of the case,**

***Noting also that* in practice, it is often difficult to establish whether the legal effects stemming from the unilateral behaviour of a State are the consequence of the intent that it has expressed or depend on the expectations that its conduct has raised among other subjects of international law,**

***Adopts* the following guiding principles which relate only to unilateral acts *stricto sensu,* i.e. those taking the form of formal declarations formulated by a State with the intent to produce obligations under international law,**

1. Declarations publicly made and manifesting the will to be bound may have the effect of creating legal obligations. When the conditions for this are met, the binding character of such declarations is based on good faith; States concerned may then take them into consideration and rely on them; such States are entitled to require that such obligations be respected;

2. Any State possesses capacity to undertake legal obligations through unilateral declarations;

3. To determine the legal effects of such declarations, it is necessary to take account of their content, of all the factual circumstances in which they were made, and of the reactions to which they gave rise;

4. A unilateral declaration binds the State internationally only if it is made by an authority vested with the power to do so. By virtue of their functions, Heads of State, Heads of Government and Ministers for Foreign Affairs are competent to formulate such declarations. Other persons representing the State in specified areas may be authorized to bind it, through their declarations, in areas falling within their competence;

5. Unilateral declarations may be formulated orally or in writing;

6. Unilateral declarations may be addressed to the international community as a whole, to one or several States or to other entities;

7. A unilateral declaration entails obligations for the formulating State only if it is stated in clear and specific terms. In the case of doubt as to the scope of the obligations resulting from such a declaration, such obligations must be interpreted in a restrictive manner. In interpreting the content of such obligations, weight shall be given first and foremost to the text of the declaration, together with the context and the circumstances in which it was formulated;

8. A unilateral declaration which is in conflict with a peremptory norm of general international law is void;

9. No obligation may result for other States from the unilateral declaration of a State. However, the other State or States concerned may incur obligations in relation to such a unilateral declaration to the extent that they clearly accepted such a declaration;

10. A unilateral declaration that has created legal obligations for the State making the declaration cannot be revoked arbitrarily. In assessing whether a revocation would be arbitrary, consideration should be given to:

(*a*) any specific terms of the declaration relating to revocation;

(*b*) the extent to which those to whom the obligations are owed have relied on such obligations;

(*c*) the extent to which there has been a fundamental change in the circumstances.

2. Text of the guiding principles with commentaries thereto adopted by the Commission at its fifty-eighth session

177. The text of the guiding principles together with commentaries[873] thereto adopted by the Commission at its fifty-eighth session is reproduced below.

GUIDING PRINCIPLES APPLICABLE TO UNILATERAL DECLARATIONS OF STATES CAPABLE OF CREATING LEGAL OBLIGATIONS

The International Law Commission,

***Noting that* States may find themselves bound by their unilateral behaviour on the international plane,**

***Noting that* behaviours capable of legally binding States may take the form of formal declarations or mere informal conduct including, in certain situations, silence, on which other States may reasonably rely,**

***Noting also that* the question whether a unilateral behaviour by the State binds it in a given situation depends on the circumstances of the case,**

---

[871] See *Yearbook ... 1997*, vol. II (Part Two), pp. 64–65, paras. 198–208.

[872] *Yearbook ... 2004*, vol. II (Part Two), p. 96, paras. 245–247. See also *Yearbook ... 2005*, vol. II (Part Two), para. 293.

[873] These commentaries are explanatory notes reviewing the jurisprudence of the ICJ and pertinent State practice analysed by several members of the Working Group and the Special Rapporteur and summarized in the eighth report of the Special Rapporteur, *Yearbook ... 2005*, vol. II (Part One), document A/CN.4/557.

***Noting also that* in practice, it is often difficult to establish whether the legal effects stemming from the unilateral behaviour of a State are the consequence of the intent that it has expressed or depend on the expectations that its conduct has raised among other subjects of international law,**

***Adopts* the following guiding principles which relate only to unilateral acts *stricto sensu*, i.e. those taking the form of formal declarations formulated by a State with the intent to produce obligations under international laws.**

1. Declarations publicly made and manifesting the will to be bound may have the effect of creating legal obligations. When the conditions for this are met, the binding character of such declarations is based on good faith; States concerned may then take them into consideration and rely on them; such States are entitled to require that such obligations be respected.

Commentary

(1) The wording of guiding principle 1, which seeks both to define unilateral acts in the strict sense and to indicate what they are based on, is very directly inspired by the *dicta* in the judgments handed down by the ICJ on 20 December 1974 in the *Nuclear Tests* case.[874] In the case concerning the *Frontier Dispute (Burkina Faso/Republic of Mali)*, the Court was careful to point out that "it all depends on the intention of the State in question".[875]

(2) Most of the cases studied illustrate this principle. Besides the declarations made by France in 1974 on the cessation of nuclear tests in the atmosphere,[876] the public nature of the declaration made by Egypt on 24 April 1957 on the Suez Canal[877] and Jordan's waiver of claims to the West Bank territories[878] represent an important indication of their authors' intention to commit themselves. The Ihlen Declaration, made during a purely bilateral meeting between the Minister for Foreign Affairs of Denmark and the Norwegian Ambassador to Copenhagen,[879] and the Colombian diplomatic note addressed solely to the Venezuelan authorities[880] are not counter-examples: they relate only to bilateral relations between the two States concerned.[881]

[874] *Nuclear Tests* (*Australia* v. *France*) and (*New Zealand* v. *France*) (see footnote 869 above), pp. 267–268, paras. 43 and 46, and pp. 472–473, paras. 46 and 49.

[875] *Frontier Dispute (Burkina Faso/Republic of Mali), Judgment, I.C.J. Reports 1986*, p. 573, para. 39.

[876] See the *Nuclear Tests* cases (*Australia* v. *France*) and (*New Zealand* v. *France*) (footnote 869 above), pp. 265–266, paras. 34 and 37, and pp. 469 and 471, paras. 35 and 40.

[877] United Nations, *Treaty Series*, vol. 265, No. 3821, p. 299. This declaration was examined by the Special Rapporteur in his eighth report, *Yearbook ... 2005*, vol. II (Part One), document A/CN.4/557, paras. 55–58; see also paras. 62–63.

[878] ILM, vol. 27 (1988), p. 1638. See also the eighth report of the Special Rapporteur (see footnote 877 above), paras. 44–45.

[879] See the decision of the PCIJ in *Legal Status of Eastern Greenland, Judgment of 5 April 1933, P.C.I.J., Series A/B, No. 53*, p. 22, at pp. 70–71. See also the eighth report of the Special Rapporteur, *Yearbook ... 2005*, vol. II (Part One), document A/CN.4/557, paras. 116–126. It should, however, be pointed out that whether this declaration constituted a unilateral act is controversial (*ibid.*, para. 122).

[880] A. Vázquez Carrizosa, *Las relaciones de Colombia y Venezuela: La historia atormentada de dos naciones*, Bogotá, Ediciones Tercer Mundo, 1983, pp. 337–339.

[881] See guiding principle 6 below.

2. Any State possesses capacity to undertake legal obligations through unilateral declarations.

Commentary

Just as "[e]very State possesses capacity to conclude treaties",[882] every State can commit itself through acts whereby it unilaterally undertakes legal obligations under the conditions indicated in these guiding principles. This capacity has been acknowledged by the ICJ.[883]

3. To determine the legal effects of such declarations, it is necessary to take account of their content, of all the factual circumstances in which they were made, and of the reactions to which they gave rise.

Commentary

(1) The wording of guiding principle 3 is also inspired by a passage in the ICJ judgments in the *Nuclear Tests* cases;[884] allusion is made to this jurisprudence in the judgments of 22 December 1986 in the *Frontier Dispute (Burkina Faso/Republic of Mali)* case[885] and of 3 February 2006 in the *Armed Activities on the Territory of the Congo* case.[886] In the *Military and Paramilitary Activities in and against Nicaragua* and *Frontier Dispute (Burkina Faso/Republic of Mali)* cases, the Court found nothing in the content of the declarations cited or the circumstances in which they were made "from which it [could] be inferred that any legal undertaking was intended to exist".[887]

(2) Generally speaking, the cases studied by the Commission confirm the relevance of this principle. In the Commission's view, it is particularly important to take account of the context and circumstances in which the declarations were made in the case of the Swiss statements concerning the privileges and immunities of United Nations staff,[888] the Egyptian declaration of 1957[889] and Jordan's waiver of claims to the West Bank territories.[890]

[882] 1969 Vienna Convention, art. 6.

[883] See the jurisprudence cited in support of guiding principles 1 and 3.

[884] *Nuclear Tests* (*Australia* v. *France*) and (*New Zealand* v. *France*) (see footnote 869 above), pp. 269–270, para. 51, and pp. 474–475, para. 53.

[885] *Frontier Dispute (Burkina Faso/Republic of Mali)* (see footnote 875 above), pp. 573–574, paras. 39–40.

[886] *Armed Activities on the Territory of the Congo* (New Application: 2002) (see footnote 637 above), p. 28, para. 49.

[887] *Military and Paramilitary Activities in and against Nicaragua (Nicaragua* v. *United States of America), Merits, Judgment, I.C.J. Reports 1986*, p. 14, at p. 132, para. 261, and *Frontier Dispute (Burkina Faso/Republic of Mali)* (see footnote 875 above), pp. 573–574, para. 39.

[888] See the eighth report of the Special Rapporteur, *Yearbook ... 2005*, vol. II (Part One), document A/CN.4/557, paras. 138–156.

[889] *Ibid.*, paras. 58–60 or 66. See also, by analogy, in the case of conduct other than unilateral statements, the courses of conduct followed by Cambodia and Thailand in the *Temple of Preah Vihear* case (*eighth report of the Special Rapporteur*, paras. 160–167) and the judgment in the case, of 15 June 1962) (*Merits, Judgment, I.C.J. Reports 1962*, p. 6, at pp. 32–34).

[890] See footnote 878 above. See also the eighth report of the Special Rapporteur, *Yearbook ... 2005*, vol. II (Part One), document A/CN.4/557, paras. 47–48.

(3) Several of these examples show the importance of the reactions of other States concerned in evaluating the legal scope of the unilateral acts in question, whether those States take cognizance of commitments undertaken[891] (or, in some cases, rights asserted[892]), or, on the contrary, object to[893] or challenge the binding nature of the "commitments" at issue.[894]

4. A unilateral declaration binds the State internationally only if it is made by an authority vested with the power to do so. By virtue of their functions, Heads of State, Heads of Government and Ministers for Foreign Affairs are competent to formulate such declarations. Other persons representing the State in specified areas may be authorized to bind it, through their declarations, in areas falling within their competence.

Commentary

(1) Guiding principle 4 is also inspired by the consistent jurisprudence of the PCIJ and the ICJ, on unilateral acts and the capacity of State authorities to represent and commit the State internationally. In its recent judgment on jurisdiction and admissibility in the case of *Armed Activities on the Territory of the Congo*, the ICJ observed, referring to the similar customary rule in the law of treaties,[895] that

> in accordance with its consistent jurisprudence (*Nuclear Tests (Australia* v. *France), Judgment, I.C.J. Reports 1974*, pp. 269–270, paras. 49–51; *Application of the Convention on the Prevention and Punishment of the Crime of Genocide (Bosnia and Herzegovina* v. *Yugoslavia), Preliminary Objections, Judgment, I.C.J. Reports 1996 (II)*, p. 622, para. 44; *Arrest Warrant of 11 April 2000 (Democratic Republic of the Congo* v. *Belgium), Judgment, I.C.J. Reports 2002*, pp. 21–22, para. 53; see also *Legal Status of Eastern Greenland (Denmark* v. *Norway), Judgment, 1933, P.C.I.J., Series A/B, No. 53*, p. 71), it is a well-established rule of international law that the Head of State, the Head of Government and the Minister for Foreign Affairs are deemed to represent the State merely by virtue of exercising their functions, including for the performance, on behalf of the said State, of unilateral acts having the force of international commitments.[896]

(2) State practice shows that unilateral declarations creating legal obligations for States are quite often made by Heads of State or Government[897] or Ministers for Foreign Affairs[898] without their capacity to commit the State being called into question. In the two examined cases in which problems relating to the extent of the speaker's authority arose, both related to compliance with the domestic law of the State concerned.[899] The statement by the King of Jordan relating to the West Bank, which some considered to be *ultra vires* under the Constitution of the Kingdom, was confirmed by subsequent domestic acts.[900] In the case of the declaration by the Colombian Minister for Foreign Affairs about Venezuelan sovereignty over the Los Monjes archipelago, the note itself was set aside in domestic law because its author had no authority to make such a commitment, yet the Colombian authorities did not challenge the validity of the commitment at the international level.[901]

(3) In its judgment of 3 February 2006,[902] the ICJ did, however, note "that with increasing frequency in modern international relations other persons representing a State in specific fields may be authorized by that State to bind it by their statements in respect of matters falling within their purview. This may be true, for example, of holders of technical ministerial portfolios exercising powers in their field of competence in the area of foreign relations, and even of certain officials".[903]

5. Unilateral declarations may be formulated orally or in writing.

Commentary

(1) It is generally accepted that the form of a unilateral declaration does not affect its validity or legal effects. The ICJ mentioned the relative unimportance of formalities[904]

---

[891] See the international community's reactions to the Egyptian statement on the Suez Canal (*ibid.*, paras. 63–64), and the reactions to Jordan's statement about the West Bank (*ibid.*, paras. 48 and 50–51).

[892] See *United States Statutes at Large*, 1945, vol. 59, part 2 (Washington D.C., United States Government Printing Office, 1946), p. 884. See the reactions of certain States to the Truman Proclamation (eighth report of the Special Rapporteur, *Yearbook ... 2005*, vol. II (Part One), document A/CN.4/557, paras. 132–134); see also the note dated 22 November 1952 by the Government of Venezuela concerning the Los Monjes archipelago (Vázquez Carrizosa, *op. cit.* (footnote 880 above), pp. 340–341, cited in the eighth report of the Special Rapporteur, para. 17); however, like the Ihlen Declaration (see footnote 879 above) this note was clearly a matter of bilateral negotiations with Colombia.

[893] See in particular Uruguay's refusal of a donation of vaccines from Cuba (eighth report of the Special Rapporteur, *Yearbook ... 2005*, vol. II (Part One), document A/CN.4/557, paras. 38–39) or the Russian protest at the law passed by Turkmenistan in 1993 on the delimitation of its internal and territorial waters in the Caspian Sea (*ibid.*, paras. 84–98).

[894] See the reactions of the non-nuclear-weapon States to the statements made in April 1995 to the Conference on Disarmament by the permanent members of the Security Council (*ibid.*, paras. 113–115); their scepticism is, incidentally, vindicated by the content of those statements (A/50/151–155; S/1995/261–265).

[895] See article 7 of the 1969 Vienna Convention.

[896] *Armed Activities on the Territory of the Congo (New Application: 2002)* (see footnote 637 above), p. 27, para. 46.

[897] See the statement made on 31 July 1988 by the King of Jordan waiving Jordan's claims to the West Bank territories (eighth report of the Special Rapporteur, *Yearbook ... 2005*, vol. II (Part One), document A/CN.4/557, para. 44), the Egyptian declaration of 24 April 1957 on the Suez Canal made by the Government of Egypt (*ibid.*, para. 55), the statements of 8 June and 25 July 1974 and the letter of 1 July 1974 by the President of the French Republic (*ibid.*, para. 71), or the statement made on 28 September 1945 by President Truman of the United States concerning the continental shelf (*ibid.*, para. 127).

[898] See the note dated 22 November 1952 from the Colombian Minister for Foreign Affairs relating to Venezuelan sovereignty over the Los Monjes archipelago (*ibid.*, para. 13), the statement from the Minister for Foreign Affairs of Cuba about the supply of vaccines to Uruguay (*ibid.*, para. 36), the statement by the French Minister for Foreign Affairs to the United Nations General Assembly on 25 September 1974 about the cessation of nuclear tests in the atmosphere (*ibid.*, para. 71), the statements made, as representatives of nuclear-weapon States, by the Minister for Foreign Affairs of the Russian Federation and the United States Secretary of State to the United Nations Security Council (*ibid.*, para. 106), and the statement by Mr. Ihlen, the Minister for Foreign Affairs of Norway (*ibid.*, para. 116).

[899] See the case of the statement made by the Colombian Minister for Foreign Affairs on 22 November 1952 (*ibid.*, paras. 24–35) and the statement by the King of Jordan about the West Bank (*ibid.*, paras. 53–54).

[900] *Ibid.*, para. 54.

[901] *Ibid.*, para. 35.

[902] *Case concerning Armed Activities on the Territory of the Congo (New Application: 2002)* (see footnote 637 above).

[903] *Ibid.*, p. 27, para. 47.

[904] See *Mavrommatis Palestine Concessions* (footnote 26 above), p. 34; and *Application of the Convention on the Prevention and Punishment of the Crime of Genocide (Bosnia-Herzegovina* v. *Yugoslavia),*

in its judgment in the *Temple of Preah Vihear* case in connection with unilateral conduct.[905] In the *Nuclear Tests* cases, the Court emphasized that

> [w]ith regard to the question of form, it should be observed that this is not a domain in which international law imposes any special or strict requirements. Whether a statement is made orally or in writing makes no essential difference, for such statements made in particular circumstances may create commitments in international law, which does not require that they should be couched in written form. Thus the question of form is not decisive.[906]

(2) State practice also shows the many different forms that unilateral declarations by States may take. The various declarations by France about the cessation of atmospheric nuclear tests took the form of a *communiqué* from the Office of the President of the Republic, a diplomatic note, a letter from the President of the Republic sent directly to those to whom the declaration was addressed, a statement made during a press conference and a speech to the General Assembly.[907] Other examples also go to show that, while written declarations prevail,[908] it is not unusual for States to commit themselves by simple oral statements.[909]

(3) France's statements on the suspension of atmospheric nuclear tests also show that a unilateral commitment by a State can come about through a series of declarations with the same general thrust, none of which might, in isolation, have bound the State. In its judgments of 1974 on the *Nuclear Tests* cases, the ICJ did not concentrate on any particular declaration by the French authorities but took them, together, to constitute a whole: "[the] statements [of the President of the French Republic], and those of members of the French Government acting under his authority, up to the last statement made by the Minister of Defence (of 11 October 1974), constitute a whole. Thus, in whatever form the statements were expressed, they must be held to constitute an engagement of the State, having regard to their intention and to the circumstances in which they were made".[910]

Preliminary Objections, Judgment, I.C.J. Reports 1996, p. 595, at p. 612, para. 24, and pp. 613–614, para. 26.

[905] See *Temple of Preah Vihear (Cambodia* v. *Thailand), Preliminary Objections, Judgment of 26 May 1961, I.C.J. Reports 1961*, p. 17, at p. 31.

[906] *Nuclear Tests* (*Australia* v. *France*) and (*New Zealand* v. *France*) (see footnote 869 above), pp. 267–268, para. 45, and p. 473, para. 48.

[907] See the eighth report of the Special Rapporteur, *Yearbook ... 2005*, vol. II (Part One), document A/CN.4/557, paras. 71–72.

[908] Consider the examples of the note dated 22 November 1952 from the Colombian Minister for Foreign Affairs (diplomatic note, *ibid.*, para. 13), the declaration by Egypt of 24 April 1957 (*ibid.*, pp. 55 *et seq.*), the protests of the Russian Federation against Azerbaijan and Turkmenistan (*ibid.*, paras. 85 and 99), the statements by the nuclear-weapon States (statements made before an international body, *ibid.*, paras. 106–107), the Truman Proclamation of 28 September 1945 (*ibid.*, para. 127) and the Swiss statements concerning the United Nations and its staff members (tax exemptions and privileges) (*ibid.*, paras. 140–142).

[909] See, for example, Jordan's waiver of its claims to the West Bank territories in a public speech (*ibid.*, para. 44), or the Ihlen Declaration (*ibid.*, para. 117; see the judgment of the PCIJ in *Legal Status of Eastern Greenland* (footnote 879 above), p. 71).

[910] *Nuclear Tests* (*Australia* v. *France*) and (*New Zealand* v. *France*) (see footnote 869 above), p. 269, para. 49, and p. 474, para. 51. See also the Swiss statements concerning the United Nations and its staff members (tax exemptions and privileges), eighth report of the Special Rapporteur, *Yearbook ... 2005*, vol. II (Part One), document A/CN.4/557, paras. 138–156.

6. Unilateral declarations may be addressed to the international community as a whole, to one or several States or to other entities.

Commentary

(1) Several of the cases examined remain within the scope of strictly bilateral relations between two States; accordingly, these unilateral declarations by a State had another State as the sole addressee. Such was the case of the Colombian diplomatic note addressed to Venezuela,[911] the Cuban declarations concerning the supply of vaccines to Uruguay,[912] the protests by the Russian Federation against Turkmenistan and Azerbaijan[913] and the Ihlen Declaration.[914]

(2) Although initially concerning a limited group of States, other declarations were addressed to the international community as a whole, containing *erga omnes* undertakings. Thus, Egypt's declaration regarding the Suez Canal was not addressed only to the States parties to the Convention between Austria-Hungary, France, Germany, Great Britain, Italy, the Netherlands, Russia, Spain and Turkey respecting the Free Navigation of the Suez Canal (Constantinople Convention) or to the States members of the Suez Canal Users' Association, but to the entire international community.[915] Similarly, the Truman Proclamation,[916] and also the French declarations regarding suspension of nuclear tests in the atmosphere, although the latter were of more direct concern to Australia and New Zealand, as well as certain neighbouring States,[917] were also made *erga omnes* and, accordingly, were addressed to the international community in its entirety.[918] The same holds for the declaration by the King of Jordan of 31 July 1988, waiving Jordan's claims to the West Bank territories, which was addressed simultaneously to the international community, to another State (Israel) and to another entity, the Palestine Liberation Organization.[919]

7. A unilateral declaration entails obligations for the formulating State only if it is stated in clear and specific terms. In the case of doubt as to the scope of the obligations resulting from such a declaration, such obligations must be interpreted in a restrictive manner. In interpreting the content of such obligations, weight shall be given first and foremost to the text of the declaration, together with the context and the circumstances in which it was formulated.

[911] Eighth report of the Special Rapporteur (footnote 910 above), paras. 15–16.

[912] *Ibid.*, para. 36.

[913] *Ibid.*, paras. 85 and 99.

[914] *Ibid.*, para. 117.

[915] *Ibid.*, para. 62.

[916] *Ibid.*, para. 127.

[917] Fiji filed an application to intervene in the proceedings. The Governments of Argentina, Fiji and Peru requested that the pleadings and annexed documents should be made available to them. See *Nuclear Tests* (*Australia* v. *France*) and (*New Zealand* v. *France*) (footnote 869 above), pp. 255–256, paras. 7 and 9, and p. 459, paras. 7 and 9.

[918] *Ibid.*, pp. 269–270, paras. 50–51, and pp. 474–475, paras. 52–53.

[919] See the eighth report of the Special Rapporteur, *Yearbook ... 2005*, vol. II (Part One), document A/CN.4/557, para. 45. Other unilateral declarations are addressed to one or more international organizations, as is the case with Switzerland's declarations concerning the United Nations and its staff (tax exemptions and privileges) (*ibid.*, paras. 138 *et seq.*)

Commentary

(1) In its judgments in the *Nuclear Tests* cases, the ICJ stressed that a unilateral declaration may have the effect of creating legal obligations for the State making the declaration only if it is stated in clear and specific terms.[920] This understanding has been adopted without change by the Court in the case concerning *Armed Activities on the Territory of the Congo*.[921]

(2) In case of doubt concerning the legal scope of the unilateral declaration, it must be interpreted in a restrictive manner, as clearly stated by the Court in its judgments in the *Nuclear Tests* cases when it held that "[w]hen States make statements by which their freedom of action is to be limited, a restrictive interpretation is called for".[922] The interpreter must therefore proceed with great caution in determining the legal effects of unilateral declarations, in particular when the unilateral declaration has no specific addressee.[923]

(3) With regard, in particular, to the method and means of the interpretation, attention is drawn to the observation by the ICJ that

> [t]he régime relating to the interpretation of declarations made under Article 36 of the Statute [of the International Court of Justice[924]] is not identical with that established for the interpretation of treaties by the Vienna Convention on the Law of Treaties ... . Spain has suggested in its pleadings that "[t]his does not mean that the legal rules and the art of interpreting declarations (and reservations) do not coincide with those governing the interpretation of treaties". The Court observes that the provisions of that Convention may only apply analogously to the extent compatible with the *sui generis* character of the unilateral acceptance of the Court's jurisdiction.[925]

Applying the Court's dictum and by analogy with article 31, paragraph 1, of the 1969 Vienna Convention, priority consideration must be given to the text of the unilateral declaration, which best reflects its author's intentions. In addition, as acknowledged by the Court in its judgment in the *Frontier Dispute* case, "to assess the intentions of the author of a unilateral act, account must be taken of all the circumstances in which the act occurred",[926] which constitutes an application by analogy of article 31, paragraph 2, of the 1969 Vienna Convention.

8. A unilateral declaration which is in conflict with a peremptory norm of general international law is void.

Commentary

The invalidity of a unilateral act which is contrary to a peremptory norm of international law derives from the analogous rule contained in article 53 of the 1969 Vienna Convention. Most members of the Commission agreed that there was no obstacle to the application of this rule to the case of unilateral declarations.[927] In its judgment in the *Armed Activities on the Territory of the Congo* case, the Court did not exclude the possibility that a unilateral declaration by Rwanda[928] could be invalid in the event that it was in conflict with a norm of *jus cogens*, which proved, however, not to be the case.[929]

9. No obligation may result for other States from the unilateral declaration of a State. However, the other State or States concerned may incur obligations in relation to such a unilateral declaration to the extent that they clearly accepted such a declaration.

Commentary

(1) It is well established in international law that obligations cannot be imposed by a State upon another State without its consent. For the law of treaties, this principle has been codified in article 34 of the 1969 Vienna Convention.[930] There is no reason why this principle should not also apply to unilateral declarations; the consequence is that a State cannot impose obligations on other States to which it has addressed a unilateral declaration unless the latter unequivocally accept these obligations resulting from that declaration.[931] In the circumstances, the State or States concerned are in fact bound by their own acceptance.

(2) The 1945 Truman Proclamation, by which the United States of America aimed to impose obligations on other States or, at least, to limit their rights on the American continental shelf, was not strictly speaking accepted by other States. All the same, as the Court has stressed, the "régime [of the continental shelf] furnishes an example of a legal theory derived from a particular source that has secured a

[920] *Nuclear Tests* (*Australia* v. *France*) and (*New Zealand* v. *France*) (see footnote 869 above), p. 267, para. 43; pp. 269–270, para. 51; p. 472, para. 46; and pp. 474–475, para. 53.

[921] *Armed Activities on the Territory of the Congo (New Application: 2002)* (see footnote 637 above), pp. 28–29, paras. 50 and 52.

[922] *Nuclear Tests* (*Australia* v. *France*) and (*New Zealand* v. *France*) (see footnote 869 above), p. 267, para. 44, and pp. 472–473, para. 47.

[923] See *Frontier Dispute (Burkina Faso/Republic of Mali)* (footnote 875 above), pp. 573–574, para. 39.

[924] Declarations accepting the compulsory jurisdiction of the ICJ made under Article 36 of the Statute of the Court lie outside the scope of the present study (see footnote 856 above). That said, the Court's reasoning is fully applicable to unilateral acts and declarations *stricto sensu*.

[925] *Fisheries Jurisdiction (Spain* v. *Canada), Jurisdiction of the Court, Judgment of 4 December 1998, I.C.J. Reports 1998*, p. 432, at p. 453, para. 46. See also *Land and Maritime Boundary between Cameroon and Nigeria (Cameroon* v. *Nigeria), Preliminary Objections, Judgment of 11 June 1998, I.C.J. Reports 1998*, p. 275, at p. 293, para. 30.

[926] *Frontier Dispute (Burkina Faso/Republic of Mali)* (see footnote 875 above), p. 574, para. 40; see also *Armed Activities on the Territory of the Congo (New Application: 2002)* (footnote 637 above), p. 29, para. 53, and *Nuclear Tests* (*Australia* v. *France*) and (*New Zealand* v. *France*) (footnote 869 above), pp. 269–270, para. 51, and pp. 474–475, para. 53.

[927] See *Yearbook ... 1999*, vol. II (Part Two), document A/54/10, p. 136, para. 557; and *Yearbook ... 2000*, vol. II (Part Two), document A/55/10, pp. 97–98, para. 597.

[928] The declaration in this case was a reservation, a unilateral act which lies outside the scope of the present guiding principles (see paragraph 174 above).

[929] See *Armed Activities on the Territory of the Congo (New Application: 2002)* (footnote 637 above), p. 33, para. 69.

[930] This article states: "A treaty does not create either obligations or rights for a third State without its consent." See also *Reservations to the Convention on the Prevention and Punishment of the Crime of Genocide* (footnote 714 above), p. 21.

[931] Or if there was a general norm authorizing States to take such action; but the unilateral acts made pursuant to a norm of this kind lie outside the scope of the present guiding principles (see paragraph 175 above).

general following".[932] In fact, the other States responded to the Truman Proclamation with analogous claims and declarations[933] and, shortly thereafter, the content of the Proclamation was taken up in article 2 of the 1958 Geneva Convention on the Continental Shelf. It could therefore be said to have been generally accepted and it marked a point of departure for a customary process leading, in a very short time, to a new norm of international law. The ICJ remarked in that context: "The Truman Proclamation however, soon came to be regarded as a starting point of the positive law on the subject, and the chief doctrine it enunciated ... came to prevail over all others, being now reflected in Article 2 of the 1958 Geneva Convention on the Continental Shelf."[934]

10. A unilateral declaration that has created legal obligations for the State making the declaration cannot be revoked arbitrarily. In assessing whether a revocation would be arbitrary, consideration should be given to:

(*a*) any specific terms of the declaration relating to revocation;

(*b*) the extent to which those to whom the obligations are owed have relied on such obligations;

(*c*) the extent to which there has been a fundamental change in the circumstances.

Commentary

(1) In its 1974 judgments in the *Nuclear Tests* cases, the ICJ stated that "the unilateral undertaking resulting from [the French] statements cannot be interpreted as having been made in implicit reliance on an arbitrary power of reconsideration".[935] This does not, however, exclude any power to terminate a unilateral act, only its arbitrary withdrawal (or amendment).

(2) There can be no doubt that unilateral acts may be withdrawn or amended in certain specific circumstances. The Commission has drawn up an open-ended list of criteria to be taken into consideration when determining whether or not a withdrawal is arbitrary.

(3) A similar situation occurs where the declaration itself stipulates the circumstances in which its author may terminate it[936] or when its addressees have relied on it in good faith and have accordingly been led "detrimentally to change position or suffer some prejudice".[937] A unilateral declaration may also be rescinded following a fundamental change of circumstances within the meaning and within the strict limits of the customary rule enshrined in article 62 of the 1969 Vienna Convention.[938]

---

[932] *North Sea Continental Shelf* (see footnote 789 above), p. 53, para. 100.

[933] See the case of Mexico, *Laws and Regulations on the Regime of the High Seas*, vol. I (United Nations publication, Sales No. 1951.V.2), p. 13. See also the eighth report of the Special Rapporteur, *Yearbook ... 2005*, vol. II (Part One), document A/CN.4/557, para. 132.

[934] *North Sea Continental Shelf* (see footnote 789 above), pp. 32–33, para. 47.

[935] *Nuclear Tests* (*Australia* v. *France*) and (*New Zealand* v. *France*) (see footnote 869 above), p. 270, para. 51, and p. 475, para. 53.

[936] When the circumstances do not exist.

[937] *Military and Paramilitary Activities in and against Nicaragua (Nicaragua* v. *United States of America), Jurisdiction and Admissibility, I.C.J. Reports 1984*, p. 392, at p. 415, para. 51.

[938] See *Fisheries Jurisdiction (Federal Republic of Germany* v. *Iceland), Jurisdiction of the Court, Judgment, I.C.J. Reports 1973*, p. 49, at p. 63, para. 36, and *Gabčikovo–Nagymaros Project* (footnote 363 above), p. 64, para. 104.

Chapter X

EFFECTS OF ARMED CONFLICTS ON TREATIES

A. Introduction

178. The Commission, at its fifty-second session, held in 2000, identified the topic "Effects of armed conflicts on treaties" for inclusion in its long-term programme of work.[939] A brief syllabus describing the possible overall structure and approach to the topic was annexed to the report of the Commission to the General Assembly on the work of its fifty-second session.[940] In paragraph 8 of its resolution 55/152 of 12 December 2000, the General Assembly took note of the topic's inclusion.

179. During its fifty-sixth session, held in 2004, the Commission decided, at its 2830th meeting, on 6 August 2004, to include the topic "Effects of armed conflicts on treaties" in its current programme of work, and to appoint Mr. Ian Brownlie as Special Rapporteur for the topic.[941] The General Assembly, in paragraph 5 of its resolution 59/41 of 2 December 2004, endorsed the decision of the Commission to include the topic in its agenda.

180. At its fifty-seventh session, held in 2005, the Commission had before it the first report of the Special Rapporteur[942] as well as a memorandum prepared by the Secretariat entitled "The effects of armed conflict on treaties: an examination of practice and doctrine".[943] At its 2866th meeting, on 5 August 2005, the Commission endorsed the Special Rapporteur's suggestion that the Secretariat be requested to circulate a note to Governments requesting information about their practice with regard to this topic, in particular the more contemporary practice as well as any other relevant information.[944]

B. Consideration of the topic at the present session

181. At the present session, the Commission had the second report of the Special Rapporteur (A/CN.4/570) before it. The Commission considered the Special Rapporteur's report at its 2895th to 2898th meetings, from 18 to 21 July 2006.

1. General remarks on the topic

(a) *Introduction by the Special Rapporteur*

182. The Special Rapporteur observed that his second report, which had to be read together with his first report,[945] focused on two matters: (*a*) considering specific elements of the debate in the Commission and the substantial points made by various Governments in the debate in the Sixth Committee at the sixtieth session of the General Assembly; and (*b*) implementing the first report by asking the Commission to consider the first seven draft articles with a view to referring them to the Drafting Committee or to a working group.

183. The Special Rapporteur noted that general support had been expressed for his view that the topic was generally part of the law of treaties and not of the law on the use of force. He also recalled the views expressed in the Sixth Committee that the subject was closely related to other domains of international law, such as international humanitarian law, self-defence and State responsibility.

(b) *Summary of the debate*

184. It was reiterated that it was not possible to maintain a strict separation between the law of treaties and other branches of international law such as that of the rules relating to prohibition of use or threat of force in international relations, international humanitarian law and the law of responsibility of States for internationally wrongful acts, which were also of relevance to the topic.

(c) *Special Rapporteur's concluding remarks*

185. The Special Rapporteur was of the view that, given the nature of the debate in the Commission and the existence of substantial differences of opinion on important aspects of the subject, it would be premature to send the matter to a working group. In addition, a working group established in the first year of the new quinquennium of the Commission in 2007 would not necessarily be familiar with the debate on the topic during the present quinquennium. Accordingly, it was proposed that the best way forward would be for the Special Rapporteur to prepare a third report on the topic which could, together with the first two reports, form the basis for consideration by a working group in the future.

2. Article 1. Scope[946]

(a) *Introduction by the Special Rapporteur*

186. The Special Rapporteur pointed to the suggestion made in the Sixth Committee that, since article 25 of the 1969 Vienna Convention allowed for the provisional application of treaties, it seemed advisable that the draft articles also cover treaties that were being provisionally

---

[939] *Yearbook ... 2000*, vol. II (Part Two), p. 131, para. 729.

[940] *Ibid.*, Annex.

[941] *Yearbook ... 2004*, vol. II (Part Two), p. 120, para. 364.

[942] *Yearbook ... 2005*, vol. II (Part One), document A/CN.4/552.

[943] Document A/CN.4/550 and Corr.1–2 (mimeographed).

[944] *Yearbook ... 2005*, vol. II (Part Two), p. 27, para. 112.

[945] See footnote 942 above.

[946] Draft article 1 reads as follows:

"*Scope*

"The present draft articles apply to the effects of an armed conflict in respect of treaties between States."

applied. He also noted that some members of the Commission had suggested that a distinction be made between contracting parties, under article 2, paragraph (1) (*f*), of the 1969 Vienna Convention, and those which are not.

(b) *Summary of the debate*

187. It was suggested that consideration be given to including within the scope of the topic the effect on the rights of third States parties to the treaty in question; the distinction between effects on different provisions of the treaty as opposed to on the entire treaty, as well as that between the effects on the treaty itself and those on the obligations arising from it; and the distinction between suspension and termination of the treaty or provisions thereof.

(c) *Special Rapporteur's concluding remarks*

188. The Special Rapporteur accepted that he would have to explore issues related to the scope of the topic more thoroughly. Nonetheless, he cautioned against drawing a distinction between the effects on the treaty and those on the obligations arising from it which could upset the balance of the topic by entering into matters outside its traditional scope. He did not favour dealing with subjects like *force majeure* and supervening impossibility of performance, which risked replicating subjects already governed by the 1969 Vienna Convention.

3. ARTICLE 2. USE OF TERMS[947]

(a) *Introduction by the Special Rapporteur*

189. As regards subparagraph (*a*), the Special Rapporteur observed that there was support for the inclusion of treaties concluded by international organizations.

190. He noted that the most problematic issue was the definition of armed conflict, in subparagraph (*b*), which had been examined in his first report. He observed that the distinction between international and non-international armed conflict was still considered to be basic in character and noted that the question provoked marked differences of opinion in the Sixth Committee. He requested that the Commission provide a general indication on the inclusion or not of non-international armed conflicts. At the same time, he cautioned that it would be inappropriate for it to seek to frame a definition of "armed conflict" for all departments of public international law.

(b) *Summary of the debate*

191. As regards subparagraph (*a*), while general support was expressed for the definition of "treaty", a preference was also expressed for including treaties entered into by international organizations. Others were of the view that international organizations were best not covered in light of their specificity. It was proposed that consideration also be given to treaties which had not yet entered into force or which had not yet been ratified by the parties to the armed conflict. In terms of another suggestion, the definition could be more flexible so as to cover agreements between an occupying power and an administration of the occupied territory, such as the regime based on the *Oslo Accords*.[948] Others preferred restricting the topic to agreements concluded within the framework of international law.

192. The definition of "armed conflict" in subparagraph (*b*) was the subject of criticism: reference was made to the inherent circularity in defining the concept as "a state of war or a conflict which involves armed operations". It was suggested that the definition expressly include internal armed conflicts which were more common in the contemporary world, and a preference was expressed for the definition employed in the *Tadić*[949] case, because it included internal conflicts where government armed forces were not involved.

193. In terms of a further view, internal conflicts do not affect relations between the States parties to the treaty directly, but may give rise to circumstances which affect the application of the treaty indirectly. These may include impossibility of performance or a change of circumstances and therefore lead to the suspension or termination of a treaty to which the State involved in the internal conflict is a party and the other States parties to the treaty are not involved, and, as such, were best analysed within the framework of the 1969 Vienna Convention.

194. Support was also expressed for the view of the Netherlands that military occupations should also be included, as envisaged in article 18 of the 1954 Convention for the Protection of Cultural Property in the Event of Armed Conflict, and reference was also made to the advisory opinion of the ICJ in the *Legal Consequences of the Construction of a Wall in the Occupied Palestinian Territory* case.[950] Others opposed this proposal, noting that military occupations should more properly be seen as a consequence of armed conflict and not part of the definition of armed conflict itself. In terms of a further suggestion, it was necessary also to deal with territories under international administration. Others were of the

[947] Draft article 2 reads as follows:

"*Use of terms*

"For the purposes of the present draft articles:

"(*a*) "Treaty" means an international agreement concluded between States in written form and governed by international law, whether embodied in a single instrument or in two or more related instruments, and whatever its particular designation;

"(*b*) "Armed conflict" means a state of war or a conflict which involves armed operations which by their nature or extent are likely to affect the operation of treaties between States parties to the armed conflict or between States parties to the armed conflict and third States, regardless of a formal declaration of war or other declaration by any or all of the parties to the armed conflict."

[948] Declaration of Principles on Interim Self-Government Arrangements, signed at Washington D.C. on 13 September 1993 by the Government of Israel and the Palestinian Liberation Organization (A/48/486, annex).

[949] *Prosecutor* v. *Duško Tadić a/k/a "Dule", Decision on the Defence Motion of Interlocutory Appeal on Jurisdiction, Case No. IT-94-1-AR72, 2 October 1995*, International Tribunal for the Former Yugoslavia, Judicial Reports 1994–1995, vol. I, Kluwer Law International (The Hague), 1999, p. 429, para. 70. See also ILM, vol. 35 (January 1996), pp. 54–55, para. 70.

[950] *Legal Consequences of the Construction of a Wall in the Occupied Palestinian Territory, Advisory Opinion, I.C.J. Reports 2004*, p. 136.

view that such situations should not be considered as they did not constitute armed conflict. In terms of another suggestion, it had to be considered whether conflicts of the "third kind", such as the "war on terrorism", should be dealt with—even if only to exclude such conflicts from the scope of the topic. Others cautioned against including the activities of non-State actors since such an approach could threaten the stability of the treaty system.

195. It was reiterated that an aggressor State could not be placed on an equal footing with the State exercising its right to self-defence, whether individual or collective, in accordance with the Charter of the United Nations. Reference was made to the 1985 resolution of the Institute of International Law which had drawn such a distinction.[951] This opinion was shared by the majority of members of the Commission.

196. It was proposed that a third subparagraph be included to define the term "effects".

(c) *Special Rapporteur's concluding remarks*

197. With regard to the inclusion of international organizations, while he preferred not to bring in material from other drafts by analogy, the Special Rapporteur acknowledged the practical point that it was not feasible to study the effects on treaties of international organizations as a separate topic, and therefore there was a case for dealing with such treaties in the present draft articles.

198. In response to comments on the definition of "armed conflict", the Special Rapporteur confirmed his willingness to refer to internal armed conflict. The concern he had related to the implication from some of the comments that what was called for was a global definition of armed conflict, whereas the purpose of subparagraph (*a*) was to provide a definition solely for the purposes of the draft articles. To his mind, the concept of the inclusion of internal armed conflicts was governed by the intention of the parties in draft article 4. One of the criteria for discerning the intention of the parties was the nature and scope of the conflict in question. As to the illegal use of force, he reiterated his position from the previous year that draft article 10 would be carefully redrafted.

4. Article 3. *Ipso facto* termination or suspension[952]

(a) *Introduction by the Special Rapporteur*

199. The Special Rapporteur noted that draft article 3 was the primary article because it was based on the central proposition that the outbreak of an armed conflict does not *ipso facto* terminate or suspend the operation of treaties. He noted that it was not strictly necessary, in the sense that draft article 4 could stand without it. Nonetheless it was useful to rebut the historical view that armed conflict, in effect, set treaties aside. He recalled that the phrase "*ipso facto*" would be replaced by "necessarily".

(b) *Summary of the debate*

200. General support was expressed for the retention of draft article 3 which was considered central to the draft articles. Support was also expressed for the Special Rapporteur's proposal to replace the phrase "*ipso facto*" with "necessarily", which would serve as an indication that in some cases armed conflict did lead to the suspension or termination of treaties, but in others it would not, i.e. different effects were possible for different treaties. Others opposed the proposed drafting change and preferred to retain the expression "*ipso facto*" to indicate that outbreak of an armed conflict does not have an automatic effect on terminating or suspending a treaty.

5. Article 4. The indicia of susceptibility to termination or suspension of treaties in case of an armed conflict[953]

(a) *Introduction by the Special Rapporteur*

201. The Special Rapporteur pointed to the reliance on the concept of the intention of the parties, which had been the subject of strong scepticism. While he shared such scepticism, he was of the view that it was the only workable concept available. He noted that it was not infrequent that decision makers and tribunals had to construct the intention of the parties. At the same time, he recognized that it was necessary to include other factors, such as the object and purpose of the treaty and the circumstances of the armed conflict.

202. There remained the question of the relationship between draft articles 4 and 7. It was his intention that the two provisions would be applicable on a basis of coordination. In addition, draft article 4 referred to articles 31 and 32 of the 1969 Vienna Convention, which was necessary since there could be no question of fashioning "designer" principles of interpretation for exclusive use in the present context.

(b) *Summary of the debate*

203. The view was expressed that the criterion of intention had lost its significance after the Second World War, apart from some specific treaties, given the strengthening of the principle of the prohibition of recourse to armed

[951] Resolution entitled "The effects of armed conflicts on treaties" (art. 7), *Yearbook of the Institute of International Law*, vol. 61-II (1986).

[952] Draft article 3 reads as follows:

"Ipso facto *termination or suspension*

"The outbreak of an armed conflict does not *ipso facto* terminate or suspend the operation of treaties as:

"(*a*) Between the parties to the armed conflict;

"(*b*) Between one or more parties to the armed conflict and a third State."

[953] Draft article 4 reads as follows:

"*The indicia of susceptibility to termination or suspension of treaties in case of an armed conflict*

"1. The susceptibility to termination or suspension of treaties in case of an armed conflict is determined in accordance with the intention of the parties at the time the treaty was concluded.

"2. The intention of the parties to a treaty relating to its susceptibility to termination or suspension shall be determined in accordance:

"(*a*) With the provisions of articles 31 and 32 of the Vienna Convention on the Law of Treaties; and

"(*b*) The nature and extent of the armed conflict in question."

force in international relations. In addition, agreement was expressed with the view that it was not realistic to think that parties contemplate the effect of an armed conflict on a treaty at the time of its conclusion. A preference was expressed for considering the viability of the continuance of the treaty, or one of its provisions, in the context of armed conflicts, as well as the legality of the actions of each of the parties to the conflict. Several members also referred to the criteria of the object and purpose of the treaty, the nature of the conflict or the situation that arises therefrom and the nature of the treaty obligation itself. It was also pointed out that it was necessary to take into account the subsequent history of the treaty as contemplated in articles 31 and 32 of the 1969 Vienna Convention.

(c) *Special Rapporteur's concluding remarks*

204. The Special Rapporteur confirmed that he intended to pursue the question of intention further. At the same time, he could not accept that intention was no longer a part of international law. It was quite common to see references to the intention of the parties or of the legislator. Indeed, the Commission itself was employing the concept in the context of reservations to treaties. Instead, the problem was the ascertainment of evidence of intention.

6. Article 5. Express provisions on the operation of treaties[954]

(a) *Introduction by the Special Rapporteur*

205. The Special Rapporteur remarked that the draft article was redundant under a strict view of drafting. However, he felt it helpful to have such a provision for the sake of clarity, and he noted that the Commission had expressed general support for it.

(b) *Summary of the debate*

206. It was suggested that the two paragraphs could be dealt with in separate draft articles. It was also proposed that paragraph 1 be replaced with the version proposed in article 35, paragraph (*a*), of the Harvard Research in International Law draft convention on the law of treaties.[955] Reference was made to the advisory opinion of the ICJ in the *Legal Consequences of the Construction of a Wall in the Occupied Palestinian Territory* case,[956] where the Court confirmed that human rights treaties were not excluded as a result of the operation of *lex specialis*.

7. Article 6. Treaties relating to the occasion for resort to armed conflict[957]

(a) *Introduction by the Special Rapporteur*

207. The Special Rapporteur confirmed that he no longer supported draft article 6 since it was not strictly necessary in light of draft article 3. It was an attempt to deal with the special case where an agreement had been the subject of conflict and then some procedure of peaceful settlement ensued.

(b) *Summary of the debate*

208. General support was expressed for the Special Rapporteur's proposal to delete the provision.

8. Article 7. The operation of treaties on the basis of necessary implication from their object and purpose[958]

(a) *Introduction by the Special Rapporteur*

209. The Special Rapporteur noted that the provision was complementary to draft article 4. It was also the main source of debate and comment by Governments. There were some convincing arguments, such as that by the United States that it was a mistaken approach to resort to the categorization of treaties. He noted some other suggestions to take into account possible guiding principles or policy elements in the discernment of the element of intention. Yet, it had to be recognized that there was customary law, or nascent customary law, supporting some if not all of the categories, and an appropriate

---

[954] Draft article 5 reads as follows:

"*Express provisions on the operation of treaties*

"1. Treaties applicable to situations of armed conflict in accordance with their express provisions are operative in case of an armed conflict, without prejudice to the conclusion of lawful agreements between the parties to the armed conflict involving suspension or waiver of the relevant treaties.

"2. The outbreak of an armed conflict does not affect the competence of the parties to the armed conflict to conclude treaties in accordance with the Vienna Convention on the Law of Treaties."

[955] Supplement to the AJIL, vol. 29 (1935), Codification of International Law, Part. III, "The Law of Treaties", p. 657, at p. 1183.

[956] See footnote 950 above.

[957] Draft article 6 reads as follows:

"*Treaties relating to the occasion for resort to armed conflict*

"A treaty, the status or interpretation of which is the subject matter of the issue which was the occasion for resort to armed conflict, is presumed not to be terminated by operation of law, but the presumption will be rendered inoperable by evidence of a contrary intention of the contracting parties."

[958] Draft article 7 reads as follows:

"*The operation of treaties on the basis of necessary implication from their object and purpose*

"1. In the case of treaties the object and purpose of which involve the necessary implication that they continue in operation during an armed conflict, the incidence of an armed conflict will not as such inhibit their operation.

"2. Treaties of this character include the following:

"(*a*) Treaties expressly applicable in case of an armed conflict;

"(*b*) Treaties declaring, creating, or regulating permanent rights or a permanent regime or status;

"(*c*) Treaties of friendship, commerce and navigation and analogous agreements concerning private rights;

"(*d*) Treaties for the protection of human rights;

"(*e*) Treaties relating to the protection of the environment;

"(*f*) Treaties relating to international watercourses and related installations and facilities;

"(*g*) Multilateral law-making treaties;

"(*h*) Treaties relating to the settlement of disputes between States by peaceful means, including resort to conciliation, mediation, arbitration and the International Court of Justice;

"(*i*) Obligations arising under multilateral conventions relating to commercial arbitration and the enforcement of awards;

"(*j*) Treaties relating to diplomatic relations;

"(*k*) Treaties relating to consular relations."

vehicle had to be found to reflect such practice. A possible approach was to include an annex containing an analysis of the State practice and case law, which could be prepared by the Secretariat with assistance from the Special Rapporteur.

(b) *Summary of the debate*

210. Different views were expressed on draft article 7. For some, the provision was useful but needed to be clarified. Reference was made to the memorandum prepared by the Secretariat entitled "The effect of armed conflict on treaties: an examination of practice and doctrine"[959] by way of suggestions for the expansion of the list. In addition, it was suggested that certain categories of treaties had to be listed in a more precise manner, e.g. multilateral law-making treaties. Support was expressed for the current inclusion of human rights treaties (para. 2 (*d*)). Others supported the proposal to delete the provision. It was pointed out that any list of examples of types of treaties created an *a contrario* presumption that treaties not covered by those categories would automatically lapse, which could amount to a potentially large, even if unintended, exception to the general rule in draft article 3. Support was expressed for the Special Rapporteur's proposal to replace the list with an annex containing State practice and jurisprudence. Still others considered it more useful to enumerate the factors which might lead to the conclusion that a treaty or some of its provisions should continue or should be suspended or terminated in the event of armed conflict.

(c) *Special Rapporteur's concluding remarks*

211. The Special Rapporteur recalled that the list of categories in draft article 7 was only meant to provide guidance for the discovery of intention in draft article 4, and reiterated that he was prepared to revisit the provision.

[959] See footnote 943 above.

Chapter XI

THE OBLIGATION TO EXTRADITE OR PROSECUTE (*AUT DEDERE AUT JUDICARE*)

A. Introduction

212. The Commission, at its fifty-sixth session (2004), identified the topic "Obligation to extradite or prosecute (*aut dedere aut judicare*)" for inclusion in its long-term programme of work.[960] A brief syllabus describing the possible overall structure and approach to the topic was annexed to the report of the Commission to the General Assembly on the work of its fifty-sixth session.[961] The General Assembly, in resolution 59/41 of 2 December 2004, took note of the Commission's report concerning its long-term programme of work.

213. During its fifty-seventh session (2005), the Commission decided, at its 2865th meeting, on 4 August 2005, to include the topic "Obligation to extradite or prosecute (*aut dedere aut judicare*)" in its current programme of work, and to appoint Mr. Zdzislaw Galicki as Special Rapporteur for the topic.[962] The General Assembly, in paragraph 5 of its resolution 60/22 of 23 November 2005, endorsed the decision of the Commission to include the topic in its programme of work.

B. Consideration of the topic at the present session

214. At the present session, the Commission had the preliminary report of the Special Rapporteur (A/CN.4/571) before it. The Commission considered the report at its 2899th to 2903rd meetings, from 25 July to 2 August 2006.

1. Introduction by the Special Rapporteur

215. The Special Rapporteur observed that his report contained a preliminary set of observations concerning the substance of the topic, marking the most important points for further consideration and including a preliminary plan of action for the future work on the topic. While it was premature to take a decision, it was useful to receive an indication from the Commission as to the possible final form of the work on the topic.

216. A key question to be considered was whether the obligation derived exclusively from the relevant treaty or whether it also reflected a general obligation under customary international law, at least with respect to specific international offences. He noted that there was no consensus in the doctrine, although a growing number of scholars supported the concept of an international legal obligation "*aut dedere aut judicare*" as a general duty based not only on the provisions of particular international treaties, but also on generally binding customary norms, at least as it concerned certain categories of crimes. In addition, it was suggested that an analysis of the link between the principle of universal jurisdiction in criminal matters and the principle *aut dedere aut judicare* should be undertaken.

217. As regards the scope of the obligation to extradite or prosecute, the Special Rapporteur noted that it was constructed in the alternative, giving a State the choice to decide which part of the obligation it was going to fulfil. It was presumed that after fulfilling a part of the obligation—either *dedere* or *judicare*—the State was released from fulfilling the other part.

218. The Special Rapporteur recalled that, while the obligation to extradite or prosecute was traditionally formulated in the alternative, there was the possibility of a "triple alternative", which contemplated the existence of a jurisdictional competence to be exercised by an international criminal tribunal.

219. As regards methodology, the Special Rapporteur stated his intention to proceed in future reports to formulate draft rules concerning the concept, structure and operation of the obligation *aut dedere aut judicare*. It was also necessary to undertake a thorough analysis of the practice of States in the area, and to compile a complete list of relevant treaty provisions reflecting the obligation. He proposed that the Commission could address a written request to Member States for information concerning their contemporary practice.

2. Summary of the debate

220. The Commission welcomed the preliminary report, including the proposed preliminary plan of action. It was suggested that the scope of the topic should be limited to the objective of the obligation, namely to reduce cases of impunity for persons suspected of having committed international crimes by depriving them of "safe havens". It was proposed that the topic could be further limited to particular categories of crimes, such as those which were particularly grave and threatened the international community as a whole. It was also suggested that a distinction be drawn between crimes under international law (defined in treaty instruments), and crimes recognized under international customary law, such as war crimes, genocide and crimes against humanity. There was general support for excluding from the scope of the study crimes that were solely foreseen under national laws.

221. In addition, it was observed that a more limited form of the obligation existed in regard to treaty crimes. For example, it was noted that many treaties, including the sectoral conventions for the suppression of international terrorism, contained a more guarded formulation, namely to submit the case to the competent authorities

---

[960] *Yearbook ... 2004*, vol. II (Part Two), p. 120, paras. 362–363.

[961] *Ibid.*, Annex, pp. 123–126.

[962] *Yearbook ... 2005*, vol. II (Part Two), p. 92, para. 500.

"for the purpose of prosecution", as opposed to an obligation "to prosecute". It was recalled that Governments typically resisted accepting an obligation "to prosecute" since the independence of prosecution was a cardinal principle in their national criminal procedures.

222. It was suggested that the Commission focus on gaps in existing treaties, such as the execution of penalties and the lack of a monitoring system with regard to compliance with the obligation to prosecute. As regards the question of the existence of a customary obligation to extradite or prosecute, it was suggested that any such obligation would have to be based on a two-tier system as in existing treaties, whereby certain States were given priority jurisdiction and other States would be obliged to exercise jurisdiction if the alleged offender was not extradited to a State having that priority jurisdiction.

223. Concerning the obligation to extradite, it was pointed out that whether such an obligation existed depended on the treaties in place between the parties and on the circumstances. In addition, since crimes were typically defined very precisely in domestic laws, the question had to be whether there was an obligation to extradite or prosecute for a precisely defined crime in precisely defined circumstances. It was also noted that most of the complex issues in extradition were solved pragmatically. Some members considered that the obligation to extradite or prosecute had acquired a customary status, at least as far as crimes under international law were concerned. Further, some considered that the procedure of deportation was relevant to the topic.

224. It was proposed that the Commission could consider the practical difficulties encountered in the process of extradition, including: problems of the sufficiency of evidence; the existence of outdated bilateral and multilateral treaties and national laws allowing multiple grounds for refusal; limitations on the extradition of nationals; and the failure to recognize specific safeguards for the protection of the rights of the extradited individual, particularly in situations where extradition could expose the individual to torture, the death penalty or even life imprisonment. It was also recalled that in the situation of international crimes some of the limitations on extradition were inapplicable.

225. Others cautioned against considering the technical aspects of extradition law. What was specific to the topic and the precise meaning of the Latin maxim "*aut dedere aut judicare*" was that, failing an extradition, an obligation to prosecute arose. The focus, therefore, should be on the conditions for triggering the obligation to prosecute. The view was expressed that the Commission should not deal with all the collateral rules on the subject, which were linked to it but not necessarily part of it. It was also proposed that the focus should be limited to the elaboration of secondary rules.

226. A general preference was expressed for drawing a clear distinction between the concepts of the obligation to extradite or prosecute and that of universal criminal jurisdiction. It was recalled that the Commission had decided to focus on the former and not the latter, even if for some crimes the two concepts existed simultaneously. It was pointed out that the topic did not necessarily require a study in extraterritorial criminal jurisdiction. If the Commission were nonetheless to embark on a consideration of the concept of universal jurisdiction, it was suggested that the different kinds of universal jurisdiction, particularly whether it was permissive or compulsory, be considered. It was also deemed worth contemplating whether such jurisdiction could only be exercised when the person was present in a particular State or whether any State could request the extradition of a person from another State on grounds of universal jurisdiction.

227. It was also suggested that the topic not include the "triple" alternative, involving the concurrent jurisdiction of an international tribunal, since the existing tribunals had their own *lex specialis* rules. According to another opinion, it would be necessary to favour that third path insofar as possible.

228. It was suggested that the Special Rapporteur undertake a systematic study of State practice, focusing on contemporary practice, including national jurisprudence.

229. On the question of the final form, while it was recognized that it was premature to consider the matter, a preference was expressed for the eventual formulation of a set of draft articles, although it was noted that if the Commission were to conclude that the obligation existed only under international treaties, then a draft of a recommendatory nature would be more appropriate.

3. Special Rapporteur's concluding remarks

230. The Special Rapporteur noted that a range of views had been expressed during the debate. In particular, he referred to the general consensus in the Commission that the scope of the topic be limited as far as possible so as to concentrate on the issues directly connected with the obligation to extradite or prosecute, as well as on an analysis of the principal elements of the obligation, i.e. "*dedere*" and "*judicare*". He supported such an approach especially with regard to drawing a clear distinction between the obligation to extradite or prosecute and the principle of universal jurisdiction, and taking a cautious approach to the existence of a "triple alternative" in the context of the jurisdiction of international criminal tribunals.

231. With regard to the issue of limiting the source of the obligation only to treaties, or extending it to customary norms or general principles of law, the Special Rapporteur noted that the Commission had opted for a cautious approach: recognizing the treaty basis of the obligation while expressing some reservations about the existence of a general customary obligation to extradite or prosecute applicable to all offences under criminal law. Support existed instead for recognizing such a customary basis in the context of certain categories of crimes in the context of which the concept of universal jurisdiction, as well as the principle *aut dedere aut judicare*, had already received general recognition among States. The Special Rapporteur expressed support for such an approach, although without prejudice to the possibility of developing general rules applicable to all crimes. He further recalled the suggestions that special attention be given to the applicability of international human rights law. Furthermore, he agreed

with the suggestion that the focus of the whole exercise be on the elaboration of secondary rules. The Special Rapporteur also agreed with the recommendation that both international and national judicial decisions should be considered.

232. As regards the title of the topic, he recalled the references in the debate to the "principle" of *aut dedere aut judicare*, but expressed a preference for retaining the existing reference to "obligation". As to the eventual form of the Commission's work on the topic, the Special Rapporteur noted that preliminary support existed for the formulation of draft articles. Accordingly, he announced his intention to proceed in future reports with the formulation of draft rules on the concept, structure and operation of the obligation *aut dedere aut judicare*.

Chapter XII

FRAGMENTATION OF INTERNATIONAL LAW: DIFFICULTIES ARISING FROM THE DIVERSIFICATION AND EXPANSION OF INTERNATIONAL LAW

A. Introduction

233. The Commission, at its fifty-fourth session (2002), decided to include the topic "Risks ensuing from fragmentation of international law" in its programme of work;[963] it established a Study Group and subsequently decided to change the title of the topic to "The fragmentation of international law: difficulties arising from the diversification and expansion of international law".[964] The Commission also agreed on a number of recommendations, including recommendations on five studies to be undertaken,[965] commencing with a study by the Chairperson of the Study Group on the question of "The function and scope of the *lex specialis* rule and the question of 'self-contained regimes'".

234. From the fifty-fifth (2003) to the fifty-seventh (2005) sessions of the Commission, the Study Group was successively reconstituted under the chairpersonship of Mr. Martti Koskenniemi and carried out several tasks. In 2003, it set a tentative schedule for work to be carried out for the remainder of the quinquennium (2003–2006), distributed among its members work on the other studies agreed upon in 2002, and decided upon the methodology to be adopted for that work.[966] In 2004, the Study Group held discussions on the study by its Chairperson on "The function and scope of the *lex specialis* rule and the question of 'self-contained regimes'", as well as discussions on the outlines prepared in respect of the other remaining studies.[967] In 2005, the Study Group held discussions on (*a*) a memorandum on regionalism in the context of the study on "The function and scope of the *lex specialis* rule and the question of 'self-contained regimes'"; (*b*) a study on the interpretation of treaties in the light of "any relevant rules of international law applicable in the relations between the parties" (article 31, paragraph 3 (*c*) of the 1969 Vienna Convention), in the context of general developments in international law and concerns of the international community; (*c*) a study on the application of successive treaties relating to the same subject matter (article 30 of the 1969 Vienna Convention); (*d*) a study on the modification of multilateral treaties between certain of the parties only (article 41 of the 1969 Vienna Convention); and (*e*) a study on hierarchy in international law: *jus cogens*, obligations *erga omnes* and Article 103 of the Charter of the United Nations, as conflict rules. It also held discussion on an informal paper on the "disconnection clause".[968]

235. The Study Group decided to approach the various studies by focusing on the substantive aspects of fragmentation in the light of the 1969 Vienna Convention, while leaving aside institutional considerations pertaining to fragmentation. It sought to attain an outcome that would be concrete and of practical value especially for legal experts in foreign offices and international organizations. Accordingly, it decided to prepare, as the substantive outcome of its work: (*a*) a relatively large analytical study on the question of fragmentation, composed on the basis of the individual outlines and studies submitted by individual members of the Study Group during 2003–2005 and discussed in the Study Group, and (*b*) a single collective document containing a set of conclusions emerging from the studies and the discussions in the Study Group. The latter was to be a concrete, practice-oriented set of brief statements that would serve, on the one hand, as the summary and conclusions of the Study Group's work and, on the other hand, as a set of practical guidelines to help think about and deal with the issue of fragmentation in legal practice.[969]

236. At its 2859th, 2860th and 2864th meetings, on 28 and 29 July and on 3 August 2005, the Commission held an exchange of views on the topic on the basis of a briefing by the Chairperson of the Study Group on the status of work of the Study Group.

B. Consideration of the topic at the present session

237. At the current session, the Study Group was reconstituted and it held 10 meetings on 17 and 26 May, on 6 June, on 4, 11, 12, 13 and 17 July 2006. The Study Group had before it a study finalized by the Chairperson of the Study

[963] The topic was included on the Commission's long-term of work at its fifty-second session, held in 2000 (see *Yearbook ... 2000*, vol. II (Part Two), p. 131, para. 729), following its consideration of a feasibility study by G. Hafner ("Risks ensuing from fragmentation of international law", *ibid.*, Annex, p. 143).

[964] *Yearbook ... 2002*, vol. II (Part Two), p. 97, paras. 492–494.

[965] The topics for further study agreed in 2002 were:

"(*a*) The function and scope of the *lex specialis* rule and the question of 'self-contained regimes';

"(*b*) The interpretation of treaties in the light of 'any relevant rules of international law applicable in the relations between the parties (article 31, paragraph 3 (*c*), of the 1969 Vienna Convention), in the context of general developments in international law and concerns of the international community;

"(*c*) The application of successive treaties relating to the same subject matter (article 30 of the Convention);

"(*d*) The modification of multilateral treaties between certain of the parties only (article 41 of the Convention);

"(*e*) Hierarchy in international law: *jus cogens*, obligations *erga omnes*, Article 103 of the Charter of the United Nations as conflict rules."

[966] *Yearbook ... 2003*, vol. II (Part Two), pp. 96–99, paras. 415–435.

[967] *Yearbook ... 2004*, vol. II (Part Two), pp. 112–119, paras. 303–358.

[968] *Yearbook ... 2005*, vol. II (Part Two), pp. 84–91, paras. 449–493.

[969] *Ibid.*, paras. 447–448. See also *Yearbook ... 2002*, vol. II (Part Two), chap. IX; *Yearbook ... 2003*, vol. II (Part Two), pp. 96–97, paras. 416–418; and *Yearbook ... 2004*, vol. II (Part Two), pp. 111–112, paras. 301–302.

Group, Mr. Martti Koskenniemi, as well as a set of draft conclusions based on that study (A/CN.4/L.682 and Corr.1 and Add.1). The document summarized and analysed the phenomenon of fragmentation on the basis of the studies prepared by the various members of the Study Group and taking into account the comments made by members of the Study Group. The addendum to the document incorporated the draft conclusions of the Study Group's work between 2002 and 2005, as well as additional draft conclusions and a section on background. The substantive work of the Study Group during the present session was focused on finalizing these conclusions. At its meeting on 17 July 2006, the Study Group completed its work and adopted its report containing 42 conclusions (see section D.2 below). The Study Group stressed the importance of the collective nature of its conclusions. It also emphasized that these conclusions had to be read in connection with the analytical study, finalized by the Chairperson, on which they are based.

238. At the 2901st and 2902nd meetings of the Commission, on 27 and 28 July 2006, the Chairperson of the Study Group introduced the report of the Study Group.

239. At its 2902nd, 2911th and 2912th meetings, on 28 July, 9 and 10 August 2006, the Commission considered the report of the Study Group (see section D below). A proposal by a member to make a distinction between positive and negative fragmentation was not endorsed by the Commission. After an exchange of views, the Commission at its 2902nd meeting decided to take note of the conclusions of the Study Group (see section D.2 below), and at its 2912th meeting commended them to the attention of the General Assembly. At its 2911th meeting, the Commission requested that, in accordance with the usual practice, the analytical study finalized by the Chairperson of the Study Group be made available on the website of the Commission and also be published in its *Yearbook*.

C. Tribute to the Study Group and its Chairperson

240. At its 2911th meeting, on 9 August 2006, the Commission adopted the following resolution by acclamation:

The International Law Commission,

Having taken note of the report and the conclusions of the Study Group on fragmentation of international law: difficulties arising from the diversification and expansion of international law,

Expresses to the Study Group and its Chairperson, Mr. Martti Koskenniemmi, its deep appreciation and warm congratulations for the outstanding contribution made in the preparation of the report on fragmentation of international law and for the results achieved in the elaboration conclusions, as well as the accompanying study on "The fragmentation of international law: difficulties arising from the diversification and expansion of international law finalized" by the Chairperson.

D. Report of the Study Group

1. Background

241. In the past half-century, the scope of international law has increased dramatically. From a tool dedicated to the regulation of formal diplomacy, it has expanded to deal with the most varied kinds of international activity, from trade to environmental protection, from human rights to scientific and technological cooperation. New multilateral institutions, regional and universal, have been set up in fields such as commerce, culture, security and development. It is difficult to imagine today a sphere of social activity that would not be subject to some type of international legal regulation.

242. However, this expansion has taken place in an uncoordinated fashion, within specific regional or functional groups of States. Focus has been on solving specific problems rather than attaining general, law-like regulation. This reflects what sociologists have called "functional differentiation", the increasing specialization of parts of society and the related autonomization of those parts. It is a well-known paradox of globalization that while it has led to increasing uniformization of social life around the world, it has also led to its increasing fragmentation—that is, to the emergence of specialized and relatively autonomous spheres of social action and structure.

243. The fragmentation of the international social world has acquired legal significance, as it has been accompanied by the emergence of specialized and (relatively) autonomous rules or rule complexes, legal institutions and spheres of legal practice. What once appeared to be governed by "general international law" has become the field of operation for such specialist systems as "trade law", "human rights law", "environmental law", "law of the sea", "European law" and even such highly specialized forms of knowledge as "investment law" or "international refugee law"—each possessing its own principles and institutions.

244. While the reality and importance of fragmentation cannot be doubted, assessments of the phenomenon have varied. Some commentators have been highly critical of what they have seen as the erosion of general international law, emergence of conflicting jurisprudence, "forum shopping" and loss of legal security. Others have seen here a predominantly technical problem that has emerged naturally with the increase of international legal activity and may be controlled by the use of technical streamlining and coordination.[970] It is in order to assess

[970] "Fragmentation" is a very frequently treated topic of academic writings and conferences today. Out of the various collections that discuss the diversification of the sources of international regulation, see for example E. Loquin and C. Kessedjian (eds.), *La mondialisation du droit*, Paris, Litec, 2000; and P. S. Berman (ed.), *The Globalization of International Law*, Aldershot, Ashgate, 2005. The activity of traditional organizations is examined in J. E. Alvarez, *International Organizations as Law-makers*, Oxford University Press, 2005. Different perspectives of non-treaty law-making today are also presented in R. Wolfrum and V. Röben (eds.), *Developments of International Law in Treaty-making*, Berlin, Springer, 2005, pp. 417–586, and R. D. Lipschutz and C. Fogel, "'Regulation for the rest of us?' Global civil society and the privatization of transnational regulation", in R. B. Hall and T. J. Biersteker (eds.), *The Emergence of Private Authority in Global Governance*, Cambridge University Press, 2002, pp. 115–140. See also "Symposium issue: the proliferation of international tribunals: piecing together the puzzle", *New York University Journal of International Law and Politics,* vol. 31, No. 4 (1999) pp. 679–933; A. Zimmermann and R. Hofmann (eds.), *Unity and Diversity of International Law—Proceedings of an International Symposium of the Kiel Walther Schücking Institute of International Law, November 4–7, 2004*, Berlin, Duncker & Humblot, 2006; and K. Wellens and R. Huesa Vinaixa (eds.), *L'influence des sources sur l'unité et la fragmentation du droit international*, Brussels, Bruylant, 2006. A strong plea for unity is contained in P.-M. Dupuy, "L'unité de l'ordre juridique internationale: cours général de droit international public", *Recueil des cours: Collected Courses of the Hague Academy of International Law,* vol. 297 (2002). For more references, see M. Koskenniemi and P. Leino, "Fragmentation of international law? Postmodern anxieties", *Leiden Journal of International Law*, vol. 15, No. 3 (2002), pp. 553–579.

the significance of the problem of fragmentation and, possibly, to suggest ways and means of dealing with it, that in 2002 the Commission established the Study Group to deal with the matter.

245. At the outset, the Commission recognized that fragmentation raises both institutional and substantive problems. The former have to do with the jurisdiction and competence of various institutions applying international legal rules and their hierarchical relations *inter se*. The Commission has decided to leave this question aside. The issue of institutional competencies is best dealt with by the institutions themselves. The Commission has instead wished to focus on the substantive question—the splitting up of the law into highly specialized "boxes" that claim relative autonomy from each other and from the general law. What are the substantive effects of specialization? How should the relationship between such "boxes" be conceived? More concretely, if the rules in two or more regimes conflict, what can be done about such conflicts?

246. Like the majority of academic commentators, the Commission has understood the subject to have both positive and negative sides, as attested to by its reformulation of the title of the topic: "The fragmentation of international law: difficulties arising from the diversification and expansion of international law". On the one hand, fragmentation does create the danger of conflicting and incompatible rules, principles, rule-systems and institutional practices. On the other hand, it reflects the expansion of international legal activity into new fields and the attendant diversification of its objects and techniques. Fragmentation and diversification account for the development and expansion of international law in response to the demands of a pluralistic world. At the same time, it may occasionally create conflicts between rules and regimes in a way that might undermine their effective implementation. Although fragmentation may create problems, they are neither altogether new nor of such nature that they could not be dealt with through techniques international lawyers have used to deal with the normative conflicts that may have arisen in the past.

247. The rationale for the Commission's treatment of fragmentation is that the emergence of new and special types of law, so-called "self-contained regimes" and geographically or functionally limited treaty systems, creates problems of coherence in international law. New types of specialized law do not emerge accidentally but seek to respond to new technical and functional requirements. The emergence of "environmental law", for example, is a response to growing concern over the state of the international environment. "Trade law" develops as an instrument to respond to opportunities created by comparative advantage in international economic relations. "Human rights law" aims to protect the interests of individuals and "international criminal law" gives legal expression to the "fight against impunity". Each rule complex or "regime" comes with its own principles, its own form of expertise and its own "ethos", not necessarily identical to the ethos of neighbouring specialization. "Trade law" and "environmental law", for example, have highly specific objectives and rely on principles that may often point in different directions. In order for the new law to be efficient, it often includes new types of treaty clauses or practices that may not be compatible with old general law or the law of some other specialized branch. Very often new rules or regimes develop precisely in order to deviate from what was earlier provided by the general law. When such deviations become general and frequent, the unity of the law suffers.

248. It is quite important to note that such deviations do not emerge as legal-technical "mistakes". They reflect the differing pursuits and preferences of actors in a pluralistic (global) society. A law that would fail to articulate the experienced differences between the interests or values that appear relevant in particular situations or problem areas would seem altogether unacceptable. But if fragmentation is a "natural" development (indeed, international law was always relatively "fragmented" due to the diversity of national legal systems that participated in it), there have likewise always been countervailing, equally natural processes leading in the opposite direction. For example, general international law has continued to develop through the application of the 1969 Vienna Convention, customary law and "general principles of law recognized by civilized nations". The fact that a number of treaties reflect rules of general international law, and in turn, certain provisions of treaties enter into the corpus of general international law, is a reflection of the vitality and synergy of the system and the pull for coherence in the law itself.

249. The justification for the Commission's work on fragmentation has been in the fact that although fragmentation is inevitable, it is desirable to have a framework through which it may be assessed and managed in a legal-professional way. That framework is provided by the 1969 Vienna Convention. One aspect that unites practically all of the new regimes (and certainly all of the most important ones) is that they claim binding force from and are understood by the relevant actors to be covered by the law of treaties. This means that the 1969 Vienna Convention already provides a unifying frame for these developments. As the organ that once prepared that Convention, the Commission is in a privileged position to analyse international law's fragmentation from that perspective.

250. In order to do that, the Commission's Study Group held it useful to have regard to the wealth of techniques in the traditional law for dealing with tensions or conflicts between legal rules and principles. What is common to these techniques is that they seek to establish meaningful relationships between such rules and principles so as to determine how they should be used in any particular dispute or conflict. The following conclusions lay out some of the principles that should be taken into account when dealing with actual or potential conflicts between legal rules and principles.

2. Conclusions of the work of the Study Group

251. The conclusions reached in the work of the Study Group are as follows:

(a) *General*

(1) *International law as a legal system.* International law is a legal system. Its rules and principles (i.e. its norms) act in relation to and should be interpreted against

the background of other rules and principles. As a legal system, international law is not a random collection of such norms. There are meaningful relationships between them. Norms may thus exist at higher and lower hierarchical levels, their formulation may involve greater or lesser generality and specificity and their validity may date back to earlier or later moments in time.

(2) In applying international law, it is often necessary to determine the precise relationship between two or more rules and principles that are both valid and applicable in respect of a situation.[971] For that purpose the relevant relationships fall into two general types:

— *Relationships of interpretation.* This is the case where one norm assists in the interpretation of another. A norm may assist in the interpretation of another norm for example as an application, clarification, updating or modification of the latter. In such a situation, both norms are applied in conjunction.

— *Relationships of conflict.* This is the case where two norms that are both valid and applicable point to incompatible decisions so that a choice must be made between them. The basic rules concerning the resolution of normative conflicts are to be found in the 1969 Vienna Convention.

(3) *The Vienna Convention on the Law of Treaties.* When seeking to determine the relationship of two or more norms to each other, the norms should be interpreted in accordance with, or analogously to, the Vienna Convention, and especially the provisions in its articles 31–33 having to do with the interpretation of treaties.

(4) *The principle of harmonization.* It is a generally accepted principle that when several norms bear on a single issue, they should, to the extent possible, be interpreted so as to give rise to a single set of compatible obligations.

(b) *The maxim* lex specialis derogat legi generali

(5) *General principle.* The maxim *lex specialis derogat legi generali* is a generally accepted technique of interpretation and conflict resolution in international law. It suggests that whenever two or more norms deal with the same subject matter, priority should be given to the norm that is more specific. The principle may be applicable in several contexts: between provisions within a single treaty, between provisions within two or more treaties, and between a treaty and a non-treaty standard, as well as between two non-treaty standards.[972] The source of the norm (whether treaty, custom or general principle of law) is not decisive for the determination of the more specific standard. However, in practice treaties often act as *lex specialis* by reference to the relevant customary law and general principles.[973]

(6) *Contextual appreciation.* The relationship between the *lex specialis* maxim and other norms of interpretation or conflict solution cannot be determined in a general way. Which consideration should be predominant—i.e. whether it is the speciality or the time of emergence of the norm—should be decided contextually.

(7) *Rationale of the principle.* That special law has priority over general law is justified by the fact that such special law, being more concrete, often takes better account of the particular features of the context in which it is to be applied than any applicable general law. Its application may also often create a more equitable result and it may often better reflect the intent of the legal subjects.

(8) *Functions of* lex specialis. Most of international law is dispositive. This means that special law may be used to apply, clarify, update or modify, as well as set aside, general law.

(9) *The effect of* lex specialis *on general law.* The application of the special law does not normally extinguish the relevant general law.[974] That general law will remain valid and applicable and will, in accordance with the principle of harmonization under conclusion (4) above, continue to give direction for the interpretation and application of the relevant special law and will become fully applicable in situations not provided for by the latter.[975]

---

[971] That two norms are *valid* in regard to a situation means that they each cover the facts of which the situation consists. That two norms are *applicable* in a situation means that they have binding force in respect to the legal subjects finding themselves in the relevant situation.

[972] For application in relation to provisions within a single treaty, see *Case concerning a dispute between Argentina and Chile concerning the Beagle Channel*, UNRIAA, vol. XXI (Sales No. E/F.95.V.2), pp. 53 *et seq.*, at pp. 99–100 (or ILR, vol. 52 (1979), pp. 97 *et seq.*, at p. 141); Case C-96/00, *Rudolf Gabriel, Judgment of 11 July 2002, Reports of Cases before the Court of Justice and the Court of First Instance, Section I, Court of Justice*, (2002-7), pp. 6367 *et seq.*, at pp. 6398–6399, paras. 35–36 and p. 6404, para. 59; *Brannigan and McBride* v. *the United Kingdom, Judgement of 26 May 1993*, European Court of Human Rights, *Series A: Judgments and Decisions*, vol. 258 (1993), pp. 34 *et seq.*, at p. 57, para. 76; *De Jong, Baljet and van den Brink* v. *the Netherlands, Judgment of 22 May 1984, ibid.*, vol. 77 (1984), pp. 6 *et seq.*, at p. 27, para. 60; *Murray* v. *the United Kingdom, Judgment of 28 October 1994, ibid.*, vol. 300 (1995), pp. 34 *et seq.*, at p. 37, para. 98; and *Nikolova* v. *Bulgaria, Application no. 31195/96, Judgment of 25 March 1999, Grand Chamber, idem., Reports of Judgments and Decisions 1999-II*, pp. 203 *et seq.*, at p. 225, para. 69. For application between different instruments, see *Mavrommatis Palestine Concessions* (footnote 26 above), p. 31. For application between a treaty and non-treaty standards, see *INA Corporation* v. *Government of the Islamic Republic of Iran*, Case No. 161, 12 August 1985, Iran–United States Claims Tribunal, *Iran–United States Claims Tribunal Reports*, vol. 8, p. 373, at p. 378. For application between particular and general custom, see *Case concerning Right of Passage over Indian Territory, Merits, Judgment of 12 April 1960, I.C.J. Reports 1960*, p. 6, at p. 44. In that case, the Court said: "Where therefore the Court finds a practice clearly established between two States which was accepted by the Parties as governing the relations between them, the Court must attribute decisive effect to that practice for the purpose of determining their specific rights and obligations. Such a particular practice must prevail over any general rules."

[973] In *Military and Paramilitary Activities in and against Nicaragua* (see footnote 887 above), the ICJ said: "In general, treaty rules being *lex specialis*, it would not be appropriate that a State should bring a claim based on a customary-law rule if it has by treaty already provided means for settlement of a such a claim" (p. 137, para. 274).

[974] Thus, in *Military and Paramilitary Activities in and against Nicaragua* (see footnote 887 above), the ICJ noted: "It will … be clear that customary international law continues to exist and to apply, separately from international treaty law, even where the two categories of law have an identical content" (p. 96, para. 179).

[975] In the *Legality of the Threat or Use of Nuclear Weapons, Advisory Opinion, I.C.J. Reports 1996*, p. 226, the ICJ described the relationship between human rights law and the laws of armed conflict in the following way: "the protection of the International Covenant of Civil and Political Rights does not cease in times of war, except by operation of article 4 of the Covenant …. The test of what is an arbitrary deprivation of life, however, then falls to be determined by the applicable *lex specialis*, namely, the law applicable in armed conflict which is designed to regulate the

(10) *Particular types of general law*. Certain types of general law[976] may not, however, be derogated from by special law. *Jus cogens* is expressly non-derogable as set out in conclusions (32), (33), (40) and (41) below.[977] Moreover, there are other considerations that may provide a reason for concluding that a general law would prevail, in which case the *lex specialis* presumption may not apply. These include the following:

— Whether such prevalence may be inferred from the form or the nature of the general law or intent of the parties, wherever applicable;

— Whether the application of the special law might frustrate the *purpose* of the general law;

— Whether third party beneficiaries may be negatively affected by the special law; and

— Whether the balance of rights and obligations established in the general law would be negatively affected by the special law.

(c) *Special ("self-contained") regimes*

(11) *Special ("self-contained") regimes as* lex specialis. A group of rules and principles concerned with a particular subject matter may form a special regime ("self-contained regime") and be applicable as *lex specialis*. Such special regimes often have their own institutions to administer the relevant rules.

(12) Three types of special regime may be distinguished:

— Sometimes violation of a particular group of (primary) rules is accompanied by a special set of (secondary) rules concerning breach and reactions to breach. This is the main case provided for under article 55 of the draft articles on responsibility of States for internationally wrongful acts.[978]

— Sometimes, however, a special regime is formed by a set of special rules, including rights and obligations, relating to a special subject matter. Such rules may concern a geographical area (e.g. a treaty on the protection of a particular river) or some substantive matter (e.g. a treaty on the regulation of the uses of a particular weapon). Such a special regime may emerge on the basis of a single treaty, several treaties or a treaty and treaties plus non-treaty developments (subsequent practice or customary law).[979]

— Finally, sometimes all the rules and principles that regulate a certain problem area are collected together so as to express a "special regime". Expressions such as "law of the sea", "humanitarian law", "human rights law", "environmental law" and "trade law" give expression to some such regimes. For interpretative purposes, such regimes may often be considered in their entirety.

(13) *Effect of the "speciality" of a regime*. The significance of a special regime often lies in the way its norms express a unified object and purpose. Thus, their interpretation and application should, to the extent possible, reflect that object and purpose.

(14) *The relationship between special regimes and general international law*. A special regime may prevail over general law under the same conditions as *lex specialis* generally (see conclusions (8) and (10) above).

(15) *The role of general law in special regimes*: *gap filling*. The scope of special laws is by definition narrower than that of general laws. It will thus frequently be the case that a matter not regulated by special law will arise in the institutions charged to administer it. In such cases, the relevant general law will apply.[980]

---

conduct of hostilities. Thus whether a particular loss of life, through the use of a certain weapon in warfare, is to be considered an arbitrary deprivation of life contrary to Article 6 of the Covenant, can only be decided by reference to the law applicable in armed conflict and not deduced from the terms of the Covenant itself" (p. 240, para. 25).

[976] There is no accepted definition of "general international law". For the purposes of these conclusions, however, it is sufficient to define what is "general" by reference to its logical counterpart, namely what is "special". In practice, lawyers are usually able to operate this distinction by reference to the context in which it appears.

[977] In the *Dispute Concerning Access to Information Under Article 9 of the OSPAR Convention between Ireland and the United Kingdom, Final Award, Decision of 2 July 2003*, UNRIAA, vol. XXIII (Sales No. E/F.04/V.15) p. 59, the tribunal observed: "[e]ven then, [the OSPAR Convention] must defer to the relevant *jus cogens* with which the Parties' *lex specialis* may be inconsistent" (p. 87, para. 84); for this case see also ILR, vol. 126 (2005), p. 364.

[978] *Yearbook ... 2001*, vol. II (Part Two) and corrigendum, p. 140–141. In *United States Diplomatic and Consular Staff in Tehran*a (see footnote 190 above), the ICJ said: "The rules of diplomatic law, in short, constitute a self-contained régime which, on the one hand, lays down the receiving State's obligations regarding the facilities, privileges and immunities to be accorded to diplomatic missions and, on the other, foresees their possible abuse by members of the mission and specifies the means at the disposal of the receiving States to counter any such abuse" (p. 40, para. 86).

[979] See *S.S. "Wimbledon", Judgments, 1923, PCIJ, Series A, No. 1*, noting that the provisions on the Kiel Canal in the 1919 Treaty of Peace between the Allied and Associated Powers and Germany (Treaty of Versailles) "differ on more than one point from those to which other internal navigable waterways of the [German] Empire are subjected ... the Kiel Canal is open to the war vessels and transit traffic of all nations at peace with Germany, whereas free access to the other German navigable waterways ... is limited to the Allied and Associated Powers alone .... The provisions relating to the Kiel Canal in the Treaty of Versailles are therefore self-contained" (pp. 23–24).

[980] Thus, in *Banković and others* v. *Belgium and others, Application no. 52207/99, Grand Chamber, European Court of Human Rights, Reports of Judgments and Decisions 2001-XII*, the Court canvassed the relationship between the European Convention on Human Rights and general international law as follows: "the Court reiterates that the principles underlying the Convention cannot be interpreted and applied in a vacuum. The Court must also take into account any relevant rules of international law when examining questions concerning its jurisdiction and, consequently, determine State responsibility in conformity with the governing principles of international law, although it must remain mindful of the Convention's special character as a human rights treaty. The Convention should be interpreted as far as possible in harmony with other principles of international law of which it forms part" (p. 351, para. 57).

Similarly, in *Korea–Measures Affecting Government Procurement*, Report of the Panel of 1 May 2000 (WT/DS163/R), the Appellate Body of the WTO noted the relationship between the WTO-covered agreements and general international law as follows: "We take note that Article 3.2 of the DSU requires that we seek within the context of a particular dispute to clarify the existing provisions of the WTO agreements in accordance with customary rules of interpretation of public international law. However, the relationship of the WTO Agreements to customary international law is broader than this. Customary international law applies generally to the economic relations between the WTO Members. Such international law applies to the extent that the WTO treaty agreements do not 'contract out' from it. To put it another way, to the extent that there is no conflict or inconsistency, or an expression in a covered WTO agreement that applies differently, we are of the view that the customary rules of international law apply to the WTO treaties and to the process of treaty formation under the WTO" (para. 7.96).

(16) *The role of general law in special regimes: failure of special regimes.* Special regimes or the institutions set up by them may fail. Failure might be inferred when the special laws have no reasonable prospect of appropriately addressing the objectives for which they were enacted. It could be manifested, for example, by the failure of the regime's institutions to fulfil the purposes allotted to them, persistent non-compliance by one or several of the parties, desuetude, or withdrawal by parties instrumental for the regime, among other causes. Whether a regime has "failed" in this sense, however, would have to be assessed above all by an interpretation of its constitutional instruments. In the event of failure, the relevant general law becomes applicable.

(d) *Article 31 (3) (c) of the Vienna Convention on the Law of Treaties*

(17) *Systemic integration.* Article 31, paragraph (3) (*c*) of the Vienna Convention on the Law of Treaties provides one means within the framework of the Convention through which relationships of interpretation (referred to in conclusion (2) above) may be applied. It requires the interpreter of a treaty to take into account "any relevant rules of international law applicable in the relations between the parties". The article gives expression to the objective of "systemic integration" according to which, whatever their subject matter, treaties are a creation of the international legal system and their operation is predicated upon that fact.

(18) *Interpretation as integration in the system.* Systemic integration governs all treaty interpretation, the other relevant aspects of which are set out in the other paragraphs of articles 31–32 of the 1969 Vienna Convention. These paragraphs describe a process of legal reasoning in which particular elements will have greater or less relevance depending upon the nature of the treaty provisions in the context of interpretation. In many cases, the issue of interpretation will be capable of resolution with the framework of the treaty itself. Article 31, paragraph (3) (*c*) deals with the case where material sources external to the treaty are relevant in its interpretation. These may include other treaties, customary rules or general principles of law.[981]

(19) *Application of systemic integration.* Where a treaty functions in the context of other agreements, the objective of systemic integration will apply as a presumption with both positive and negative aspects:

(*a*) the parties are taken to refer to customary international law and general principles of law for all questions which the treaty does not itself resolve in express terms;[982]

(*b*) in entering into treaty obligations, the parties do not intend to act inconsistently with generally recognized principles of international law.[983]

Of course, if any other result is indicated by ordinary methods of treaty interpretation, that should be given effect, unless the relevant principle were part of *jus cogens*.

(20) *Application of custom and general principles of law.* Customary international law and general principles of law are of particular relevance to the interpretation of a treaty under article 31, paragraph (3) (*c*), especially where:

(*a*) the treaty rule is unclear or open-textured;

(*b*) the terms used in the treaty have a recognized meaning in customary international law or under general principles of law;

(*c*) the treaty is silent on the applicable law and it is necessary for the interpreter, applying the presumption in conclusion (19) (*a*) above, to look for rules developed in another part of international law to resolve the point.

(21) *Application of other treaty rules.* Article 31, paragraph (3) (*c*) also requires the interpreter to consider other treaty-based rules so as to arrive at a consistent meaning. Such other rules are of particular relevance where parties to the treaty under interpretation are also parties to the other treaty, where the treaty rule has passed into or expresses customary international law or where they provide evidence of the common understanding of the parties as to the object and purpose of the treaty under interpretation or as to the meaning of a particular term.

(22) *Inter-temporality.* International law is a dynamic legal system. A treaty may convey whether in applying article 31, paragraph (3) (*c*) the interpreter should refer only to rules of international law in force at the time of the conclusion of the treaty or may also take into account subsequent changes in the law. Moreover, the meaning of a treaty provision may also be affected by subsequent developments, especially where there are subsequent developments in customary law and general principles of law.[984]

---

[981] In the *Oil Platforms* case (*Islamic Republic of Iran* v. *United States of America*), *Judgment, I.C.J. Reports 2003*, p. 161, the Court spoke of the relations between a bilateral treaty and general international law by reference to article 31 (3) (*c*) as follows: "Moreover, under the general rules of treaty interpretation, as reflected in the 1969 Vienna Convention on the Law of Treaties, interpretation must take into account 'any relevant rules of international law applicable in the relations between the parties' (Art. 31, para. 3 (*c*)). The Court cannot accept that Article XX, paragraph 1 (*d*), of the 1955 Treaty was intended to operate wholly independently of the relevant rules of international law … . The application of the relevant rules of international law relating to this question thus forms an integral part of the task of interpretation entrusted to the Court by … the 1955 Treaty" (p. 182, para. 41).

[982] *Georges Pinson*, French–Mexican Claims Commission, UNRIAA, vol. V (Sales No. 1952.V.3), p. 327, at p. 422. It was noted that parties are taken to refer to general principles of international law for questions which the treaty does not itself resolve in express terms or in a different way.

[983] In the *Case concerning Right of Passage over Indian Territory, Preliminary Objections, Judgment of 26 November 1957, I.C.J. Reports 1957*, p. 125, the Court stated: "It is a rule of interpretation that a text emanating from a Government must, in principle, be interpreted as producing and as intended to produce effects in accordance with existing law and not in violation of it" (p. 142).

[984] The traditional rule was stated by Judge Huber in the *Island of Palmas* case *(the Netherlands/United States of America)*, UNRIAA, vol. II (Sales No. 1949.V.1), p. 829, in the context of territorial claims: "a juridical fact must be appreciated in the light of the law contemporary with it, and not the law in force at the time when a dispute in regard

(23) *Open or evolving concepts*. Rules of international law subsequent to the treaty to be interpreted may be taken into account, especially where the concepts used in the treaty are open or evolving. This is the case, in particular, where: (*a*) the concept is one which implies taking into account subsequent technical, economic or legal developments;[985] (*b*) the concept sets up an obligation for further progressive development for the parties; or (*c*) the concept has a very general nature or is expressed in such general terms that it must take into account changing circumstances.[986]

(e) *Conflicts between successive norms*

(24) *Lex posterior derogat legi priori*. According to article 30 of the 1969 Vienna Convention, when all the parties to a treaty are also parties to an earlier treaty on the same subject, and the earlier treaty is not suspended or terminated, then it applies only to the extent its provisions are compatible with those of the later treaty. This is an expression of the principle according to which "later law supersedes earlier law".

(25) *Limits of the* lex posterior *principle*. The applicability of the *lex posterior* principle is, however, limited. It cannot, for example, be automatically extended to the case where the parties to the subsequent treaty are not identical to the parties of the earlier treaty. In such cases, as provided in article 30, paragraph (4) of the of the 1969 Vienna Convention, the State that is party to two incompatible treaties is bound *vis-à-vis* both of its treaty parties separately. If it cannot fulfil its obligations under both treaties, it risks being responsible for the breach of one of them unless the concerned parties agree otherwise. In such a case, article 60 of the Convention may also become applicable. The question which of the incompatible treaties should be implemented and the breach of which should attract State responsibility cannot be answered by a general rule.[987] Conclusions (26)–(27) below lay out considerations that might then be taken into account.

(26) *The distinction between treaty provisions that belong to the same "regime" and provisions in different "regimes"*. The *lex posterior* principle is at its strongest in regard to conflicting or overlapping provisions that are part of treaties that are institutionally linked or otherwise intended to advance similar objectives (i.e. that form part of the same regime). In case of conflicts or overlaps between treaties in different regimes, the question of which of them is later in time would not necessarily express any presumption of priority between them. Instead, States bound by the treaty obligations should try to implement them as far as possible with the view of mutual accommodation and in accordance with the principle of harmonization. However, the substantive rights of treaty parties or third party beneficiaries should not be undermined.

(27) *Particular types of treaties or treaty provisions*. The *lex posterior* presumption may not apply where the parties have intended otherwise, which may be inferred from the nature of the provisions or the relevant instruments, or from their object and purpose. The limitations that apply in respect of the *lex specialis* presumption in conclusion (10) may also be relevant with respect to the *lex posterior*.

(28) *Settlement of disputes within and across regimes*. Disputes between States involving conflicting treaty

---

to it arises or falls to be settled. … The same principle which subjects the act creative of a right to the law in force at the time the right arises, demands that the existence of the right, in other words, its continued manifestation, shall follow the conditions required by the evolution of law" (p. 845).

[985] In *Gabčíkovo–Nagymaros Project* (see footnote 363 above), the Court observed: "By inserting these evolving provisions in the Treaty, the parties recognized the potential necessity to adapt the Project. Consequently, the Treaty is not static, and is open to adapt to emerging norms of international law. By means of Articles 15 and 19, new environmental norms can be incorporated in the Joint Contractual Plan" (pp. 67–68, para. 112).

In the arbitral award in the *Arbitration regarding the Iron Rhine ("Ijzeren Rijn") Railway (Belgium/Netherlands)* of 24 May 2005 (UNRIAA, vol. XXVII (Sales No. E/F.06.V.8), p. 35), at issue was not a conceptual or generic term, but a new technical development relating to the operation and capacity of a railway. Evolutive interpretation was used to ensure the effective application of the treaty in terms of its object and purpose. The Tribunal observed that: "The object and purpose of the 1839 Treaty of Separation was to resolve the many difficult problems complicating a stable separation of Belgium and the Netherlands: that of Article XII was to provide for transport links from Belgium to Germany, across a route designated by the 1842 Boundary Treaty. This object was not for a fixed duration and its purpose was 'commercial communication'. It necessarily follows, even in the absence of specific wording, that such works, going beyond restoration to previous functionality, as might from time to time be necessary or desirable for contemporary commerciality, would remain a concomitant of the right of transit that Belgium would be able to request. That being so, the entirety of Article XII, with its careful balance of the rights and obligations of the Parties, remains in principle applicable to the adaptation and modernisation requested by Belgium" (p. 38, para. 83).

[986] See *Legal Consequences for States of the Continued Presence of South Africa in Namibia (South West Africa) notwithstanding Security Council Resolution 276 (1970)* (footnote 51 above). The Court said that the concept of "sacred trust" was by definition evolutionary. "The parties to the Covenant must consequently be deemed to have accepted [it] as such. That it is why, viewing the institutions of 1919, the Court must take into consideration the changes which have occurred in the supervening half-century, and its interpretation cannot remain unaffected by the subsequent development of law, through the Charter of the United Nations and by way of customary international law. Moreover, an international instrument has to be interpreted and applied within the framework of the entire legal system prevailing at the time of the interpretation" (p. 31, para. 53).

In *Gabčíkovo–Nagymaros Project*, (see footnote 363 above), the ICJ noted that "the Court wishes to point out that newly developed norms of environmental law are relevant for the implementation of the Treaty and that the parties could, by agreement, incorporate them … [in] … the Treaty. These articles do not contain specific obligations of performance but require the parties, in carrying out their obligations to ensure that the quality of water in the Danube is not impaired and that nature is protected, to take new environmental norms into consideration when agreeing upon the means to be specified in the Joint Contractual Plan" (p. 67, para. 112).

[987] There is not much case law on conflicts between successive norms. However, the situation of a treaty conflict arose in *Slivenko and others* v. *Latvia, Application no. 48321/99, Decision as to the admissibility of 23 January 2002, Grand Chamber, European Court of Human Rights, Reports of Judgments and Decisions 2002-II*, p. 467, in which the Court held that a prior bilateral treaty between Latvia and the Russian Federation could not be invoked to limit the application of the European Convention on Human Rights: "It follows from the text of Article 57 § 1 of the [European Convention on Human Rights], read in conjunction with Article 1, that ratification of the Convention by a State presupposes that any law then in force in its territory should be in conformity with the Convention. … In the Court's opinion the same principles must apply as regards any provisions of international treaties which a Contracting State has concluded prior to the ratification of the Convention and which might be at variance with certain of its provisions" (pp. 482–483, paras. 60–61).

provisions should be normally resolved by negotiation between parties to the relevant treaties. However, when no negotiated solution is available, recourse ought to be had, where appropriate, to other available means of dispute settlement. When the conflict concerns provisions within a single regime (as defined in conclusion (26) above), then its resolution may be appropriate in the regime-specific mechanism. However, when the conflict concerns provisions in treaties that are not part of the same regime, special attention should be given to the independence of the means of settlement chosen.

(29) Inter se *agreements*. The case of agreements to modify multilateral treaties by certain of the parties only (*inter se* agreements) is covered by article 41 of the 1969 Vienna Convention. Such agreements are an often-used technique for the more effective implementation of the original treaty between a limited number of treaty parties that are willing to take more effective or more far-reaching measures for the realization of the object and purpose of the original treaty. *Inter se* agreements may be concluded if this is provided for by the original treaty or it is not specifically prohibited and the agreement "(i) does not affect the enjoyment by the other parties of their rights under the treaty or the performance of their obligations; (ii) does not relate to a provision, derogation from which is incompatible with the effective execution of the object and purpose of the treaty as a whole" (article 41, paragraph (1) (*b*) of the 1969 Vienna Convention).

(30) *Conflict clauses*. When States enter into a treaty that might conflict with other treaties, they should aim to settle the relationship between such treaties by adopting appropriate conflict clauses. When adopting such clauses, it should be borne in mind that:

(*a*) they may not affect the rights of third parties;

(*b*) they should be as clear and specific as possible. In particular, they should be directed to specific provisions of the treaty and they should not undermine the object and purpose of the treaty;

(*c*) they should, as appropriate, be linked with means of dispute settlement.

(f) *Hierarchy in international law:* jus cogens, *obligations* erga omnes, *Article 103 of the Charter of the United Nations*

(31) *Hierarchical relations between norms of international law*. The main sources of international law (treaties, custom and general principles of law as laid out in Article 38 of the Statute of the International Court of Justice) are not in a hierarchical relationship *inter se*.[988] Drawing analogies from the hierarchical nature of domestic legal systems is not generally appropriate owing to the differences between the two systems. Nevertheless, some rules of international law are more important than other rules and for this reason enjoy a superior position or special status in the international legal system. This is sometimes expressed by the designation of some norms as "fundamental" or as expressive of "elementary considerations of humanity"[989] or "intransgressible principles of international customary law".[990] What effect such designations may have is usually determined by the relevant context or instrument in which that designation appears.

(32) *Recognized hierarchical relations by the substance of the rules*: jus cogens. A rule of international law may be superior to other rules on account of the importance of its content as well as the universal acceptance of its superiority. This is the case of peremptory norms of international law (*jus cogens*, Article 53 of the 1969 Vienna Convention), that is, norms "accepted and recognized by the international community of States as a whole from which no derogation is permitted".[991]

(33) *The content of* jus cogens. The most frequently cited examples of *jus cogens* norms are the prohibition of aggression, slavery and the slave trade, genocide, racial discrimination, apartheid and torture, as well as basic rules of international humanitarian law applicable in armed conflict and the right to self-determination.[992] Also, other rules may have a *jus cogens* character inasmuch as they are "accepted and recognized by the international community of States as a whole as norms from which no derogation is permitted".

(34) *Recognized hierarchical relations by virtue of a treaty provision*: *Article 103 of the Charter of the United Nations*. A rule of international law may also be superior to other rules by virtue of a treaty provision. This is the case of Article 103 of the United Nations Charter by virtue of which "[i]n the event of a conflict between the obligations of the Members of the United Nations under the … Charter and their obligations under any other international agreement, their obligations under the … Charter shall prevail".

(35) *The scope of Article 103 of the Charter of the United Nations*. The scope of Article 103 of the Charter of the United Nations extends not only to the Articles of the Charter but also to binding decisions made by United Nations organs such as the Security Council.[993] Given the

[988] In addition, Article 38, paragraph (1) (*d*) mentions "judicial decisions and the teachings of the most highly qualified publicists of the various nations, as subsidiary means for the determination of rules of law".

[989] *Corfu Channel* (see footnote 197 above), p. 22.

[990] *Legality of the Threat or Use of Nuclear Weapons* (see footnote 975 above), p. 257, para. 79.

[991] Article 53 of the 1969 Vienna Convention: "A treaty is void if, at the time of its conclusion, it conflicts with a peremptory norm of general international law. For the purposes of the present Convention, a peremptory norm of general international law is a norm accepted and recognized by the international community of States as a whole as a norm from which no derogation is permitted and which can be modified only by a subsequent norm of general international law having the same character."

[992] See *Yearbook … 2001*, vol. II (Part Two) and corrigendum, pp. 112–113 (commentary to article 40 of the draft articles on State responsibility, paras. (4)–(6)). See also *ibid.*, p. 85 (commentary to article 26, para. (5)). See also *Armed Activities on the Territory of the Congo (New Application: 2002)* (footnote 637 above), pp. 31–32, para. 64.

[993] See *Questions of Interpretation and Application of the 1971 Montreal Convention arising from the Aerial Incident at Lockerbie (Libyan Arab Jamahiriya* v. *United States), Provisional Measures, Order of 14 April 1992, I.C.J. Reports 1992*, p. 114, at p. 126, para. 42; and *Questions of Interpretation and Application of the 1971 Montreal Convention arising from the Aerial Incident at Lockerbie (Libyan Arab Jamahiriya* v. *United Kingdom), Provisional Measures, Order of 14 April 1992*, *ibid.*, p. 3, at p. 15, paras. 39–40.

character of some Charter provisions, the constitutional character of the Charter and the established practice of States and United Nations organs, Charter obligations may also prevail over inconsistent customary international law.

(36) *The status of the Charter of the United Nations*. It is also recognized that the Charter of the United Nations itself enjoys special character owing to the fundamental nature of some of its norms, particularly its principles and purposes and its universal acceptance.[994]

(37) *Rules specifying obligations owed to the international community as a whole: obligations* erga omnes. Some obligations enjoy a special status owing to the universal scope of their applicability. This is the case of obligations *erga omnes*, that is obligations of a State towards the international community as a whole. These rules concern all States and all States can be held to have a legal interest in the protection of the rights involved.[995] Every State may invoke the responsibility of the State violating such obligations.[996]

(38) *The relationship between* jus cogens *norms and obligations* erga omnes. It is recognized that while all obligations established by *jus cogens* norms, as referred to in conclusion (33) above, also have the character of *erga omnes* obligations, the reverse is not necessarily true.[997] Not all *erga omnes* obligations are established by peremptory norms of general international law. This is the case, for example, of certain obligations under "the principles and rules concerning the basic rights of the human person",[998] as well as of some obligations relating to the global commons.[999]

(39) *Different approaches to the concept of obligations* erga omnes. The concept of *erga omnes* obligations has also been used to refer to treaty obligations that a State owes to all other States parties (obligations *erga omnes partes*)[1000] or to non-party States as third party beneficiaries. In addition, issues of territorial status have frequently been addressed in *erga omnes* terms, referring to their opposability to all States.[1001] Thus, boundary and territorial treaties have been stated to "represent[] a legal reality which necessarily impinges upon third States, because they have effect *erga omnes*".[1002]

(40) *The relationship between* jus cogens *and the obligations under the Charter of the United Nations*. The Charter of the United Nations has been universally accepted by States and thus a conflict between *jus cogens* norms and Charter obligations is difficult to contemplate. In any case, according to Article 24, paragraph (2) of the Charter, the Security Council shall act in accordance with the Purposes and Principles of the United Nations which include norms that have been subsequently treated as *jus cogens*.

(41) *The operation and effect of* jus cogens *norms and Article 103 of the Charter of the United Nations*:

(*a*) a rule conflicting with a norm of *jus cogens* becomes thereby *ipso facto* void;

(*b*) a rule conflicting with Article 103 of the Charter of the United Nations becomes inapplicable as a result of such conflict and to the extent of such conflict.

---

[994] See Article 2, paragraph (6) of the Charter of the United Nations.

[995] In the words of the ICJ, "an essential distinction should be drawn between the obligations of a State towards the international community as a whole, and those arising *vis-à-vis* another State in the field of diplomatic protection. By their very nature the former are the concern of all States. In view of the importance of the rights involved, all States can be held to have a legal interest in their protection; they are obligations *erga omnes*" (*Barcelona Traction, Second Phase* (see footnote 35 above), p. 32, para. 33). Or, in accordance with the definition by the Institute of International Law, an obligation *erga omnes* is "an obligation under general international law that a State owes in any given case to the international community, in view of its common values and its concern for compliance, so that a breach of that obligation enables all States to take action" (*Yearbook of the Institute of International Law*, Session of Krakow 2005—Second Part, vol. 71-II (2006), p. 297, resolution I ("Obligations *erga omnes* in the International Law"), art. 1 (*a*)).

[996] See *Yearbook ... 2001*, vol. II (Part Two) and corrigendum, p. 126 (article 48, paragraph (1) (*b*) of the draft articles on responsibility of States for internationally wrongful acts). This would include common article 1 of the Geneva Convention for the Amelioration of the Condition of the Wounded and Sick in Armed Forces in the Field (Convention I), the Geneva Convention for the Amelioration of the Condition of the Wounded, Sick and Shipwrecked Members of Armed Forces at Sea (Convention II), the Geneva Convention relative to the Treatment of Prisoners of War (Convention III), and the Geneva Convention relative to the Protection of Civilian Persons in Time of War (Convention IV), all of 12 August 1949.

[997] According to the ICJ, "[s]uch obligations derive, for example, in contemporary international law, from the outlawing of acts of aggression, and of genocide, as also from the principles and rules concerning the basic rights of the human person, including protection from slavery and racial discrimination. Some of the corresponding rights of protection have entered into the body of general international law … ; others are conferred by international instruments of a universal or quasi-universal character" (*Barcelona Traction (Second Phase), Judgment*, (footnote 35 above), p. 32, para. 34). See also *East Timor (Portugal* v. *Australia), Judgment, I.C.J. Reports 1995*, p. 90, at p. 102, para. 29. See also *Legal Consequences of the Construction of a Wall in the Occupied Palestinian Territory* (footnote 950 above), pp. 199 and 200, paras. 155 and 159 (including as *erga omnes* obligations "certain … obligations under international humanitarian law" as well as the right of self-determination). For the prohibition of genocide as an *erga omnes* obligation, see *Application of the Convention on the Prevention and Punishment of the Crime of Genocide (Bosnia and Herzegovina* v. *Yugoslavia)* (footnote 904 above), pp. 615–616, para. 31, and *Armed Activities on the Territory of the Congo (New Application: 2002)* (footnote 637 above), pp. 31–32, para. 64. In the *Furundžija* case, torture was defined as both a peremptory norm and an obligation *erga omnes*, see *Prosecutor* v. *Anto Furundžija, Case No. IT-95-17/1-T, Trial Chamber II, Judgement of 10 December 1998*, ILR, vol. 121 (2002), p. 260, para. 151.

[998] *Barcelona Traction (Second Phase), Judgment* (footnote 35 above), p. 32, para. 34.

[999] The obligations are illustrated by article 1 of the Treaty on principles governing the activities of States in the exploration and use of outer space, including the moon and other celestial bodies and article 136 of the United Nations Convention on the Law of the Sea.

[1000] See *Yearbook of the Institute of International Law* (footnote 995 above), resolution I, article 1 (*b*).

[1001] "In my view, when a title to an area of maritime jurisdiction exists—be it to a continental shelf or (*arguendo*) to a fishery zone—it exists *erga omnes*, i.e., is opposable to all States under international law" (separate opinion of Vice-President Oda, *Maritime Delimitation in the Area between Greenland and Jan Mayen, Judgment, I.C.J. Reports 1993*, p. 38, at p. 100, para. 40). See also the separate opinion of Judge De Castro in *Legal Consequences for States of the Continued Presence of South Africa in Namibia (South-West Africa) notwithstanding Security Council Resolution 276 (1970)* (footnote 51 above): "a legal status—like the *iura in re* with which it is sometimes confused—is effective *inter omnes* and *erga omnes*" (p. 177). See also the dissenting opinion of Judge Skubiszewski, in *East Timor* (footnote 997 above), at p. 248, paras. 78–79.

[1002] *Government of the State of Eritrea* v. *the Government of the Republic of Yemen (Phase One: Territorial Sovereignty and Scope of the Dispute)*, Arbitration Tribunal, 9 October 1998, ILR, vol. 114 (1999), p. 1, at p. 48, para. 153.

(42) *Hierarchy and the principle of harmonization.* Conflicts between rules of international law should be resolved in accordance with the principle of harmonization, as laid out in conclusion (4) above. In the case of conflict between one of the hierarchically superior norms referred to in this section and another norm of international law, the latter should, to the extent possible, be interpreted in a manner consistent with the former. In case this is not possible, the superior norm will prevail.

Chapter XIII

OTHER DECISIONS AND CONCLUSIONS OF THE COMMISSION

A. Expulsion of aliens

252. The Commission had before it the second report of the Special Rapporteur for the topic, Mr. Maurice Kamto (A/CN.4/573) and a memorandum prepared by the Secretariat (A/CN.4/565 and Corr.1). The Commission decided to consider the report at its next session in 2007.

B. Programme, procedures and working methods of the Commission and its documentation

253. At its 2899th meeting, held on 25 July 2006, the Commission established a Planning Group for the current session.[1003]

254. The Planning Group held three meetings. It had before it Section I of the topical summary of the discussion held in the Sixth Committee of the General Assembly during its sixtieth session, prepared by the Secretariat and entitled "Other decisions and conclusions of the Commission" (A/CN.4/560), and General Assembly resolution 60/22, in particular paragraphs 6, 7, 8, 13 and 16 on the report of the International Law Commission on the work of its fifty-seventh session. It also had before it the proposed strategic framework for the period 2008–2009, concerning Programme 6: Legal Affairs, sub-programme 3 (Progressive development and codification of international law), of which it took note.

255. At its 2907th meeting, held on 7 August 2006, the Commission took note of the report of the Planning Group.

1. Long-term Programme of Work

256. The Working Group on the Long-term Programme of Work, established by the Planning Group during the fifty-fourth session of the Commission (2002), with Mr. Alain Pellet as Chairperson, was reconstituted during the current session.[1004] The Working Group submitted its report to the Planning Group on 27 July 2006. The Working Group, in accordance with the established practice, was requested to report at the end of the quinquennium, at the fifty-eighth session (2006) of the Commission. During the quinquennium, the Working Group considered a number of topics, and requested members of the Working Group, other members of the Commission and the Secretariat to prepare drafts on those topics. The Working Group was guided by the recommendation of the Commission, at its forty-ninth session (1997), regarding the criteria for the selection of the topics:

(*a*) the topic should reflect the needs of the States in respect of the progressive development and codification of international law;

(*b*) the topic should be sufficiently advanced in stage in terms of State practice to permit progressive development and codification;

(*c*) the topic is concrete and feasible for progressive development; [and]

... the Commission should not restrict itself to traditional topics, but could also consider those that reflect new developments in international law and pressing concerns of international community.[1005]

257. Bearing in mind the criteria above, during the present quinquennium the Planning Group recommended and the Commission endorsed the inclusion of the following topics in the long-term programme of work of the Commission:

(*a*) the obligation to extradite or prosecute (*aut dedere aut judicare*);

(*b*) immunity of State officials from foreign criminal jurisdiction;

(*c*) jurisdictional immunity of international organizations;

(*d*) protection of persons in the event of disasters;

(*e*) protection of personal data in transborder flow of information; and

(*f*) extraterritorial jurisdiction.

258. The syllabuses on the topics that have been recommended for inclusion in the long-term programme of work, except for the topic "The obligation to extradite or prosecute (*aut dedere aut judicare*)", are annexed to the present report. It will be recalled, with respect to the topic "The obligation to extradite or prosecute (*aut dedere aut judicare*)", that an interim report, together with a syllabus, was submitted during the Commission's fifty-sixth session (2004) and its inclusion was recommended in the long-term programme of work.[1006] At the same session, the Commission agreed with the inclusion of this topic in its long-term programme of work.[1007]

[1003] For the membership of the Planning Group, see paragraph 6 above.

[1004] *Yearbook ... 2002*, vol. II (Part Two), p. 102, para. 521. For the membership of the Working Group, see paragraph 10 above.

[1005] *Yearbook ... 1997*, vol. II (Part Two), pp. 71–72, para. 238.

[1006] *Yearbook ... 2004*, vol. II (Part Two), p. 120, para. 362, and Annex.

[1007] *Ibid.*, para. 363.

259. Regarding the topic "The most-favoured-nation clause", on which the Planning Group did not make a final recommendation, the Commission decided to seek the views of Governments as to the utility of further work by the Commission on this topic (see chapter III, paragraph 33 above).[1008]

260. The consolidated list included in the long-term programme of work since the forty-fourth session of the Commission (1992) is as follows:[1009]

(*a*) law and practice relating to reservations to treaties;[1010]

(*b*) State succession and its impact on the nationality of natural and legal persons;[1011]

(*c*) diplomatic protection;[1012]

(*d*) ownership and protection of wrecks beyond the limits of national maritime jurisdiction;[1013]

(*e*) unilateral acts of States;[1014]

(*f*) responsibility of international organizations;[1015]

(*g*) shared natural resources of States;[1016]

(*h*) risks ensuing from fragmentation of international law;[1017]

(*i*) effects of armed conflict on treaties;[1018]

(*j*) expulsion of aliens;[1019]

(*k*) the obligation to extradite or prosecute (*aut dedere aut judicare*);[1020]

(*l*) immunity of State officials from foreign criminal jurisdiction;[1021]

(*m*) jurisdictional immunity of international organizations;[1022]

(*n*) protection of persons in the event of disasters;[1023]

(*o*) protection of personal data in transborder flow of information;[1024] and

(*p*) extraterritorial jurisdiction.[1025]

261. The Commission expressed its appreciation for the valuable assistance rendered by the Codification Division in the preparation of proposals on "Protection of persons in the event of disasters", "Protection of personal data in transborder flow of information", "Extraterritorial jurisdiction", and "Acquiescence and its effects on the legal rights and obligations of States", at the request, and for the consideration, of the Working Group of the long-term programme of work.

2. Documentation and publications

262. The Commission considered the issue of timely submission of reports by Special Rapporteurs. Bearing in

---

[1008] The Commission included the topic "The most-favoured-nation clause" in its programme of work at its twentieth session, in 1967 (*Yearbook ... 1967*, vol. II, p. 369, para. 48) and appointed Mr. Endre Ustor (*ibid.*) and Mr. Nikolaï Ushakov (*Yearbook ... 1977*, vol. II (Part Two), p. 124, para. 77) as the successive Special Rapporteurs. The Commission completed the second reading of the topic at its thirtieth session, in 1978 (*Yearbook ... 1978*, vol. II (Part Two), pp. 16–73, para. 74). The General Assembly at its thirty-fifth, thirty-sixth, thirty-eighth, fortieth and forty-third sessions (1980, 1981, 1983, 1985 and 1988) invited comments from Governments and intergovernmental organizations, on the draft articles proposed by the Commission. At its forty-sixth session (1991), the General Assembly, in its decision 46/416 of 9 December 1991, took note with appreciation of the work of the Commission as well as views and comments by Governments and intergovernmental organizations and decided to bring the draft articles to the attention of Member States and intergovernmental organizations for their consideration in such cases and to the extent they deemed appropriate.

[1009] In order to establish a global view of the main fields of public international law, the Commission, at its forty-eighth session (1996) established a general scheme of topics classified under 13 main fields. The list was not intended to be exhaustive and was to serve as a general reference. For the list, see *Yearbook ... 1996*, vol. II (Part Two), Annex II.

[1010] *Yearbook ... 1993*, vol. II (Part Two), para. 427. The Commission included this topic on its agenda at its forty-fifth session (1993), *ibid.*, para. 440. See also General Assembly resolution 48/31 of 9 December 1993. The title was subsequently changed to "Reservations to treaties", *Yearbook ... 1995*, vol. II (Part Two), para. 487 (*a*).

[1011] *Yearbook ... 1993*, vol. II (Part Two), para. 427. The Commission included this topic on its agenda at its forty-fifth session (1993), *ibid.*, para. 440. See also General Assembly resolution 48/31. The title was subsequently changed to "Nationality in relation to the succession of States", *Yearbook ... 1996*, vol. II (Part Two), para. 83. See also General Assembly resolution 51/160 of 11 December 1996.

[1012] *Yearbook ... 1995*, vol. II (Part Two), para. 501. Pursuant to General Assembly resolution 51/160, the Commission included this topic on its agenda at its forty-ninth session (1997), *Yearbook ... 1997*, vol. II (Part Two), paras. 169–171.

[1013] *Yearbook ... 1996*, vol. II (Part Two), para. 248.

[1014] *Ibid.* Pursuant to General Assembly resolution 51/160, the Commission included this topic on its agenda at its forty-ninth session (1997), *Yearbook ... 1997*, vol. II (Part Two), paras. 191–194.

[1015] *Yearbook ... 2000*, vol. II (Part Two), para. 729. The Commission included this topic on its agenda at its fifty-fourth session (2002), *Yearbook ... 2002*, vol. II (Part Two), para. 517 (*b*).

[1016] *Yearbook ... 2000*, vol. II (Part Two), para. 729. The Commission included this topic on its agenda at its fifty-fourth session (2002), *Yearbook ... 2002*, vol. II (Part Two), para. 518 (*a*).

[1017] *Yearbook ... 2000*, vol. II (Part Two), para. 729. The Commission included this topic on its agenda at its fifty-fourth session (2002), *Yearbook ... 2002*, vol. II (Part Two), para. 518 (*b*). The title was subsequently changed to "The fragmentation of international law: difficulties arising from the diversification and expansion of international law", see *ibid.*, para. 494.

[1018] *Yearbook ... 2000*, vol. II (Part Two), para. 729. The Commission included this topic on its agenda at its fifty-sixth session (2004), *Yearbook ... 2004*, vol. II (Part Two), para. 364.

[1019] *Yearbook ... 2000*, vol. II (Part Two), para. 729. The Commission included this topic on its agenda at its fifty-sixth session (2004), *Yearbook ... 2004*, vol. II (Part Two), para. 364.

[1020] *Ibid.*, paras. 362–363, and Annex.

[1021] See para. 257 above, and Annex I below.

[1022] *Ibid.*, and Annex II below.

[1023] *Ibid.*, and Annex III below. It would be recalled that a proposal entitled "International protection of persons in critical situations" (2004) was prepared by Mr. M. Kamto for the consideration of the Working Group on the long-term programme of work. Copies are on file with the Codification Division.

[1024] See para. 257 above, and Annex IV below.

[1025] *Ibid.*, and Annex V below. It would be recalled that a proposal entitled "Extra-territorial application of national legislation" (1993) was prepared by Mr. Pemmaraju Sreenivasa Rao for the consideration of the Working Group on the long-term programme of work. Copies are on file with the Codification Division.

mind the rules and regulations relating to the submission of documents in the United Nations as well as the heavy workload of the relevant services of the Organization, the Commission emphasized once more the importance that it attaches to the timely submission of reports by Special Rapporteurs in view of both their processing and their distribution sufficiently in advance to allow members to study the reports.

263. The Commission reiterated the importance of providing and making available all evidence of State practice and other sources of international law relevant to the performance of the Commission's function of progressive development and codification of international law. While the Commission is aware of the advantages of being as concise as possible, it strongly believes that an *a priori* limitation cannot be placed on the length of its documentation and research projects, in particular reports of Special Rapporteurs.

264. The Commission expressed its appreciation for the valuable assistance of the Codification Division in its substantive servicing of the Commission and in the preparation of research projects, by providing legal materials and their analysis. In particular, appreciation should be expressed for the extensive research reflected in the Secretariat memorandum on expulsion of aliens.

265. The Commission requested the Secretariat to provide it with information on publications that relate to the work of the Commission.

266. Taking into account the usefulness of the publication "Work of the International Law Commission" and the fact that the sixth edition was published in 2004, the Commission requested the Codification Division to prepare the seventh edition of the publication.

267. The Commission expressed its appreciation for the results of activity of its Secretariat in establishing the Commission's new website.[1026] The new site constitutes an invaluable resource for the Commission in undertaking its work and represents an information tool for research on the work of the Commission, thereby contributing to the overall strengthening of the teaching, study, dissemination and wider appreciation of international law. The Commission encouraged the Secretariat to continue to develop the electronic database on the work of the Commission (including the Commission's new website) and to explore further options for its electronic dissemination.

3. Meeting with United Nations human rights experts

268. In accordance with article 25, paragraph 1 of its Statute,[1027] the Commission recommended that the Secretariat, in consultation with the Special Rapporteur on reservations to treaties, organize a meeting during the fifty-ninth session of the Commission with United Nations experts in the field of human rights, including representatives from human rights treaty bodies, in order to hold a discussion on issues relating to reservations to human rights treaties.

4. Honoraria

269. The Commission reiterated once more its views concerning the question of honoraria, resulting from the adoption by the General Assembly of its resolution 56/272 of 27 March 2002, which were expressed in its previous reports.[1028] The Commission emphasized again that the above resolution especially affects the Special Rapporteurs, in particular those from developing countries, as it compromises support for their research work. The Commission urges the General Assembly to reconsider this matter, with a view to restoring, at this stage, the honoraria for Special Rapporteurs.

C. Date and place of the fifty-ninth session of the Commission

270. The Commission decided that the fifty-ninth session of the Commission be held in Geneva from 7 May to 8 June and 9 July to 10 August 2007.

D. Cooperation with other bodies

271. At its 2899th meeting, on 25 July 2006, Judge Rosalyn Higgins, President of the International Court of Justice, addressed the Commission and informed it of the Court's recent activities and of the cases currently before it.[1029] An exchange of views followed.

272. The Asian–African Legal Consultative Organization was represented at the present session of the Commission by its Secretary-General, Mr. Wafik Z. Kamil, who addressed the Commission at its 2898th meeting, on 21 July 2006.[1030] An exchange of views followed.

273. The Inter-American Juridical Committee was represented at the present session of the Commission by its Vice-President, Mr. Jean-Paul Hubert, who addressed the Commission at its 2904th meeting, on 3 August 2006.[1031] An exchange of views followed. The Commission also decided to express its congratulations to the Committee on the occasion of its centennial celebration and that it should be presented at the commemorative ceremony by M. João Baena Soares.

274. The European Committee on Legal Co-operation and the Committee of Legal Advisers on Public International Law of the Council of Europe were represented at the present session of the Commission by the Director General of Legal Affairs of the Council of Europe, Mr. Guy De Vel, who addressed the Commission at its 2904th meeting, on 3 August 2006.[1032] An exchange of views followed.

[1026] Located at www.un.org/law/ilc/.

[1027] Article 25, paragraph 1 of Statute provides: "The Commission may consult, if it considers it necessary, with any of the organs of the United Nations on any subject which is within the competence of that organ."

[1028] *Yearbook ... 2002*, vol. II (Part Two), pp. 102–103, paras. 525–531; *Yearbook ... 2003*, vol. II (Part Two), p. 101, para. 447; *Yearbook ... 2004*, vol. II (Part Two), pp. 120–121, para. 369; and *Yearbook ... 2005*, vol. II (Part Two), p. 92, para. 501.

[1029] This statement is recorded in the summary record of that meeting, *Yearbook ... 2006*, vol. I.

[1030] *Ibid.*

[1031] *Ibid.*

[1032] *Ibid.*

E. Representation at the sixty-first session of the General Assembly

275. The Commission decided that it should be represented at the sixty-first session of the General Assembly by its Chairperson, Mr. Guillaume Pambou-Tchivounda.

276. The Commission expressed regrets that due to budgetary constraints, it was not possible for a Special Rapporteur to attend the sixty-first session of the General Assembly.

F. International Law Seminar

277. Pursuant to General Assembly resolution 60/22, the forty-second session of the International Law Seminar was held at the Palais des Nations from 3 to 21 July 2006, during the present session of the Commission. The Seminar is intended for advanced students specializing in international law and for young professors or government officials pursuing an academic or diplomatic career or in posts in the civil service in their country.

278. Twenty-five participants of different nationalities, mostly from developing countries, were able to take part in the session.[1033] The participants in the Seminar observed plenary meetings of the Commission, attended specially arranged lectures, and participated in working groups on specific topics.

279. The Seminar was opened by Mr. Guillaume Pambou-Tchivounda, Chairperson of the Commission. Mr. Ulrich von Blumenthal, Senior Legal Adviser of the United Nations Office at Geneva, was responsible for the administration, organization and conduct of the Seminar, assisted by Mr. Vittorio Mainetti, Legal Consultant at the United Nations Office at Geneva.

280. The following lectures were given by members of the Commission: Mr. Giorgio Gaja: "Responsibility of international organizations"; Mr. Pemmaraju Sreenivasa Rao: "International Liability for injurious consequences arising out of acts not prohibited by international law"; Mr. Chusei Yamada: "Shared Natural Resource"; Mr. Zdzislaw Galicki: "*Aut dedere aut judicare*"; Mr. Ian Brownlie: "The Work of the ICJ"; Mr. John Dugard: "Diplomatic Protection"; Mr. Djamchid Momtaz: "The Darfour Case before the ICC"; Mr. Martti Koskenniemi: "Fragmentation of international law".

281. Lectures were also given by Mr. Vittorio Mainetti, Assistant to the Director of the International Law Seminar: "*Introduction to the Work of the ILC*"; Ms. Maria Isabel Torres-Cazorla, Professor of International Law at the University of Malaga: "*Unilateral Acts of States*"; Mr. Betrand Ramcharan, Former Deputy and Acting High Commissioner for Human Rights: "*The OHCHR and the New Human Rights Council*"; Ms. Jelena Pejic, Legal Adviser at the ICRC: "*Current Challenges to International Humanitarian Law*"; Ms. Brigitte Stern, Judge at the United Nations Administrative Tribunal: "*The work of the UNAT*". A meeting was also organized with Mr. Nicolas Michel, United Nations Legal Counsel, who addressed seminar participants and spoke about the activities of the Office of Legal Affairs.

282. Seminar participants were invited to visit the European Organization for Nuclear Research (CERN). The discussion focused on legal matters related to CERN. A morning was also devoted to the visit of the WTO, upon invitation of Mr. Georges Abi-Saab, Chairperson of the WTO Appellate Body, and Mr. Werner Zdouc, Director of the WTO Appellate Body Secretariat. The discussion focused on the WTO dispute settlement system and on the case law of the Appellate Body.

283. In addition, a Conference-Debate was organized in the premises of the UNHCR, in the presence of Mr. Helmut Buss, Chief, Legal Affairs Section, and Mr. Stevenson Wolfson, Senior Legal Officer, Protection Operations and Legal Advice Section. The discussion focused on the structure and mandate of the UNHCR and on refugee law.

284. Seminar participants also visited the OHCHR, at the Palais Wilson. After a briefing by Mr. Markus Schmidt (OHCHR) on the work of the Human Rights Committee, they attended the presentation of the report of the United Nations Interim Administration Mission in Kosovo (UNMIK) before the Human Rights Committee.

285. Each Seminar participant was assigned to one of three working groups on "*Fragmentation of international law*", "*Unilateral acts of States*" and "*Diplomatic protection*". The Chairperson of the Study Group and the Special Rapporteurs of the Commission for these subjects, Mr. Martti Koskenniemi, Mr. Víctor Rodriguez Cedeño and Mr. John Dugard, provided guidance for the working groups. Moreover, two former Seminar participants, Ms. Maria Isabel Torres-Cazorla, University of Malaga, and Ms. Annemarieke Künzli, University of Leiden, assisted in the organization and coordination of the working groups. The groups presented their findings to the Seminar. Each participant was also assigned to submit a written summary report on one of the lectures. A collection of the reports was compiled and distributed to all participants.

286. The Republic and Canton of Geneva offered its traditional hospitality to the participants with a guided visit of the Alabama Room at the City Hall followed by a reception.

287. Mr. Guillaume Pambou-Tchivounda, Chairperson of the Commission, Mr. Ulrich von Blumenthal, Director

---

[1033] The following persons participated in the forty-second session of the International Law Seminar: Mr. Andy Aron (Indonesia), Ms. Shakira Maria Bedoya-Sanchez (Peru), Mr. Kemoko Diakité (Senegal), Ms. Sasha Franklin (Trinidad and Tobago), Ms. Sandra García-Loredo (Mexico), Ms. Syuzanna Gevorgyan (Armenia), Mr. Henok Teferra (Ethiopia), Mr. Tamás Hoffmann (Hungary), Mr. Dan Oduor Juma (Kenya), Ms. Tomdwsam Kadjika (Togo), Mr. Andrey Kalinin (Russia), Ms. Chie Kojima (Japan), Ms. Sanaa Kourkmadi (Morocco), Mr. Emad Masalmeh (Jordan), Ms. Godelive Mbomakonga (Congo), Mr. Malefetsane Seth Moseme (Lesotho), Ms. Ilona Nieminen (Finland), Mr. Vasileios Pergantis (Greece), Mr. Dahai Qi (China), Mr. Yannick Radi (France), Mr. Emanuele Rebasti (Italy), Mr. Gustavo Ribeiro (Brazil), Ms. Myrtelle Rochette (Haiti), Mr. Visal Som (Cambodia) and Ms. Cassandra Steer (Australia). The Selection Committee, chaired by Mr. Jean-Marie Dufour (President of the Geneva International Academic Network), met on 9 May 2006 and selected 26 candidates out of 150 applications for participation in the Seminar. At the last minute, the twenty-sixth candidate selected was unable to attend.

of the Seminar, and Ms. Cassandra Steer, on behalf of the participants, addressed the Commission and the participants at the close of the Seminar. Each participant was presented with a certificate attesting to his or her participation in the forty-second session of the Seminar.

288. The Commission noted with particular appreciation that the Governments of Austria, China, Cyprus, Czech Republic, Finland, Germany, Ireland, Norway, Sweden and Switzerland had made or pledged voluntary contributions to the United Nations Trust Fund for the International Law Seminar. The financial situation of the Fund allowed awarding a sufficient number of fellowships to deserving candidates from developing countries in order to achieve adequate geographical distribution of participants. This year, full fellowships (travel and subsistence allowance) were awarded to 18 candidates and a partial fellowship (subsistence only) was awarded to one candidate.

289. Since 1965, year of the Seminar's inception, 952 participants, representing 157 nationalities, have taken part in the Seminar. Of them, 576 have received a fellowship.

290. The Commission stresses the importance it attaches to the Seminar, which enables young lawyers, especially from developing countries, to familiarize themselves with the work of the Commission and the activities of the many international organizations which have their headquarters in Geneva. The Commission recommends that the General Assembly should again appeal to States to make voluntary contributions in order to secure the holding of the Seminar in 2007 with as broad participation as possible.

291. The Commission noted with satisfaction that in 2006 comprehensive interpretation services were made available to the Seminar. It expresses the hope that the same services would be provided at the next session, within the constraints of existing resources.

Annex I

IMMUNITY OF STATE OFFICIALS FROM FOREIGN CRIMINAL JURISDICTION

(Roman A. Kolodkin)

A. A topical issue

1. The question of the immunity of State officials from foreign criminal jurisdiction has begun to attract greater attention in recent years. This is connected to a large extent with the growth of the concept of protection of human rights, a decline in willingness to tolerate gross violations of human rights, and efforts to combat terrorism, transnational crime, corruption and money laundering. Society no longer wishes to condone impunity on the part of those who commit these crimes, whatever their official position in the State. At the same time it can hardly be doubted that immunity of State officials is indispensable to keep stable inter-State relations.

2. Academic and public discussion as well as State practice, including domestic case law, in this area was given a substantial boost following consideration of the case of former Chilean dictator General Augusto Pinochet in the United Kingdom.[1] Between 1998 and 2001, more than 20 attempts were made to institute criminal proceedings in domestic courts against senior incumbent and former officials of foreign States.[2] Specifically, there were attempts to prosecute President Laurent-Désiré Kabila of the Democratic Republic of the Congo in Belgium and France in 1998; Israeli Prime Minister Ariel Sharon in Belgium in 2001–2002; President Muamar Al-Qadhafi of Libya, President Denis Sassou Nguesso of the Republic of the Congo and Cuban leader Fidel Castro in 2000–2001 in France; and former President of Chad Hissène Habré in Senegal in 2001.[3]

3. In 2002, the ICJ rendered a judgment in the case concerning the *Arrest Warrant of 11 April 2000*.[4] This judgment contains a valuable assessment of the state of international law in this field.

4. Currently before the ICJ is a case concerning *Certain Criminal Proceedings in France (Republic of the Congo* v. *France)*, the focus of which is also the immunity of senior State officials from foreign criminal jurisdiction. In 2003, the Court issued an order on the question of provisional measures which is of interest in the context of the matter under discussion.[5]

5. Following the above-mentioned judgment of the ICJ, a number of rulings were issued by national courts which are also of significance for the consideration of this issue. For example, in 2004 appeal courts in the United States rendered final decisions in cases involving President Robert Mugabe of Zimbabwe and former Chinese leader Jiang Zemin.[6] Although both of these judgements concerned immunity from civil jurisdiction, they are also of interest when considering the issue of immunity from foreign criminal jurisdiction.

6. It should be pointed out that the position of various State organs, including those representing the executive branch, on the issue under consideration from the viewpoint of international law was expressed on several occasions recently, both during consideration of the above-mentioned court cases and independently of judicial procedures.[7]

7. The issue of the immunity of State officials from foreign criminal jurisdiction most often provokes a significant public response when it is intended to indict such persons for gross violations of human rights (such as torture or genocide) and international humanitarian law. In relation

---

[1] See United Kingdom High Court of Justice, Queen's Bench Division (Divisional Court): *In Re Augusto Pinochet Ugarte*, ILM, vol. 38 (1999), pp. 68 *et seq.*, at pp. 68–90; United Kingdom House of Lords: *Regina* v. *Bartle and the Commissioner of Police for the Metropolis and Others–Ex Parte Pinochet*, *ibid.*, vol. 37 (1998), pp. 1302 *et seq.*, at pp. 1302–1339; and United Kingdom House of Lords: *Regina* v. *Bartle and the Commissioner of Police for the Metropolis and Others–Ex Parte Pinochet*, *ibid.*, vol. 38 (1999), pp. 581 *et seq.*, at pp. 581–663.

[2] See, for example, A. Borghi, *L'immunité des dirigeants politiques en droit international*, Basel, Helbing & Lichtenhahn, 2003, pp. 361–369.

[3] "Several cases that hit the headlines in the late 1990s raised the question of the limits of the immunity available to the heads of State or former heads of State" (P. Daillier and A. Pellet, *Droit international public (Nguyen Quoc Dinh)*, 7th ed., Paris, Librairie générale de droit et de jurisprudence, 2002, p. 453).

[4] *Arrest Warrant of 11 April 2000 (Democratic Republic of Congo* v. *Belgium), Judgment, I.C.J. Reports 2002*, p. 3. The text of the judgment is also available at www.icj-cij.org.

[5] *Certain Criminal Proceedings in France (Republic of the Congo* v. *France), Provisional Measure, Order of 17 June 2003, I.C.J. Reports 2003*, p. 102. The text of the order can also be found at www.icj-cij.org.

[6] *Tachiona* v. *United States*, 386 F.3d 205, 2004 U.S. App. LEXIS 20879 (2d Cir., 6 October 2004) (Tachiona II); *Wei Ye* v. *Jiang Zemin*, 383 F.3d 620, 2004 U.S. App. LEXIS 18944 (7th Cir., 8 September 2004). For commentaries on these cases, see, for example, S. Andrews, "U.S. courts rule on absolute immunity and inviolability of foreign Heads of State: the cases against Robert Mugabe and Jiang Zemin", The American Society of International Law, *Insights (November 2004)*, www.asil.org/insights_2004.cfm.

[7] For example, in 2005, in connection with a planned visit to the Russian Federation by Prime Minister Yulia Timoshenko of Ukraine, against whom criminal proceedings had been instituted in the Russian Federation long before her appointment to the post, the official position on the question of her immunity from criminal jurisdiction in the Russian Federation was publicly formulated by the Prosecutor-General of the Russian Federation. In particular, he pointed out that Prime Minister Yulia Timoshenko of Ukraine would have no problem if she wished to visit the Russian Federation, since senior State leaders—including Heads of Government—enjoy immunity. At the same time he added that the criminal proceedings against Ms. Timoshenko would be extended. It was only on 26 December 2006 that the Main Military Prosecution of the Russian Federation announced the closing of the criminal case against the former Prime Minister of Ukraine because of the expiration of the statute of limitations (http://genproc.gov.ru).

to such crimes, some States have recently been trying to exercise universal jurisdiction. However, this issue arises not only in connection with the exercise of universal jurisdiction in respect of international crimes (or crimes under international law), but also in the exercise of other types of jurisdiction. This happens, for example, when a State tries to prosecute under its own criminal law officials or former officials of another State who are suspected of crimes which are not connected with massive and gross violations of human rights but are nevertheless directed against the State exercising jurisdiction, or its nationals.

8. Originally, long before the issue of human rights became topical, the problem of the immunity of a State, its representatives or property arose from the conflict between, on the one hand, the rights of such a State stemming from the principle of the sovereign equality of States, and on the other hand, the rights of the State on whose territory these representatives or property were located, stemming from the principle of the full territorial jurisdiction of the latter. It seems that this conflict of rights and principle remains significant today. Indeed, it is obviously possible to say that it now displays new shades of meaning related to the development of universal and other types of domestic criminal jurisdiction, including extraterritorial jurisdiction, in the context of efforts to combat gross human rights violations, terrorism, transnational crime, money laundering, etc., against a background of globalization.

9. Nevertheless, despite the interrelation, issues of immunity and jurisdiction have an independent nature, and are regulated by different legal norms. As the ICJ pointed out in the above-mentioned judgment,

> rules governing the jurisdiction of national courts must be carefully distinguished from those governing jurisdictional immunities: jurisdiction does not imply absence of immunity, while absence of immunity does not imply jurisdiction. Thus, although various international conventions on the prevention and punishment of certain serious crimes impose on States obligations of prosecution or extradition, thereby requiring them to extend their criminal jurisdiction, such extension of jurisdiction in no way affects immunities under customary international law.[8]

In one of the recent publications on the topic it was also rightly noted that "a court faced with the violation of international law must first distinguish between jurisdictional immunities and the rules governing criminal jurisdictions of municipal courts".[9] Immunity is an obstacle to jurisdiction[10] and as such deserves a separate analysis.

10. The issue of the immunity of senior State officials from foreign criminal jurisdiction was examined by the Institute of International Law at the end of the last century. It adopted a resolution containing 16 articles[11] which, together with the corresponding *travaux préparatoires*, constitutes an important doctrinal source for the establishment of the content of international law in this field.

11. In 2004, by its resolution 59/38 of 2 December 2004, the United Nations General Assembly adopted the United Nations Convention on Jurisdictional Immunities of States and Their Property. Under article 2, paragraph 1 (*b*) (i) and (iv), of the Convention, the term "State" includes "various organs of government" and also "representatives of the State acting in that capacity". At the same time, article 3, paragraph 2, of the Convention states that it is "without prejudice to privileges and immunities accorded under international law to heads of State *ratione personae*". It is not entirely clear what this means for the immunity *ratione personae* of other officials and, in particular, such senior officials as Heads of Government and Ministers for Foreign Affairs.[12] However, in any case, paragraph 2 of the above-mentioned resolution states that the General Assembly agrees with the general understanding reached in the Ad Hoc Committee on Jurisdictional Immunities of States and Their Property that the United Nations Convention on Jurisdictional Immunities of States and Their Property does not cover criminal proceedings.[13] The Chairperson of the Ad Hoc Committee, when presenting its report at the fifty-ninth session of the General Assembly, pointed out that the Convention did not apply where there was a special immunity regime, including immunities *ratione personae* (*lex specialis*).[14]

12. The charters and statutes of *ad hoc* international criminal tribunals (Nuremberg, Tokyo, the former Yugoslavia, Rwanda) and the Statute of the International Criminal Court contain provisions which deprive State officials, including senior State officials, of immunity from the jurisdiction of these international organs.[15] However, here it is a question of international criminal jurisdiction.[16]

[8] *Arrest Warrant of 11 April 2000* (see footnote 4 above), pp. 24–25, para. 59.

[9] E. K. Bankas, *The State Immunity Controversy in International Law: Private Suits Against Sovereign States in Domestic Courts*, Berlin, Springer, 2005, p. 296.

[10] It was stated in the draft article 2 of the Draft Declaration on Rights and Duties of States: "Every State has the right to exercise jurisdiction over its territory and over all persons and things therein, subject to the immunities recognized by international law" (*Yearbook ... 1949*, p. 287, and annex to General Assembly resolution 375 (IV) of 6 December 1949; see also *The Work of the International Law Commission*, 6th ed., vol. I (United Nations publication, Sales No. E.04.V.6), Annex IV, p. 262).

[11] *Yearbook of the Institute of International Law*, Session of Vancouver, 2000–2001, vol. 69 (2001), Paris, Pedone, 2001, pp. 442–709.

[12] The Commission's commentary to article 3 of the draft articles adopted by the Commission in 1991 states the following: "Paragraph 2 is designed to include an express reference to the immunities extended under existing international law to foreign sovereigns or other heads of State in their private capacities, *ratione personae*. Jurisdictional immunities of States in respect of sovereigns or other heads of State acting as State organs or State representatives are dealt with under article 2. Article 2, paragraph 1 (*b*) (i) and (v) [subparagraph (iv) in the Convention] covers the various organs of the Government of a State and State representatives, including heads of State ... The reservation of article 3, paragraph 2, therefore refers exclusively to the private acts or personal immunities and privileges recognized and accorded in the practice of States, without any suggestion that their status should in any way be affected by the present articles. The existing customary law is left untouched" (*Yearbook ... 1991*, vol. II (Part Two), p. 22).

[13] The recommendation on this subject appears in paragraph 14 of the Ad Hoc Committee's report, *Official Records of the General Assembly, Fifty-ninth Session, Supplement No. 22* (A/59/22).

[14] *Ibid., Sixth Committee, 13th meeting* (A/C.6/59/SR.13), para. 37.

[15] Article 7 of the Charter of the International Military Tribunal (see United Nations, *Treaty Series*, vol. 82, No. 251, p. 288); article 6 of the Charter of the International Military Tribunal for the Far East (see *Documents on American Foreign Relations*, vol. VIII, Princeton University Press, 1948, p. 354); article 7, paragraph 2, of the Statute of the International Tribunal for the Former Yugoslavia (see S/25704, Annex); article 6, paragraph 2, of the Statute of the International Tribunal for Rwanda (see Security Council resolution 955 (1994) of 8 November 1994, Annex); and article 27 of the Rome Statute of the International Criminal Court.

[16] In the *Arrest Warrant* case, the ICJ, it seems, drew a clear distinction between the situation as regards the immunity of senior State

13. As regards the immunity of State officials from foreign national criminal jurisdiction, the corresponding provisions on this subject of the 1961 Vienna Convention on Diplomatic Relations, the 1963 Vienna Convention on Consular Relations, the 1969 Convention on special missions, the 1973 Convention on the prevention and punishment of crimes against internationally protected persons, including diplomatic agents, and the 1975 Vienna Convention on the Representation of States in Their Relations with International Organizations of a Universal Character are well known. However, these instruments concern only some specific aspects of the issue under consideration. The principal source of international law in relation to the immunity of State officials from foreign criminal jurisdiction is international custom.

B. The topic of immunity of State officials in the work of the International Law Commission

14. The Commission has addressed this topic more than once in one form or another. This took place during work on: the Draft Declaration on Rights and Duties of States;[17] the draft Principles of International Law Recognized in the Charter of the Nürnberg Tribunal;[18] the draft code of offences against the peace and security of mankind of 1954;[19] the draft Code of Crimes against the Peace and Security of Mankind of 1996;[20] the draft articles on diplomatic[21] and consular[22] relations and immunities; the draft articles on special missions;[23] the draft articles on the representation of States in their relations with international organizations;[24] the draft articles on the prevention and punishment of crimes against diplomatic agents and other internationally protected persons;[25] and, as already mentioned, draft articles on jurisdictional immunities of States and their property.[26]

15. However, the Commission has never examined the issue of the immunity of State officials from foreign criminal jurisdiction in a separate and focused manner.[27]

officials from international criminal jurisdiction, on the one hand, and from domestic criminal jurisdiction on the other (see *Arrest Warrant of 11 April 2000* (footnote 4 above), paras. 56–58).

[17] See in particular draft article 2 and the commentary thereto (footnote 10 above).

[18] See in particular draft principle III and the commentary thereto, *Yearbook ... 1950*, vol. II, p. 192.

[19] See in particular draft article 3 and the commentary thereto, *Yearbook ...1954*, vol. II, pp. 119–120.

[20] See in particular draft article 7 and the commentary thereto, *Yearbook ... 1996*, vol. II (Part Two), pp. 26–27.

[21] *Yearbook ... 1958*, vol. II, pp. 89–105.

[22] *Yearbook ... 1961*, vol. II, pp. 89–128.

[23] See in particular draft article 21 and the commentary thereto, *Yearbook ... 1967*, vol. II, p. 359.

[24] *Yearbook ...1971*, vol. I, pp. 287 *et seq.*; *Yearbook ... 1971*, vol. II (Part Two), pp. 101–110.

[25] *Yearbook ... 1972*, vol. II, pp. 309–323.

[26] See footnote 12 above.

[27] At a certain stage it was proposed to include in the draft articles on jurisdictional immunities of States and their property a provision on the immunity of sovereigns or Heads of State from criminal jurisdiction. See in particular draft article 25 in the seventh report of the Special Rapporteur on this topic, Mr. Sompong Sucharitkul, *Yearbook ... 1985*, vol. II (Part One), pp. 44–45.

C. Should the International Law Commission examine the issue of the immunity of State officials from foreign criminal jurisdiction?

16. It seems that State practice as well as the rulings of domestic courts, the above-mentioned conventions, the judgment of the ICJ in the *Arrest Warrant of 11 April 2000* case and the work of the Commission hitherto bear witness to the fact that customary international law in this field exists. Although there is a variety of views on the subject, this conclusion, in our opinion, is also confirmed by international legal doctrine.[28]

17. It is undoubtedly important that State officials, and first and foremost senior State officials, who have committed crimes, especially massive and gross violations of human rights or international humanitarian law, should bear responsibility, including criminal responsibility. It is important that, where the rights of its nationals have been violated by criminal acts, a State should be able to exercise its criminal jurisdiction in respect of the suspected perpetrators. However, it is also crucially important that inter-State relations based on generally recognized principles of international law, and in particular the principle of the sovereign equality of States, should be stable and predictable, and, correspondingly, that officials acting on behalf of their States should be independent *vis-à-vis* other States.

18. The Commission could make a contribution to ensuring a proper balance between these concepts through the codification and progressive development of international law, if it examined the issue of the immunity of State officials from foreign criminal jurisdiction and formulated its vision of the content of international law in this area.

D. Possible scope of consideration of the proposed topic

19. When analysing this topic in the Commission, it would be appropriate to examine the following issues in particular.

(1) The discussion should cover only immunity from domestic jurisdiction. The legal regime of this institution, as noted above, is distinct from the legal regime of immunity from international jurisdiction.

It is suggested that the analysis should be limited to issues of immunity from criminal jurisdiction. (At the same time, one might think about adding issues of immunity *ratione personae* from foreign civil and administrative jurisdiction to issues of immunity from foreign criminal jurisdiction, as, for example, in the above-mentioned draft articles of the Institute of International Law.[29])

Of course, the focus should be immunity from foreign jurisdiction (it is well known that domestic legal systems provide for the immunity of certain State officials from the jurisdiction of the same State) and immunity under international and not domestic law.

[28] A short list of publications on this topic is attached.

[29] See footnote 11 above.

(2) It will perhaps be necessary first to examine the concept of immunity (including the issue of immunity *ratione materiae* and immunity *ratione personae*) and the concept of criminal jurisdiction (including the issue of the principles on which it is based) for the purposes of this topic, and the relationship between them. There is a view that consideration of the issue of jurisdiction must precede consideration of the issue of immunity, since, in particular, the issue of immunity from jurisdiction arises only when the State has the requisite jurisdiction.[30]

It is worth defining the Commission's position concerning the nature of immunity—whether it is procedural or material in nature—and also, perhaps, concerning the question of whether it is peremptory in nature. The study of this latter question may be useful in the context of examination of the relations between immunity of State officials from foreign criminal jurisdiction and rules prohibiting torture, genocide, etc., which have the status of *jus cogens*.[31]

Here it would be worth examining the question of the relations between jurisdictional immunity and other legal doctrines which have similar consequences, such as the doctrine of the "act of State" and the doctrine of "non-justiciability".[32]

It is also desirable to look at the relations between immunity of State officials and immunity of the State itself and diplomatic immunity.

It is also necessary to analyse the relations between the concepts of "jurisdictional immunity", "inviolability", "immunity from procedural enforcement" and "immunity from execution".

It would be important to include in the final product of the Commission's work on the topic (whatever form it might take) provisions relating to the differences between the institution of immunity of officials from jurisdiction, on the one hand, and the institution of criminal responsibility, on the other. Immunity does not mean impunity.[33]

(3) At the beginning of the study it is important to examine the question of the foundation, the rational root of the immunity of State officials from foreign criminal jurisdiction. For example, does immunity derive only from a functional necessity, i.e. is it linked exclusively to the functions performed by State officials? Or is it not only the functional component which is significant but also, for example, the fact that the official is acting on behalf of a sovereign State, which participates on an equal footing with other States in international relations, in ensuring the stability in which all States have an interest? Is the immunity of the officials of a State a manifestation of the rights of that State, stemming from its sovereignty? Or is the immunity of State officials from foreign criminal jurisdiction the result of the consent of a State possessing such jurisdiction not to exercise it in view of the acknowledged practical need to respect international courtesy?[34] Can the foundation of the immunity of State officials be the same as the foundation of the immunity of the State itself?[35] The logic governing consideration of this topic will depend to a large extent on the concept that is behind the immunity of State officials from foreign criminal jurisdiction.

(4) It is necessary to define which State officials enjoy this immunity. The judgment of the ICJ in *Arrest Warrant of 11 April 2000* refers to the immunity of Ministers for Foreign Affairs and Heads of State and Government, and these persons are cited as examples of senior State officials who enjoy immunity from foreign jurisdiction.[36] The draft articles of the Institute of International Law speak only of Heads of State and Government.

The Commission may try to examine the issues of immunity of senior State officials, including Heads of State and Government and Ministers for Foreign Affairs (in such cases, however, it must bear in mind the difficulties which will obviously arise in defining precisely which officials fall in the category of senior State officials). The other option is to examine the question of the immunity not only of senior but also of any other State officials.

However, it would seem to be better for the Commission to confine itself at first to Heads of State and Government and Ministers for Foreign Affairs. At least in respect of this group of officials a sufficient body of State (including judicial) practice and doctrine exists.

The issue of immunity must be examined in respect of both present officials and former officials.

---

[30] See in particular *Arrest Warrant of 11 April 2000* (footnote 4 above), Joint Separate Opinion of Judges Higgins, Kooijmans and Buergenthal, paras. 3–5.

[31] On the question of these relations, see, for example the judgement on the merits delivered by the Grand Chamber in *Al-Adsani* v. *The United Kingdom, Application no. 35763/97, Judgement of 21 November 2001*, Grand Chamber, European Court of Human Rights, *Reports of Judgments and Decisions 2001-XI*, paras. 57–67; and especially the Joint Dissenting Opinion of Judges Rozakis and Caflisch, joined by Judges Wildhaber, Costa, Cabral Barreto and Vajić.

[32] "It is, however, important to bear in mind that state immunity may appear as a doctrine of inadmissibility or non-justiciability rather than an immunity in a strict sense" (I. Brownlie, *Principles of Public International Law*, 5th ed., Oxford University Press, 1998, p. 326). See also, for example, A. Bianchi, "*Immunity versus human rights: the Pinochet case*", *European Journal of International Law*, vol. 10, No. 2 (1999), pp. 266–270.

[33] See on this subject *Arrest Warrant of 11 April 2000* (footnote 4 above), para. 60.

[34] Caplan, for example, considers the foundation of State immunity to be the manifestation of "practical courtesy" on the part of the State possessing territorial jurisdiction (see L. M. Caplan, "State immunity, human rights and *jus cogens*: a critique of the normative hierarchy theory", AJIL, vol. 97, No. 4 (2003), pp. 741 *et seq.*, at pp. 745–757).

[35] Concerning the foundations of immunity, including the immunity of officials, in the practice of the ICJ, see for example V. S. Vereshchetin and C. J. Le Mon, "Immunities of individuals under international law in the jurisprudence of the International Court of Justice", *The Global Community: Yearbook of International Law and Jurisprudence, 2004*, vol. I, pp. 77–89.

[36] "[I]n international law it is firmly established that, as also diplomatic and consular agents, certain holders of high-ranking office in a State, such as Head of State, Head of Government and Minister for Foreign Affairs, enjoy immunities from jurisdiction in other States, both civil and criminal" (*Arrest Warrant of 11 April 2000* (footnote 4 above), para. 51).

In addition, it would also be worth examining the issue of the immunity of members of the families of those officials whose immunity will be the subject of consideration by the Commission.

(5) It seems appropriate to analyse the relevance in the context of this topic of the issue of recognition of foreign States and Governments and their Heads. For example, in the case of *M. A. Noriega*, the Court of Appeals pointed out that "[t]he district court rejected Noriega's head-of-state immunity claim because the United States government never recognized Noriega as Panama's legitimate, constitutional ruler".[37]

(6) The central issue in this topic is the scope or limits of immunity of State officials from foreign criminal jurisdiction. Here a number of questions can be identified.

First, the period of time during which a person enjoys immunity (the period when he or she occupies the corresponding post; the period after he or she leaves the post).

Secondly, the acts of the State official covered by immunity from foreign criminal jurisdiction. Acts in an official capacity, acts in a private capacity. Criteria for distinguishing between these categories of acts. Acts carried out before, during and after the occupation of a post. Here it is also appropriate to examine the question of whether criminally punishable acts, in particular international crimes, can be regarded as having been committed in an official capacity.[38]

Thirdly, does the solution of the question of the immunity of a State official from foreign criminal jurisdiction depend on whether he or she committed the crime in the territory of the State exercising jurisdiction, or outside it? Does it depend on whether, at the time of the exercise of foreign criminal jurisdiction, he or she is in the territory of the State exercising jurisdiction, or outside it?

Fourthly, does immunity depend on the nature of the presence of the official in the territory of the foreign State exercising jurisdiction (official visit, private visit, exile, etc.)?

Fifthly, does the immunity of a State official from foreign criminal jurisdiction signify that a foreign State cannot pursue any criminal procedures in relation to this person, or does it preclude only specific criminal procedures (specifically, only those procedural acts which directly affect the person enjoying immunity, and restrict his or her ability to perform his or her official functions)? For example, judging by the order on provisional measures in *Certain Criminal Proceedings in France (Republic of the Congo v. France),* the ICJ does not consider that the immunity of a Head of State from foreign criminal jurisdiction is an obstacle to any criminal procedures pursued by a foreign State.[39]

Sixthly, does immunity depend on the gravity of the crime of which the official is suspected? This question, which is obviously crucial, can also be considered as the question of whether exceptions exist to immunity.

The view that immunity, including the immunity of current State officials, does not exist in the case of the most serious crimes under international law was set out, for example, in the House of Lords in the United Kingdom during consideration of the Pinochet case and, in considerable detail, in the Belgian memorandum in Arrest Warrant of 11 April 2000 before the ICJ.[40] It is even held that there is a principle of "absence of immunity" from foreign criminal jurisdiction in respect of international crimes.[41]

However, in the opinion of the ICJ, immunity is an obstacle to the exercise of foreign criminal jurisdiction in respect of a current senior State official irrespective of the gravity of the crime of which he or she is suspected.[42] Where current Heads of State and Government are concerned, this view was also reflected in the draft articles prepared by the Institute of International Law.[43]

Note that the issues relating to the scope or limits of the immunity must be considered separately in relation to current officials and former officials.

(7) If it is decided that the immunity of a State official from foreign criminal jurisdiction does not include the inviolability of this official, immunity from procedural enforcement and immunity from execution, the question arises whether these topics should also be considered in the framework of the subject. Here it would be possible to consider the question of immunity from procedural enforcement and execution in respect of the property of an official located in the territory of the foreign State exercising criminal jurisdiction.

---

[37] *United States* v. *Noriega* (117 F.3d 1206; 47 Fed. R. Evid. Serv. (Callaghan) 786; 11 Fla. L. Weekly Fed. C 103).

[38] See, for example, *Arrest Warrant of 11 April 2000* (footnote 4 above), Joint Separate Opinion of Judges Higgins, Kooijmans and Buergenthal, para. 85.

[39] In any case, the Court did not consider those criminal procedures in respect of officials of the Republic of the Congo which were applied in France, and the cessation of which was demanded by the Republic of the Congo, as violating its rights arising from the immunity of those persons. Accordingly, the Court did not consider it necessary for these procedures to be halted (see *Certain Criminal Proceedings in France (Republic of the Congo* v. *France), Provisional Measure, Order of 17 June 2003, I.C.J. Reports 2003*, p. 102, at pp. 109–110, paras. 30–35).

[40] United Kingdom House of Lords: *Regina* v. *Bartle and the Commissioner of Police for the Metropolis and Others–Ex Parte Pinochet* (see footnote 1 above), pp. 581–663, at p. 651 (Lord Millett) and p. 661 (Lord Phillips of Worth Matravers); *Arrest Warrant of 11 April 2000 (Democratic Republic of Congo* v. *Belgium)*, Counter Memorial of the Kingdom of Belgium, 28 September 2001, www.icj-cij.org, paras. 3.5.10–3.5.150. See also, for example, A. Watts, "The legal position in international law of Heads of States, Heads of Governments and Foreign Ministers", *Collected Courses of the Hague Academy of International Law, 1994-III*, vol. 247, pp. 82–84 (it must be borne in mind, however, that this section of Sir Arthur Watts's lecture is devoted to the international responsibility of the Head of State). See also *Arrest warrant of 11 April 2000, Judgment* (footnote 4 above), Dissenting Opinion of Judge Al-Khasawneh, paras. 5–7.

[41] Borghi, *op. cit.* (footnote 2 above), pp. 287–331.

[42] *Arrest Warrant of 11 April 2000, Judgment* (footnote 4 above), paras. 56–61.

[43] See footnote 11 above. See in particular article 2 of the resolution adopted by the Institute.

(8) It will be necessary to examine the question of waiver of immunity. It is obvious that it is not the official but the State which has the right to waive his or her immunity. The question concerns which organ of State (which law is applicable in determining it—domestic or international?) and in what manner the State has the right to waive the immunity of its official (explicit waiver, implied waiver, *ad hoc* waiver, waiver of a general nature, for example, through the conclusion of an international treaty, etc.).

(9) It is necessary to consider the question of the form which the final product of the Commission's work on the proposed topic should take.

If the Commission decides to draw up draft articles, then it would be appropriate to consider whether to include in them provisions relating to the following two issues:

(10) *Lex specialis*. It would seem that any draft articles should contain a provision defining their relationship with special treaty regimes which provide for a different manner of regulating the issue at hand.

(11) Dispute settlement. The Commission may consider it desirable to set up a special regime for the settlement of disputes between governments regarding the immunity of State officials from foreign criminal jurisdiction.

Selected bibliography

AKANDE, D. "International law immunities and the International Criminal Court", AJIL, vol. 98 (2004), 407–433.

ALEBEEK, R. VAN. "The *Pinochet* case: international human rights law on trial", BYBIL, vol. 71 (2000), 29–70.

AMBOS, K. "Impunity and international criminal law: a case study on Colombia, Peru, Bolivia and Argentina", *Human Rights Law Journal*, vol. 18, No. 1–4 (1997), 1–15.

ASCENSIO, H., E. Decaux and A. Pellet (eds.). *Droit international pénal*, Paris, Pedone, 2000, 26–27, 84–87, 183–237.

AVELLÁN HONRUBIA, V. "La responsabilité international de l'individu et les principes généraux du droit international", *Collected Courses of the Hague Academy of International Law, 1999*, vol. 280 (2000), 219–230.

BAKER, B. "Twilight of impunity for Africa's presidential criminals", *Third World Quarterly*, vol. 25, No. 8 (2004), 1487–1499.

BANKAS, E. K. *The State Immunity Controversy in International Law: Private Suits Against Sovereign States in Domestic Courts*, Heidelberg/Berlin, Springer, 2005.

BARKER, J. C. "State immunity, diplomatic immunity and act of State: a triple protection against legal action?", *International and Comparative Law Quarterly*, vol. 47 (1998), 950–958.

BASS, P. E. "Ex-Head of State immunity: a proposed statutory tool of foreign policy", *Yale Law Journal*, vol. 97, No. 2 (1987), 299–319.

BASSIOUNI, Ch. *Introduction to International Criminal Law*, Ardsley (New York). Transnational Publishers, 2003, 64–89, 712–715.

BIANCHI, A. "Immunity versus human rights: the *Pinochet* case", *European Journal of International Law*, vol. 10, No. 2 (1999), 237–277.

———. "Serious violations of human rights and foreign States' accountability before municipal courts", in L. Ch. Vohrah *et al.* (eds.), *Man's Inhumanity to Man: Essays on International Law in Honour of Antonio Cassese*, The Hague/London/New York, Kluwer Law International, 2003, 149–181.

BOISTER, N. and R. Burchill. "The implications of the Pinochet decisions for the extradition or prosecution of former South African Heads of State for crimes committed under apartheid", *African Journal of International and Comparative Law/Revue Africaine de droit international et comparé*, vol. 11 (1999), 619–637.

BOJIC, M. "Immunity of High State Representatives with regard to international crimes: are Heads of State, Heads of Government and Foreign Ministers still untouchable?", Master thesis, Faculty of Law, University of Lund, 2005.

BORGHI, A. *L'immunité des dirigeants politiques en droit international*, Geneva, Helbing & Lichtenhahn, 2003.

BOUTRUCHE, T. "L'affaire Pinochet ou l'internationalisation balbutiante de la justice", *L'Observateur des Nations Unies*, vol. 6 (1999), 77–103.

BRÖHMER, J. *State Immunity and the Violation of Human Rights*, The Hague/Boston/London, Martinus Nijhoff, 1997, 29–32.

BULLIER, A. J. "Y a-t-il encore une immunité pour chefs d'État et chefs de guerre en Afrique?", *Afrique contemporaine*, vol. 194 (2000), 47–51.

CAFLISCH, L. "Immunité de juridiction et respect des droits de l'homme", in L. Boisson De Chazournes and V. Gowlland-Debbas (eds.), *The International Legal System in Quest of Equity and Universality: Liber Amicorum Georges Abi-Saab*, The Hague/London/Boston, Martinus Nijhoff, 2001, 651–676.

CALLAN, E. M. "In re Mr. and Mrs. Doe: witnesses before the Grand Jury and the Head of State immunity doctrine", *New York University Journal of International Law and Politics*, vol. 22 (1989), 117–139.

CAPLAN, L. M. "State immunity, human rights, and *jus cogens*: a critique of the normative hierarchy theory", AJIL, vol. 97 (2003), 741–781.

CARA, J.-Y. "L'affaire Pinochet devant la Chambre des Lords", *Annuaire français de droit international*, vol. 45 (1999), 72–100.

CASEY, L. A. and D. B. Rivkin, JR. "The limits of legitimacy: the Rome Statute's unlawful application to non-State parties", *Virginia Journal of International Law*, vol. 44 (2003–2004), 63–89.

CASSESE, A. *International Criminal Law*, New York, Oxford University Press, 2003, 264–274.

———. "Peut-on poursuivre des hauts dirigeants des États pour des crimes internationaux? À propos de l'affaire *Congo c/ Belgique* (C.I.J.)", *Revue de science criminelle et de droit pénal comparé*, vol. 3 (2002), 479–499.

———. and M. Delmas-Marty, *Juridictions nationales et crimes internationaux*, Paris, Presses Universitaires de France, 2002.

CHINKIN, C. M., *et al.* "*In re Pinochet*", AJIL, vol. 93 (1999), 690–711.

COMMITTEE OF LEGAL ADVISERS ON PUBLIC INTERNATIONAL LAW. *Meeting Report*, 23rd meeting (Strasbourg, 4–5 March 2002).

COSNARD, M. "Les immunités du chef d'Etat", in Société française pour le droit international, *Colloque de Clermont-Ferrand: le chef d'État et le droit international*, Paris, Pedone, 2002, 189–268.

———. "Quelques observations sur les décisions de la Chambre des Lords du 25 novembre 1998 et du 24 mars 1999 dans l'affaire Pinochet", *Revue générale de droit international public* (1999–2), 309–328.

COT, J.-P. "Éloge de l'indécision. La Cour et la compétence universelle", *Revue belge de droit international*, vol. 35 (2002), 546–553.

DANILENKO, G. M. "The Statute of the International Criminal Court and third States", *Michigan Journal of International Law*, vol. 21, No. 3 (2000), 445–494.

DAY, A. "Crimes against humanity as a nexus of individual and State responsibility: why the ICJ got *Belgium* v. *Congo* wrong", *Berkeley Journal of International Law*, vol. 22 (2004), 489–512.

DE SENA, P. "Immunity of State organs and defence of superior orders as an obstacle to the domestic enforcement of international human rights", in B. Conforti and F. Francioni (eds), *Enforcing International Human Rights in Domestic Courts*, The Hague, Martinus Nijhoff, 1997, 367–403.

———. *et al.* (eds.): "Italian practice relating to international law: judicial decisions", *Italian Yearbook of International Law*, vol. 8 (1988–1992), 43–57.

DE SMET, L. and F. Naert. "Making or breaking international law? An international law analysis of Belgium's Act concerning the punishment of grave breaches of international humanitarian law", *Revue belge de droit international*, vol. 35 (2002), 471–511.

DE SMET, S. "The immunity of Heads of States in US courts after the decision of the International Court of Justice", *Nordic Journal of International Law*, vol. 72, No. 3 (2003), 313–339.

DELLAPENNA, J. W. "Head-of-state immunity—Foreign Sovereign Immunities Act—suggestion by the Department of State", AJIL, vol. 88 (1994), 528–532.

DOMINICÉ, Ch. "Quelques observations sur l'immunité de juridiction pénale de l'ancien chef d'Etat", *Revue générale de droit international public* (1999–2), 297–308.

DU PLESSIS, M. and S. Bosch. "Immunities and universal jurisdiction—the World Court steps in (or on?)", *South African Yearbook of International Law*, vol. 28 (2003), 246–262.

DUPUY, P.-M. "Crimes et immunités, ou dans quelle mesure la nature des premiers empêche l'exercice des secondes", *Revue générale de droit international public* (1999-2), 289–296.

FASSBENDER, B. "*S.* v. *Berlin Court of Appeal and District Court of Berlin-Tiergarten*", AJIL, vol. 92, No. 1 (1998), 74–78.

FENET, A. "La responsabilité pénale internationale du chef d'État", *Revue générale de droit*, vol. 32 (2002), 585–615.

FITZGERALD, A. "The Pinochet case: Head of State immunity within the United States", *Whittier Law Review*, vol. 22, No. 4 (2001), 987–1028.

FLAUSS, J.-F. "Droit des immunités et protection internationale des droits de l'homme", *Revue suisse de droit international et de droit européen*, vol. 10 (2000), 299–324.

FOX, H. "The first *Pinochet* case: immunity of a former Head of State", *International and Comparative Law Quarterly*, vol. 48 (1999), 207–216.

———. "The resolution of the Institute of International Law on the immunities of Heads of State and Government", *International and Comparative Law Quarterly*, vol. 51 (2002), 119–125.

———. "Some aspects of immunity from criminal jurisdiction of the State and its officials: the *Blaškić* case", in L. Ch. Vohrah *et al.* (eds.), *Man's Inhumanity to Man: Essays on International Law in Honour of Antonio Cassese*, The Hague/London/New York, Kluwer Law International, 2003, 297–307.

———. *The Law of State Immunity*, Oxford/New York, Oxford University Press, 2002.

GAETA, P. "Official capacity and immunities", in A.Cassese *et al.* (eds.) *The Rome Statute of the International Criminal Court: a Commentary*, vol. I, New York, Oxford University Press, 2002, 975–1002.

GARNETT, R. "State immunity triumphs in the European Court of Human Rights", *The Law Quarterly Review*, vol. 118 (2002), 367–373.

GEORGE, S. V. "Head-of-State immunity in the United States courts: still confused after all these years", *Fordham Law Review*, vol. 64, No. 3 (1995), 1051–1088.

GROSSCUP, S. "The trial of Slobodan Milosevic: the demise of Head of State immunity and the specter of victor's justice", *Denver Journal of International Law and Policy*, vol. 32, No. 2 (2004), 355–381.

HENZELIN, M. "L'immunité pénale des chefs d'État en matière financière. Vers une exception pour les actes de pillage de ressources et de corruption?", *Revue suisse de droit international et de droit européen*, vol. 12 (2002), 179–212.

HICKEY, Ch. E. "The dictator, drugs and diplomacy by indictment: Head-of-State immunity in *United States* v. *Noriega*", *Connecticut Journal of International Law*, vol. 4, No. 3 (1989), 729–765.

HOPKINS, J. "Immunity–Head of foreign State", *The Cambridge Law Journal*, vol. 57 (1998), 4–6.

———. "Former Head of foreign State–Extradition–Immunity", *The Cambridge Law Journal*, vol. 58, No. 3 (1999), 461–465.

HOPKINS, K. "The International Court of Justice and the question of sovereign immunity: why the *Yerodia case* is an unfortunate ruling for the development of public international law", *South African Yearbook of International Law*, vol. 27 (2002), 256–263.

INSTITUT DE DROIT INTERNATIONAL. "L'immunité de juridiction et d'exécution forcée des États étrangers", in H. Wehberg (ed.), *Tableau général des résolutions (1873–1956)*, Basel, Editions juridiques et sociologiques, 1957, 14–18.

———. *Annuaire*, vol. 69 (2000–2001), *Session of Vancouver, 2001*, Paris, Pedone, 441–709.

INTERNATIONAL LAW ASSOCIATION. "Final report on the exercise of universal jurisdiction in respect of gross human rights offences", *Report of the Sixty-ninth Conference held in London 25–29th July 2000*, London, 2000, 403–431.

JACKSON, V. C. "Suing the Federal Government: sovereignty, immunity, and judicial independence", *George Washington International Law Review*, vol. 35 (2003), 521–609.

KAMTO, M. "Une troublante 'Immunité totale' du ministre des Affaires étrangères (Sur un aspect de l'arrêt du 14 février 2002 dans l'affaire relative au *Mandat d'arrêt du 11 avril 2000*)", *Revue belge de droit international*, vol. 35 (2002), 518–530.

KITTICHAISAREE, K. *International Criminal Law*, New York, Oxford University Press, 2001, 43–63.

KLINGBERG, V. "(Former) Heads of State before international(ized) criminal courts: the case of Charles Taylor before the Special Court for Sierra Leone", *German Yearbook of International Law*, vol. 46 (2003), 537–564.

KNOOPS, G.-J. *Defenses in Contemporary International Criminal Law*, New York, Transnational Publishers, 2001, 70–72.

KOFELE-KALE, N. *International Law of Responsibility for Economic Crimes: Holding Heads of State and Other High Ranking State Officials Individually Liable for Acts of Fraudulent Enrichment*, The Hague/London/Boston, Kluwer Law International, 1995.

KOIVU, V. "Head-of-State immunity v. individual criminal responsibility under international law", *Finnish Yearbook of International Law*, vol. 12 (2001), 305–330.

KOLLER, D. S. "Immunities of Foreign Ministers: paragraph 61 of the *Yerodia* judgment as it pertains to the Security Council and the International Criminal Court", *American University International Law Review*, vol. 20, No. 1 (2004–2005), 7–42.

LABUSCHAGNE, J. M. T. "Diplomatic immunity: a jurisdictional or substantive-law defence?", *South African Yearbook of International Law*, vol. 27 (2002), 291–295.

LANSING, P. and J. King Perry. "Should former government leaders be subject to prosecution after their term in office? The case of South African President P. W. Botha", *California Western International Law Journal*, vol. 30, No. 1 (1999), 91–115.

LLOYD JONES, D. "Article 6 ECHR and immunities arising in public international law", *International and Comparative Law Quarterly*, vol. 52 (2003), 463–472.

MALLORY, J. L. "Resolving the confusion over Head of State immunity: the defined rights of kings", *Columbia Law Review*, vol. 86 (1986), 169–197.

MANGU, A. "Immunities of Heads of State and Government: a comment on the indictment of Liberia's president Charles Taylor by the Special Court for Sierra Leone and the reaction of the Ghanaian Government", *South African Yearbook of International Law*, vol. 28 (2003), 238–245.

MCLACHLAN, C. "The influence of international law on civil jurisdiction", *Hague Yearbook of International Law/Annuaire de La Haye de droit international*, vol. 6 (1993), 125–144.

———. "*Pinochet* revisited", *International and Comparative Law Quarterly*, vol. 51 (2002), 959–966.

MITCHELL, A. D. "Leave your hat on? Head of State immunity and Pinochet", *Monash University Law Review*, vol. 25 (1999), 225–256.

MOREAU DEFARGES, Ph. "Punir les tyrans", *Défense nationale*, vol. 55 (1999), 46–54.

MURPHY, S. D. (ed.), "Contemporary practice of the United States relating to international law", AJIL, vol. 95 (2001), 873–903.

———. "Head-of-State immunity for former Chinese President Jiang Zemin", AJIL, vol. 97 (2003), 974–977.

NEIER, A. "Accountability for State crimes: the past twenty years and the next twenty years", *Case Western Reserve Journal of International Law*, vol. 35 (2003), 351–362.

NICHOLLS, C. "Reflections on Pinochet", *Virginia Journal of International Law*, vol. 41, No. 1 (2000), 140–151.

O'NEILL, K. C. "A new customary law of Head of State immunity?: Hirohito and Pinochet", *Stanford Journal of International Law*, vol. 38, No. 2 (2002), 289–317.

ORREGO VICUÑA, F. "Diplomatic and consular immunities and human rights", *International and Comparative Law Quarterly*, vol. 40 (1991), 34–48.

PANHUYS, H. F. VAN. "In the borderland between the act of State doctrine and questions of jurisdictional immunities", *International and Comparative Law Quarterly*, vol. 13 (1964), 1193–1213.

PENROSE, M. M. "It's good to be the king!: Prosecuting Heads of State and former Heads of State under international law", *Columbia Journal of Transnational Law*, vol. 39, No. 1 (2000), 193–220.

PIERSON, Ch. "Pinochet and the end of immunity: England's House of Lords holds that a former Head of State is not immune for torture", *Temple International and Comparative Law Journal*, vol. 14 (2000), 263–326.

PROUVÈZE, R. "Les tribunaux pénaux internationaux à l'aube du XXIème siècle: l'affaire *Milosevic* ou la difficile recherche d'un véritable rôle de juridiction pénale internationale", *L'Observateur des Nations Unies*, No. 11 (2001), 201–221.

———. "L'affaire relative au Mandat d'arrêt du 11 avril 2000 (RDC c. Belgique): Quelle contribution de la Cour internationale de justice au droit international pénal?", *L'Observateur des Nations Unies*, No. 12 (2002), 285–309.

PRZETACZNIK, F. "Protection of foreign officials", *Revue égyptienne de droit international*, vol. 33 (1977), 113–151.

———. "Basic principles of international law concerning the protection of officials of foreign States", *Revue de droit international, de sciences diplomatiques et politiques*, vol. 69 (1991), 51–81.

RANDALL, K. C. "Book Review: *Universal Jurisdiction: National Courts and the Prosecution of Serious Crimes Under International Law*", AJIL, vol. 99 (2005), 293–298.

RAU, M. "After *Pinochet*: foreign sovereign immunity in respect of serious human rights violations—the decision of the European Court of Human Rights in *Al-Adsani* case", *German Law Journal*, vol. 3, No. 6 (2002).

ROBERTSON, G. *Crimes against Humanity: the Struggle for Global Justice*, London, Allen Lane the Penguin Press, 1999, 190–224, 342–407.

RODLEY, N. S. "Breaking the cycle of impunity for gross violations of human rights: the Pinochet case in perspective", *Nordic Journal of International Law*, vol. 69 (2000), 11–26.

ROUSSEAU, Ch. *Droit international public. Tome IV: Les relations internationales*, Paris, Sirey, 1980, 8–19, 123–126, 171–210, 247–263.

SALMON, J. "Libres propos sur l'arrêt de la C.I.J. du 14 février 2002 dans l'affaire relative au *Mandat d'arrêt du 11 avril 2000 (R.D.C. c. Belgique)*", *Revue belge de droit international*, vol. 35 (2002), 512–517.

———. and E. David. "Chef d'Etat, Chef de Gouvernement, ministre des Affaires étrangères", in N. Angelet (ed.), "La pratique du pouvoir exécutif et le contrôle des chambres législatives en matière de droit international (1995–1999)", *Revue belge de droit international*, vol. 35 (2002), 122–125.

SANDS, Ph. "What is the ICJ for?", *Revue belge de droit international*, vol. 35 (2002), 537–545.

———. "After Pinochet: the role of national courts", in Ph. Sands (ed.), *From Nuremberg to The Hague: the Future of International Criminal Justice*, Cambridge University Press, 2003, 68–108.

———. "International law transformed? From Pinochet to Congo…?", *Leiden Journal of International Law*, vol. 16 (2003), 37–53.

SASSOLI, M. "*L'arrêt Yerodia: quelques remarques sur une affaire au point de collision entre les deux couches du droit international*", *Revue générale de droit international public*, vol. 106 (2002), 797–817.

SEARS, J. M. "Confronting the 'culture of impunity': immunity of Heads of State from Nuremberg to *ex parte Pinochet*", *German Yearbook of International Law*, vol. 42 (1999), 125–146.

SHAW, M. N. "The *Yerodia* case: remedies and judicial function", *Revue belge de droit international*, vol. 35 (2002), 554–559.

———. *International Law*, 5th ed., Cambridge University Press, 2003, 655–667.

SHELTON, D. *Remedies in International Human Rights Law*, New York, Oxford University Press, 1999, 64–92.

SIMBEYE, Y. *Immunity and International Criminal Law*, Aldershot/Burlington, Ashgate, 2004.

SISON, G. "A king no more: the impact of the *Pinochet* decision on the doctrine of Head of State immunity", *Washington University Law Quarterly*, vol. 78 (2000), 1583–1602.

SOCIÉTÉ FRANÇAISE POUR LE DROIT INTERNATIONAL. *Colloque de Clermont-Ferrand: le Chef d'État et le droit international*, Paris, Pedone, 2002.

STONE, C. R. "Head of State immunity. New standard on a narrow issue. Waiver of Head of State immunity *In re: Grand Jury Proceedings, John Doe #700*", *Suffolk Transnational Law Journal*, vol. 12 (1988–1989), 491–502.

SUMMERS, M. A. "The International Court of Justice's decision in *Congo* v. *Belgium*: how has it affected the development of a principle of universal jurisdiction that would obligate all States to prosecute war criminals?", *Boston University International Law Journal*, vol. 21, No. 1 (2003), 63–100.

THOMAS, K. R. and J. Small. "Human rights and State immunity: is there immunity from civil liability for torture?", *Netherlands International Law Review*, vol. 50 (2003), 1–30.

TOMONORI, M. "The individual as beneficiary of State immunity: problems of the attribution of *ultra vires* conduct", *Denver Journal of International Law and Policy*, vol. 29, No. 3/4 (2001), 261–287.

TOMUSCHAT, C. "*General course on public international law*", *Collected Courses of the Hague Academy of International Law, 1999*, vol. 281 (2001), 176–183.

TONER, P. J. "Competing concepts of immunity: the (r)evolution of the Head of State immunity defense", *Penn State Law Review*, vol. 108, No. 3 (2004), 899–927.

TRIFFTERER, O. (ed.). *Commentary on the Rome Statute of the International Criminal Court: Observers' Notes, Article by Article*, Baden-Baden, Nomos, 1999, 501–514.

TUNKS, M. A. "Diplomats or defendants? Defining the future of Head of State immunity", *Duke Law Journal*, vol. 52, No. 3 (2002), 651–682.

VERHOEVEN, J. "Quelques réflexions sur l'affaire relative au *Mandat d'arrêt du 11 avril 2000*", *Revue belge de droit international*, vol. 35 (2002), 531–536.

VILLALPANDO, S. "L'affaire Pinochet: beaucoup de bruit pour rien? L'apport au droit international de la décision de la Chambre des Lords du 24 mars 1999", *Revue Générale de droit international public*, vol. 104 (2000), 393–427.

WALSH, N. M. "The President and Foreign Minister of Zimbabwe are entitled to Head-of-State immunity under United States and international law, but their political party is not immune and was properly served by notice of process on it in New York", *New York International Law Review*, vol. 15, No. 2 (2002), 91–99.

WARBRICK, C. "Immunity and international crimes in English law", *International and Comparative Law Quarterly*, vol. 53 (2004), 769–774.

WATTS, A. "The legal position in international law of Heads of States, Heads of Governments and Foreign Ministers", *Collected Courses of the Hague Academy of International Law, 1994-III*, vol. 247 (1995), 52–63.

WELLER, M. "On the hazards of foreign travel for dictators and other international criminals", *International Affairs*, vol. 75, No. 3 (1999), 599–617.

WEYEMBERGH, A. "Sur l'ordonnance du juge d'instruction Vandermeersch rendue dans l'affaire *Pinochet* le 6 novembre 1998", *Revue belge de droit international*, vol. 32 (1999), 178–204.

WHITE, M. "Pinochet, universal jurisdiction, and impunity", *Southwestern Journal of Law and Trade in the Americas*, vol. 7 (2000), 209–226.

WHOMERSLEY, C. A. "Some reflections on the immunity of individuals for official acts", *International and Comparative Law Quarterly*, vol. 41 (1992), 848–858.

WICKREMASINGHE, C. "Difference relating to immunity from legal process of a Special Rapporteur of the Commission on Human Rights", *International and Comparative Law Quarterly*, vol. 49 (2000), 724–730.

WILSON, R. A. "Diplomatic immunity from criminal jurisdiction: essential to effective international relations", *Loyola of Los Angeles International and Comparative Law Journal*, vol. 7, No. 1 (1984), 113–138.

WILSON, R. J. "Prosecuting Pinochet: international crimes in Spanish domestic law", *Human Rights Quarterly*, vol. 21, No. 4 (1999), 927–979.

WOUTERS, J. "The judgement of the International Court of Justice in the *Arrest Warrant* case: some critical remarks", *Leiden Journal of International Law*, vol. 16 (2003), 253–267.

YANG, X. "Immunity for international crimes: a reaffirmation of traditional doctrine", *The Cambridge Law Journal*, vol. 61 (2002), 242–246.

———. "State immunity in the European Court of Human Rights: reaffirmations and misconceptions", BYBIL, vol. 74 (2003), 333–408.

ZAPPALÀ, S. "Do Heads of State in office enjoy immunity from jurisdiction for international crimes? The *Ghaddafi* case before the French *Cour de Cassation*", *European Journal of International Law*, vol. 12, No. 3 (2001), 595–612.

ZIMAN, G. M. "Holding foreign Governments accountable for their human rights abuses: a proposed amendment to the Foreign Sovereign Immunities Act of 1976", *Loyola of Los Angeles International and Comparative Law Journal*, vol. 21, No. 1 (1999), 185–213.

ZUPPI, A. L. "Immunity v. universal jurisdiction: the *Yerodia Ndombasi* decision of the International Court of Justice", *Louisiana Law Review*, vol. 63, No. 2 (2003), 309–339.

Annex II

JURISDICTIONAL IMMUNITY OF INTERNATIONAL ORGANIZATIONS

(Giorgio Gaja)

1. The adoption of the 1969 Vienna Convention on the Law of Treaties and of the draft articles on State responsibility for internationally wrongful acts, in 2001, prompted the Commission to take up parallel studies with regard to international organizations. The recent adoption through General Assembly resolution 59/38, of 2 December 2004, of the United Nations Convention on Jurisdictional Immunities of States and Their Property gives the opportunity for the Commission to reconsider whether it should undertake a study of the jurisdictional immunity of international organizations.

2. The subject was for thirty years on the agenda of the Commission, as part of the study of "Relations between States and international organizations". For the second part of the topic, entitled "Status, privileges and immunities of international organizations and their agents", Mr. Abdullah El-Erian and Mr. Leonardo Díaz González successively acted as Special Rapporteurs. Draft articles were referred to the Drafting Committee but were not referred back to the Plenary. In 1992, the Commission decided "to put aside for the moment the consideration of a topic which does not seem to respond to a pressing need of States or of international organizations".[1]

3. It is true that many constituent instruments of international organizations, protocols on privileges and immunities or headquarters agreements provide for immunity. However, those provisions are often very general. Moreover, the question of immunity arises not infrequently before courts of States which are not bound by any treaty in this regard. The relevance of the topic also depends on the ever-increasing activities of many international organizations. Some problems are raised, for instance, by the practice of arranging meetings outside the territory of States with whom headquarters agreements are in force.

4. The existence of an obligation under general international law to grant immunity to international organizations has been asserted by several courts. According to the Labour Court of Geneva in *ZM* v. *Permanent Delegation of the League of Arab States to the United Nations*,[2] "international organizations, whether universal or regional, enjoy absolute jurisdictional immunity". The Netherlands Supreme Court held in *Iran–United States Claims Tribunal* v. *AS*, that "even in cases where there is no treaty … it follows from unwritten international law that an international organization is entitled to the privilege of immunity from jurisdiction on the same footing as generally provided for in the treaties referred to above, in any event in the State in whose territory the organization has its seat, with the consent of the government of the State".[3] In *T. M.* v. *Ligue des États Arabes*, the Belgian Court of Cassation referred to immunity granted to international organizations either by a general principle of international law or by special agreements.[4]

5. Similar decisions were taken by the Court of Appeals for the District of Columbia in the United States in *Weidner* v. *International Telecommunications Satellite Organization*,[5] and in a string of judgements by the Supreme Court of the Philippines. For instance, in *Southeast Asian Fisheries Development Center* v. *Acosta*, the latter Court said that "[o]ne of the basic immunities of an international organization is immunity from local jurisdiction, i.e., that it is immune from the legal writs and processes issued by the tribunals of the country where it is found".[6]

6. Precedents like those referred to above suggest the need for a thorough inquiry into State practice with a view to reaching appropriate conclusions, whether on the basis of codification or progressive development.

7. A study on the jurisdictional immunity of international organizations would not simply involve ascertaining the extent to which rules governing State immunity may also be applied with regard to international organizations. Immunity of the latter has to be studied in the context of remedies that are available for bringing claims against an organization, according to the rules of that organization or to arbitration agreements. There is a need to avoid the risk of a denial of justice. Thus, for example, in the above-mentioned judgement of the Labour Court of Geneva, the Court considered whether there was a "real possibility of recourse to the administrative tribunal of the defendant Organization".[7] More recently, in *Pistelli* v. *Istituto universitario europeo*, the Italian Court of Cassation ruled that the immunity of an international organization from jurisdiction is admissible when the rules of the organization assure "jurisdictional protection of the same rights and interests in front of an independent and impartial court".[8]

---

[1] *Yearbook … 1992*, vol. II (Part Two), p. 53, para. 362.

[2] *ZM* v. *Permanent Delegation of the League of Arab States to the United Nations, Judgement of 17 November 1993*, ILR, vol. 116, pp. 643 *et seq.*, at p. 647.

[3] *Iran–United States Claims Tribunal* v. *AS, Judgement of 20 December 1985, ibid.*, vol. 94, pp. 327 *et seq.*, at p. 329.

[4] *T. M.* v. *Ligue des États Arabes, Judgement of 3 December 2001*, available at www.cassonline.be.

[5] *Weidner* v. *International Telecommunications Satellite Organization, Judgement of 21 September 1978*, ILR, vol. 63, p. 191 *et seq.*

[6] *Southeast Asian Fisheries Development Center* v. *Acosta, Judgement of 2 September 1993*, available at www.lawphil.net.

[7] *ZM* v. *Permanent Delegation of the League of Arab States to the United Nations* (see footnote 2 above), p. 649.

[8] *Pistelli* v. *Istituto universitario europeo, Judgement of 28 October 2005*, Rivista di Diritto Internazionale, vol. 89 (2006), pp. 248 *et seq.*, at p. 254.

8. Major issues raised by the topic

— Definition of international organizations which the study is intended to consider.

— Immunity from contentious jurisdiction. In particular: modalities to giving effect to immunity, consent to exercise of jurisdiction, effects of participation in a proceeding before a court, counterclaims; questions relating to commercial transactions, contracts of employment, property cases, participation in companies or other collective bodies; effect of an arbitration agreement.

— Immunity from measures of constraint in connection with proceedings before a court.

— Protection of the rights of natural and legal persons in relation to jurisdictional immunities of international organizations. In particular, the role of alternative means of settling disputes.

9. Applicable treaties, general principles or relevant legislation or judicial decisions

A few references to trends in treaties and national legislation and judicial decisions were made above. While treaties and legislation refer to a limited number of organizations, some judicial decisions considered also the question of jurisdictional immunity of international organizations in general terms.

10. Existing doctrine

Current views on the existence of rules of general international law covering immunities of international organizations are divided. While some studies still deny the existence of any such rule,[9] the prevailing trend in recent works is more favourable to admitting that some form of immunity[10]—sometimes, even absolute immunity—is part of international law. Immunity of jurisdiction from execution is more widely admitted.[11] A selected bibliographical note is attached.

11. Advantages of preparing a draft convention

Given the number of instances in which treaties concerning immunities of international organizations do not apply and given also the general character of most treaty provisions, it would be in the interest of all concerned that the rules of international law governing immunities of international organizations be more easily ascertainable. Due consideration should be made, where appropriate, to the need for progressive development. The increased importance of economic activities of international organizations, often in direct competition with the private sector, adds urgency to the matter.

Should the topic be retained, it would lend itself to the preparation of a draft convention. This would apply alongside the United Nations Convention on Jurisdictional Immunities of States and Their Property.

[9] See P. Glavinis, *Les litiges relatifs aux contrats passés entre organisations internationales et personnes privées*, Paris, Librairie générale de droit et de jurisprudence, 1990, p. 122; S. De Bellis, *L'immunità delle organizzazioni internazionali dalla giurisdizione*, Bari, Cacucci Editore, 1992, p. 18; P. Klein, *La responsabilité des organisations internationales dans les ordres juridiques internes et en droit des gens*. Brussels, Bruylant, 1998, p. 230; and H. Fox, *The Law of State Immunity*, Oxford University Press, 2002, p. 469.

[10] See J.-F. Lalive, "L'immunité de juridiction des Etats et des organisations internationales", *Collected Courses of the Hague Academy of International Law, 1953–III*, vol. 84 (1955), pp. 209 *et seq.*, at p. 304; E. H. Fedder, "The functional basis of international privileges and immunities: a new concept in international law and organization", *American University Law Review*, vol. 9 (1960), pp. 60–69.; and B. Conforti, *Diritto internazionale*, Naples, Editoriale Scientifica, 2002, p. 259. Dominicé held that a customary rule has come in to existence only with regard to the United Nations and the specialized agencies (see Ch. Dominicé, "L'immunité de juridiction et d'exécution des organisations internationales", *Collected Courses of the Hague Academy of International Law, 1984-IV*, vol. 187 (1985), pp. 145 *et seq.*, at p. 220).

[11] See F. Schröer, "Sull'applicazione alle organizzazioni internazionali dell'immunità statale dalle misure esecutive", *Rivista di diritto internazionale privato e processuale*, vol. 13 (1977), pp. 575 *et seq.*, at p. 584; Dominicé, *loc. cit.* (see footnote 10 above), p. 225; J. Moussé, *Le contentieux des organisations internationales et de l'Union européenne*, Brussels, Établissements Émile Bruylant, 1997, pp. 376–377; and C. Zanghì, *Diritto delle organizzazioni internazionali*, Turin, G. Giappichlli Editore, 2001, p. 330.

Selected bibliography*

ABRAHAMSON, N. G. "Waiver of immunity for World Bank denied: *Mendaro* v. *The World Bank*", *Suffolk Transnational Law Journal*, vol. 8 (1984), 413–422.

AHLUWALIA, K. *The Legal Status, Privileges and Immunities of the Specialized Agencies of the United Nations and Certain Other International Organizations*, The Hague, Martinus Nijhoff, 1964, 230 p.

AKEHURST, M. "Settlement of claims by individuals and companies against international organisations", *Yearbook of Association of Attenders and Alumni of the Hague Academy of International Law (1967–1968)*, vol. 37/38 (1969), 69–98.

AMERASINGHE, C. F. *The Law of the International Civil Service as Applied by International Administrative Tribunals*, Oxford University Press, 1994.

———. *Principles of the Institutional Law of the International Organizations*, Cambridge University Press, 1996, 519 p.

ARCHER, C. *International Organizations*, London/New York, Routledge, 1992, 205 p.

ARISTODEMOU, M. "Applicability of article VI, section 22, of the Convention on the Privileges and Immunities of the United Nations", *International and Comparative Law Quarterly*, vol. 41 (1992), 695–701.

ARSANJANI, M. H. "Claims against international organizations: *quis custodiet ipsos custodes*", *The Yale Journal of World Public Order*, vol. 7, No. 2 (1981), 131–176.

AUFRICHT, H. "The expansion of the concept of sovereign immunity: with special reference to international organizations", *Proceedings of the American Society of International Law at its Forty-sixth Annual Meeting held at Washington, D.C. (April 24–26, 1952)*, Washington D.C., American Society of International Law, 1952, 85–100.

BARDOS, R. "Judicial abstention through the act of State doctrine. *International Association of Machinists* v. *Organization of Petroleum Exporting Countries*", *The International Trade Law Journal*, vol. 7, No. 1 (1981–1982), 177–192.

BATTAGLIA, R. M. "Jurisdiction over NATO employees", *The Italian Yearbook of International Law*, vol. 4 (1978–1979), 166–184.

BAXTER, R. R. "Jurisdiction over visiting forces and the development of international law", *Proceedings of the American Society of International Law at its Fifty-second Annual Meeting held at Washington, D.C. (April 24–26, 1958)*, Washington D.C., American Society of International Law, 1958, 174–180.

BEDERMAN, D. J. "The souls of international organizations: legal personality and the lighthouse at Cape Spartel", *Virginia Journal of International Law*, vol. 36 (1995), 275–377.

BEKKER, P. *The Legal Position of Intergovernmental Organization: a Functional Necessity Analysis of their Legal Status and Immunities*, Dordrecht/Boston, Martinus Nijhoff, 1994, 265 p.

BENTIL, J. K. "Involvement of an international organization in litigation in England", *Litigation*, vol. 8, No. 3 (1989), 90–97.

———. "Suing an international organisation for debt payment", *The Solicitor's Journal*, vol. 134 (1990), 475–479.

BERTRAND, C. "La nature juridique de l'Organisation pour la Sécurité et la Cooperation en Europe (OSCE)", *Revue générale de droit international public*, vol. 102, No. 2 (1998), 365–406.

BISCOTTINI, G. *Il diritto delle organizzazioni internazionali*, vol. I, Padova, CEDAM, 1971, 185 p.

BOWETT, D. *The Law of International Institutions*, 4th ed., London, Stevens, 1982, 431 p.

BRADLOW, D. D. "International organizations and private complaints: the case of the World Bank Inspection Panel", *Virginia Journal of International Law*, vol. 34 (1994), 553–613.

BROWER, C. H., II. "International immunities: some dissident views on the role of municipal courts", *Virginia Journal of International Law*, vol. 41 (2000), 1–92.

BYK, C. "Case note to *Hintermann* v. *UEO*", *Journal du droit international*, vol. 124 (1997), 141–151.

CAHIER, Ph. *Étude des accords de siège conclus entre les organisations internationales et les Etats où elles résident*, Milan, A Giuffrè, 1959, 449 p.

CANE, P. "Prerogative acts, acts of State and justiciability", *International and Comparative Law Quarterly*, vol. 29 (1980), 680–700.

CASSESE, A. "L'immunité de juridiction des organisations internationales dans la jurisprudence italienne", *Annuaire français de droit international*, vol. 30 (1984), 556–566.

CHANDRASEKHAR, S. "Cartel in a can: the financial collapse of the International Tin Council", *Northwestern Journal of International Law and Business*, vol. 10, No. 2 (1989), 309–332.

CHEN, K. "The legal status, privileges and immunities of the specialized agencies", AJIL, vol. 42 (1948), 900–906.

CHEYNE, I. "Status of international organisations in English law", *International and Comparative Law Quarterly*, vol. 40 (1991), 981–983.

CULLY, K. "Jurisdictional immunities of intergovernmental organizations", *The Yale Law Journal*, vol. 91, No. 6 (1982), 1167–1195.

D'ARGENT, P. "Jurisprudence belge relative au droit international public (1993–2003)", *Revue belge de droit international*, vol. 36, No. 2 (2003).

DAVID, E. " Ligue des Etats arabes c. T… M… (Observations)", *Journal des tribunaux*, No. 6020 (2001), 610–613.

———. "Bruxelles (9e ch.) 4 mars 2003 (Observations: Une décision historique?)", *Journal des tribunaux*, No. 6110 (2003), 686–687.

DE BELLIS, S. *L'immunità delle organizzazioni internazionali dalla giurisdizione*, Bari, Cacucci Editore, 1992.

DE VISSCHER, P. "De l'immunité de juridiction de l'Organisation des Nations Unies et du caractère discrétionnaire de la compétence de protection diplomatique", *Revue critique de jurisprudence belge* (1971), 456–462.

DISTEFANO, G. "La CICR et l'immunité de juridiction en droit international contemporain: fragments d'investigation autour d'une notion centrale de l'organisation internationale", *Revue suisse de droit international et de droit européen*, vol. 3 (2002), 355–370.

DOMINICÉ, C. "L'immunité de juridiction et d'exécution des organisations internationales", *Collected Courses of the Hague Academy of International Law*, vol. 187 (1984), 145–238.

———. "L'arbitrage et les immunités des organisations internationales", in C. Dominicé, R. Patry, C. Reymond (eds.), *Études de droit international en l'honneur de Pierre Lalive*, Basel, Helbing and Lichtenhahn, 1993, 483–497.

* Prepared by Stefano Dorigo, PhD candidate at the University of Pisa (Italy).

———. "Problèmes actuels des immunités juridictionelles internationales", in J. Cardona Llorens (ed.), *Cours Euro-Méditerranéens Bancaja de Droit international*, vol. II (1998), Castellón de la Plana, Aranzadi, 1999, 305–348.

———. "Observations sur le contentieux des organisations internationales avec des personnes privées", *Annuaire français de droit international*, vol. 45 (1999), 623–648.

DROUILLAT, R. "*L'actualité judiciaire. L'immunité de juridiction des organismes internationaux*", *Recueil Sirey. Jurisprudence* (1954), 97.

DUFFAR, J. *Contribution à l'étude des privilèges et immunités des organisations internationales*, Paris, Librairie générale de droit et de jurisprudence, 1982, 392 p.

DURANTE, F. and E. Spatafora. *Gli Accordi di Sede. Immunità et privilegi degli enti e dei funzionari internazionali in Italia*, Milan, Giuffrè, 1993, 512 p.

EBENROTH, C. T. "Shareholders' liability in international organizations—the settlement of the International Tin Council case", *Leiden Journal of International Law*, vol. 4 (1991), 171–183.

EHRENFELD, A. "United Nations immunity distinguished from sovereign immunity", *Proceedings of the American Society of International Law at its Fifty-second Annual Meeting held at Washington, D.C. (April 24–26, 1958)*, Washington D.C., American Society of International Law, 1958, 88–94.

EISEMANN, P. M. "Crise du Conseil international de l'étain et insolvabilité d'une organisation intergouvernmentale", *Annuaire français de droit international*, vol. 31 (1985), 730–746.

FARRUGIA, A. "*Boiman* v. *United Nations General Assembly*: international organizations immunity is absolutely not restrictive", *Brooklyn Journal of International Law*, vol. 15, No. 2 (1989), 497–525.

FEDDER, E. H. "The functional basis of international privileges and immunities: a new concept in international law and organization", *American University Law Review*, vol. 9, No. 1 (1960), 60–69.

FISCHER, G. "Organisation internationale du travail. Privilèges et immunités", *Annuaire français de droit international* (1955), 385–392.

FLAUSS, J.-F. "Contentieux de la fonction publique européenne et Convention européenne des droits de l'homme", in J.-F. Flauss and P. Wachsmann (eds.), *Le droit des organisations internationales. Recueil d'études à la mémoire de Jacques Schwob*, Brussels, Bruylant, 1997, 157–173.

———. "Droit des immunités et protection internationale des droits de l'homme", *Revue suisse de droit international et de droit européen* (2000), 299–324.

FOX, H. *The Law of State Immunity*, Oxford University Press, 2002, 572 p.

FREYMOND, P. "Remarques sur l'immunité de juridiction des organisations internationales en matière immobilière", *Die Friedens-Warte. Blätter für internationale Verständigung und zwischenstaatliche Organisation*, vol. 53, No. 4 (1956), 365–379.

GAILLARD, E. "Convention d'arbitrage et immunités de juridiction et d'exécution des Etats et des organisations internationales", *Bulletin de l'Association Suisse d'Arbitrage*, vol. 18, No. 3 (2000), 471–481.

GAJA, G. "L'esecuzione su beni di Stati esteri: l'Italia paga per tutti?", *Rivista di diritto internazionale*, vol. 68, No. 2 (1985), 345–347.

GLAVINIS, P. *Les litiges relatifs aux contrats passés entre organisations internationales et personnes privées*, Paris, Librairie générale de droit et de jurisprudence, 1990, 271 p.

GLAZER, J. H. "A functional approach to the international finance corporation", *Columbia Law Review*, vol. 57, No. 8 (1957), 1089–1112.

GLENN, G. H., M. M. Kearney and D. J. Padilla, "Immunities of international organizations", *Virginia Journal of International Law*, vol. 22, No. 2 (1982), 247–290.

GOETTEL, J. G. "Is the International Olympic Committee amenable to suit in a United States Court?", *Fordham International Law Journal*, vol. 7, No. 1 (1983–1984), 61–82.

GORDON, M. "International organizations: immunity—*Broadbent* v. *Organization of American States*", *Harvard International Law Journal*, vol. 21, No. 2 (1980), 552–561.

GREGORIDES, F. *Die Privilegien und Immunitäten der internationalen Beamten, mit besonderer Berücksichtigung der Rechtslage in Österreich*, Vienna, [s.n.], 1972, 214 p.

GRIFFITH, J. C., Jr. "Restricting the immunity of international organizations in labor disputes: reforming an obsolete shibboleth", *Virginia Journal of International Law*, vol. 25, No. 4 (1985), 1007–1033.

HABSCHEID, W. J. "Die Immunität internationaler Organisationen im Zivilprozess", *Zeitschrift für Zivilprozess* (1997), 269–286.

HAILBRONNER, K. "Immunity of international organizations from German national jurisdiction", *Archiv des Völkerechts* (2004), 329–342.

HAMMERSCHLAG, D. "*Morgan* v. *International Bank for Reconstruction and Development*", *Maryland Journal of International Law and Trade*, vol. 16, No. 2 (1992), 279–303.

HENDERSON, F. W. "How much immunity for international organizations? *Mendaro* v. *World Bank*", *North Carolina Journal of International Law and Commercial Regulation*, vol. 10 (1985), 487–497.

JENKS, C. W. *International Immunities*, London, Stevens and Sons, 1961.

KING, J. K. *The Privileges and Immunities of the Personnel of International Organizations*, Odense, Strandberg Bogtryk, 1949.

KLABBERS, J. *An Introduction to International Institutional Law*, Cambridge University Press, 2002.

KLEIN, P. *La responsabilité des organisations internationales dans les ordres juridiques internes et en droit des gens*, Brussels, Bruylant, 1998.

KNAPP, B. "Les privilèges et immunités des organisations internationales et de leurs agents devant les tribunaux internationaux", *Revue générale de droit international public* (1965), 615–681.

KUNZ, J. L. "Privileges and immunities of international organizations", AJIL, vol. 41 (1947), 828–862.

LALIVE, J. F. "L'immunité de juridiction des États et des organisations internationales", *Collected Courses of the Hague Academy of International Law, 1953–III*, vol. 84 (1955), 209–396.

LA ROSA, R. "Immunità delle organizzazioni internazionali dall'esecuzione e principi costituzionali", *Rivista di diritto internazionale privato e processuale* (1987), 453–474.

LEE, K. R. "International organizations. Immunity. Personnel decision of international organizations are not 'commercial activities' and thus may not form the basis for an action against the organization", *Virginia Journal of International Law*, vol. 20, No. 4 (1980), 913–923.

LEWIS, R. P. "Sovereign immunity and international organizations: *Broadbent* v. *OAS*", *Journal of International Law and Economics*, vol. 13, No. 3693 (1978–1979), 675–693.

LIANG, Yuen-Li. "The legal status of the United Nations in the United States", *The International Law Quarterly*, vol. 2, No. 4 (1948–1949), 577–602.

MACGLASHAN, M. E. "The International Tin Council: should a trading organisation enjoy immunity?", *The Cambridge Law Journal*, vol. 46 (1987), 193–195.

MERKATZ, H. J. VON. "Les privilèges et immunités des organisations internationales et de leurs agents", *Revue de droit international et de sciences diplomatiques et politiques*, vol. 46, No. 2 (1968), 147–164.

MICHAELS, D. B. *International Privileges and Immunities. A Case for a Universal Statute*, The Hague, Martinus Nijhoff, 1971, 249 p.

MITRANY, D. *A Working Peace System: An Argument for the Functional Development of International Organization (and other essays)*, London, Oxford University Press for the Royal Institute of International Affairs, 1943, 56 p.

MORGENSTERN, F. *Legal Problems of International Organizations*, Cambridge, Grotius, 1986, 147 p.

MOUSSÉ, J. *Le contentieux des organisations internationales et de l'Union européenne*, Bruxelles, Bruylant, 1997, 828 p.

MULLER, A. S. *International Organizations and their Host States: Aspects of their Legal Relationship*, The Hague, Kluwer Law International, 1995, 317 p.

NAKAMURA, O. "The status, privileges and immunities of international organizations in Japan", *Japanese Annual of International Law*, vol. 35 (1992), 116–129.

NGUYEN, Q. D. "Les privilèges et immunités des organismes internationaux d'après les jurisprudences nationales depuis 1945", *Annuaire français de droit international*, vol. 3, No. 3 (1957), 262–304.

OPARIL, R. J. "Immunity of international organizations in United States Courts: absolute or restrictive?", *Vanderbilt Journal of Transnational Law*, vol. 24, No. 4 (1991), 689–710.

O'TOOLE, T. J. "Sovereign immunity redivivus: suits against international organizations", *Suffolk Transnational Law Journal*, vol. 4 (1979–1980), 1–16.

PATEL, B. N. "The accountability of international organisations: a case study of the Organisation for the Prohibition of Chemical Weapons", *Leiden Journal of International Law*, vol. 13 (2000), 571–597.

PERRENOUD, G. *Régime des privilèges et immunités des missions diplomatiques étrangères et des organisations internationales en Suisse*, Lausanne, F. Rouge, 1949, 253 p.

PESCATORE, P. "Les relations extérieures des communautés européennes: contribution à la doctrine de la personnalité des organisations internationales", *Collected Courses of the Hague Academy of International Law, 1961–II*, vol. 103 (1962), 1–244.

PINGEL-LENUZZA, I. "Autonomie juridictionnelle et employeur privilégié: concilier les contraires", *Revue générale de droit international public* (2000), 445–464.

———. and E. Gaillard, "International organisations and immunity from jurisdiction: to restrict or to bypass", *International and Comparative Law Quarterly*, vol. 51 (2002), 1–15.

PINGEL-LENUZZA, I. (ed.), *Droit des immunités et exigences du procès équitable: actes du colloque du 30 avril 2004*, Paris, Pedone, 2004, 162 p.

PISILLO MAZZESCHI, R. "Immunità giurisdizionale delle organizzazioni internazionali e Costituzione italiana", *Rivista di diritto internazionale*, vol. 59, No. 3 (1976), 489–521.

PREUSS, L. "The International Organizations Immunities Act", AJIL, vol. 40 (1946), 332–345.

PUSTORINO, P. "Immunità giurisdizionale delle organizzazioni internazionali e tutela dei diritti fondamentali: le sentenze della Corte europea nei casi *Waite et Kennedy* e *Beer et Regan*", *Rivista di diritto internazionale*, vol. 83, No. 1 (2000), 132–150.

REINISCH, A. *International Organizations before National Courts*, Cambridge University Press, 2000, 449 p.

———. and U. A. Weber. "In the shadow of Waite and Kennedy—the jurisdictional immunity of international organizations, the individual's right of access to the courts and administrative tribunals as alternative means of dispute settlement", *International Organizations Law Review*, vol. 1, No. 1 (2004), 59–110.

SALMON, J. "Immunités et actes de la fonction", *Annuaire français de droit international*, vol. 38 (1992), 314–357.

SCHNEIDER, M. E. "International organizations and private persons: the case for a direct application of international law", in C. Dominicé, R. Patry and C. Reymond (eds.), *Études de droit international en l'honneur de Pierre Lalive*, Basel, Helbing and Lichtenhahn, 1993, 345–358.

SCHREUER, C. H. "Concurrent jurisdiction of national and international tribunals", *Houston Law Review*, vol. 13, No. 3 (1976), 508–526.

SCHRÖER, F. "De l'application de l'immunité juridictionnelle des Etats étrangers aux organisations internationales", *Revue générale de droit international public* (1971), 712–741.

———. "Sull'applicazione alle organizzazioni internazionali dell'immunità statale dalle misure esecutive", *Rivista di diritto internazionale privato e processuale*, vol. 13 (1977), 575.

SCOBBIE, I. "International organizations and internal relations", in R. J. Dupuy (ed.), *A Handbook on International Organizations* , 2nd ed., Dordrecht, Martinus Nijhoff, 1998, 831–896.

SEIDL-HOHENVELDERN, I. "L'immunité de juridiction et d'exécution des Etats et des organisations internationales", in P. Weil (ed.), *Cours et travaux de l'Institut des hautes études internationales de Paris. Droit International 1*, Paris, Pedone, 1981, 109–167.

———. "L'immunité de juridiction des Communautés européennes", *Revue du Marché commun et de l'Union européenne*, vol. 338 (1990), 475–479.

———. "Functional immunity of international organizations and human rights", in W. Benedek, *et al.* (eds.), *Development and Developing International and European law: Essays in Honour of Konrad Ginther on the Occasion of his 65th Birthday*, Frankfurt am Main, Peter Lang, 1999, 137–149.

———. and G. Loibl. *Das Recht der Internationalen Organisationen einschließlich der Supranationalen Gemeinschaften*, Cologne, C. Heymanns, 1996, 414 p.

SEYERSTED, F. "Jurisdiction over organs and officials of States, the Holy See and intergovernmental organisations", *International and Comparative Law Quarterly*, vol. 14 (1965), 31–82.

SINCLAIR, I. M. "The law of sovereign immunity: recent developments", *Collected Courses of the Hague Academy of International Law, 1980-II*, vol. 167 (1980), 113–284.

SINGER, M. "Jurisdictional immunity of international organizations: human rights and functional necessity concerns", *Virginia Journal of International Law*, vol. 36, No. 1 (1995), 53–165.

TIGROUDJA, H. "L'immunité de juridiction des organisations internationales et le droit d'accès à un tribunal", *Revue trimestrielle des droits de l'homme*, vol. 41 (2000), 83–106.

VERHOEVEN, J. (ed.). *Le droit international des immunités: contestation ou consolidation?*, Brussels/Paris, Larcier/Librairie générale de droit et de jurisprudence, 2004, 283 p.

WENCKSTERN, M. *Die Immunität internationaler Organisationen*, Tübingen, Mohr, 1994, 399 p.

WHITE, N. D. *The Law of International Organisations*, Manchester/New York, Manchester University Press, 1996, 285 p.

ZACKLIN, R. "Diplomatic relations: status, privileges and immunities", in R. J. Dupuy (ed.), *A Handbook on International Organizations*, 2nd ed., Dordrecht, Martinus Nijhoff, 1998, 179–198.

ZANGHÌ, C. *Diritto delle organizzazioni internazionali*, Turin, G. Giappichelli Editore, 2001.

Note: "The status of international organizations under the law of the United States", *Harvard Law Review*, vol. 71 (1957–1958), 1300–1324.

Annex III

PROTECTION OF PERSONS IN THE EVENT OF DISASTERS

(Secretariat)

A. Introduction

1. The topic "Protection of persons in the event of disasters" would fall within the category of "new developments in international law and pressing concerns of the international community as a whole" as contemplated by the Commission, at its forty-ninth session, upon establishing guidelines for the inclusion of topics in the long-term programme of work.[1] The focus of the topic would, at the initial stage, be placed on the protection of persons in the context of natural disasters or natural disaster components of broader emergencies, through the undertaking of activities aimed at the prevention, and mitigation of the effects, of natural disasters as well as through the provision of humanitarian relief in the immediate wake of natural disasters. In light of the present state of development of existing international law regulating disaster relief, as well as the perceived need for a systematization of such law, particularly from among the ranks of the disaster relief community (both within and beyond the United Nations), the consideration of such a topic by the Commission is merited.

2. Natural disasters are, however, a subset of a broader range of types of disasters, which include man-made and other technological disasters. A further distinction can be made between emergencies arising from the onset of a single (natural or other type of) disaster, and "complex emergencies" which may involve multiple disasters, including natural and man-made (such as armed conflict).[2] Furthermore, it is appreciated that such a distinction between natural and other types of disasters, such as technological disasters, is not always maintained in existing legal and others texts dealing with disasters, nor that it is always possible to sustain a clear delineation. Accordingly, while it is proposed that the more immediate need may be for a consideration of the activities undertaken in the context of a natural disaster, this would be without prejudice to the possible inclusion of the consideration of the international principles and rules governing actions undertaken in the context of other types of disasters.

B. Background

Natural disasters

3. Leaving aside considerations of the impact of human activities on the environment, and their potential causal link to the frequency and severity of natural disasters, such disasters are distinguished by the fact that they emanate from naturally occurring episodes in the geological or hydrometeorological, as the case may be, history of the planet. Such "natural hazards" include: earthquakes, floods, volcanic eruptions, landslides, hurricanes (typhoons and cyclones), tornadoes, tsunamis (tidal waves), droughts and plagues. They are also typically costly in terms of loss of life and destruction of property.[3] Earthquakes often happen without warning and with widespread destruction and loss of life owing to the collapse of buildings, landslides or tsunamis.[4] While hurricanes (typhoons and cyclones), tornadoes and even volcanic eruptions may be predicted in advance, their onset can be sudden, violent and destructive over a large geographic area, resulting in widespread dislocation, disruption in food and clean water supply and the outbreak of epidemics. In contrast, drought, food shortage or crop failure leading to famine have a slow onset but have equally devastating ramifications. By undermining development gains in a short period of time, such disasters also constitute a major impediment to sustainable development and poverty reduction.[5]

4. The fact that such events become "disasters" speaks more to the susceptibility of human beings to the adverse effects of natural hazards.[6] Indeed, with the burgeoning presence of human settlements in historically disaster-prone zones, such as floodplains, coastal areas and on geological faults (so-called earthquake "hotspots"), the risks of loss and destruction have increased commensurately. In addition, nature knows no political boundaries. Many natural disasters affect several States at a time, or even entire regions, a point demonstrated by the 2004 tsunami. In such cases, disaster relief efforts take on an international dimension and character.

Contemporary activities in the provision of disaster relief

5. While in a disaster the responsibility for response and coordination lies with the affected State, international

---

[1] *Yearbook ... 1997*, vol. II (Part Two), pp. 71–72, para. 238.

[2] Complex emergencies have been defined as "a humanitarian crisis in a country, region or society where there is a total or considerable breakdown of authority resulting from internal or external conflict and which requires an international response that goes beyond the mandate or capacity of any single agency and/or the ongoing United Nations programme" (Working Paper on the Definition of Complex Emergency, Inter-Agency Standing Committee, December 1994).

[3] According to one estimate, in 2004 alone, "there were 360 disasters affecting more than 145 million people and causing more than [US]$103 billion in material damage" (Report of the Secretary-General on the "Strengthening of the coordination of emergency humanitarian assistance of the United Nations", 2005, document A/60/87–E/2005/78, para. 4).

[4] *Ibid.* It is estimated that the massive earthquake that took place off the coast of Sumatra on 26 December 2004 and the resulting tsunami wave, which affected 12 countries across the entire Indian Ocean, killed more than 240,000 people and displaced well over a million more.

[5] Hyogo Declaration, adopted at the World Conference on Disaster Reduction, on 22 January 2005 (A/CONF.206/6 and Corr.1, resolution 1).

[6] See footnote 45 below for a discussion of the term "hazard" and its link to "disasters".

assistance may be requested by such a State. Indeed, the involvement of the international community is not limited to multinational disasters, but may be specifically requested by individual States seeking assistance in coping with the outcome of catastrophic events which take place entirely within their borders. Today, a diverse group of entities, including international organizations such as the United Nations and its specialized agencies, the major donor community and non-governmental organizations, devote a substantial amount of resources to providing assistance to States and their populations which have been adversely affected by disasters.[7]

6. The General Assembly, in resolution 46/182 of 19 December 1991, recognized the key activities undertaken in this area as being: disaster prevention and mitigation; preparedness including through enhanced early-warning capacities; improving standby capacity such as contingency funding arrangements; issuing consolidated appeals for assistance; and providing coordination, cooperation and leadership in the provision of disaster relief.[8] Such a classification of activities remains largely relevant today, even though the type of activities undertaken have evolved considerably since 1991.

7. At the operational level, time is of the essence in the wake of a disaster, with on-site coordination of response assets in real time being of particular importance.[9] Yet, humanitarian relief staff typically face a number of challenges in carrying out their mandates. These include: difficulties with sectoral coordination (both within and between sectors); limitations on the ability to mobilize technical expertise within the necessary timeframe; capacity gaps in water and sanitation, and shelter and camp management and protection; limitations on the availability of adequate and prompt funding; difficulties with national and local preparedness and response capacity deficiencies; and deliberate targeting and killing of humanitarian staff.

8. While some obstacles are of a technical nature, others are legal, where a regulatory framework would substantially expedite technical arrangements. Examples include inadequacies in existing regulatory frameworks, often designed for times of normalcy but ill-suited or ill-equipped to facilitate response measures during emergency situations. Expedited access for humanitarian relief personnel to the theatre of disaster may be impeded by visa, immigration and customs formalities, as well as overflight and landing rights procedures and clearances. Logistical bottlenecks and delays at trans-shipment points may arise from the imposition of export and import controls as well as documentation and customs duties. Questions may arise relating to immunities and privileges as well as to the delimitation of liability. In addition, the safety of humanitarian relief staff, particularly United Nations and associated personnel, has recently been a matter of interest for the international legal community.[10] In complex emergencies, these problems may be compounded by the prevailing political situation in the State confronted by a natural disaster.

PROTECTION OF VICTIMS

9. Humanitarian assistance, including disaster relief, is undertaken, *inter alia*, within the broader policy context of the question of the protection of victims of disasters, including natural disasters—an issue which continues to be the subject of discussion within the disaster relief community.[11] The present proposal is nonetheless also to be viewed as located within contemporary reflection on an emerging principle entailing the responsibility to protect,[12] which, although couched primarily in the context of conflict, may also be of relevance to that of disasters.

10. Of the three specific responsibilities identified in 2004 by the High-Level Panel on Threats, Challenges and Change as implicit in the overall responsibility to protect, the responsibility of the international community to prevent is considered the most pertinent to the topic at hand.[13] The principle of prevention, including through risk reduction, is well established in the field of disaster relief and was, most recently, reaffirmed in the Hyogo Declaration[14] adopted at the World Conference on Disaster Reduction held in January 2005. While recognizing the importance of involving all stakeholders, including regional and international organizations and financial institutions, civil society, including non-governmental organizations and volunteers, the private sector and the scientific community, the declaration affirms the primary responsibility of States to protect the people and property on their territory from hazards, whether natural or induced by human processes.[15]

C. Brief survey of existing norms and rules

11. The various activities undertaken at the international level in response to the incidence of disasters have come to be regulated by a series of legal norms which, taken

[7] Within the United Nations, the responsibility for coordination of international response to disasters devolves to the United Nations Relief Coordinator who is also the Under-Secretary General for Humanitarian Affairs responsible for the Office for the Coordination of Humanitarian Affairs (OCHA).

[8] The resolution further recognizes the link between relief, rehabilitation and development.

[9] See A. Katoch, "International natural disaster response and the United Nations", in V. Bannon (ed.), *International Disaster Response Laws, Principles and Practice: Reflections, Prospects and Challenges*, Geneva, IFRC, 2003, p. 48.

[10] See the Convention on the Safety of United Nations and Associated Personnel, adopted in 1994, as well as the Optional Protocol to the Convention on the Safety of United Nations and Associated Personnel, adopted by the General Assembly, in resolution 60/42 of 8 December 2005 (extending the scope of the 1994 Convention to cover United Nations operations established, *inter alia*, for the purposes of delivering emergency humanitarian assistance subject to the possibility that host States may make a declaration "opting out" of such a regime where humanitarian assistance is delivered for the sole purpose of responding to a natural disaster).

[11] See "Humanitarian Response Review: an independent report commissioned by the United Nations Emergency Relief Coordinator and Under-Secretary-General for Humanitarian Affairs" (August 2005), para. 4.2, pp. 30–31.

[12] See Report of the High-Level Panel on Threats, Challenges and Change, *A More Secure World: Our Shared Responsibility*, 2004, document A/59/565 and Corr.1.

[13] It is proposed that the International Law Commission, in accordance with its traditional approach of focusing on the peaceful interaction between States, not consider the question of the responsibility to react in response, including through coercive measures and, in extreme cases, military intervention.

[14] See footnote 5 above, resolution 1.

[15] *Ibid.*, operative paragraphs 2 and 4, respectively.

collectively, have been referred to as "international disaster response law".[16] International disaster response law is not an entirely new area of international law.[17] Its origins may be traced back at least to the mid-eighteenth century, when Emer de Vattel wrote:

> when the occasion arises, every Nation should give its aid to further the advancement of other Nations and save them from disaster and ruin, so far as it can do so without running too great a risk.[18]
>
> [I]f a Nation is suffering from famine, all those who have provisions to spare should assist it in its need, without, however, exposing themselves to scarcity. … To give assistance in such dire straits is so instinctive an act of humanity that hardly any civilized Nation is to be found which would absolutely refuse to do so. … Whatever be the calamity affecting a Nation, the same help is due to it.[19]

12. In its modern form, international disaster response law denotes those rules and principles for international humanitarian assistance that apply in the context of a disaster, whether natural or technological, in peacetime.[20] More specifically the "core" of international disaster response law has been described as being "[t]he laws, rules and principles applicable to the access, facilitation, coordination, quality and accountability of international disaster response activities in times of non-conflict related disasters, which includes preparedness for imminent disaster and the conduct of rescue and humanitarian assistance activities".[21]

13. In themselves, disasters have not been viewed as a direct source of international rights and obligations. However, they have on occasion led to the conclusion of international agreements.[22] Today, international disaster response law is composed of a relatively substantial body of conventional law, including a number of multilateral (both global and regional)[23] agreements as well as a significant network of bilateral treaties which has emerged in Europe and elsewhere.[24] Many of these agreements relate to the provision of mutual assistance, regulating requests for, and offers of, assistance, facilitation of entry into sovereign territory, technical cooperation, information sharing and training. Other common provisions relate to the regulation of access of personnel and equipment and their internal movement, entry of relief goods and customs, status, immunity and protection of personnel, and costs relating to disaster relief operations.[25]

14. A further source of rules can be found in a substantial number of memoranda of understanding and headquarters agreements, typically entered into between intergovernmental or non-governmental organizations, and States. While many of these instruments tend to be context-specific, it is still possible to discern a number of general or common provisions that have come to be accepted as reflecting the received view as a matter of international law.

15. In addition, a significant amount of the development of international disaster response law has occurred in the realm of "soft law" in the context of, *inter alia*, resolutions of the General Assembly, the Economic and Social Council of the United Nations and other bodies such as the International Conference of the Red Cross; political declarations; and codes of conduct, operational guidelines, and internal United Nations rules and regulations which provide interpretative tools for preparedness, mobilization, coordination, facilitation and delivery of humanitarian assistance in times of disaster.[26]

---

[16] The title of the present proposal refers to disaster "relief" by way of clarifying the broader scope of the topic, i.e. not limited to the "response" phase. However, to the extent that the reference to "response" may include other related actions such as pre-disaster risk-mitigation activities, the two phrases might be used interchangeably.

[17] See M. H. Hoffman, "What is the scope of international disaster response law?", in V. Bannon (ed.), *International Disaster Response Laws, Principles and Practice: Reflections, Prospects and Challenges*, Geneva, IFRC, 2003, p. 13.

[18] E. de Vattel, *The Law of Nations or the Principles of Natural Law Applied to the Conduct and to the Affairs of Nations and of Sovereigns*, Text of 1758, volumes I, II, III, IV, translation by Charles G. Fenwick with an introduction by Albert de Lapradelle, Carnegie Institution of Washington, 1916, vol. III, p. 114.

[19] *Ibid.*, p. 115. He noted at the same time that if that State can pay for the provisions furnished they may be sold for a fair price, noting that "there is no duty of giving it what it can obtain for itself, and consequently no obligation of making a present of things which it is able to buy".

[20] See Hoffman, *loc. cit.* (footnote 17 above), p. 13.

[21] IFRC, "International Disaster Response Laws (IDRL): Project Report 2002–2003", 2003, p. 14.

[22] See J. H. W. Verzijl, *International Law in Historical Perspective*, Leiden, A. W. Sijthoff, 1973, p. 47.

[23] While only two major multilateral agreements dealing specifically with disaster relief have been adopted in the post-war era, namely the 1986 Convention on assistance in the case of nuclear accident or radiological emergency and the 1998 Tampere Convention on the Provision of Telecommunication Resources for Disaster Mitigation and Relief Operations (adopted at the Intergovernmental Conference on Emergency Telecommunications, held at Tampere, Finland, from 16 to 18 June 1998), several other multilateral treaties may also be of relevance in that they deal with some aspects of disaster relief in the context of land, air and maritime transportation as well as customs procedures. Examples include the 1946 Convention on the Privileges and Immunities of the United Nations; the 1980 Convention concerning International Carriage by Rail; the 1944 Convention on International Civil Aviation; the 1965 Convention on facilitation of international maritime traffic; the 1990 Convention on temporary admission; the Convention on the simplification and harmonization of Customs procedures (adopted at Kyoto in 1973 under the auspices of the Customs Cooperation Council), as well as the (revised) International Convention on the Simplification and Harmonization of Customs Procedures (adopted at Kyoto in 1999 under the auspices of the World Customs Organization), which include provisions aimed at facilitating departure, entry or transit of relief supplies as well as easing customs procedures. Also of some relevance is the 1994 Convention on the Safety of United Nations and Associated Personnel and its 2005 Optional Protocol (footnote 10 above), which, *inter alia,* establishes the duty of States to prevent and punish crimes against a specific class of protected personnel.

[24] Regional agreements include the 1987 Council of Europe Open Partial Agreement for the Prevention of, Protection Against and Organisation of Relief in Major Natural and Technological Disasters, Resolution (87) 2 (adopted by the Committee of Ministers on 20 March 1987) and 1960 Agreement on the temporary importation, free of duty, of medical, surgical and laboratory equipment for use on free loan in hospitals and other medical institutions for purposes of diagnosis or treatment; the 1991 Inter-American Convention to Facilitate Disaster Assistance (adopted at the twenty-first regular session of the General Assembly of the Organization of American States, held at Santiago, on 6 July 1991); and the 2005 Association of Southeast Asian Nations (ASEAN) Agreement on Disaster Management and Emergency Response (adopted at Vientiane on 26 July 2005).

[25] See "International Disaster Response Laws (IDRL): Project Report 2002–2003" (footnote 21 above), p. 16.

[26] See, for example, the "Measures to Expedite International Relief", adopted at the 23rd International Conference of the Red Cross, res. 6, in ICRC/IFRC, *Handbook of the International Red Cross and Red Crescent Movement*, 13th ed., Geneva, 1994, p. 811–815); resolution 2102 (LXIII) of the Economic and Social Council, of 3 August 1977; the Declaration of principles for international humanitarian relief to the civilian population in disaster situations of 1969, adopted by the 21st

The contemporary "cornerstone" resolution is General Assembly resolution 46/182 of 19 December 1991, which, together with other instruments such as the resolution of the International Conference of the Red Cross on measures to expedite international relief,[27] is a key component of an expanding regulatory framework which built upon, and has been supplemented by, a series of General Assembly resolutions[28] as well as other instruments, the most recent being the Hyogo Framework for Action.[29]

Applicability of international humanitarian law and other relevant rules of international law

16. Usually, commentators point to international humanitarian law as a point of reference and comparison in any efforts to develop international disaster response law.[30] The linkages between the two fields reflect a common heritage in the humanitarian impulse and relate to the unique respective missions of the ICRC and the IFRC. While it is doubtful whether international disaster response law would develop along similar lines as that in international humanitarian law,[31] there exist examples of rules of international humanitarian law which would be applicable to the provision of disaster relief, even if only by analogy.

17. Similarly, some principles and aspects of other rules of international law, such as those dealing with the environment, human rights, refugees and internally displaced persons, may be of relevance to a broader legal framework for disaster relief.

Systematization through codification and progressive development

18. While there is a growing recognition of the existence of international disaster response law, there also exists an appreciation that the field largely lacks coherence as a set of rules constituting a single body of law.[32] Proposals for codification can be traced as far back as the late nineteenth century to unsuccessful suggestions to extend the "Geneva Law", regulating international humanitarian law, also to victims of disasters. The establishment of the International Relief Union in 1927,[33] under the auspices of the League of Nations, signalled the first major attempt in the twentieth century to provide a legal and institutional framework for the provision of international relief for disasters. The preamble of the Convention establishing the Union specifically envisaged as one of its purposes "to further the progress of international law in [the] field".

19. Although the Union proved largely ineffective and was superseded by the United Nations and its specialized agencies, several proposals for the codification of some aspects of international disaster response law have continued to be made in subsequent years.[34] In the United Nations, as early as 1971, the General Assembly, in resolution 2816 (XXVI), invited potential recipient countries to consider appropriate legislative and other measures to facilitate the receipt of aid, including overflight and landing rights and necessary privileges and immunities for relief units. In the early 1980s, a study was undertaken, on the initiative of the United Nations Disaster Relief Coordinator, on the possibility of negotiating an instrument on disaster relief operations. It was subsequently examined in 1983 by a group of international legal experts, chaired by the then-Chairperson of the International Law Commission, and resulted in a proposal by the Secretary-General for a draft international convention on expediting the delivery of emergency relief.[35] The proposal was not considered further after its initial presentation in the Economic and Social Council in 1984, nor did a subsequent proposal for a convention on the duty of humanitarian assistance, in the late 1980s, meet with approval, owing largely to resistance from several major non-governmental organizations.[36] A similar initiative was made at the fifteenth session of the World Food Council (of the World Food Programme), held in Cairo in 1989, which had before it a proposal for an international agreement on safe passage

International Conference of the Red Cross, resolution 26, *Handbook of the International Red Cross and Red Crescent Movement*, p. 808; the Recommendation of the Customs Co-operation Council to Expedite the Forwarding of Relief Consignments in the Event of Disasters, of 8 June 1970, document T2-423 (available at www.wcoomd.org/); *The Sphere Project: Humanitarian Charter and Minimum Standards in Disaster Response*, Geneva, Sphere Project, 2004; and the Code of Conduct for the International Red Cross and Red Crescent Movement and NGOs in Disaster Relief, Annex VI to the resolutions of the 26th International Conference of the Red Cross and Red Crescent, *International Review of the Red Cross*, No. 310 (January–February 1996), pp. 119 *et seq.*

[27] See footnote 26 above.

[28] See General Assembly resolutions 2816 (XXVI) of 14 December 1971; 36/225 of 17 December 1981; 37/144 of 17 December 1982; 39/207 of 17 December 1984; 41/201 of 8 December 1986; 45/221 of 21 December 1990; 48/57 of 14 December 1993; 49/139 of 20 December 1994; 51/194 of 17 December 1996; 52/12 of 12 November 1997; 52/172 of 16 December 1997; 54/233 of 22 December 1999; 55/163 of 14 December 2000; 56/103 of 14 December 2001; 56/164 of 19 December 2001; 56/195 of 21 December 2001; 57/150 of 16 December 2002; 57/153 of 16 December 2002; 58/177 of 22 December 2003; and 59/231 of 22 December 2004.

[29] Hyogo Framework for Action 2005–2015: Building the Resilience of Nations and Communities to Disasters, adopted on 22 January 2005 at the World Conference on Disaster Reduction (A/CONF.206/6 and Corr.1, resolution 2).

[30] See Hoffman, *loc. cit.* (footnote 17 above), pp. 14–15.

[31] *Ibid.* p. 15.

[32] See IFRC, "International Disaster Response Law: A Preliminary Overview and Analysis of Existing Treaty Law. Summary of the study on existing treaty law prepared by Professor Horst Fischer, Bochum University, Germany" (January 2003), p. 2.

[33] Created by the Convention and Statute establishing an International Relief Union, which entered into force in 1932 with 30 States parties. See B. Morse, "Practice, Norms and Reform of International Rescue Operations", *Collected Courses of the Hague Academy of International Law, 1997-IV*, vol. 157 (1980), pp. 121–194, at pp. 132–133.

[34] For example, in 1980, the International Law Association, at its fifty-ninth conference, in Belgrade, adopted a report containing a draft agreement for cooperation in disaster relief. See International Law Association, *Report of the Fifty-ninth Conference, Belgrade, 17–23 August 1980*, London, 1982, p. 5.

[35] See document A/39/267/Add.1–E/1984/96/Add.1.

[36] See document A/45/587, at paras 43–44. A similar resistance had been earlier expressed to a proposal for the consideration of a "new international humanitarian order", which entailed, *inter alia*, the elaboration of an internationally recognized framework of comprehensive legal principles governing relations among peoples and nations in times of war and peace; see A/40/348.

of emergency food aid to people affected by civil strife, war and natural disasters.[37]

20. Summing up the situation in 1990, the Secretary-General, in his report on humanitarian assistance to victims of natural disasters and similar emergency situations, again acknowledged the perceived desirability of new legal instruments in order to overcome the obstacles in the way of humanitarian assistance, but limited his suggestions to "new legal instruments such as declarations of the rights of victims of disaster to relief and bilateral agreements between donors and recipient countries as well as between recipient countries".[38]

21. The idea of developing a legal framework for international assistance in the wake of natural disasters and environmental emergencies has been revived in recent years. In his 2000 report on "Strengthening of the coordination of emergency humanitarian assistance of the United Nations",[39] the Secretary-General noted that such a framework may outline responsibilities of States receiving and providing assistance. Accordingly, he suggested that Member States consider drafting a convention on the deployment and utilization of international urban search and rescue teams, asserting that:

> [s]uch a convention would provide a working framework for complex issues, such as utilization of air space, customs regulations for import of equipment, respective responsibilities of providing and recipient countries, that have to be resolved prior to international response to a sudden-onset natural disaster.[40]

22. Similarly, the *World Disasters Report 2000*, issued by the IFRC, also lamented generally the limited legal progress. After noting that elements of law which assist in humanitarian relief work exist in some treaties, the report described the situation as follows:

> [a]t the core is a yawning gap. There is no definitive, broadly accepted source of international law which spells out legal standards, procedures, rights and duties pertaining to disaster response and assistance. No systematic attempt has been made to pull together the disparate threads of existing law, to formalize customary law or to expand and develop the law in new ways.[41]

23. Moreover, increased emphasis has been placed on the risk reduction and prevention components of the topic following the adoption of the Hyogo Declaration, and the Hyogo Framework for Action 2005–2015 which specifically calls for consideration to be given to, *inter alia*, the strengthening of relevant international legal instruments related to disaster risk reduction.[42]

D. Proposal for consideration of the topic by the Commission

24. The objective of the proposal would be the elaboration of a set of provisions which would serve as a legal framework for the conduct of international disaster relief activities, clarifying the core legal principles and concepts and thereby creating a legal "space" in which such disaster relief work could take place on a secure footing. A possible model would be the 1946 Convention on the Privileges and Immunities of the United Nations which, on the narrow aspect of privileges and immunities, serves as the basic reference point for the prevailing legal position, and which is routinely incorporated by reference into agreements between the United Nations and States and other entities. Similarly, the envisaged text regulating disaster relief could serve as the basic reference framework for a host of specific agreements between the various actors in the area, including, but not limited to, the United Nations.

25. Given the nature of what is a rapidly developing field, it is anticipated that the work on the topic would be primarily limited to the codification of existing norms and rules, with emphasis on progressive development as appropriate. The focus would thus be on the concretization of existing rules to facilitate activities being undertaken on the ground, as opposed to unnecessarily developing new norms which may inadvertently constrain such operational activities in an unforeseen manner.

Brief substantive overview

(a) *Scope*

26. As already mentioned (paras. 1–2 above), it is proposed that the Commission initially limit the scope *ratione materiae* of the topic to natural disasters (disasters linked to natural hazards), or natural disaster components of broader emergencies. At the same time, some reflection might be had as to the implications of drawing such distinction between natural and other disasters, even if by way of a "without prejudice" clause. In addition, various natural disasters have different distinguishing features: an

---

[37] See *Official Records of the General Assembly, Forty-fourth Session, Supplement No. 19* (A/44/19), Part One. At its sixteenth session in Bangkok in 1990, the Council's Executive Director was requested by Council Ministers to "further consult with all concerned institutions on the development of guidelines for more effective measures to ensure the safe passage of emergency food aid" (*ibid., Forty-fifth Session, Supplement No. 19* (A/45/19), para. 31). It also recommended that the Secretary-General consider endorsement by the General Assembly of an international draft agreement (*ibid.*).

[38] Document A/45/587, paras. 41 and 45.

[39] Document A/55/82–E/2000/61.

[40] *Ibid.*, para. 135 (*m*).

[41] P. Walker and J. Walker (eds.), *World Disasters Report 2000*, Geneva, IFRC, 2000, p. 145. In 2001, the IFRC initiated a study on the adequacy of existing legal and other mechanisms to facilitate humanitarian activities in response to natural and technological disasters. The study seeks to identify the most common legal problems in international disaster response, analyse the scope and implementation of existing international standards and propose solutions for gap areas. See IFRC, *International Disaster Response Law: Briefing Paper*, April 2003, p. 2, and *Revised IDRL Strategic Plan*, 2005–2007, available at www.ifrc.org/idrl. In the preamble of its resolution 57/150 of 16 December 2002, the General Assembly noted this development and stressed the need for intergovernmental oversight, particularly with regard to principles, scope and objectives. In 2003, the 28th International Conference of the Red Cross and Red Crescent (comprised of all components of the Red Cross/Red Crescent Movement and the States parties to the 1949 Geneva Conventions for the protection of war victims) mandated the IFRC and national societies to "lead collaborative efforts, involving States, the United Nations and other relevant bodies, in conducting research and advocacy activities" in this area and to report back to the International Conference in 2007 (IFRC, *28th International Conference of the Red Cross and Red Crescent, Geneva, 2–6 December 2003. Declaration, Agenda for Humanitarian Action, Resolutions*, p. 25 (*Final Goal 3.2.6*)). For a different perspective on the efficacy of the resort to international law in this area, see D. P. Fidler, "Disaster relief and governance after the Indian Ocean tsunami: what role for international law?", *Melbourne Journal of International Law*, vol. 6, No. 2 (2005), pp. 458 *et seq.*, at pp. 471–473.

[42] Hyogo Framework for Action 2005–2015 (see footnote 29 above), para. 22.

analysis of such features may have to be undertaken in the process of delineating the scope *ratione materiae*.

27. As regards the scope *ratione loci*, the topic would cover primarily those rules governing the theatre of the disaster, but would also extend to where the planning, coordination and monitoring efforts occur. *Ratione temporis*, the scope of the topic, would include not only the "response" phases of the disaster, but also the pre- and the post-disaster phases.[43]

28. Concerning the scope *ratione personae*, it is in the nature of the topic that, while State practice exists, it is primarily through the organs of intergovernmental organizations, such as the United Nations, as well as through the activities of non-governmental organizations and other non-State entities, such as the IFRC, that much of the activity occurs and, accordingly, where a large part of the development of legal norms takes place. While earlier instruments tend to exclude non-governmental organizations from their scope of application, whether explicitly or implicitly, it is proposed that the Commission adopt a broader approach to also cover the staff of such entities. This would accord with current trends, as evidenced by the approach taken in the Tampere Convention on the Provision of Telecommunication Resources for Disaster Mitigation and Relief Operations, which extends, for example, the provisions on privileges and immunities to staff members of non-governmental organizations involved in the provision of telecommunication assistance as envisaged in the Convention.[44] It would also accord with the contemporary reality that a significant portion of the operational component of disaster relief operations is undertaken by non-governmental organizations.

29. Since existing international human rights obligations apply in the context of natural disasters, subject to the possibility of derogation in the situation of emergencies to the extent permissible under applicable international law, it may also be necessary to consider the human rights implications of the plight of victims of such disasters, particularly as regards the right to protection and access to disaster relief and basic needs. This may be limited to a reaffirmation of the affected State's obligation to respect and ensure the human rights of all individuals within its territory. Such reaffirmation may also be a factor in determining the emphasis to be placed on the scope of the topic *ratione personae*.

(b) *Definitions*

30. Defining the main concepts to be covered by a future text would be an important component of the work to be undertaken. Defining the terms "natural disaster" and "natural hazards"[45] would serve to distinguish other types of disasters, such as "technological disasters".

31. Examples of terms that have been defined in various texts relating, *inter alia*, to the provision of disaster relief include: "disaster relief personnel", "possessions of disaster relief personnel", "relief consignment", "United Nations relief operation", "international disaster relief assistance", "assisting State or organization", "receiving State", "transit State", "military and civil defence assets", "relief supplies", "relief services", "disaster mitigation", "disaster risk", "health hazard", "non-governmental organization", "non-State entities" and "telecommunications".

32. In addition, consideration might be given to the inclusion of specific technical terms relating to particular operational aspects of disaster relief, to the extent that it is decided to deal with such matters.

(c) *Core principles*

33. A number of core principles underpin contemporary activities in the realm of the protection of persons in the event of disasters. Many are a reflection of existing principles for humanitarian assistance, i.e., applicable in a context not limited to disaster relief for emergencies arising out of natural disasters, but nonetheless equally applicable. Others are taken from other fields such as international human rights law. While General Assembly resolution 46/182 of 19 December 1991, which adopted, *inter alia*, a set of Guiding Principles for emergency humanitarian assistance, is widely regarded as the key instrument, other similar pronunciations of principles also exist.[46] All share a common appreciation for the importance of humanitarian assistance for the victims of natural disasters and other emergencies.

34. Such principles include:[47]

— *The principle of humanity.* Human suffering is to be addressed wherever it exists, and the dignity and rights of all victims should be respected and protected;

— *The principle of neutrality.* The provision of humanitarian assistance takes place outside of the political, religious, ethnic or ideological context;

— *The principle of impartiality.* The provision of humanitarian assistance is based on needs assessments undertaken in accordance with internationally

[43] See footnote 16 above.

[44] Similarly, in the context of the protection regime established by the Convention on the Safety of United Nations and Associated Personnel, the General Assembly in resolution 58/82 of 9 December 2003, *inter alia*, took note of the development by the Secretary-General of a standardized provision for incorporation into the agreements concluded between the United Nations and humanitarian non-governmental organizations or agencies for the purposes of clarifying the application of the Convention to persons deployed by those organizations or agencies; see A/58/187.

[45] The Hyogo Framework for Action 2005–2015 (see footnote 29 above) places emphasis on the reduction of vulnerability and risk to a "hazard" which is defined as "[a] potentially damaging physical event, phenomenon or human activity that may cause the loss of life or injury, property damage, social and economic disruption or environmental degradation. Hazards can include latent conditions that may represent future threats and can have different origins: natural (geological, hydrometeorological and biological) or induced by human processes (environmental degradation and technological hazards)" (para. 1, footnote 2).

[46] See, for example, the Code of Conduct for the International Red Cross and Red Crescent Movement and NGOs in Disaster Relief (footnote 26 above).

[47] Without prejudice to the applicability of some of the principles at a more general level.

recognized standards, giving priority to the most urgent cases of distress and in accordance with the principle of non-discrimination;

— *The principle of full respect for the sovereignty and territorial integrity of States, in accordance with the Charter of the United Nations.* Humanitarian assistance is provided with the consent of the affected country;

— *The principle of access.* States whose populations are in need of humanitarian assistance are to facilitate the work of intergovernmental and non-governmental organizations in implementing humanitarian assistance, in particular the supply of food, medicines, shelter and health care, for which unrestricted access to affected areas and victims is essential;

— *The principle of non-discrimination.* The provision of relief is to be undertaken without discrimination of any kind as to race, colour, sex, language, religion, political or other opinion, national or social origin, property, birth, age, disability or other status;

— *The principle of accountability.* Humanitarian assistance agencies and other entities providing humanitarian assistance are accountable to the people they assist and to those from whom they accept resources;

— *The principle of cooperation.* International cooperation[48] should be provided in accordance with international law and respect for national laws;

— *The principle of protection.* It is the primary responsibility of each State to take care of the victims of natural disasters and other emergencies occurring on its territory;

— *The principle of security.* The safety and security of humanitarian staff and their cargo and property is the basis upon which such assistance is provided;

— *The principle of prevention.* States are to review existing legislation and policies to integrate disaster risk reduction strategies into all relevant legal, policy and planning instruments, both at the national and international levels, in order to address vulnerability to disasters;

— *The principle of mitigation.* States are to undertake operational measures to reduce disaster risks at the local and national levels with a view to minimizing the effects of a disaster both within and beyond their borders.

35. It would have to be considered both the extent to which these principles are reflections of existing specific legal obligations of States and rights of individuals or whether they apply at a more general level.

(d) *Specific provisions*

36. It is proposed that the Commission also consider a number of specific legal questions relating to the operational aspects of the provision of disaster relief. These would not be limited to lacunae in the current legal framework. Instead, the approach would be more holistic, with a view to covering most of the legal aspects of the activities being undertaken in this area—even if only at a generalized level.

37. The following appendix sets out an outline of the issues that would require consideration in any legal instrument in this field.

[48] Both among States and between the affected State and the entities involved in the international humanitarian relief operation.

Appendix

PROPOSED OUTLINE

1. General provisions
   (*a*) Scope of application
   (*b*) Definitions
2. Applicable principles
   (*a*) Humanity
   (*b*) Neutrality
   (*c*) Impartiality
   (*d*) Sovereignty and territorial integrity of States, in accordance with the Charter of the United Nations
   (*e*) Access
   (*f*) Non-discrimination
   (*g*) Accountability
   (*h*) Cooperation
   (*i*) Protection
   (*j*) Security
   (*k*) Prevention
   (*l*) Mitigation
3. Disaster relief and protection
   (*a*) Right of victims to protection, safety and security
   (*b*) Right of victims to access to disaster relief and basic needs
   (*c*) Obligation of receiving State to protect disaster relief staff, their property, premises, facilities means of transport, relief consignments and equipment to be used in connection with the assistance
4. Provision of disaster relief
   (*a*) Conditions for the provision of assistance
   (*b*) Offers and requests for assistance
   (*c*) Coordination
   (*d*) Communications and exchange of information
   (*e*) Distribution and use of relief assistance
   (*f*) Costs relating to disaster response operations
   (*g*) Conformity with national laws, standards and regulations
   (*h*) Liability
   (*i*) Insurance
5. Access
   (*a*) Staff
      (i) Visas, entry and work permits
      (ii) Recognition of professional qualifications
      (iii) Freedom of movement
      (iv) Status
      (v) Identification
      (vi) Privileges and immunities
      (vii) Notification requirements
   (*b*) Relief consignments
      (i) Customs, duties, tariffs and quarantine
      (ii) Status
      (iii) Transportation and transit of goods
      (iv) Notification requirements
      (v) Identification
6. Disaster prevention and risk reduction
   (*a*) Early warning
   (*b*) Coordination activities
   (*c*) Training and information exchange

Selected bibliography

1. Books

ALEXANDER, D. *Natural Disasters*, London, UCL Press, 1993, 632 p.

———. *Confronting Catastrophe: New Perspectives on Natural Disasters*, New York, Oxford University Press, 2000, 282 p.

BEIGBEDER, Y. *The Role and Status of International Humanitarian Volunteers and Organizations: the Right and Duty to Humanitarian Assistance*, Dordrecht, Martinus Nijhoff, 1991.

BROWN, B. J. *Disaster Preparedness and the United Nations: Advance Planning for Disaster Relief*, New York, Pergamon Press, 1979, 147 p.

DYNES, R. R. *Organized Behavior in Disaster*, Lexington (Massachusetts), Heath Lexington Books, 1974.

EL BARADEI, M. *Model Rules for Disaster Relief Operations*, New York, United Nations Institute for Training and Research, 1982, 68 p.

FIDLER, D. P. *International Law and Infectious Diseases*, New York, Oxford University Press, 1999.

GREEN, S. *International Disaster Relief: Toward A Responsive System*, New York, McGraw-Hill, 1977.

HOLBORN, L. W. *The International Refugee Organization: a Specialized Agency of the United Nations: its History and Work, 1946–1952*, London/New York, Oxford University Press, 1956.

KÄLIN, W. *Guiding Principles on Internal Displacement: Annotations*, Studies in Transnational Legal Policy, Washington D.C., The American Society of International Law and the Brookings Institution, vol. 32, 2000.

MACALISTER-SMITH, P. *International Humanitarian Assistance: Disaster Relief Actions in International Law and Organization*, Dordrecht, Martinus Nijhoff, 1985.

PAN AMERICAN HEALTH ORGANIZATION. *Humanitarian Assistance in Disaster Situations: a Guide for Effective Aid*, PAHO/WHO Emergency Preparedness and Disaster Relief Coordination Program, Washington D.C., 1999.

POSNER, R. A. *Catastrophe: Risk and Response*, New York, Oxford University Press, 2004.

RAMCHARAN, B. G. *The International Law and Practice of Early-Warning and Preventive Diplomacy: the Emerging Global Watch*, Dordrecht, Martinus Nijhoff, 1991, 185 p.

UNITED NATIONS. INTERNATIONAL STRATEGY FOR DISASTER REDUCTION (ISDR): *Living with Risk: a Global Review of Disaster Reduction Initiatives*, vols. I and II (2004).

2. Articles and other documents

ALEXANDER, D. "The study of natural disasters, 1977–1997: some reflections on a changing field of knowledge", *Disasters*, vol. 21, No. 4 (1997), 284–304.

AWOONOR, K. N. "The concerns of recipient nations", in K. M. Cahill (ed.), *A Framework for Survival: Health, Human Rights and Humanitarian Assistance in Conflicts and Disasters*, 2nd rev. ed., London/New York, Routledge, 1999, 63–81.

BANNON, V. and D. Fisher: "Legal lessons in disaster relief from the tsunami, the Pakistan earthquake and Hurricane Katrina", The American Society of International Law, *ASIL Insights*, vol. 10, No. 6 (March 2006), www.asil.org/insights.cfm.

BAUDOT-QUÉGUINER, E. "The laws and principles governing preparedness, relief and rehabilitation operations: the unique case of the International Federation of Red Cross and Red Crescent Societies", in V. Bannon (ed.), *International Disaster Response Laws, Principles and Practice: Reflections, Prospects and Challenges*, Geneva, IFRC, 2003, 128–137.

BERRAMDANE, A. "L'obligation de prévention des catastrophes et risques naturels", *Revue du droit public et de la science politique en France et à l'étranger*, vol. 113 (1997), 1717–1751.

BETTATI, M. "Un droit d'ingérence?", *Revue générale de droit international public*, vol. 95 (1991), 639–670.

BOTHE, M. "Rapport spécial sur un projet d'acccord-type relative aux actions de secours humanitaires", *International Law Association, Report on the 58th Conference, Manila, 27 August–2 September 1978*, London, 1980, 461–466.

———. "Rapport spécial sur un projet d'accord-type relative aux actions de secours humanitaires", *International Law Association, Report on the 59th Conference, Belgrade, 17–23 August 1980*, London, 1982, 520–527.

———. "Relief actions: the position of the recipient State", in F. Kalshoven (ed.), *Assisting the Victims of Armed Conflicts and Other Disasters: Papers Delivered at the International Conference on Humanitarian Assistance in Armed Conflict, The Hague, 22–24 June 1988*, Dordrecht, Martinus Nijhoff, 1989, 91–97.

———. "Relief actions", in R. Bernhardt (ed.), *Encyclopedia of Public International Law*, vol. 4, Amsterdam, Elsevier, 2000, 168–173.

BROWN, B. J. "An overview of the structure of the current system", in L. H. Stephens and S. J. Green (eds.), *Disaster Assistance: Appraisal, Reform and New Approaches*, New York, New York University Press, 1979, 3–27.

BURLEY, L. A. "Disaster relief administration in the Third World", *International Development Review*, vol. 15, No. 1 (1973), 8–12.

CALLAMARD, A. "Accountability to disaster-affected populations", in V. Bannon (ed.), *International Disaster Response Laws, Principles and Practice: Reflections, Prospects and Challenges*, Geneva, IFRC, 2003, 153–164.

CARON, D. D. "Addressing catastrophes: conflicting images of solidarity and separateness", in D. D. Caron and C. Leben (eds.), *The International Aspects of Natural and Industrial Catastrophes*, The Hague/Boston/London, Martinus Nijhoff, 2001, 3–29.

COURSEN-NEFF, Z. "Preventive measures pertaining to unconventional threats to the peace such as natural and humanitarian disasters", *New York University Journal of International Law and Politics*, vol. 30 (1998), 645–707.

EBERSOLE, J. M. "The Mohonk criteria for humanitarian assistance in complex emergencies: Task Force on Ethical and Legal Issues in Humanitarian Assistance", *Human Rights Quarterly*, vol. 17, No. 1 (1995), 192–208.

EL-KHAWAS, M. "A reassessment of international relief programs", in M. H. Glantz (ed.), *The Politics of Natural Disaster: the Case of the Sahel Drought*, New York, Praeger, 1976, 77–100.

FARAH, A. A. "Responding to emergencies: a view from within", in K. M. Cahill (ed.), *A Framework for Survival: Health, Human Rights and Humanitarian Assistance in Conflicts and Disasters*, 2nd rev. ed., London/New York, Routledge, 1999, 259–274.

FIDLER, D. P. "The Indian Ocean tsunami and international law", The American Society of International Law, *ASIL Insights* (January 2005), www.asil.org/insights.cfm.

———. "Disaster relief and governance after the Indian Ocean tsunami: what role for international law?", *Melbourne Journal of International Law*, vol. 6 (May 2005), 458–473.

FINUCANE, A. "The changing roles of voluntary organizations", in K. M. Cahill (ed.), *A Framework for Survival: Health, Human Rights and Humanitarian Assistance in Conflicts and Disasters*, 2nd rev. ed., London/New York, Routledge, 1999, 175–190.

FISCHER, H. "International disaster response law treaties: trends, patterns and lacunae", in V. Bannon (ed.), *International Disaster Response Laws, Principles and Practice: Reflections, Prospects and Challenges*, Geneva, IFRC, 2003, 24–44.

FONROUGE, J. M. "Droit international: approche des problèmes liés à la survenue des catastrophes technologiques ou naturelles", *Médecine de catastrophe—urgences collectives*, vol. 1, Nos. 4/5 (December 1998), 113–123.

GOLD, J. "Natural disasters and other emergencies beyond control: assistance by the IMF", *The International Lawyer*, vol. 24 (1990), 621–641.

GOLDSTEIN, R. J. "Proposal for institutionalization of emergency response to global environmental disasters", *Pace Yearbook of International Law*, vol. 4 (1992), 219–240.

GOSTELOW, L. "The Sphere Project: the implications of making humanitarian principles and codes work", *Disasters: The Journal of Disaster Studies, Policy and Management*, vol. 23, No. 4 (1999), 316–325.

GREEN, S. J. "Expanding assistance for national preparedness and prevention programs", in L. H. Stephens and S. J. Green (eds.), *Disaster Assistance: Appraisal, Reform and New Approaches*, New York, New York University Press, 1979, 83–103.

GUNN, S. W. A. "The language of disasters: a brief terminology of disaster management and humanitarian action", in K. M. Cahill (ed.), *Basics of International Humanitarian Missions*, New York, Fordham University Press and the Center for International Health and Cooperation, 2003, 35–46.

HARDCASTLE, R. J. and A. T. L. Chua: "Humanitarian assistance: towards a right of access to victims of natural disasters", *International Review of the Red Cross*, No. 325 (December 1998), 589–609.

———. and A. T. L. Chua: "Victims of natural disasters: the right to receive humanitarian assistance", *The International Journal of Human Rights*, vol. 1, No. 4 (1997), 35–49.

HELTON, A. C. "The legality of providing humanitarian assistance without the consent of the Sovereign", *International Journal of Refugee Law*, vol. 4, No. 3 (1992), 373–375.

———. "Legal dimensions of responses to complex humanitarian emergencies", *International Journal of Refugee Law*, vol. 10, No. 3 (1998), 533–546.

HOFFMAN, M. "Towards an international disaster response law", in P. Walker and J. Walker (eds.), *World Disasters Report 2000*, Geneva, IFRC, 2000, 144–157.

———. "What is the scope of international disaster response law?", in V. Bannon (ed.), *International Disaster Response Laws, Principles and Practice: Reflections, Prospects and Challenges*, Geneva, IFRC, 2003, 13–20.

HOLLAND, G. L. "Observations on the International Decade for Natural Disaster Reduction", *Natural Hazards*, vol. 2, No. 1 (1989), 77–82.

INTERNATIONAL FEDERATION OF RED CROSS AND RED CRESCENT SOCIETIES: "International Disaster Response Law: A Preliminary Overview and Analysis of Existing Treaty Law. Summary of the study on existing treaty law prepared by Professor Horst Fischer, Bochum University, Germany" (January 2003).

JAKOVLJEVIĆ, B. "The right to humanitarian assistance: legal aspects", *International Review of the Red Cross*, vol. 27, No. 260 (September–October 1987), 469–484.

———. "International disaster relief law", *Israel Yearbook on Human Rights*, vol. 34 (2004), 251–286.

———. and J. Patrnogic: "Protection of human beings in disaster situations—a proposal for guiding principles", in *Collection of Publications*, No. 8, Sanremo, International Institute of Humanitarian Law, 1989.

KALSHOVEN, F. "Assistance to the victims of armed conflicts and other disasters", in *Assisting the Victims of Armed Conflicts and Other Disasters: Papers Delivered at the International Conference on Humanitarian Assistance in Armed Conflict, The Hague, 22–24 June 1988*, Dordrecht, Martinus Nijhoff, 1989, 13–26.

KATOCH, A. "International disaster response and the United Nations", in V. Bannon (ed.), *International Disaster Response Laws, Principles and Practice: Reflections, Prospects and Challenges*, Geneva, IFRC, 2003, 47–56.

LA PRADELLE, P. de: "L'organisation des secours en cas de désastre naturel", *International Law Association, Report of the Fifty-fifth Conference, New York, 21–26 August 1972*, London, 1974, 317–327.

———. "L'organisation des secours en cas de désastre naturel", *International Law Association, Report on the Fifty-seventh Conference, Madrid, 30 August–4 September 1976*, London, 1978, 309–320.

LEBEN, C. "Vers un droit international des catastrophes?", in D. D. Caron and C. Leben (eds.), *The International Aspects of Natural and Industrial Catastrophes*, The Hague/Boston/London, Martinus Nijhoff, 2001, 31–91.

LIENHARD, C. "Pour un droit des catastrophes", *Recueil Dalloz Sirey de doctrine, de jurisprudence et de législation*, No. 13 (1995), 91–98.

MACALISTER-SMITH, P. "Disaster relief: reflections on the role of international law", *Zeitschrift für ausländisches öffentliches Recht und Völkerrecht*, vol. 45 (1985), 25–43.

———. "The International Relief Union: reflections on the Convention Establishing an International Relief Union of July 12, 1927", *The Legal History Review*, vol. 54 (1986), 363–374.

———. "Les organisations non gouvernementales et la coordination de l'assistance humanitaire", *Revue internationale de la Croix-Rouge*, No. 767 (September–October 1987), 524–531.

———. "The right to humanitarian assistance in international law", *Revue de droit international, de sciences diplomatiques et politiques (The International Law Review)*, vol. 66, No. 3 (July–September 1988), 211–233.

———. *International Guidelines for Humanitarian Assistance Operations*, Max Planck Institute for Comparative Public Law and International Law (1991).

OKERE, B. and E. M. Makawa: "Global solidarity and the international response to disasters", in D. D. Caron and C. Leben (eds.), *The International Aspects of Natural and Industrial Catastrophes*, The Hague/Boston/London, Martinus Nijhoff, 2001, 429–456.

OWEN, D. "Obligations and responsibilities of donor nations", in K. M. Cahill (ed.), *A Framework for Survival: Health, Human Rights and Humanitarian Assistance in Conflicts and Disasters*, 2nd rev. ed., London/New York, Routledge, 1999, 52–62.

PATRNOGIC, J. "Some reflections on humanitarian principles applicable in relief actions", in C. Swinarski (ed.), *Studies and Essays on International Humanitarian Law and Red Cross Principles in Honour of Jean Pictet*, Geneva/The Hague, Martinus Nijhoff, 1984, 925–936.

PETIT, E. W. "Les actions d'urgence dans les catastrophes: evolution des activités des organisations interétatiques et des organisations non gouvernementales", in D. D. Caron and C. Leben (eds.), *The International Aspects of Natural and Industrial Catastrophes*, The Hague/Boston/London, Martinus Nijhoff, 2001, 537–589.

RABIN, R. L. "Dealing with disasters: some thoughts on the adequacy of the legal system", *Stanford Law Review*, vol. 30 (1977–1978), 281–298.

ROMANO, C. P. R. "L'obligation de prevention des catastrophes industrielles et naturelles", in D. D. Caron and C. Leben (eds.), *The International Aspects of Natural and Industrial Catastrophes*, The Hague/Boston/London, Martinus Nijhoff, 2001, 379–428.

SAMUELS, J. W. "Organized responses to natural disasters", in R. S. J. Macdonald, D. M. Johnston and G. L. Morris (eds.), *The International Law and Policy of Human Welfare*, Alphen aan den Rijn, Sijthoff and Noordhoff, 1978, 675–690.

———. "The relevance of international law in the prevention and mitigation of natural disasters", in L. H. Stephens and S. J. Green (eds.), *Disaster Assistance: Appraisal, Reform and New Approaches*, New York, New York University Press, 1979, 245–266.

SÉGUR, Ph. "La catastrophe et le risque naturels: essai de définition juridique", *Revue du droit public et de la science politique en France et a l'étranger*, vol. 113 (1997), 1693–1716.

SHIBATA, A. "Creating an international urgent assistance mechanism in case of natural and industrial catastrophes", in D. D. Caron and C. Leben (eds.), *The International Aspects of Natural and Industrial Catastrophes*, The Hague/Boston/London, Martinus Nijhoff, 2001, 457–535.

SLIM, H. "By what authority? The legitimacy and accountability of non-governmental organisations", *The Journal of Humanitarian Assistance*, vol. 10, No. 1 (2002), www.jha.ac.

THOUVENIN, J.-M. "L'internationalisation des secours en cas de catastrophe naturelle", *Revue générale de droit international public*, vol. 102 (1998), 327–363.

TOMAN, J. "Towards a disaster relief law: legal aspects of disaster relief operations", in F. Kalshoven (ed.), *Assisting the Victims of Armed Conflicts and Other Disasters: Papers Delivered at the International Conference on Humanitarian Assistance in Armed Conflict, The Hague, 22–24 June 1988*, Dordrecht, Martinus Nijhoff, 1989, 181–199.

TSUI, E. "Initial response to complex emergencies and natural disasters", in K. M. Cahill (ed.), *Emergency Relief Operations*, New York, Fordham University Press and the Center for International Health and Cooperation, 2003, 32–54.

WALKER, P. "Victims of natural disaster and the right to humanitarian assistance: a practitioner's view", *International Review of the Red Cross*, vol. 325 (December 1998), 611–617.

WALTER, J. (ed.): "Risk reduction: challenges and opportunities", in *World Disasters Report 2002*, Geneva, IFRC, 2002, 9–39.

———. "Accountability: a question of rights and duties", in *World Disasters Report 2002*, Geneva, IFRC, 2002, 149–169.

WESTGATE, K. N. and P. O'Keefe: *Some Definitions of Disaster*, University of Bradford Disaster Research Unit, Occasional Paper No. 4 (June 1976).

3. Selected United Nations documents

General Assembly. Assistance in cases of natural disaster, Report of the Secretary-General, 5 January 1965 (A/5845).

Economic and Social Council. Assistance in cases of natural disaster, Comprehensive report of the Secretary-General, 13 May 1971 (E/4994).

General Assembly. Office of the United Nations Disaster Relief Co-ordinator, Report of the Secretary-General, 12 May 1977 (A/32/64).

General Assembly. New International Humanitarian Order. Report of the Secretary-General, 3 June and 9 October 1985 (A/40/348 and Add.1).

General Assembly. New International Humanitarian Order. Humanitarian assistance to victims of natural disasters and similar emergency situations, Report of the Secretary-General, 24 October 1990 (A/45/587).

General Assembly. Economic and Social Council. Strengthening of the coordination of emergency humanitarian assistance of the United Nations, Report of the Secretary-General, Addendum, 1 November 1994 (A/49/177/Add.1–E/1994/80/Add.1).

General Assembly. Economic and Social Council. Strengthening of the coordination of emergency humanitarian assistance of the United Nations, Report of the Secretary-General, 15 June 1999 (A/54/154–E/1999/94).

General Assembly. Economic and Social Council. Strengthening of the coordination of emergency humanitarian assistance of the United Nations, Report of the Secretary-General, 30 May 2000 (A/55/82–E/2000/61).

General Assembly. Economic and Social Council. Implementation of the International Strategy for Disaster Reduction, Report of the Secretary-General, 8 May 2001 (A/56/68–E/2001/63).

General Assembly. Strengthening of the coordination of emergency humanitarian assistance of the United Nations, Report of the Secretary-General, 18 June 2001 (A/56/95–E/2001/85).

General Assembly. International cooperation on humanitarian assistance in the field of natural disasters, from relief to development, Report of the Secretary-General, 20 August 2001 (A/56/307).

General Assembly. Economic and Social Council. Strengthening of the coordination of emergency humanitarian assistance of the United Nations, Report of the Secretary-General, 14 May 2002 (A/57/77–E/2002/63).

General Assembly. Emergency response to disasters, Report of the Secretary-General, 16 August 2002 (A/57/320).

General Assembly. International cooperation on humanitarian assistance in the field of natural disasters, from relief to development, Report of the Secretary-General, 29 October 2002 (A/57/578).

General Assembly. International cooperation on humanitarian assistance in the field of natural disasters, from relief to development, Report of the Secretary-General, 14 October 2003 (A/58/434).

General Assembly. Economic and Social Council. Strengthening of the coordination of emergency humanitarian assistance of the United Nations, Report of the Secretary-General, 11 June 2004 (A/59/93–E/2004/74).

General Assembly. Implementation of the International Strategy for Disaster Reduction, Report of the Secretary-General, 11 August 2004 (A/59/228).

General Assembly. International cooperation on humanitarian assistance in the field of natural disasters, from relief to development, Report of the Secretary-General, 21 September 2004 (A/59/374).

General Assembly. Economic and Social Council. Strengthening of the coordination of emergency humanitarian assistance of the United Nations, Report of the Secretary-General, 23 June 2005 (A/60/87–E/2005/78).

General Assembly. Implementation of the International Strategy for Disaster Reduction, Report of the Secretary-General, 1 August 2005 (A/60/180).

Report of the Secretary-General on the work of the Organization, *Official Records of the General Assembly, Sixtieth Session, Supplement No. 1*, 8 August 2005 (A/60/1).

General Assembly. International cooperation on humanitarian assistance in the field of natural disasters, from relief to development, Report of the Secretary-General, 12 August 2005 (A/60/227).

General Assembly. Human rights and mass exoduses, Report of the Secretary-General, 1 September 2005 (A/60/325).

General Assembly. Letter dated 31 January 2006 from the Secretary-General addressed to the President of the General Assembly, 2 February 2006 (A/60/664).

General Assembly. Economic and Social Council. Strengthening of the coordination of emergency humanitarian assistance of the United Nations, Report of the Secretary-General, 2 June 2006 (A/61/85–E/2006/81).

Annex IV

PROTECTION OF PERSONAL DATA IN TRANSBORDER FLOW OF INFORMATION

(Secretariat)

1. It is proposed that the International Law Commission consider including the topic "Protection of personal data in the transborder flow of information" in its long-term programme of work.

A. Nature of the problem

2. Data collection or storage is not a new phenomenon. Public institutions and private entities, including natural and legal entities, have collected and kept data and records since time immemorial.[1] However, the radical and unimaginable changes brought about by advances in science and technology since the Second World War[2] and, more particularly, in information and communication technologies (ICTs),[3] from the 1960s on, have redefined ways in which information and personal data are generated, collected, stored, filed, disseminated and transferred. In particular, the Internet has proved a powerful global information infrastructure transcending the traditional physical boundaries, thereby challenging traditional conceptions of State sovereignty.[4] The electronic movement of data between States has become easier, cheaper, almost instantaneous and omnipresent. Time and space have been reduced remarkably. The data generated is detailed, processable, indexed to the individual and permanent.[5] The various actors—Governments, industry, other businesses and organizations and individual users—increasingly depend on ICTs for the provision of essential goods and services, the conduct of business and the exchange of information in a multitude of activities of human endeavour.[6] On a daily basis, personal data are collected in respect of individuals, for a variety of reasons, by various means and by a panoply of actors and kept by them in the public and private sectors.[7] When such data is shared or circulated by different actors, serious questions about the respect of the individual's right to privacy arise, although these concerns are not new.[8]

3. Public policy concerns over the invasion of privacy have ratcheted up the debate as new technologies have made identification and tracing of sources easier.[9] Improved technology in data surveillance, digital audio technology, integrated services digital network (ISDN), digital telephones, including mobile-phone location data, DNA and biometrics, black boxes, Radio Frequency Identification (RFID) chips and implantable GPS chips and their wide accessibility have commentators and civil libertarians warning, in Orwellian metaphor,[10] of the risk of turning into a surveillance society.[11]

4. Not surprisingly, the international community, most recently the World Summit on the Information Society (WSIS), has expressed concerns in the confidence

---

[1] Daniel J. Solove, in "Privacy and power: computer databases and the metaphors for information privacy", *Stanford Law Review*, vol. 53 (2000–2001), pp. 1393–1462, notes on page 1400 that in the eleventh century, William the Conqueror collected information about his subjects for taxation purposes. Many, if not all States, now conduct censuses periodically during which a variety of questions about personal details are asked.

[2] *Ibid*., p. 1402. The emergence of the mainframe computer in 1946 revolutionalized the collection of information.

[3] These include computers, cameras, sensors, wireless communication, the Global Positioning System (GPS), biometrics, remote sensing and other technologies.

[4] See J. S. Bauchner, "State sovereignty and the globalizing effects of the Internet: a case study of the privacy debate", *Brooklyn Journal of International Law*, vol. 26 (2000–2001), pp. 689–722.

[5] See J. Kang, "Information privacy in cyberspace transactions", *Stanford Law Review*, vol. 50 (1997–1998), pp. 1193–1294, at p. 1199.

[6] See General Assembly resolution 57/239 of 20 December 2002 on the creation of a global culture of cybersecurity. See also General Assembly resolution 59/220 of 22 December 2004, and paragraph 6 of the 2000 Ministerial declaration of the high-level segment [of the substantive session of 2000 of the Economic and Social Council] submitted by the President of the Council, *Official Records of the General Assembly, Fifth-fifth Session, Supplement No. 3* (A/55/3/Rev.1), chap. III.

[7] For example, information stored in computerized data files affecting individuals concerning banking, payroll, travel records, social security, insurance, as well as various subscriptions to membership clubs, newspapers and all other mundane social activities, are now easily filed and processed.

[8] The possibility that privacy issues may arise in horizontal relationships between natural persons or legal persons *qua* natural persons seems to distinguish the contemporary concerns from those of earlier decades when the vertical relationship concerns between the State and private individuals were dominant; see generally the 1974 report of the Secretary-General on the uses of electronics which may affect the rights of the person and the limits which should be placed on such uses in a democratic society (E/CN.4/1142 [and Corr.1] and Add.1–2). See also the 1973 report of the Secretary-General on respect for the privacy of individuals and integrity and sovereignty of nations in the light of advances in recording and other techniques (E/CN.4/1116 [and Corr.1] and Add.1–3 [and Add.3/Corr.1] and Add.4).

[9] See generally S. Hetcher, "Changing the social meaning of privacy in cyberspace", *Harvard Journal of Law and Technology*, vol. 15 (2001–2002), pp. 149–209. See also Asia–Pacific Economic Cooperation, *APEC Privacy Framework*, Singapore, APEC, 2005, preamble, para. 1. It may be noted that the increase in interconnectivity has also exposed information systems and networks to a growing number and wider variety of threats and vulnerabilities, heightening calls for cybersecurity. Computer hackers have challenged the integrity of networks. The Internet has been employed to engage in hate speech and different forms of criminality, including child pornography and identity theft.

[10] George Orwell, in *Nineteen Eighty-Four* (1949), used the metaphor "Big Brother".

[11] See the report of the American Civil Liberties Union, by Jay Stanley and Barry Steinhardt, "Bigger Monster, Weaker Chains: The Growth of an American Surveillance Society" (2003), available at www.aclu.org.

and security in the use of ICTs and has sought ways to strengthen the "trust framework", including through the enhancement of the protection of personal information, privacy and data.[12] Moreover, an appeal has been made to the United Nations to prepare a legally binding instrument which sets out in detail the rights to data protection and privacy as enforceable human rights.[13]

5. Sceptics have questioned whether there was no more a law of "cyberspace" than there is a "law of the horse".[14] This debate—whether the cyberspace can or should be regulated—has essentially waned and is largely a historical milestone.[15] Nevertheless, a number of themes emerge and one of them has been what rights and expectations the users of the electronic and digital space have by virtue of their participation in cyberspace and their increasing reliance on ICTs.[16] Three different legal responses are discernible in dealing with computer-related problems.[17] Evidently, these responses are not so easily distinguishable and there are overlaps. In the first place, the existing law has often been applied to new situations; secondly, the existing law may not be adequate but is nevertheless adapted and applied to respond to new situations; thirdly, new problems demand the creation of new law.[18] In this law of cyberspace, various fields of law have been applied or adapted for application to address problems posed by ICTs.[19] On the one hand, the law of contracts, torts, evidence, intellectual property or conflict of laws is germane in resolving questions posed by the application and use of ICTs; and on the other, data protection has emerged as an example of the third type of legal response: a new law to be applied to a new situation.[20] The present proposal focuses on this aspect. Data protection is defined as the protection of the rights and freedoms and essential interests of individuals with respect to the processing of personal information relating to them, particularly in situations where ICTs aid the processing procedures.[21] Data protection aspires to ensure that the data is not abused and that the data-subjects have and retain the ability to correct errors.[22]

---

[12] World Summit on the Information Society, Outcome Documents, Geneva 2003–Tunis 2005. The WSIS was held in two phases in Geneva on 10–12 December 2003, and in Tunis on 16–18 November 2005. The Geneva Declaration of Principles, the Geneva Plan of Action, the Tunis Commitment and the Tunis Agenda for the Information Society constitute the Outcome Documents and are available at www.itu.int/wsis.

[13] Montreux Declaration on "the protection of personal data and privacy in a globalised world: a universal right respecting diversity", adopted by Data Protection and Privacy Commissioners assembly in Montreux (Switzerland) for their Twenty-seventh International Conference of Data Protection and Privacy Commissioners, 14–16 September 2005, available at www.privacyconference2005.org. See also the interest in the subject as reflected in paragraph 51 of the declaration of the Heads of Governments and States of countries which share the French language at their summit in Ouagadougou, in November 2004:

> "Nous sommes convenus d'attacher une importance particulière à la protection des libertés et des droits fondamentaux des personnes, notamment de leur vie privée, dans l'utilisation des fichiers et traitements des données à caractère personnel. Nous appelons à créer ou consolider les règles assurant cette protection. Nous encourageons la coopération internationale entre les autorités indépendantes chargées dans chaque pays de contrôler le respect de ces règles." [We agreed to pay particular attention to the protection of freedoms and fundamental rights of persons, including of their private lives, in the use of files and the processing of data of a personal nature. We call to create or strengthen rules ensuring this protection. We encourage international cooperation between independent authorities responsible in each country for monitoring compliance with these rules.]

The Internet Governance Forum has also identified data protection as one of the issues requiring discussion, see generally www.intgov forum.org.

[14] F. H. Easterbrook, "Cyberspace and the law of the horse", *University of Chicago Legal Forum* (1996), pp. 207–216.

[15] See R. S. R. Ku, M. A. Faber and A. J. Cockfield, *Cyberspace Law: Cases and Materials*, New York, Aspen Law and Business, 2002, p. 37, quoted by V. N. Nguy in "Using architectural constraints and game theory to regulate international cyberspace behavior", *San Diego International Law Journal*, vol. 5 (2004), pp. 431–463, at p. 432.

[16] Other themes relate to governance: who should govern and ergo regulate the electronic and digital space offered by improved ICTs, how should this electronic and digital space be regulated and what tools can be applied to regulate it? Generally, the discursive response to the governance of electronic and digital space among the various actors has taken one of the following three positions: (*a*) a more traditional Statist approach, with the Government as the main regulator of Internet and ICT activities; (*b*) a *laissez faire* approach that perceives the Internet and ICT activities as a new social frontier where the traditional rules are inapplicable and inappropriate; instead self-rule and self-regulation are the dominant operational mantras; and finally (*c*) a more internationalist posture. The latter approach considers the global and interconnected nature of the Internet and the emergence of an information society as much more suited for regulation by international law. These responses overlap, interrelate and are mutually reinforcing. See generally V. Mayer-Schönberger, "The shape of governance: analyzing the world of Internet regulation", *Virginia Journal of International Law*, vol. 43 (2002–2003), pp. 605–673, who suggests these three types of cyberlaw discourses and terms them as (*a*) the State-based traditionalist discourse; (*b*) the cyber-separatist discourse; and (*c*) the cyber-internationalist discourse and provides a critique of each of these approaches (p. 612). The other theme is how should this electronic and digital space be regulated and what tools can be applied to regulate it?

[17] See F. W. Hondius, "Data law in Europe", *Stanford Journal of International Law*, vol. 16 (1980), pp. 87–111, at p. 88. The four kinds of constraints on human behaviour in ordinary life—the "real space", namely the law, social norms, the market and the "architecture," have all been deployed and interplay and interact in providing an analytical understanding of the law of the "cyberspace". Typically, the various actors involved in the transborder flow of data have used these tools to provide regulation at different levels. For example, the Government may pass a law on privacy and the providers of transmission lines and facilities may agree on a framework for technical compatibility standards, tariffs and protocols; the service providers may have their own privacy code; the users may conduct themselves in accordance with certain Internet etiquette; and the manufacturers may agree on certain codes by which compatibility and networking is assured. See generally L. Lessig, "The law of the horse: what cyberlaw might teach", *Harvard Law Review*, vol. 113 (1999–2000), pp. 501–549, who defines the architecture as "the physical world as 'we find it'" or "'how it has been made'" (p. 507). The architecture of the cyberspace is its code: "the software and the hardware that make the cyberspace the way it is" (p. 509).

[18] Hondius, *loc. cit.* (footnote 17 above), p. 88.

[19] The ITU focuses on the institutional infrastructure and technical functioning of transborder flows of data and other organizations are involved in the elaboration of standards for data processing, data transmission and data safety, see M. Bothe, "Data, transborder flow and protection", in R. Bernhardt (ed.), *Encyclopedia of Public International Law*, vol. 1, Amsterdam, Elsevier, 1992, pp. 950–961, at p. 954. UNCITRAL adopted in 1985 a recommendation on the legal value of computer records (*Official Records of the General Assembly, Fortieth Session, Supplement No. 17* (A/40/17), chap. VI, para. 360). In its resolution 40/71 of 11 December 1985, the General Assembly commended UNCITRAL on its recommendation. See also United Nations Convention on the Use of Electronic Communications in International Contracts. See also, for example, Directive 2001/29/EC of the European Parliament and of the Council of 22 May 2001 on the harmonisation of certain aspects of copyright and related rights in the information society (*Official Journal of the European Communities*, No. L 167, 22 June 2001, p. 10) and the United States Digital Millennium Copyright Act of 1998.

[20] Hondius, *loc. cit.* (footnote 17 above), p. 88.

[21] *Ibid.*, p. 89.

[22] See B. P. Smith, review of *Policing Across National Boundaries, Yale Journal of International Law,* vol. 20 (1995), pp. 215–217, at pp. 216–217.

B. Brief survey of existing norms and rules

6. Data protection has been a concern of the international community since the late 1960s.[23] The general orientation has been to assure the free flow of information.[24] This general disposition has implications for the flow of international trade, protection of intellectual property and the protection of human rights, in particular the right to privacy. The various approaches taken by States or the industry tend to accentuate the differences in emphasis attached to the various values. A variety of binding and non-binding instruments, national legislations and judicial decisions regulate this area. Earlier efforts within the United Nations, the Council of Europe and the OECD culminated in the adoption of "first generation" instruments and provided synergies at the domestic level in the promulgation of "first generation" legislation, beginning in the 1970s.[25] These instruments recognize as the basic issue the conflict between the ideal of data protection and the ideal of free flow of information between States.[26] The state of Hesse in Germany was the first to enact general data protection legislation in 1970,[27] while Sweden was the first country to do so in 1973.[28] Some other States elected to adopt more sectoral, subject-specific legislation.[29]

7. Disparities and divergences in the implementation of the "first generation" legislation prompted action and further developments within the context of the European Union, and elsewhere. These led to the subsequent adoption of "second generation" instruments,[30] some of which,

[23] Paragraph 18 of the Proclamation of Teheran and resolution XI concerning human rights and scientific and technological developments of 12 May 1968 adopted by the International Conference on Human Rights (Final Act of the International Conference on Human Rights held in Teheran from 22 April to 13 May 1968 (United Nations publication, Sales No. E.68.XIV.2), A/CONF.32/41, pp. 5 and 12, respectively) expressed concern that recent scientific discoveries and technological advances, while opening vast prospects for economic, social and culture progress, may endanger the rights and freedoms of individuals and peoples. In its resolution 2450 (XXIII) of 19 December 1968, the General Assembly invited the Secretary-General to undertake a study of the problems in connection of human rights arising from developments in science and technology. See the reports referred to in footnote 8 above. The Commission on Human Rights was eventually seized with the matter; see, for example, Commission on Human Rights resolution 10 (XXVII) of 18 March 1971. The Council of Europe established the Committee of Experts on the Harmonisation of the Means of Programming Legal Data into Computers in 1968 and also constituted within the OECD was its first expert group, the Data Bank Panel in 1969. The subsequent expert group, the Group of Experts on Transborder Data Barriers and Privacy Protection, was established in 1978.

[24] The right to seek, receive and impart information and ideas regardless of frontiers is recognized in the Universal Declaration of Human Rights (art. 19) and the International Covenant on Civil and Political Rights (art. 19), as well as regional human rights instruments. See also article 10 of the 1950 European Convention on Human Rights; article 13 of the 1969 American Convention on Human Rights: "Pact of San José, Costa Rica"; article 9 of the 1981 African Charter on Human and People's Rights; the Concluding Document of Vienna Meeting 1986 of representatives of the participating States of the Conference on Security and Co-operation in Europe (ILM, vol. 28, No. 2 (1989), pp. 531 *et seq.*, at pp. 540–541, paras. 34–46); the Document of the Copenhagen Meeting of the Conference on the Human Dimension of the Conference on Security and Cooperation in Europe, of 29 June 1990 (*ibid.*, vol. 29, No. 5 (1990), pp. 1305 *et seq.*, at p. 1311, para. 9); the Document of the Moscow Meeting of the Conference on the Human Dimension of the Conference on Security and Cooperation in Europe, of 3 October 1991 (*ibid.*, vol. 30, No. 6 (1991), pp. 1671 *et seq.*, at para. 26); and article 23 of the Cairo Declaration on Human Rights in Islam, adopted at the Islamic Conference of Foreign Ministers held in Cairo from 31 July to 5 August 1990.

[25] In 1973 the Council of Europe first adopted a resolution (Resolution (73) 22E, of 26 September 1973) on the protection of the privacy of individuals *vis-à-vis* electronic data banks in the private sector, and later, in 1974, another resolution (Resolution (74) 29E, of 20 September 1974) on the protection of the privacy of individuals *vis-à-vis* electronic data banks in the public sector. The OECD adopted the Guidelines on the Protection of Privacy and Transborder Flows of Personal data in 1980 and the Council of Europe adopted the Convention for the protection of individuals with regard to automatic processing of personal data in 1981. The efforts within the United Nations took longer to mature. The Commission on Human Rights in its resolution 10B (XXXIII), of 11 March 1977, requested the Sub-Commission on Prevention of Discrimination and Protection of Minorities to engage in a second study on relevant guidelines in the field of computerized personal files. Mr. Louis Joinet served as the Special Rapporteur of the Sub-Commission. The report recommended for consideration possible options for preparing minimum standards to be established by national and international legislation (see E/CN.4/Sub.2/1983/18). In resolution 45/95 of 14 December 1990, the General Assembly adopted the United Nations Guidelines concerning computerized personal data files, contained in resolution 1990/38 of 25 May 1990 of the Economic and Social Council. For follow-up developments concerning the implementation of the guidelines, see for example document E/CN.4/1995/75, prepared pursuant to decision 1993/113 of the Commission on Human Rights, of 10 March 1993; document E/CN.4/1997/67, prepared pursuant to decision 1995/114 of the Commission on Human Rights, of 8 March 1995; and document E/CN.4/1999/88 prepared pursuant to decision 1997/122 of the Commission on Human Rights, of 16 April 1997. In its decision 1999/109 on 28 April 1999, the Commission on Human Rights decided, without a vote: (*a*) to remove the question from its agenda, since the applicable guidelines are progressively being taken into consideration by States; and (*b*) to request the Secretary-General to entrust the competent inspection bodies with the task of ensuring the implementation of the guidelines by the organizations concerned within the United Nations system.

[26] See J. Bing, "The Council of Europe Convention and the OECD guidelines on data protection", *Michigan Yearbook of International Legal Studies,* vol. 5 (1984), pp. 271–303, at p. 273.

[27] Data protection derives its name from German "*Datenschutz*". Sweden: Data Act of 1973 (*Datalagen*, 1973:289), in force as of 1 July 1974. See also for example, Norway: Personal Data Registers Act of 1978 ((*lov om personregistre mm av 9 juni 1978 nr 48*), in force as of 1 January 1980; Denmark: Private Registers Act of 1978 (*lov nr 293 af 8 juni 1978 om private registre mv*) and Public Authorities' Registers Act of 1978 (*lov nr 294 af 8 juni 1978 om offentlige myndigheders registre*), both in force as of 1 January 1979; Canada: Human Rights Act of 1977 and the 1982 Federal Privacy Act; Germany: Federal Data Protection Act (*Bundesdatenschutzgesetz (BDSG)*) of 1977; France: Act No. 78–17 of 6 January 1978 on Data Processing, Files and Individual Liberties; United Kingdom: Data Protection Act 1984.

[28] Bing, *loc. cit.* (footnote 26 above), p. 271.

[29] In the United States, for example, the following pieces of legislation were passed: the Privacy Act of 1974, Pub. L. No. 93–579 (1974); the Fair Credit Reporting Act, Pub. L. No. 91–508 (1970); the Right to Financial Privacy Act, Pub. L. No. 95–630 (1978); the Cable Communications Policy Act of 1984, Pub. L. No. 98–549 (1984); and the Family Educational Rights and Privacy Act, Pub. L. No. 93–380 (1974).

[30] Article XIV, on general exceptions, of the 1994 WTO General Agreement on Trade in Services (Annex to the Marrakesh Agreement Establishing the World Trade Organization), envisages, *inter alia*, the possible adoption of enforcement of measures "necessary to secure compliance with laws or regulations which are not inconsistent with the provisions of this Agreement including those relating to: … (ii) the protection of the privacy of individuals in relation to the processing and dissemination of personal data and the protection of confidentiality of individual records and accounts". See also the 1995 Directive 95/46/EC of the European Parliament and of the Council of 24 October 1995 on the protection of individuals with regard to the processing of personal data and the free movement of such data, which provides a detailed privacy regulatory structure intended to be adopted by European Union member States domestically, *Official Journal of the European Communities*, No. L. 281, 23 November 1995, p. 31. See also the 2001 Additional Protocol to the Convention for the protection of individuals with regard to automatic processing of personal data, regarding supervisory authorities and transborder data flows; Directive 2002/58/EC of the European Parliament and of the Council of 12 July 2002

(*Continued on next page.*)

like the European Union Directive, have implications for third States,[31] and "second generation" legislation.[32] Efforts have also been made to promote the enactment of legislation on the basis of model legislation prepared in a multilateral framework.[33] Some other States remain disposed towards the enactment of sectoral, subject-specific legislation.[34] The preferred options taken by States are deeply embedded in historical, legal and political traditions.[35] More generally, the laws adopted within the

(*Footnote 30 continued.*)

concerning the processing of personal data and the protection of privacy in the electronic communications sector, *Official Journal of the European Communities*, No. L 201, 31 July 2002, p. 37, which repeals the earlier Directive 97/66/EC of the European Parliament and of the Council of 15 December 1997 concerning the processing of personal data and the protection of privacy in the telecommunications sector, *ibid.*, No. L 24, 30 January 1998, p. 1. See also Directive 2006/24/EC of the European Parliament and of the Council of 15 March 2006 on the retention of data generated or processed in connection with the provision of publicly available electronic communications services or of public communications networks and amending Directive 2002/58/EC, *ibid.*, No. L 105, 13 April 2006, p. 54. Article 8 of the Charter of Fundamental Rights of the European Union proclaimed on 7 December 2000, not yet into force, contains a specific provision on the protection of personal data:

"1. Everyone has the right to the protection of personal data concerning him or her.

"2. Such data must be processed fairly for specified purposes and on the basis of the consent of the person concerned or some other legitimate basis laid down by law. Everyone has the right of access to data which has been collected concerning him or her, and the right to have it rectified.

"3. Compliance with these rules shall be subject to control by an independent authority." (*Ibid.*, No. C 364, 18 December 2000, p. 1.)

In 2004, APEC also adopted an Asia–Pacific Economic Cooperation Privacy Framework to promote a consistent approach in information privacy as a means of ensuring the free flow of information in the Asia–Pacific region (see footnote 9 above).

[31] Article 25 of Directive 95/46/EC of the European Parliament and of the Council (see footnote 30 above) addresses the transfer of personal data to third countries on the basis of adequate level of protection, and article 26 sets forth circumstances in which derogations are permissible. In response to that Directive, the United States Department of Commerce adopted the Safe Harbor Privacy Principles encouraging companies to cooperate. The Safe Harbor Privacy Principles were issued by the United States Department of Commerce on 21 July 2000 (see *Federal Register*, vol. 65, Nos. 142 and 182 (2000); see also www.ita.doc.gov). European Commission decision 2000/520/EC of 26 July 2000 recognized these principles as providing adequate protection, *Official Journal of the European Communities*, No. L 215, 25 August 2000, p. 7. The adequacy of the level of protection appertaining to the transfer of data to the United States is a matter on which the Court of Justice of the European Communities rendered a judgment on 30 May 2006, in joined cases C-317/04 and C-318/04 (see *ibid.*, No. C 178, 29 July 2006, p. 1). The European Parliament *inter alia* sought the annulment of decision 2004/535/EC of 14 May 2004 of the Commission of European Communities, which authorized the transfer of air Passenger Name Records (PNR) data to United States Bureau of Customs and Border Protection, *ibid.*, No. L 235, 6 July 2004, p. 11. The Court annulled the decision of the Council on a technicality that the matter fell out of Community competence.

[32] Argentina: Ley de protección de los datos personales (Personal Data Protection Act) (Act No. 25.326) of 4 October 2000; Australia: 1988 Privacy Act and the 2000 Privacy Amendment Act (Private Sector); Austria: Personal Data Protection Act of 17 August 1999 and *Länder* legislation to implement the European Union Directive; Belgium: Law on Privacy Protection in relation to the Processing of Personal Data of 8 December 1992, modified by the implementation law of 11 December 1998 and Secondary Legislation of 13 February 2001; Brazil: Anteprojeto de Lei (draft law) No. 61/1996, and Anteprojeto de Lei (draft law) No. 151; Canada: 2001 Personal Information Protection and Electronic Document Acts (PIPEDA); Chile: Ley No. 19.628 sobre la protección de la vida privida (law on on the protection of private life) of 28 August 1999; Cyprus: Processing of Personal Data (Protection of the Individual) Law of 2001, as amended in 2003, and the Regulation of Electronic Communications and Postal Services Law of 2004; Czech Republic: Personal Data Protection Act of 4 April 2000; Denmark: Act on Processing of Personal Data (Act No. 429) of 31 May 2000; Germany: Federal Data Protection Act (*Bundesdatensschutzgesetz*) of 18 May 2001, and *Länder* data protection laws adopted to implement the European Union Directive; Estonia: Data Protection Act of 12 February 2003; Finland: Finnish Personal Data Act (No. 523/1999) of 22 April 1999, as amended on 1 December 2000, and Finnish Data Protection Act in Working Places of 2004; France: Law No. 2004-801 modifying Law No. 78-17 of 6 January 1978; Greece: Implementation Law No. 2472 on the protection of individuals with regard to the processing of personal data, which entered into force on 10 April 1997; Hungary: Act No. LXIII on the Protection of Personal Data and Public Access to Data of Public Interest of 1992, Act No. IV of 1978 on the Criminal Code on misuse of personal data and misuse of personal information, and Data Protection Act No. XXVI of 14 December 2001, as amended by Act No. XXXI of 2002; Ireland: Data Protection Act of 1998, amended by the Data Protection Act of 2003 of 10 April 2003; Israel: data protection law enacted in 1981 and amended in 1996; Italy: Act No. 675 on the protection of individuals and other subjects with regard to the processing of personal data of 31 December 1996, and the New Data Protection Code, which entered into force on 1 January 2004; Japan: Act of the Protection of Personal Information, Act No. 57 of 2003; Latvia: Personal Data Protection Law amended by the Law of 24 October 2004; Lithuania: Law No. IX–1296 on Legal Protection of Personal Data of 21 January 2003, with amendments of 13 April 2004; Luxembourg: Data Protection Law of 2 August 2002; the Netherlands: Personal Data Protection Act of 6 July 2000 (the former sectoral codes of conduct are under review to become legislation); New Zealand: Privacy Act of 1 July 1993; Paraguay: data protection law in Paraguay, Act No. 1682 regulating private information; Poland: Act on the Protection of Personal Data of 29 August 1997, amended on 1 January 2004; Portugal: personal data protection law No. 67/98 of 26 October 1998; Republic of Korea: Act on the Protection of Personal Data maintained by Public Agencies (Act No. 4734) of 1994, Act on the Promotion and Protection of Information Infrastructure (Act No. 5835) of 1999; Russian Federation: Federal Law on Information, Informatization and Protection of Information of 25 January 1995; Slovakia: Act No. 428/2002 Coll. on Protection of Personal Data, as amended by Act No. 602/2003 Coll., Act No. 576/2004 Coll. and Act No. 90/2005 Coll.; Slovenia: 1999 Personal Data Protection Act (based on the Council of Europe Convention) and Act Amending the Personal Data Protection Act of July 2001; Spain: Ley orgánica No. 15/1999 de protección de datos de carácter personal (organic law on the protection of personal data) of 13 December 1999; Sweden: Personal Data Act 1998:204 of 29 April 1998, and Regulation 1998:1191 of 3 September 1998; Switzerland: Federal Act on Data Protection No. 235.1 (DPA) of 19 June 1992; Tunisia: personal data protection law No. 2004-63 of 27 July 2004; and United Kingdom: Data Protection Act of 16 July 1998, completed by legislation of 17 February 2000.

[33] The 2002 Meeting of the Commonwealth Law Ministers' Conference in Kingstown (Saint Vincent and Grenadines) proposed two draft models bills on privacy (for the private and the public sectors). The model law was influenced by the Canadian system of personal data protection and the 1998 United Kingdom Data Protection Act which implements the European Union Directive, as well as the OECD Guidelines.

[34] In the United States, the following legislation was passed: Privacy Act, 5 U.S.C. § 552a (2001); Fair Credit Reporting Act, 15 U.S.C. § 1681 (2001); Video Privacy Protection Act, 18 U.S.C. § 2710–2711 (2000); Cable Communications Policy Act of 1984, 47 U.S.C. § 551 (2000); Drivers Privacy Protection Act, 18 U.S.C. § 2721–2725 (2000); Telephone Consumer Protection Act, 47 U.S.C. § 227 (2000); Family Educational Rights and Privacy Act, 20 U.S.C. § 1232 (2000); Health Insurance Portability and Accountability Act of 1996, Pub. L. No. 104–191 (1996); and Children Online Privacy Protection Act, 15 U.S.C. § 6501–6506 (2000).

[35] See Hondius, *loc. cit.* (footnote 17 above), pp. 87–111. States have adopted either a single piece of legislation covering both the public and the private sectors equally (e.g. European Union member States, Argentina, Chile, Israel, the Russian Federation and Switzerland); a single Act addressing the public and private sectors in separate chapters, or two separate Acts covering the public and private sectors separately (e.g. Australia, Canada, Paraguay and Tunisia); or an Act covering the public sector and separate pieces of legislation for various aspects of private sector activities (e.g. Japan and the Republic of Korea). In some instances, general legislation is accompanied by alternative codes of conduct for various sectors (e.g. New Zealand).

European context establish limits on the collection of data.[36] They require *ex ante* notification of purposes for which the data are required. Moreover, any subsequent use of the data, unless authorized by the consent of the data subject or otherwise provided by law, must accord with the specified purposes. Secondly, the legislation imposes controls *ex post*, aimed at ensuring the continued reliability of the data. Notification about the existence of such data records, access and an opportunity to make corrections to erroneous data are elements of such reliability.[37] Thirdly, such legislation regulates aspects concerning security and protection of such data by making provision for storage and usage, including procedures for securing against loss, destruction and an unauthorized disclosure. Any use or disclosure must be recorded and the data-subject notified in the event of any unauthorized use or disclosure.[38] A framework is established to address these matters. Fourthly, a regime for grievance and redress is also contemplated.

8. On the other hand, the approach—particularly in the United States—is sectoral, relying on a combination of legislation, regulation and self-regulation,[39] and the responses are more market-driven. The legislation covers essentially the public sector or specialized areas of it; the data-subjects afforded protection are citizens and resident aliens. Moreover, there is no single agency charged with questions of enforcement.

9. It may also be noted that the industry has taken an active role in adopting self-regulatory codes to protect personal data.[40]

10. Case law has also recognized the importance of data protection. The European Court of Justice in the *Fisher* case confirmed that principles of data protection constituted general principles of Community law. It asserted that the Directive 95/46/EC of the European Parliament and of the Council adopted, at the Community level, general principles which already formed part of the law of member States in the area in question.[41] In the *Rechnungshof case*, the Court noted that the provisions of the Directive, insofar as they govern the processing of personal data liable to infringement, in particular the right to privacy, must necessarily be interpreted in the light of the fundamental rights, which form an integral part of the general principles of community law. It also deemed that "[a]rticles 6 (1) (*c*) and 7 (*c*) and (*e*) of Directive 95/46 are directly applicable, in that they may be relied on by an individual before the national courts to oust the application of rules of national law which are contrary to those provisions".[42] The European Court of Human Rights has expressly recognized the protection of personal data as a fundamental right as it is included in the right to privacy established under article 8 of the European Convention on Human Rights.[43]

11. The international binding and non-binding instruments, as well as the national legislation adopted by States, and judicial decisions reveal a number of core principles, including: (*a*) lawful and fair data collection and processing; (*b*) accuracy; (*c*) purpose specification and limitation; (*d*) proportionality; (*e*) transparency; (*f*) individual participation and in particular the right to access; (*g*) non-discrimination; (*h*) responsibility; (*i*) supervision and legal sanction; (*j*) data equivalency in the case of transborder flow of personal data; and (*k*) the principle of derogability.

C. Elaboration of proposal for consideration of the Commission

12. The objective of the present proposal would be to elaborate general principles that are attendant in the protection of personal data. The overview of existing norms and rules suggests that although there are differences in approach, there is a commonality of interests in a number of core principles. The precedents and other relevant material, including treaties, national legislation, judicial decisions and non-binding instruments, point to the possibility of elaboration of a set of provisions that flesh out the issues relevant in data protection in light of contemporary practice. Such an exercise would facilitate the preparation of a set of internationally acceptable best practices guidelines and would assist Governments in the development of national legislation. It would also assist the industry in devising models for self-regulation. The elaboration of a "third generation" of privacy principles would augur well with increasing calls for an international response on this matter. Although this is an area which is technical and

---

[36] See G. M. Epperson, "Contracts for transnational information services: securing equivalency of data protection", *Harvard International Law Journal*, vol. 22 (1981) pp. 157–175, at p. 162.

[37] *Ibid.*

[38] *Ibid.*

[39] Comments of the United States on Internet Governance, Released by the Bureau of Economic and Business Affairs, 15 August 2005: "*Data protection and privacy rights: …* Any effective approach to ensuring protection of personal information includes: appropriate laws to protect consumer privacy in highly sensitive areas such as financial, medical, and children's privacy; government enforcement of these laws; and encouragement of private sector efforts to protect consumer privacy" (WSIS-II/PC-3/DT/7E, p. 24); these comments are available on the website of the ITU, www.itu.int, "Compilation of comments received on the Report of the Working Group on Internet Governance (WGIG)", 30 August 2005.

[40] The International Chamber of Commerce is playing a lead role in this regard. See for example its Toolkit for Policymakers, at www.rfid-in-action.eu/public/rfid-knowledge-platform/all-rfid-documents/guidelines-on-privacy/iccwbo_privacy-toolkit. Accessed 27 November 2012.

[41] *The Queen* v. *Minister of Agriculture, Fisheries and Food* ex parte Fisher (Case No. C-369/98), Judgement of the European Court of Justice of 14 September 2000, *Official Journal of the European Communities,* No. C 355, 25 November 2000, p. 4. With regard to Directive 95/46/CE, see footnote 30 above.

[42] Joined Cases C-465/00, C-138/01 and C-139/01 (Reference for a preliminary ruling from the *Verfassungsgerichtshof* and *Oberster Gerichtshof*): *Rechnungshof* (C-465/00) v. *Österreichischer Rundfunk and Others* and between *Christa Neukomm* (C-138/01), *Joseph Lauermann* (C-139/01) *and Österreichischer Rundfunk* ("Protection of individuals with regard to the processing of personal data–Directive 95/46/EC–Protection of private life–Disclosure of data on the income of employees of bodies subject to control by the *Rechnungshof*"), Judgement of the European Court of Justice of 20 May 2003, *Official Journal of the European Union*, No. C 171, 19 July 2003, p. 3, para. 2.

[43] See also *Amann* v. *Switzerland, Application no. 27798/95, Judgement of 16 February 2000*, Grand Chamber, European Court of Human Rights, *Reports of Judgments and Decisions 2000-II*, pp. 245 *et seq.*; *Leander case, Judgement of 26 March 1987*, European Court of Human Rights, *Series A: Judgements and Decisions*, vol. 116, pp. 6 *et seq.*; *Rotaru* v. *Romania, Application no. 28341/95, Judgement of 4 May 2000*, Grand Chamber, European Court of Human Rights, *Reports of Judgments and Decisions 2000-V*, pp. 109 *et seq.*; *Turek* v. *Slovakia, Application no. 57986/00, Judgement of 14 February 2006*, European Court of Human Rights, *Reports of Judgments and Decisions 2006-II*, pp. 41 *et seq.*

specialized, it is also an area in which State practice is not yet extensive or fully developed. By applying its working methods, the Commission may nevertheless be able to identify emerging trends in legal opinion and practice which are likely to shape any global legal regime which would finally emerge.

DELINEATING THE SCOPE OF THE TOPIC

13. There is a link between privacy and data protection. The right to privacy has centuries-old provenance and has attained constitutional status and recognition in many jurisdictions,[44] as well as in international binding and non-binding instruments.[45] However, the right to privacy is not absolute and its parameters and penumbras are not always easy to fathom and delineate. From philosophical and analytical perspectives, privacy conjures a variety of possibilities and ideas which may fall into one or cross-cut any of the following clusters: (*a*) spatial; (*b*) decisional; (*c*) informational;[46] and (*d*) privacy of communications.

14. Although the four clusters implicate and have a bearing on the other, the scope of the present proposal does not address the general question of privacy and would be narrower and more restricted in four respects.

15. First, its main focus is on the third cluster: the informational subset of privacy, which is concerned with the individual's control over the processing of personal information—its acquisition, disclosure and use,[47] a concept usefully referred to as "fair record management".[48] It would be necessary to consider the rights that the data-subject and users possess.

16. Secondly, it would address the protection to be afforded to the means of communication, that is to say, those aspects of the fourth cluster concerning the privacy of communications insofar as there is a connection in securing informational privacy: the security and privacy of mail, telephony, e-mail and other forms of ICTs. With improved technologies, the availability of information in the public domain challenges the traditional paradigm of privacy as one "protecting one's hidden world".[49] Data security, location data and traffic data have become elements within the penumbra of protection. Data security goes to the physical security of the data, an effort that seeks to ensure that data are not destroyed or tampered with in the place where they are located. Data are also always in a state of flux and movement and easily found in the custody of third parties. Where one is located (location data)[50] and what is being sent to another (traffic data)[51] are matters whose anonymity can no longer be guaranteed. The type and nature of protection to be given to the data—whether stationary or in traffic—are matters that would fall within the purview of the topic. However, the protection offered has to be weighed against society's need for tools that would ensure effective law enforcement, including in combating international terrorism and organized crime.

17. Thirdly, it would be restricted to addressing personal data flows.[52] Transborder data flows may involve different kinds of data, such as (*a*) operational data;[53] (*b*) actual financial transactions;[54] (*c*) scientific or technical information;[55] and (*d*) personally identifiable information relating for example to credit, medical history, criminal records, travel reservations, or it may simply be a name or an identification number. Only personally identifiable

[44] For example, in 1361, the Justices of the Peace Act 34 Edw. 3 c.1 in England provided for the arrest of peeping toms and eavesdroppers; a 1776 Public Records Act of Sweden required that all information held by Government be used for legitimate purposes; in the United States, in 1890, Samuel D. Warren and Louis D. Brandeis, in "The right to privacy", *Harvard Law Review*, vol. 4, No. 5 (1890), pp. 193–220, wrote that a right to privacy was "the right 'to be let alone'" (p. 195). In *Griswold v. Connecticut*, the United States Supreme Court gave an expansive interpretation of the Bill of Rights and averred that an individual had a constitutional right to privacy, United States Reports, vol. 381 (1965), p. 479.

[45] Article 12 of the Universal Declaration of Human Rights and article 17 of the International Covenant on Civil and Political Rights. See also articles V, IX and X of the American Declaration of the Rights and Duties of Man, adopted by the Ninth International Conference of American States, held at Bogotá in 1948; article 8 of the 1950 European Convention on Human Rights Fundamental Freedoms; article 11 of the 1969 American Convention on Human Rights: "Pact of San José, Costa Rica"; the 1990 African Charter on the Rights and Welfare of the Child; and article 18 of the 1990 Cairo Declaration on Human Rights in Islam. See also article 18 of the 1981 African Charter on Human and Peoples' Rights. In the area of medical ethics, see, for example, the Nuremberg Code on Directions for Human Experimentation (*Trials of War Criminals before the Nuernberg Military Tribunals under Control Council Law No. 10 (Nuernberg, October 1946–April 1949)*, 15-volume series, vol. II, Washington D.C., United States Government Printing Office, 1949–1953, p. 180), the 1948 Declaration of Geneva (World Medical Association, *Handbook of Declarations* (October 1996), 17.A) and the 1964 Declaration of Helsinki (*ibid.*, 17.C, or "World Medical Association Declaration of Helsinki. Ethical Principles for Medical Research Involving Human Subjects", *Bulletin of the World Health Organization*, 2001, 79 (4), p. 373).

[46] See Kang, *loc. cit.* (footnote 5 above), at pp. 1202–1203. In *Whalen* v. *Roe* (429 U.S 589 (1977)), the United States Supreme Court extended the substantive due process protection of privacy to information privacy.

[47] Kang, *loc. cit.* (footnote 5 above), at p. 1203.

[48] Epperson, *loc. cit.* (footnote 36 above): "Data protection does not, however, mean that all such privacy interests will be fully protected. The term refers less to absolute prohibition of the accumulation and usage of data than to the establishment of procedures guaranteeing to data-subjects the opportunity to know of the existence of data concerning them and of the uses to which such data will be put" (pp. 160–161).

[49] D. J. Solove, "Privacy and Power …", *loc. cit.* (footnote 1 above), at p. 1437.

[50] The latitude, longitude and altitude of the terminal equipment of the user, the direction of travel, the level and accuracy of the location information, the identification of the network cell and the time the location information was made are easily recordable.

[51] The routing, duration, time or volume of communication, the protocol used, the location of the terminal equipment of the sender or recipient, the network on which the communication originates or terminates, the beginning, end or duration of a communication, the format of conveyance of the communication are easily identifiable pieces in the traffic of data.

[52] See E. J. Novotny, "Transborder data flows and international law: a framework for policy-oriented inquiry", *Stanford Journal of International Law*, vol. 16 (1980), pp. 141 *et seq.* "Data" and "information" are used sometimes as synonymous terms. However, from a technical perspective:

> "'data' refers to a set of organized symbols capable of machine processing and information. 'Information' implies a higher class of data intelligible to a human being. The purpose of transborder data flows is to create, store, retrieve, and use information; at times information is reduced to data for intermediate purposes" (p. 144, footnote 7).

[53] *Ibid.*, p. 156. These are intended to support the organizational decisions or that sustain certain administrative functions.

[54] *Ibid.*, p. 157. These involve credits, debits and transfers of money.

[55] *Ibid.*, p. 158. These reflect results of experiments, surveys, environmental or meteorological measurements or economic statistics.

data is intended to fall within the scope of the present proposal, although such data may also appear in the form of operational or financial transactions[56] as well as part of scientific and technical surveys, including demographic surveys.

18. What is personally identifiable information may bear on (*a*) authorship in relation to the individual; (*b*) a descriptive relation to the individual; or (*c*) an instrumental mapping in relation to the individual.[57] It is these aspects that may require protection from disclosure. Natural persons are ordinarily associated with personally identifiable information. In some States, legal persons and other entities may be affected.[58] The scope of the topic *ratione personae* would have to determine the treatment to be given to other entities other than natural persons.

19. Data flows include flows among the various actors, and these may include Governments, intergovernmental organizations, non-governmental organizations and the private sector, such as multinational corporations and enterprises, some of which provide data processing services. The span of activities in the public or private sector that may be involved would have to be taken into account in the treatment of the topic.

20. Fourthly, there are restrictions and exceptions and competing interests recognized in the protection of informational data. Indeed, the privacy protections offered by national Constitutions and in judicial decisions and international human rights instruments recognize possible restrictions and exceptions, in the form of derogations or limitations.

Definitions

21. Transborder flow of data has been defined as "the electronic transmission of data across political boundaries for processing and/or storage in [ICT] files".[59] The scope of the topic *ratione materiae* would be a matter that would require careful consideration, in particular whether it should be only automated computerized data, or any kind of data, including manually generated and processed data; and whether the scope should be defined through the technology used or through any kind of data involved regardless of the technology.

22. It would be necessary to define such terms as data; data-subject; data user; data file; data retention; data preservation; personally identifiable data; sensitive data; traffic data; location data; transborder flow of personal data; processing of personal data; communication; third party user; registration and transactional data; clickstream data. The definitions are only illustrative; they need to take into account the technological advances that are continuously taking place in the network environment.

Core principles

23. A number of core principles are discernible from developments in this field over almost forty years. Such principles include the following:[60]

— *Lawful and fair data collection and processing.* This principle presupposes that the collection of personal data would be restricted to a necessary minimum. In particular, such data should not be obtained unlawfully or through unfair means.

— *Accuracy.* The information quality principle is a qualitative requirement and entails a responsibility that the data is accurate and necessarily complete and up-to-date for the purpose intended.

— *Purpose specification and limitation.* This principle establishes the requirement that the purpose for which the data are collected should be specified to the data-subject. Data should not be disclosed, made available or otherwise used for purposes other than those specified. It has to be done with the consent or knowledge of the data-subject or under the operation of the law. Any subsequent use is limited to such purpose, or any other that is not incompatible with such purpose. Differences lie in the approaches taken by States. Some jurisdictions perceive the obligation for consent to be *ex ante*.

— *Proportionality.* Proportionality requires that the necessary measure taken should be proportionate to the legitimate claims being pursued.

— *Transparency.* Transparency denotes a general policy of openness regarding developments, practices and policies with respect to protection of personal data.

— *Individual participation and in particular the right to access.* This principle may be the most important for purposes of data protection. The individual should have access to such data as well as to the possibility of determining whether or not the keeper of the file has data concerning him and of obtaining such information or having

[56] *Ibid.*, p. 157. See also a pending case (*Segerstedt-Wiberg and others* v. *Sweden, Application No. 62332/00*), which was declared admissible on 20 September 2005. The European Court of Human Rights had to determine whether the collection and storage of information about individuals which are "in connection with their public activities", "already in the public domain" and which are accurate and collected on national security grounds, might constitute an infringement of the right to privacy. It also entails the right to refuse to advise the individuals concerned of the full extent of the information collected. See in this regard the Court's judgement of 6 June 2006, *Reports of Judgments and Decisions 2006-VII*, pp. 131 *et seq.* The Supreme Court of Iceland in its judgement No. 151/2003 of 27 November 2003, *Guðmundsdóttir* v. *Iceland,* addressed the question on the definition of "personal data" in the context of DNA data and questions of identifiability as linked to a relation who was deceased. See R. Gertz, "An analysis of the Icelandic Supreme Court judgment on the Health Sector Database Act", *SCRIPTed–A Journal of Law, Technology and Society*, vol. 1, No. 2 (June 2004), pp. 241–258.

[57] Kang, *loc. cit.* (footnote 5 above), at pp. 1207–1208.

[58] Novotny, *loc. cit.* (footnote 52 above), at p. 157.

[59] International Barriers to Data flows, Background Report, Committee on Interstate and Foreign Commerce, House of Representatives, Ninety-Sixth Congress, First Session, April 1979, quoted by the panel on Legal Issues of Transborder Data Transmission, *American Society of International Law Proceedings*, vol. 74 (1980), p. 175.

[60] See generally M. D. Kirby, "Transborder data flows and the 'basic rules' of data privacy", *Stanford Journal of International Law*, vol. 16 (1980), pp. 27–66. See also J. M. Eger, "The global phenomenon of teleinformatics: an introduction", *Cornell International Law Journal*, vol. 14 (1981) pp. 203–236. See also Secretary's Advisory Committee on Automated Personal Data Systems, United States Department of Health, Education and Welfare, *Records, Computers and the Rights of Citizens* (1973), Appendix A, p. 147.

it communicated to him in a form, in a manner and at a cost that is reasonable. This holds with the right of an individual to know about the existence of any data file and its contents, to challenge the data and to have it corrected, amended or erased.

— *Non-discrimination.* This principle connotes that data likely to give rise to unlawful and arbitrary discrimination should not be compiled. This includes information collated on racial or ethnic origin, colour, sex life, political opinions, religious, philosophical and other beliefs as well as membership in an association or trade union.

— *Responsibility.* This principle embraces data security; data should be protected by reasonable and appropriate measures to prevent their loss, destruction, unauthorized access, use, modification or disclosure and the keeper of the file should be accountable for it.

— *Independent supervision and legal sanction.* Supervision and sanction require that there should be a mechanism for ensuring due process and accountability. There should be an authority legally accountable for giving effect to the requirements of data protection.

— *Data equivalency in the case of transborder flow of personal data.* This is a principle of compatibility; it is intended to avoid the creation of unjustified obstacles and restrictions to the free flow of data, as long as the circulation is consistent with the standard or deemed adequate for that purpose.

— *The principle of derogability.* This entails power to make exceptions and impose limitations if they are necessary to protect national security, public order, public health or morality or to protect the rights of others.

DEROGABILITY

24. While privacy concerns are of critical importance, such concerns have to be balanced with other value-interests. The privacy values to avoid embarrassment, construct intimacy and protect against misuse associated with the need to protect the individual have to be weighed against other counter-values against individual control over personal information, such as the need not to disrupt the flow of international trade and commerce and the flow of information and the importance of securing the truth, as well as the need to live in a secure environment.[61] There are allowable restrictions and exceptions, for example, with respect to national security, public order (*ordre public*),[62] public health or morality[63] or in order to protect the rights and freedoms of others, as well as the need for effective law enforcement and judicial cooperation in combating crimes at the international level, including the threats posed by international terrorism and organized crime.

25. The processing of personal data must be interpreted in accordance with human rights principles.[64] Accordingly, any of the objectives in the public interest would justify interference with private life if it is (*a*) in accordance with the law, (*b*) necessary in a democratic society for the pursuit of legitimate aims, and (*c*) not disproportionate to the objective pursued.[65] The phrase "in accordance with the law" goes beyond the formalism of having in existence a legal basis in domestic law: it requires that the legal basis be "accessible" and "foreseeable".[66] Foreseeability necessitates sufficiency of precision in formulation of the rule to enable any individual to regulate his conduct.[67]

26. A number of issues still arise in the practice of States. The first relates to *data retention and data preservation*. In the cyberworld, there are two basic ways in which personal information is collected: (*a*) through direct solicitation from users (registration and transactional data)[68]; and (*b*) surreptitiously through tracking the way people surf the Internet (clickstream data).[69] One way in which States have used the law to monitor activities in the cyberspace for purposes of law enforcement is to promulgate *data retention* legislation.[70] Essentially, Internet service providers are required to clickstream, collect and store data on the activities of their customers in the cyberspace. This has raised particular concerns because it

> "rearchitects" the Internet from a context of relative obscurity to one of greater transparency. This manipulation of context influences what values flourish on the Internet. Specifically, data retention, by making it easier to link acts to actors, promotes the value of accountability, while diminishing the values of privacy and anonymity.[71]

---

[61] See generally C. Crump, "Data retention: privacy, anonymity, and accountability online, *Stanford Law Review*, vol. 56 (2003–2004), pp. 191–229.

[62] See, for example, the Convention on cybercrime adopted by the Council of Europe at Budapest on 23 November 2001.

[63] For example, UNESCO adopted the Universal Declaration on the Human Genome and Human Rights on 11 November 1997 (UNESCO, *Records of the General Conference, Twenty-ninth Session*, vol. I, *Resolutions*, resolution 16), endorsed by General Assembly resolution 53/152 of 9 December 1998. See also the 1997 Convention for the Protection of Human Rights and Dignity of the Human Being with regard to the Application of Biology and Medicine, and the 1998 Additional Protocol to the Convention for the Protection of Human Rights and Dignity of the Human Being with regard to the Application of Biology and Medicine, on the Prohibition of Cloning Human Beings.

[64] Joined Cases C-465/00, C-138/01 and C-139/01 (see footnote 42 above).

[65] See *Fressoz and Roire* v. *France, Application no. 29183/95, Judgement of 21 January 1999*, Grand Chamber, European Court of Human Rights, *Reports of Judgments and Decisions 1999-I*, pp. 1 *et seq*. For example, when reviewing proportionality, the extent to which the data affect private life is taken into account. Data relating to private intimacy, health, family life or sexuality must be protected more strongly than data relating to income and taxes, which, while also personal, concern identity to a lesser extent and are therefore less sensitive.

[66] *Amann* v. *Switzerland* (see footnote 43 above), paras. 55–62.

[67] *Malone* v. *United Kingdom, Application no. 8691/79, Judgement of 2 August 1984*, European Court of Human Rights, *Series A: Judgments and Decisions*, vol. 82, pp. 31–32, para. 66.

[68] D. J. Solove, "Privacy and power…", *loc. cit.* (footnote 1 above), at p. 1408.

[69] *Ibid.*, p. 1411.

[70] For example, Commission decision 2004/535/EC of 14 May 2004 (see footnote 31 above). Swiss Internet service providers are legally required to record the time, date, sender identity and receiver identity of all e-mails. Spain also requires Internet service providers to retain some types of data on their customers for one year. See also Directive 2006/24/EC of the European Parliament and of the Council of 15 March 2006 on the retention of data generated or processed in connection with the provision of publicly available electronic communications services or of public communications networks and amending Directive 2002/58/EC (footnote 30 above).

[71] C. Crump, *loc. cit.* (footnote 61 above), p. 194.

27. Unlike data retention, *data preservation* has a more limited remit as a tool to enable law enforcement to preserve records and other evidence in respect of a particular customer under investigation pending the issuance of a court order.[72] Protection of personal data in a form that permits identification of the data-subject may in some cases require that, once the purpose has expired, the data be destroyed, properly archived or reidentified. The longer the data are retained or the more general the edict for retention is, the higher the concerns are from a perspective of privacy in accordance with human rights principles.

28. A second related aspect is accessibility of Governments to private and public databases: the ability of Governments to purchase information on individuals for use in law enforcement from private databases. Such databases are often voluntarily compiled and shared voluntarily with governmental authorities.[73]

29. It may be necessary to identify safeguards that would assure that data retention or data preservation and accessibility to databases do not render the essence of privacy inoperable.

30. There is also recognition of limitations in respect of use of files for statistical uses or scientific research or in respect of journalistic purposes or for artistic or literary expression. The importance of securing the truth and the importance of the free flow of information necessitate that certain data files be treated differently even if they may relate to personally identifiable data. The use of files for statistical, technical or scientific research or concerning journalistic pursuits or artistic or literary expression falls into this category. The right of access to information may be restricted, provided such restrictions are based on law and are necessary in order to respect the rights and reputation of others, for the protection of national security or of public order (*ordre public*) or of public health or morals.

Data adequacy/equivalency

31. The transfer of data from one State to another raises questions of security and protection, such as whether and in what circumstances transfer should occur when the other State cannot ensure adequate levels of protection, what would be the applicable law and how problems that could arise would be resolved. Accordingly, data adequacy or data equivalency issues may need some treatment within the topic.

32. The following appendix outlines, for indicative purposes only, the issues that may have to be addressed:

Appendix

Scope: Protection of personal data and privacy of communications

Scope ratione personae: personal data

Scope ratione materiae: private and public sectors: query whether international organizations should be included

Possible exclusions: purely personal and household activities

Definitions: data; data-subject; data user; data file; data retention; data preservation; personally identifiable data; sensitive data; traffic data; location data; transborder flow of personal data; processing of personal data; communication; third party user; registration and transactional data; clickstream data

Core principles: lawful and fair data collection and processing; accuracy; purpose specification and limitation; proportionality; transparency; individual participation and in particular the right to access; non-discrimination; responsibility; independent supervision and legal sanction; data equivalency in the case of transborder flow of personal data; derogability

Restrictions to right of access: maintenance of public order; defence and security of the State; public health, etc.

Confidentiality and security: confidentiality of communications; security of sensitive data

Rights in respect of the data subject: to be informed; to withhold consent; access; rectification; to object to processing of data for a legitimate reason; to a remedy

Data processing: fairness and lawfulness; accountability

Criteria for legitimate data processing: consent; contractual obligation; other legal obligation; necessary to protect vital interest of data-subject; necessary in the public interest; necessary for the purposes of legitimate interest

Exceptions and limitations: national security; defence; public security; criminal law enforcement; fiscal concerns and economic well-being; protection of data-subject and others

Policymaking (census, population registers, surveys): scientific, research and statistics; journalistic and artistic activities

Sanction and remedy: administrative; judicial

Adequacy of level of transborder protection: principle of adequacy; determination of adequacy; derogations

Implementation: legislation; regulation; self-regulation

---

[72] The Uniting and Strengthening America by Providing Appropriate Tools Required to Intercept and Obstruct Terrorism (USA Patriot Act) Act of 2001 establishes numerous amendments to legislation in order to increase the investigative and surveillance capacities of the law enforcement agencies in the United States. The Wiretap Act, the Electronic Communications Privacy Act of 1986, the Computer Fraud and Abuse Act of 1986, the Foreign Intelligence Surveillance Act of 1978, Family Education Rights and Privacy Act, the Pen Registers and Trap and Trace Devices Statute, the Money Laundering Control Act of 1986, the Immigration and Nationality Act, the Bank Secrecy Act of 1970, the Right to Financial Privacy Act of 1978 and the Fair Credit Reporting Act have been amended by the USA Patriot Act.

[73] See generally D. J. Solove, "Digital dossiers and the dissipation of Fourth Amendment privacy", *Southern California Law Review,* vol. 75 (2002), pp. 1083–1167. The *New York Times*, in its edition of 21 March 2006, B.6 (A. L. Cowan, "Librarian is still John Doe, despite Patriot Act Revision"), notes that 30,000 national security letters are issued in a year demanding patron records. See also *John Doe, American Civil Liberties Union and American Civil Liberties Union Foundation* v. *Attorney-General, et al.*, United States Southern District Court of New York, opinion, decision and order of Judge Victor Marrero.

Selected bibliography

All European Academies: *Privacy Protection in the Information Society*, Amsterdam, Allea, 2002.

Bauchner, J. S. "State sovereignty and the globalizing effects of the Internet: a case study of the privacy debate", *Brooklyn Journal of International Law,* vol. 26 (2000–2001), 689–722.

———. and R. Ramani: *International Regulatory Devices: Legal Research Guides to the EU Data Protection Directive and the Convention on Biological Diversity*, Buffalo (New York), Hein, 2001.

Beardwood, J. and D. Fabiano: "Approaches to 'extra-jurisdictional' data transfers in Canadian and European outsourcing: a comparative approach", *Computer Law Review International*, vol. 6 (2005), 166–177.

Becker, R. K. A. "Transborder data flows: personal data—recommendations of the Organisation for Economic Co-operation and Development concerning guidelines governing the protection of privacy and transborder flows of personal data, O.E.C.D. Doc. C(80)58 (Oct. 1, 1980)", *Harvard International Law Journal*, vol. 22 (1981) 241–247.

Belleil, A: *e-Privacy—Le marché des données personnelles: protection de la vie privée à l'âge d'Internet*, Paris, Dunod, 2001.

Bergkamp, L. *European Community Law for the New Economy*, Antwerp/Oxford/New York, Intersentia, 2003.

Beyleveld, D., *et al.* (eds.): *The Data Protection Directive and Medical Research across Europe*, Ashgate, Aldershot, 2004.

Bignami, F. "Transgovernmental networks vs. democracy: the case of the European information privacy network", *Michigan Journal of International Law*, vol. 26 (2004–2005), 807–868.

Bing, J. "The Council of Europe Convention and the OECD guidelines on data protection", *Michigan Yearbook of International Legal Studies*, vol. 5 (1984), 271–303.

Bothe, M. "Transborder data flows: do we mean freedom or business?", *Michigan Journal of International Law*, vol. 10 (1989), 333–344.

———. "Data, transborder flow and protection", in R. Bernhardt (ed.), *Encyclopedia of Public International Law*, vol. 1, Amsterdam, Elsevier, 1992, 950–961.

Bourgeos, C. "L'anonymat et les nouvelles technologies de l'information", Paris, Université René Descartes, 2003 (unpublished doctoral thesis; J. Huet, advisor).

Boyle, D. C. "Proposal to amend the United States Privacy Act to extend its protections to foreign nationals and non-resident aliens", *Cornell International Law Journal*, vol. 22 (1989), 285–305.

Brulin, H. "La protection des données: quête et errements dans le troisième pilier", *Actualités de droit pénal européen*, Brussels, La Charte, 2003, 133–152.

Burke, M. E., *et al.* "Information services, technology, and data protection", *International Lawyer (ABA),* vol. 39 (2005), 403–416.

Carr, J. G. "Wiretapping in West Germany", *The American Journal of Comparative Law*, vol. 29 (1981), 607–645.

Chassigneux, C. "L'encadrement juridique du traitement des données personnelles sur les sites de commerce en ligne", Ann Arbor (Michigan), UMI Dissertation Services, 2004 (doctoral thesis of the Université Panthéon-Assas (Paris II) and the Université de Montréal).

Chatillon, G. (ed.): *Le droit international de l'internet: Actes du colloque organisé à Paris, les 19 et 20 novembre 2001 par le Ministère de la Justice, l'Université Paris-I Panthéon-Sorbonne et l'Association Arpeje*, Brussels, Bruylant, 2002.

Chene, T. "La protection des données personnelles face aux fichiers des renseignements généraux", Paris, Université Panthéon-Assas (Paris II), 2005 (mémoire de DESS, Droit du multimédia et de l'informatique de Paris II; G. Kostic, advisor).

Chung, Ch.-M. and I. Shin: "On-line data protection and cyberlaws in Korea", *Korean Journal of International and Comparative Law,* vol. 27 (December 1999), 21–43.

Commission nationale de l'informatique et des libertés: *Voix, image et protection des données personnelles*, Paris, La documentation française, 1996.

Crump, C. "Data retention: privacy, anonymity, and accountability online", *Stanford Law Review,* vol. 56 (2003–2004), 191–229.

Damon, L. J. "Freedom of information versus national sovereignty: the need for a new global forum for the resolution of transborder data flow problems", *Fordham International Law Journal,* vol. 10 (1986–1987), 262–287.

Daniel-Paczosa, A. "Data protection and the right to privacy in the United States and West Germany", *Arizona Journal of International and Comparative Law* (1987), 154–163.

De Graaf, F. "The protection of privacy in Dutch law", *Human Rights*, vol. 5 (1975–1976), 177–192.

De Schutter, B. "Data protection in the area of freedom, security and justice", *Collegium*, No. 22 (December 2001), *Proceedings of the Conference Integrated Security in Europe: a Democratic Perspective, Bruges, 14–17 November 2001*, Bruges, College of Europe, 2001, 51–55.

De Schutter, O. "Article II–68: Protection des données à caractère personnel", *Traité établissant une Constitution pour l'Europe*, vol. 2, Brussels, Bruylant, 2005, 122–152.

Dempsey, J. X. and L. M. Flint. "Commercial data and national security", *George Washington Law Review,* vol. 72 (2003–2004), 1459–1502.

Dhont, J. and M. V. Pérez Asinari. "New physics and the law. A comparative approach to the EU and US privacy and data protection regulation", in F. R. Van der Mensbrugghe (ed.), *L'utilisation de la méthode comparative en droit européen*, Namur, Presses universitaires de Namur, 2003, 67–97.

Dilascio, T. "How safe is the safe harbor?: U.S. and E.U. data privacy law and the enforcement of the FTC's Safe Harbor program", *Boston University International Law Journal*, vol. 22 (2004), 399–424.

Easterbrook, F. H. "Cyberspace and the law of the horse", *University of Chicago Legal Forum* (1996), 207–216.

Eger, J. M. "The global phenomenon of teleinformatics: an introduction", *Cornell International Law Journal,* vol. 14 (1981), 203–236.

Eguiguren Praeli, F. J. "El Hábeas Data y su desarrollo en el Perú," in *Liber Amicorum Héctor Fix-Zamudio*, vol. 1, San José, Secretaría de la Corte Interamericana de Derechos Humanos, 1998, 611–625.

Elmajzoub, M. "*La gestion des données personnelles dans le secteur de la police en Europe*", Montpellier, Université de Montpellier I, UFR Droit, 2004 (unpublished doctoral thesis; J. Frayssinet, advisor).

Epperson, G. M. "Contracts for transnational information services: securing equivalency of data protection", *Harvard International Law Journal*, vol. 22 (1981), 157–175.

Estadella-Yuste, O. "The draft directive of the European Community regarding the protection of personal data", *International and Comparative Law Quarterly*, vol. 41 (1992), 170–179.

Evans, A. C. "European data protection law", *The American Journal of Comparative Law,* vol. 29 (1981), 571–605.

FENOLL-TROUSSEAU, M.-P. and G. Haas (eds.). *Internet et protection des données personnelles*, Paris, Litec, 2000.

FISHMAN, W. L. "Introduction to transborder data flows", *Stanford Journal of International Law,* vol. 16 (1980), 1–26.

———."Some policy and legal issues in transborder data flow", *American Society of International Law Proceedings*, vol. 74 (1980), 179–188.

FRAZIER, L. E. "Extraterritorial enforcement of PIPEDA: a multi-tiered analysis", *George Washington International Law Review*, vol. 36 (2004), 203–225.

GAO, F. "The e-commerce legal environment in China: status quo and issues", *Temple International and Comparative Law Journal*, vol. 18 (2004), 51–75.

GARCÍA BELAUNDE, D. "El *Habeas Data* y su configuración normativa (con algunas referencias a la Constitución peruana de 1993)," in *Liber Amicorum Héctor Fix-Zamudio*, vol. 1, San José, Secretaría de la Corte Interamericana de Derechos Humanos, 1998, 715–722.

GERARDS, J. H., A. W. Heringa and H. L. Janssen. *Genetic Discrimination and Genetic Privacy in a Comparative Perspective*, Antwerp, Intersentia, 2005.

GEVERS, S. "Human tissue research, with particular reference to DNA banking", in J. K. M. Gevers, E. H. Hondius and J. H. Hubben (eds.), *Health Law, Human Rights and the Biomedicine Convention: Essays in Honour of Henriette Roscam Abbing*, Leiden, Martinus Nijhoff, 2005, 231–243.

GILBERT, F. "Emerging issues in global AIDS policy: preserving privacy", *Whittier Law Review*, vol. 25 (2003–2004), 273–306.

GOEMANS, C. and J. Dumortier. "Enforcement issues—mandatory retention of traffic data in the EU: possible impact on privacy and on-line anonymity", in C. Nicoll, J. E. J. Prins and M. J. M. van Dellen (eds.), *Digital Anonymity and the Law: Tensions and Dimensions*, The Hague, T.M.C. Asser Press, 2003, 161–183.

GOURAS, E. K. "The reform of West German data protection law as a necessary correlate to improving domestic security", *Columbia Journal of Transnational Law*, vol. 24 (1985–1986), 597–621.

GROETKER, R. "Looking for Mohammed: data screening in search of terrorists", in G. Meggle, *et al.* (eds.), *Ethics of Terrorism and Counter-terrorism*, Frankfurt, Ontos, 2005, 301–318.

GUBITZ, A. S. "The U.S. Aviation and Transportation Security Act of 2001 in conflict with the E.U. data protection laws: how much access to airline passenger data does the United States need to combat terrorism?", *New England Law Review*, vol. 39 (2004–2005), 431–475.

HEISENBERG, D. *Negotiating Privacy: the European Union, the United States, and Personal Data Protection*, Boulder, Lynne Rienner, 2005.

HERRÁN ORTIZ, A. I. *El derecho a la protección de datos personales en la sociedad de la información*, Bilbao, Universidad de Deusto, 2003.

HETCHER, S. "Changing the social meaning of privacy in cyberspace", *Harvard Journal of Law & Technology,* vol. 15 (2001–2002), 149–209.

HONDIUS, F. W. *Emerging Data Protection in Europe*, Amsterdam/New York, North Holland/Elsevier, 1975.

———. "Data law in Europe", *Stanford Journal of International Law*, vol. 16 (1980), 87–111.

HOOFNAGLE, C. J. "Big Brother's little helpers: how ChoicePoint and other commercial data brokers collect and package your data for law enforcement", *North Carolina Journal of International Law and Commercial Regulation,* vol. 29 (2003–2004), 595–637.

INSTITUT INTERNATIONAL D'ADMINISTRATION PUBLIQUE. *La protection des données personnelles*, Paris, Institut international d'administration publique, 1999.

INTERNATIONAL LABOUR ORGANIZATION. *Protection des données personnelles des travailleurs*, Geneva, ILO, 1997 (Recueil de directives pratiques du BIT).

IVASCANU, D. "Legal issues in electronic commerce in the Western hemisphere", *Arizona Journal of International and Comparative Law,* vol. 17 (2000), 219–255.

KANG, J. "Information privacy in cyberspace transactions", *Stanford Law Review*, vol. 50 (1997–1998), 1193–1294.

KIRBY, M. D. "Transborder data flows and the 'basic rules' of data privacy", *Stanford Journal of International Law,* vol. 16 (1980), 27–66.

KOSSICK, R. "The Internet in Latin America: new opportunities, developments, & challenges", *American University International Law Review*, vol. 16 (2000–2001), 1309–1341.

LEHDONVIRTA, V. "European Union data protection Directive: adequacy of data protection in Singapore", *Singapore Journal of Legal Studies* (2004), 511–546.

LEMAY, V. "La protection des données personnelles face aux nouvelles conditions d'entrée aux Etats-Unis", Paris, Université Panthéon-Assas (Paris II), 2004 (mémoire de DESS, Droit du multimédia et de l'informatique de Paris II; G. Kostic, advisor).

LESSIG, L. "The law of the horse: what cyberlaw might teach", *Harvard Law Review*, vol. 113 (1999–2000), 501–549.

LIPOWICZ, I. "Right to information versus data protection: a challenge for modern constitution and modern society", in G. Amato, G. Braibant and E. Venizelos (eds.), *The Constitutional Revision in Today's Europe*, London, Esperia, 2002, 479–482.

LOBATO DE FARIA, M. P. M. G. *Données génétiques informatisées: un nouveau défi à la protection du droit à la confidentialité des données personnelles de santé*, Villeneuve d'Ascq, Presses universitaires du Septentrion, 1999.

LOWTHER, R. "U.S. privacy regulations dictated by EU law: how the healthcare profession may be regulated", *Columbia Journal of Transnational Law*, vol. 41 (2002–2003), 435–454.

LUJÁN FAPPIANO, O. "*Habeas Data*: una aproximación a su problemática y a su posible solución normative", in *Liber Amicorum Héctor Fix-Zamudio*, vol. 1, San José, Corte Interamericana de Derechos Humanos, 1998, 643–666.

MANLEY, T. J. and S. M. Hobby. "Globalization of work: offshore outsourcing in the IT age", *Emory International Law Review*, vol. 18 (2004), 401–419.

MARCELIN, F. "*La protection des données personnelles et la régulation*", Avignon, Université d'Avignon et des Pays de Vaucluse, 2002 (unpublished doctoral thesis; J.-M. Bruguière, advisor).

MARKS, S. P. "Tying Prometheus down: the international law of human genetic manipulation", *Chicago Journal of International Law*, vol. 3 (2002), 115–136.

MARLIAC-NEGRIER, C. *La protection des données nominatives informatiques en matière de recherche médicale*, Aix-Marseille, Presses universitaires d'Aix-Marseille, 2001.

MAYER-SCHÖNBERGER, V. "The shape of governance: analyzing the world of Internet regulation", *Virginia Journal of International Law*, vol. 43 (2002–2003), 605–673.

MERL, S. R. "Internet communication standards for the 21st century: international terrorism must force the U.S. to adopt 'carnivore' and new electronic surveillance standards", *Brooklyn Journal of International Law*, vol. 27 (2001–2002), 245–284.

MINISTÈRE DE LA FONCTION PUBLIQUE ET DE LA RÉFORME DE L'ETAT (P. Truche, J.-P. Faugère and P. Flichy; rapporteur général M. Ronai; conseiller juridique J.-Ph. Mochon). *Administration électronique et protection des données personnelles: livre blanc. Rapport au Ministre de la fonction publique et de la réforme de l'État*, Paris, La documentation française, 2002.

MONCAYO VON HASE, A. "El comercio electrónico: problemas y tendencias en materia de protección de la propiedad intelectual y de los datos personales desde una perspectiva argentina e internacional", in C. M. Correa (ed.), *Temas de derecho industrial y de la competencia. Derecho del comercio internacional: acuerdos regionales y OMC*, Buenos Aires, Ciudad Argentina, 2004, 275–342.

Monnier, G. *Le droit d'accès aux données personnelles traitées par un média: droit suisse de la personnalité; aspects de droit constitutionnel, de droit pénal et de droit de procédure*, Bern, Stæmpfli, 1999.

Muñoz, R. "La protection des données des passagers", *Revue du droit de l'Union européenne* (2004), 771–795.

Nguy, V. N. "Using architectural constraints and game theory to regulate international cyberspace behavior", *San Diego International Law Journal*, vol. 5 (2004), 431–463.

Novotny, E. J. "Transborder data flows and international law: a framework for policy-oriented inquiry", *Stanford Journal of International Law*, vol. 16 (1980), 141–180.

Oble-Laffaire, M.-L. *Protection des données à caractère personnel*, Paris, Editions d'Organisation, 2005.

Orengo, E. "*La protection des personnes dans le cadre des flux transfrontières de données personnelles*", Paris, Université Panthéon-Assas, 2002 (unpublished doctoral thesis; J. Huet and G. Kostic, advisors).

Page, G. *Le droit d'accès et de contestation dans le traitement des données personnelles: étude de base en droit privé suisse et américain*, Zurich, Schulthess, 1983.

Palazzi, P. A. *La transmisión internacional de datos personales y la protección de la privacidad, Argentina, América Latina, Estados Unidos y la Unión Europea*, Buenos Aires, Ad-Hoc, 2002.

Panel on Trade in Services: "The case of transborder data flows, *American Society of International Law Proceedings*, vol. 79 (1985), 246–260.

Panel on Legal issues of Transborder Data Transmission: *American Society of International Law Proceedings*, vol. 74 (1980), 175–178.

Pérez Asinari, M. V. "Legal constraints for the protection of privacy and personal data in electronic evidence handling", *International Review of Law, Computers and Technology*, vol. 18 (2004), 231–250.

Perrin, J.-F. "La notion d' 'effectivité' en droit européen, international et comparé de la protection des données personnelles", in Faculté de droit de l'Université de Lausanne (ed.), *Mélanges en l'honneur de Bernard Dutoit*, Geneva, Librairie Droz, 2002, 197–208.

Pierre-Beausse, C. *La protection des données personnelles*, Luxemburg, Promoculture, 2005.

Ploem, C. "Freedom of research and its relation to the right to privacy", in J. K. M. Gevers, E. H. Hondius and J. H. Hubben (eds.), *Health Law, Human Rights and the Biomedicine Convention: Essays in Honour of Henriette Roscam Abbing*, Leiden, Martinus Nijhoff, 2005, 161–173.

Pool, I. de S. and R. J. Solomon: "Intellectual property and transborder data flows", *Stanford Journal of International Law*, vol. 16 (1980), 113–139.

Poullet, Y. and M. V. Péres Asinan: "Données des voyageurs aériens: le débat Europe–Etats-Unis", in *Journal des tribunaux: Droit européen*, vol. 12, No. 105 (January 2004), 266–274.

Quilleré-Majzoub, F. "Les individus face aux systèmes d'information de l'Union européenne: l'impossible équation du contrôle juridictionnel et de la protection des données personnelles au niveau européen?," in *Journal du droit international*, vol. 132 (2005), 609–635.

Rehder, J. and E. C. Collins: "The legal transfer of employment-related data to outside the European Union: is it even still possible?", *International Lawyer*, vol. 39 (2005), 129–160.

Renard, A. "Les enjeux mondiaux de la protection des données personnelles dans le cadre de la communication en ligne", Paris, Université Panthéon-Sorbonne, 2002 (mémoire de DESS, Gestion européenne et internationale).

Ribs, J. "20 ans de protection des données, ou les droits de l'homme de la troisième génération", in M. Balado and J. A. García Regueiro (eds.), *La Declaración Universal de los Derechos Humanos en su 50 aniversario*, Barcelona, Bosch, 1998, 597–611.

Salbu, S. R. "Regulation of borderless high-technology economies: managing spillover effects", *Chicago Journal of International Law*, vol. 3 (2002), 137–153.

Seitz, N. "Transborder search: a new perspective in law enforcement?", *Yale Journal of Law and Technology*, vol. 7 (2004–2005), 23–50.

Senat, Service des affaires européennes: *Etude de législation comparée No. 62: La protection des données personnelles*, Paris, Le Sénat, 1999.

Shaffer, G. "Globalization and social protection: the impact of EU and international rules in the ratcheting up of U.S. privacy standards", *Yale Journal of International Law*, vol. 25 (2000), 1–88.

———. "The power of EU collective action: the impact of EU data privacy regulation on US business practice", in P. S. Berman (ed.), *The Globalization of International Law*, Aldershot, Ashgate, 2005, 497–515.

Siegenthaler, J. "La protection des données à caractère personnel en Europe: spécificité de l'Union européenne et régime suisse", in T. Balmelli (ed.), *La Suisse saisie par l'Union européenne. Thèmes choisis sur le droit et les politiques de l'UE*, Fribourg, Edis, 2003, 213–249.

Siemen, B. "The EU–US agreement on passenger name records and EC-law: data protection, competences and human rights issues in international agreements of the Community", *German Yearbook of International Law*, vol. 47 (2004), 629–665.

Sihanya, B. "Infotainment and cyberlaw in Africa: regulatory benchmarks for the Third Millennium", *Transnational Law & Contemporary Problems*, vol. 10 (2000), 583–640.

Société de législation comparée. "La protection des données personnelles. Etat de la législation et tendances de la jurisprudence/3èmes Journées franco-suisses, Dijon, 13–15 octobre 1986", *Revue internationale de droit comparé*, vol. 39, No. 3 (July–September 1987).

Solove, D. J. "Privacy and power: computer databases and metaphors for information privacy", *Stanford Law Review*, vol. 53 (2000–2001), 1393–1462.

Soma, J. T., S. D. Rynerson and B. D. Beall-Eder. "An analysis of the use of bilateral agreements between transnational trading groups: the U.S./EU e-commerce privacy safe harbor", *Texas International Law Journal*, vol. 39 (2004), 171–214.

Sussmann, M. A. "The critical challenges from international high-tech and computer-related crime at the Millennium", *Duke Journal of Comparative & International Law*, vol. 9 (1998–1999), 451–489.

Swire, P. P. and R. E. Litan. *None of Your Business: World Data Flows, Electronic Commerce, and the European Privacy Directive*, Washington D.C., Brookings Institution Press, 1998.

Tabatoni, P. *La protection de la vie privée dans la société d'information*, Paris, Presses universitaires de France, 2002.

Taussig, E. A. "European Union data protection Directive", in A. P. Morriss and S. Estreicher (eds.), *Cross-Border Human Resources, Labor and Employment Issues: Proceedings of the New York University 54th Annual Conference on Labor Law*, The Hague, Kluwer Law International, 2005, 327–337.

Turn, R. "Privacy protection and security in transnational data processing systems", *Stanford Journal of International Law*, vol. 16 (1980), 67–86.

Wakana, J. M. "The future of online privacy: a proposal for international legislation", *Loyola of Los Angeles International and Comparative Law Review*, vol. 26 (2003–2004), 151–179.

Walden, I. "Anonymising personal data under European law", in C. Nicoll, J. E. J. Prins and M. J. M. van Dellen (eds.), *Digital Anonymity and the Law: Tensions and Dimensions*, The Hague, T.M.C. Asser Press, 2003, 147–159.

Yarn, D. "The development of Canadian law on transborder data flow", *Georgia Journal of International and Comparative Law*, vol. 13 (1983), 825–855.

Zgajewski, T. "L'échange des données personnelles des passagers áeriens entre l'Union européenne et les États-Unis: une mise en lumière des faiblesses de l'Union européenne dans la lutte contre le terrorisme", in *Studia diplomatica*, vol. 57, Nos. 4–5 (2004), 117–158.

Annex V

EXTRATERRITORIAL JURISDICTION

(Secretariat)

A. Background

1. Traditionally, the exercise of jurisdiction by a State was primarily limited to persons, property and acts within its territory and to relatively exceptional situations in which its nationals travelled beyond its borders. Today, the exercise of extraterritorial jurisdiction by a State with respect to persons, property or acts outside its territory has become an increasingly common phenomenon largely as a consequence of: (*a*) the increase in the movement of persons beyond national borders;[1] (*b*) the growing number of multinational corporations; (*c*) the globalization of the world economy,[2] including international banking and international stock exchanges; (*d*) the increase in transnational criminal activities, including drug trafficking, money laundering, securities fraud and international terrorism; (*e*) the increase in illegal migration;[3] and (*f*) the increasing use of the Internet across national borders for legal or illegal purposes, such as electronic contracts, e-commerce and cybercrimes.

2. The assertion of extraterritorial jurisdiction by a State is an attempt to regulate by means of national legislation, adjudication or enforcement the conduct of persons, property or acts beyond its borders which affect the interests of the State in the absence of such regulation under international law. The exercise of extraterritorial jurisdiction by a State tends to be more common with respect to particular fields of national law in view of the persons, property or acts outside its territory which are more likely to affect its interests, notably criminal law and commercial law.

3. The topic "extraterritorial jurisdiction" is in an advanced stage in terms of State practice, and is concrete. Although there appears to be a strong need for codification in this field, some may question whether the practice is sufficiently uniform or widespread to support a codification effort at this time. However, recent developments in this regard indicate that practice may be converging towards a more uniform view of the law. Moreover, innovations in communications and transportation make the codification and progressive development of the limits of the extraterritorial jurisdiction of States a timely and important endeavour.

B. Brief survey of existing norms and rules

1. The notion of extraterritorial jurisdiction

4. The notion of extraterritorial jurisdiction may be understood as referring to the exercise of sovereign power or authority by a State outside of its territory. There are three aspects of this notion which may require consideration, namely, jurisdiction, extraterritoriality and applicable law.

5. The jurisdiction of a State may be understood as generally referring to the sovereign power or authority of a State.[4] More specifically, the jurisdiction of a State may be divided into three categories, namely, prescriptive jurisdiction, adjudicative jurisdiction and enforcement jurisdiction.[5] Prescriptive jurisdiction refers to the authority of a State to adopt legislation providing norms of conduct which govern persons, property or conduct. Adjudicative jurisdiction refers to the authority of a State to determine the rights of parties under its law in a particular case. Enforcement jurisdiction refers to the authority of a State to ensure compliance with its law. The consideration of the various types of jurisdiction may be important for two reasons. First, the internationally valid exercise of

[1] "Since 1965, the number of international migrants has doubled. As of the year 2000, there were approximately 175 million migrants throughout the world" (J.-D. Gerber, "Foreword", in A. T. Aleinikoff and V. Chetail (eds.), *Migration and International Legal Norms*, The Hague, T.M.C. Asser Press, 2003, p. vii).

[2] "The world has been transformed by the process of globalization. States, societies, economies and cultures in different regions of the world are increasingly integrated and interdependent. New technologies enable the rapid transfer of capital, goods, services, information and ideas from one country and continent to another" (*Migration in an Interconnected World: New Directions for Action*, report of the Global Commission on International Migration, October 2005, p. 1, para. 1).

[3] "An estimated 2.5 to 4 million migrants cross international borders without authorization each year" (*ibid*, p. 85).

[4] See, for example, B. H. Oxman, "Jurisdiction of States", in R. Bernhardt (ed.), *Encyclopedia of Public International Law*, vol. 3, Amsterdam, Elsevier, 1997, pp. 55–60, at p. 55.

[5] "The term 'jurisdiction' is most often used to describe the lawful power of a State to define and enforce the rights and duties, and control the conduct, of natural and juridical persons. A State exercises its jurisdiction by establishing rules (sometimes called the exercise of legislative jurisdiction or prescriptive competence), by establishing procedures for identifying breaches of the rules and the precise consequences thereof (sometimes called judicial jurisdiction or adjudicative competence), and by forcibly imposing consequences such as loss of liberty or property for breaches or, pending adjudication, alleged breaches of the rules (sometimes called enforcement jurisdiction or competence)" (Oxman, *loc. cit.* (footnote 4 above), at p. 55). See also R. O'Keefe, "Universal jurisdiction: clarifying the basic concept", *Journal of International Criminal Justice*, vol. 2, No. 1 (March 2004), pp. 735–760, at pp. 736–740; F. A. Mann, "The doctrine of jurisdiction in international law", *Recueil des cours* ... vol. 111 (1964–I), pp. 1–162, at p. 1; D. W. Bowett, "Jurisdiction: changing patterns of authority over activities and resources", BYBIL, vol. 53 (1982), pp. 1–26, at pp. 1 *et seq.*; I. Brownlie, *Principles of Public International Law,* 6th ed., Oxford University Press, 2003, at p. 297; and M. N. Shaw, *International Law*, 4th ed., Cambridge University Press, 1997, at p. 452. See, with respect to French-speaking literature, P. Daillier and A. Pellet, *Droit international public (Nguyen Quoc Dinh)*, 6th ed., Paris, Librairie générale de droit et de jurisprudence, 1999, pp. 501 and 504, paras. 334 and 336; P.-M. Dupuy, *Droit international public*, 7th ed., Paris, Dalloz, 2004, at pp. 78 *et seq.*; and J. Combacau and S. Sur, *Droit international public,* 6th ed., Paris, Montchrestien, 2004, at pp. 343 *et seq.*

prescriptive jurisdiction in the adoption of a law is a prerequisite for the valid exercise of adjudicative or enforcement jurisdiction with respect to that law.[6] Secondly, the requirements for the lawful exercise of different types of jurisdiction may differ.[7] The potential interference resulting from the extraterritorial exercise of prescriptive jurisdiction is less than that resulting from either adjudicative or enforcement jurisdiction.

6. The notion of extraterritoriality may be understood in relation to a State as encompassing the area beyond its territory, including its land, internal waters and territorial sea, as well as the adjacent airspace. The area beyond the territory of a State may fall within the territory of another State or may be outside the territorial jurisdiction of any State, namely the high seas and adjacent airspace[8] as well as outer space.[9] From a practical as well as a legal perspective, the organs of a State generally perform legislative, judicial or enforcement functions only within the territory of a State.[10] Principles of international law relating to the territorial integrity and independence of States prevent the organs of one State from being physically present or performing their functions in the territory of another State without the consent of the latter State.[11] Moreover, the exceptional cases in which a State has attempted to exercise its jurisdiction within the territory of another State by sending its officials to that State without consent are generally considered to be a violation of the territorial integrity and independence of the other State.[12] Certain special situations in which the authorities of a State are physically present and exercise jurisdiction in the territory of another State, for example, in the case of diplomatic premises, consular premises and military bases located in the territory of another State, are governed by specific rules of international law[13] rather than by international law concerning extraterritorial jurisdiction.

7. As regards the applicable law, the notion of extraterritorial jurisdiction may be understood as referring to the exercise of jurisdiction by a State with respect to its national law in its own national interest rather than the application of *foreign law* or *international law*. A State's application of foreign law or international law rather than its own national law would therefore be excluded from the scope of this topic since these situations would not constitute the exercise of extraterritorial jurisdiction by a State in relation to its national law based on its national interests.

2. Principles of extraterritorial jurisdiction

8. The exercise of the jurisdiction or sovereign authority of a State is often provided for in the national law of a State. However, the lawfulness of the exercise of this jurisdiction or authority—including extraterritorial jurisdiction—is determined by international law.[14]

9. The decision of the Permanent Court of International Justice in the *Lotus* case may be regarded as the starting point for the consideration of the rules of international law governing the extraterritorial exercise of jurisdiction by a State.[15] The Court indicated that the jurisdiction of a

---

[6] "If the substantive jurisdiction is beyond lawful limits, then any consequent enforcement jurisdiction is unlawful" (Brownlie, *op. cit.* (footnote 5 above), p. 308); "It is widely assumed that a State may not enforce its rules unless it has jurisdiction to prescribe those rules" (Oxman, *loc. cit.* (footnote 4 above), at p. 55; "A state may employ judicial or nonjudicial measures to induce or compel compliance or punish non-compliance with its laws or regulations, provided it has jurisdiction to prescribe..." (*Restatement of the Law Third, Restatement of the Law: The Foreign Relations Law of the United States*, vol. 1, St. Paul (Minnesota), American Law Institute Publishers, 1987, para. 431.(1), p. 321). With respect to criminal law: "A court cannot exercise jurisdiction in respect of an offence which the United States (or a State of the United States) could not constitutionally prescribe" (*ibid.*, para. 422, comment *c*, p. 314). There are different views concerning the distinction between the second and third types of jurisdiction in view of the close relationship between the two. See, for instance, with respect to literature addressing the adjudicative jurisdiction distinction, *Oppenheim's International Law,* 9th ed., vol. I, *Peace*, R. Y. Jennings and A. Watts (eds.), Harlow, Longman, 1992, p. 456; M. Akehurst, "Jurisdiction in international law", BYBIL, vol. 46 (1972–1973), pp. 145–257, at pp. 145 *et seq.*; and Oxman, *loc. cit.* (footnote 4 above), at p. 55.

[7] "These distinctions can be important in determining the limits of jurisdiction. The requisite contacts with a State necessary to support the exercise of jurisdiction differ depending on the nature of the jurisdiction being exercised" (Oxman, *loc. cit.* (footnote 4 above), at p. 55).

[8] Most of this matter is governed by treaties, for example, article 8 of the 1940 Treaty on International Penal Law; articles 1, 3 and 4 of the 1952 International Convention for the unification of certain rules relating to penal jurisdiction in matters of collision or other incidents of navigation; articles 5, 6 and 11 of the Convention on the High Seas; and articles 19 and 21 of the 1958 Convention on the Territorial Sea and the Contiguous Zone.

[9] However, it should be noted that outer space law constitutes a separate field of international law which would not be appropriate for consideration under the present topic.

[10] In exceptional cases, a court of one State may sit in the territory of another State on the basis of an agreement between the States concerned. See the *Lockerbie case*, Security Council resolution 1192 (1998), 27 August 1998, paragraph 4; verdict and the appeal of the Scottish Court, of 31 January 2001 and 14 March 2002 respectively, available at www.scotcourts.gov.uk/search-judgments/lockerbie-trial. Accessed 27 November 2012.

[11] The principles of the territorial integrity and the political independence of States are among those recognized in Article 2, paragraph 4, of the Charter of the United Nations. In the *Island of Palmas* case, the sole arbitrator, Max Huber, observed as follows: "Sovereignty in the relations between States signifies independence. Independence in regard to a portion of the globe is the right to exercise therein, to the exclusion of any other State, the functions of a State. The development of the national organisation of States during the last few centuries and, as a corollary, the development of international law, have established this principle of the exclusive competence of the State in regard to its own territory in such a way as to make it the point of departure in settling most questions that concern international relations" (*Island of* Palmas case *(Netherlands/United States of America), Award of 4 April 1928*, UNRIAA, vol. II (Sales No. 1949.V.I), pp. 829–871, at p. 838). "The governing principle is that a state cannot take measures on the territory of another state by way of enforcement of national laws without the consent of the latter" (Brownlie, *op. cit.* (footnote 5 above), at p. 306).

[12] "There are many cases in which states have claimed the right to their own law enforcement abroad. But the (open or secret) performance of state acts on the territory of another state without its consent, such as the kidnapping of the Nazi criminal Eichmann in Argentina by Israel in 1960 and the kidnapping in the *Alvarez-Machain* case by US agents, or the sinking of *Rainbow Warrior* by French agents in a New Zealand harbour, although some are disputed, generally constitute violations of the principles of territorial integrity and non-intervention" (P. Malanczuk, *Akehurst's Modern Introduction to International Law*, 7th rev. ed., London, Routledge, 1997, at p. 110).

[13] Special agreements govern the exercise of jurisdiction by the sending or the receiving State with respect to military or civilian aliens present on a military base; see H. Rumpf, "Military bases on foreign territory", in R. Bernhardt (ed.), *Encyclopedia of Public International Law*, vol. 3, Amsterdam, Elsevier, 1997, pp. 381–388, at pp. 381–382.

[14] See the *Case of the S.S. "Lotus" (France* v. *Turkey), Judgment No. 9 of 7 September 1927, P.C.I.J. Reports 1928, Series A, No. 10*, at pp. 18–19.

[15] *Ibid.* The *Lotus* case involved the exercise of adjudicative jurisdiction by Turkey with respect to the criminal responsibility of a French national on a French vessel for the deaths of Turkish nationals on a

State is territorial in nature and that a State cannot exercise jurisdiction outside its territory in the absence of a permissive rule of international law to the effect. However, the Court distinguished between the exercise of jurisdiction by a State outside its territory and the exercise of jurisdiction by a State within its territory with respect to persons, property or acts outside its territory. The Court indicated that States have broad discretion with respect to the exercise of jurisdiction in the latter sense as follows:

> Now the first and foremost restriction imposed by international law upon a State is that—failing the existence of a permissive rule to the contrary—it may not exercise its power in any form in the territory of another State. In this sense jurisdiction is certainly territorial; it cannot be exercised by a State outside its territory except by virtue of a permissive rule derived from international custom or from a convention.
>
> It does not, however, follow that international law prohibits a State from exercising jurisdiction in its own territory, in respect of any case which relates to acts which have taken place abroad, and in which it cannot rely on some permissive rule of international law.
>
> ...
>
> In these circumstances all that can be required of a State is that it should not overstep the limits which international law places upon its jurisdiction; within these limits, its title to exercise jurisdiction rests in its sovereignty.[16]

10. There have been a number of significant developments with respect to the extraterritorial jurisdiction of a State since the *Lotus* case was decided by the PCIJ in 1927. In particular, there are a number of principles of jurisdiction which may be asserted under contemporary international law in order to justify the extraterritorial jurisdiction of a State, including: (*a*) the "objective" territoriality principle; (*b*) the "effects doctrine"; (*c*) the protective principle; (*d*) the nationality principle; and (*e*) the passive personality principle. The common element underlying the various principles for the extraterritorial exercise of jurisdiction by a State under international law is the valid interest of the State in asserting its jurisdiction in such a case on the basis of a sufficient connection to the persons, property or acts concerned.

11. The *objective territoriality principle* may be understood as referring to the jurisdiction that a State may exercise with respect to persons, property or acts outside its territory when a constitutive element of the conduct sought to be regulated occurred in the territory of the State.

12. The *effects doctrine* may be understood as referring to jurisdiction asserted with regard to the conduct of a foreign national occurring outside the territory of a State which has a substantial effect within that territory. This basis, while closely related to the objective territoriality principle, does not require that an element of the conduct take place in the territory of the regulating State.

13. The *protective principle* may be understood as referring to the jurisdiction that a State may exercise with respect to persons, property or acts abroad which constitute a threat to the fundamental national interests of a State, such as a foreign threat to the national security of a State. This principle of jurisdiction may be viewed as a specific application of the objective territoriality principle or the effects doctrine.

14. The *nationality principle* may be understood as referring to the jurisdiction that a State may exercise with respect to the activities of its nationals abroad, including natural persons as well as corporations, aircraft or ships.[17] This well-established principle of jurisdiction is based on the sovereign authority of a State with respect to its nationals.

15. The *passive personality* principle may be understood as referring to the jurisdiction that a State may exercise with respect to conduct abroad which injures one or more of its nationals. This principle of jurisdiction, which was contested by some States in the past, has gained greater acceptance in recent years.[18]

16. The *universality principle* may be understood as referring to the jurisdiction that any State may exercise with respect to certain crimes under international law in the interest of the international community. A State may exercise such jurisdiction even in situations where it has no particular connection to the perpetrator, the victim or the *locus situs* of the crime. Thus, a State may exercise such jurisdiction with respect to a crime committed by a foreign national against another foreign national outside its territory. However, a State exercises such jurisdiction in the interest of the international community rather than exclusively in its own national interest, and thus, this principle of jurisdiction would fall outside of the scope of the present topic.

17. The principles relating to the extraterritorial jurisdiction of a State will be considered briefly in relation to fields of national law which are of particular relevance in this respect, namely, criminal law and commercial law.[19]

3. Extraterritorial jurisdiction with respect to particular fields of law

(a) *Criminal law*

18. The assertion of prescriptive or adjudicative jurisdiction by States in criminal law matters has traditionally been based on a number of well-established principles of jurisdiction. Although the territoriality principle is considered

Turkish vessel resulting from a collision of the two vessels on the high seas after the French vessel had arrived at Istanbul.

[16] *Ibid.*, pp. 18–19.

[17] The nationality of a person, corporation, aircraft or ship depends upon the relevant rules of municipal law as well as international law. These rules have been addressed by the International Law Commission in its consideration of other topics.

[18] With respect to criminal law, see the joint separate opinion of Judges Higgins, Kooijmans and Buergenthal in *Arrest Warrant of 11 April 2000 (Democratic Republic of the Congo* v. *Belgium), Judgment, I.C.J. Reports 2002*, p. 3, at pp. 76–77, para. 47. See also article 4 of the 1963 Convention on offences and certain other acts committed on board aircraft and article 5 of the 1979 International Convention against the taking of hostages.

[19] Extraterritorial jurisdiction may also be of growing relevance in the fields of immigration law and environmental law. The extraterritorial application of immigration laws has occurred with increasing frequency in recent years with respect to the interdiction of illegal aliens attempting to reach the shores of another State by sea as well as aliens suspected of terrorist activities. With regard to environmental law, a State may be tempted to regulate conduct or situations possibly producing harmful environmental effects on its own territory or at the global level, which occur in the high seas or in the territory of another State. See, for example, A. L. Parrish, "*Trail Smelter* déjà vu: extraterritoriality, international environmental law, and the search for solutions to Canadian–U.S. transboundary water pollution disputes", *Boston University Law Review*, vol. 85 (2005), pp. 363–429.

the primary basis for jurisdiction in criminal law matters,[20] the objective territorial principle and the nationality principle are also well established.[21] In contrast, reliance on other principles such as the passive personality principle, the protective principle and the effects doctrine, has been more controversial. More recently, however, the practice of States indicates a general tendency to broaden the classical bases for criminal jurisdiction in relation to certain specific types of crimes committed abroad, which have a particularly international scope and effect, such as terrorism, cybercrimes and drug offences.[22]

19. The passive personality principle, according to which States have jurisdiction over crimes committed abroad against one of their nationals, although disputed in the past[23] is "now reflected ... in the legislation of various countries ... and today meets with relatively little opposition, at least so far as a particular category of offences is concerned".[24] In the field of terrorism, in particular, some States that were originally reluctant to apply the passive personality principle now acknowledge it as an appropriate basis for jurisdiction. Recent United States statutes[25] and jurisprudence[26] relating to terrorism constitute paradigmatic examples in this respect.

20. The protective principle, which allows States to exercise jurisdiction over aliens who have committed an act abroad which is deemed to constitute a threat to some fundamental national interests, although usually limited to very specific crimes and to political acts,[27] may be of particular relevance to new types of cybercrimes and terrorist offences. In this regard, some States have broadened their interpretation of the concept of "vital interests" in order to address terrorism security concerns and introduced the protective principle in their legislation[28] and applied it in some court cases.[29]

21. The "effects doctrine", which justifies a State's exercise of jurisdiction when a conduct performed abroad has substantial effects within that State's territory, has also

---

[20] See the *Lotus* case (footnote 14 above), at p. 20.

[21] Common law countries tend to restrict the crimes over which they will exercise jurisdiction over their nationals abroad to very serious ones (such as treason, murder or bigamy), but they have never protested against the extensive use of the nationality principle as a basis for criminal jurisdiction. It is interesting to note in this respect that an Act was recently adopted by the United States Congress which establishes federal jurisdiction for crimes committed by civilians who accompany military forces outside the United States, as well as crimes by former members of the military who leave active duty before being prosecuted by courts martial. This Act, the Military Extraterritorial Jurisdiction Act of 2000 (Publ. L. No. 106-523, 114 Stat. 2488 (2000) (codified at 18 U.S.C. 3261-67 (2002)) was intended to fill a jurisdictional gap with regard to crimes such as rape, arson, robbery, larceny and fraud (see M. J. Yost and D. S. Anderson, "The Military Extraterritorial Jurisdiction Act of 2000: closing the gap", AJIL, vol. 95 (2001), pp. 446–454). See, for cases in common law countries, *United States* v. *Bowman* (260 U.S. 94 (1922)), *Blackmer* v. *United States* (284 U.S. 421 (1932)) or *United States* v. *Boshell* (952 F.2d 1101 (9th Cir. 1991)).

[22] See, for such general enlargement regarding money laundering, the International Money Laundering Abatement and Anti-Terrorist Financing Act of 2001 (Pub. L. No. 107-56, 115 Stat. 272 (2001)).

[23] Particularly the United States and the United Kingdom: see for instance *United States* v. *Columba-Colella* (604 F.2d 356 (5th Cir. 1979)) and *United States* v. *Vasquez-Velasco* (15 F.3d 833 (9th Cir. 1994)); see also the *Cutting* case (in J. B. Moore, *A Digest of International Law, vol. 2,* Washington D.C., United States Government Printing Office, 1906, pp. 228–242) in which the United States strongly protested Mexico's assertion of jurisdiction over a crime committed by a United States citizen against a Mexican national in the United States. See, however, the rejection by France in 1974 of the Israel's request for extradition of a Palestinian terrorist on the ground that this request was based on the passive personality principle (*see* E. Cafritz and O. Tene, "Article 113-7 of the French Penal Code: the passive personality principle", *Columbia Journal of Transnational Law,* vol. 41 (2002–2003), pp. 585–599, at p. 594).

[24] Joint separate opinion of Judges Higgins, Kooijmans and Buergenthal in the *Arrest Warrant of 11 April 2000* (see footnote 18 above), at pp. 76–77, para. 47. Indeed, international practice shows that most States, the United States included, give effect to this principle but limit its application to particular crimes (regarding terrorism, see below). With respect to the United States, see for example *Restatement of the Law Third...* (footnote 6 above), para. 402, at p. 240) which states that the passive personality principle has not been generally accepted for ordinary torts or crimes; China, Denmark and Italy limit the exercise of passive personality jurisdiction to certain classes of crimes or to crimes with a certain minimum degree of punishment; the dual criminality requirement is a statutory precondition to passive personality jurisdiction in Finland, Greece, Norway, and Sweden; the Norwegian Penal Code provides that only the king may commence legal proceedings based on passive personality jurisdiction; and Finland, Italy and Sweden also require executive consent for the application of the principle (see Cafritz and Tene (footnote 23 above), at pp. 596–598). Indeed, see in this respect the new article 113-7 of the French Penal Code which provides for the application of the passive personality principle to any kind of crime.

[25] See, for example, 18 U.S.C. 2332A (*a*)(1) (2004) concerning the use of weapons of mass destruction in relation to terrorism; 18 U.S.C. 2332F (*b*)(2)(B) (2002) concerning the bombing of places of public use, Government facilities, public transportation systems and infrastructure facilities in relation to terrorism. With respect to France, see, for example, an Act passed in 1975, Law No. 75-624 of 11 July 1975, *Journal officiel de la République française*, 13 July 1975, at p. 7219.

[26] See, for example, *United States* v. *Yunis* (681 F. Supp. 896 (1988)) and *United States* v. *Vasquez-Velasco* (footnote 23 above).

[27] See Harvard Law School, *Harvard Research in International Law*, Supplement to the AJIL, vol. 29 (1935), Codification of International Law, Part. II, "Jurisdiction with Respect to Crime" (draft convention on jurisdiction with respect to crime), pp. 435–651, at pp. 543 and 561); this draft convention links the concept of "protection" to those of "security of the State" and "counterfeiting". The protective principle is also usually applied to crimes such as currency, immigration or economic offenses (see Brownlie, *op. cit.* (footnote 5 above), at p. 302). See, for example, with regard to national applications of the protective principle, decisions of United States and United Kingdom courts, respectively *United States* v. *Pizzarusso*, 388 F.2d 8 (2nd Cir. 1968); *United States* v. *Egan*, 501 F. Supp. 1252 (S.D.N.Y. 1980); *Naim Molvan* v. *A.G. for Palestine* ((1948) AC 531, *Annual Digest/ILR*, vol. 15 (1948), p. 115); and *Joyce* v. *D.P.P.* ((1946) AC 347, *ibid.*, p. 91).

[28] See, for example, 18 U.S.C. 2332F (*b*)(2)(E) (2002) concerning the bombing of places of public use, Government facilities, public transportation systems and infrastructure facilities in relation to terrorism; and 18 U.S.C. 2332G (*b*)(4) (2004) concerning missile systems designed to destroy aircraft in relation to terrorism.

[29] See, for a recent case, *United States* v. *Bin Laden* (92 F. Supp. 2d 189 (S.D.N.Y. 2000)), in which the United States court concluded that extraterritorial jurisdiction under the Antiterrorism Act was justified by the protective principle under international law (*see* J. T. Gathii, "Torture, extraterritoriality, terrorism, and international law", *Albany Law Review*, vol. 67 (2003–2004), pp. 335–370, at p. 343); see, for older cases related to "terrorism", *Wechsler* (Conseil de Guerre de Paris, 20 July 1917, *Journal du droit international*, vol. 44, at p. 1745); *In re Urios* ([1919–1922] *Annual Digest/ILR*, vol. 1, p. 107 (No. 70 (Cour de Cassation, France, 1920)), or *Journal de droit international*, vol. 47 (1920), p. 195); *In re Bayot* ([1923–1924] *Annual Digest/ILR, vol. 2*, p. 109 (No. 54) (Cour de Cassation, France, 1923)), or *Recueil périodique et critique de jurisprudence, de législation et de doctrine en matière civile, commerciale, criminelle, administrative et de droit public, 1924*, p. 136); *Nusselein* v. *Belgian State* ([1950] *Annual Digest/ILR*, vol. 17, p. 136 (No. 35) (Cour de Cassation, Belgium, 1950)), or *Pasicrisie Belge. Recueil général de la jurisprudence des cours et tribunaux et du Conseil d'Etat de Belgique, 1950*, p. 450).

recently been applied in criminal matters.[30] The national legislation of some States provides for an extraterritorial effect by allowing such legislation to apply to persons who merely conspire or intend to import drugs from abroad although no conduct has been performed on the territory of the State asserting jurisdiction.[31]

22. With regard to the jurisdiction to enforce, a State may not enforce its criminal law, that is, investigate crimes or arrest suspects, in the territory of another State without that other State's consent.[32] However, in some instances, States have sent representatives into the territory of another State in order to enforce their criminal law, by *inter alia* conducting investigations[33] or arresting suspects on the territory of other countries[34] with respect to terrorism, cybercrimes and drug trafficking.[35]

(b) *Commercial law*

23. The increased globalization of the world economy has led States to rely increasingly on extraterritorial assertions of jurisdiction to protect their economic interests *vis-à-vis* multinational corporations and other global actors. Although the assertion of extraterritorial jurisdiction through national laws in the commercial sphere has engendered substantial resistance, in certain fields, such as competition law/antitrust law, there is some indication that such measures are slowly gaining acceptance. While the United States[36] remains the most active promulgator of extraterritorial measures in this field, other States and regional organizations such as the European Union,[37] France,[38] Germany[39] and, most recently, the Republic of Korea,[40] have also adopted laws with extraterritorial application.

---

[30] Although in the jurisprudence of some States (mainly coming from the Western European States), the territoriality principle seems to be the main basis of jurisdiction relied upon for combating cybercrimes, it is interpreted in such a broad way that it may resemble an application of the effects doctrine or the protective principle. See, for apparent applications of the territoriality principle, the judgement of a British court regarding a pornographic content of a website, Southwark Crown Court, *R.* v. *Graham Waddon [2000]*, 30 June 1999, [2002] All ER (D) 502, 30 June 1999) and the judgement of the Australian High Court, *Dow Jones & Company Inc.* v. *Gutnick*, HCA 56, 10 December 2002. But see, for broad interpretations of the territoriality principle resembling applications of the effects doctrine or the protective principle, the decision of the German Federal Court of Justice in the *Töben* case (BGH 46, 212, decision of 12 December 2000) concerning Holocaust denial on the Internet, and the decision of a French court, the *Yahoo!* case (*Yahoo! Inc.* v. *La Ligue contre le Racisme et l'Antisémitisme*, 169 F. Supp. 2d 1181 (N.D. Cal. 2001)). See Y. A. Timofeeva, "Worldwide prescriptive jurisdiction in Internet content controversies: a comparative analysis", *Connecticut Journal of International Law*, vol. 20 (2005), pp. 199–225, at pp. 202 *et seq.*

[31] See the statutes applied by the United States Court in the *Noriega* case (*United States* v. *Noriega*, 117 F.3d 1206, at pp. 1515–1519 (11th Cir. 1997)); see also the United States Travel Act, 18 U.S.C. 1952 (*a*) (3) (2002).

[32] It should be noted, however, that the inability of a State to enforce its jurisdiction has been held by some national courts not to affect its ability to legislate or adjudicate the matter in question. See, for instance, the judgement of the Federal Court of Justice in Germany in the *Töben* case (footnote 30 above) and the *Yahoo!* case (*ibid.*).

[33] For instance, the United States acknowledged having conducted recent investigations on Russian territory to search for some data on the ground that would otherwise have been lost (for further details, see P. L. Bellia, "Chasing bits across borders", *University of Chicago Legal Forum* (2001), pp. 35–101, at p. 40).

[34] The important issue raised by these abductions was whether courts or tribunals had jurisdiction to judge people illegally brought before them. Case law is largely divided on this issue: regarding the United States courts, see *Ker* v. *Illinois* (119 U.S. 436 (1886)), *Frisbie* v. *Collins* (342 U.S. 519 (1952)), *United States* v. *Yunis* (924 F.2d 1086 (D.C. Cir. 1991)) and *United States* v. *Álvarez-Machain* (504 U.S. 655 (1992)); but see, for another solution given by a United States court, *United States* v. *Toscanino* (500 F.2d 267 (2nd Cir. 1974)); regarding other States: in Israel, the *Eichmann* case (*Attorney General of Israel* v. *Eichmann* (1961), District Court of Jerusalem, 12–15 December 1961, ILR, vol. 36 (1968), p. 5); in England, *Ex parte Susannah Scott* (1829) (*The English Reports*, vol. 109 (1910), p. 166); but see, for another solution given by a British court, *R.* v. *Horseferry Road Magistrates' Court (Ex parte Bennett)* (1993, 3 P, 138 (H.L)); in Canada, see *In re Hartnett* (1973, 1 O.R. (2d) 206, 207 (Can)); in Germany, see the decision of the Federal Constitutional Court in which the Court ruled that an abducted person only needs to be returned when the victim nation objects to the abduction (39 Neue Juritische Wochenschrift 1427 (1986) (German Federal Constitutional Court 1985)); in South Africa, see *State (South Africa)* v. *Ebrahim* (ILR, vol. 95, p. 417); see, in this respect, Timofeeva, *loc. cit.* (footnote 30 above), at pp. 202 *et seq.*

[35] It is usually asserted that such actions constitute a violation of the States' sovereignty, protected by Article 2, paragraph 4 of the Charter of the United Nations and, as far as abductions are concerned, an infringement of article 5 of the European Convention on Human Rights, provided that European States are involved (see, regarding the latter case, *Stocké* v. *Germany, Application no. 11755/85, Judgement of 19 March 1991*, European Court of Human Rights, *Series A: Judgments and Decisions*, vol. 199 (1991), p. 5, and *Öcalan* v. *Turkey, Application no. 46221/99, Judgement of 12 May 2005*, Grand Chamber, European Court of Human Rights, *Reports of Judgments and Decisions 2005-IV*).

[36] In this regard, two commercial laws of the United States can be highlighted: the Sherman Antitrust Act of 1890 and the Sarbanes-Oxley Act of 2002. The first is the leading American antitrust law, which prohibits any contract, trust or conspiracy aiming to restrain interstate or foreign trade and any attempt or actual monopolization of any part of this commerce. It provides for financial sanctions for engaging in any of those acts. The Sarbanes-Oxley Act of 2002 regulates the corporate governance of companies listed on the United States stock exchange and "calls for application to all companies that list stock on the U.S. capital markets" without any exception for foreign companies. See C. A. Falencki, "Sarbanes-Oxley: ignoring the presumption against extraterritoriality", *George Washington International Law Review*, vol. 36 (2004), pp. 1211–1238, at p. 1216.

[37] The European Union, despite its original resistance to extraterritorial jurisdiction and harsh criticisms towards American practice in this regard, also *de facto* extended its jurisdiction to control mergers, acquisitions and joint ventures outside the territories of its member States. Indeed, the Court of Justice of the European Communities recognized its own jurisdiction on some foreign corporations and their activities abroad and it applied to them the competition provision of articles 81 and 82 of the Treaty Establishing the European Economic Community (formerly articles 85 and 86) and the Council Regulation (EEC) No. 4064/89 of 21 December 1989 on the control of concentrations between undertakings amended by Council Regulation (EC) No. 1310/97 of 30 June 1997. See D. J. Feeney, "The European Commission's extraterritorial jurisdiction over corporate mergers", *Georgia State University Law Review*, vol. 19 (2002–2003), pp. 425–491, at p. 427.

[38] The best-known example of this is the highly criticized provision of the French Civil Code on the adjudication by French courts of contracts signed abroad between a French person and a foreigner. See Combacau and Sur, *op. cit.* (footnote 5 above), at p. 354.

[39] The German Act Against Restraints of Competition was initially enacted in 1957 and had several major revisions, the last one in 1998, with a last amendment in 1999: article 130 (2) states that "this Act shall apply to all restraints of competition which have effect in the area in which this Act applies, even if they result from acts done outside such area". Therefore, all prohibitions and notification requirements apply to activities which have a direct, reasonably foreseeable and significant (not necessarily substantial) effect. The Act has been regularly applied to foreign enterprises (see www.antitrust.de). See also A.V. Lowe, "The problems of extraterritorial jurisdiction: economic sovereignty and the search for a solution", *International and Comparative Law Quarterly*, vol. 34 (1985), pp. 724–746, at p. 736, citing also D. J. Gerber, "The extraterritorial application of the German antitrust laws", AJIL, vol. 77 (1983), pp. 756–783.

[40] The Republic of Korea has also recently given an extraterritorial application of its national antitrust law. On 1 April 2005, the amended Monopoly Regulation and Fair Trade Act, providing for an extraterritorial application of the Act, entered into force. This legal amendment

24. In commercial law, States have based their extraterritorial jurisdiction to prescribe primarily on the nationality principle and the "effects doctrine". The European Union, for example, has relied on an enlarged theory of nationality with respect to multinational corporations with local subsidiaries to establish jurisdiction over their activities.[41] The United States, on the other hand, has increasingly relied upon the "effects doctrine" to establish jurisdiction over the conduct of foreign actors abroad, as long as it is intended to and actually has an effect on the United States domestic market,[42] although with some international opposition.[43]

25. The extension of extraterritorial jurisdiction of a State and of the "effects doctrine" to cover activities contrary to the foreign policy interest of a State has proven particularly controversial. An example of this is the attempts by the United States to enforce economic sanctions against Cuba and Libya through extraterritorial measures such as the Helms-Burton Act[44] and the D'Amato-Kennedy Act[45] of 1996. Such measures provoked diplomatic protests, the adoption of blocking statutes and the institution of dispute resolution proceedings in the WTO by potentially affected States (see, below, the proposed outline for an instrument on extraterritorial jurisdiction, section E.7). Eventually, it was agreed that the enforcement of the extraterritorial provisions of these measures would be suspended indefinitely.

26. Reliance by a State on the passive personality principle to establish adjudicative jurisdiction in the commercial law context has also proven controversial with regard to a provision of the French Civil Code allowing for any dispute arising from a contract between a French national and a foreigner to be adjudicated in a French court.[46]

aimed to make the law consistent with the recent practice of some Korean courts since 2002, to apply the domestic antitrust act to some foreign manufacturers. See Korea Fair Trade Commission decision of 4 April 2002 (case 2-77), confirmed by the Seoul High Court Decision of 26 August 2003 (2002nu 14647) and Korea Fair Trade Commission decision of 29 April 2003 (case 3-98); see also Y. Jung, "Korean competition law: first step towards globalization", *Journal of Korean Law*, vol. 4, No. 2 (2005), pp. 177–199, and W. Kim, "The extraterritorial application of U.S. antitrust law and its adoption in Korea", *Singapore Journal of International and Comparative Law*, vol. 7 (2003), pp. 386–411.

[41] *Imperial Chemical Industries Ltd.* v. *Commission of the European Communities, Case 48-69, Judgement of 14 July 1972, European Court Reports 1972, p. 619*; *Europemballage Corp. and Continental Can Co.* v. *Commission of the European Communities, Case 6-72, Judgement of 21 February 1973, European Court Reports 1973*, p. 215; *Istituto Chemioterapico Italiano S.p.A. and Commercial Solvents Corporation* v. *Commission of the European Communities, Joined Cases 6 and 7-73, Judgement of 6 March 1974, European Court Reports 1974*, p. 223. See also Feeney, *loc. cit.* (footnote 37 above), at p. 426, and J. J. Norton, "The European Court of Justice judgment in *United Brands*: extraterritorial jurisdiction and abuse of dominant position", *Denver Journal of International Law and Policy*, vol. 8 (1979), pp. 379–414.

[42] See, for example, *F. Hoffman-LaRoche, Ltd.* v. *Empagran* (542 U.S. 155, 124 S. Ct. 2359 (2004)).

[43] "[T]he so-called 'effects' doctrine of territorial jurisdiction [whatever its precise content and criteria] has developed considerable controversy in international legal circles, and has been the subject of heated discussion within the Community" (Norton, *loc. cit.* (footnote 41 above), at p. 385).

[44] Cuban Liberty and Democratic Solidarity (LIBERTAD) Act of 1996, Pub. L. No. 104-114 (1996).

[45] Iran and Libya Sanctions Act of 1996 (H. R. 3107).

[46] See Combacau and Sur, *op. cit.* (footnote 5 above), at p. 354.

27. As regards enforcement jurisdiction, although the extraterritorial assertion of enforcement jurisdiction without the consent of the territorial State is generally prohibited under international law, States have in some instances concluded international agreements to allow for the extraterritorial enforcement of their commercial and competition laws.[47]

C. Consequences of the invalid assertion of extraterritorial jurisdiction

28. The assertion of extraterritorial jurisdiction by a State is entitled to recognition by other States only to the extent that it is consistent with international law. In the event that one State exercises extraterritorial jurisdiction that another State judges excessive, the other State may oppose such an exercise of jurisdiction in a number of different ways. Examples of such opposition have included diplomatic protests;[48] non-recognition of laws, orders and judgments;[49] legislative measures such as "blocking

[47] See the Convention concerning judicial competence and the execution of decisions in civil and commercial matters as amended (among European Community member States); the Convention on jurisdiction and the enforcement of judgments in civil and commercial matters (among member States of the European Community and the European Free Trade Association); Inter-American Convention on Extraterritorial Validity of Foreign Judgments and Arbitral Awards (among OAS members); Inter-American Convention on Jurisdiction in the International Sphere for the Extraterritorial Validity of Foreign Judgments; and Council [of the European Union] Regulation (EC) No. 44/2001 of 22 December 2000 on jurisdiction and the recognition and enforcement of judgments in civil and commercial matters, *Official Journal of the European Communities* No. L 12, 16 January 2001, p. 1. See also the Articles of Agreement of the International Monetary Fund, which provide under article VIII.2(*b*) that "[e]xchange contracts which involve the currency of any member and which are contrary to the exchange control regulations of that member maintained or imposed consistently with this Agreement shall be unenforceable in the territories of any member". See also Lowe, "The problems of extraterritorial jurisdiction…", *loc. cit.* (footnote 39 above), at p. 732.

[48] For example, both the European Community and the United Kingdom submitted protests when the United States amended its Export Administration Regulations in such a way as to prohibit the export of oil or natural gas exploitation equipment to the Soviet Union. The comments of the European Community laid out the provisions of the disputed measures and stated, *inter alia*: "The U.S. measures as they apply in the present case are unacceptable under international law because of their extra-territorial aspects. They seek to regulate companies not of U.S. nationality in respect of their conduct outside the United States and particularly the handling of property and technical data of these companies not in the United States"; see Note and Comments of the European Community on the Amendments of 22 June 1982 to the Export Administration Act, presented to the United States Department of State on 12 August 1982; Note on the same subject presented by the Government of the United Kingdom on 18 October 1982; and a further *aide-mémoire* presented by the European Community on 14 March 1983, in A. V. Lowe, *Extraterritorial Jurisdiction: an Annotated Collection of Legal Materials*, Cambridge, Grotius, 1983, p. 197, at p. 201. Other examples of diplomatic protests made in response to extraterritorial exertions of jurisdiction include: *Aides-mémoire* by Japan of 23 August 1960 and 20 March 1961 to the United States Department of State, *ibid.*, at p. 121 (extract); and *Aide-mémoire* by the United Kingdom of 20 October 1969 to the Commission of the European Communities, *ibid.*, at p. 144.

[49] "Where a state or its courts have acted contrary to international law, including the rules relating to the exercise of jurisdiction, other states are in international law entitled (but not compelled) to refuse to give effect to the illegal act … . In practice most states, in their rules of private international law, ensure that a foreign state's laws and decisions which exceed the limits of jurisdiction permitted by international law are not recognised or enforced abroad" (*Oppenheim's International Law* (see footnote 6 above), at p. 485). In particular, some States generally decline to give effect to the public laws of other States, such as revenue, penal and confiscatory law. See generally *ibid.*, at pp. 488–498.

statutes"[50] and "claw-back statutes";[51] judicial measures such as injunctions;[52] and the institution of international proceedings.[53] The limitation on the recognition of extraterritorial jurisdiction as well as possible responses to invalid assertions of such jurisdiction could be addressed in the draft.

D. Priority in the event of competing valid jurisdictions

29. There may be situations in which the State asserting extraterritorial jurisdiction is the only State that has any connection to the relevant person, property or situation which is beyond the territory of any State. In such a case, the State would have exclusive jurisdiction. More often the extraterritorial jurisdiction of a State coincides with the jurisdiction of one or more other States—notably the territorial State. The concurrent jurisdiction of States may give rise to disputes concerning priority of jurisdiction. The question arises as to the relationship between extraterritorial jurisdiction and territorial jurisdiction in terms of priority.[54] In this regard, it may be necessary to distinguish between legislative or adjudicative jurisdiction and enforcement jurisdiction.

30. Questions of priority in the event of competing jurisdictions as a consequence of the assertion of extraterritorial jurisdiction most frequently arise with respect to legislative or adjudicative jurisdiction. Some States have developed general principles or rules for resolving these situations. For example, the national court of one State may be called upon to apply extraterritorially the legislation of another State. In order to minimize the likelihood of conflicts and to show deference to foreign States, national courts in some States have adopted a presumption against the extraterritorial application of their own national law.[55] Thus, unless there is a specific indication that a certain law or regulation was intended to apply to foreign nationals for actions committed abroad, a court will consider that no such intent existed on the part of the legislature. Such a rule is based in part on principles of comity and non-interference in the domestic affairs of other States, as well as practical considerations.

31. Another rule developed by courts to deal with competing assertions of jurisdiction resulting from extraterritorial measures is the foreign State compulsion doctrine. The foreign State compulsion doctrine provides that a party should not be held criminally or civilly liable for undertaking an activity in another State that is required under the laws of that State.[56] Therefore, an extraterritorial measure in direct conflict with a criminal law of the territorial State would not be applied by a competent court, even if it determined that the assertion of jurisdiction was reasonable.

32. Questions of competing jurisdiction do not often arise with respect to enforcement jurisdiction. As a general rule, States are not allowed to enforce their laws in the

[50] A blocking statute is a law adopted by State disputing the validity of the exertion of jurisdiction designed to impede the enforcement of the disputed provision, often by creating a direct conflict of laws. Such provisions may, *inter alia*, prohibit cooperation in foreign court proceedings or investigations, prohibit compliance with extraterritorial laws of other States, declare judgements based on such measures unenforceable, and allow the recovery of damages suffered as a result of such measures. As a result of the foreign State compulsion doctrine discussed below, blocking statutes may have the additional effect of limiting the enforceability of an extraterritorial measure even in the State promulgating such a measure. In States that apply this doctrine, a national court would not require compliance with the extraterritorial measure in question, since compliance would involve a violation of the laws of the territorial State. For example, several States adopted protective measures in response to the United States' adoption of the Cuban Liberty and Democratic Solidarity (LIBERTAD) Act of 1996 (also known as the "Helms-Burton Act" (see footnote 44 above)), which sought to penalize non-United States companies for doing business with Cuba. Canada amended its Foreign Extraterritorial Measures Act (R.S.C., ch. F-29, para. 3 (1985), amended by ch. 28, 1996 S.C. (Can.)); Mexico adopted the Law of Protection of Commerce and Investments from Foreign Policies that Contravene International Law (www.diputados .gob.mx/LeyesBiblio/pdf/63.pdf); and the European Union adopted Council Regulation (EC) No. 2271/96 of 22 November 1996 protecting against the effects of the extra-territorial application of legislation adopted by a third country, and actions based thereon or resulting therefrom, *Official Journal of the European Communities, No. L 309*, 29 November 1996, p. 1. See J. W. Boscariol, "An anatomy of a Cuban pyjama crisis: reconsidering blocking legislation in response to extraterritorial trade measures of the United States", *Law and Policy in International Business*, vol. 30, No. 3 (1999), pp. 439–499, at pp. 441–442 and 471–474 (describing Canada's Foreign Extraterritorial Measures Act); A. Layton and A. M. Parry, "Extraterritorial jurisdiction—European responses", *Houston Journal of International Law*, vol. 26, No. 2 (2004), pp. 309–325, at pp. 311–312 (describing the United Kingdom's Protection of Trading Interests Act of 1980, c. 11 § 1(1)(*b*)(Eng.)); H. L. Clark, "Dealing with U.S. extraterritorial sanctions and foreign countermeasures", *University of Pennsylvania Journal of International Economic Law*, vol. 20 (1999), pp. 61–96, at pp. 81–92. See also Lowe, *Extraterritorial Jurisdiction..., op. cit.* (footnote 48 above), at pp. 79–219 (containing texts of blocking statutes from various States).

[51] See, for example, Council Regulation (EC) No. 2271/96, article 6 (footnote 50 above); and Canada's Foreign Extraterritorial Measures Act, article 9(1)(*a*) (*ibid.*).

[52] For example, in *U.S.* v. *Imperial Chemical Industries*, a British company was able to obtain an injunction from a British court restraining a party in the case from enforcing an extraterritorial order of the United States court. See *Oppenheim's International Law* (footnote 6 above), at p. 477, footnote 50 (citing, *inter alia, U.S.* v. *Imperial Chemical Industries* (1952), 105 F.Supp. 215).

[53] "In principle excess of jurisdiction gives rise to state responsibility even in absence of an intention to harm another state" (Brownlie, *op. cit.* (footnote 5 above), at p. 312). Thus, States have been able to seek redress in international forums for improper exercises of jurisdiction. The most relevant example of such recourse is the *Lotus* case (see footnote 14 above), where France sought damages for Turkey's allegedly excessive assertion of jurisdiction. In the *Eichmann* case (see footnote 34 above), the dispute over Israel's assertion of enforcement jurisdiction in Argentina was brought before the Security Council, and a settlement was reached between the two States.

[54] See *Oppenheim's International Law* (footnote 6 above), at p. 458 ("Territoriality is the primary basis for jurisdiction; even if another state has a concurrent basis for jurisdiction, its right to exercise is limited if to do so would conflict with the rights of the state having territorial jurisdiction"). See also Daillier and Pellet, *op. cit.* (footnote 5 above), at p. 502 ("La rigidité des solutions théoriques résultant de la hiérarchie des compétences et, en particulier, de la primauté de la souveraineté territoriale sur la compétence personnelle, qui exclut en principe toute application, au moins forcée, du droit national à l'étranger" [The rigidity of theoretical solutions resulting from the hierarchy of competencies and, in particular, from the primacy of territorial sovereignty over personal jurisdiction, which precludes in principle any application, at least forced, of national law abroad]).

[55] See Mann, *loc. cit.* (footnote 5 above), at pp. 63–64; and *F. Hoffman-LaRoche* v. *Empagran* (footnote 42 above): "*First*, this Court ordinarily construes ambiguous statutes to avoid unreasonable interference with other nations' sovereign authority" (p. 4).

[56] See Clark, *loc. cit.* (footnote 50 above), at pp. 92–93; Brownlie, *op. cit.* (footnote 5 above), at p. 308 (citing Judge R. Y. Jennings, "Extraterritorial jurisdiction and the United States antitrust laws", BYBIL, vol. 33 (1957), pp. 146–175, at p. 151); R. K. Gardiner, *International Law*, London, Pearson, 2003, at p. 325; and *Oppenheim's International Law* (footnote 6 above), at pp. 464–465.

territory of another State without the *consent* of the territorial State. As the PCIJ stated in the *Lotus* case, "a State … may not exercise its power in any form in the territory of another State".[57] Thus, when Israel captured Adolf Eichmann on Argentine soil and subsequently transferred him to Israel for trial, the Security Council requested the Government of Israel to make appropriate reparation to Argentina.[58]

E. Elaboration of an instrument

33. An instrument on this topic could aim at setting forth general principles and more specific rules governing the assertion of extraterritorial jurisdiction under public international law. The overview of the existing norms and rules indicates that there is a considerable amount of State practice relating to the assertion of extraterritorial jurisdiction upon which the Commission could draw in the elaboration of such an instrument.

34. Recent developments in technology and the globalization of the world economy, which limit the ability of States to protect their national interests by relying solely on traditional principles of jurisdiction, have contributed to the increasing level of disagreement and uncertainty with respect to certain aspects of the law governing extraterritorial jurisdiction. The elaboration of a draft instrument on the topic may therefore require substantial progressive development of the law in addition to codification. State practice indicates several strong trends in the emergence of new rules or the extension of traditional rules which may guide the Commission in resolving the areas of disagreement and thereby provide greater clarity and certainty in an area of international law which is of increasing practical importance, yet the elaboration of a draft instrument on the topic could prove to require some progressive development of the law.

1. Scope of the topic

35. The delimitation of the scope of the topic will be important in light of the breadth of the topic of jurisdiction in general. While some attempts at codification have considered extraterritorial jurisdiction from the broader perspective of jurisdiction in general,[59] the topic may be limited to extraterritorial assertions of jurisdiction only. Moreover, the topic may be restricted only to national law applied extraterritorially.

36. There are some fields of law in which questions of extraterritorial jurisdiction are likely to arise which are regulated to some extent by special regimes. Paramount amongst these are the law of the sea, outer space law, international humanitarian law and tax law. In addition, assertions of extraterritorial jurisdiction with respect to judicial and police assistance and cooperation as well as the recognition and enforcement of foreign judgments are, for the most part, regulated by existing international, regional or bilateral agreements. While these special rules may provide some guidance in the elaboration of general principles and rules with respect to extraterritorial jurisdiction, the draft instrument would be without prejudice to existing legal regimes.

37. Although the extraterritorial assertion of jurisdiction by States can often result in concurrent or conflicting attempts to exercise jurisdiction, it would not be necessary to revisit the rules of private international law developed by States to resolve such conflicts. However, it may be useful to include general principles of comity that are of particular relevance to the resolution of disputes resulting from assertions of extraterritorial jurisdiction.

38. One aspect of the topic which has not been fully addressed in previous codification efforts is the consequences of invalid assertions of extraterritorial jurisdiction. Although this aspect is to some extent addressed by the articles on the responsibility of States for internationally wrongful acts, there is also a sizeable body of State practice in this regard that could be explored in an effort to establish rules and procedures for resolving the specific issues that may arise in disputes relating to invalid assertions of extraterritorial jurisdiction.

2. Definitions

39. Defining the main concepts to be contained in an instrument would be one of the essential elements of the study. Definitions of the terms "jurisdiction" and "extraterritorial" are crucial to determining the scope of the draft text. Further consideration of the topic may indicate additional terms that would also need to be clearly defined in the draft.

40. The notion of the *jurisdiction* of a State may be understood as generally referring to the sovereign power or authority of a State. In this regard, a distinction could be drawn between three types of jurisdiction, namely prescriptive, adjudicative and enforcement jurisdiction.

41. The notion of *extraterritoriality* may be understood as referring to the area beyond the territory of a State, including its land, internal waters, territorial sea as well as the adjacent airspace. Such an area could fall within the territory of another State or outside the territorial jurisdiction of any State.

3. Core principles of extraterritorial jurisdiction

42. It is generally accepted that in order for a State to validly assert its jurisdiction over a natural or legal person, property or situation, it must have some connection to such person, property or situation. The types of connections that may constitute a sufficient basis for the exercise of extraterritorial jurisdiction are reflected in the general principles of international law which govern the exercise of such jurisdiction by a State. These principles are as follows:

---

[57] The *Lotus* case (footnote 14 above), p. 18.

[58] Security Council resolution 138 (1960) of 23 June 1960. However, see the *Eichmann* case (footnote 34 above), and the *Alvarez-Machain* case (*ibid.*).

[59] See Harvard Law School, *Harvard Research in International Law,* Codification of International Law… (footnote 27 above), p. 439; and American Law Institute, *Restatement of the Law (Third)…* (footnote 6 above). It should be noted that the Restatement, in particular, is of limited relevance for present purposes since it focuses primarily on United States practice.

— Territoriality principle as it relates to extraterritorial jurisdiction:

— Objective territoriality principle

— Effects doctrine

— Nationality principle

— Passive personality principle

— Protective principle

43. Any assertion of extraterritorial jurisdiction must be based on at least one of the above-mentioned principles to be valid under international law. More than one of the above principles may be relevant in determining the validity of extraterritorial jurisdiction in a particular case, depending on the circumstances.

4. Rules relating to the assertion of extraterritorial jurisdiction

44. The degree of the connection that a State must have with a person, property or situation in order to validly assert its jurisdiction extraterritorially may vary according to the type of jurisdiction the State is attempting to exercise. Accordingly, it would be necessary to indicate the extent to which the various jurisdictional principles may provide a valid basis for the extraterritorial assertion of prescriptive, adjudicative or enforcement jurisdiction. The exercise of extraterritorial jurisdiction may also raise special issues with respect to particular fields of law, such as those relating to cybercrimes in the field of criminal law, or e-commerce in the field of commercial law. It may be therefore also be useful to include specific provisions to address these types of special issues which may not be adequately addressed by the formulation of general principles and rules.

5. Limitations on the rights of States to assert extraterritorial jurisdiction

45. Assertions of extraterritorial jurisdiction are subject to limitations based on certain fundamental principles of international law such as the sovereign equality of States, the principle of the territorial integrity of a State and the principle of non-intervention in the domestic affairs of other States, as enshrined in the Charter of the United Nations. Considerations of comity should also be taken into account in the application of assertions of extraterritorial jurisdiction.

6. Consequences of invalid assertions of extraterritorial jurisdiction

46. In the event of an assertion of extraterritorial jurisdiction by one State which another State considers invalid under international law, States have a general obligation to cooperate to resolve the dispute. A legal instrument on this subject should also envisage a procedure for resolving such a dispute that would involve: giving notice that the assertion of jurisdiction is considered invalid; reviewing the validity of the assertion by the enacting State in light of the core principles; and taking into account the objections of the affected State.

7. Proposed outline for an instrument on extraterritorial jurisdiction

I. General provisions

1. Scope of application
2. Relationship to other legal regimes
   (*a*) *lex specialis*
   (*b*) pre-existing treaty regimes
3. Use of terms

II. Principles of jurisdiction

1. Territoriality principle
   (*a*) objective territoriality principle
   (*b*) effects doctrine
2. Nationality principle
3. Passive personality principle
4. Protective principle

III. Extraterritorial assertion of jurisdiction

1. Prescriptive jurisdiction
2. Adjudicative jurisdiction
3. Enforcement jurisdiction
4. Specific fields of law

IV. Limitations on the extraterritorial assertion of jurisdiction

1. Sovereignty, territorial integrity and non-intervention
2. Comity
   (*a*) presumption against extraterritoriality
   (*b*) foreign State compulsion doctrine
   (*c*) principle of reasonableness

V. Dispute resolution

1. General duty to cooperate
2. Duty to give notice
3. Duty to review extraterritorial measures
4. General right to countermeasures
5. Dispute resolution mechanism

Selected bibliography

A. International jurisprudence

1. Judicial organs

(a) *Permanent Court of International Justice*

Case of the S.S. "Lotus" (France v. *Turkey), Judgment No. 9 of 7 September 1927, P.C.I.J. Reports 1928, Series A. No. 10.*

(b) *International Court of Justice*

Arrest Warrant of 11 April 2000 (Democratic Republic of the Congo v. *Belgium), Judgment, I.C.J. Reports 2002*, p. 3 (Joint Separate Opinion of Judges Higgins, Kooijmans and Buergenthal).

(c) *European Court of Human Rights*

Stocké v. *Germany, Application no. 11755/85, Judgement of 19 March 1991*, European Court of Human Rights, *Series A: Judgments and Decisions*, vol. 199.

Loizidou v. *Turkey, Application no. 15318/89, Judgement of 18 December 1996 (Merits)*, European Court of Human Rights, *Reports of Judgments and Decisions, 1996-VI*, p. 2216.

Öcalan v. *Turkey, Application no. 46221/99, Judgement of 12 May 2005*, Grand Chamber, European Court of Human Rights, *Reports of Judgments and Decisions 2005-IV*.

(d) *Court of Justice of the European Communities*

Imperial Chemical Industries Ltd. v. *Commission of the European Communities, Case 48-69, Judgement of 14 July 1972, European Court Reports 1972, p. 619.*

Europemballage Corp. and Continental Can Co. v. *Commission of the European Communities, Case 6-72, Judgement of 21 February 1973, European Court Reports 1973*, p. 215.

Istituto Chemioterapico Italiano S.p.A. and Commercial Solvents Corporation v. *Commission of the European Communities, Joined Cases 6 and 7-73, Judgement of 6 March 1974, European Court Reports 1974*, p. 223.

2. Arbitral tribunals

Fur Seal Arbitration, J. B. Moore, History and Digest of the International Arbitrations to which the United States has been a Party, vol. I, Washington D.C., United States Government Printing Office, 1898, pp. 755–961.

Cutting, J. B. Moore, *A Digest of International Law*, vol. II, Washington D.C., United States Government Printing Office, 1906, pp. 228–242.

B. National jurisprudence

Ex parte *Susannah Scott, The English Reports*, vol. 109 (1910), p. 166.

Ker v. *Illinois* (119 U.S. 436 (1886)).

In re Urios ([1919–1922] *Annual Digest/ILR*, vol. 1, p. 107 (No. 70 (Cour de Cassation, France, 1920)); *Journal de droit international*, vol. 47 (1920), p. 195.

United States v. *Bowman* (260 U.S. 94 (1922)).

In re Bayot ([1923–1924] *Annual Digest/ILR*, vol. 2, p. 109 (No. 54) (Cour de Cassation, France, 1923)); *Recueil périodique et critique de jurisprudence, de législation et de doctrine en matière civile, commerciale, criminelle, administrative et de droit public, 1924*, p. 136.

Joyce v. *D.P.P.* ((1946) AC 347, *Annual Digest/ILR, vol.* 15, p. 91).

Wechsler (Conseil de Guerre de Paris, 20 July 1947, *Journal de droit international*, vol. 44, p. 1745).

Naim Molvan v. *A.G. for Palestine* ((1948) AC 531, *Annual Digest/ILR*, vol. 15 (1948), p. 115).

Nusselein v. *Belgian State* ([1950] *Annual Digest/ILR*, vol. 17, p. 136 (No. 35) (Cour de Cassation, Belgium, 1950)); *Pasicrisie Belge. Recueil général de la jurisprudence des cours et tribunaux et du Conseil d'Etat de Belgique, 1950*, p. 450.

Attorney General of the Government of Israel v. *Adolf Eichmann*, District Court of Jerusalem, 12–15 December 1961, ILR, vol. 36 (1968), p. 5.

In re Harnett (1973, 1 O.R. (2d) 206, 207 (Can)).

United States v. *Columba-Colella* (604 F.2d 356 (5th Cir. 1979)).

Tel-Oren v. *Libyan Arab Republic* (726 F.2d 774 (D.C. Cir. 1984)).

Federal Constitutional Court (39 Neue Juritische Wochenschrift 1427 (1986) (Ger. Fed. Const. Ct. 1985).

United States v. *Yunis* (681 F. Supp. 896 (1988)).

State (South Africa) v. *Ebrahim*, ILR, vol. 95, p. 417.

United States v. *Yunis* (924 F.2d 1086 (D.C. Cir. 1991)).

United States v. *Álvarez-Machain* (504 U.S. 655 (1992)).

R. v. *Horseferry Road Magistrates' Court* (*Ex parte Bennett*) (1993, 3 P, 138 (H.L)).

United States v. *Vasquez-Velasco* (15 F.3d 833, 838–839 (9th Cir. 1994)).

United States v. *Noriega* (117 F.3d 1206, 1515–1519 (11th Cir. 1997)).

Bangoura v. *Washington Post* ([2004] 235 D.L.R. (4th) 564) and the Italian Court of Cassation (Corte de Cassazione, closed session, sect. V, 27 December 2000, Judgment No. 4741).

Töben case (BGH 46, 212, decision of 12 December 2000).

United States v. *Bin Laden* (92 F. Supp. 2d 189 (S.D.N.Y. 2000)).

Estate of Cabello v. *Fernandez-Larios* (157 F. Supp. 2d 1345 (S.D. Fla. 2001)).

United States v. *Bustos-Useche* (273 F.3d 622 (5th Cir. 2001), *cert. denied*, 535 U.S. 1071 (2002)).

Yahoo! Inc. v. *La Ligue contre le Racisme et l'Antisémitisme* (169 F. Supp. 2d 1181 (N.D. Cal. 2001)).

Aguinda v. *Texaco, Inc.* (303 F.3d 470 (2nd Cir. 2002)).

Korea Fair Trade Commission decision of 4 April 2002 (case 2-77), confirmed by the Seoul High Court Decision of 26 August 2003 (2002nu 14647) and KFTC decision of 29 April 2003 (case 3-98).

Sinaltrainal v. *Coca-Cola Co.* (256 F. Supp. 2d 1345 (S.D. Fla. 2003)).

F. Hoffman-LaRoche, Ltd. v. *Empagran* (542 U.S. 155, 124 S. Ct. 2359 (14 June 2004)).

C. International organizations

1. United Nations

Security Council resolution 1192 (1998) of 27 August 1998.

2. Council of Europe

Recommendation No. R (97) 11 of the Committee of Ministers to member States on the amended model plan for the classification of documents concerning State practice in the field of public international law, 12 June 1997, Appendix, Part Eight (II).

D. Literature

Akehurst, M. "Jurisdiction in international law", *The British Yearbook of International Law*, vol. 46 (1972–1973), 145–257.

Bellia, P. L. "Chasing bits across borders", *University of Chicago Legal Forum*, vol. 2001 (2001), 35–101.

Boscariol, J. W. "An anatomy of a Cuban pyjama crisis: reconsidering blocking legislation in response to extraterritorial trade measures of the United States", *Law and Policy in International Business*, vol. 30, No. 3 (1999), 439–499.

Bowett, D. W. "Jurisdiction: changing patterns of authority over activities and resources", *The British Year Book of International Law*, vol. 53 (1982), 1–26.

Cafritz, E. and O. Tene. "Article 113-7 of the French Penal Code: the passive personality principle", *Columbia Journal of Transnational Law,* vol. 41 (2002–2003), 585–599.

Clark, H. L. "Dealing with U.S. extraterritorial sanctions and foreign countermeasures", *University of Pennsylvania Journal of International Economic Law*, vol. 20 (1999), 61–96.

Dunning, T. S. "D'Amato in a china shop: problems of extraterritoriality with the Iran and Libya Sanctions Act of 1996", *University of Pennsylvania Journal of International Economic Law*, vol. 19 (1998), 169–199.

Falencki, C. A. "Sarbanes-Oxley: ignoring the presumption against extraterritoriality", *George Washington International Law Review*, vol. 36 (2004), 1211–1238.

Feeney, D. J. "The European Commission's extraterritorial jurisdiction over corporate mergers", *Georgia State University Law Review*, vol. 19 (2002–2003), 425–491.

Fernandes, S. "*F. Hoffman-Laroche, Ltd.* v. *Empagran* and the extraterritorial limits of United States antitrust jurisdiction: where comity and deterrence collide", *Connecticut Journal of International Law*, vol. 20 (2005), 267–317.

Gathii, J. T. "Torture, extraterritoriality, terrorism, and international law", *Albany Law Review*, vol. 67 (2003–2004), 335–370.

Gerber, D. J. "The extraterritorial application of the German antitrust laws", *American Journal of International Law*, vol. 77 (1983), 756–783.

Jung, Y. "Korean competition law: first step towards globalization", *Journal of Korean Law*, vol. 4, No. 2 (2005), 177–199.

Kim, W. "The extraterritorial application of U.S. antitrust law and its adoption in Korea", *Singapore Journal of International and Comparative Law*, vol. 7 (2003), 386–411.

Layton, A. and A. M. Parry. "Extraterritorial jurisdiction—European reponses", *Houston Journal of International Law*, vol. 26, No. 2 (2004), 309–325.

Meng, W. "Extraterritorial effects of administrative, judicial and legislative acts", in R. Bernhardt (ed.), *Encyclopedia of Public International Law*, vol. 2, Amsterdam, Elsevier, 1995, 337–343.

Norton, J. J. "The European Court of Justice judgment in *United Brands*: extraterritorial jurisdiction and abuse of dominant position", *Denver Journal of International Law and Policy*, vol. 8 (1979), 379–414.

O'Keefe, R. "Universal jurisdiction: clarifying the basic concept", *Journal of International Criminal Justice*, vol. 2, No. 3 (September 2004), 735–760.

Timofeeva, Y. A. "Worldwide prescriptive jurisdiction in Internet content controversies: a comparative analysis", *Connecticut Journal of International Law,* vol. 20 (2005), 199–225.

Whitman, C. B. (ed.). "Extraterritorial jurisdiction and jurisdiction following forcible abductions: a new Israeli precedent in international law", *Michigan Law Review*, vol. 72 (1973–1974), 1087–1113.

Yost, M. J. and D. S. Anderson. "The Military Extraterritorial Jurisdiction Act of 2000: closing the gap", *American Journal of International Law*, vol. 95 (2001), 446–454.

E. Other documents

Harvard Law School, *Harvard Research in International Law, Supplement to the American Journal of International Law*, vol. 29 (1935), Codification of International Law, Part II, "Jurisdiction with Respect to Crime", 435–651.

CHECKLIST OF DOCUMENTS OF THE FIFTY-EIGHTH SESSION

Document	*Title*	*Observations and references*
A/CN.4/559	Provisional agenda	Mimeographed. For agenda as adopted, see p.18.
A/CN.4/560	Topical summary of the discussion held in the Sixth Committee of the General Assembly during its sixtieth session, prepared by the Secretariat	Mimeographed.
A/CN.4/561 and Add.1–2	Diplomatic protection: comments and observations received from Governments	Reproduced in *Yearbook ... 2006*, vol. II (Part One).
A/CN.4/562 and Add.1	International liability for injurious consequences arising out of acts not prohibited by international law (international liability in case of loss from transboundary harm arising out of hazardous activities): comments and observations received from Governments	*Idem.*
A/CN.4/563 and Add.1	Filling of casual vacancies in the Commission (article 11 of the statute): note by the Secretariat	A/CN.4/563 reproduced in *Yearbook ... 2006*, vol. II (Part One). A/CN.4/563/Add.1 mimeographed.
A/CN.4/564 and Add.1–2	Fourth report on responsibility of international organizations, by Mr. Giorgio Gaja, Special Rapporteur	Reproduced in *Yearbook ... 2006*, vol. II (Part One).
A/CN.4/565 [and Corr.1]	Expulsion of aliens: memorandum by the Secretariat	Mimeographed. Available on the website of the Commission.
A/CN.4/566	Third report on the legal regime for the allocation of loss in case of transboundary harm arising out of hazardous activities, by Mr. Pemmaraju Sreenivasa Rao, Special Rapporteur	Reproduced in *Yearbook ... 2006*, vol. II (Part One).
A/CN.4/567	Seventh report on diplomatic protection, by Mr. John Dugard, Special Rapporteur	*Idem.*
A/CN.4/568 and Add.1	Responsibility of international organizations: comments and observations received from international organizations	*Idem.*
A/CN.4/569 and Add.1	Ninth report on unilateral acts of States, by Mr. Víctor Rodríguez Cedeño, Special Rapporteur	*Idem.*
A/CN.4/570 [and Corr.1]	Second report on the effects of armed conflicts on treaties, by Mr. Ian Brownlie, Special Rapporteur	*Idem.*
A/CN.4/571	Preliminary report on the obligation to extradite or prosecute ("*aut dedere aut judicare*"), by Mr. Zdzislaw Galicki, Special Rapporteur	*Idem.*
A/CN.4/572 [and Corr.1]	Reservations to treaties: note on draft guideline 3.1.5 (Definition of the object and purpose of the treaty), by Mr. Alain Pellet, Special Rapporteur	*Idem.*
A/CN.4/573 [and Corr.1]	Second report on the expulsion of aliens, by Mr. Maurice Kamto, Special Rapporteur	*Idem.*
A/CN.4/574	Eleventh report on reservations to treaties, by Mr. Alain Pellet, Special Rapporteur	*Idem.*
A/CN.4/575	Diplomatic protection: comments and observations received from Governments	*Idem.*
A/CN.4/L.682 [and Corr.1] and Add.1	Fragmentation of international law: difficulties arising from the diversification and expansion of international law: report of the Study Group of the Commission, finalized by Martti Koskenniemi	Mimeographed. Available on the website of the Commission. The final text will appear as an annex to *Yearbook ... 2006*, vol. II (Part One).
A/CN.4/L.683	Working Group on Shared natural resources (groundwaters): report of the Working Group	Mimeographed.

Document	*Title*	*Observations and references*
A/CN.4/L.684 [and Corr.1–2]	Diplomatic protection: titles and texts of the draft articles on diplomatic protection adopted by the Drafting Committee on second reading	See the summary record of the 2881st meeting (para. 1), in *Yearbook ... 2006*, vol. I.
A/CN.4/L.685 [and Corr.1]	Reservations to treaties: titles and texts of the draft guidelines adopted by the Drafting Committee	Mimeographed.
A/CN.4/L.686 [and Corr.1]	International liability for injurious consequences arising out of acts not prohibited by international law: title and texts of the preamble and the draft principles on the allocation of loss arising out of hazardous activities adopted by the Drafting Committee on second reading	*Idem.*
A/CN.4/L.687 and Add.1 [and Corr.1]	Responsibility of international organizations: titles and texts of the draft articles adopted by the Drafting Committee	*Idem.*
A/CN.4/L.688	Shared natural resources: titles and texts of the draft articles adopted by the Drafting Committee on first reading	*Idem.*
A/CN.4/L.689	Draft report of the Commission on the work of its fifty-eighth session: chapter I (Introduction)	*Idem.* For the adopted text, see *Official Records of the General Assembly, Sixty-first Session, Supplement No. 10* (A/61/10). For the final text, see p. 17 above.
A/CN.4/L.690	*Idem*: chapter II (Summary of the work of the Commission on the work of its fifty-eighth session)	*Idem*, p. 19 above.
A/CN.4/L.691	*Idem*: chapter III (Specific issues on which comments would be of particular interest to the Commission)	*Idem*, p. 21 above.
A/CN.4/L.692 and Add.1	*Idem*: chapter IV (Diplomatic protection)	*Idem*, p. 23 above.
A/CN.4/L.693 and Add.1	*Idem*: chapter V (International liability for injurious consequences arising out of acts not prohibited by international law (international liability in case of loss from transboundary harm arising out of hazardous activities))	*Idem*, p. 56 above.
A/CN.4/L.694 and Add.1 [and Corr.1]	*Idem*: chapter VI (Shared natural resources)	*Idem*, p. 91 above.
A/CN.4/L.695 [and Corr.1] and Add.1 [and Corr.1] and Add.2	*Idem*: chapter VII (Responsibility of international organizations)	*Idem*, p. 116 above.
A/CN.4/L.696 [and Corr.1] and Add.1 [and Corr.1] and Add.2–3	*Idem*: chapter VIII (Reservations to treaties)	*Idem*, p. 133 above.
A/CN.4/L.697 and Add.1 [and Corr.1] and Add.2	*Idem*: chapter IX (Unilateral acts of States)	*Idem*, p. 159 above.
A/CN.4/L.698	*Idem*: chapter X (Effects of armed conflicts on treaties)	*Idem*, p. 167 above.
A/CN.4/L.699	*Idem*: chapter XI (Obligation to extradite or prosecute ("*aut dedere aut judicare*"))	*Idem*, p. 172 above.
A/CN.4/L.700	*Idem*: chapter XII (Fragmentation of international law: difficulties arising from the diversification and expansion of international law)	*Idem*, p. 175 above.
A/CN.4/L.701 and Add.1	*Idem*: chapter XIII (Other decisions and conclusions of the Commission)	*Idem*, p. 185 above.
A/CN.4/L.702	Fragmentation of international law: difficulties arising from the diversification and expansion of international law: report of the study group of the Commission	*Idem.*
A/CN.4/L.703	Unilateral acts of States—report of the Working Group: conclusions of the Commission	Mimeographed.
A/CN.4/L.704	Programme, procedures and working methods of the Commission, and its documentation: report of the Planning Group	*Idem.*
A/CN.4/SR.2867–A/CN.4/SR.2913	Provisional summary records of the 2867th to 2913th meetings	*Idem.* The final text appears in *Yearbook ... 2006*, vol. I.